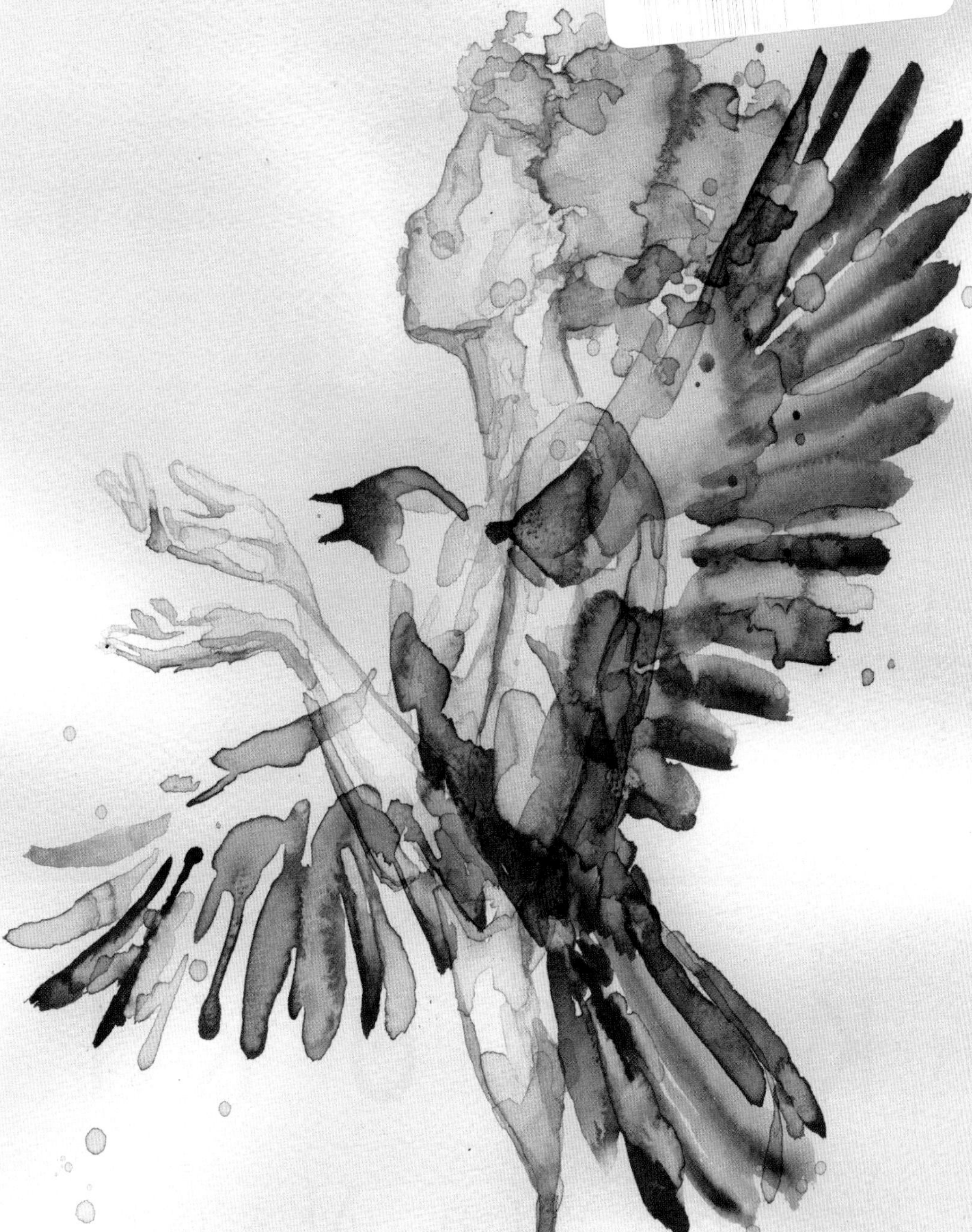

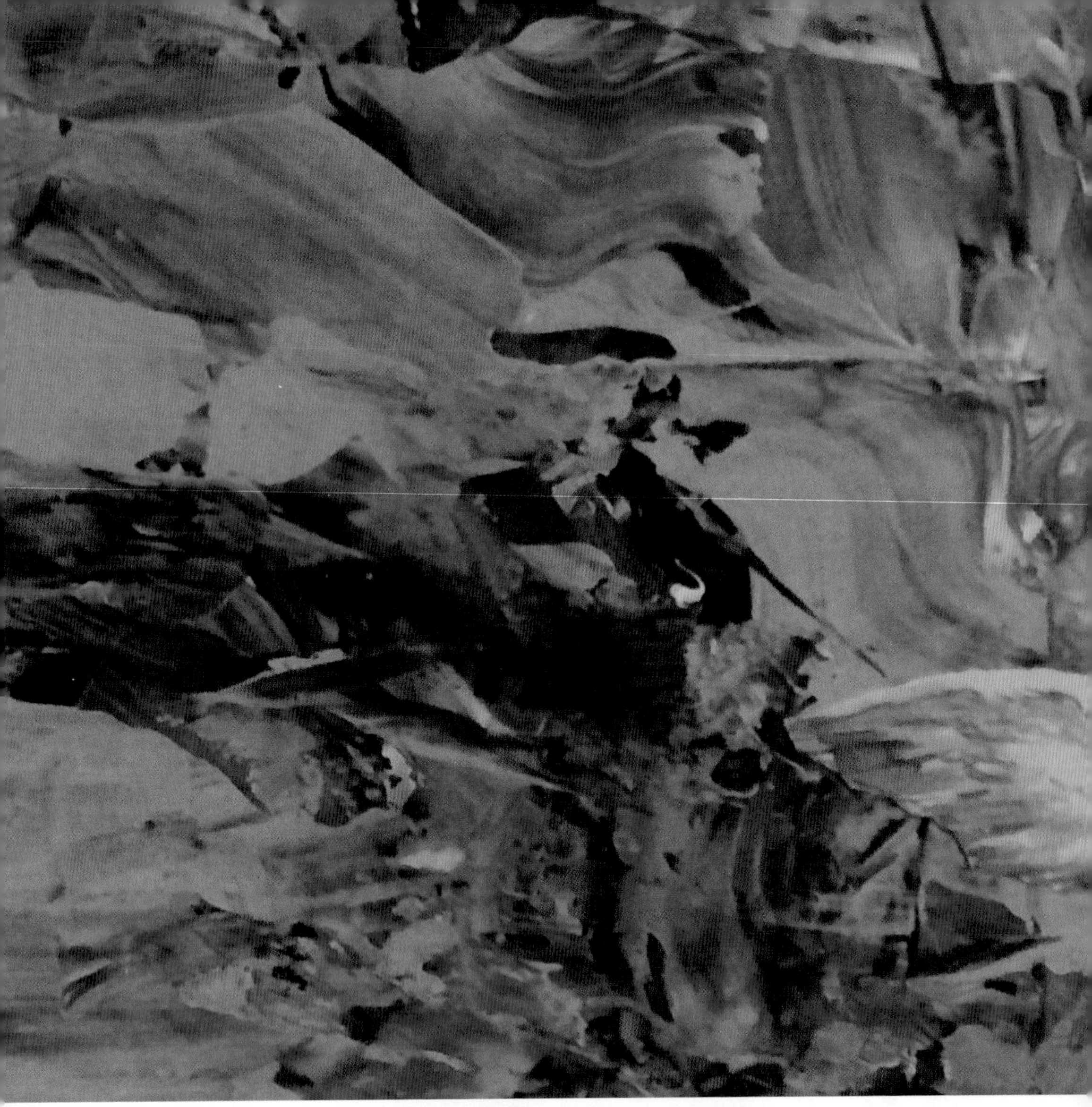

KABUKI

DAVID MACK

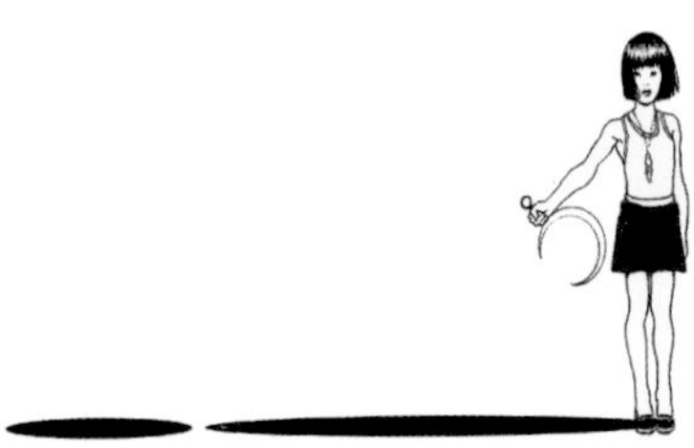

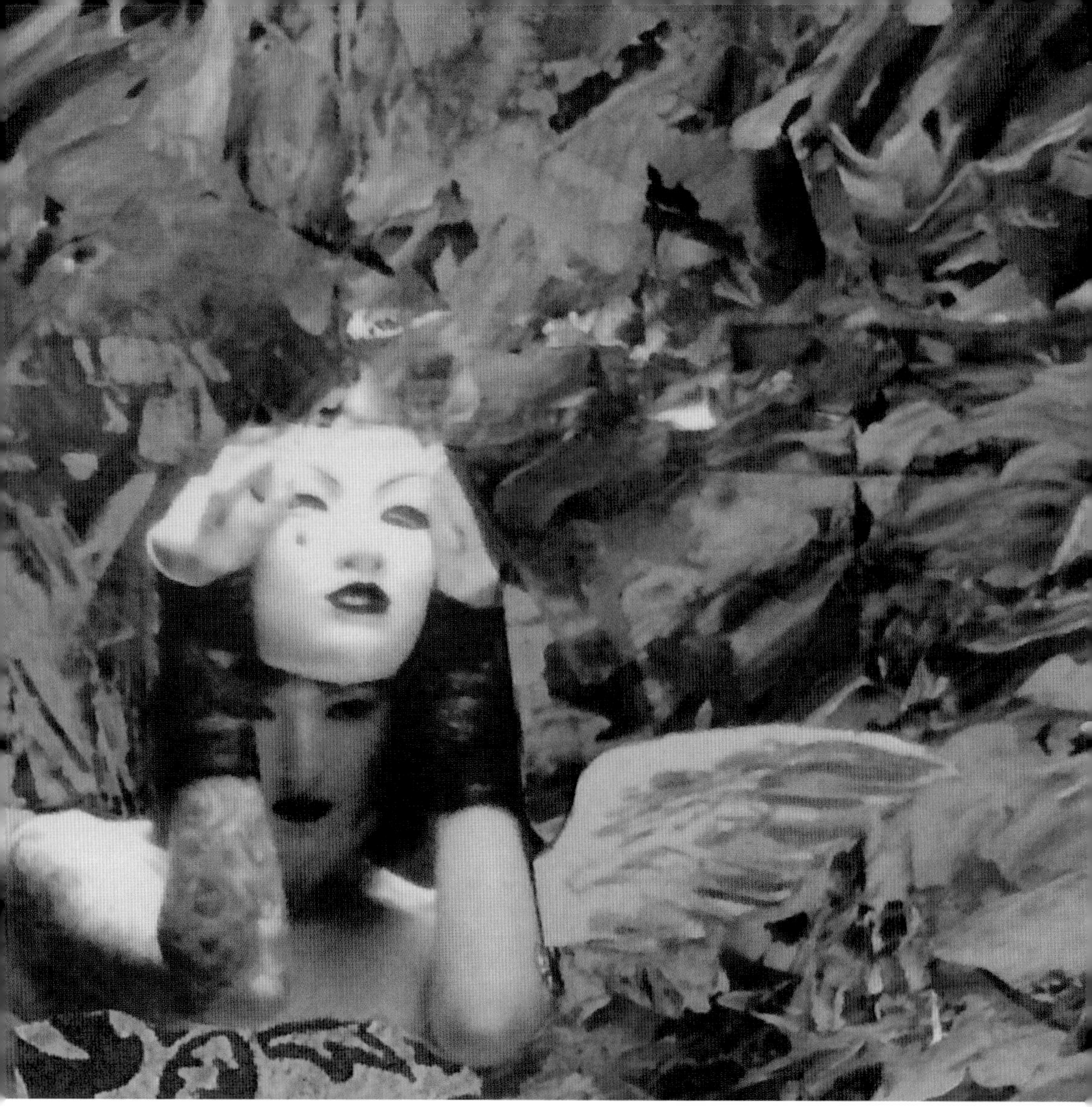

"Scars show us where we have been,
they do not dictate where we are going."

- D. Rossi

Kabuki Omnibus Vol. 3
By David Mack

 Dark Horse Books®

President and Publisher   Mike Richardson
Editor   Shantel LaRocque
Assistant Editor   Brett Israel
Designers   David Mack and Skyler Weissenfluh
Digital Art Technician   Allyson Haller

Neil Hankerson Executive Vice President • Tom Weddle Chief Financial
Officer • Randy Stradley Vice President of Publishing • Nick McWhorter
Chief Business Development Officer • Dale LaFountain Chief Information
Officer • Matt Parkinson Vice President of Marketing • Vanessa Todd-Holmes
Vice President of Production and Scheduling • Mark Bernardi Vice President
of Book Trade and Digital Sales • Ken Lizzi General Counsel • Dave Marshall
Editor in Chief • Davey Estrada Editorial Director • Chris Warner Senior
Books Editor • Cary Grazzini Director of Specialty Projects • Lia Ribacchi Art
Director • Matt Dryer Director of Digital Art and Prepress • Michael Gombos
Senior Director of Licensed Publications • Kari Yadro Director of Custom
Programs • Kari Torson Director of International Licensing • Sean Brice
Director of Trade Sales

Published by Dark Horse Books
A Division of Dark Horse Comics LLC
10956 SE Main Street
Milwaukie, OR 97222

First Omnibus Edition: June 2020
Ebook ISBN 978-1-50671-612-1
ISBN 978-1-50671-608-4

10 9 8 7 6 5 4 3 2 1
Printed in China

To find a comics shop in your area, visit comicshoplocator.com

Kabuki Omnibus volume 3
Kabuki™ © 2004-2007, 2009, 2016, 2020 David Mack. Dark Horse Books®
and the Dark Horse logo are trademarks of Dark Horse Comics LLC,
registered in various categories and countries. All rights reserved. No
portion of this publication may be reproduced or transmitted, in any form
or by any means, without the express written permission of Dark Horse
Comics LLC. Names, characters, places, and incidents featured in this
publication either are the product of the author's imagination or are used
fictitiously. Any resemblance to actual persons (living or dead), events,
institutions, or locales, without satiric intent, is coincidental.

This edition reprints Kabuki Library volume 3 containing Kabuki: The
Alchemy.

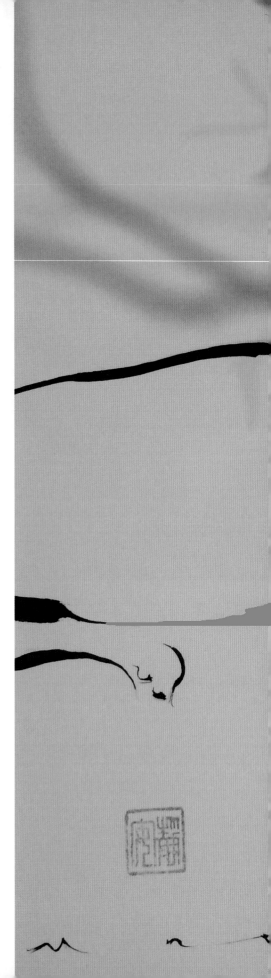

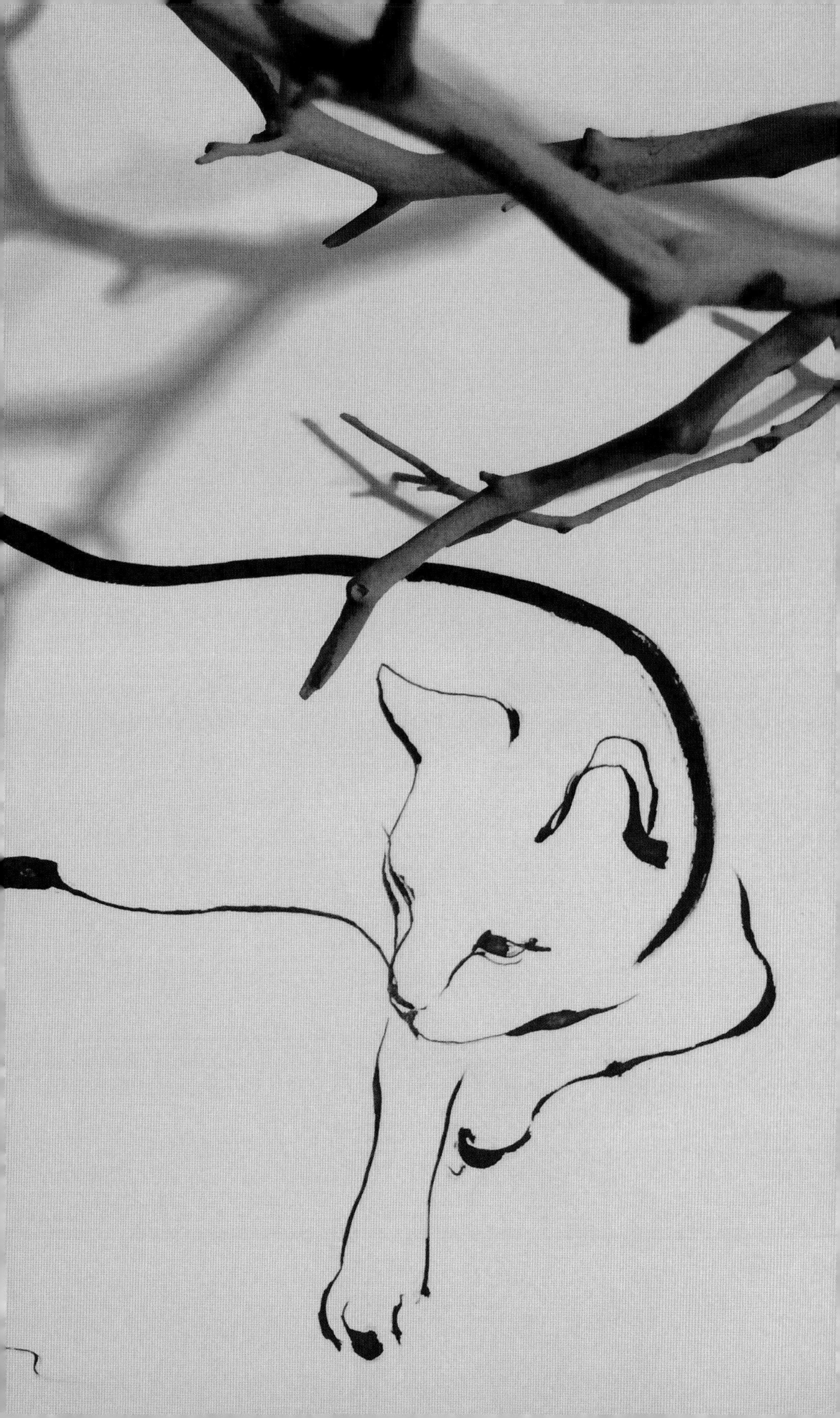

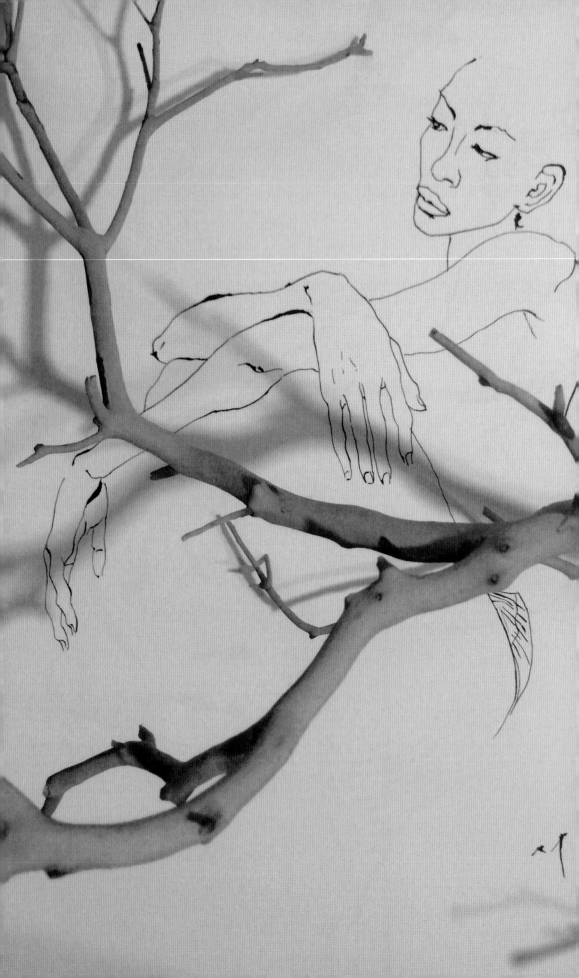

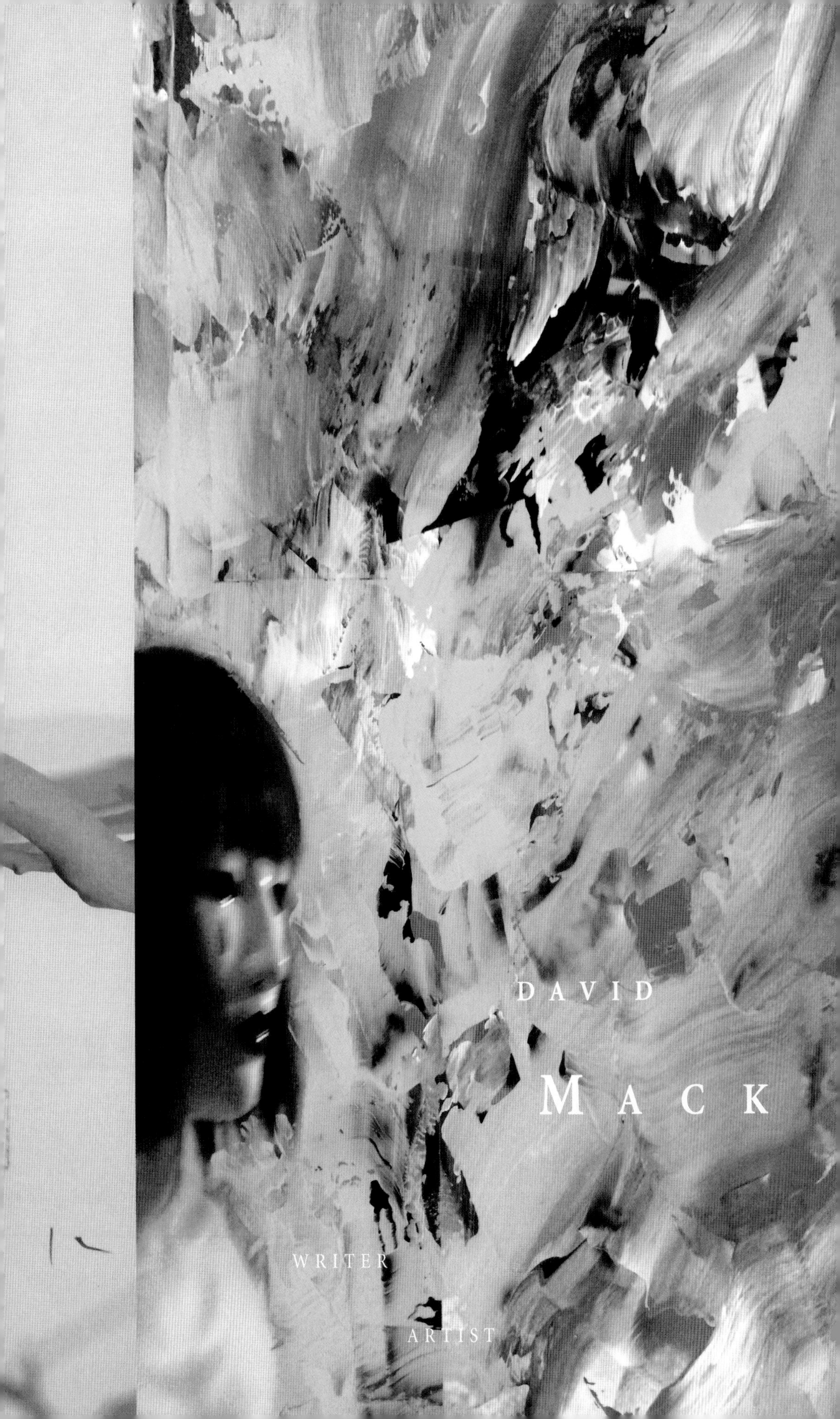
DAVID
MACK
WRITER
ARTIST

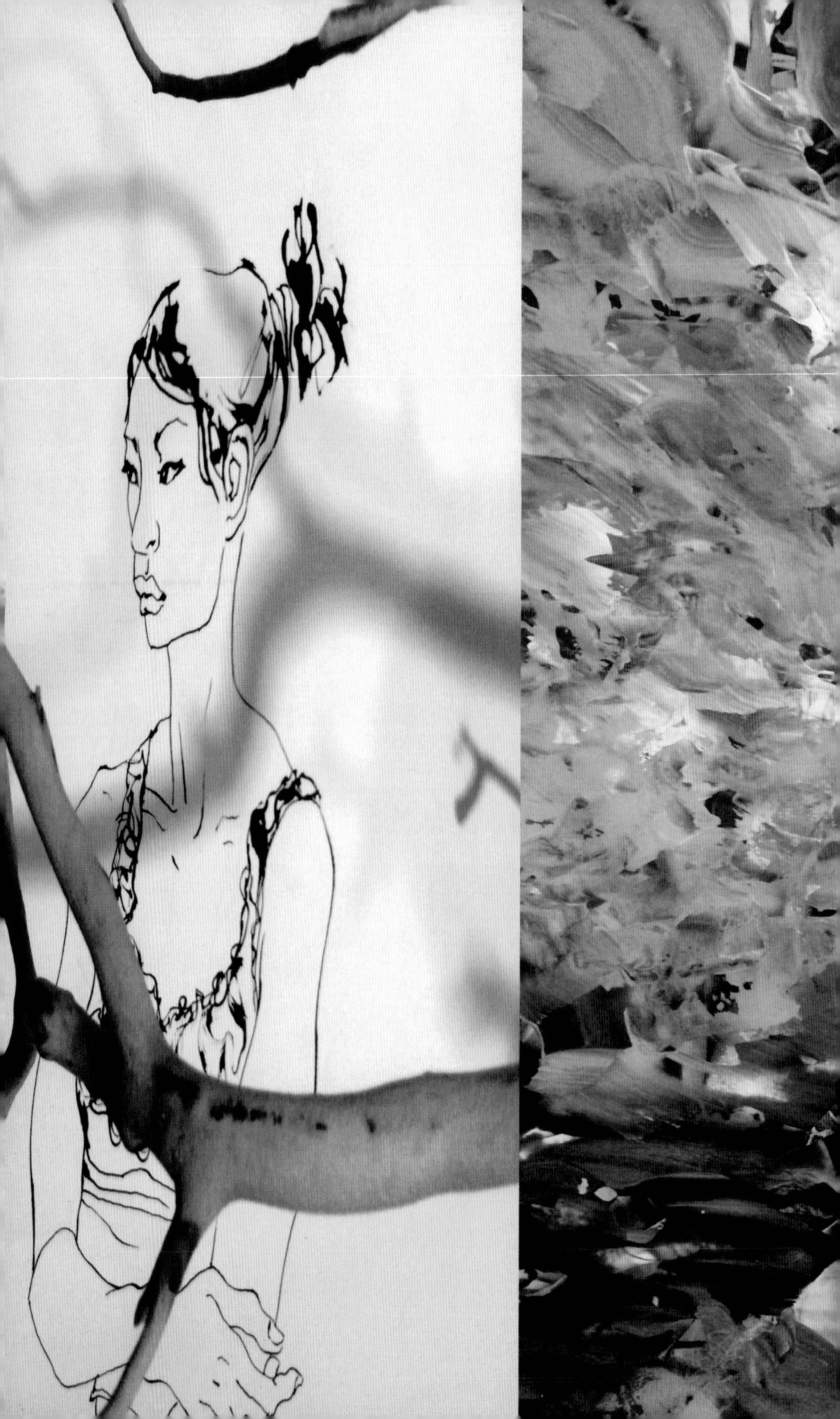

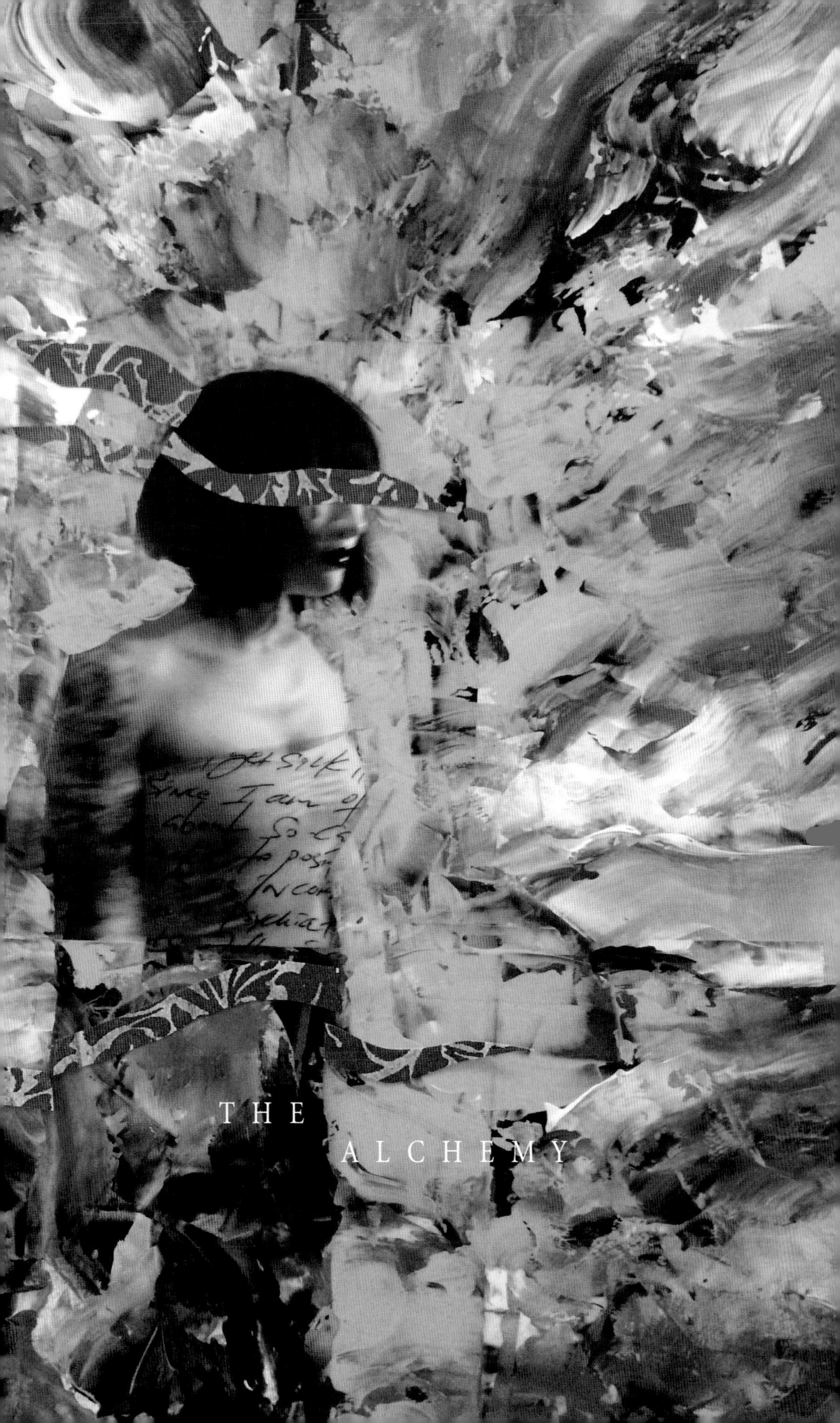
THE
ALCHEMY

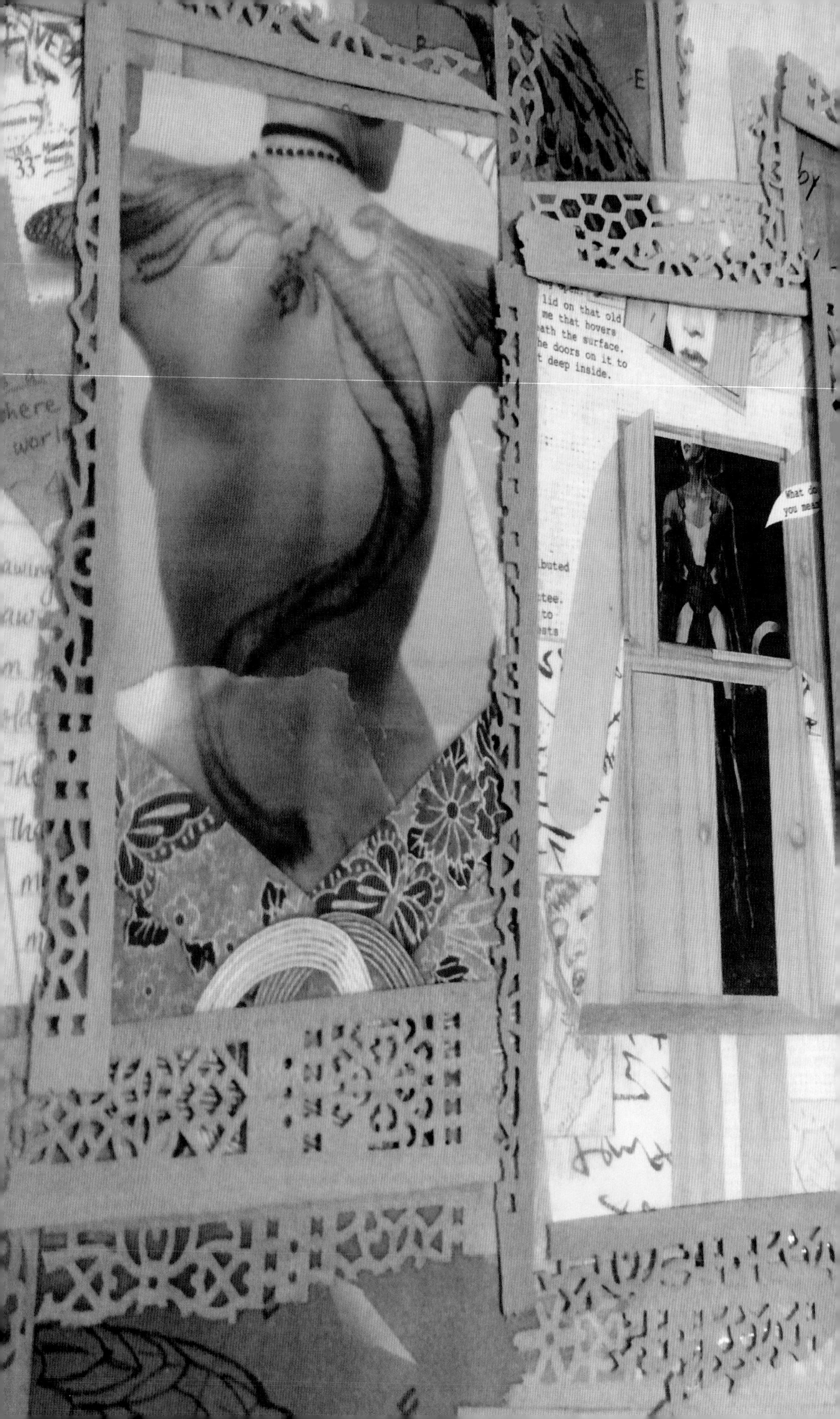
lid on that old
me that hovers
ath the surface.
he doors on it to
t deep inside.
What do
you mean

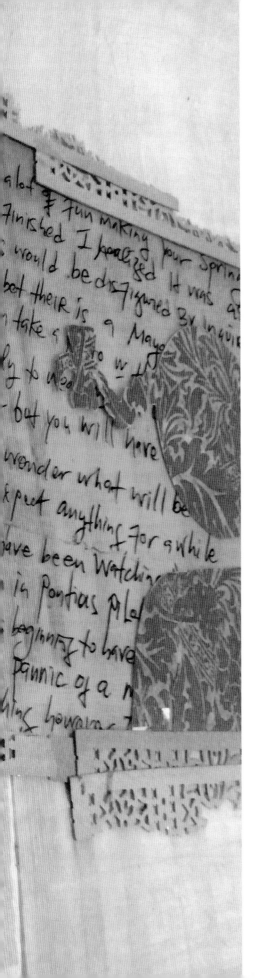

For my mother

I d a   M a c k

1946 - 1995

*My earliest and most
formative artistic influence…*

SELF-FULFILLING

PROPHECY

(or Reverse Engineering)

This *Alchemy* story began with ideas that I would jot down while working on the previous *Kabuki* books. I considered myself primarily a writer or storyteller when working on *Kabuki* and comic books. I had written the first *Kabuki* story. I had looked for an artist to draw the story. At one point in 1993 Brian Michael Bendis was going to be the artist on that very first story. Eventually I kind of tricked myself into drawing the first story and it was successful enough that I could keep making *Kabuki* stories.

As I was making the art pages for each story that I had written, my mind was still moving ahead, visualizing, imagining the scenes and story lines of future chapters. As those ideas would come I'd jot them down and put them in a file, excited about these future moments that the characters would eventually find themselves in. When it came time to begin writing this story in detail (after years of completing the others), I pulled that file out. Inside were all these little pieces of paper, scraps, napkins, post-its, with notes. Ideas I'd forgotten that I'd written. The previous version of me had given the current version of me a gift of all these little handwritten notes that I didn't even remember writing.

At this time I had completed six volumes of *Kabuki* books (the first as my senior thesis in literature) and three *Daredevil* stories for Marvel, and I had been doing them all at a breakneck pace for ten years.

Looking back on that time, those years of making those books, I realized that through trial and error, instinct and naiveté, research and willpower, I had developed certain disciplines, principles, and creative rhythms that were useful to generate ideas; to materialize ideas to fruition in a timely and continuous manner; and, perhaps most importantly, to cultivate creating work at an optimum level of my current potential–and learning to grow that potential.

Through the act of making stories on a regular basis, the daily exercise of starting with a blank page (be it writing or drawing)–putting something there and building on it–that exercise had revealed things to me in my very early formative years. The consistent ACT of making answered questions that I had puzzled over in my high school and college years, and in my professional work.

These questions:
What is my place in life?
What are practical steps to figuring that out?
Once I figure that out, what are practical steps to achieving that?
How to generate and cultivate personal ideas?
What are the practical applications to turning the ideas into reality?
How do I keep the ideas (and the making of them) flowing?

For this *Alchemy* story, the Kabuki character had come to a point in her life that I was at when I created the first *Kabuki* book. She was in a transitional state. A place that a lot of people find themselves in when they are between jobs, or relationships, or starting school, or completing school. The character was in a place where she was facing those integral questions.

In writing the story, I found myself encrypting some principles that I had reverse engineered from my own years of work. In a sense, I was writing the book that I would have wanted to read when I was starting out.

Looking at it now, this book was a kind of laboratory or playground for me to let those ideas dance and breathe, to assimilate personal experiences and far-flung research with whimsical idea approach and expression. It was also a learning process. So I see things that I would improve or finesse if I was making it now.

But as each chapter of this book was coming out, issue by issue, readers wrote to say they connected personally to the characters. Some said they also found themselves in a transitional state like Kabuki was in. Many readers wrote to say they found something personally useful or inspiring from the story.

I hope you will find it useful or inspiring too.

David Mack

2016

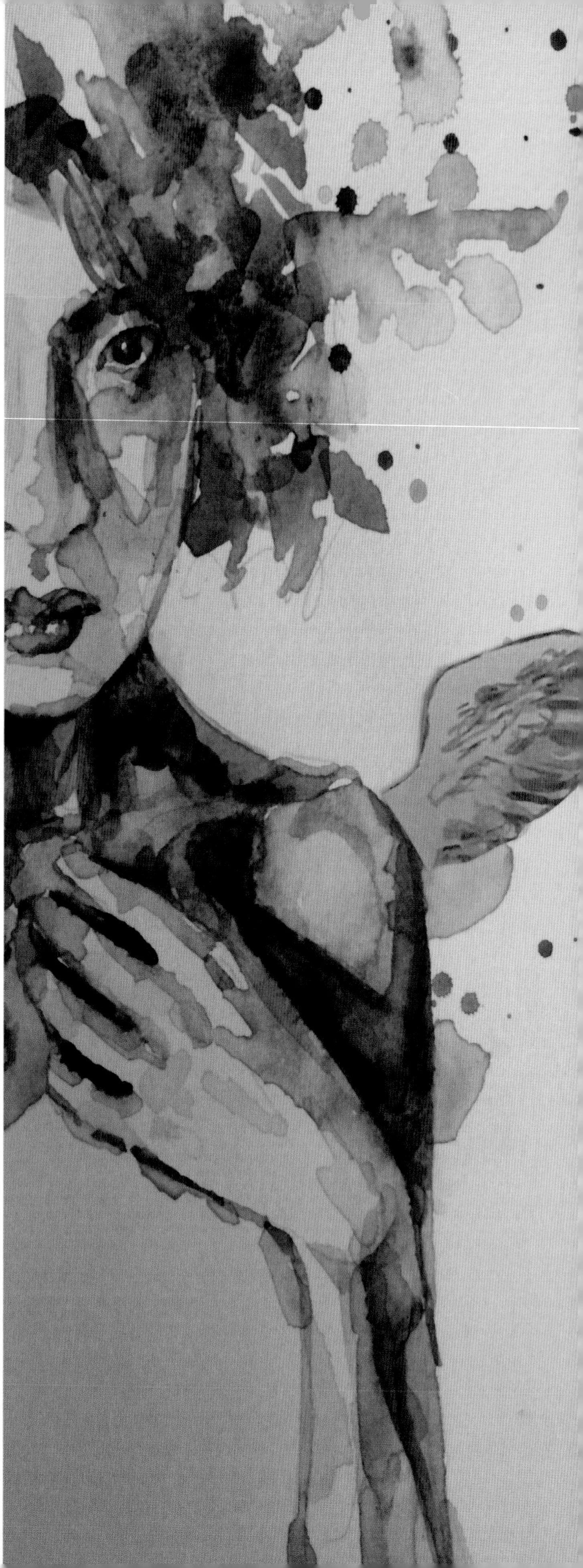

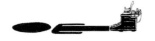

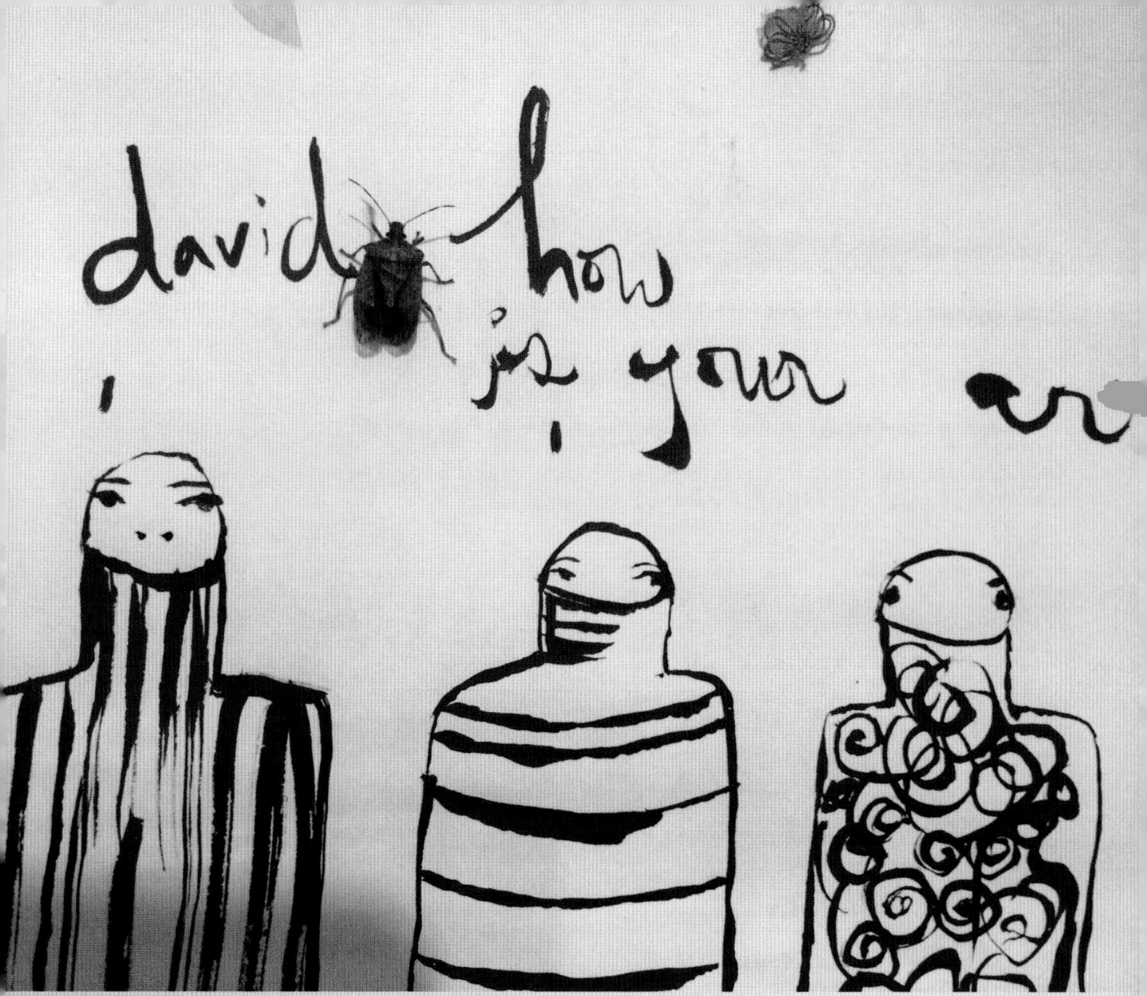
david how
is your

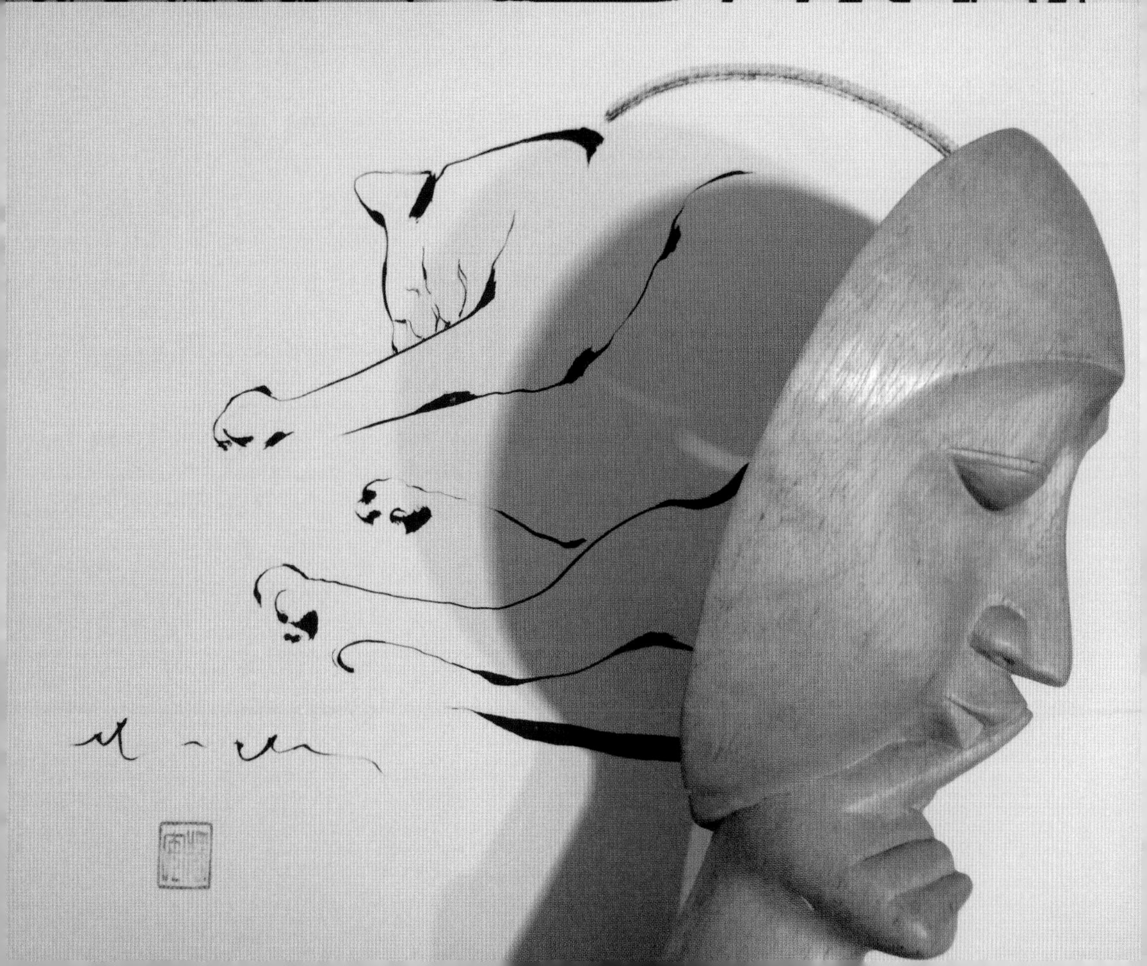

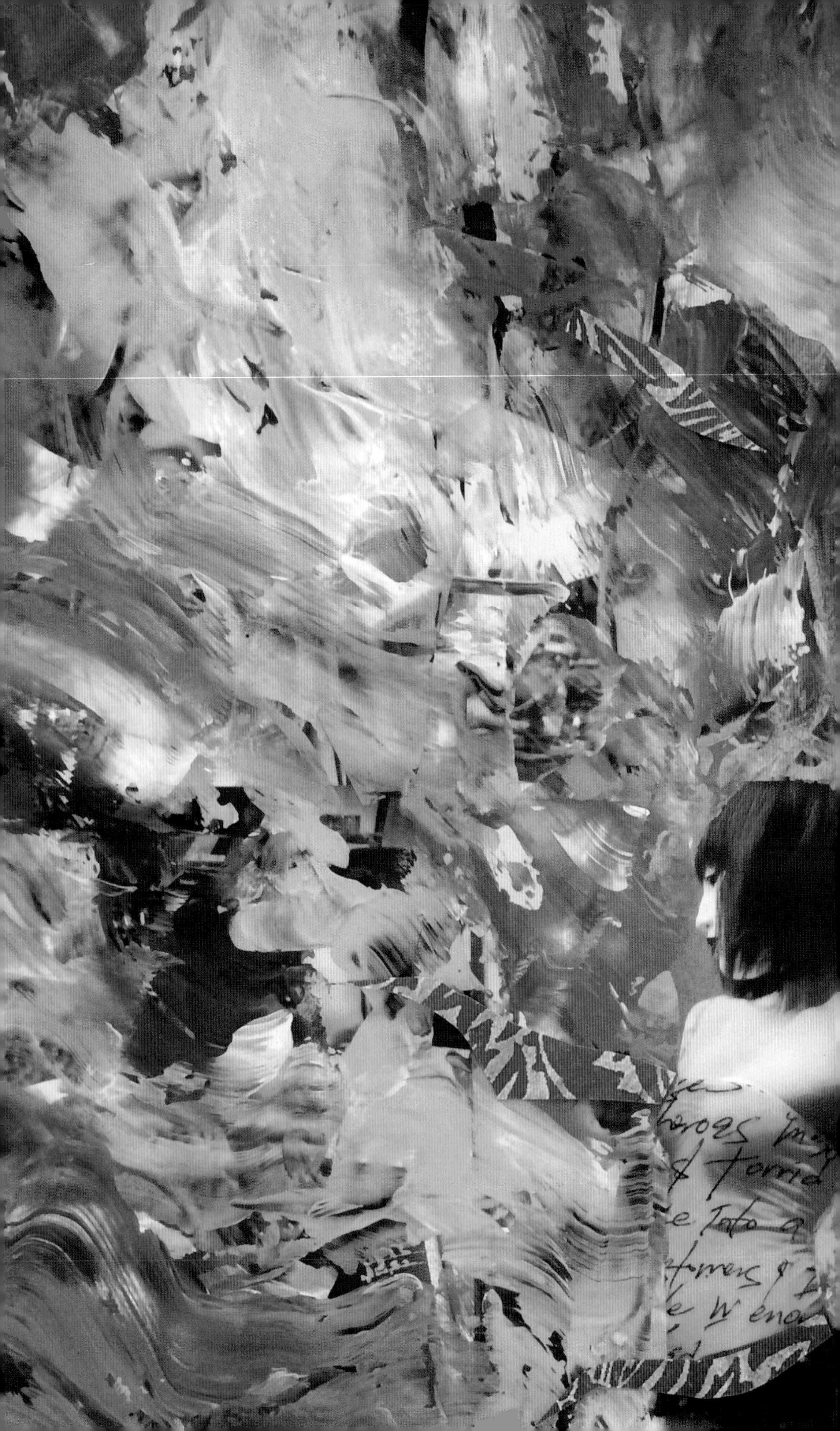

Introduction
Chuck Palahniuk

...unusual equipment ...ss, use it properly. ☺

You will be successful through innovation and determination.

Your many hidden talents will become obvious to those around you.
Lucky Numbers 4, 5, 7, 17, 24, 44

A window of opportunity won't open itself.
Lucky Numbers 37, 21, 10, 44, 35, 9

...ciples understood
☺ You will make many changes before settling satisfactorily. ☺

His martial

luminescent

Use your abilities at this time to stay focused on your goal. You will succeed.

You are the controller of your destiny.

A new wardrobe brings great joy and change to your life.
Lucky Numbers 11, 13, 16, 17, 35, 37

from one craft

and apply it to the

When you gather all your resources together, Goals are accomplished.

...ning to draw me

learning

That

You will stop on the soil of many countries in your lifetime.

Introduction

CHUCK PALAHNIUK

First Impressions

My first job after college, I bolted together the chassis frames of Freightliner trucks. Eighteen to twenty-six trucks per night shift, depending on the optional bells and whistles. And on my first night, my foreman sent me on an errand to recover a tool called a "Squeegee sharpener." Another work area – axle build-up or radiator hang or fifth-wheel assembly – had borrowed the tool and my task was to find the sharpener and bring it back.

My college degree was a B.A. in Journalism, and I'd be repaying my student loans for most of the next decade. Freightliner paid a starting wage of nine dollars per hour, and I planned to build trucks only long enough to bankroll my search for a real job as a newspaper reporter.

That first shift, I asked everybody I met about the lost tool. I asked the guys drilling and riveting together rough truck cabs. I asked the guys in the paint booth. The foreman at Axle Hang. The guys running wiring harnesses. The brake drum guys. The engine build-up crew. And they all shouted back in my face, spitting anger, veins bursting until their faces glowed red, denying they had the Squeegee sharpener. Shaking their fists or holding lady-foot pry bars – picture a smaller version of a crow bar – poised to whack out my fucking, asshole, dumb-ass, new-hire brains. Of all the insults at Freightliner, that was the worst, being called a "new hire."

For eight hours I wandered from one shouting, swearing maniac to the next lunatic grease monkey in coveralls who'd shove his fist under my chin and tell me the Squeegee sharpener was his property, and I'd only get it back by prying it from his cold, dead hand.

By the time I punched the clock, at the end of that first shift, my foreman took me aside and said... there was no such tool as a Squeegee anything. It didn't exist.

After eight hours, I wasn't all that surprised. So many jobs have some initiation ritual. People tell me, at Wal-Mart or Target stores, you might be sent to find the "shelf stretchers." In

restaurant or bar jobs, the snipe hunt is to find the "banana peeler." In warehouses or foundries, you search after a "sky hook."

Every time I told the story of my first day at Freightliner Trucks, somebody told me about a worse rite of passage. In Toronto, a man working in a brick factory was sent to fetch a bucket of hot steam. A veteran brick maker even trained him how to invert the bucket above a live steam valve, collect the scalding white vapor, then race to where the steam was needed – fast, sprinting past everyone with a blistering-hot metal bucket held upside-down. Then, breathless and blistered, be cursed because the steam had cooled and disappeared. Bucket after bucket after bucket, running for eight hours.

Everyone laughs as this happens to every new hire.

In Las Vegas, a man told how television stations send their new-hires on a similar fools errand. Television production uses colored sheets of clear plastic to tint spotlights. The sheets of red or yellow or blue plastic are called "gels" because they were originally made of thin, fragile sheets of hardened gelatin. Most television stations still have a few old sheets of the gelatin, and the boss tells you how expensive the "gels" are, how fragile and tough to replace – then tells you to carefully, cautiously take the gels to a sink and wash them. The instructions are meticulous: don't tear the edges, don't scratch the surfaces, and only use the coldest water possible or the colored sheets might warp. Any damage to the fragile, precious gels, and you're fired.

The man in Las Vegas barely breathed as he ran the cold water into the sink. Still, no matter how cold he ran the wash, no matter how lightly he touched the sheets, the moment the first gel touched the water – it dissolved into red liquid and vanished down the drain. He spent the rest of his first day hiding from the boss. As does everyone on their first day.

Now, he's the boss.

A pediatrician said how, during his residency in a huge teaching hospital, the staff waited for him to lie down on a gurney and catch a midnight nap. This was after he'd been on-call for days, eating only vending machine snack food, and the moment he fell asleep, the public address system announced his name. "Doctor So-and-so to room such-and-such, STAT! Code Blue!" Again and again, calling him as he raced through the hospital's still, late-night hallways, arriving at an isolated patient room. Even in the hallway, he could hear a woman screaming, just screaming over the code blue announcement, and the moment he threw open the door, there she was...

A woman, naked in a hospital bed, covered with blood, screaming. The room is screened strangely, folding screens and curtains are pulled to hide the walls, and the lights are placed low, near the floor, to throw everything into nightmare shadows. The moment this pediatrician throws open the door, something hits him in the ribcage. Something wet, he catches automatically and clutches to his chest. The naked, bloody woman screams, "You bastard! You bastard, you killed my baby!"

And what you're holding -- your heart pounding, your name still blaring loud over the public address system – is a cold, naked baby covered in blood. Thick, sticky blood.

You see -- in comparison, my Squeegee story fades to nothing.

For all the pediatric residents, this is tradition. The woman in bed is a nurse. The room is screened so oddly because every doctor on staff who's ever caught a cold, bloody baby wants to be present in this tiny room to watch you catch this one.

The dead baby feels so... convincing – the perfect weight and size – because it's an anatomical doll designed to teach cardiopulmonary resuscitation.

The blood feels so real because... well, it's human blood.

Worldwide, your first day at anything can suck.

In the Italian army, they cram you inside a metal locker, then kick the steel sides, demanding you sing popular songs as your fellow soldiers piss through the vents around your face. It's called "playing the jukebox." In Germany, the rite of passage involves slicing open your cheeks, then packing the wounds with horse hair to mimic traditional upper-class "dueling scars."

In France, I told my little story about Freightliner. I told about the banana peeler, the bucket full of steam, the colored gels. I told about the bloody baby and playing the jukebox, and a stranger stepped up and introduced himself as a veterinarian. A doctor of veterinary medicine, according to his business card. And he said how the French academy of veterinary sciences accept very few new students each year. This man had applied for six years to be accepted into the program, and on the year he finally began his studies his peers threw a small party to celebrate. It was a tradition of the academy, to throw a small drinking party. All of the new student's professors and advisors drink wine with you, and you drink and drink and drink wine. And if you don't pass out from the wine, your colleagues sneak an animal tranquilizer into your glass.

To guarantee that you do black out.

Then, they get to work. They strip off all of your clothing. They fold your arms and legs, bunching your sleeping, nude body into a small, naked ball. And they very carefully sew you into the gutted belly of a dead horse.

Then, your professors, your advisors and fellow students continue the drinking party around the horse.

Soon enough, when you wake up... the man says, you have no idea where you're at. Your head pounds with pain, and your stomach churns from the wine and drugs. You're shaking with cold and coated with stiff, sticky fluids. You're blind, sealed inside some tight, suffocating darkness. It stinks, and you can still hear your peers, drinking wine and shouting.

With your first movement, when they see you twist or shift inside the horse's dead skin, the party begins to shout. You must fight! They shout, you must fight to be part of their program! You must fight if you want to become a doctor of animals.

Hearing them, you twist and push. You claw and scratch against the stinking darkness until your finger breaks through, then your hand, then your arm. Then, as you stretch an arm into the world, birthing yourself from this cold, dead thing, someone puts a glass of wine in your bloody hand. You've made it. You're one of the select few, officially accepted into the academy.

Officially, you've survived the worst event of your career. No matter how many puppies or kitties die on any single day in your future, it will still beat the crap out of waking up inside a dead horse. No matter how awful your day as a pediatrician, it still beats being pelted with a dead infant. Even in summer, when the Freightliner truck assembly plant heats to steam-bucket temperatures, it will still beat being cursed, being threatened and spat on by hundreds of angry grease monkeys.

And everyone you work with – veterinarians or pediatricians or television news anchors – they know that worst-case scenario. You already have that horror in common.

Artists should practice this kind of ritual initiation.

Whether you're a singer or an actor, a writer or musician or painter, a big part of your job is to express what your audience can't. The people who enjoy your work, they're not stupid. Chances are they're just not fully aware of their feeling, the nagging, unformed ideas that haunt their lives. Maybe they're too young. Most people are too busy for reflection. Something might bother them, worry them, but they can't quite put a finger on it. That's your job. Or, your audience might not have the courage to express an idea. Each of them might feel afraid that the idea or concern or horrible experience is isolated to only them. Or, they lack the skill to communicate the idea, to express it effectively to another person.

That's why we have love songs on the radio, stand-up comics, greeting cards, slasher films, tent revival preachers, tango dancers, movie stars, Stephen King, music videos, architecture, totem poles, frescoes, Hello Kitty and cake decorating...

David Mack and *Kabuki*.

Art is the lie that tells the truth better than the truth. And in *Kabuki*, David Mack tells you more about his life than he could ever tell you in person. Using his past instead of being used by it. Building a metaphor that allows people to see and explore their own experience.

It's the job of any creative person to explore and express what other people can't.

You're always seeing your life as something within a larger pattern. Your experience is never just yours – it's only one aspect of something occurring in a million, zillion other lives. You become a listener, a watcher, a witness, pulling together the stories of other people to illustrate a larger theme.

My first day, I never did find that Squeegee sharpener, but I learned the layout of the entire factory. Met every co-worker. Introduced myself to every foreman. Instead of a couple months, I worked at Freightliner for 13 years. And every few weeks, a stranger would step up next to me and ask, "Dude, you have some tool called a 'Squeegee something-or-other'?"

The good news is -- We've all found ourselves inside that cold, dead horse. That tight, stinking darkness. The headache and abuse and terror.

The truth is, you will survive even this awful moment.

Chuck Palahniuk

2008

Chuck Palahniuk is the award winning author of Fight Club (made into a film directed by David Fincher), Choke, Rant, Diary, Survivor, Invisible Monsters, & many other novels. He is working with David Mack on the Fight Club graphic novels.

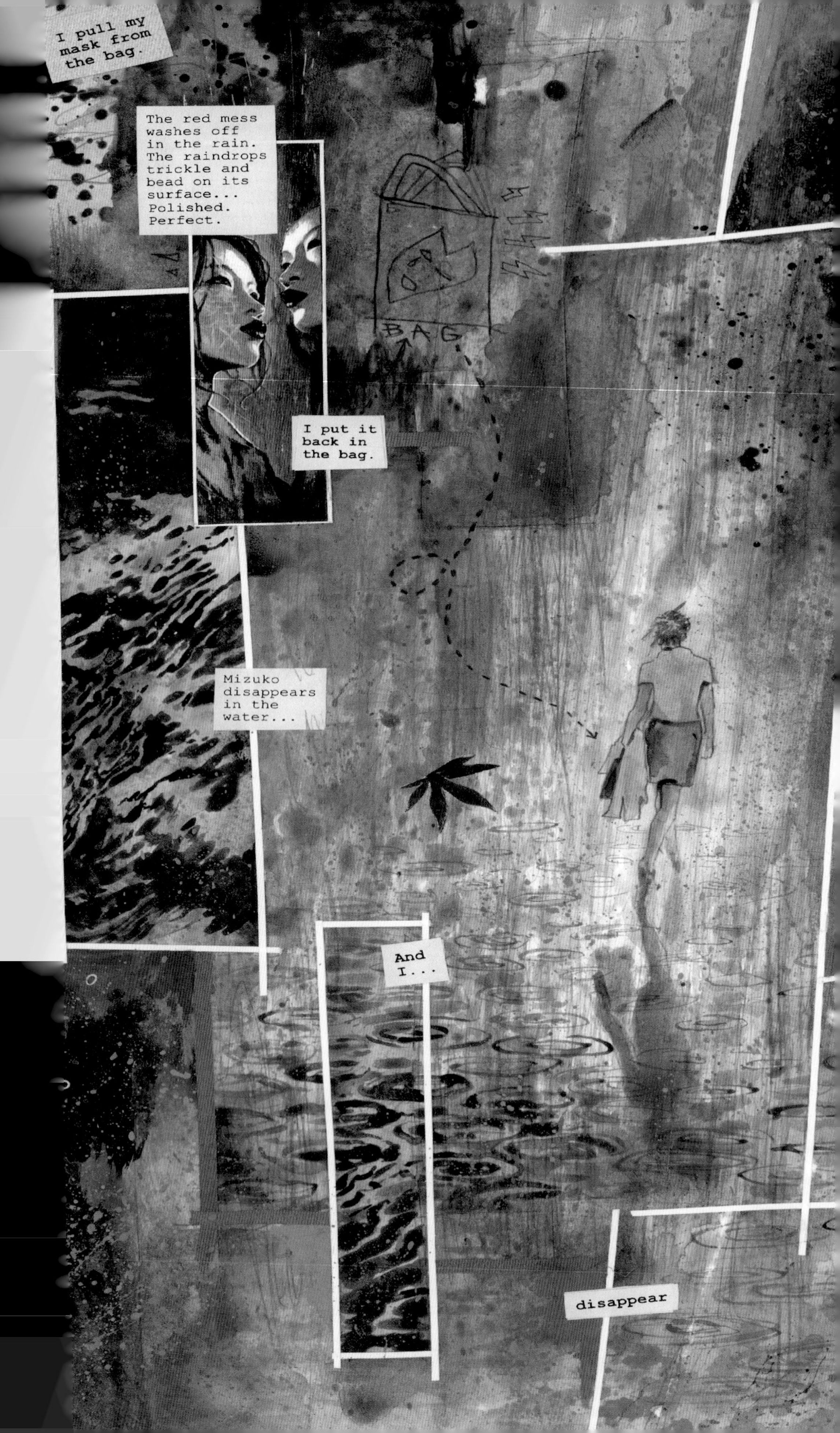
I pull my mask from the bag.
The red mess washes off in the rain. The raindrops trickle and bead on its surface... Polished. Perfect.
BAG
I put it back in the bag.
Mizuko disappears in the water...
And I...
disappear

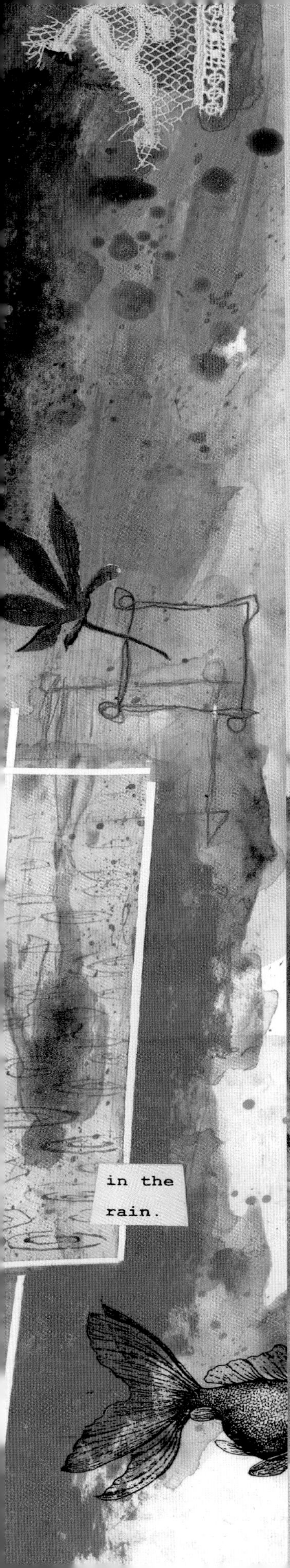
in the
rain.

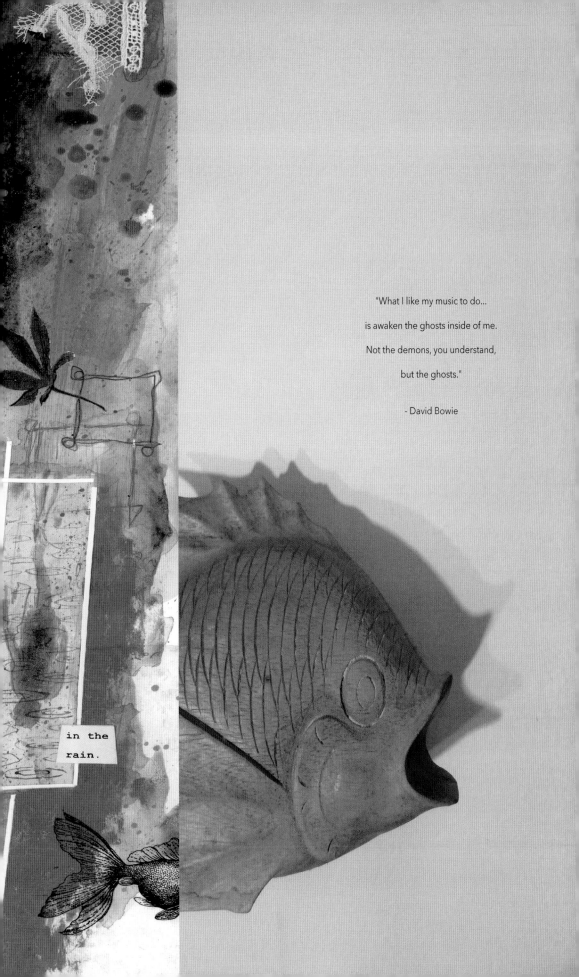

"What I like my music to do...

is awaken the ghosts inside of me.

Not the demons, you understand,

but the ghosts."

- David Bowie

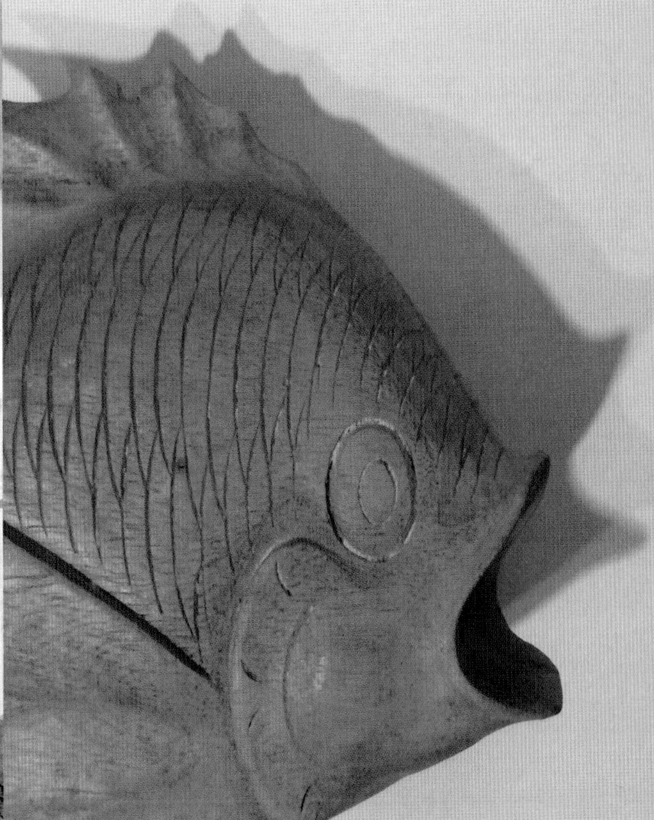

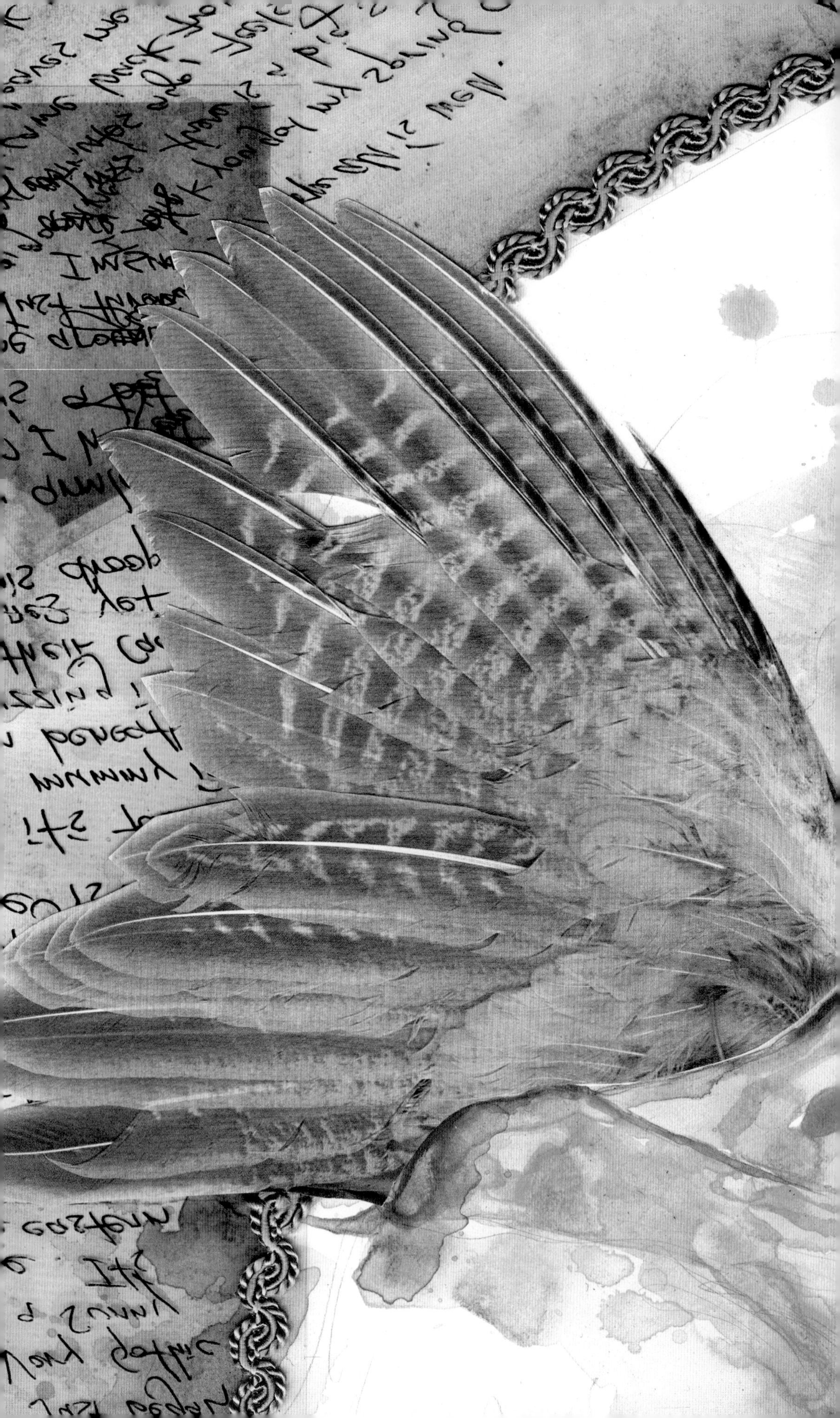

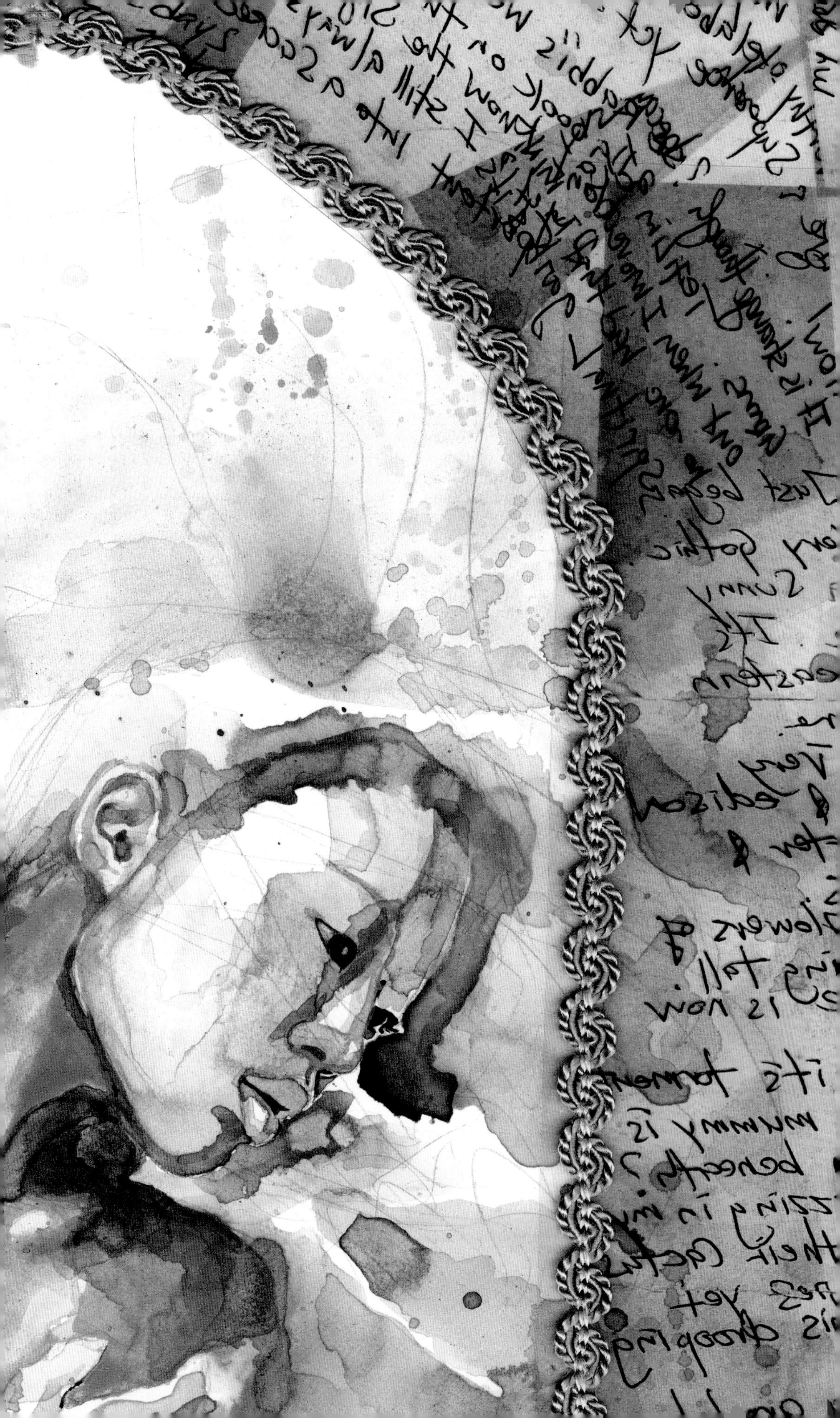

It is strange though
Just began
Sunny
It's
eastern
Madison
flowers
is now
it's torment
mummy is
beneath
zzing in my
their cactu
is drooping

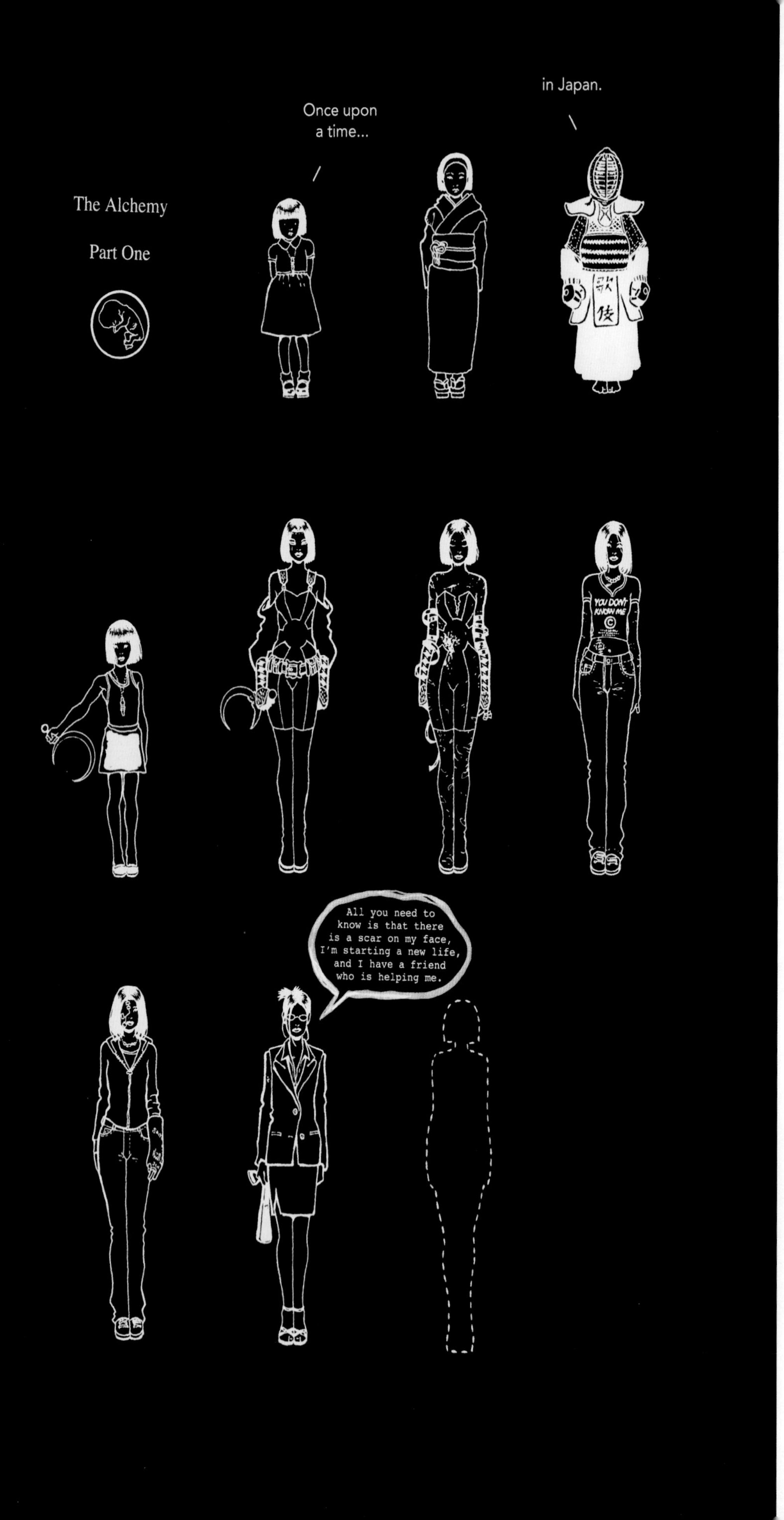
The Alchemy
Part One
Once upon a time...
in Japan.
YOU DON'T KNOW ME
All you need to know is that there is a scar on my face, I'm starting a new life, and I have a friend who is helping me.

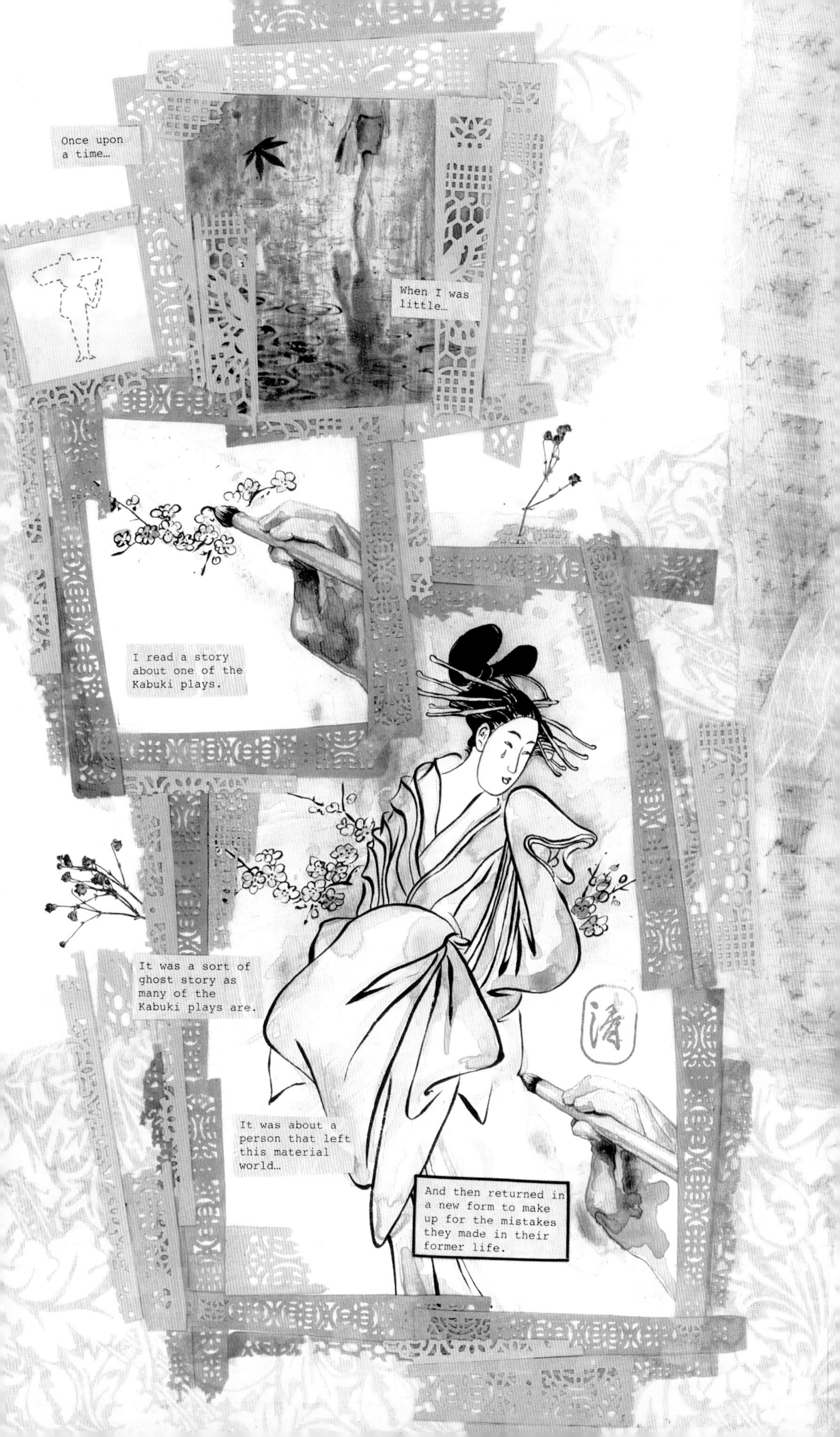

Once upon a time…
When I was little…
I read a story about one of the Kabuki plays.
It was a sort of ghost story as many of the Kabuki plays are.
It was about a person that left this material world…
And then returned in a new form to make up for the mistakes they made in their former life.

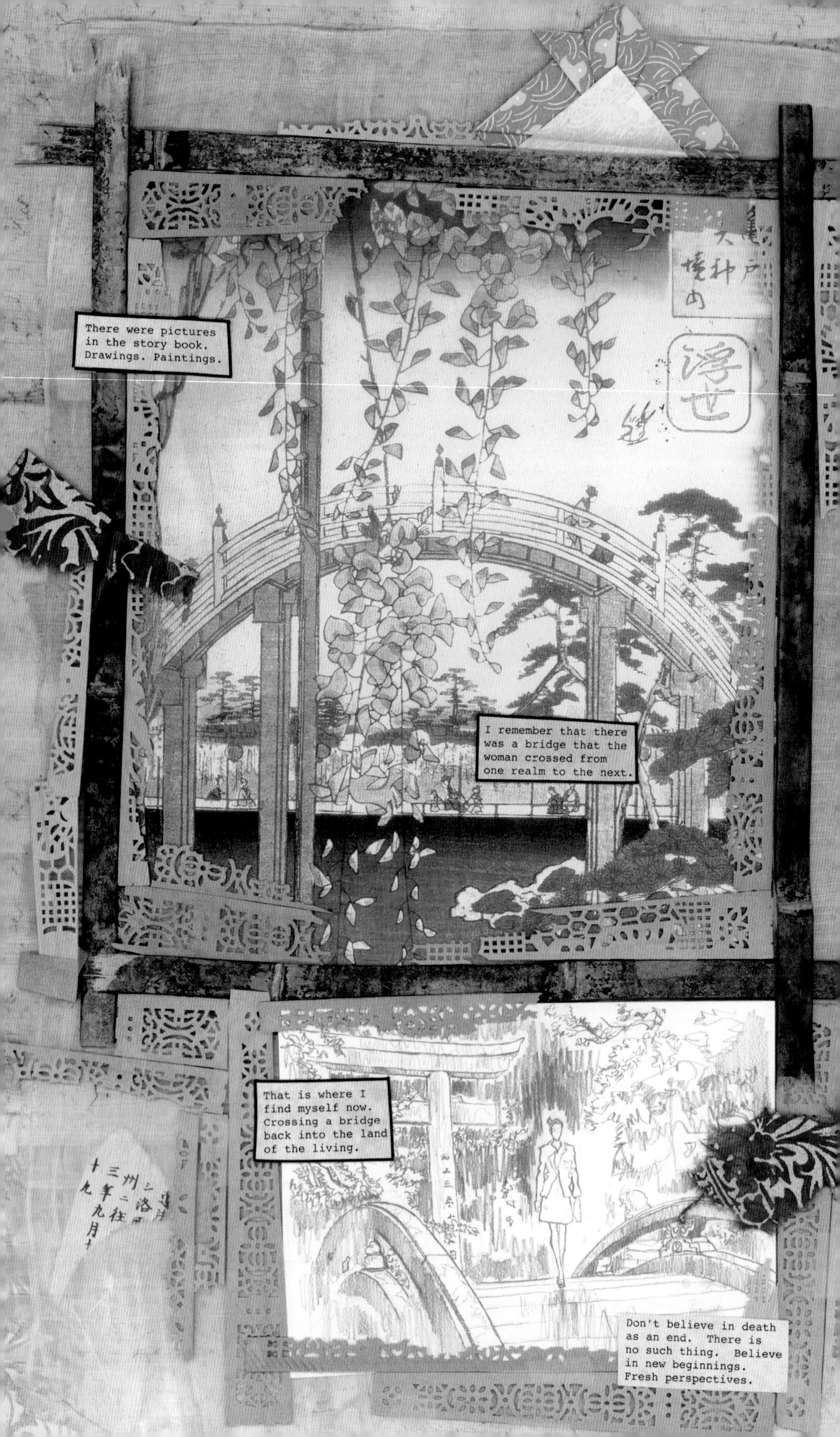

There were pictures in the story book. Drawings. Paintings.
浮世
I remember that there was a bridge that the woman crossed from one realm to the next.
That is where I find myself now. Crossing a bridge back into the land of the living.
Don't believe in death as an end. There is no such thing. Believe in new beginnings. Fresh perspectives.

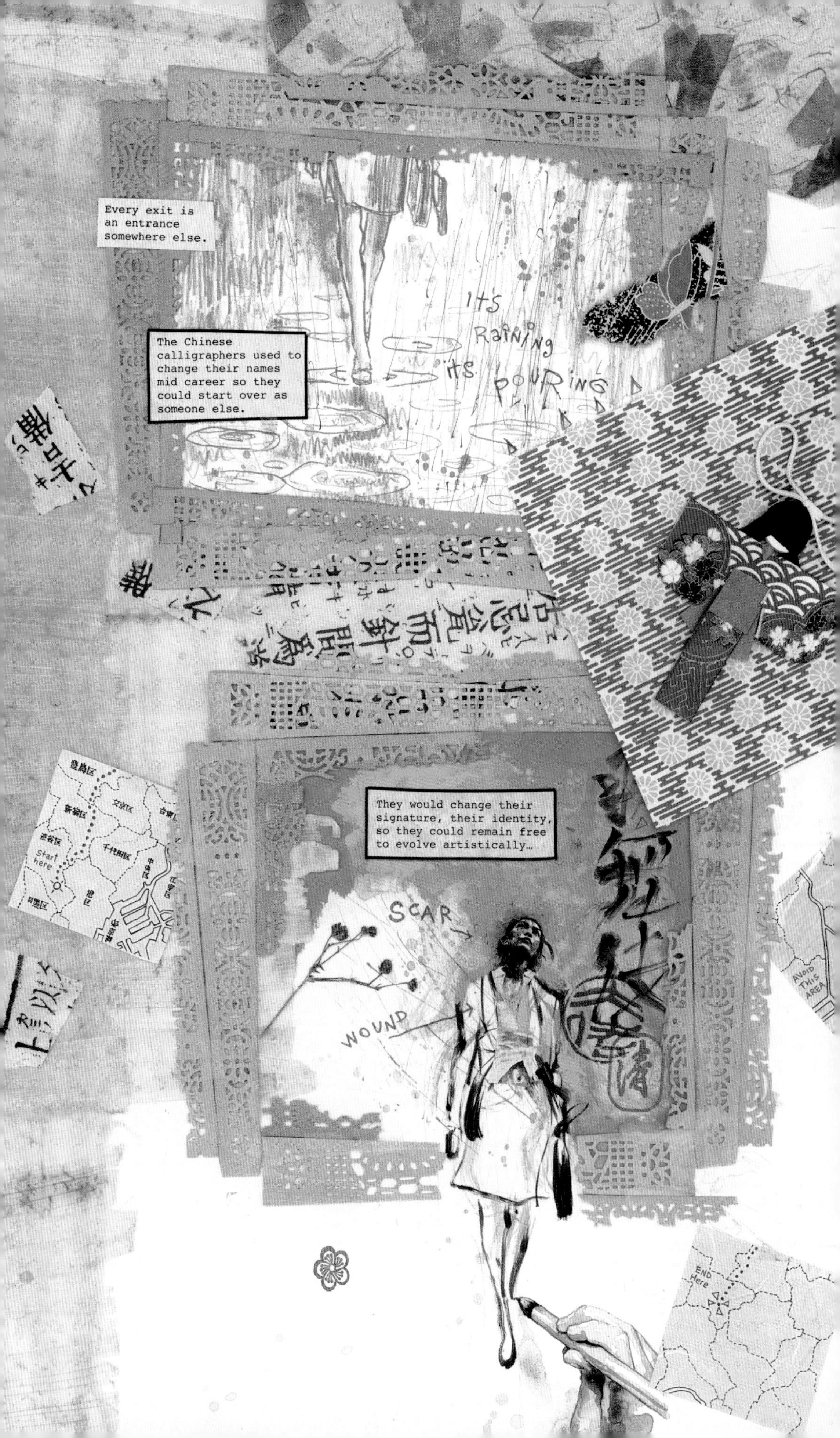
Every exit is an entrance somewhere else.
ITS RAINING ITS POURING
The Chinese calligraphers used to change their names mid career so they could start over as someone else.
Start here
They would change their signature, their identity, so they could remain free to evolve artistically…
SCAR
WOUND
AVOID THIS AREA
END Here

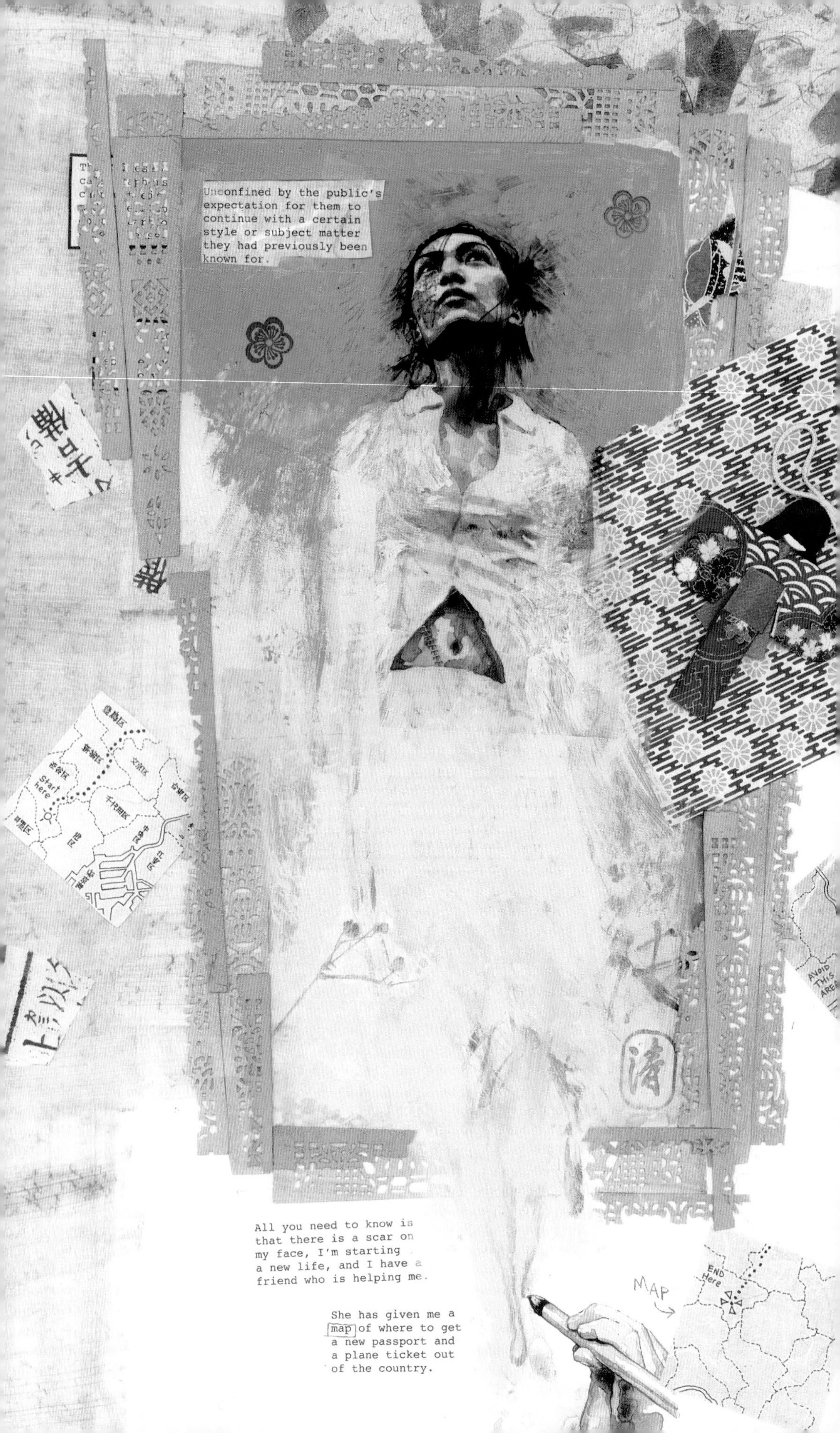

Unconfined by the public's expectation for them to continue with a certain style or subject matter they had previously been known for.
Start here
All you need to know is that there is a scar on my face, I'm starting a new life, and I have a friend who is helping me.
She has given me a map of where to get a new passport and a plane ticket out of the country.
MAP
END Here
AVOID THIS AREA

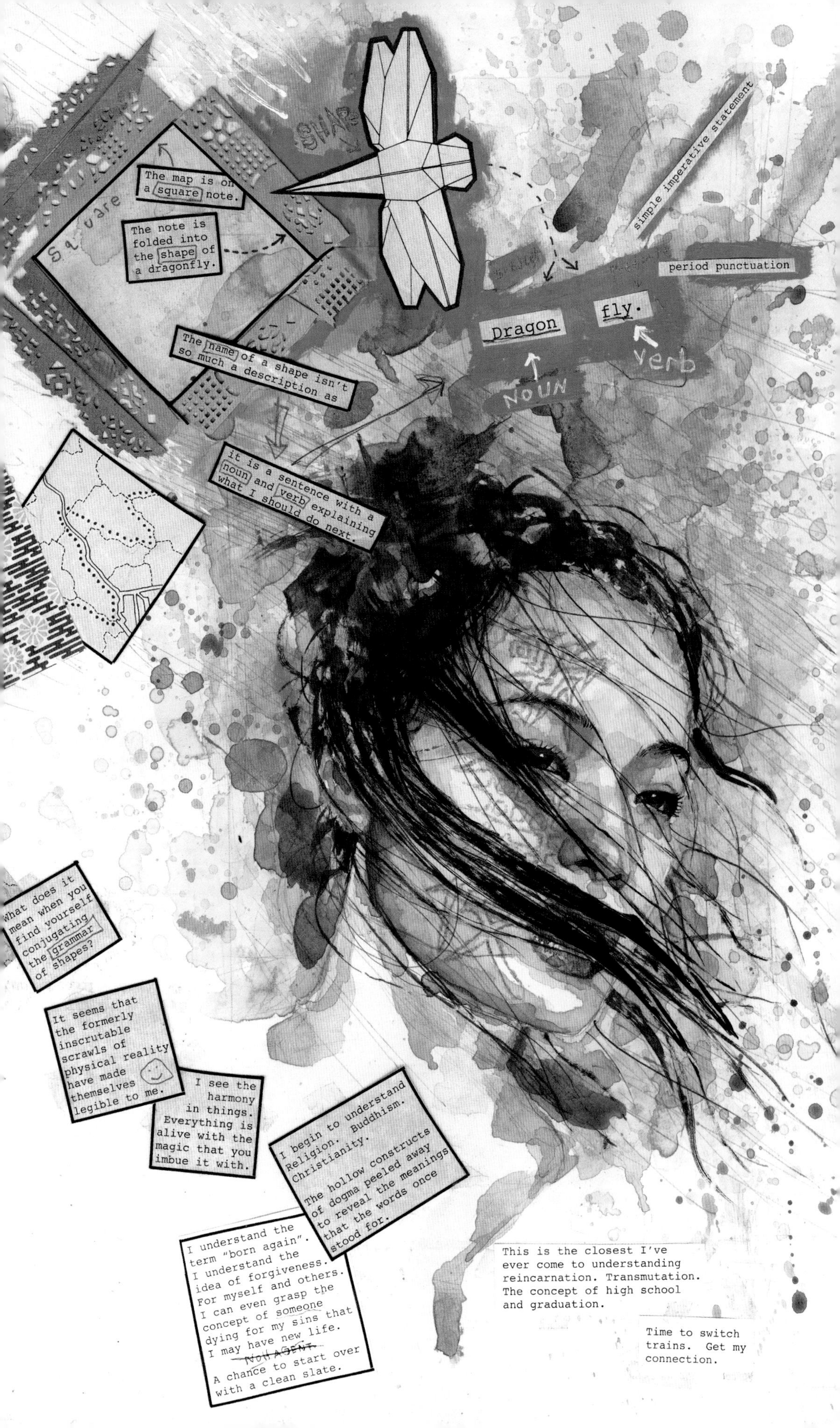

square
SHAPE
The map is on a square note.
The note is folded into the shape of a dragonfly.
The name of a shape isn't so much a description as
it is a sentence with a noun and verb explaining what I should do next.
simple imperative statement
period punctuation
Dragon fly.
NOUN
verb
What does it mean when you find yourself conjugating the grammar of shapes?
It seems that the formerly inscrutable scrawls of physical reality have made themselves legible to me.
I see the harmony in things. Everything is alive with the magic that you imbue it with.
I begin to understand Religion. Buddhism. Christianity.
The hollow constructs of dogma peeled away to reveal the meanings that the words once stood for.
I understand the term "born again". I understand the idea of forgiveness. For myself and others. I can even grasp the concept of someone dying for my sins that I may have new life.
A chance to start over with a clean slate.
This is the closest I've ever come to understanding reincarnation. Transmutation. The concept of high school and graduation.
Time to switch trains. Get my connection.

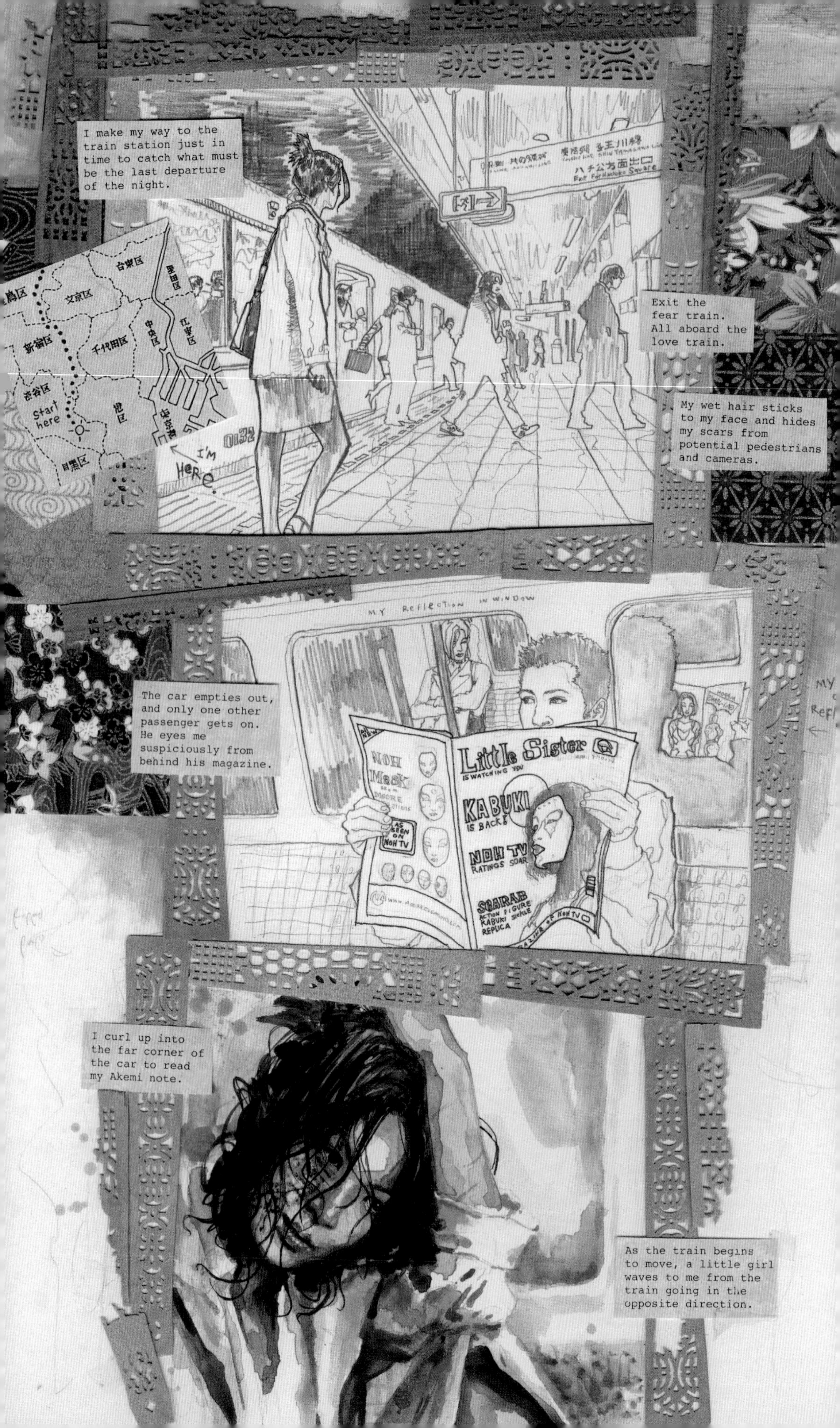
I make my way to the train station just in time to catch what must be the last departure of the night.
Start here
I'M HeRe
Exit the fear train. All aboard the love train.
My wet hair sticks to my face and hides my scars from potential pedestrians and cameras.
MY REFLECTION IN WINDOW
The car empties out, and only one other passenger gets on. He eyes me suspiciously from behind his magazine.
Little Sister IS WATCHING YOU
NOH Mask
AS SEEN ON NOH TV
KABUKI IS BACK!
NOH TV RATINGS SOAR
SCARAB ACTION FIGURE
I curl up into the far corner of the car to read my Akemi note.
As the train begins to move, a little girl waves to me from the train going in the opposite direction.

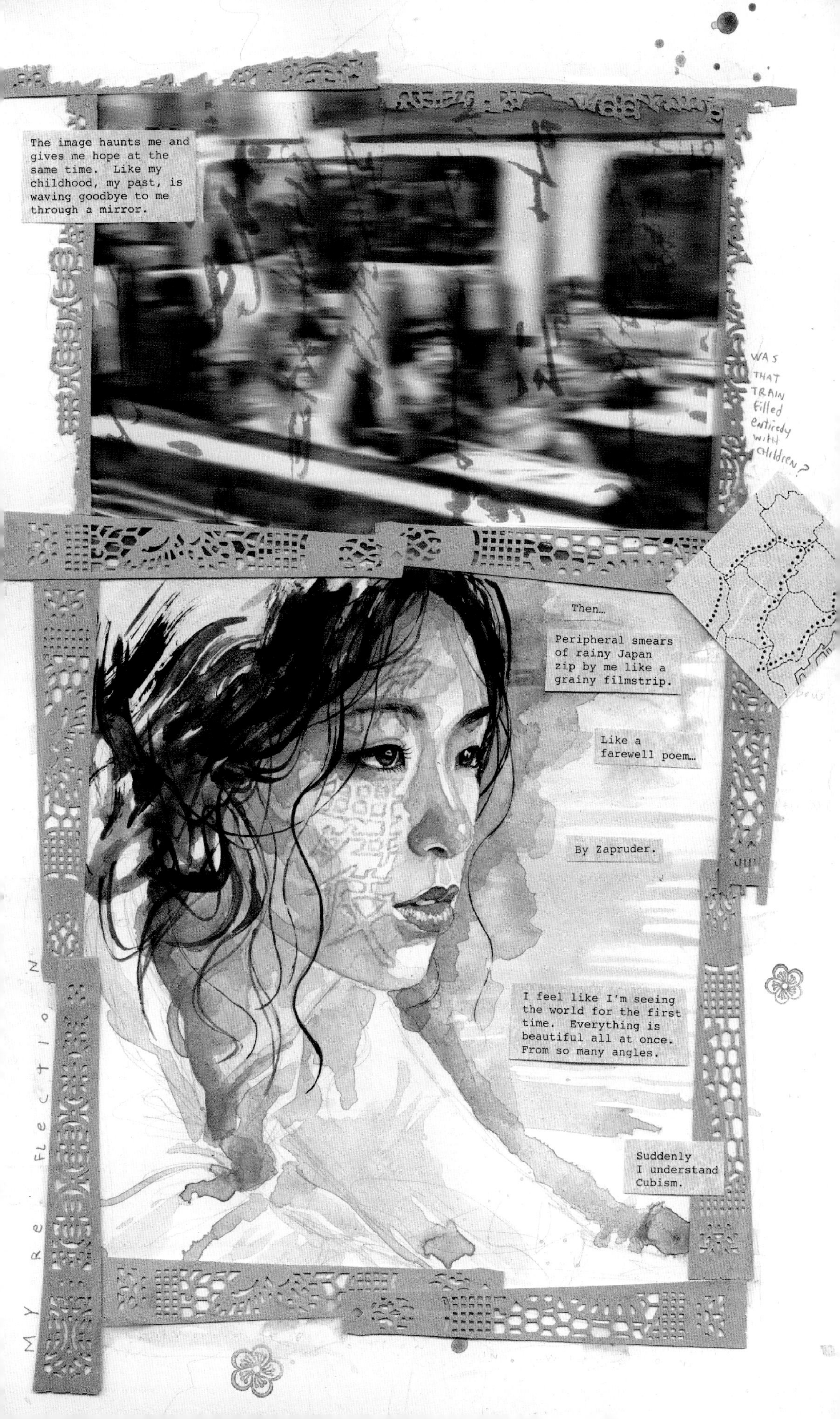
The image haunts me and gives me hope at the same time. Like my childhood, my past, is waving goodbye to me through a mirror.
WAS THAT TRAIN filled entirely with children?
Then...
Peripheral smears of rainy Japan zip by me like a grainy filmstrip.
Like a farewell poem...
By Zapruder.
I feel like I'm seeing the world for the first time. Everything is beautiful all at once. From so many angles.
Suddenly I understand Cubism.
MY REFLECTION

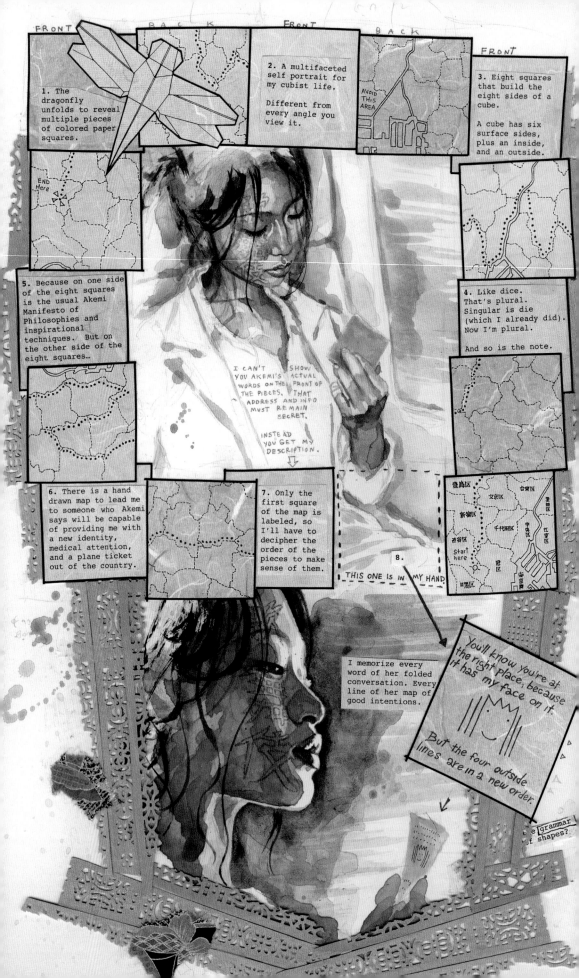

1. The dragonfly unfolds to reveal multiple pieces of colored paper squares.

2. A multifaceted self portrait for my cubist life.

Different from every angle you view it.

AVOID THIS AREA

3. Eight squares that build the eight sides of a cube.

A cube has six surface sides, plus an inside, and an outside.

END Here

5. Because on one side of the eight squares is the usual Akemi Manifesto of Philosophies and inspirational techniques. But on the other side of the eight squares...

I CAN'T SHOW YOU AKEMI'S ACTUAL WORDS ON THE FRONT OF THE PIECES, THAT ADDRESS AND INFO MUST REMAIN SECRET.

INSTEAD YOU GET MY DESCRIPTION.

4. Like dice. That's plural. Singular is die (which I already did). Now I'm plural.

And so is the note.

6. There is a hand drawn map to lead me to someone who Akemi says will be capable of providing me with a new identity, medical attention, and a plane ticket out of the country.

7. Only the first square of the map is labeled, so I'll have to decipher the order of the pieces to make sense of them.

8.

THIS ONE IS IN MY HAND

豊島区 文京区 台東区
新宿区   墨田区
千代田区 中央区 江東区
渋谷区
          港区 Start here
目黒区

I memorize every word of her folded conversation. Every line of her map of good intentions.

You'll know you're at the right place, because it has my face on it.

But the four outside lines are in a new order.

e grammar f shapes?

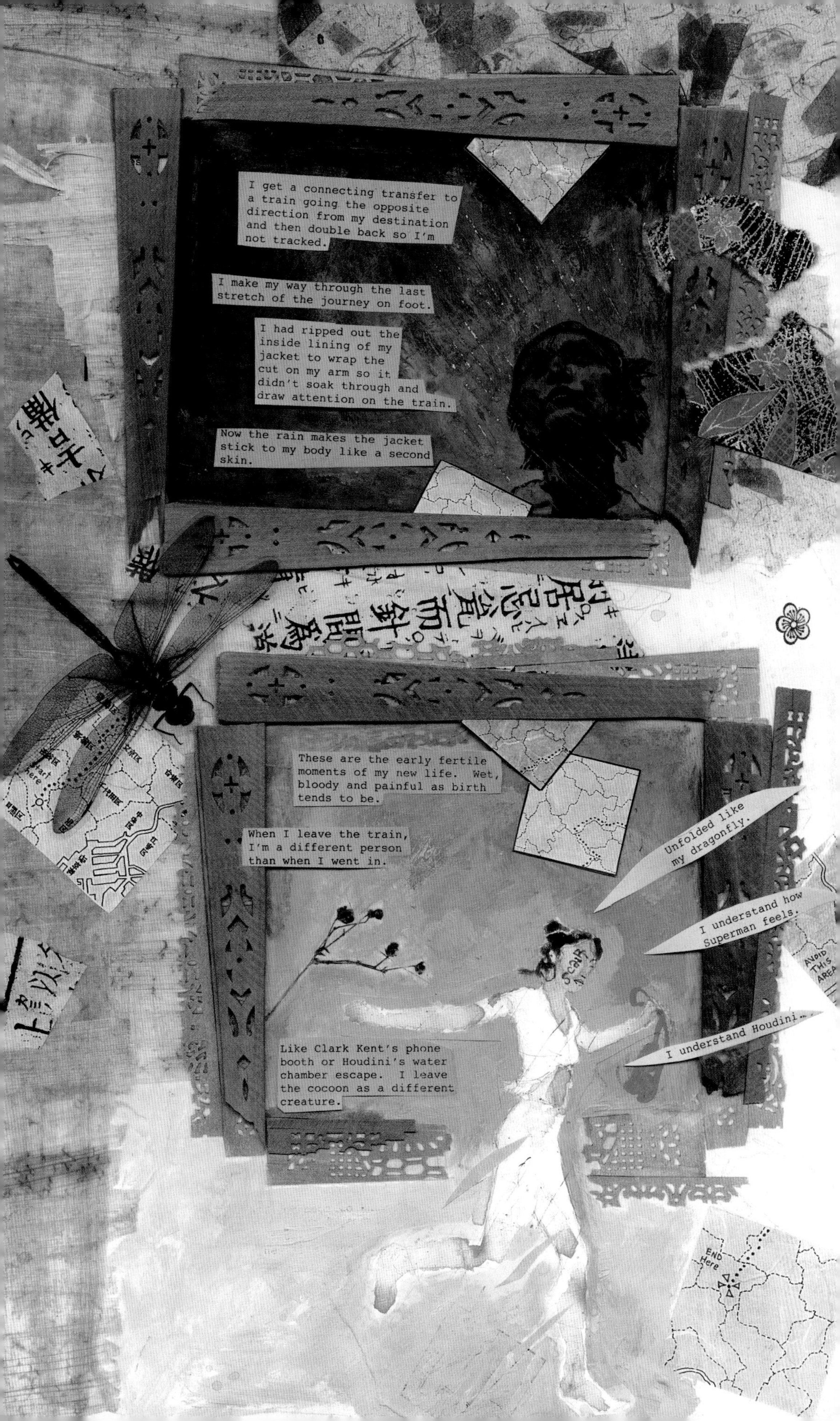
I get a connecting transfer to a train going the opposite direction from my destination and then double back so I'm not tracked.
I make my way through the last stretch of the journey on foot.
I had ripped out the inside lining of my jacket to wrap the cut on my arm so it didn't soak through and draw attention on the train.
Now the rain makes the jacket stick to my body like a second skin.
These are the early fertile moments of my new life. Wet, bloody and painful as birth tends to be.
When I leave the train, I'm a different person than when I went in.
Unfolded like my dragonfly.
I understand how Superman feels.
AVOID THIS AREA
Like Clark Kent's phone booth or Houdini's water chamber escape. I leave the cocoon as a different creature.
I understand Houdini...
END Here

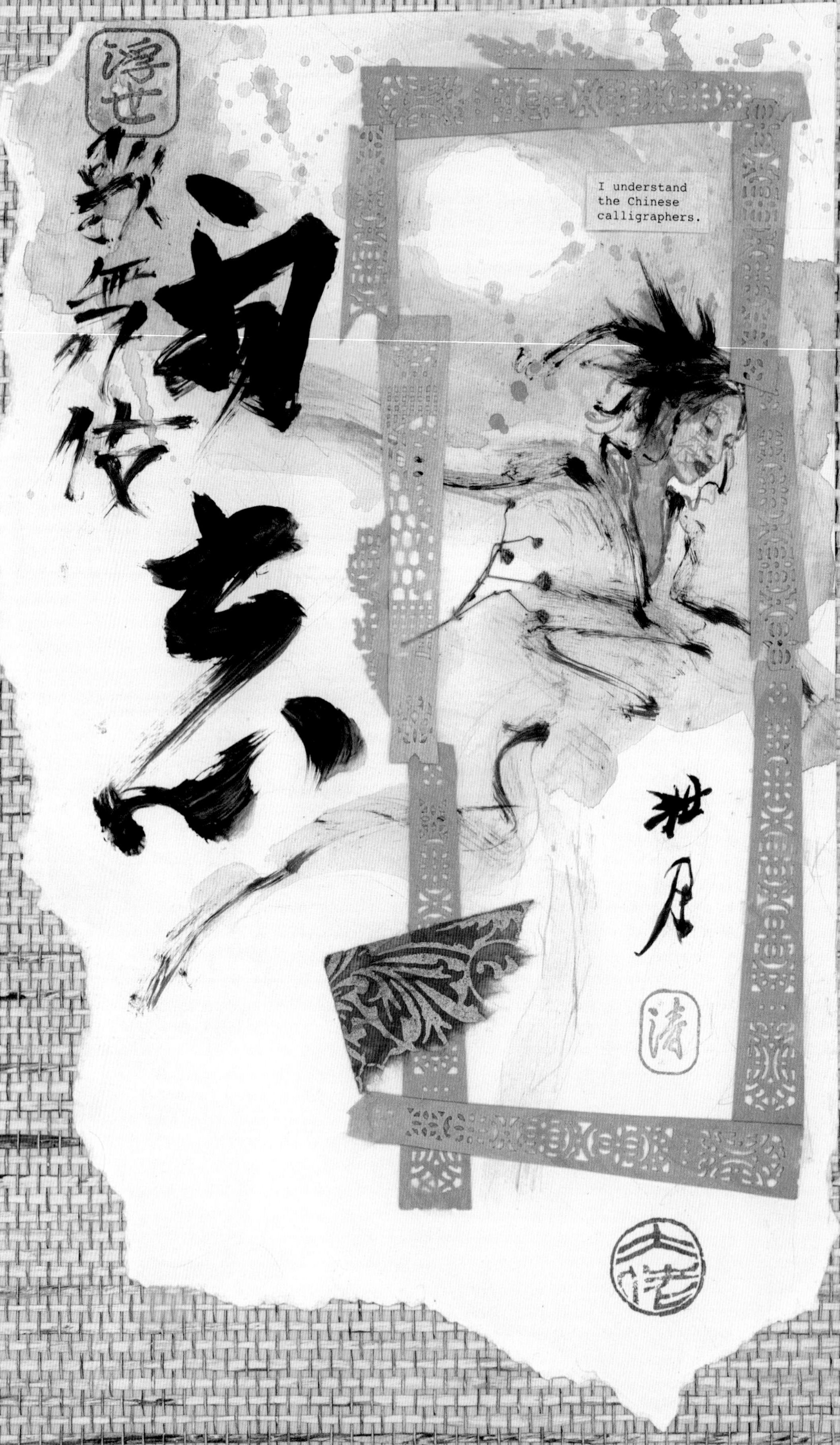
I understand the Chinese calligraphers.

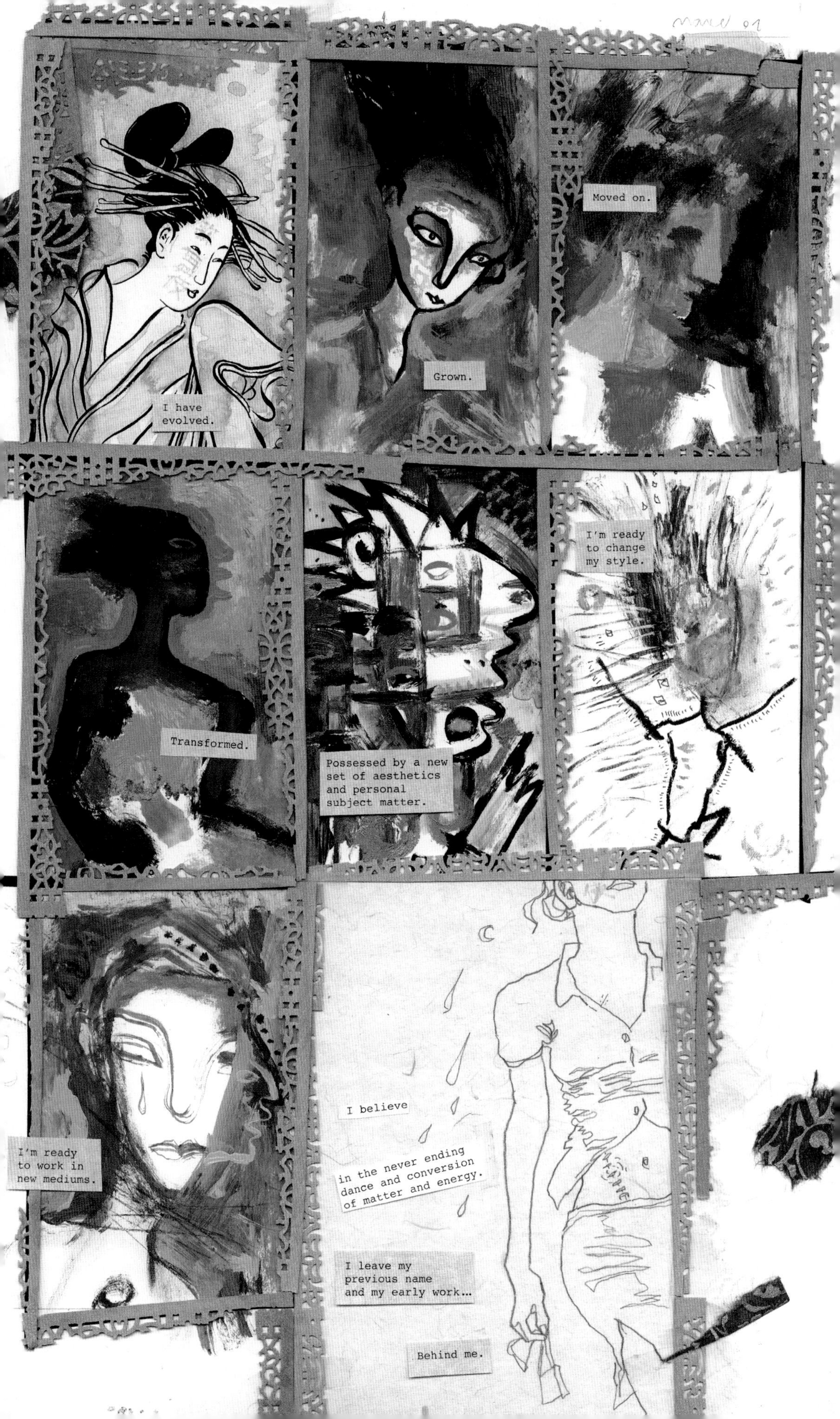
I have evolved.
Grown.
Moved on.
Transformed.
Possessed by a new set of aesthetics and personal subject matter.
I'm ready to change my style.
I'm ready to work in new mediums.
I believe
in the never ending dance and conversion of matter and energy.
I leave my previous name and my early work...
Behind me.

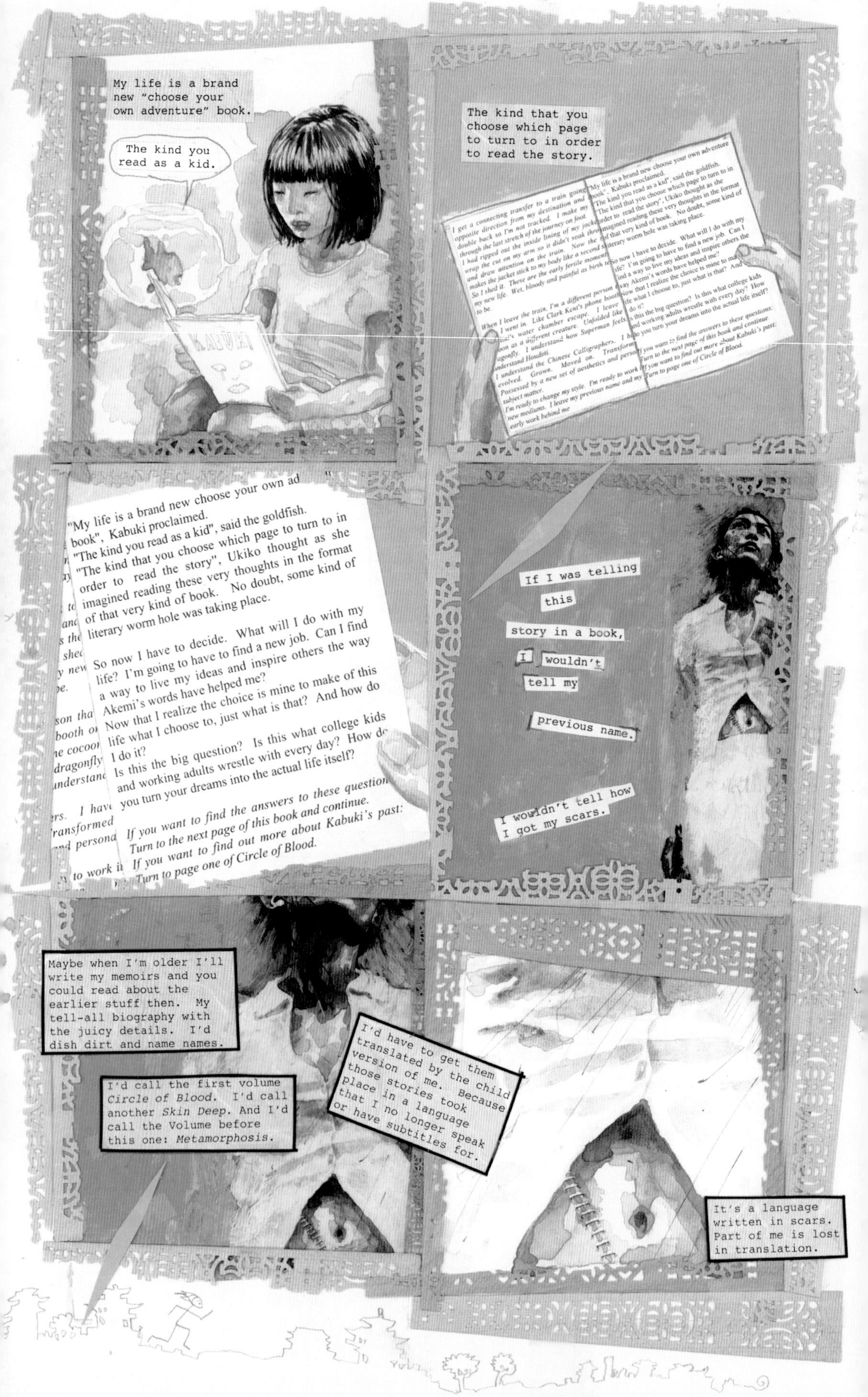

My life is a brand new "choose your own adventure" book.
The kind you read as a kid.
The kind that you choose which page to turn to in order to read the story.
"My life is a brand new choose your own ad book", Kabuki proclaimed.
"The kind you read as a kid", said the goldfish.
"The kind that you choose which page to turn to in order to read the story", Ukiko thought as she imagined reading these very thoughts in the format of that very kind of book. No doubt, some kind of literary worm hole was taking place.
So now I have to decide. What will I do with my life? I'm going to have to find a new job. Can I find a way to live my ideas and inspire others the way Akemi's words have helped me?
Now that I realize the choice is mine to make of this life what I choose to, just what is that? And how do I do it?
Is this the big question? Is this what college kids and working adults wrestle with every day? How do you turn your dreams into the actual life itself?
If you want to find the answers to these question
Turn to the next page of this book and continue.
If you want to find out more about Kabuki's past:
Turn to page one of Circle of Blood.
If I was telling this story in a book, I wouldn't tell my previous name.
I wouldn't tell how I got my scars.
Maybe when I'm older I'll write my memoirs and you could read about the earlier stuff then. My tell-all biography with the juicy details. I'd dish dirt and name names.
I'd call the first volume *Circle of Blood*. I'd call another *Skin Deep*. And I'd call the Volume before this one: *Metamorphosis*.
I'd have to get them translated by the child version of me. Because those stories took place in a language that I no longer speak or have subtitles for.
It's a language written in scars. Part of me is lost in translation.

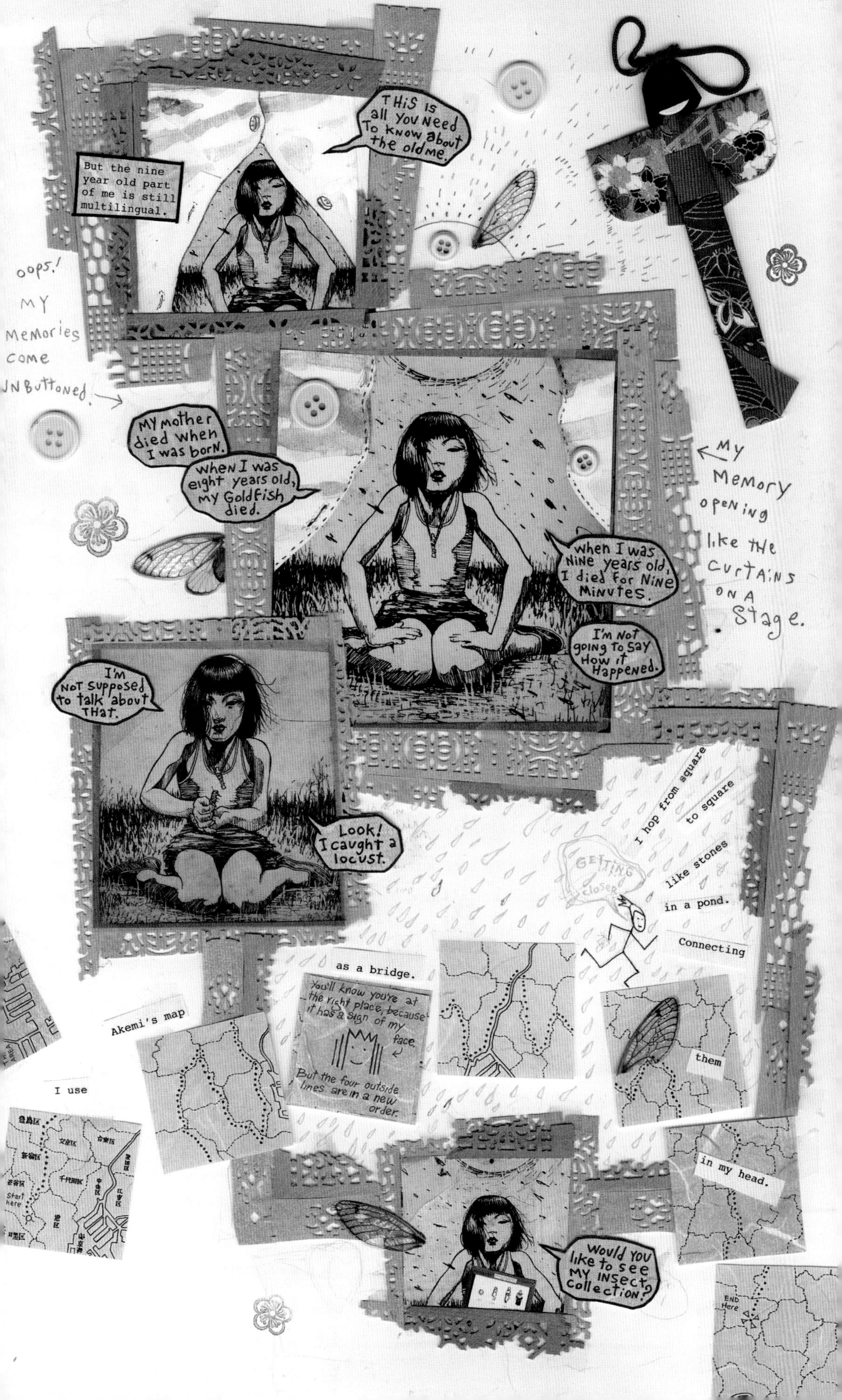
THIS is all you Need To know about the old me.
But the nine year old part of me is still multilingual.
oops.! My memories come unbuttoned.
My mother died when I was born.
when I was eight years old, my Goldfish died.
when I was Nine years old, I died for Nine Minutes.
I'm Not going to say How it Happened.
My memory opening like the curtains on a stage.
I'm Not supposed to talk about THaT.
Look! I caught a locust.
I hop from square
to square
like stones
in a pond.
GETTING closer
Connecting
as a bridge.
Akemi's map
You'll know you're at the right place, because it has a sign of my face.
But the four outside lines are in a new order.
them
I use
in my head.
Start here
END Here
Would you like to see my insect collection?

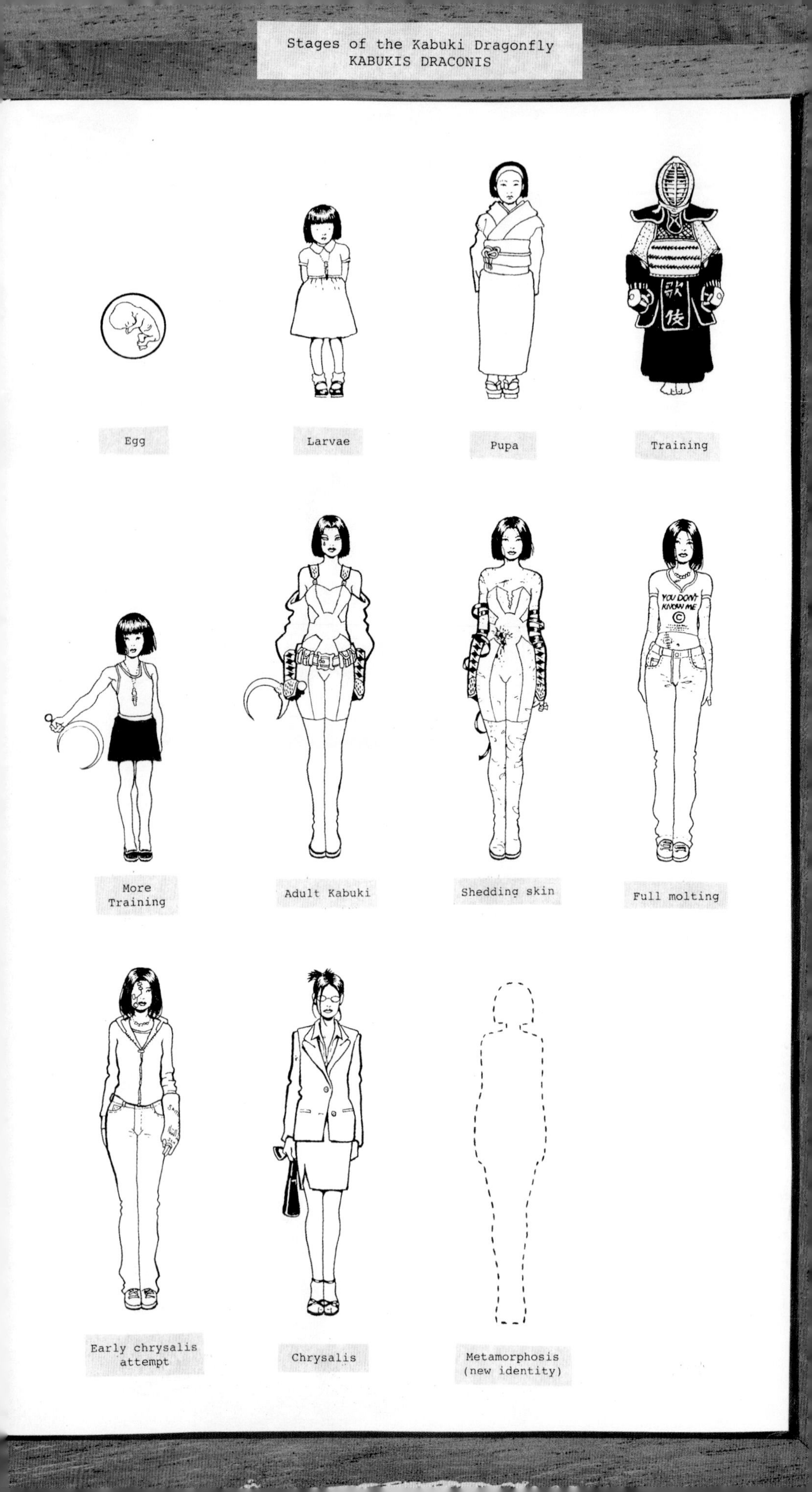
Stages of the Kabuki Dragonfly
KABUKIS DRACONIS
歌
伎
Egg
Larvae
Pupa
Training
YOU DON'T KNOW ME
©
More Training
Adult Kabuki
Shedding skin
Full molting
Early chrysalis attempt
Chrysalis
Metamorphosis (new identity)

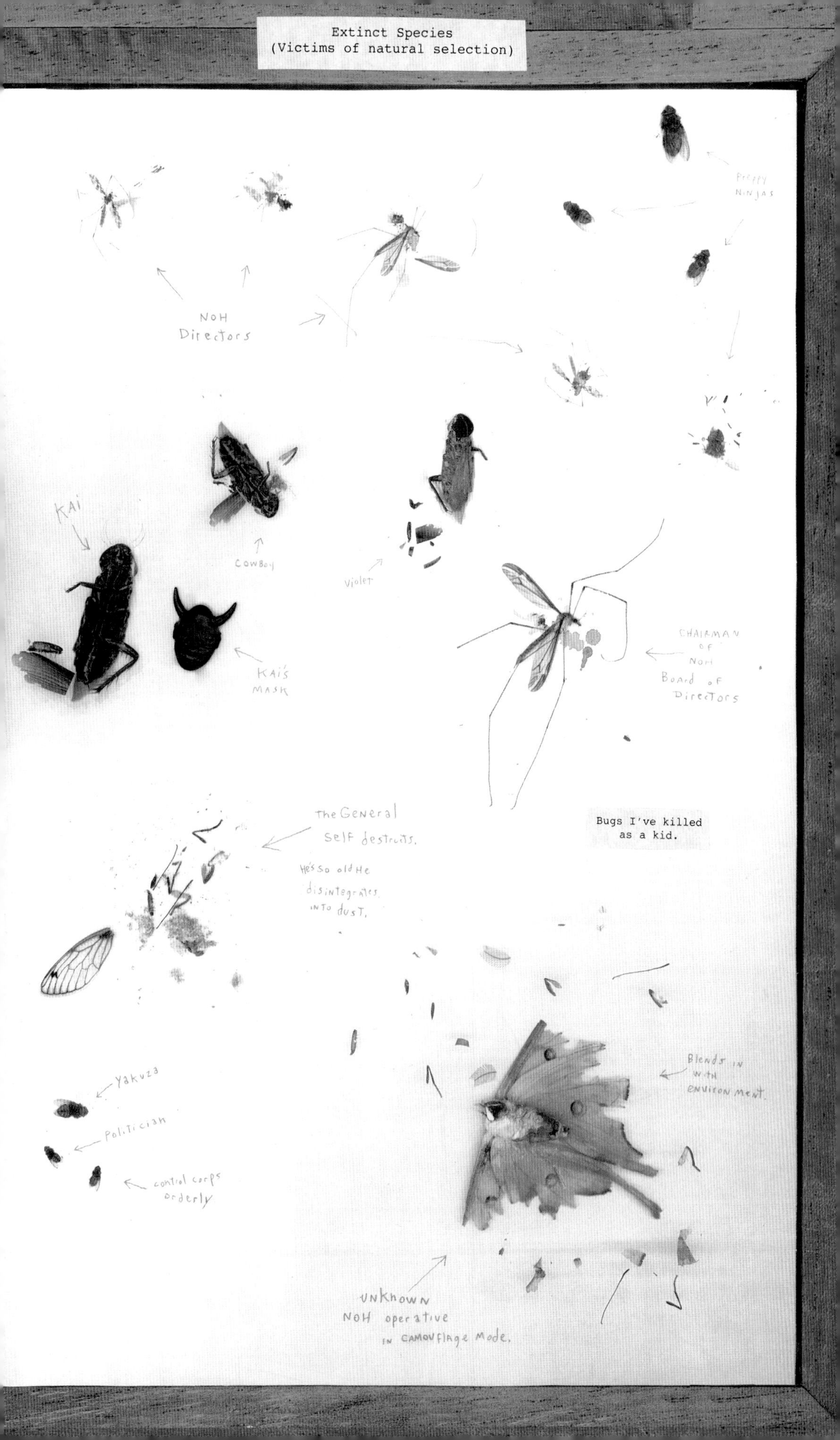

Extinct Species
(Victims of natural selection)
Pretty Ninjas
NOH Directors
KAI
COWBOY
Violet
KAI'S MASK
CHAIRMAN of NOH Board of Directors
The General self destructs.
He's so old He disintegrates into dust.
Bugs I've killed as a kid.
Yakuza
Politician
control corps orderly
Blends in with environment.
UNKNOWN NOH operative in CAMOUFLAGE Mode.

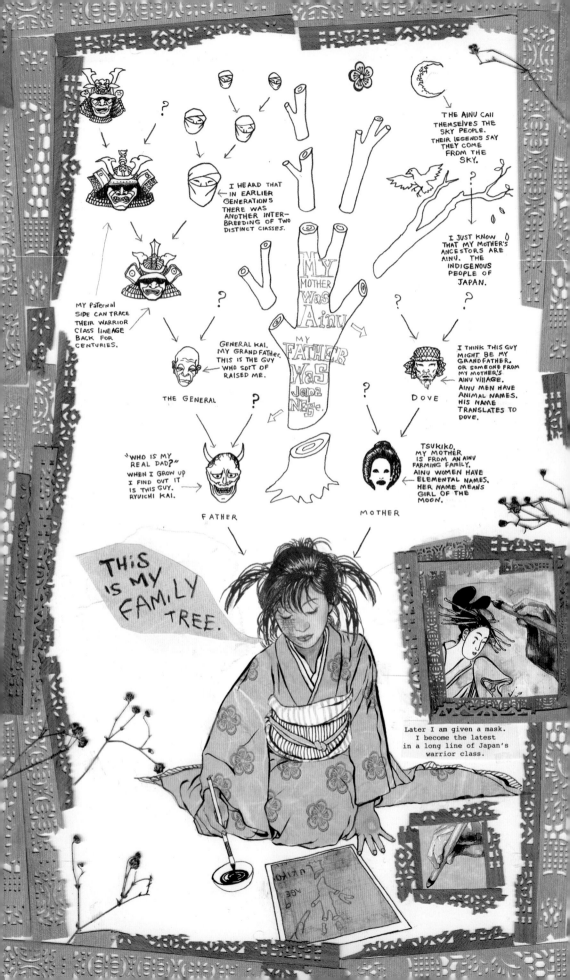

THE AINU CALL THEMSELVES THE SKY PEOPLE. THEIR LEGENDS SAY THEY COME FROM THE SKY.

I HEARD THAT IN EARLIER GENERATIONS THERE WAS ANOTHER INTER-BREEDING OF TWO DISTINCT CLASSES.

I JUST KNOW THAT MY MOTHER'S ANCESTORS ARE AINU. THE INDIGENOUS PEOPLE OF JAPAN.

MY PATERNAL SIDE CAN TRACE THEIR WARRIOR CLASS LINEAGE BACK FOR CENTURIES.

MY MOTHER WAS Ainu
MY FATHER WaS JapaNESe.

GENERAL KAI. MY GRANDFATHER. THIS IS THE GUY WHO SORT OF RAISED ME.

THE GENERAL

I THINK THIS GUY MIGHT BE MY GRANDFATHER. OR SOMEONE FROM MY MOTHER'S AINU VILLAGE. AINU MEN HAVE ANIMAL NAMES. HIS NAME TRANSLATES TO DOVE.

DOVE

"WHO IS MY REAL DAD?" WHEN I GROW UP I FIND OUT IT IS THIS GUY. RYUICHI KAI.

FATHER

TSUKIKO. MY MOTHER IS FROM AN AINU FARMING FAMILY. AINU WOMEN HAVE ELEMENTAL NAMES. HER NAME MEANS GIRL OF THE MOON.

MOTHER

THIS IS MY FAMILY TREE.

Later I am given a mask. I become the latest in a long line of Japan's warrior class.

The evolution of JAPAN'S WARRIOR CLASS

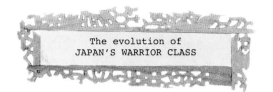

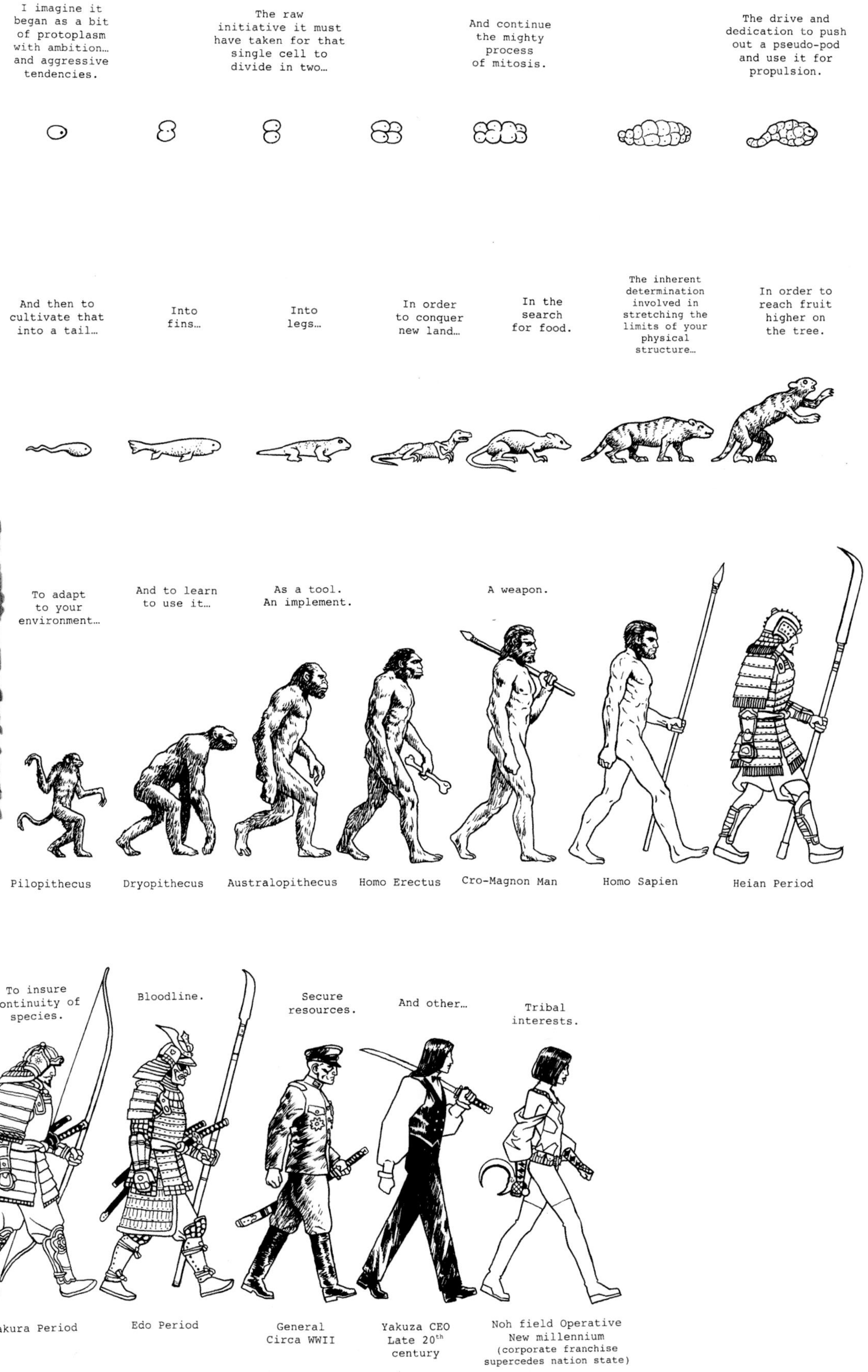
I imagine it began as a bit of protoplasm with ambition... and aggressive tendencies.
The raw initiative it must have taken for that single cell to divide in two...
And continue the mighty process of mitosis.
The drive and dedication to push out a pseudo-pod and use it for propulsion.
And then to cultivate that into a tail...
Into fins...
Into legs...
In order to conquer new land...
In the search for food.
The inherent determination involved in stretching the limits of your physical structure...
In order to reach fruit higher on the tree.
To adapt to your environment...
And to learn to use it...
As a tool. An implement.
A weapon.
Pilopithecus
Dryopithecus
Australopithecus
Homo Erectus
Cro-Magnon Man
Homo Sapien
Heian Period
To insure continuity of species.
Bloodline.
Secure resources.
And other...
Tribal interests.
Kamakura Period
Edo Period
General Circa WWII
Yakuza CEO Late 20th century
Noh field Operative New millennium (corporate franchise supercedes nation state)

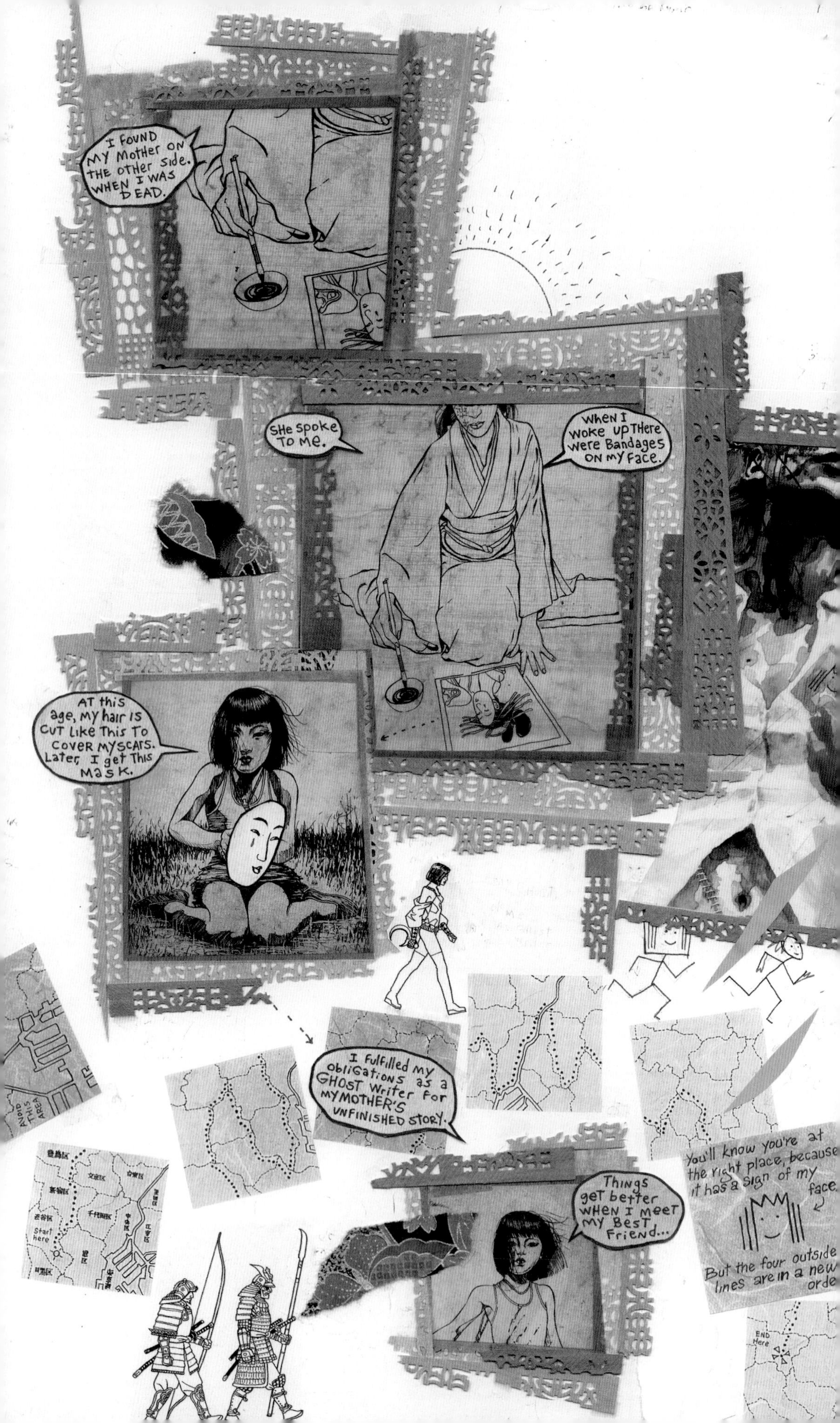
I FOUND MY Mother ON THE other side. WHEN I WAS DEAD.
SHe spoke TO me.
WHEN I woke up There were Bandages ON MY Face.
AT this age, my hair is cut like This To cover myscars. Later, I get This MASK.
AVOID THIS AREA
I fulfilled my obligations as a GHOST Writer for MY MOTHER'S UNFINISHED STORY.
Start here
Things get better WHEN I MEET MY BEST Friend...
You'll know you're at the right place, because it has a sign of my face.
But the four outside lines are in a new orde
END Here

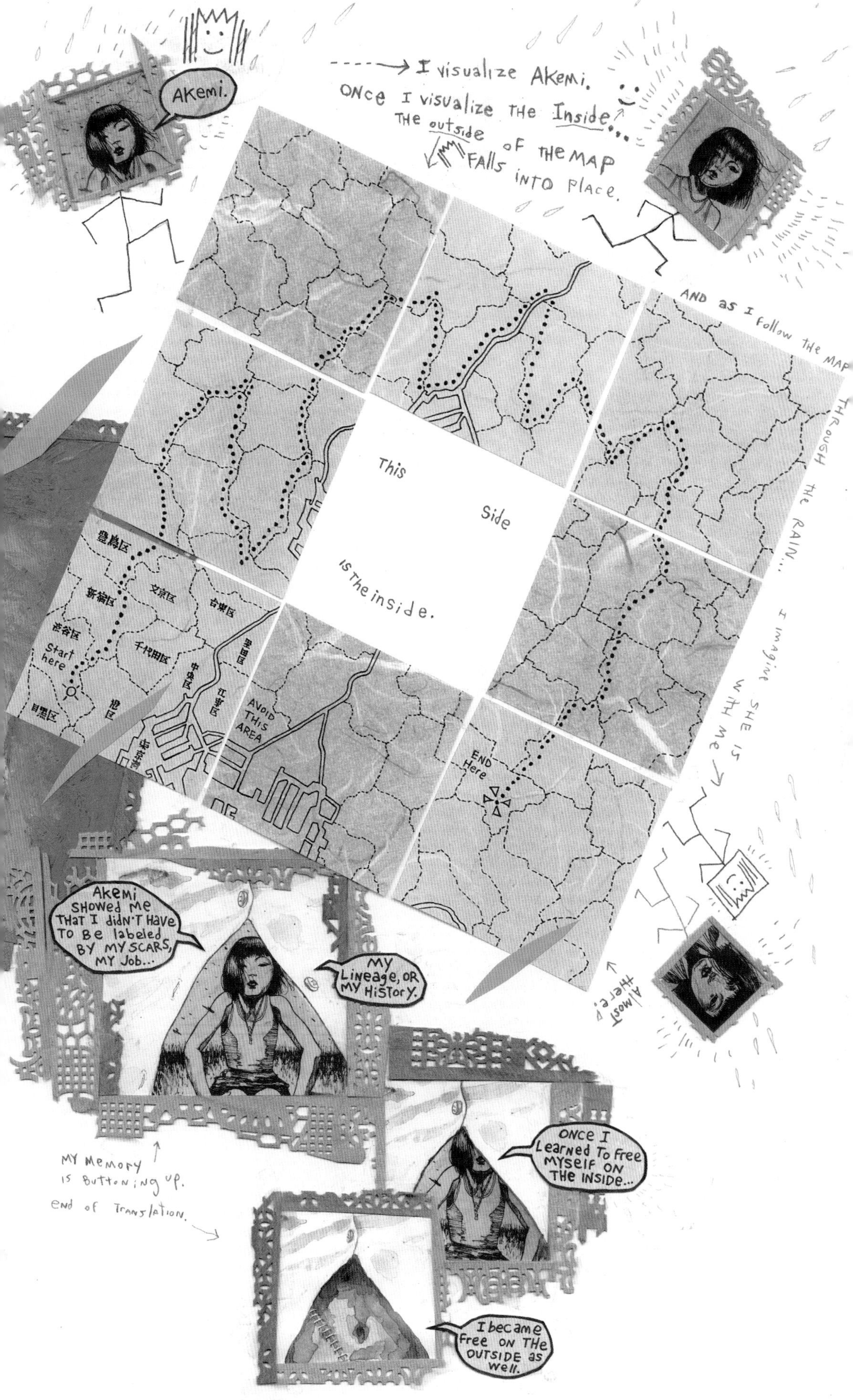
Akemi.
I visualize Akemi.
Once I visualize the Inside...
The outside of the map falls into place.
And as I follow the map through the rain...
This side is the inside.
豊島区
新宿区
文京区
台東区
渋谷区
千代田区
墨田区
中央区
江東区
港区
目黒区
Start here
AVOID THIS AREA
END Here
I imagine she is with me
Almost there!
Akemi showed me that I didn't have to be labeled by my scars, my job...
My lineage, or my history.
My memory is buttoning up.
end of translation.
Once I learned to free myself on the inside...
I became free on the outside as well.

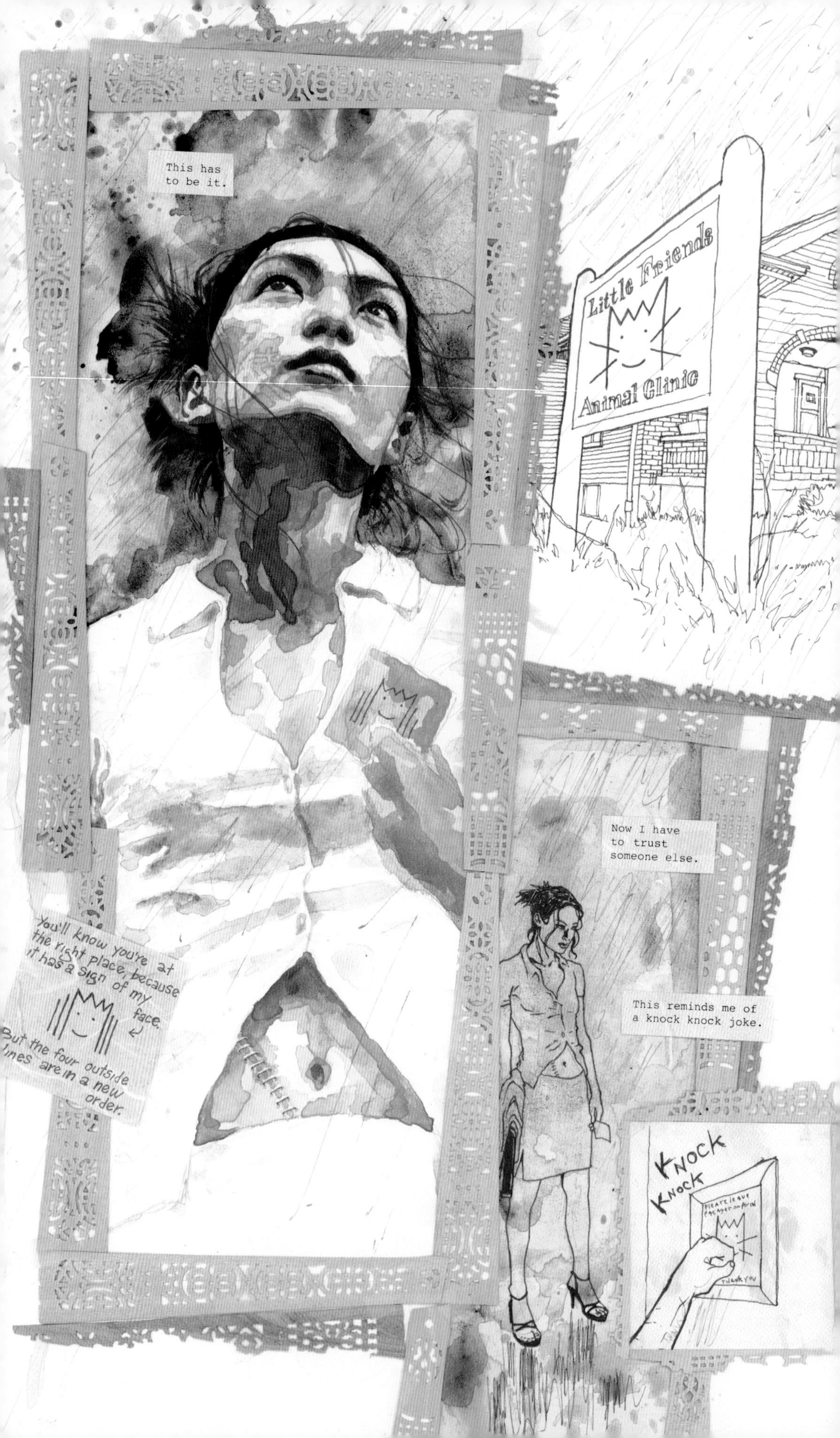
This has to be it.
Little Friends Animal Clinic
You'll know you're at the right place, because it has a sign of my face.
But the four outside lines are in a new order.
Now I have to trust someone else.
This reminds me of a knock knock joke.
KNOCK KNOCK

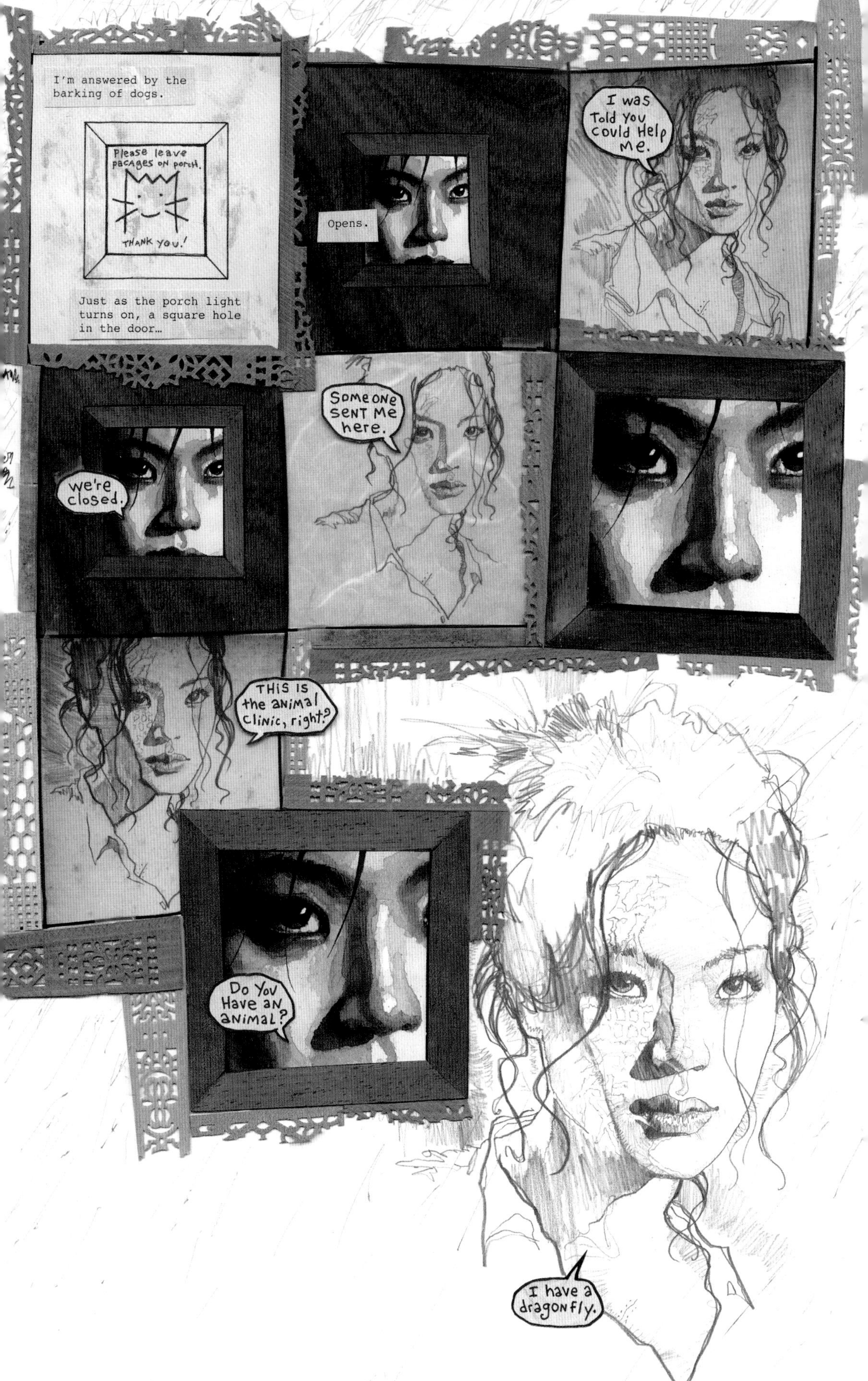
I'm answered by the barking of dogs.
Please leave pacages on porch.
THANK YOU!
Just as the porch light turns on, a square hole in the door…
Opens.
I was Told you could Help me.
we're closed.
Someone sent me here.
THIS is the animal clinic, right?
Do You Have an animal?
I have a dragonfly.

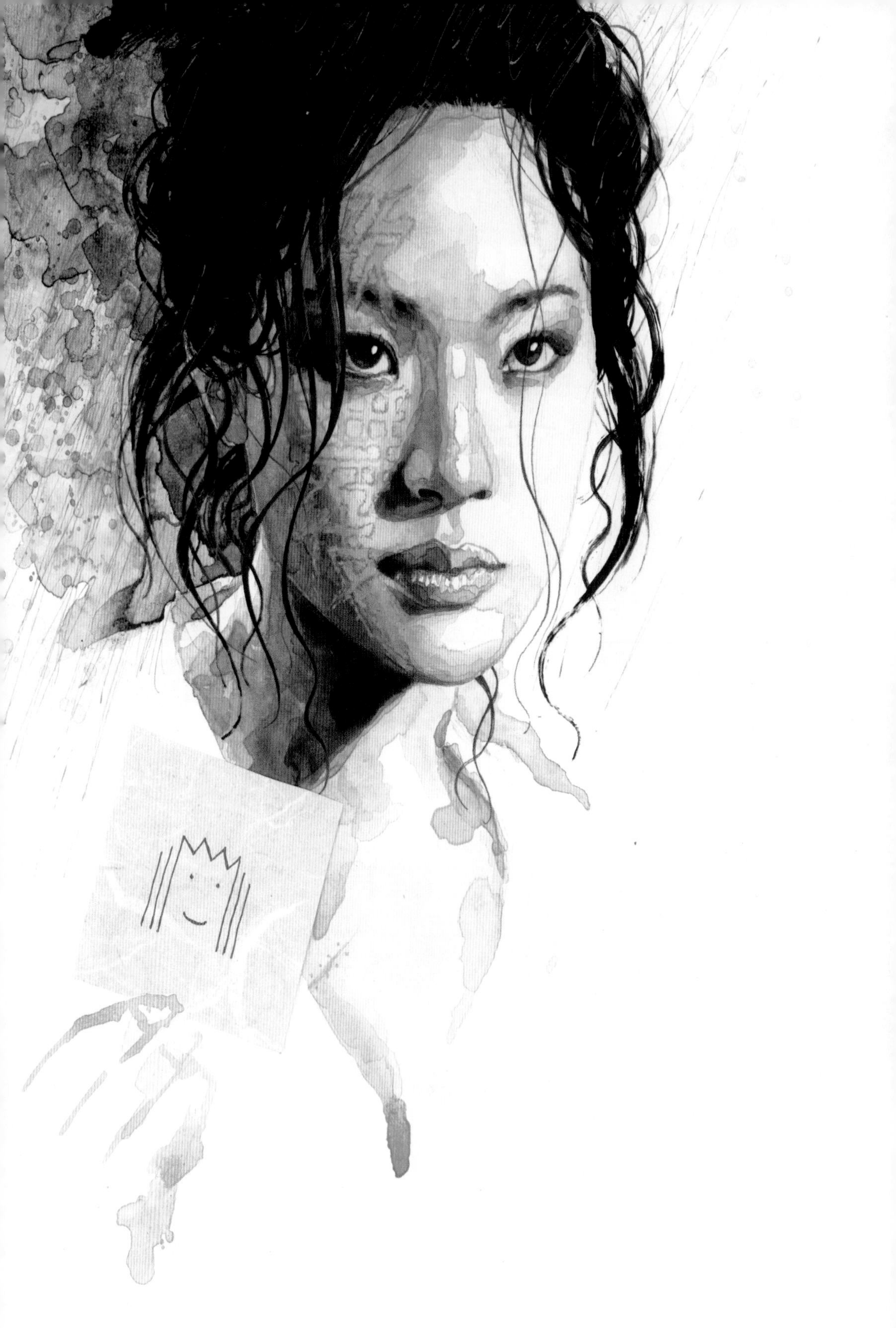

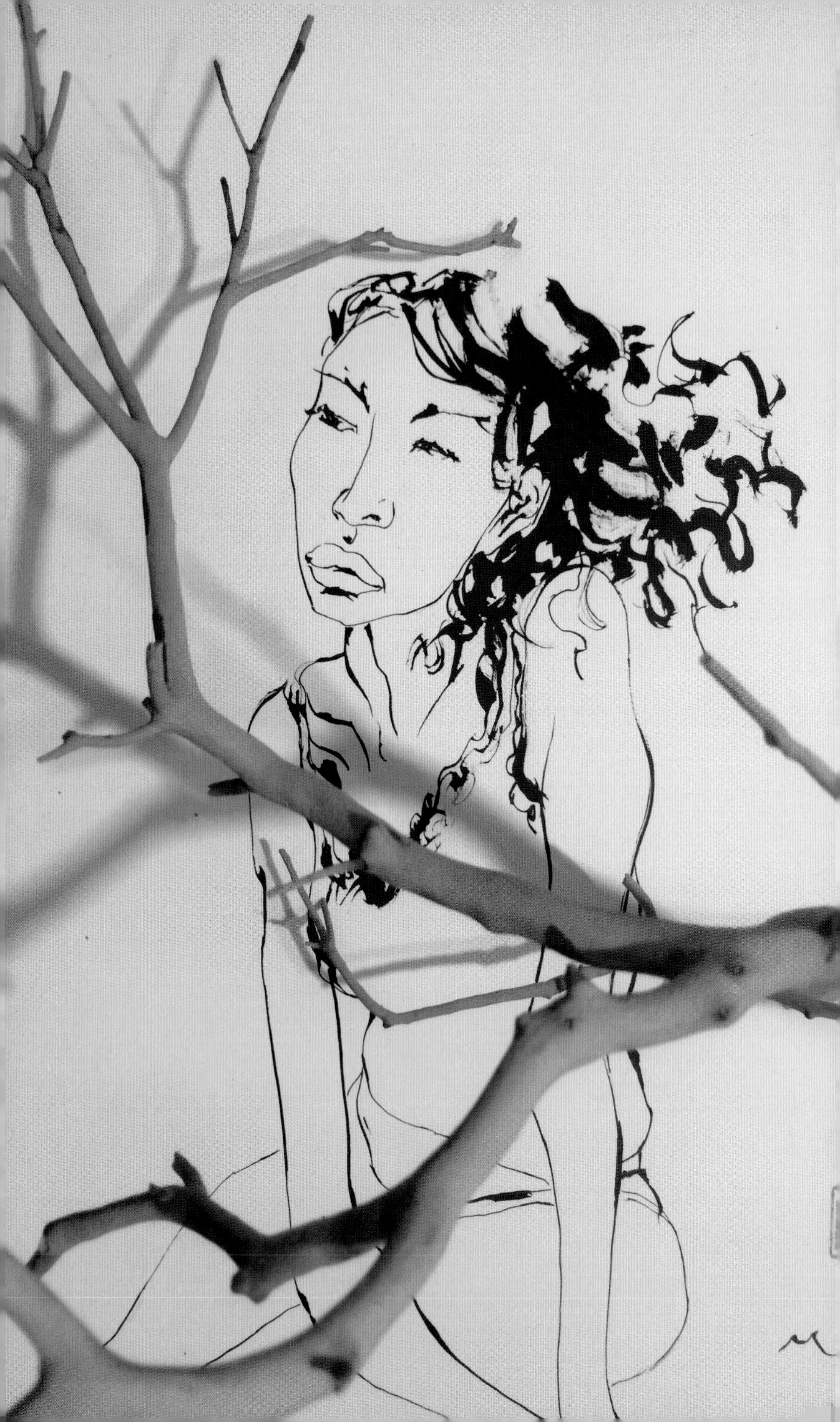

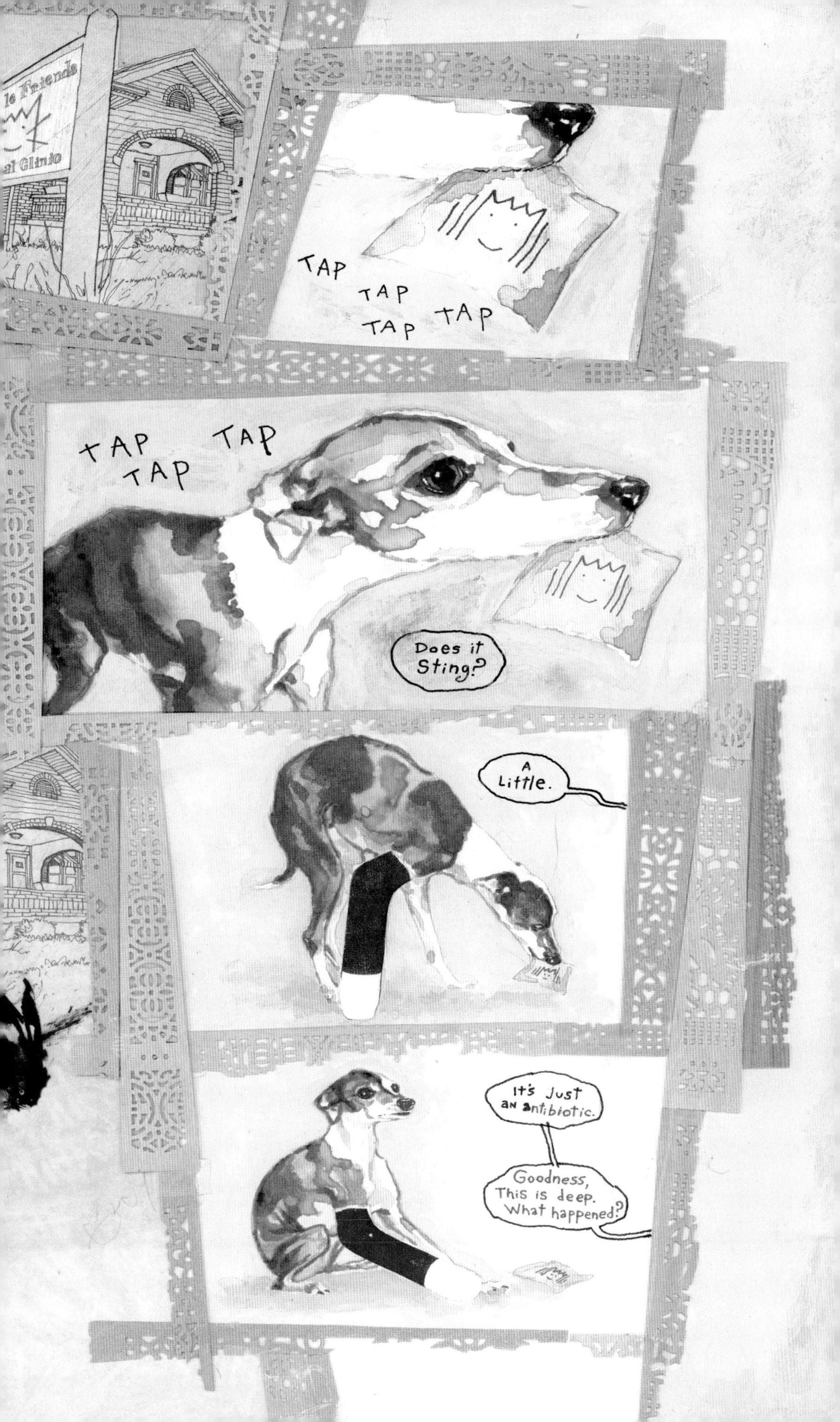

...le Friends
...al Clinic
TAP TAP TAP TAP
TAP TAP TAP
Does it Sting?
A Little.
It's Just an antibiotic.
Goodness, This is deep. What happened?

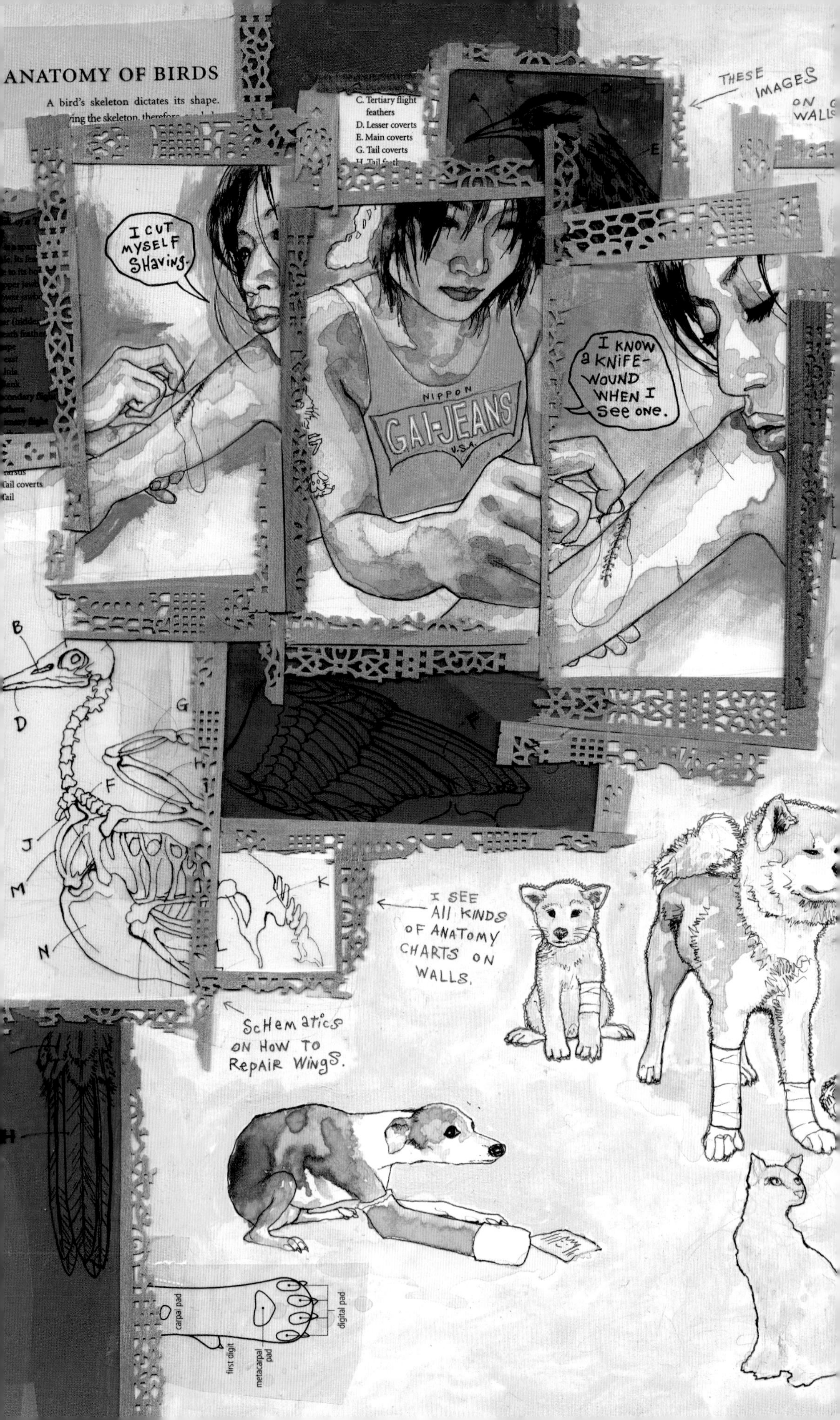

ANATOMY OF BIRDS
A bird's skeleton dictates its shape.
C. Tertiary flight feathers
D. Lesser coverts
E. Main coverts
G. Tail coverts
THESE IMAGES ON WALLS
I CUT MYSELF SHAVING.
NIPPON
GAI-JEANS
U.S.A.
I KNOW A KNIFE-WOUND WHEN I SEE ONE.
I SEE ALL KINDS OF ANATOMY CHARTS ON WALLS.
SCHEMATICS ON HOW TO REPAIR WINGS.
carpal pad
digital pad
first digit
metacarpal pad

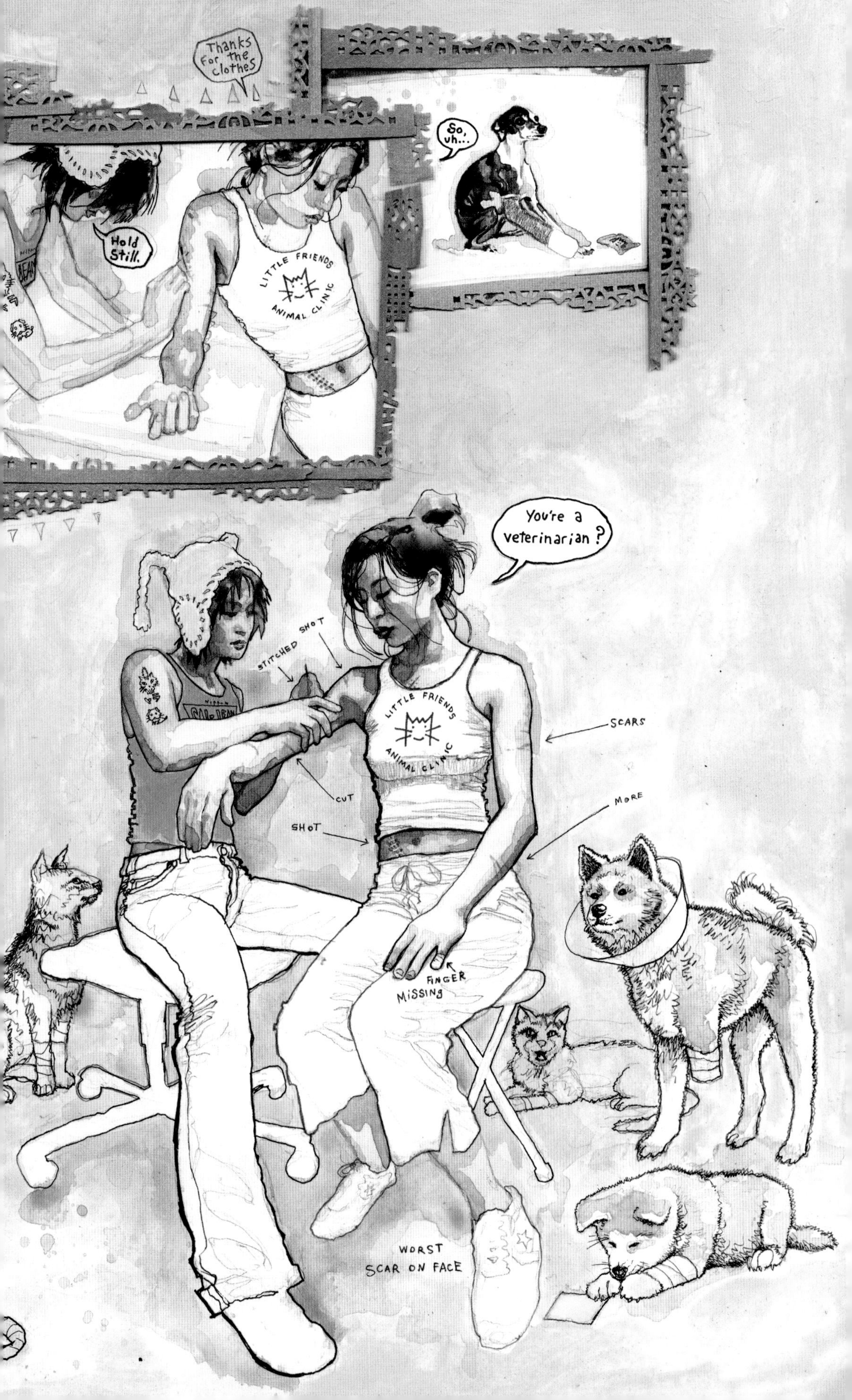

Thanks for the clothes
Hold Still.
LITTLE FRIENDS ANIMAL CLINIC
So, uh...
You're a veterinarian?
STITCHED
SHOT
LITTLE FRIENDS ANIMAL CLINIC
SCARS
CUT
SHOT
MORE
FINGER MISSING
WORST SCAR ON FACE

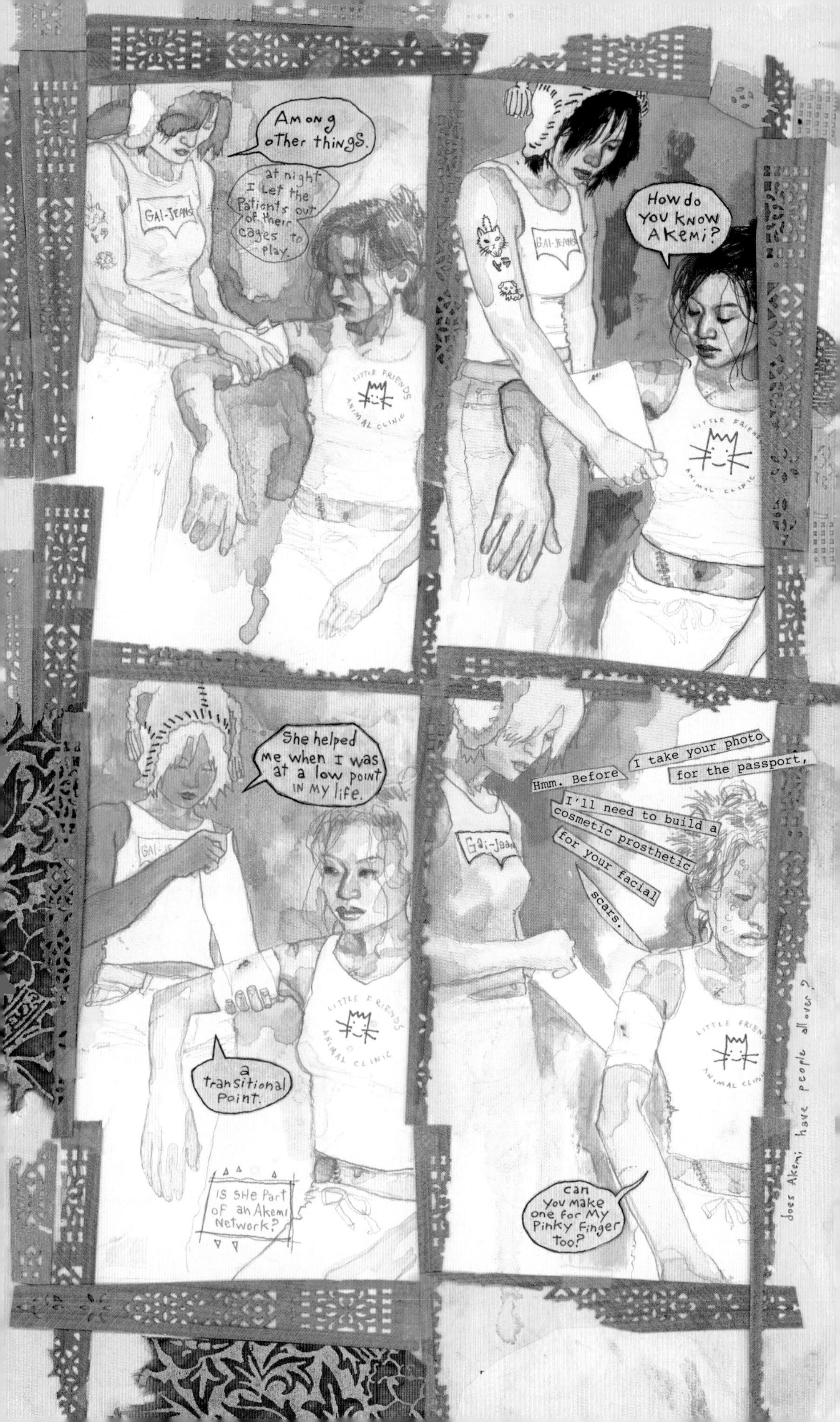

Among other things.
at night I let the Patients out of their cages to play.
How do you know Akemi?
She helped me when I was at a low point in my life.
a transitional Point.
Is she Part of an Akemi Network?
Hmm. Before I take your photo for the passport,
I'll need to build a cosmetic prosthetic for your facial scars.
can you make one for my Pinky Finger too?
does Akemi have people all over?

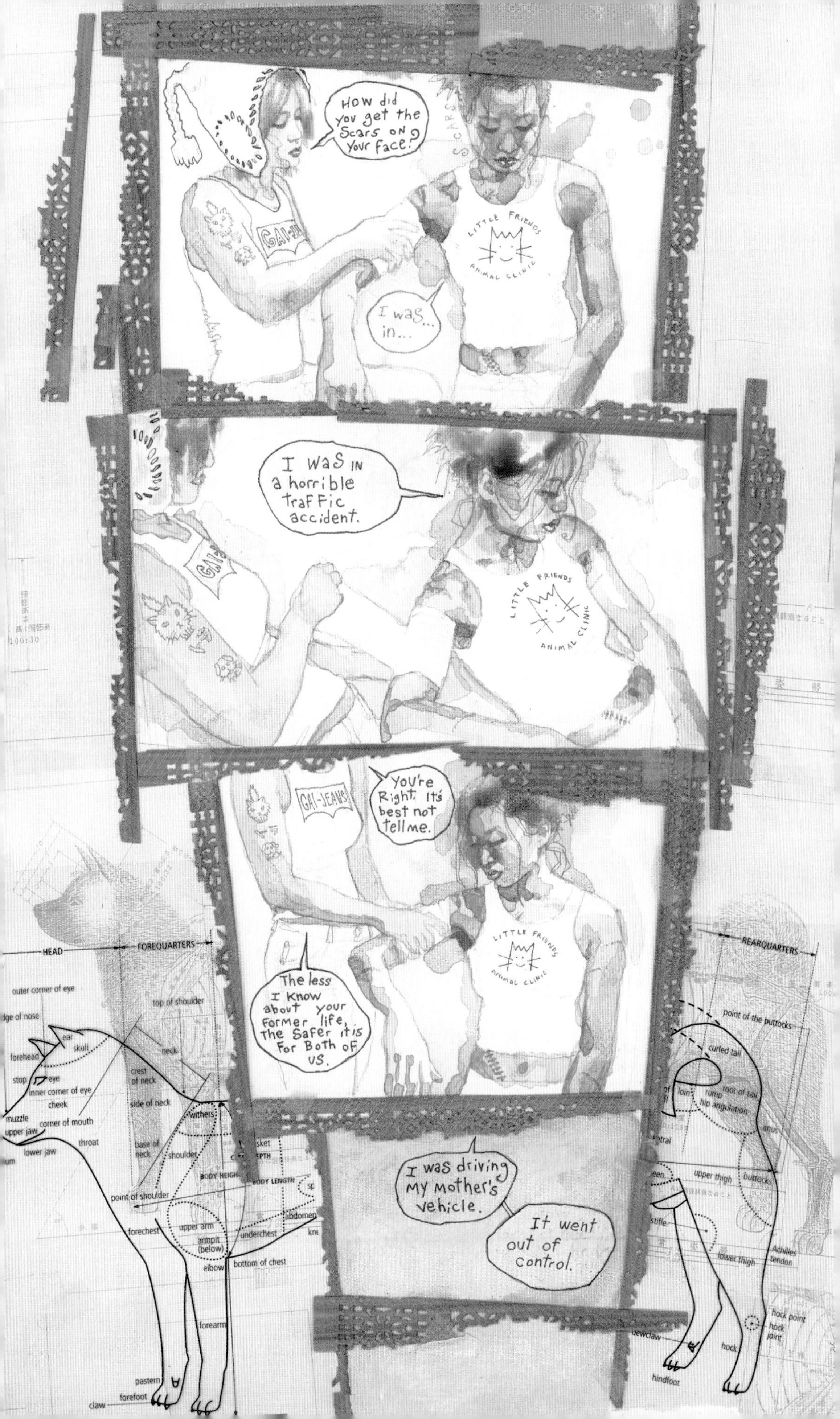
How did you get the Scars on your face?
SCARS
GAI-JEANS
LITTLE FRIENDS ANIMAL CLINIC
I was... in...
I was in a horrible traffic accident.
You're Right. It's best not tell me.
The less I know about your former life, the Safer it is for Both of us.
I was driving my mother's vehicle.
It went out of control.
HEAD
FOREQUARTERS
REARQUARTERS
outer corner of eye
top of shoulder
ear
skull
forehead
neck
crest of neck
stop
eye
inner corner of eye
cheek
side of neck
muzzle
corner of mouth
withers
upper jaw
throat
lower jaw
base of neck
shoulder
point of shoulder
forechest
upper arm
armpit (below)
underchest
abdomen
elbow
bottom of chest
forearm
pastern
forefoot
claw
point of the buttocks
curled tail
loin
rump
root of tail
hip angulation
anus
upper thigh
buttocks
stifle
lower thigh
Achilles tendon
hock point
hock joint
hock
hindfoot

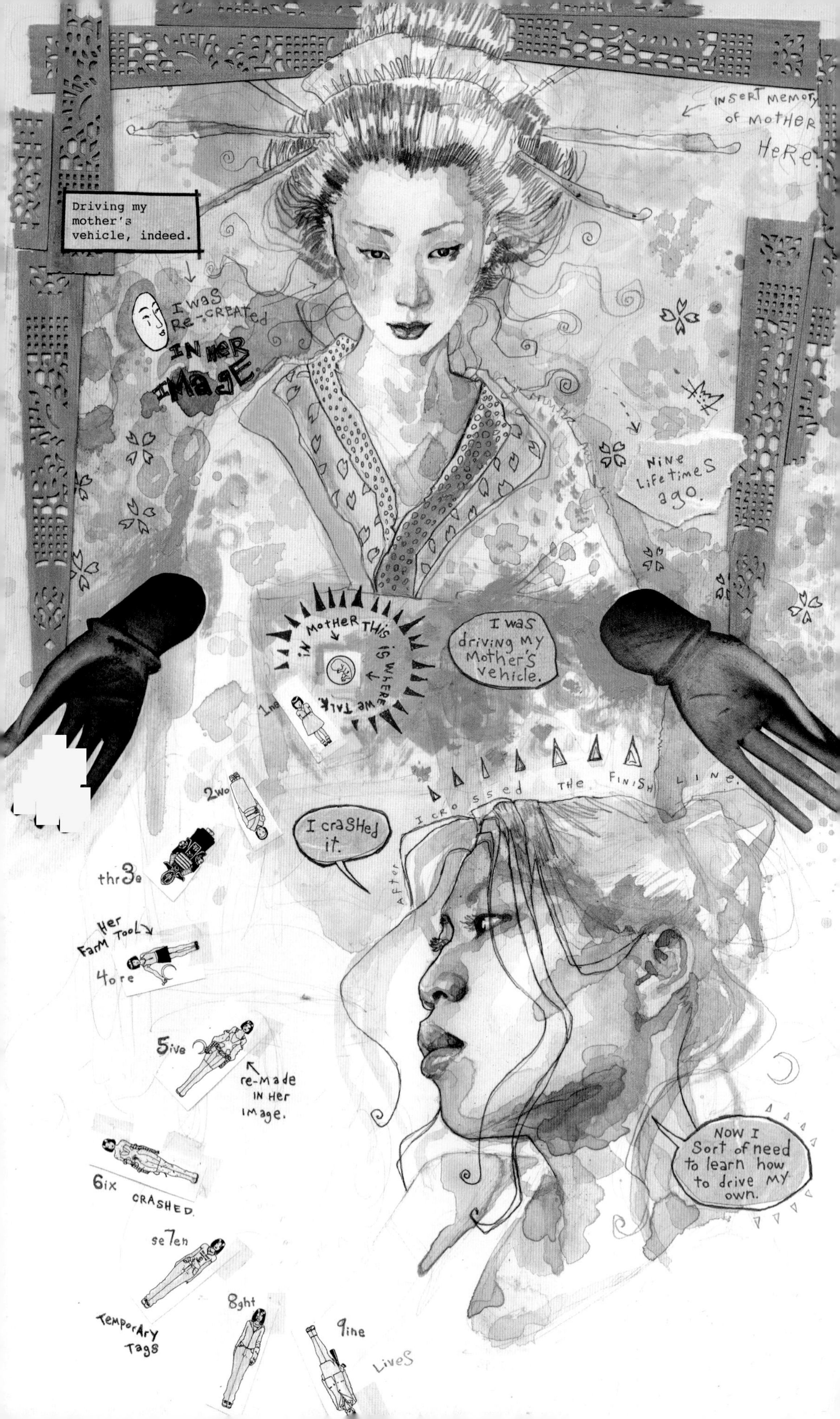
Driving my mother's vehicle, indeed.
INSERT MEMORY OF MOTHER HERE.
I WAS RE-CREATED IN HER IMAGE.
NINE LIFETIMES AGO.
THIS IS WHERE WE TALK. IN MOTHER
I WAS DRIVING MY MOTHER'S VEHICLE.
1ne
2wo
AFTER I CROSSED THE FINISH LINE.
I CRASHED IT.
thr3e
HER FARM TOOL
4ore
5ive
RE-MADE IN HER IMAGE.
6ix
CRASHED.
se7en
TEMPORARY TAGS
8ght
9ine
LIVES
NOW I SORT OF NEED TO LEARN HOW TO DRIVE MY OWN.

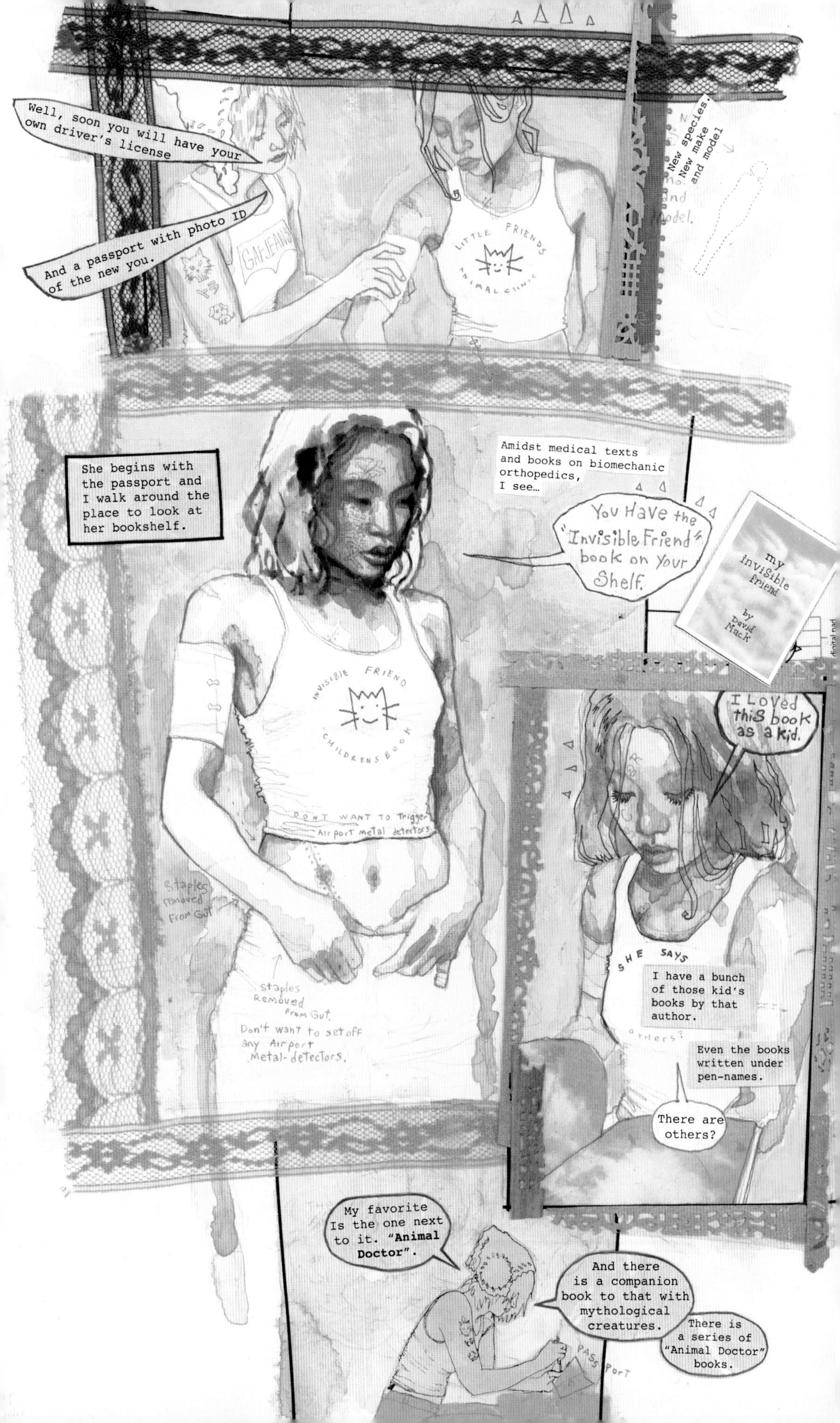

Well, soon you will have your own driver's license
And a passport with photo ID of the new you.
New species. New make and model
LITTLE FRIENDS ANIMAL CLINIC
She begins with the passport and I walk around the place to look at her bookshelf.
Amidst medical texts and books on biomechanic orthopedics, I see…
You Have the "Invisible Friend" book on Your Shelf.
my invisible friend by David Mack
INVISIBLE FRIEND CHILDRENS BOOK
DON'T WANT TO Trigger Airport metal detectors
Staples removed From Gut
Staples Removed From Gut. Don't want to set off any Airport Metal-detectors.
I Loved this book as a kid.
SHE SAYS
I have a bunch of those kid's books by that author.
Even the books written under pen-names.
There are others?
My favorite Is the one next to it. "Animal Doctor".
And there is a companion book to that with mythological creatures.
There is a series of "Animal Doctor" books.
PASSPORT

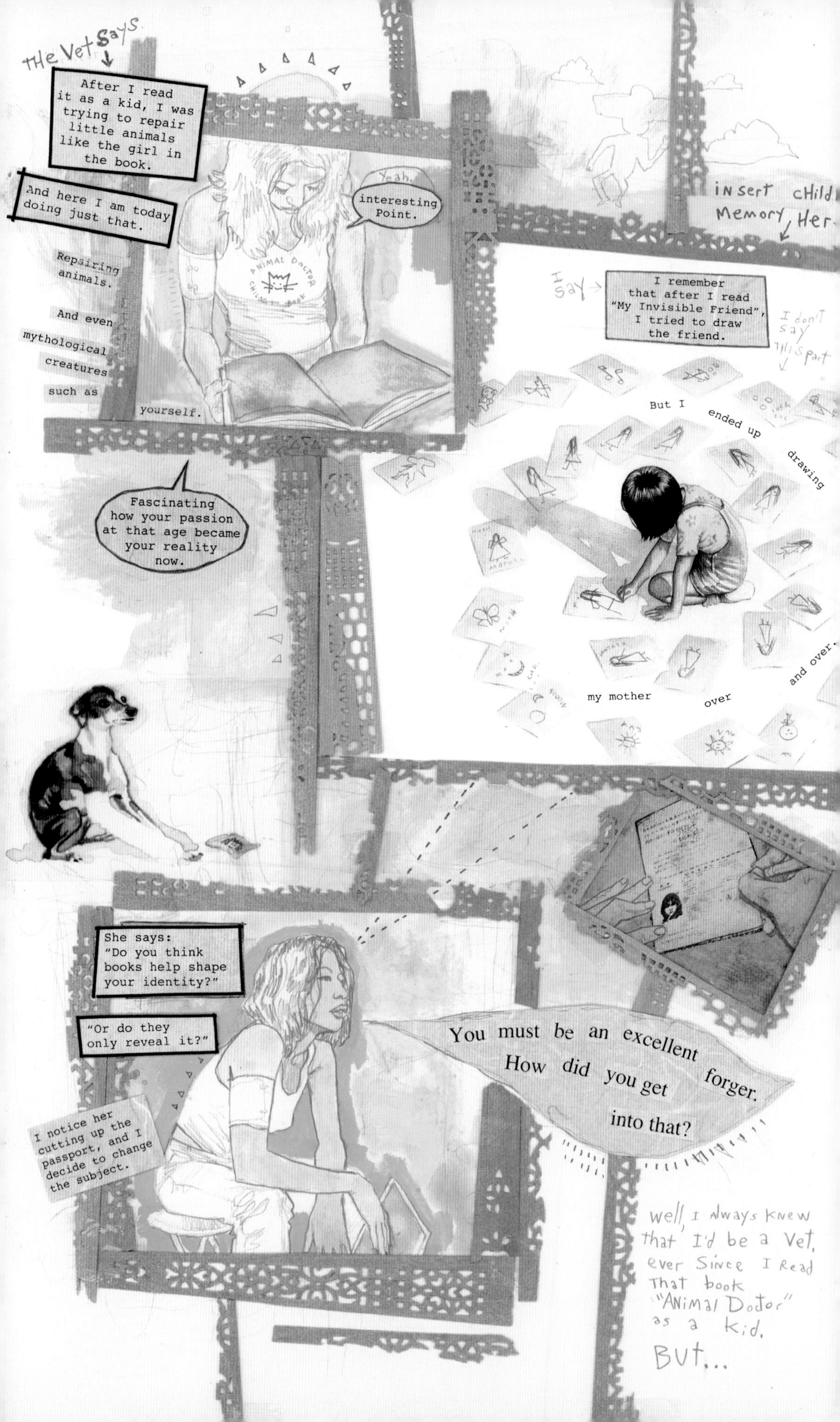
THE Vet Says
After I read it as a kid, I was trying to repair little animals like the girl in the book.
And here I am today doing just that.
Repairing animals.
And even mythological creatures such as yourself.
Yeah. interesting Point.
ANIMAL DOCTOR
insert cHild Memory Her
I say
I remember that after I read "My Invisible Friend", I tried to draw the friend.
I don't say this part
But I ended up drawing my mother over and over.
Fascinating how your passion at that age became your reality now.
She says: "Do you think books help shape your identity?"
"Or do they only reveal it?"
I notice her cutting up the passport, and I decide to change the subject.
You must be an excellent forger. How did you get into that?
Well, I always knew that I'd be a Vet, ever Since I Read That book "ANIMAL Doctor" as a kid. BUT...

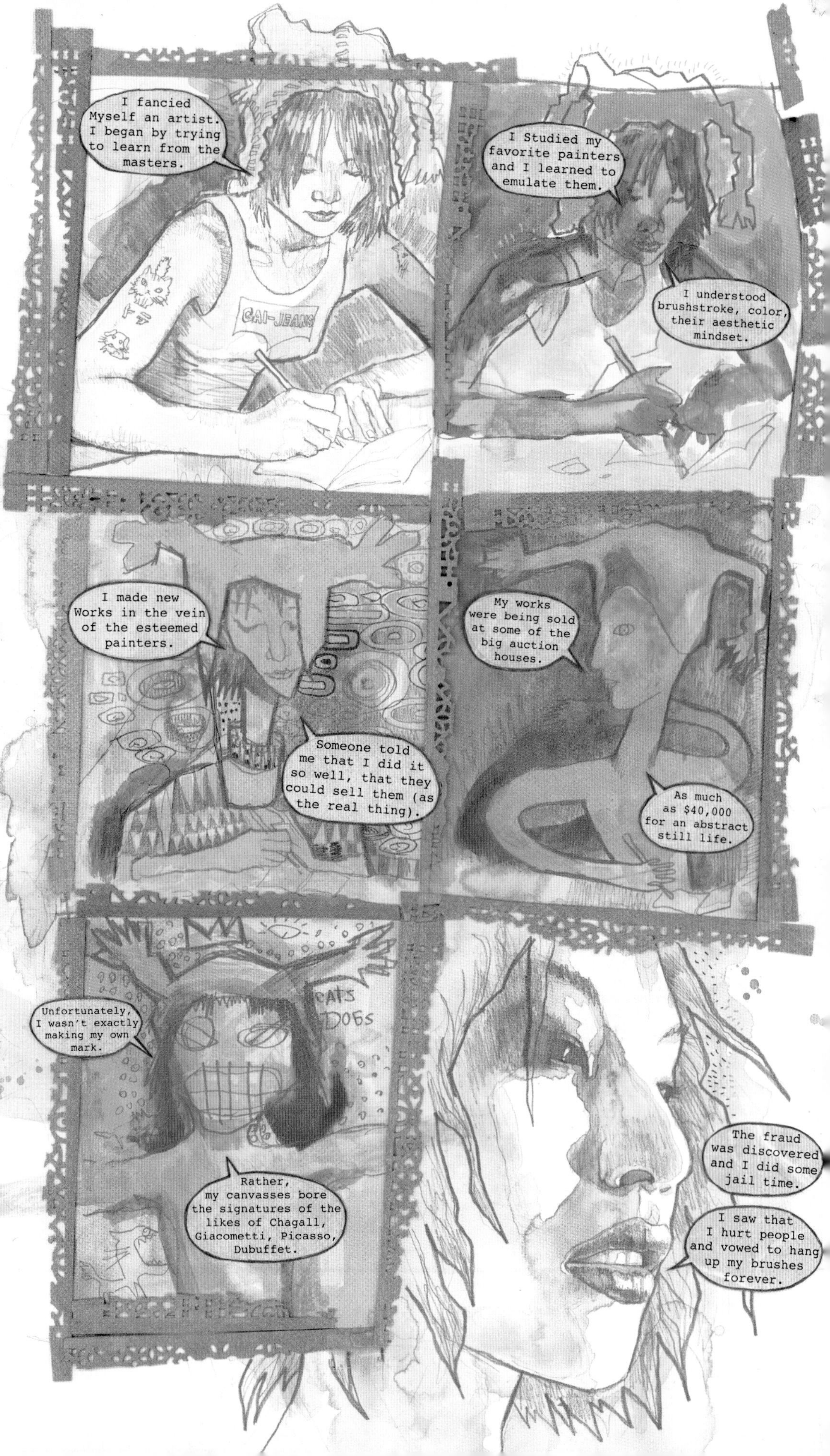
I fancied Myself an artist. I began by trying to learn from the masters.
I Studied my favorite painters and I learned to emulate them.
I understood brushstroke, color, their aesthetic mindset.
GAI-JEANS
I made new Works in the vein of the esteemed painters.
Someone told me that I did it so well, that they could sell them (as the real thing).
My works were being sold at some of the big auction houses.
As much as $40,000 for an abstract still life.
Unfortunately, I wasn't exactly making my own mark.
CATS DOGS
Rather, my canvasses bore the signatures of the likes of Chagall, Giacometti, Picasso, Dubuffet.
The fraud was discovered and I did some jail time.
I saw that I hurt people and vowed to hang up my brushes forever.

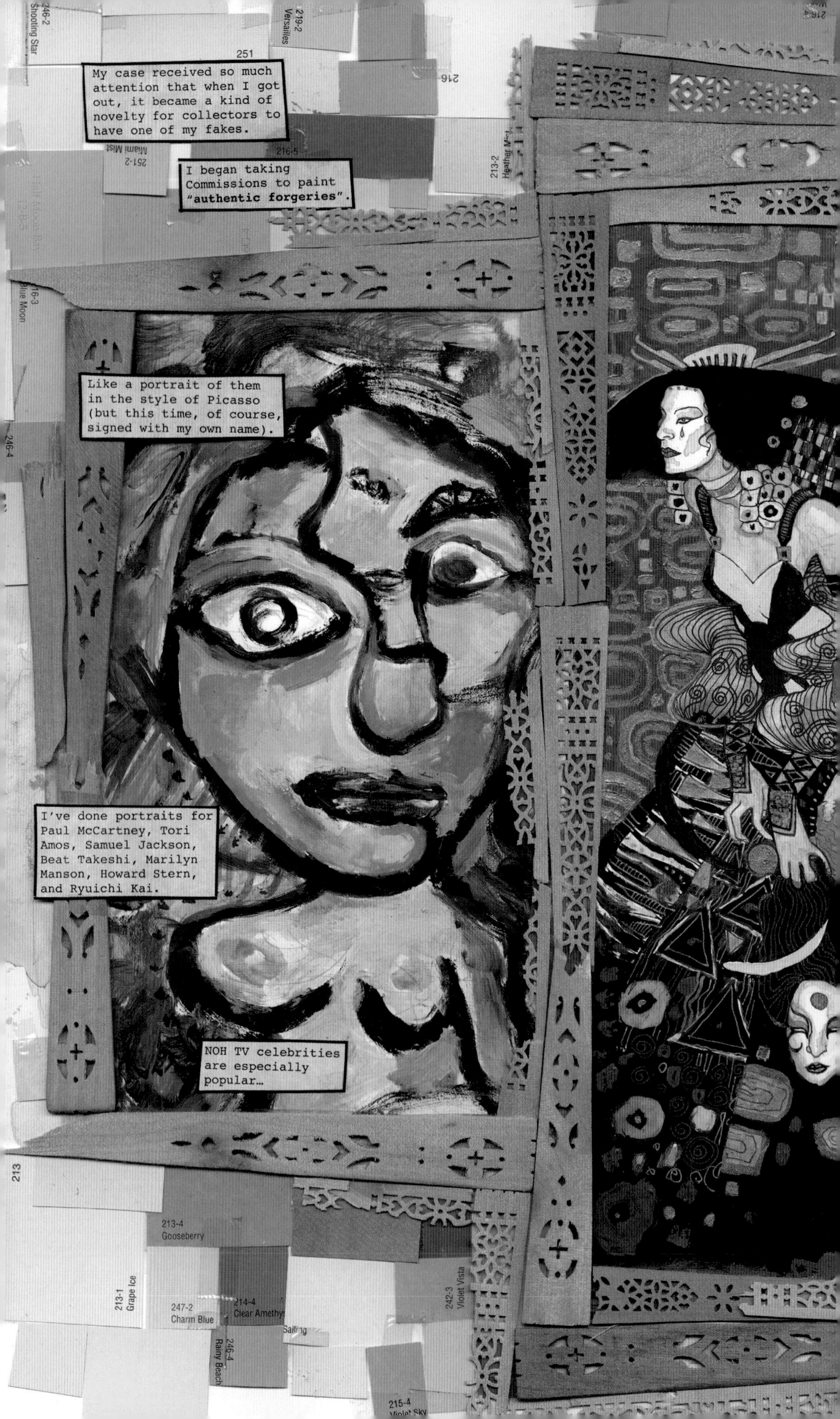
My case received so much attention that when I got out, it became a kind of novelty for collectors to have one of my fakes.
I began taking Commissions to paint **"authentic forgeries"**.
Like a portrait of them in the style of Picasso (but this time, of course, signed with my own name).
I've done portraits for Paul McCartney, Tori Amos, Samuel Jackson, Beat Takeshi, Marilyn Manson, Howard Stern, and Ryuichi Kai.
NOH TV celebrities are especially popular...

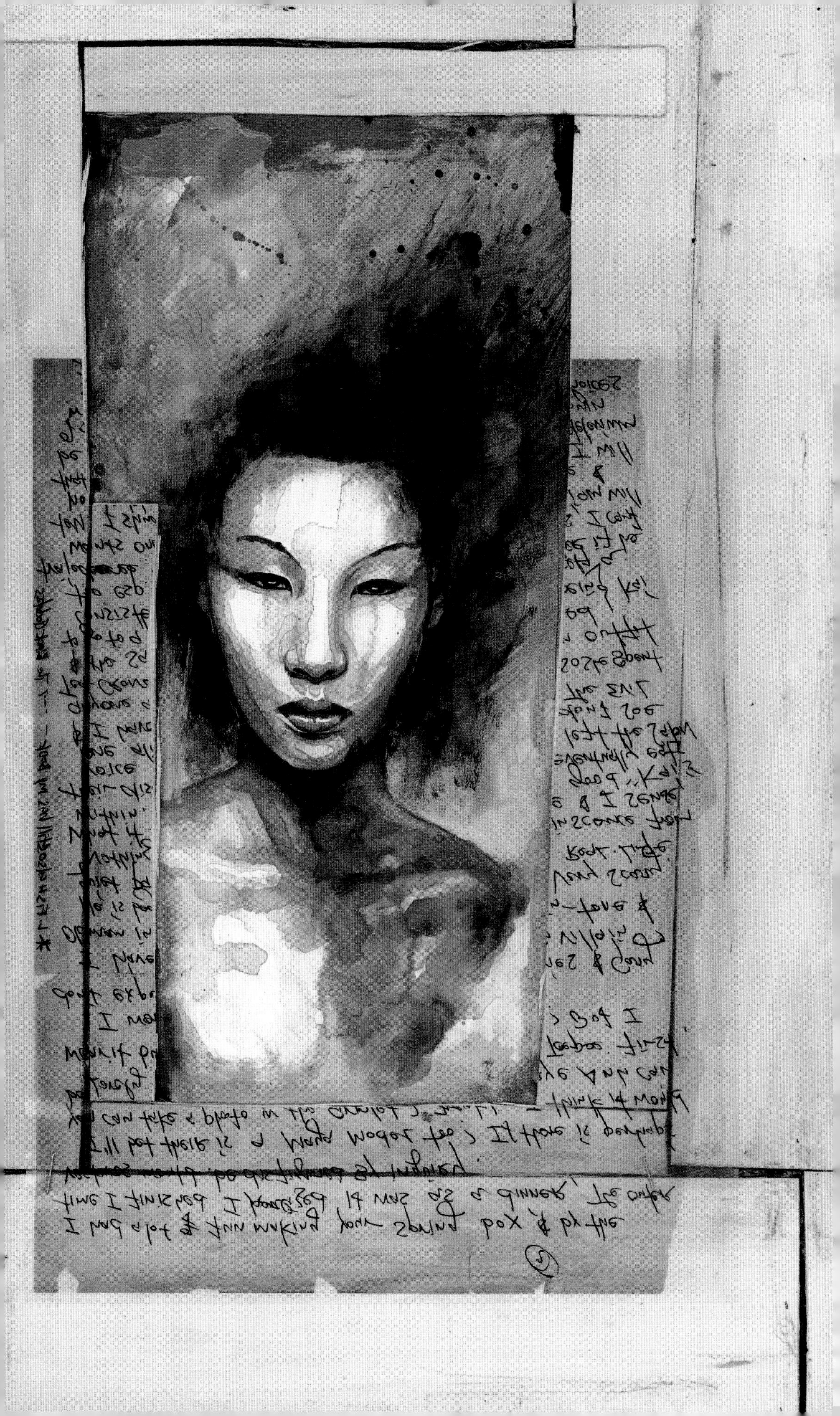

The Alchemy

Part Two

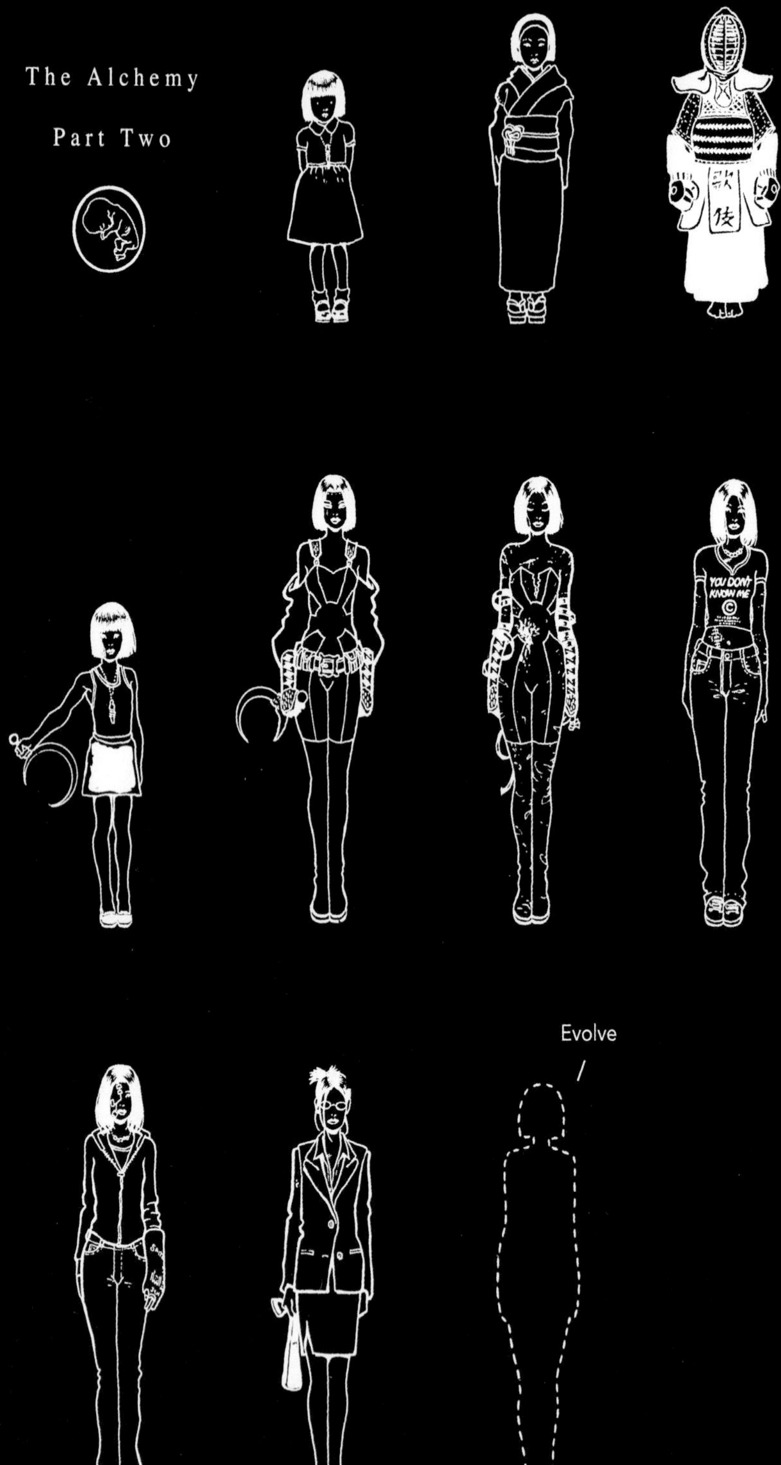
YOU DON'T KNOW ME
Evolve

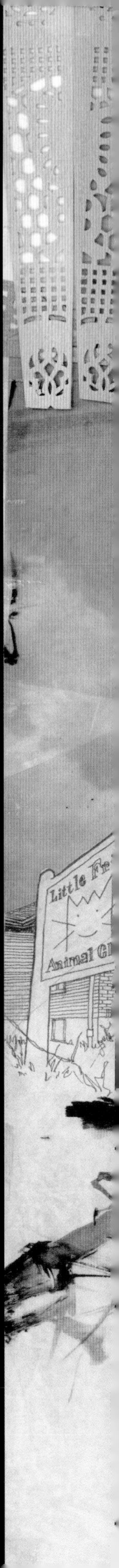

(or Reconstructing Akemi)
(or Animal Doctor)

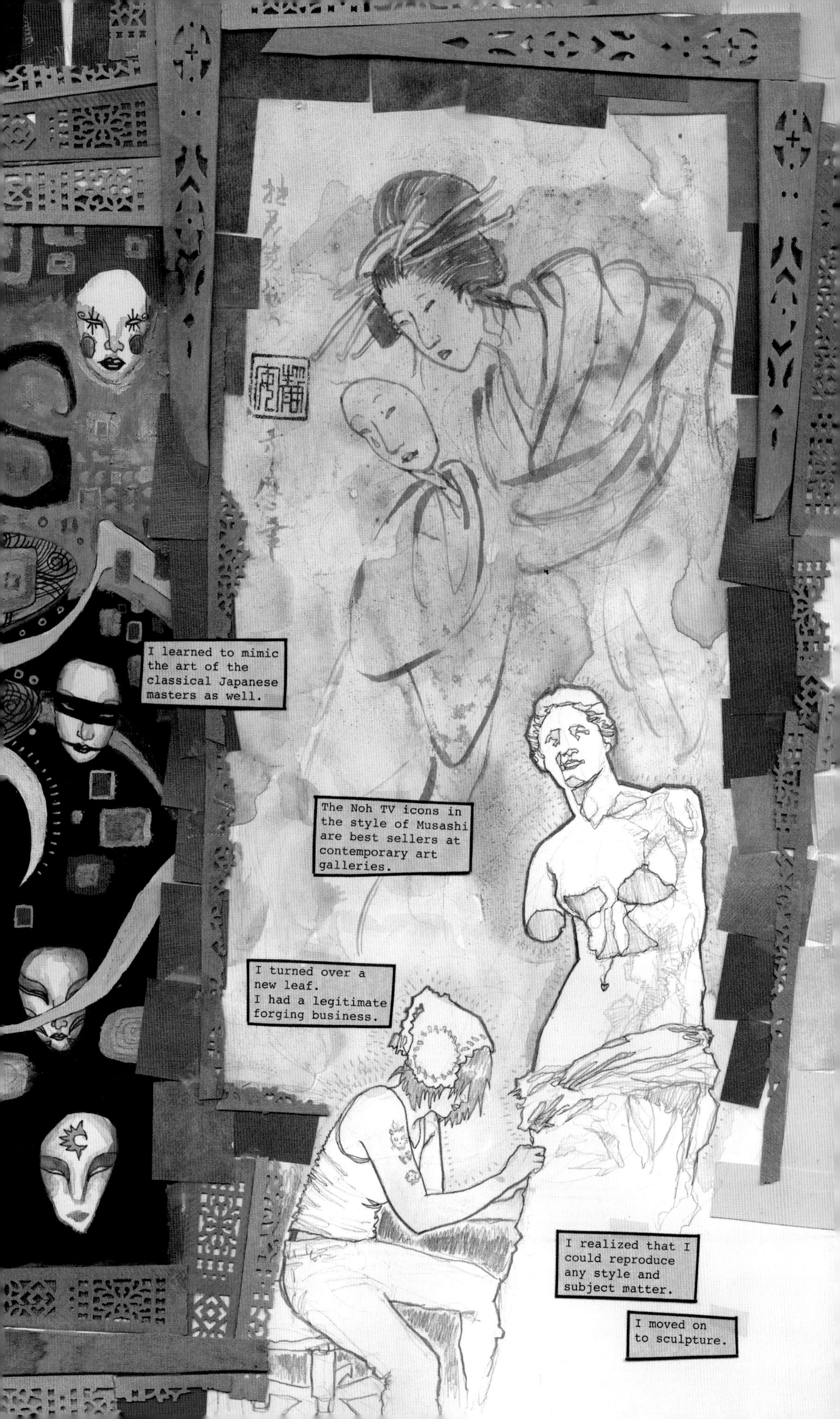
I learned to mimic the art of the classical Japanese masters as well.
The Noh TV icons in the style of Musashi are best sellers at contemporary art galleries.
I turned over a new leaf.
I had a legitimate forging business.
I realized that I could reproduce any style and subject matter.
I moved on to sculpture.

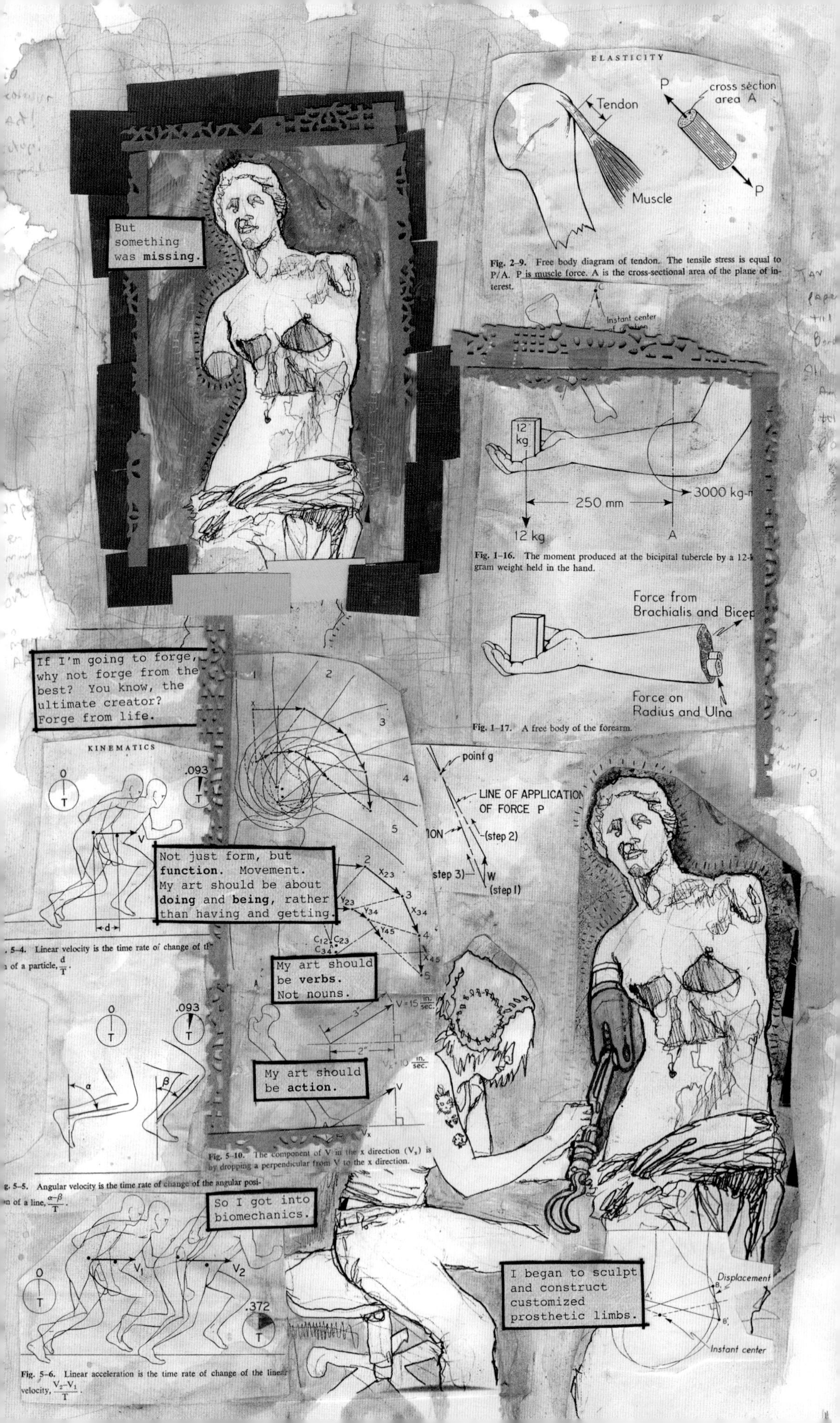
But something was **missing**.
ELASTICITY
Tendon
P
cross section area A
Muscle
Fig. 2–9. Free body diagram of tendon. The tensile stress is equal to P/A. P is muscle force. A is the cross-sectional area of the plane of interest.
Instant center
12 kg
250 mm
3000 kg-m
A
Fig. 1–16. The moment produced at the bicipital tubercle by a 12-kilogram weight held in the hand.
Force from Brachialis and Bicep
Force on Radius and Ulna
Fig. 1–17. A free body of the forearm.
If I'm going to forge, why not forge from the best? You know, the ultimate creator? Forge from life.
KINEMATICS
0
T
.093
V
d
Linear velocity is the time rate of change of the position of a particle, $\frac{d}{T}$.
point g
LINE OF APPLICATION OF FORCE P
(step 2)
(step 3)
W
(step 1)
Not just form, but **function**. Movement. My art should be about **doing** and **being**, rather than having and getting.
My art should be **verbs**. Not nouns.
V = 15 in./sec.
V_x = 10 in./sec.
My art should be **action**.
Fig. 5–10. The component of V in the x direction (V_x) is found by dropping a perpendicular from V to the x direction.
Fig. 5–5. Angular velocity is the time rate of change of the angular position of a line, $\frac{\alpha-\beta}{T}$.
So I got into biomechanics.
V_1
V_2
.372
Fig. 5–6. Linear acceleration is the time rate of change of the linear velocity, $\frac{V_2-V_1}{T}$.
I began to sculpt and construct customized prosthetic limbs.
Displacement
Instant center

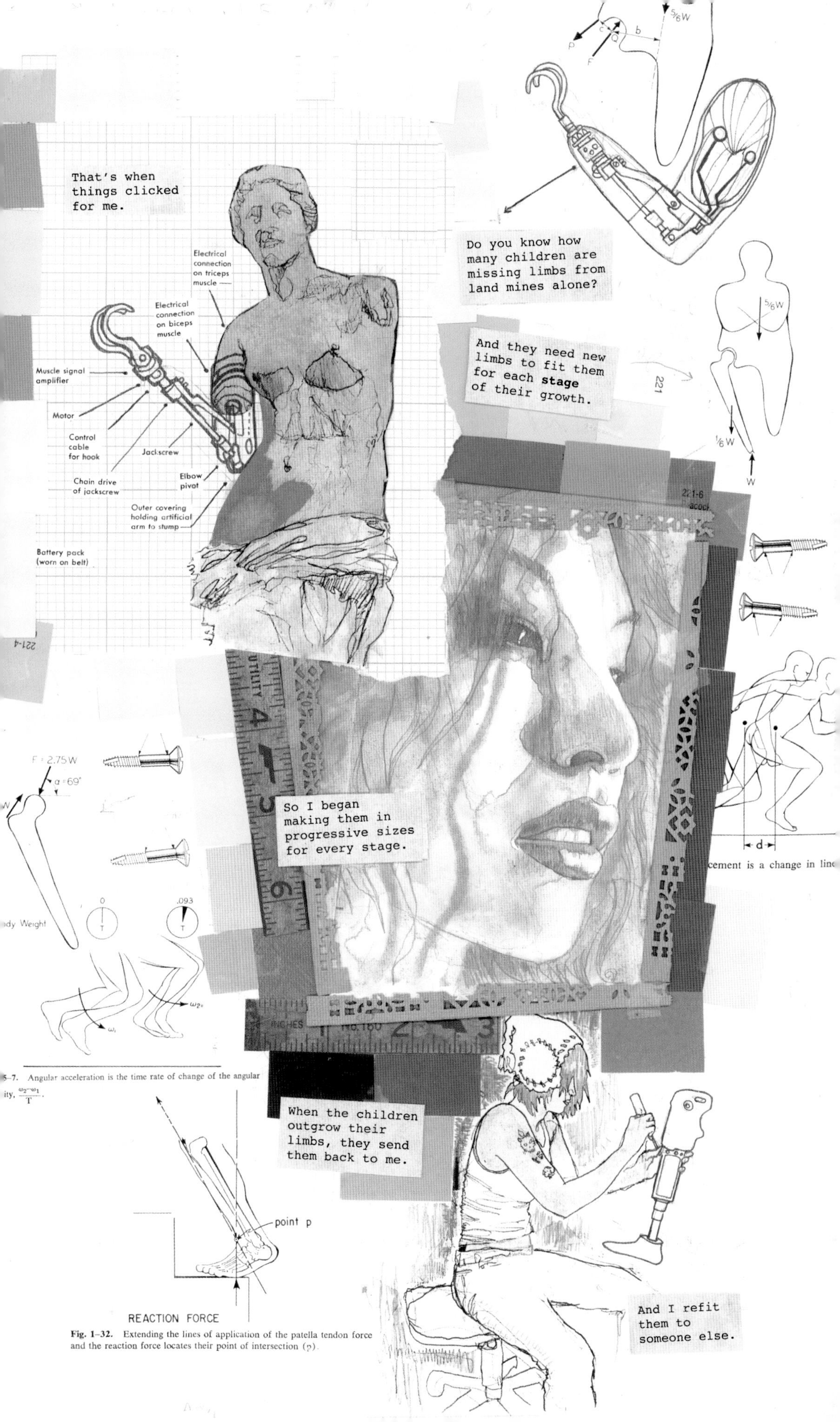
That's when things clicked for me.
Do you know how many children are missing limbs from land mines alone?
And they need new limbs to fit them for each **stage** of their growth.
So I began making them in progressive sizes for every stage.
When the children outgrow their limbs, they send them back to me.
And I refit them to someone else.
Electrical connection on triceps muscle
Electrical connection on biceps muscle
Muscle signal amplifier
Motor
Control cable for hook
Jackscrew
Chain drive of jackscrew
Elbow pivot
Outer covering holding artificial arm to stump
Battery pack (worn on belt)
221-4
221
221-6
5/6W
1/6 W
W
F = 2.75 W
α = 69°
.093
dy Weight
cement is a change in line
5–7. Angular acceleration is the time rate of change of the angular
point p
REACTION FORCE
Fig. 1–32. Extending the lines of application of the patella tendon force and the reaction force locates their point of intersection (p).

The outgrown prosthetics
that are obsolete or
unsalvageable have become
the artifacts of the new
work that I am known for.

Kiyomi's arm
8 yrs old

Kiyomi's arm
13 yrs old

Carolee's arm
12 yrs old

Jean-Michel's leg
9 yrs old

Feryal Khan's arm
11 yrs old

They are shown in
Galleries and sell
better than my
previous forgeries
ever did.

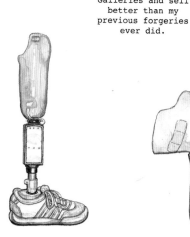

Afaq's leg
7 yrs old

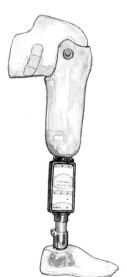

Goran's leg
14 yrs old

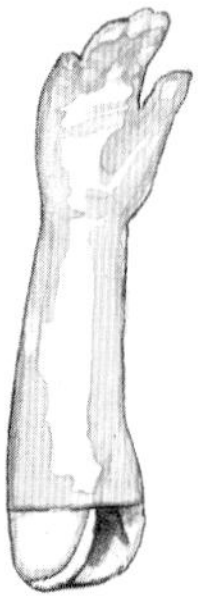

Pablo's arm
9 yrs old

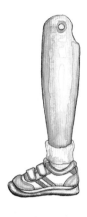

Maria's leg
8 yrs old

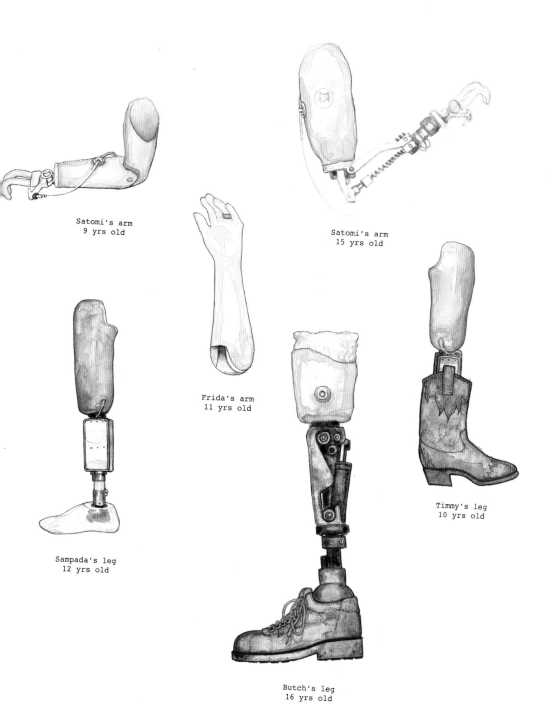

Satomi's arm
9 yrs old

Satomi's arm
15 yrs old

Frida's arm
11 yrs old

Sampada's leg
12 yrs old

Butch's leg
16 yrs old

Timmy's leg
10 yrs old

OUTGROWN PROSTHETICS FROM VARIOUS STAGES OF AGE

Sculpture / Mixed Media
Private collection

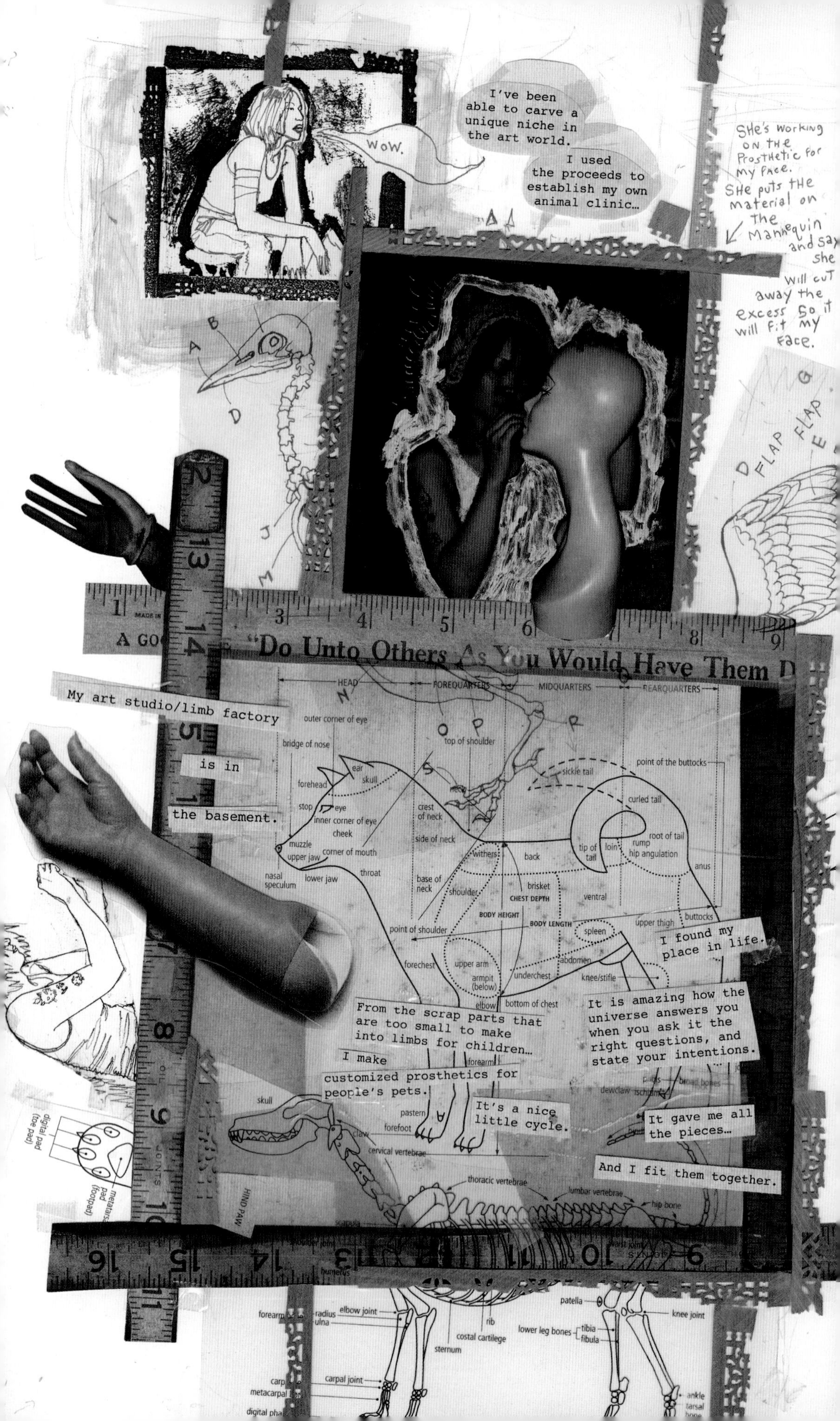
WoW.
I've been able to carve a unique niche in the art world.
I used the proceeds to establish my own animal clinic...
SHe's working on the Prosthetic for my face. SHe puts the material on the Mannequin and says she will cut away the excess so it will fit my face.
FLAP FLAP
"Do Unto Others As You Would Have Them D
My art studio/limb factory
is in
the basement.
HEAD
FOREQUARTERS
MIDQUARTERS
REARQUARTERS
outer corner of eye
bridge of nose
top of shoulder
point of the buttocks
sickle tail
curled tail
ear
skull
forehead
stop
eye
inner corner of eye
cheek
muzzle
upper jaw
corner of mouth
throat
lower jaw
nasal speculum
crest of neck
side of neck
neck
withers
back
loin
tip of tail
rump
root of tail
hip angulation
anus
base of neck
shoulder
brisket
CHEST DEPTH
ventral
BODY HEIGHT
BODY LENGTH
point of shoulder
spleen
upper thigh
buttocks
forechest
upper arm
armpit (below)
underchest
abdomen
knee/stifle
elbow
bottom of chest
I found my place in life.
It is amazing how the universe answers you when you ask it the right questions, and state your intentions.
From the scrap parts that are too small to make into limbs for children...
I make
customized prosthetics for people's pets.
It's a nice little cycle.
It gave me all the pieces...
And I fit them together.
skull
pastern
forefoot
claw
cervical vertebrae
thoracic vertebrae
lumbar vertebrae
hip bone
dewclaw
digital pad (toe pad)
metatarsal pad (footpad)
HIND PAW
forearm
radius
ulna
elbow joint
rib
costal cartilage
sternum
patella
knee joint
lower leg bones
tibia
fibula
carpal joint
metacarpal
digital pha
ankle
tarsal

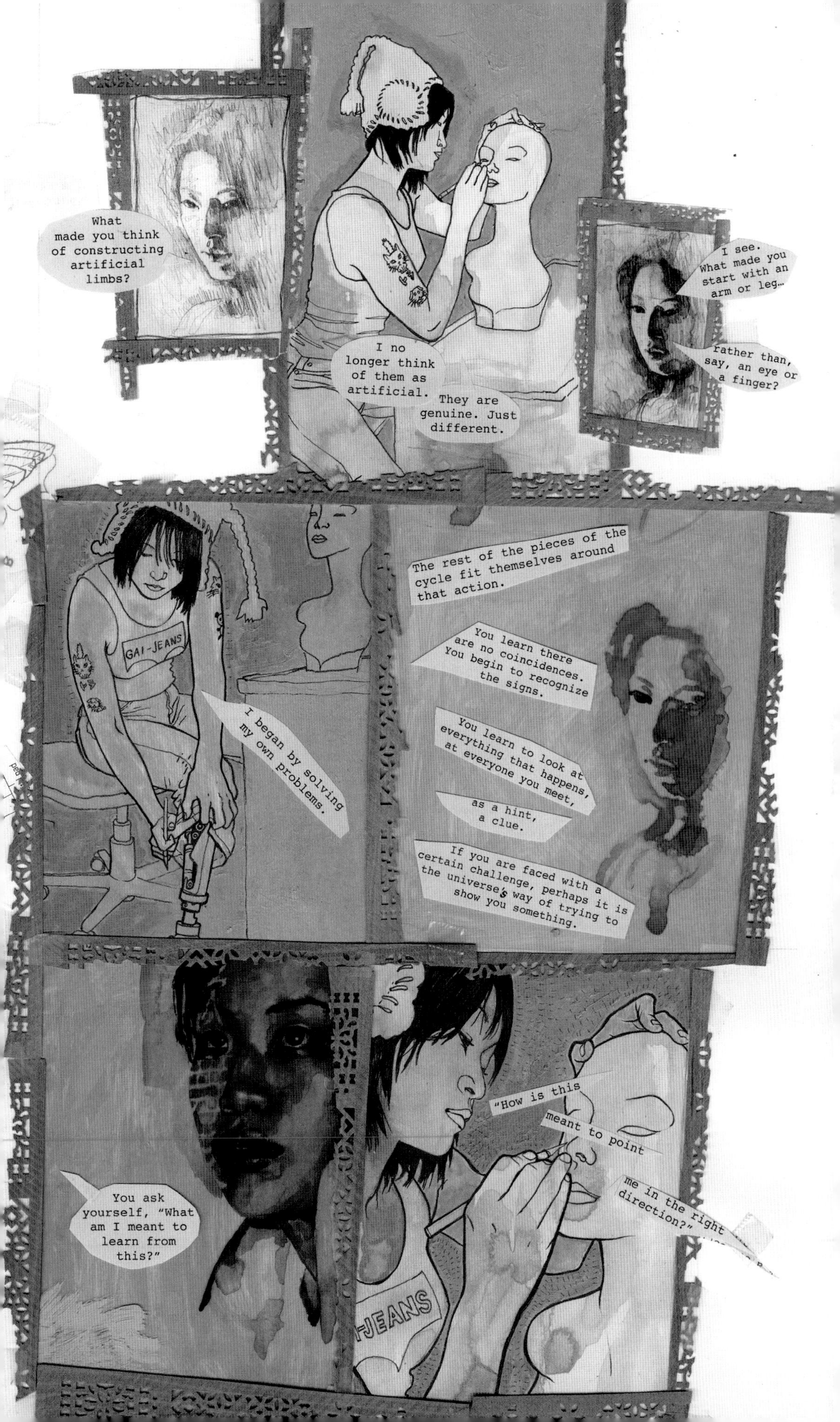
What made you think of constructing artificial limbs?
I no longer think of them as artificial.
They are genuine. Just different.
I see. What made you start with an arm or leg…
rather than, say, an eye or a finger?
I began by solving my own problems.
GAI-JEANS
The rest of the pieces of the cycle fit themselves around that action.
You learn there are no coincidences. You begin to recognize the signs.
You learn to look at everything that happens, at everyone you meet,
as a hint, a clue.
If you are faced with a certain challenge, perhaps it is the universe's way of trying to show you something.
You ask yourself, "What am I meant to learn from this?"
"How is this
meant to point
me in the right direction?"
I-JEANS

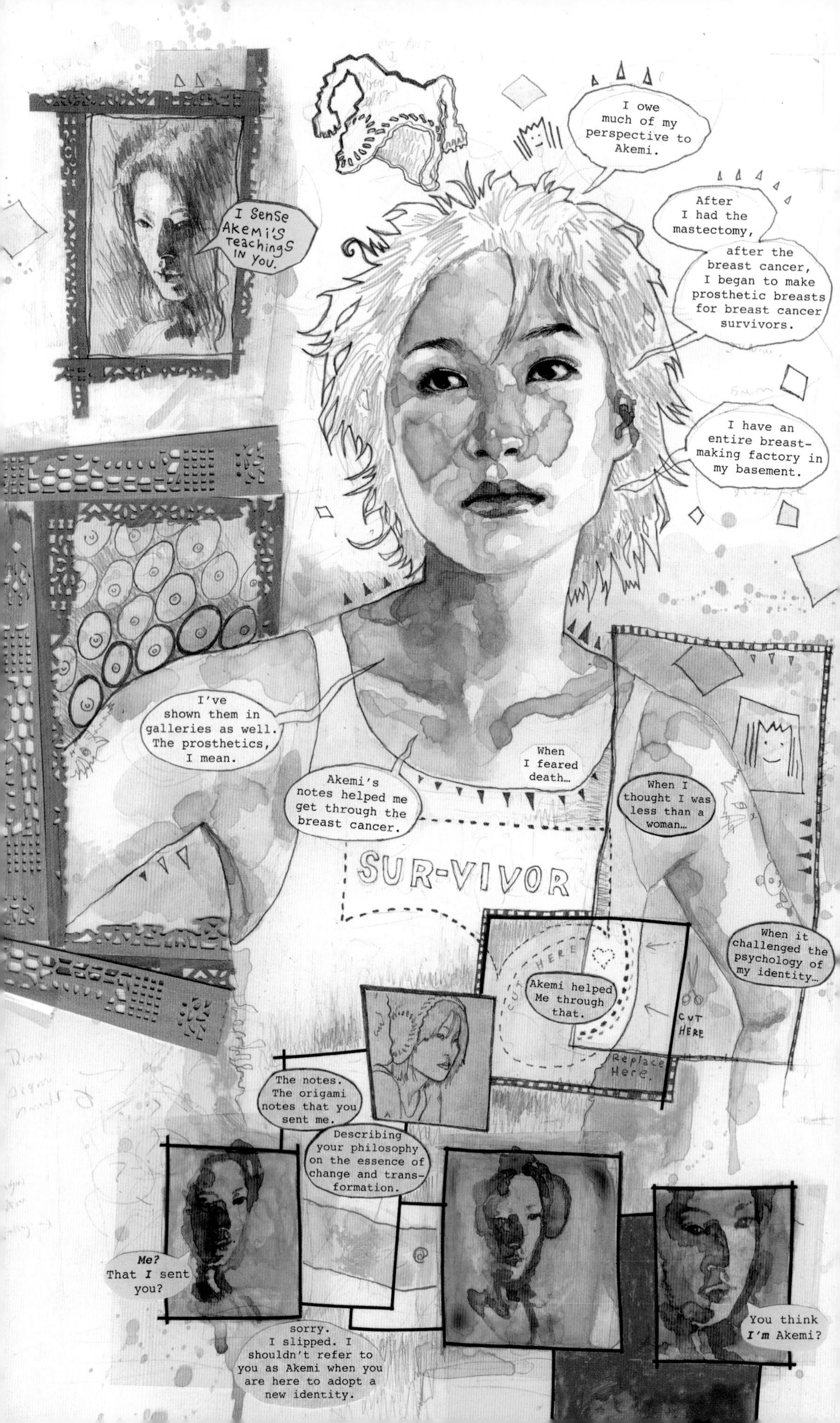
I owe much of my perspective to Akemi.
I sense Akemi's teachings in you.
After I had the mastectomy,
after the breast cancer, I began to make prosthetic breasts for breast cancer survivors.
I have an entire breast-making factory in my basement.
I've shown them in galleries as well. The prosthetics, I mean.
Akemi's notes helped me get through the breast cancer.
When I feared death...
When I thought I was less than a woman...
SUR-VIVOR
When it challenged the psychology of my identity...
CUT HERE
Akemi helped Me through that.
CUT HERE
Replace Here.
The notes. The origami notes that you sent me.
Describing your philosophy on the essence of change and transformation.
Me? That I sent you?
sorry. I slipped. I shouldn't refer to you as Akemi when you are here to adopt a new identity.
You think I'm Akemi?

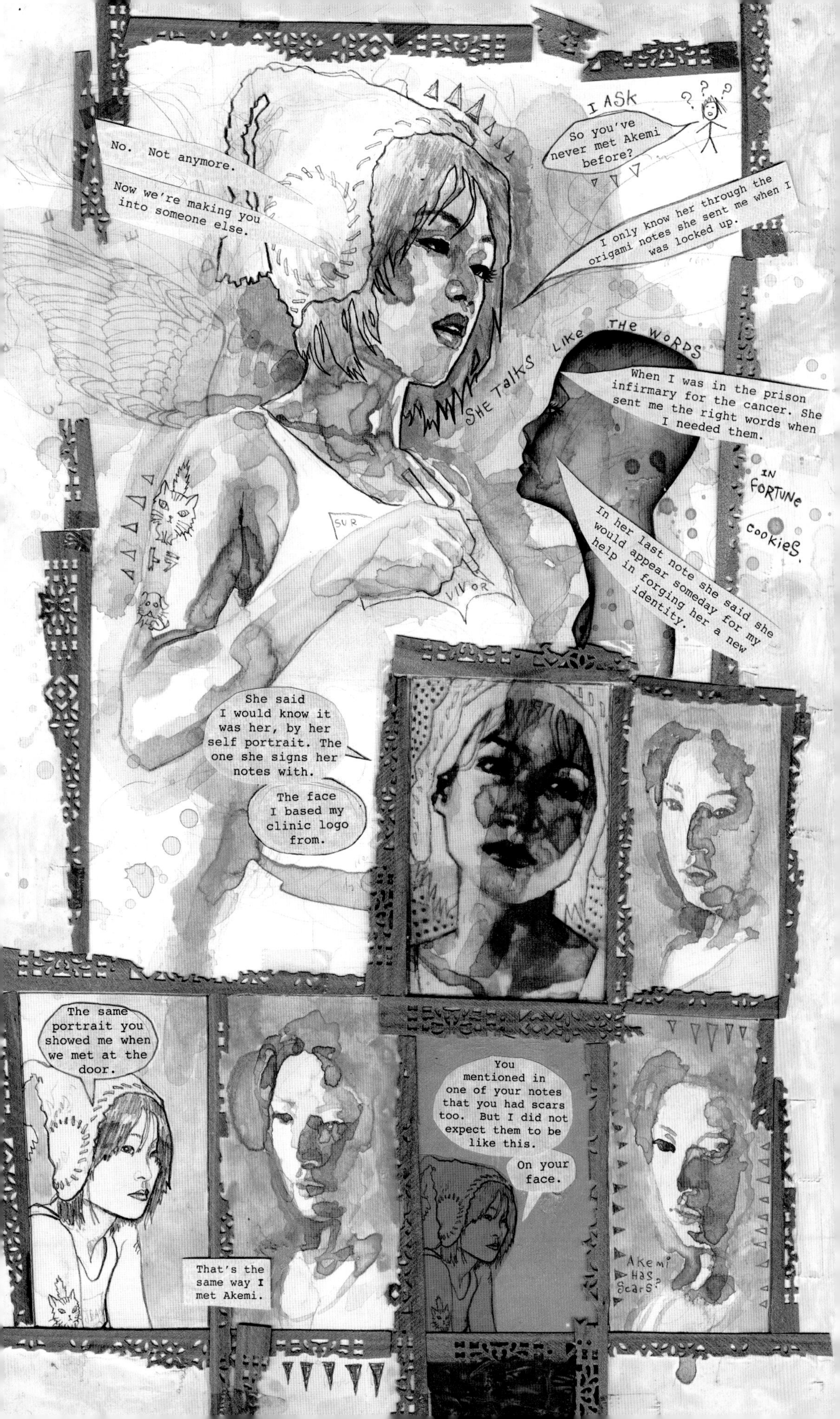

I ASK
So you've never met Akemi before?
No. Not anymore.
Now we're making you into someone else.
I only know her through the origami notes she sent me when I was locked up.
SHE TALKS LIKE THE WORDS
When I was in the prison infirmary for the cancer. She sent me the right words when I needed them.
IN FORTUNE COOKIES.
In her last note she said she would appear someday for my help in forging her a new identity.
SUR
VIVOR
She said I would know it was her, by her self portrait. The one she signs her notes with.
The face I based my clinic logo from.
The same portrait you showed me when we met at the door.
That's the same way I met Akemi.
You mentioned in one of your notes that you had scars too. But I did not expect them to be like this.
On your face.
Akemi HAS Scars?

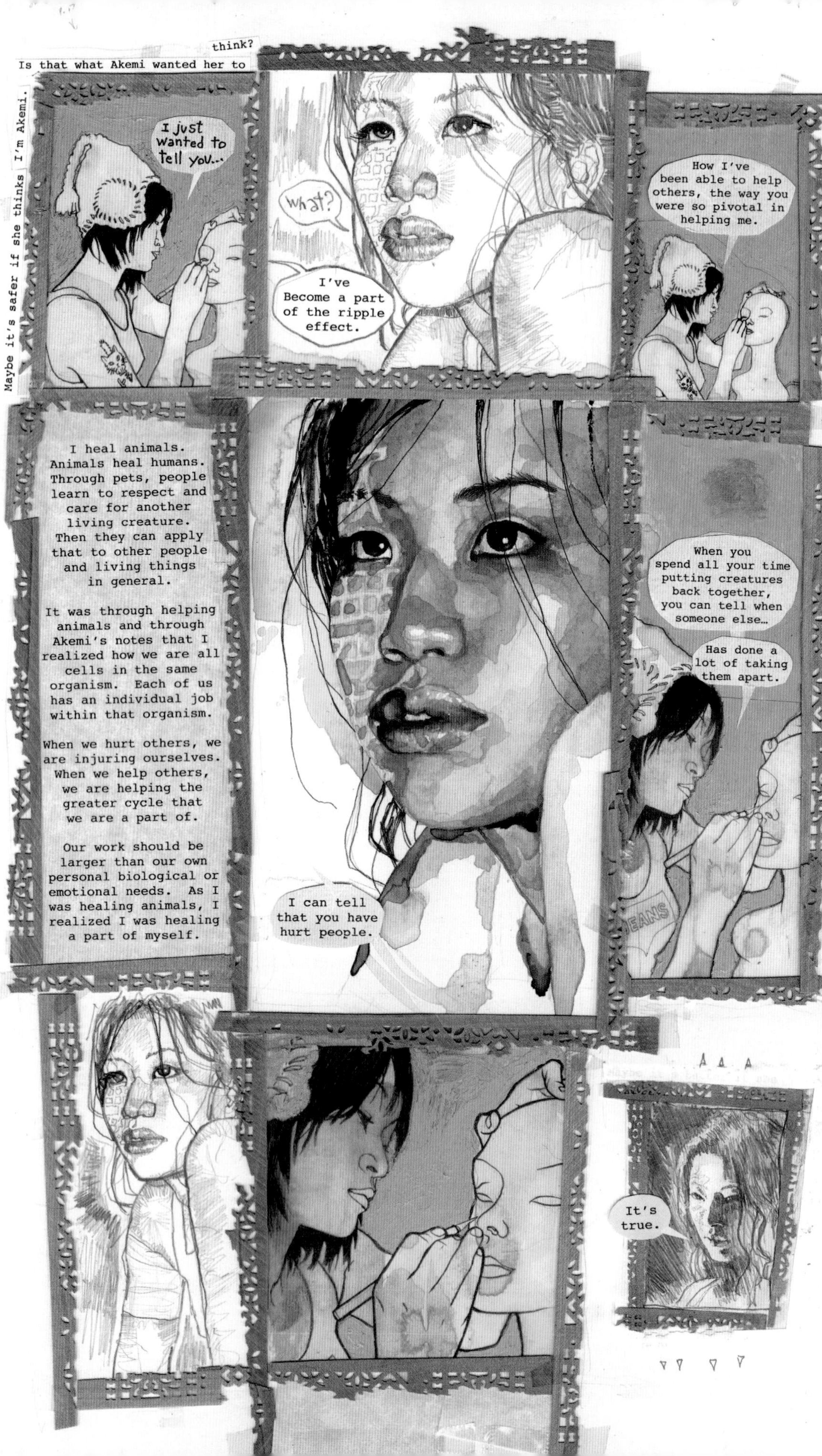
Is that what Akemi wanted her to think?
Maybe it's safer if she thinks I'm Akemi.
I just wanted to tell you...
what?
I've Become a part of the ripple effect.
How I've been able to help others, the way you were so pivotal in helping me.
I heal animals. Animals heal humans. Through pets, people learn to respect and care for another living creature. Then they can apply that to other people and living things in general.
It was through helping animals and through Akemi's notes that I realized how we are all cells in the same organism. Each of us has an individual job within that organism.
When we hurt others, we are injuring ourselves. When we help others, we are helping the greater cycle that we are a part of.
Our work should be larger than our own personal biological or emotional needs. As I was healing animals, I realized I was healing a part of myself.
I can tell that you have hurt people.
When you spend all your time putting creatures back together, you can tell when someone else...
Has done a lot of taking them apart.
It's true.

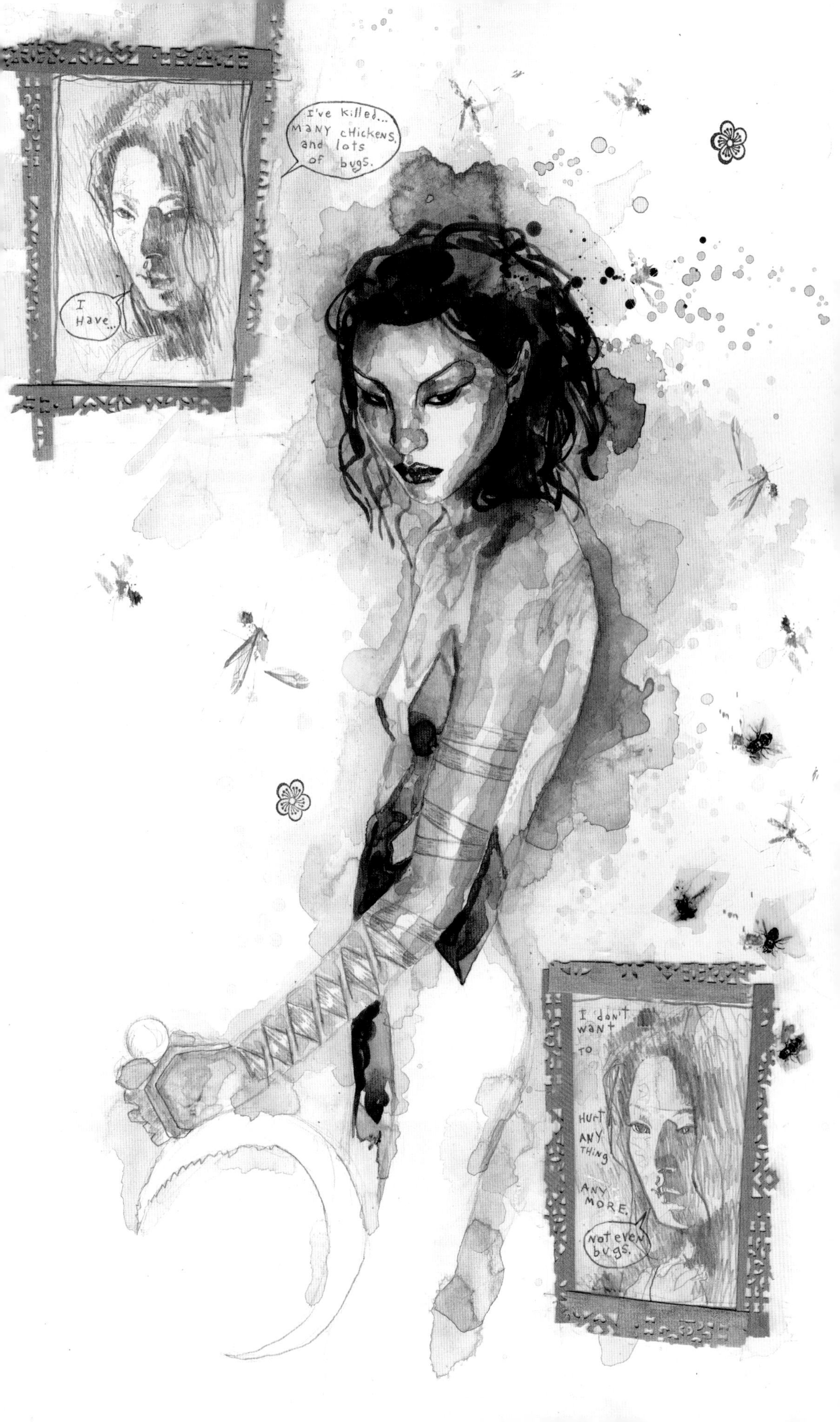
I Have...
I've killed... MANY cHickens, and lots of bugs.
I don't want to HurT ANY THing ANY MORE.
not even bugs.

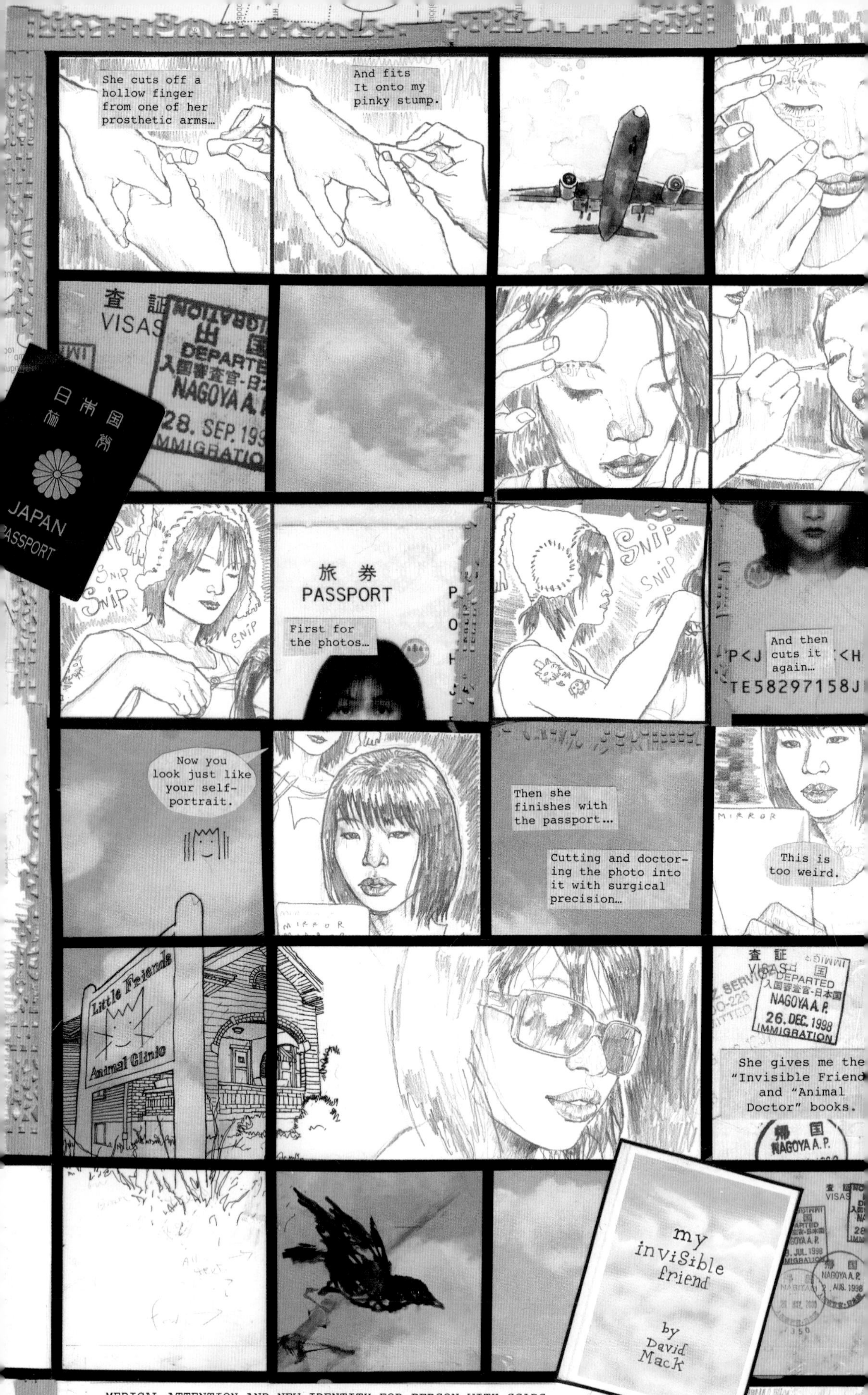
She cuts off a hollow finger from one of her prosthetic arms...
And fits It onto my pinky stump.
査証
VISAS
出国
DEPARTED
入国審査官-日本
NAGOYA A.P.
28. SEP. 19
IMMIGRATION
日本国
旅券
JAPAN
PASSPORT
SNIP
SNIP
SNIP
旅券
PASSPORT
First for the photos...
SNIP
SNIP
And then cuts it again...
P<J
<H
TE58297158J
Now you look just like your self-portrait.
MIRROR
Then she finishes with the passport...
Cutting and doctoring the photo into it with surgical precision...
MIRROR
This is too weird.
Little Friends
Animal Clinic
査証
VISAS
帰国
DEPARTED
入国審査官-日本国
NAGOYA A.P.
26. DEC. 1998
IMMIGRATION
She gives me the "Invisible Friend" and "Animal Doctor" books.
帰国
NAGOYA A.P.
my invisible friend
by David Mack

MEDICAL ATTENTION AND NEW IDENTITY FOR PERSON WITH SCARS

Sculpture / Photography / Mixed Media
Private collection

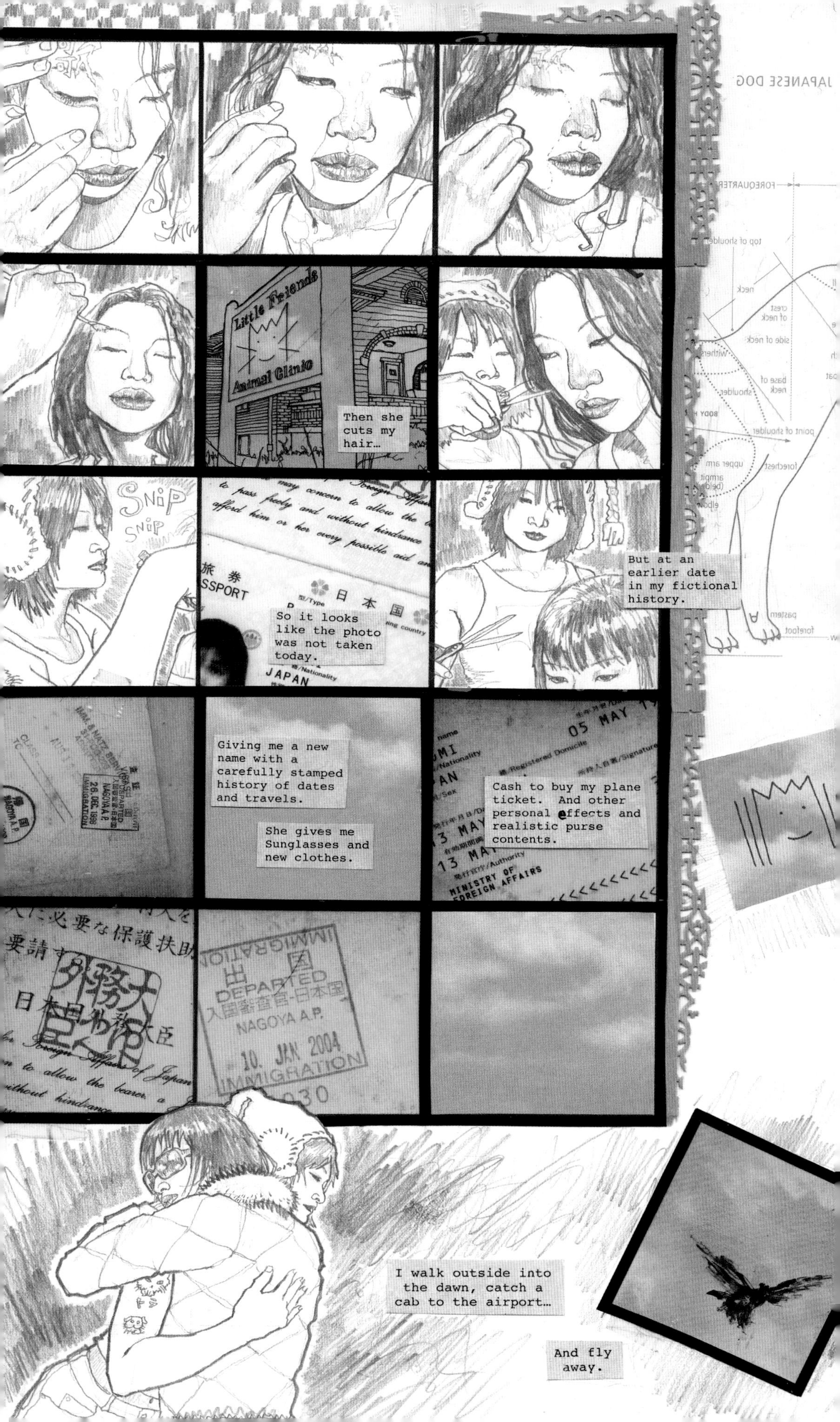
Little Friends Animal Clinic
Then she cuts my hair…
SNiP SNiP
to pass freely and without hindrance
旅券
日本国
So it looks like the photo was not taken today.
JAPAN
But at an earlier date in my fictional history.
Giving me a new name with a carefully stamped history of dates and travels.
She gives me Sunglasses and new clothes.
05 MAY
Cash to buy my plane ticket. And other personal effects and realistic purse contents.
MINISTRY OF FOREIGN AFFAIRS
IMMIGRATION
出国
DEPARTED
NAGOYA A.P.
10. JAN 2004
IMMIGRATION
I walk outside into the dawn, catch a cab to the airport…
And fly away.

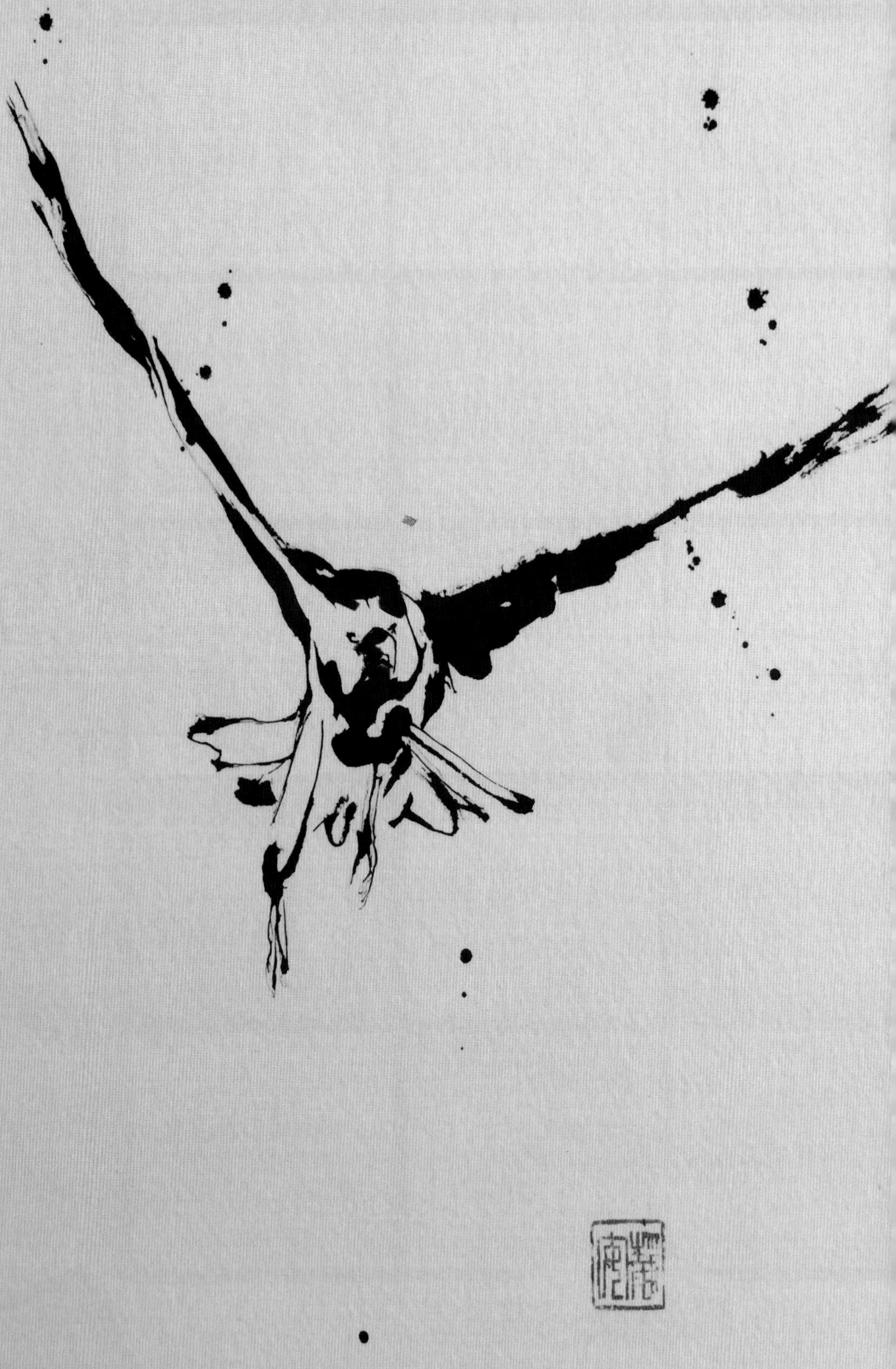

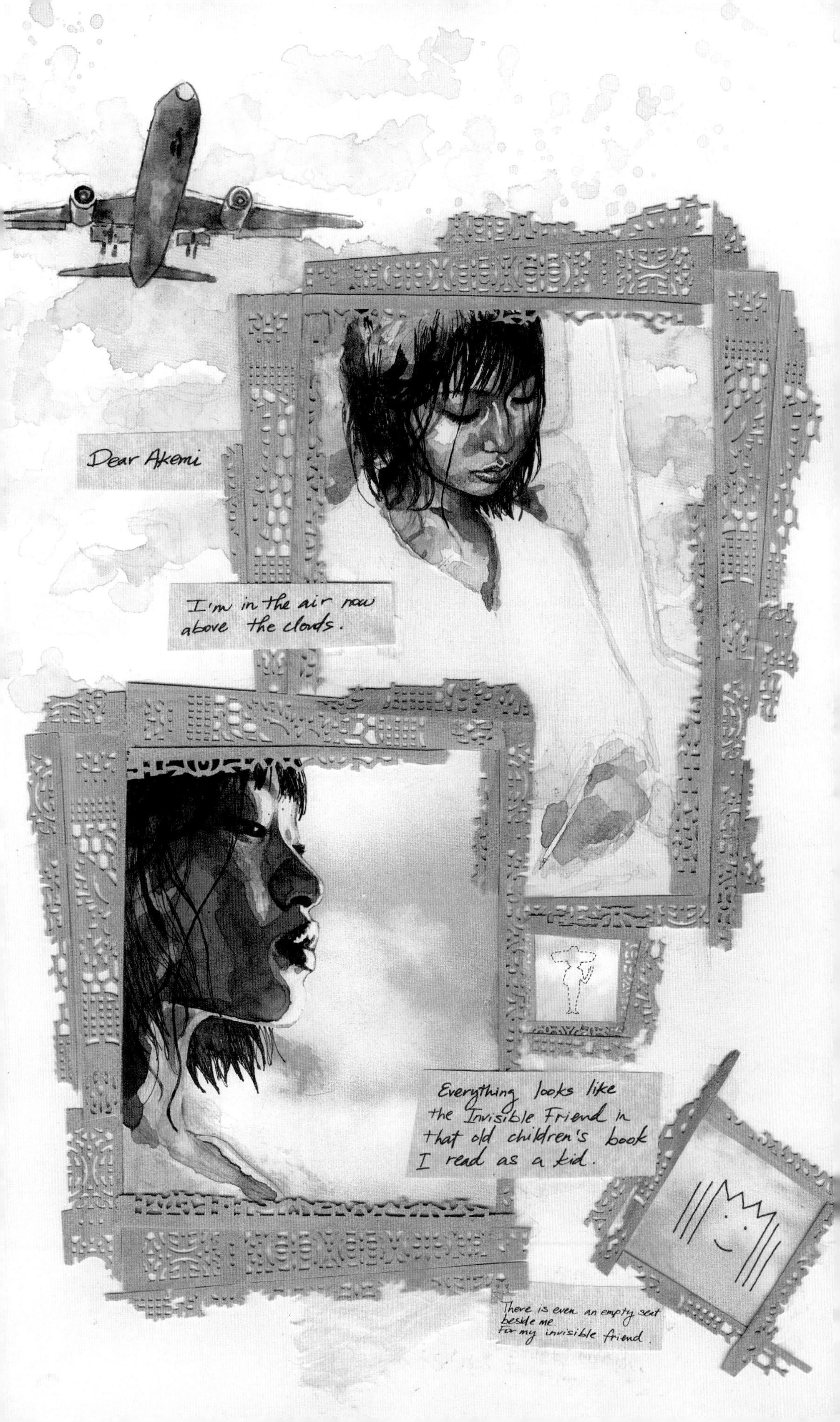
Dear Akemi
I'm in the air now above the clouds.
Everything looks like the Invisible Friend in that old children's book I read as a kid.
There is even an empty seat beside me. For my invisible friend.

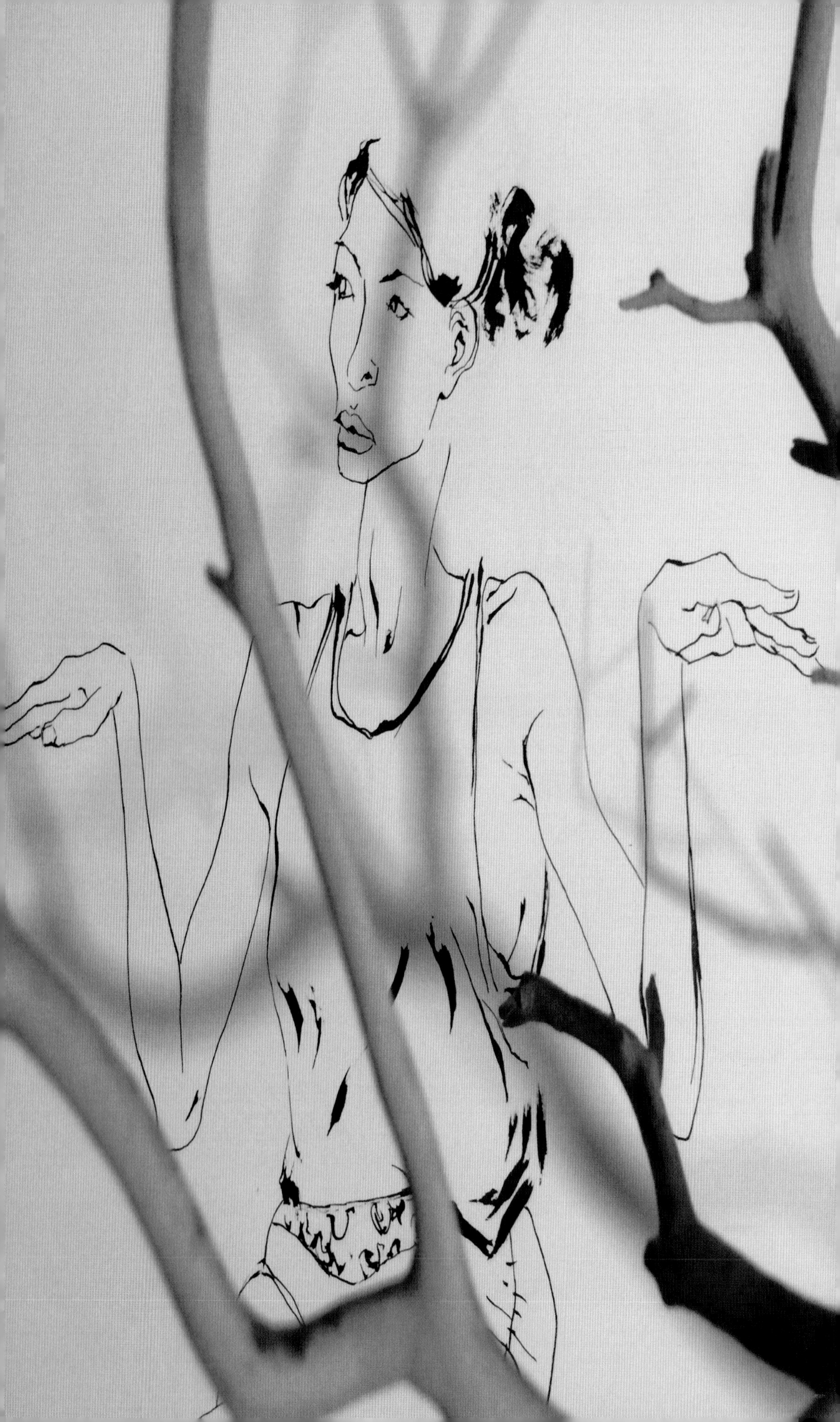

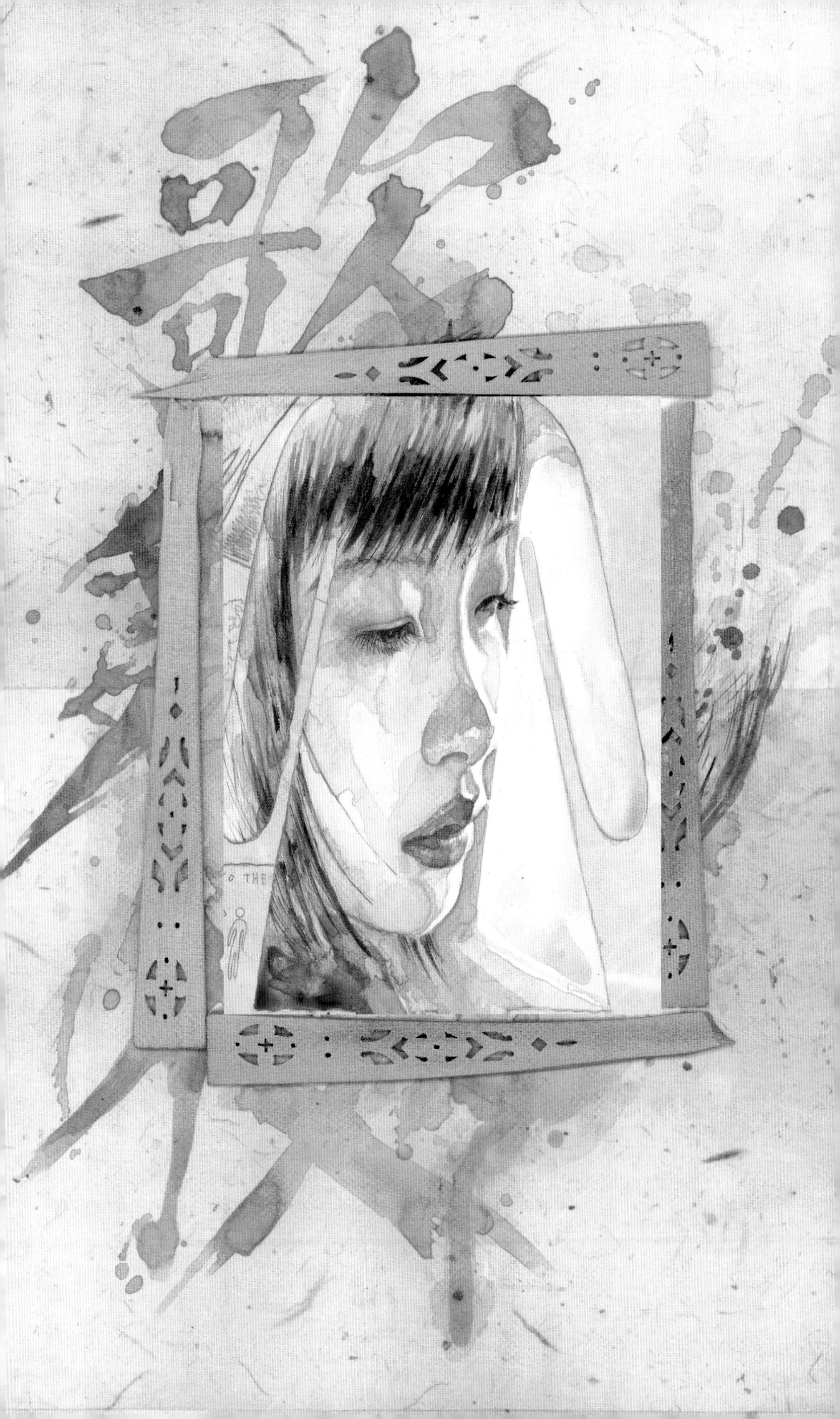

The Alchemy

Part Three

"I was painfully shy...
I didn't really have the nerve
to sing my songs...
I decided to do them in disguise."

- David Bowie

The Shy
Creatures

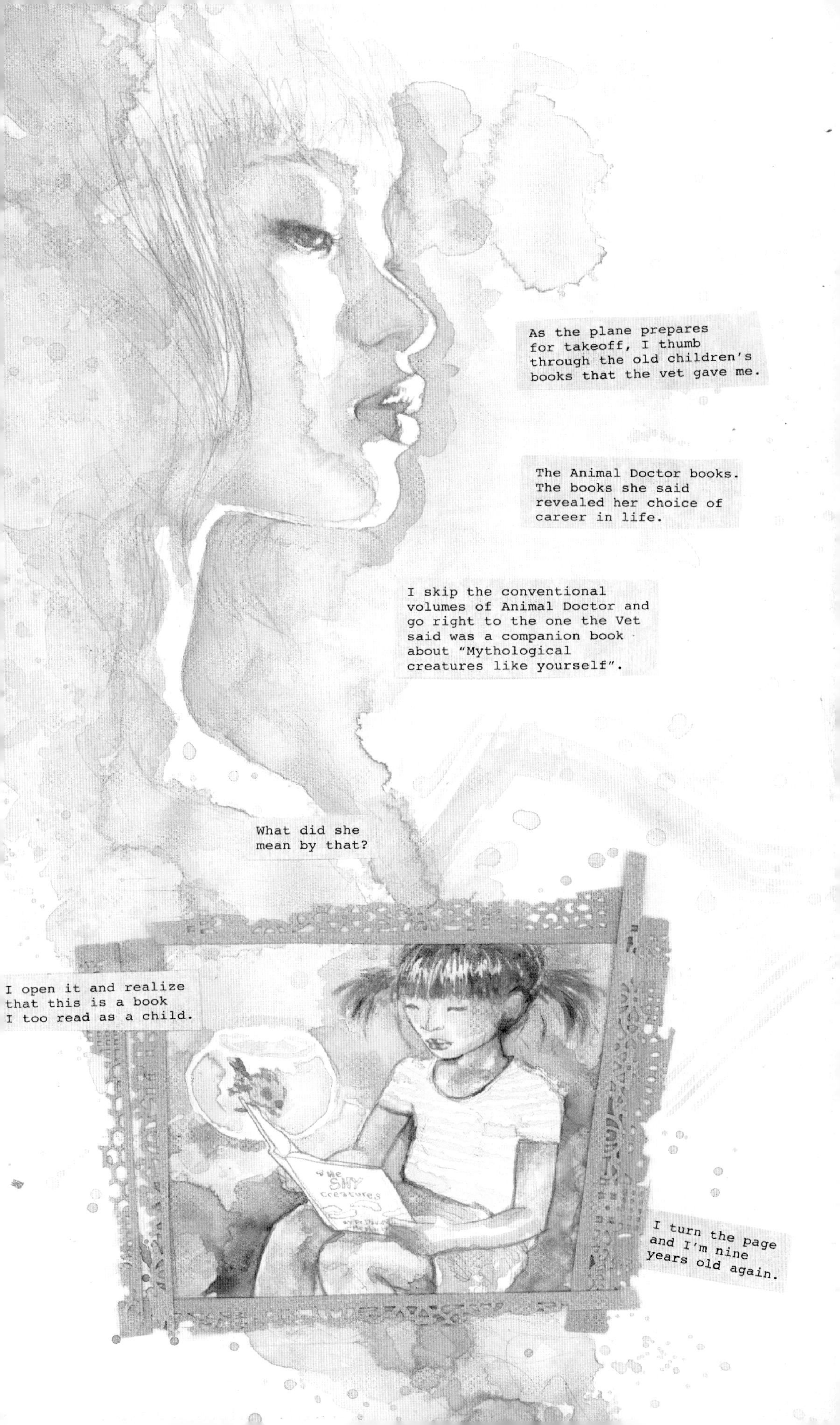
As the plane prepares for takeoff, I thumb through the old children's books that the vet gave me.
The Animal Doctor books. The books she said revealed her choice of career in life.
I skip the conventional volumes of Animal Doctor and go right to the one the Vet said was a companion book about "Mythological creatures like yourself".
What did she mean by that?
I open it and realize that this is a book I too read as a child.
the SHY creatures
I turn the page and I'm nine years old again.

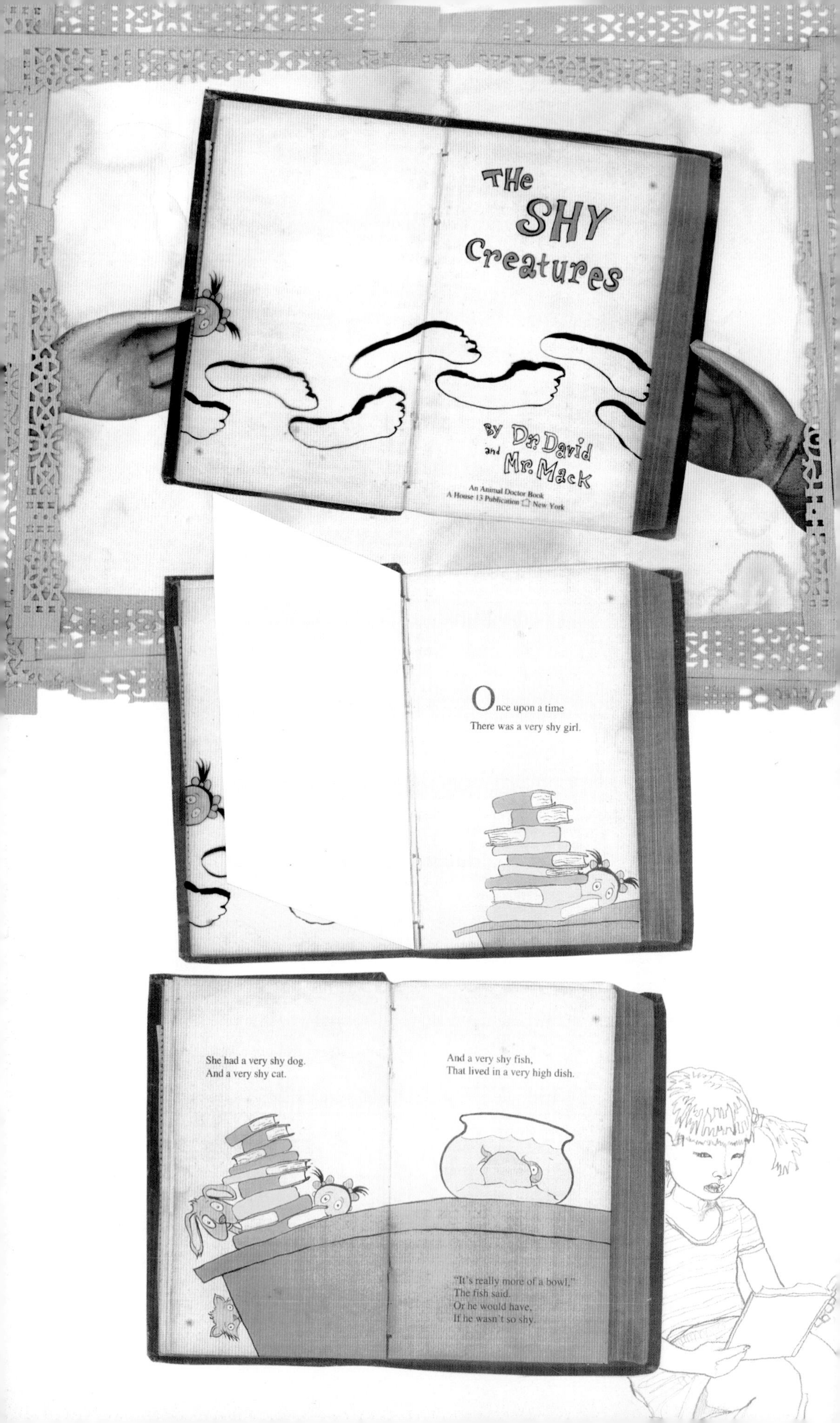
The SHY Creatures
By Dr. David and Mr. Mack
An Animal Doctor Book
A House 13 Publication New York
Once upon a time
There was a very shy girl.
She had a very shy dog.
And a very shy cat.
And a very shy fish,
That lived in a very high dish.
"It's really more of a bowl,"
The fish said.
Or he would have,
If he wasn't so shy.

"What do you want to be
When you grow up?"
Her teacher asked,
One day in school,
To the shy girl's class.

"A doctor", said Larry.
"A fireman", said Terry.
"A teacher", said Mary.

"I want to be a doctor
To the shy creatures,"
Said the shy girl.

Or she would have,
If she wasn't so shy.

"What do you mean?"
The teacher would have sighed,
If the shy girl said
What she would have said,
If she wasn't so shy.

"I would help the creatures
That most people can't see,"
Said the shy girl happily.

"HAHAHA!"
The children would have laughed.
If the shy girl said
What she would have said,
If she wasn't so shy instead.

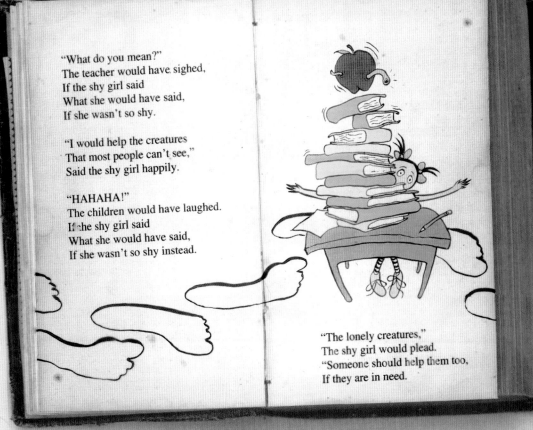

"The lonely creatures,"
The shy girl would plead.
"Someone should help them too,
If they are in need.

"What do you *mean*?"
The teacher would scream.

"Like Bigfoot,"
The shy girl would explain.

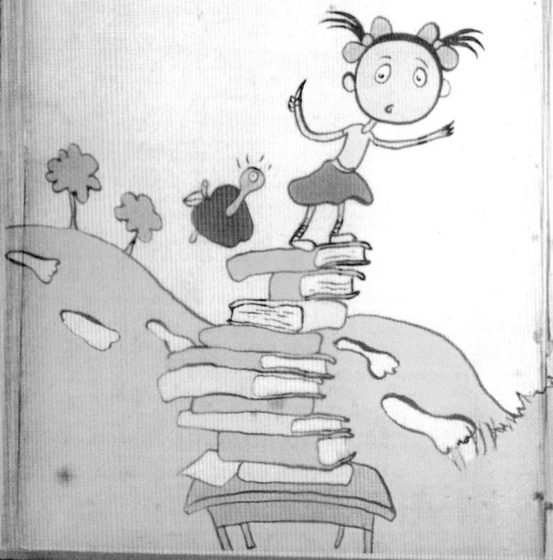

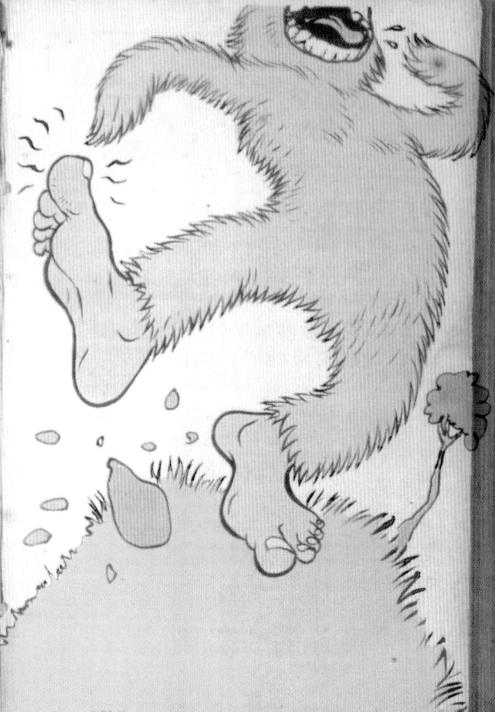

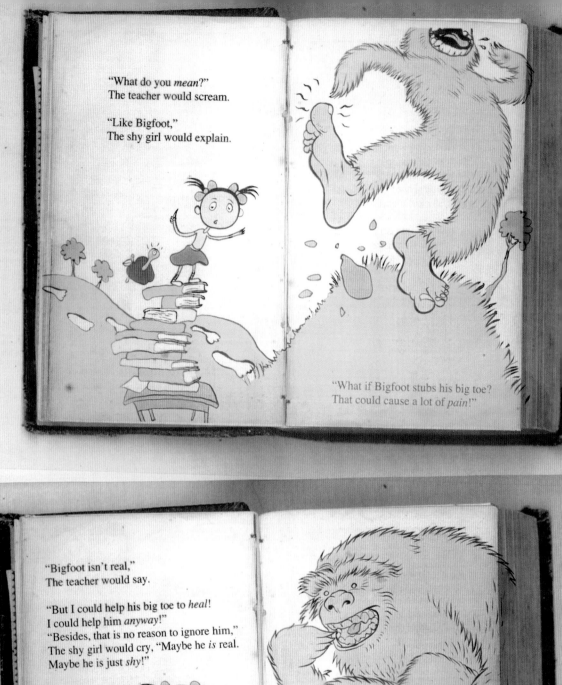

"What if Bigfoot stubs his big toe?
That could cause a lot of *pain*!"

"Bigfoot isn't real,"
The teacher would say.

"But I could help his big toe to *heal*!
I could help him *anyway*!"
"Besides, that is no reason to ignore him,"
The shy girl would cry, "Maybe he *is* real.
Maybe he is just *shy*!"

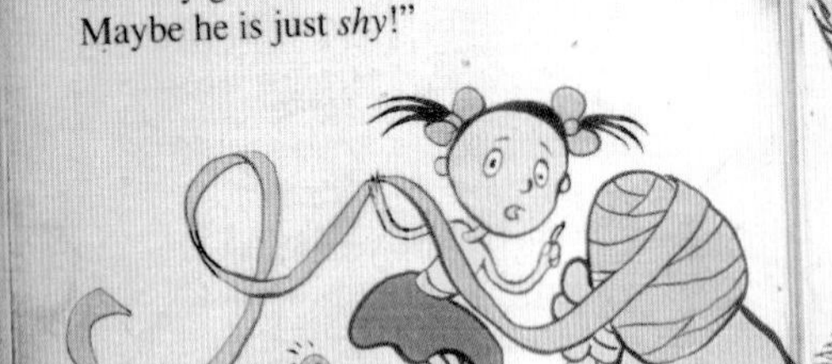

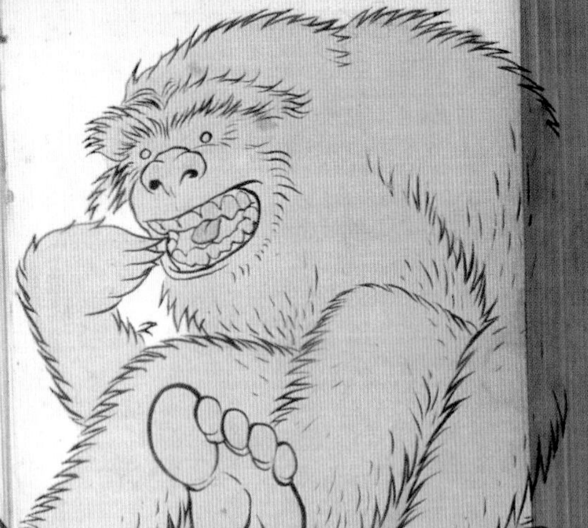

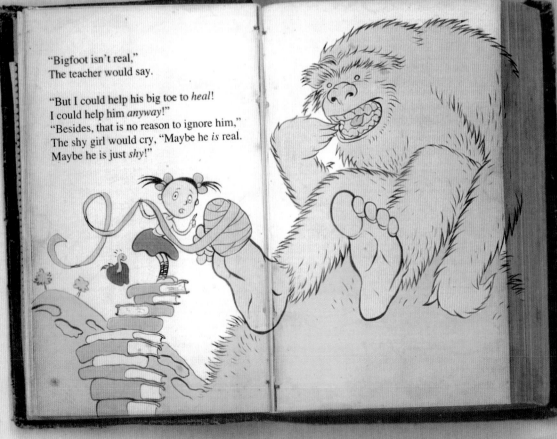

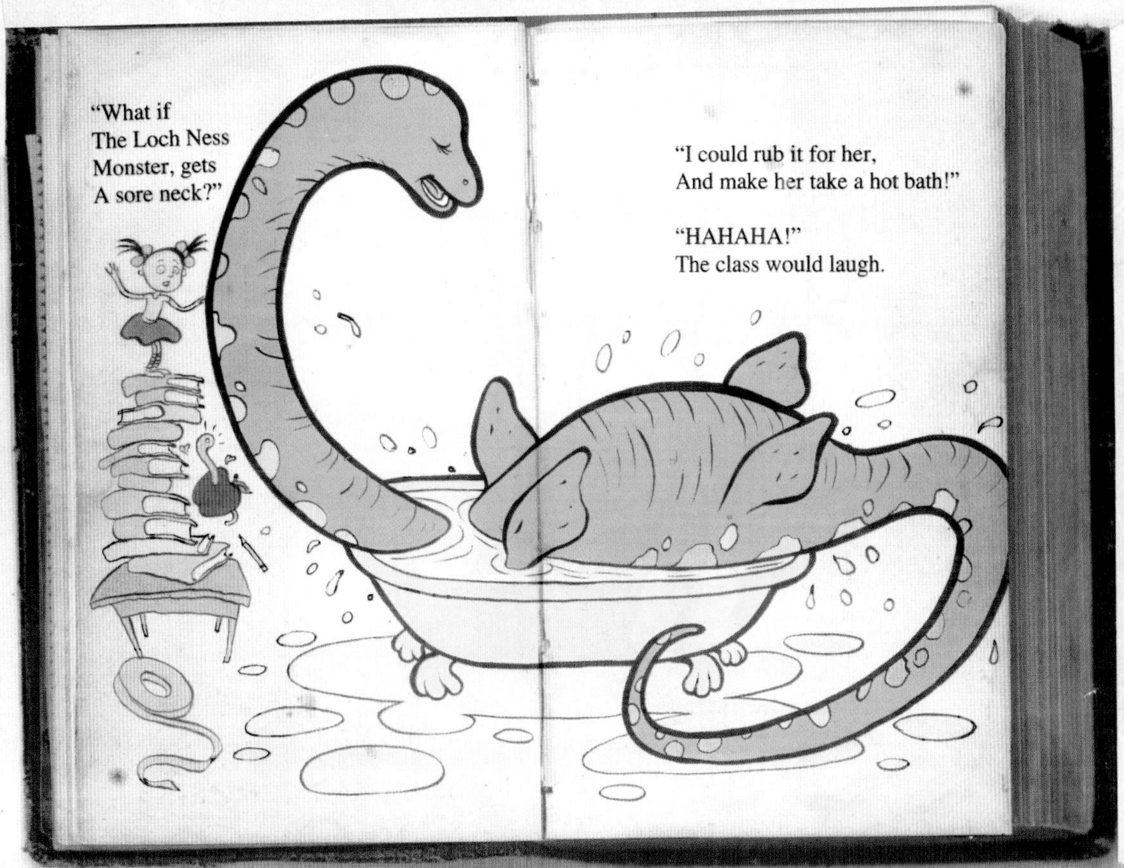
"What if
The Loch Ness
Monster, gets
A sore neck?"
"I could rub it for her,
And make her take a hot bath!"
"HAHAHA!"
The class would laugh.

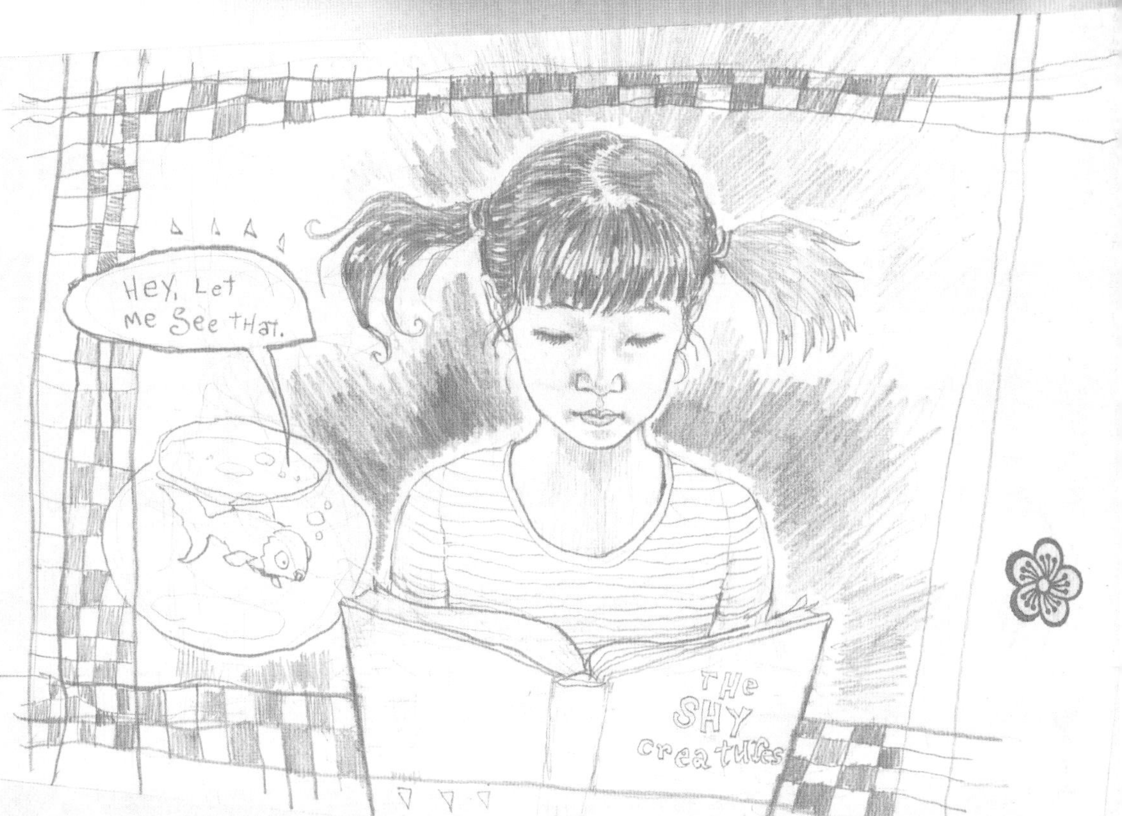
Hey, Let me See that.
THE SHY creatures

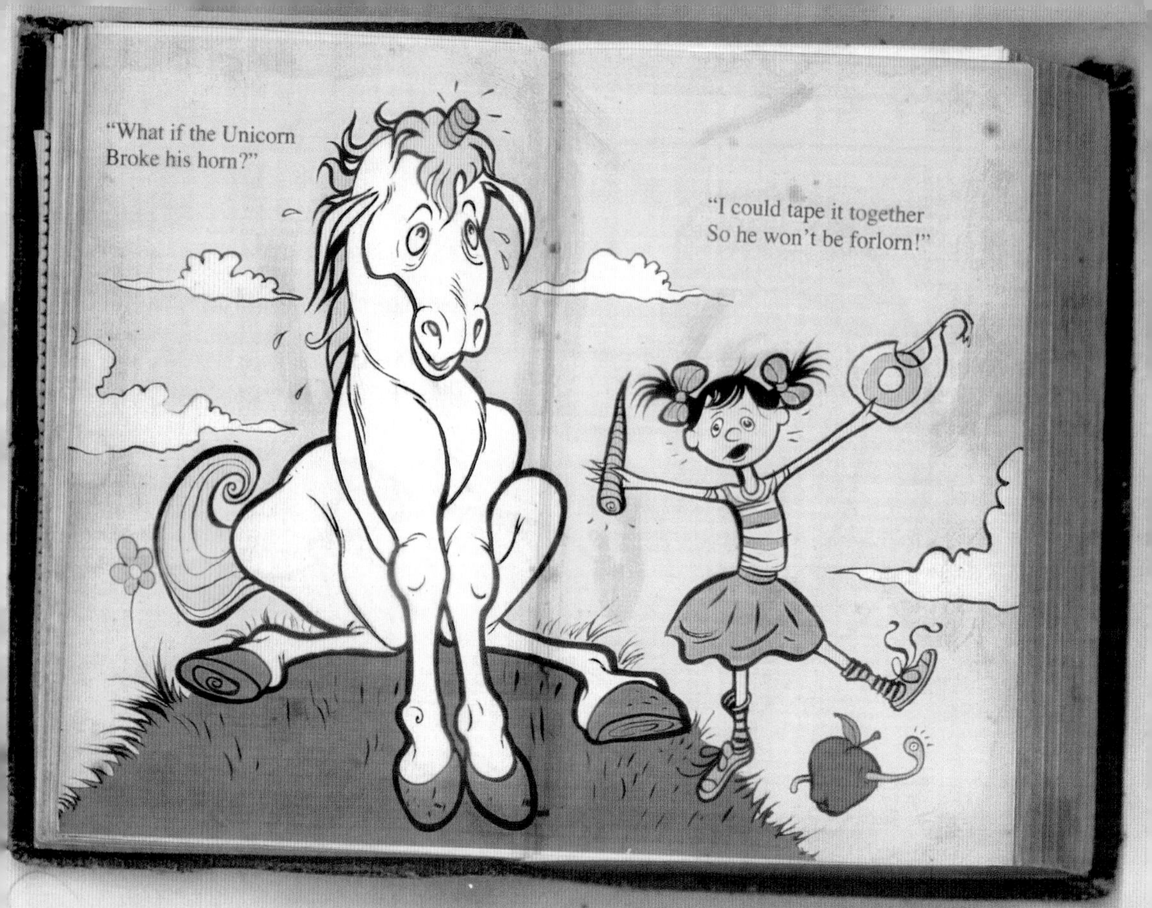
"What if the Unicorn
Broke his horn?"
"I could tape it together
So he won't be forlorn!"

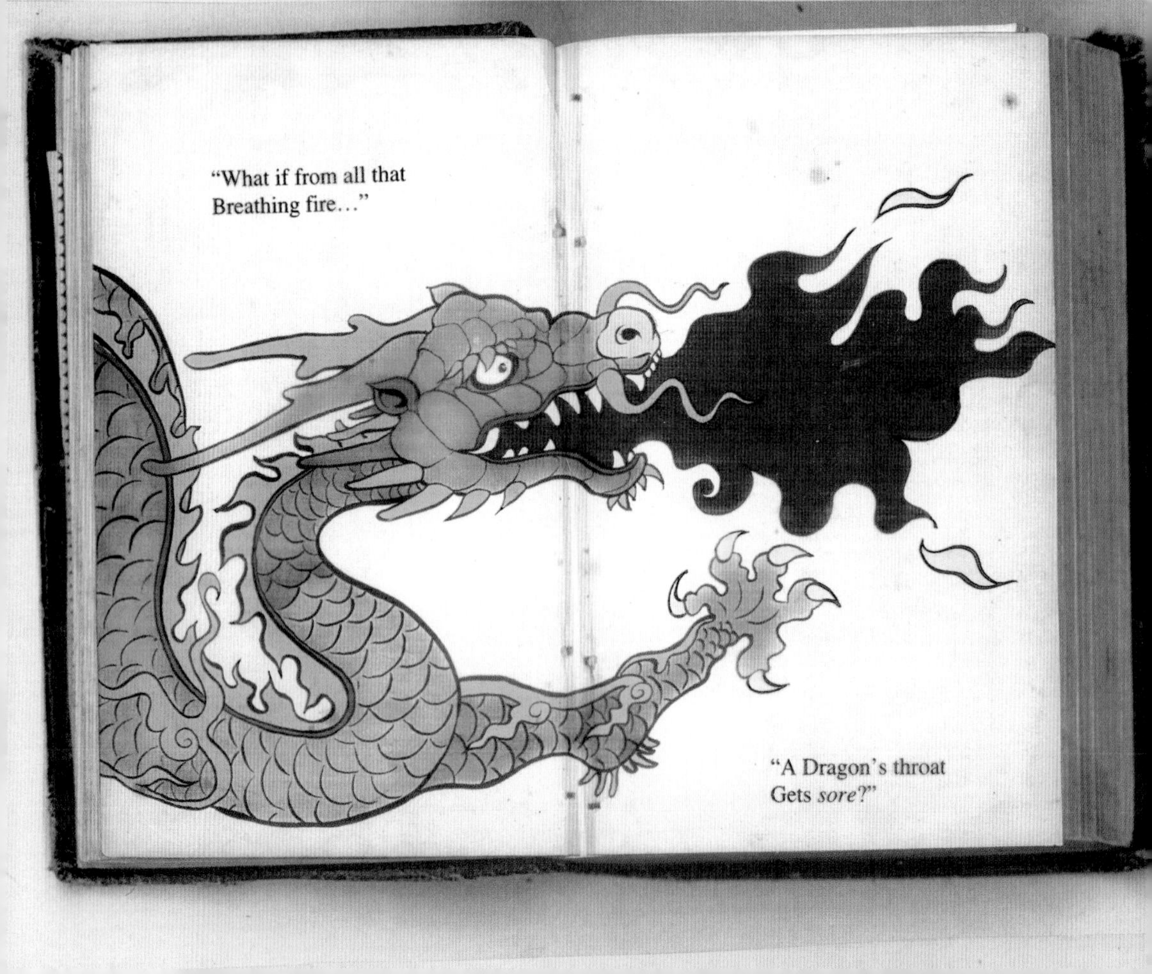
"What if from all that
Breathing fire…"
"A Dragon's throat
Gets *sore*?"

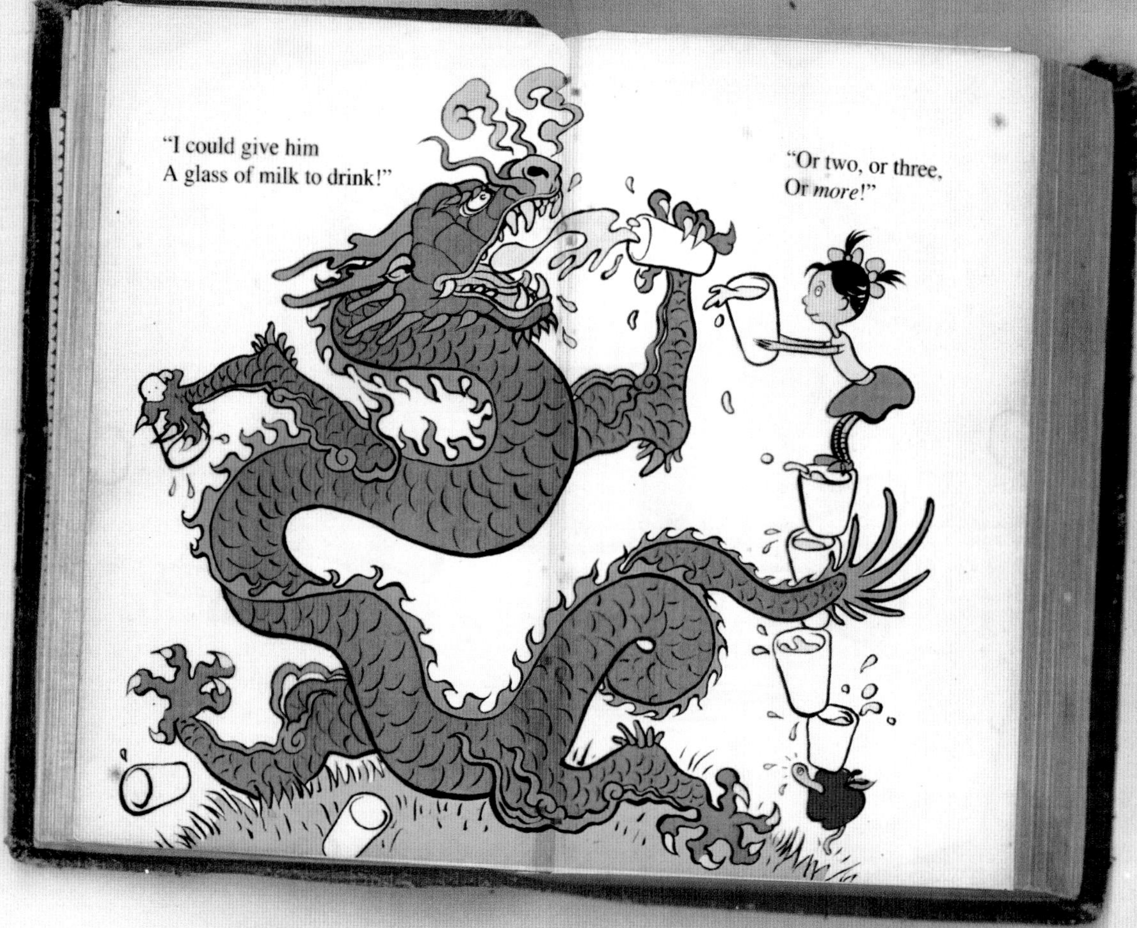
"I could give him
A glass of milk to drink!"
"Or two, or three,
Or *more*!"

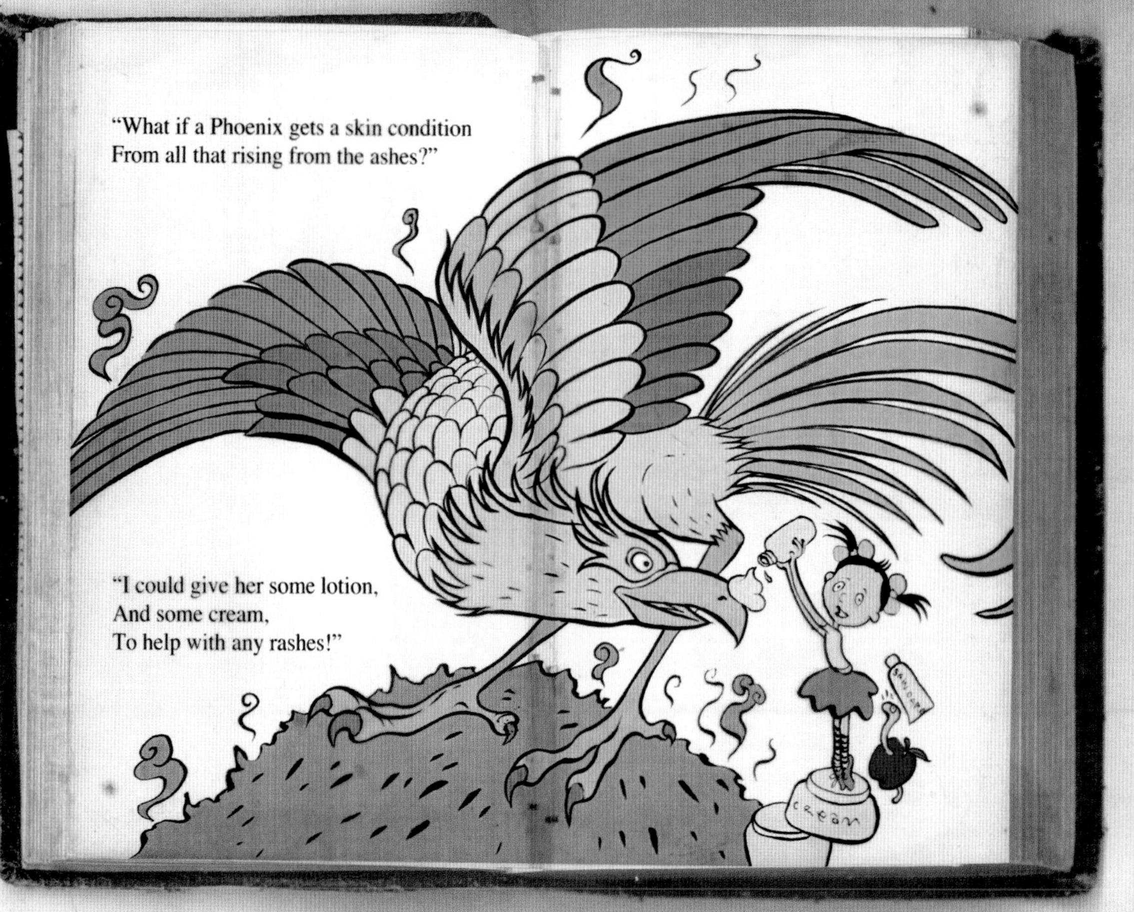
"What if a Phoenix gets a skin condition
From all that rising from the ashes?"
"I could give her some lotion,
And some cream,
To help with any rashes!"

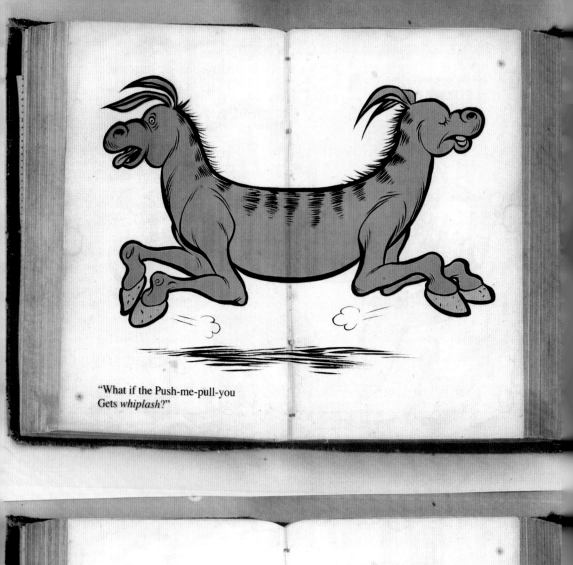

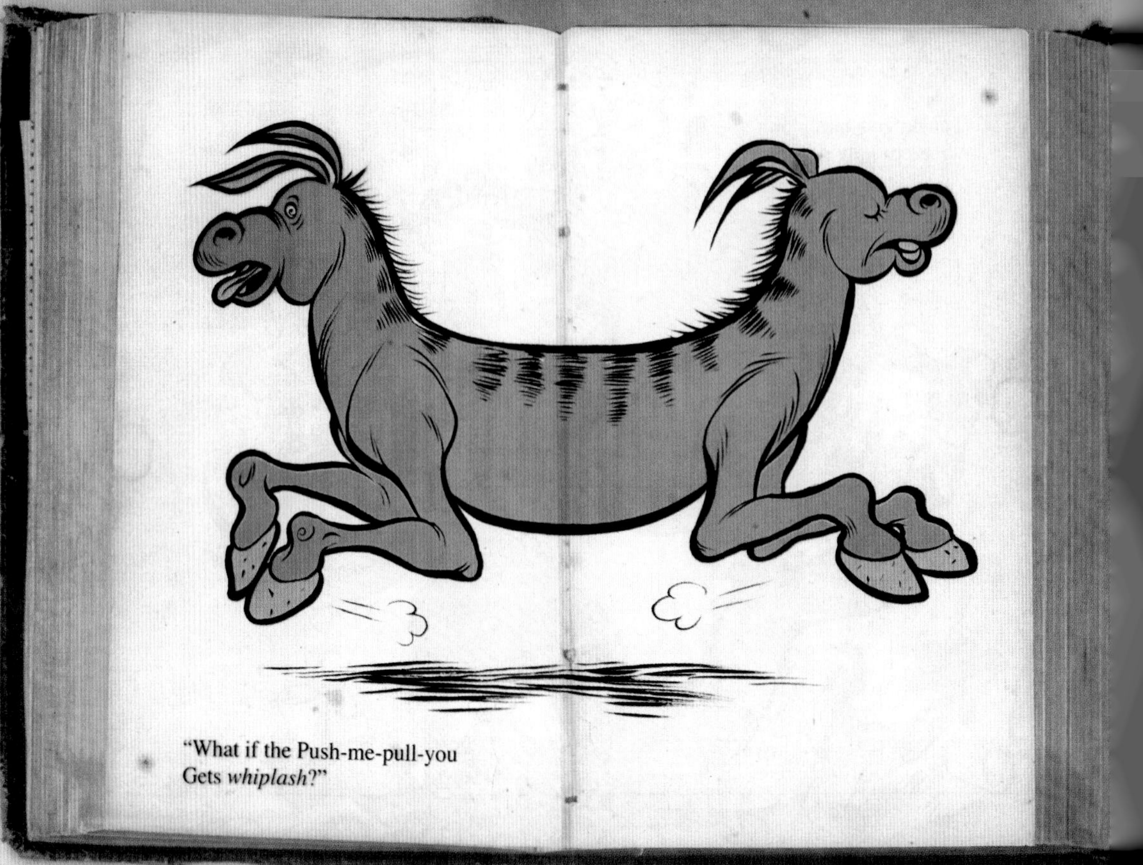
"What if the Push-me-pull-you
Gets *whiplash*?"

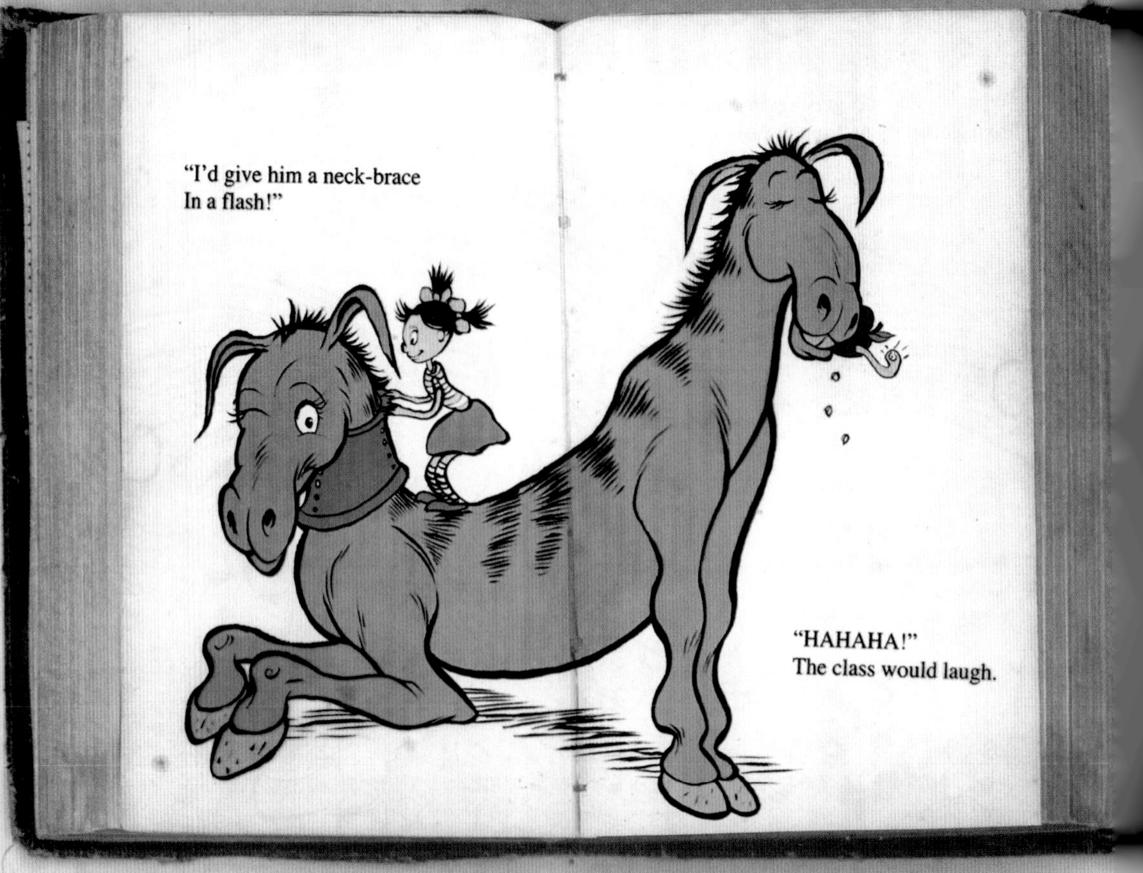
"I'd give him a neck-brace
In a flash!"
"HAHAHA!"
The class would laugh.

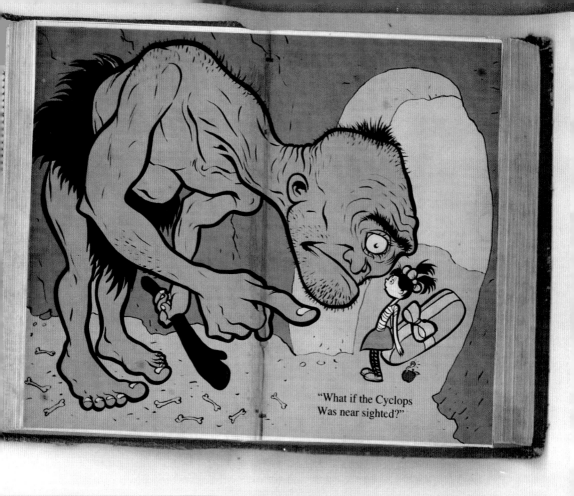

"What if the Cyclops
Was near sighted?"

I could make him glasses!

"HAHAHA!"
The kids'd be *delighted*!
They'd laugh in all the classes!"

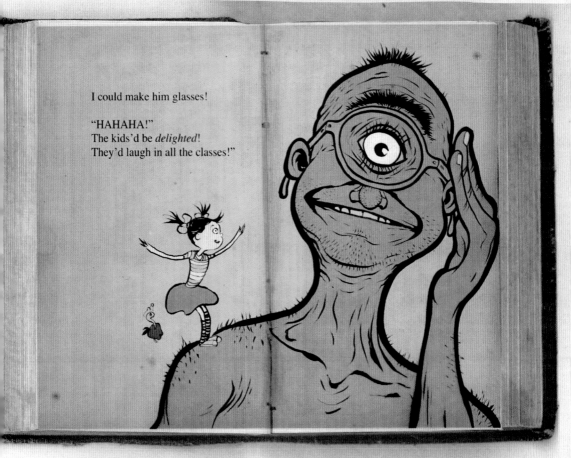

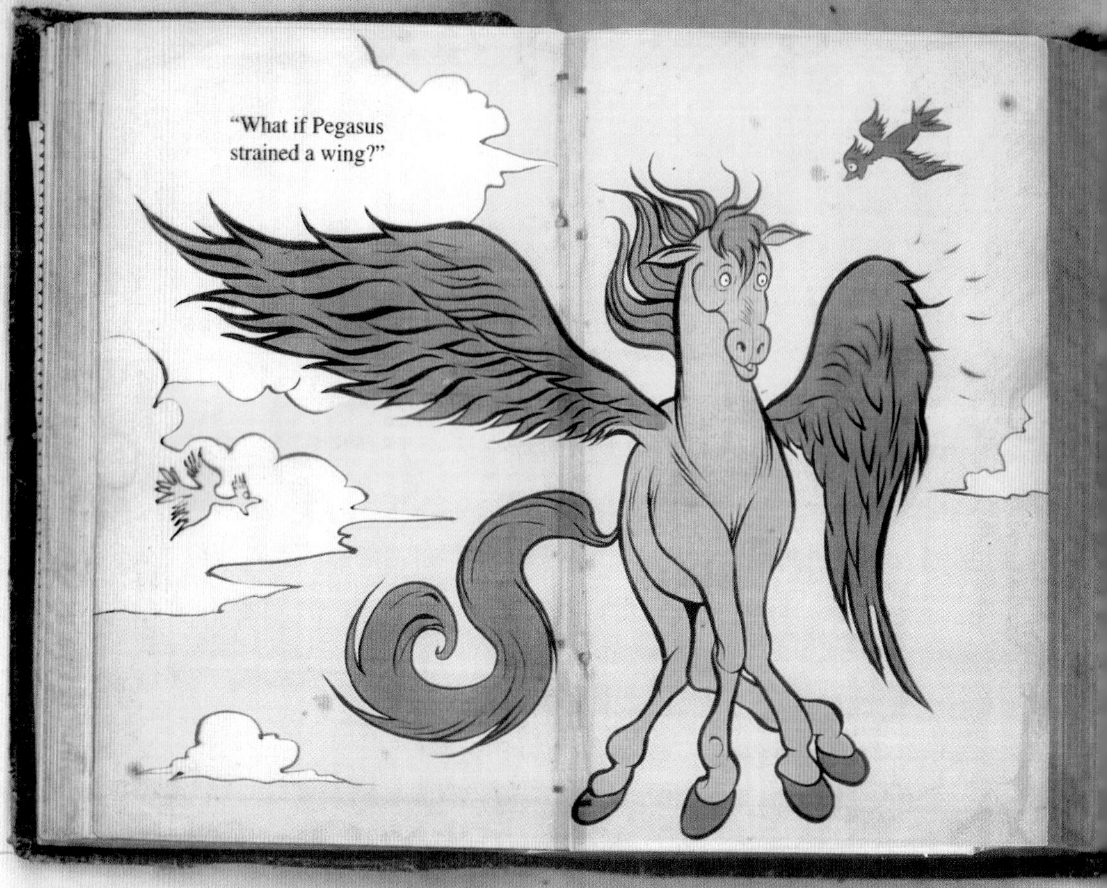
"What if Pegasus
strained a wing?"

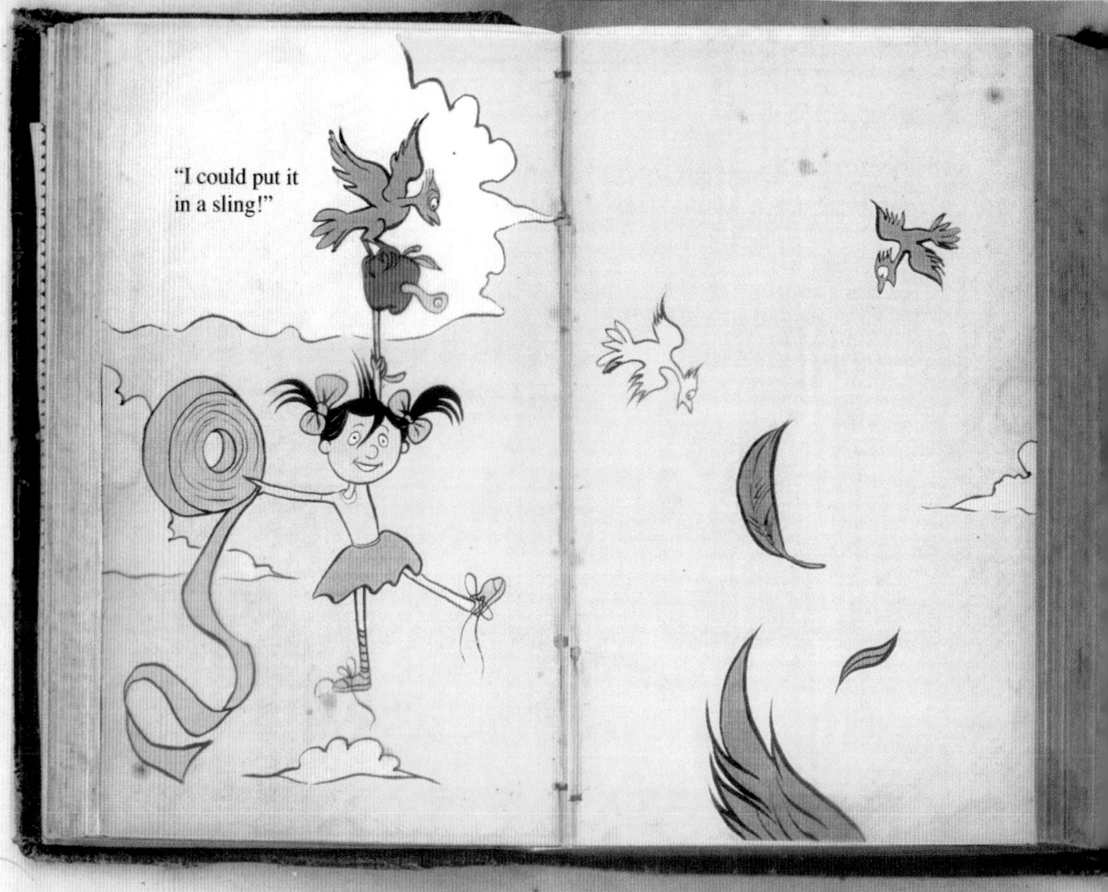
"I could put it
in a sling!"

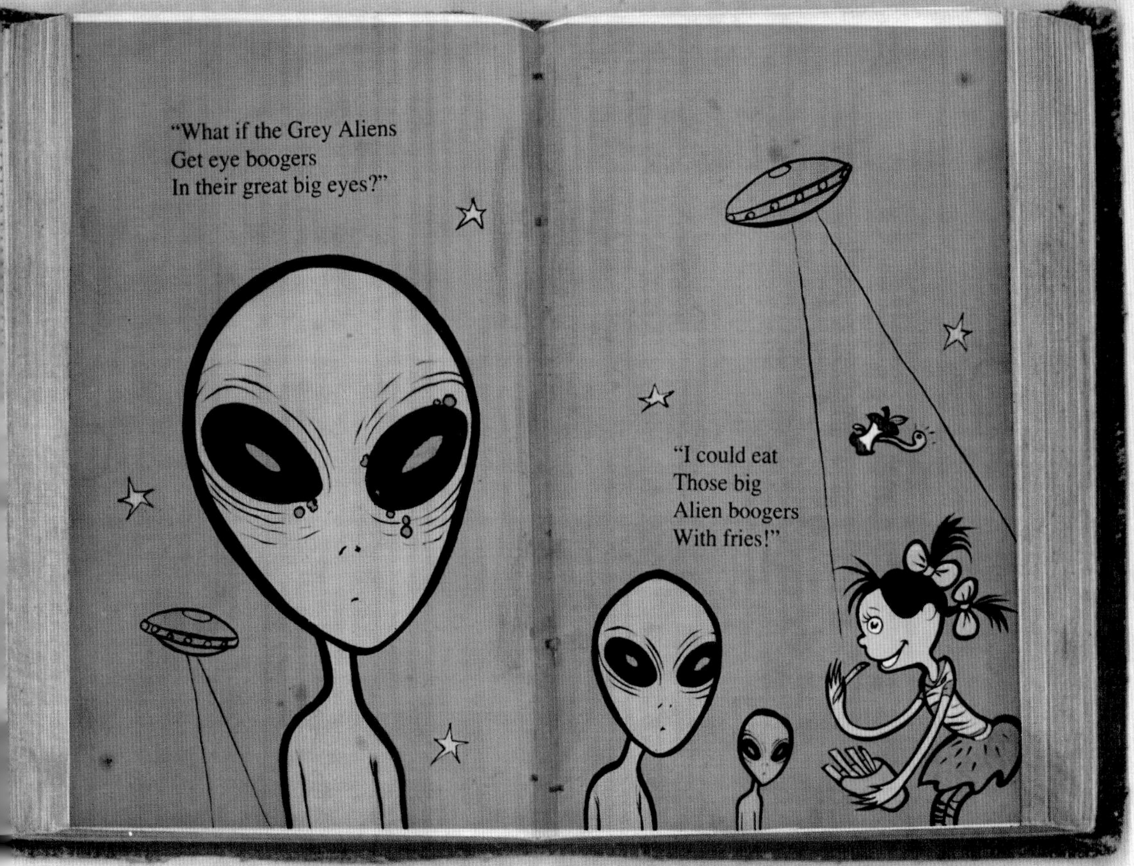
"What if the Grey Aliens
Get eye boogers
In their great big eyes?"
"I could eat
Those big
Alien boogers
With fries!"

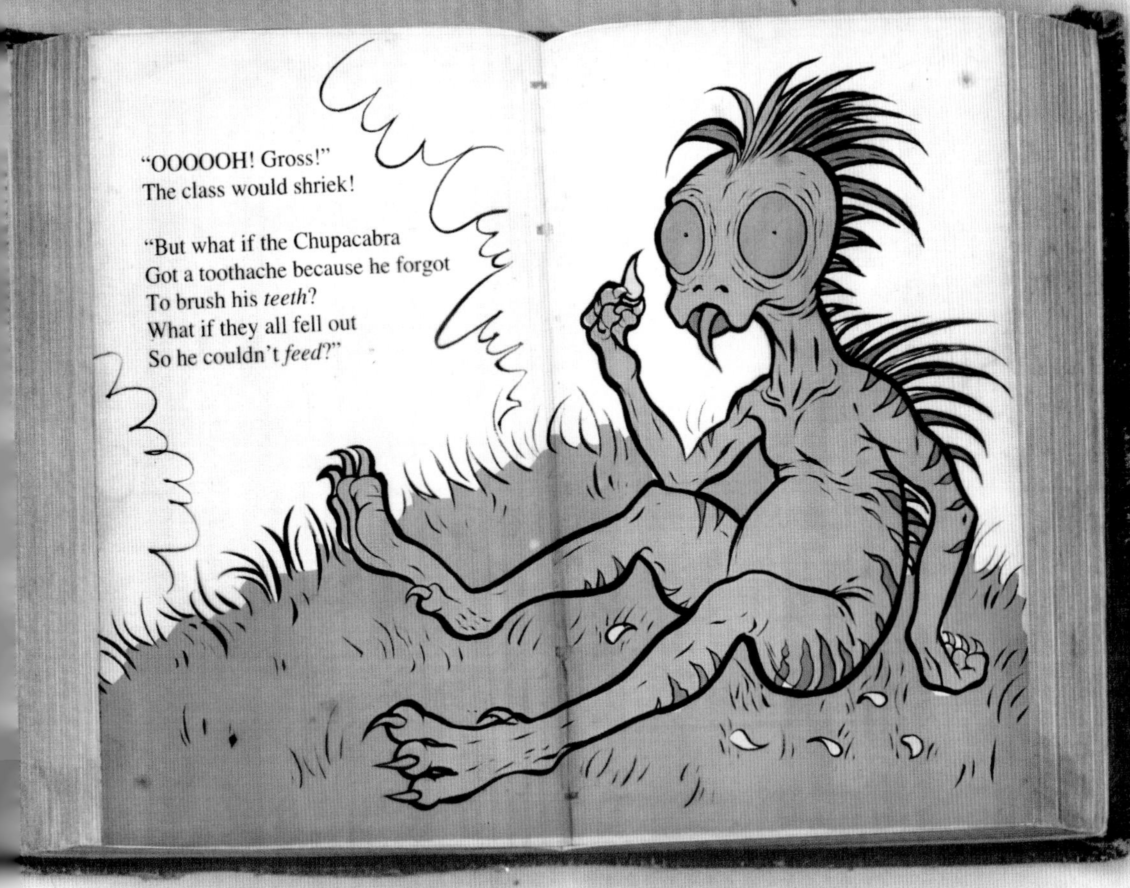
"OOOOOH! Gross!"
The class would shriek!
"But what if the Chupacabra
Got a toothache because he forgot
To brush his *teeth*?
What if they all fell out
So he couldn't *feed*?"

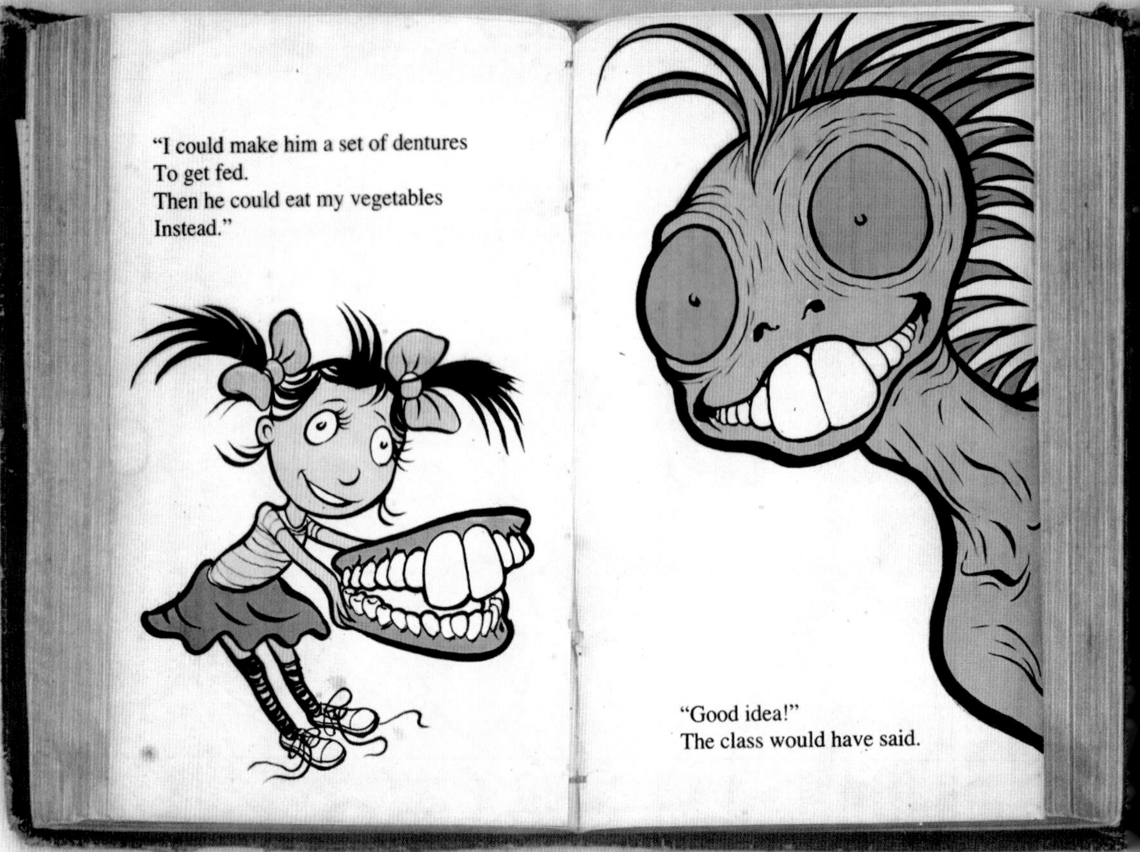

"I could make him a set of dentures
To get fed.
Then he could eat my vegetables
Instead."

"Good idea!"
The class would have said.

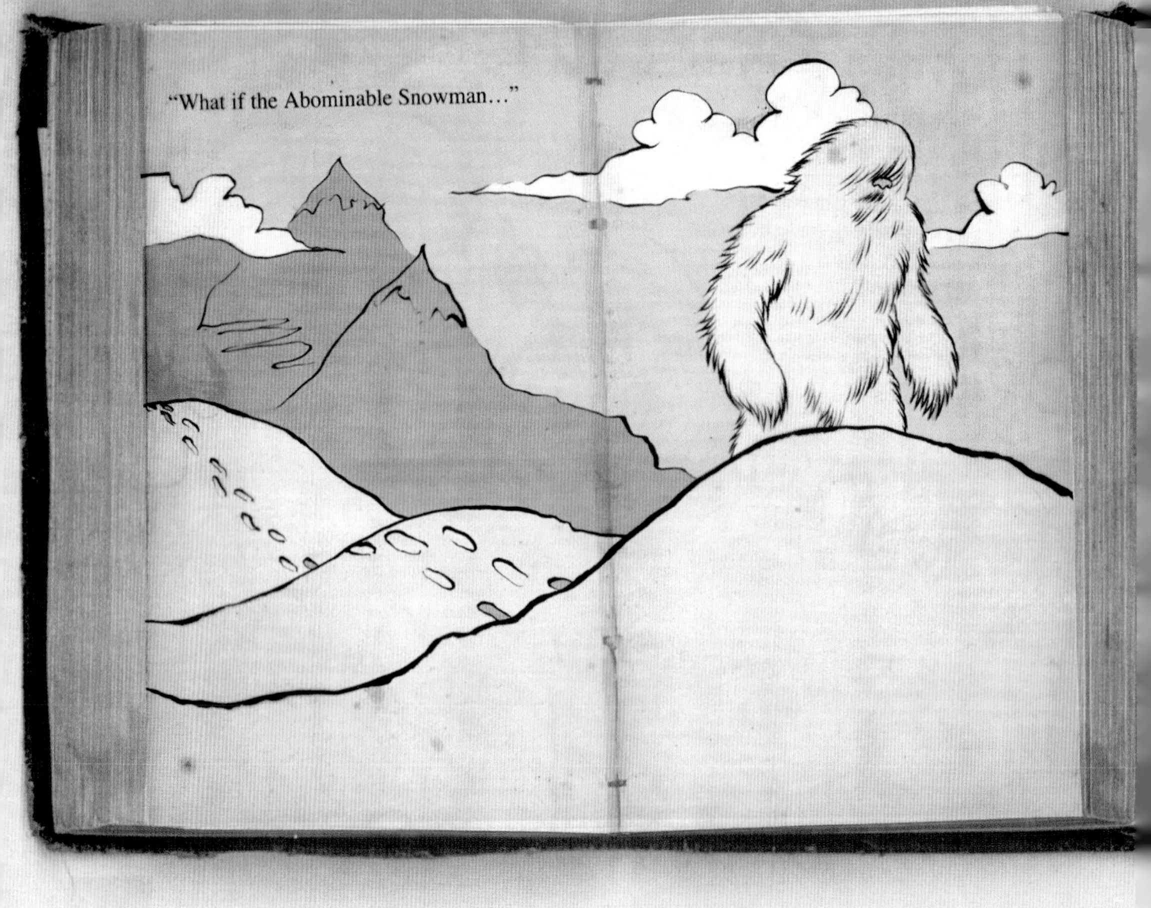

"What if the Abominable Snowman…"

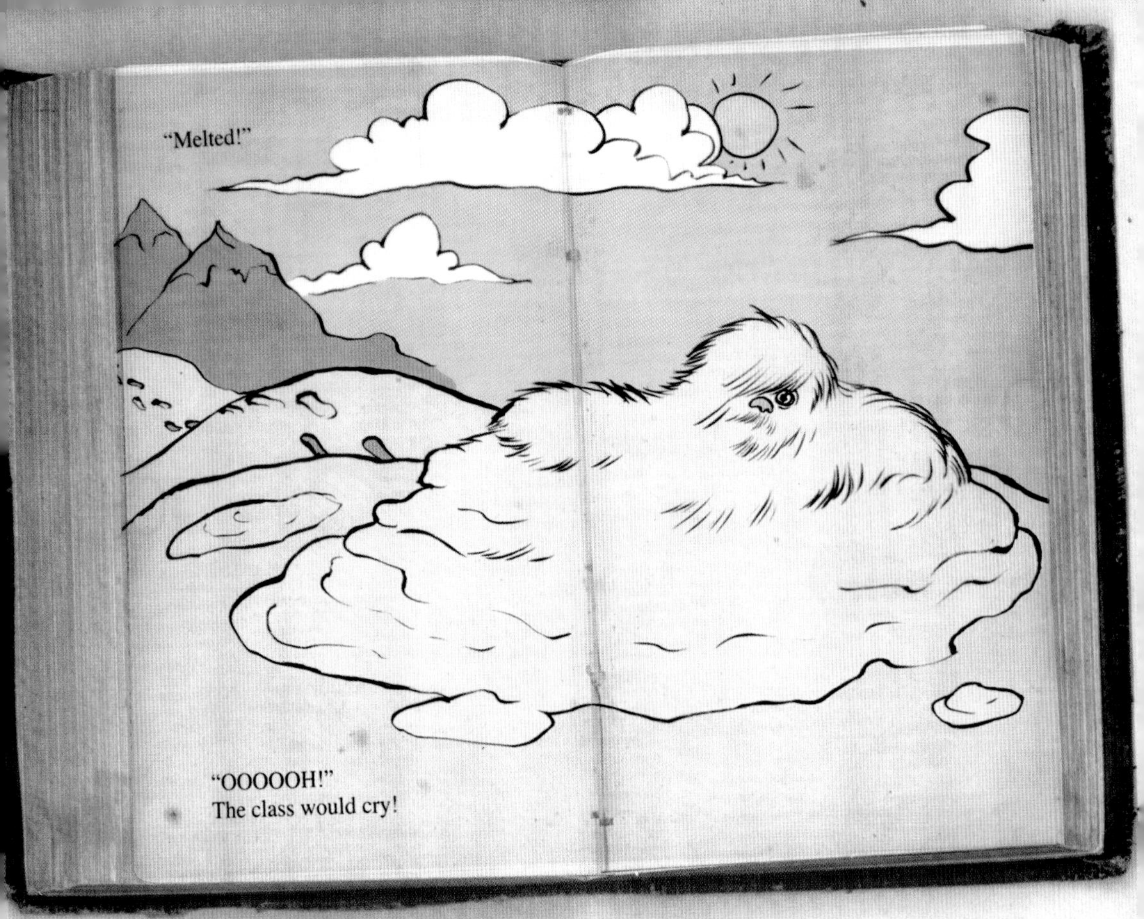
"Melted!"
"OOOOOH!"
The class would cry!

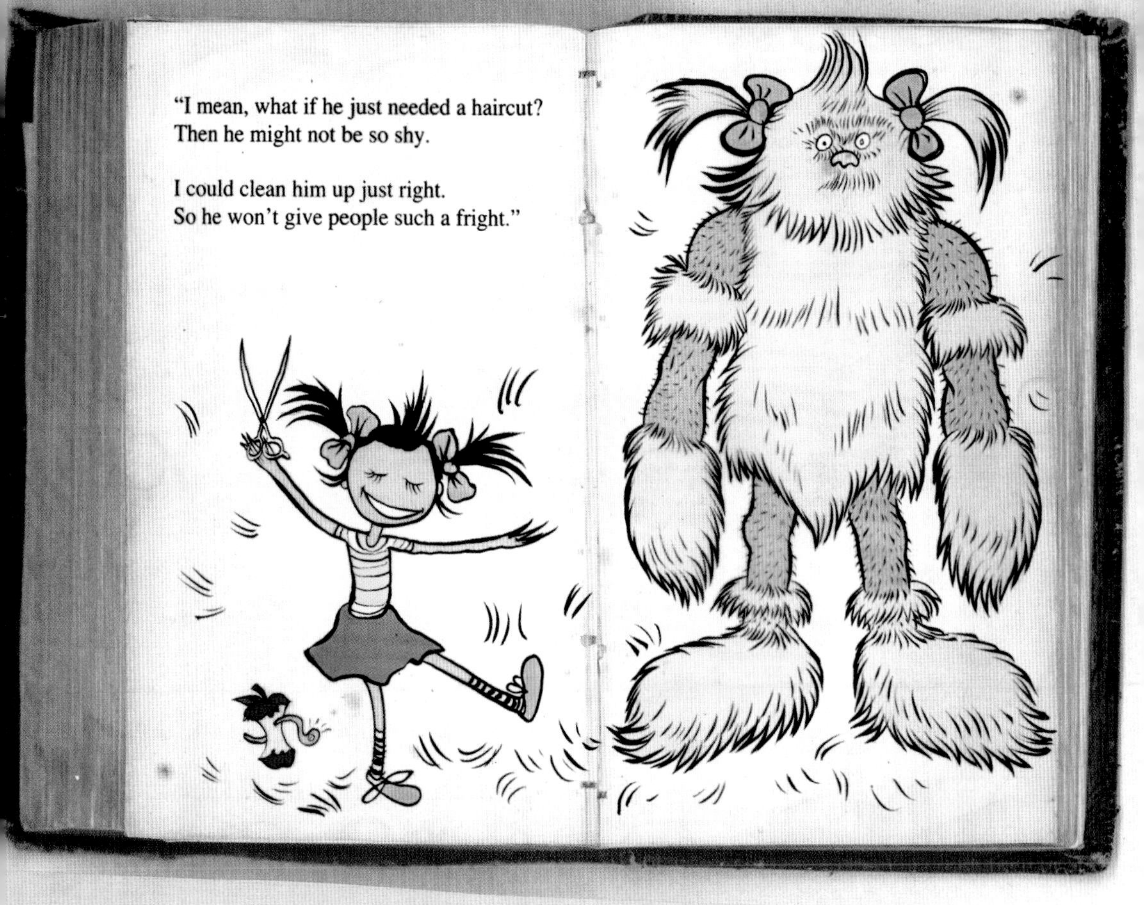
"I mean, what if he just needed a haircut?
Then he might not be so shy.
I could clean him up just right.
So he won't give people such a fright."

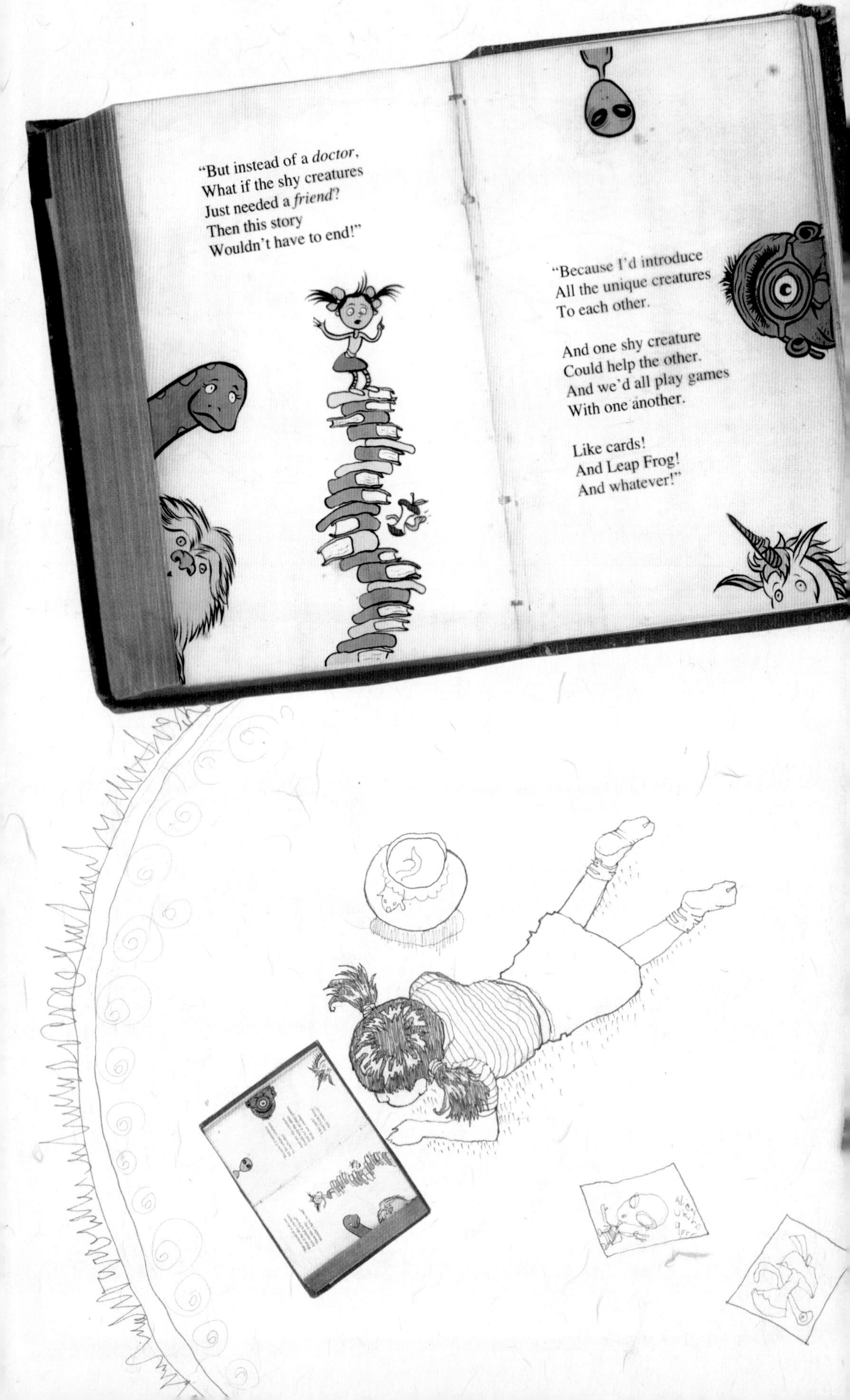
"But instead of a *doctor*,
What if the shy creatures
Just needed a *friend*?
Then this story
Wouldn't have to end!"
"Because I'd introduce
All the unique creatures
To each other.
And one shy creature
Could help the other.
And we'd all play games
With one another.
Like cards!
And Leap Frog!
And whatever!"

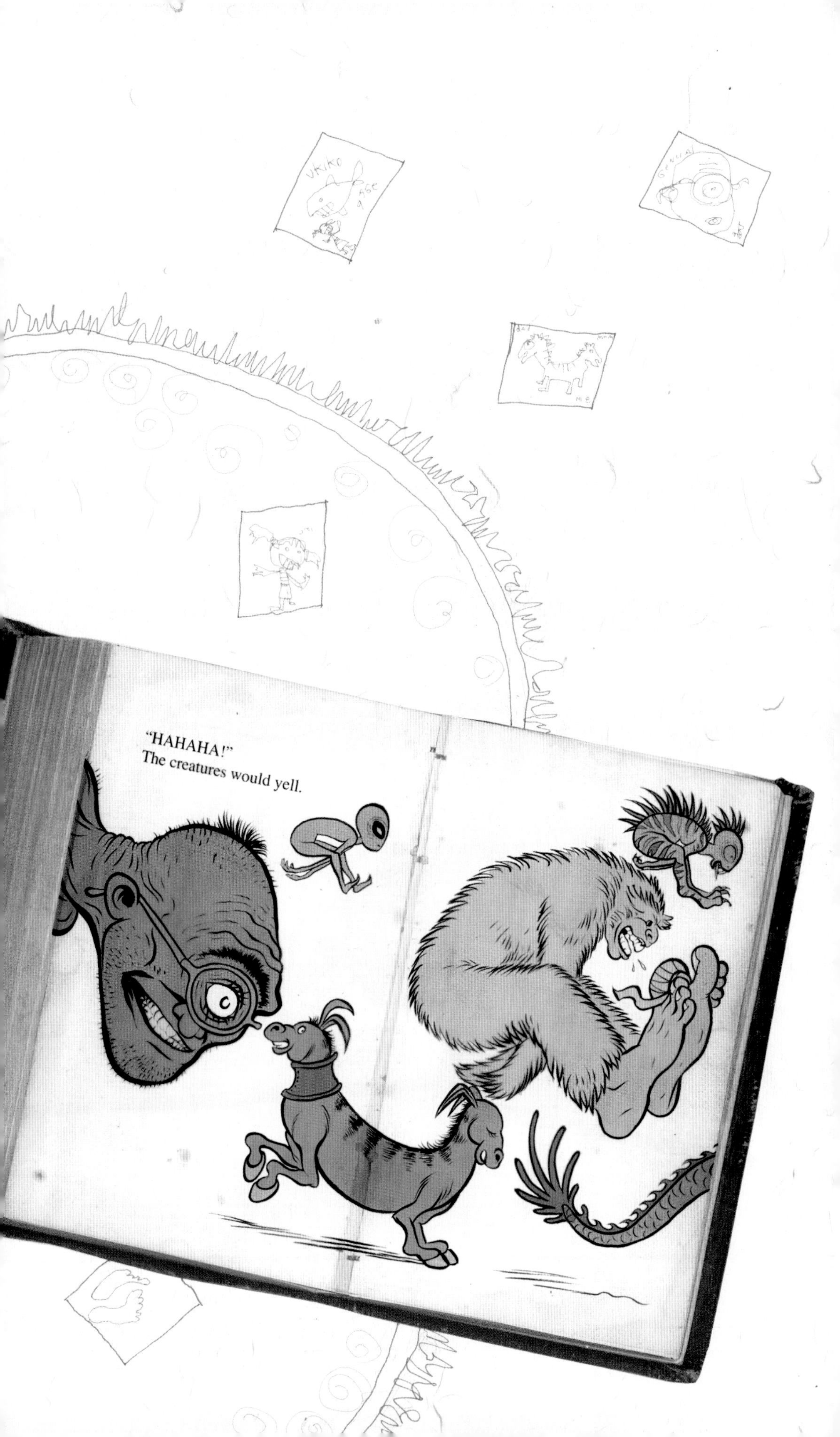
"HAHAHA!"
The creatures would yell.

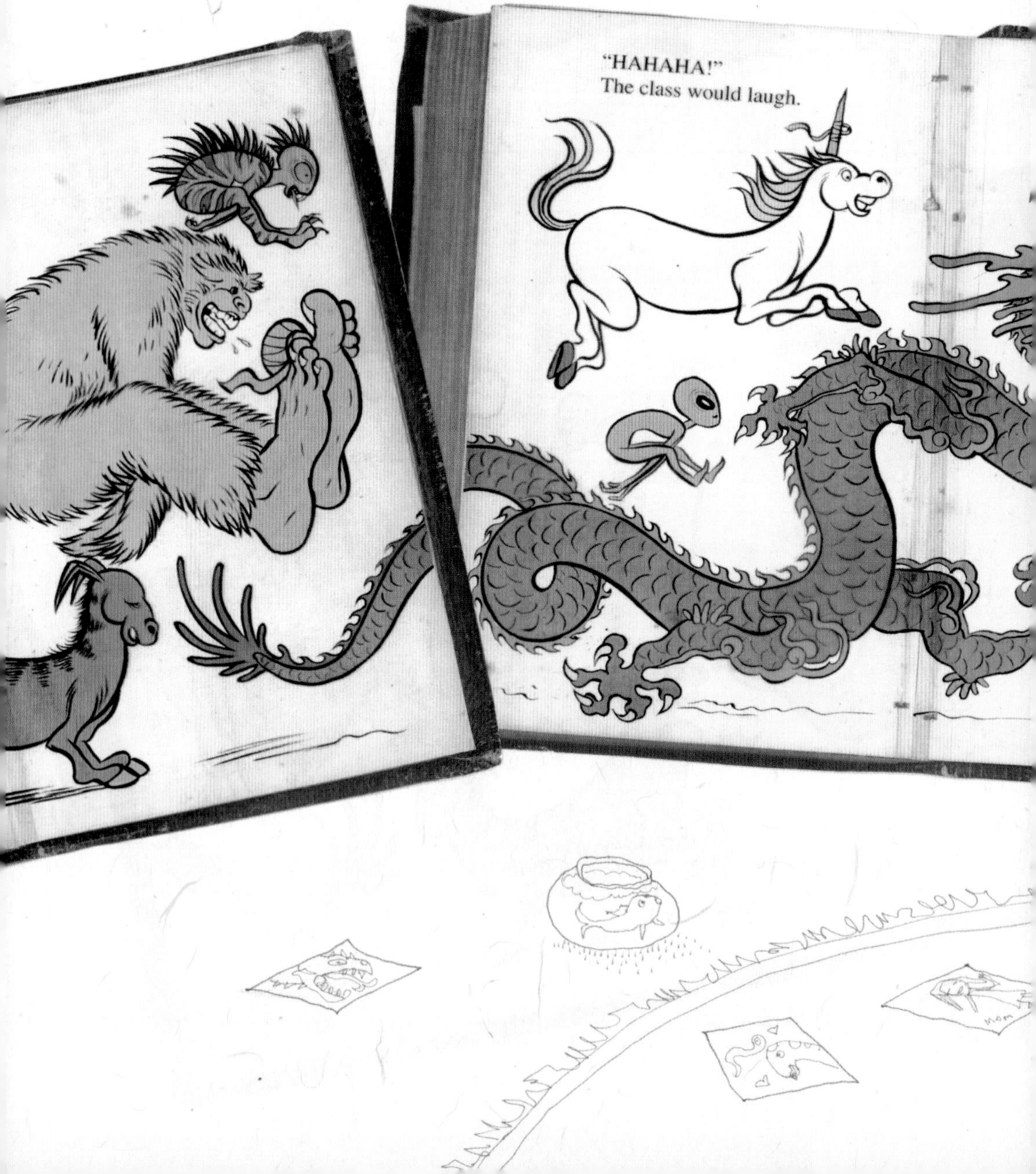
"HAHAHA!"
The class would laugh.

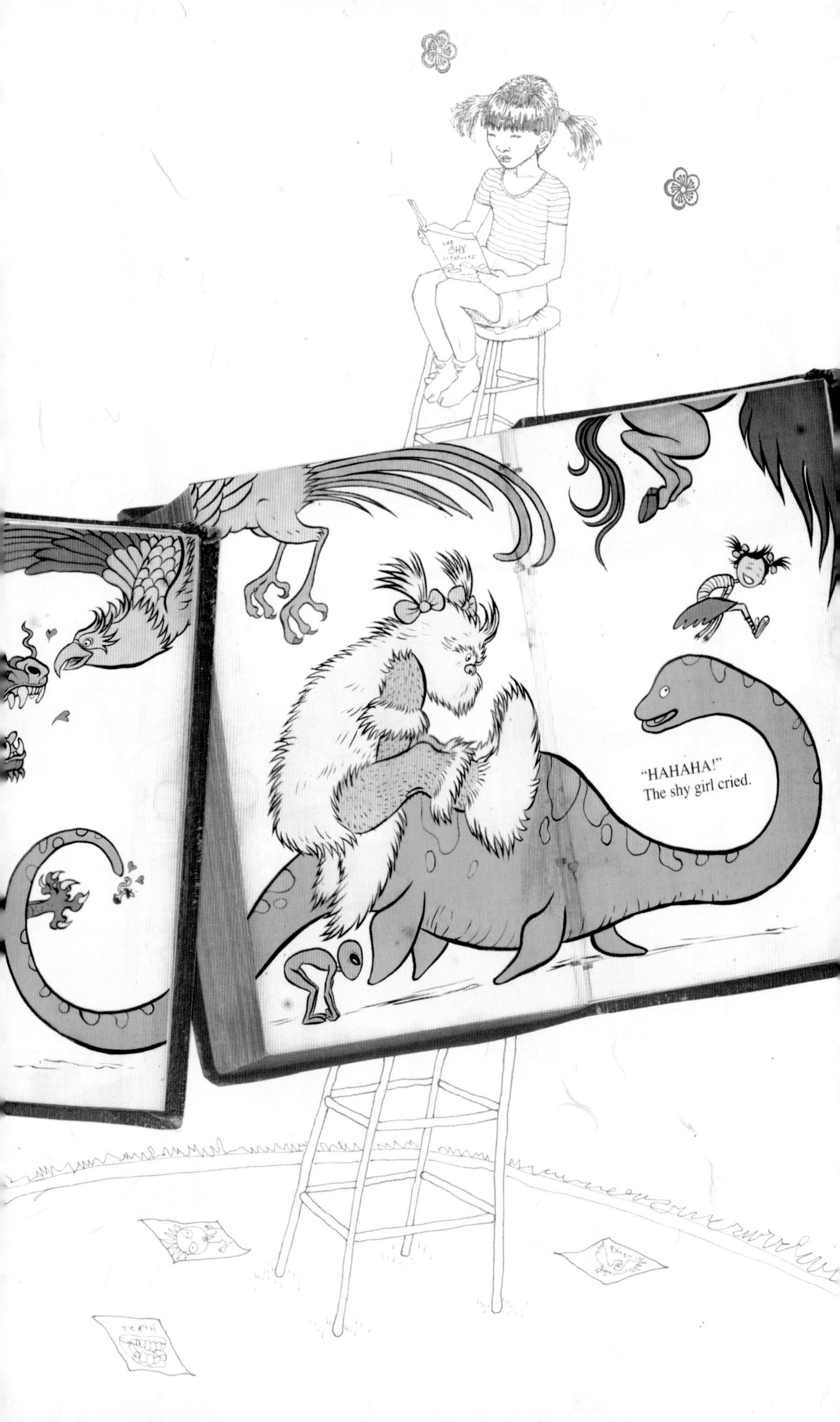
"HAHAHA!"
The shy girl cried.

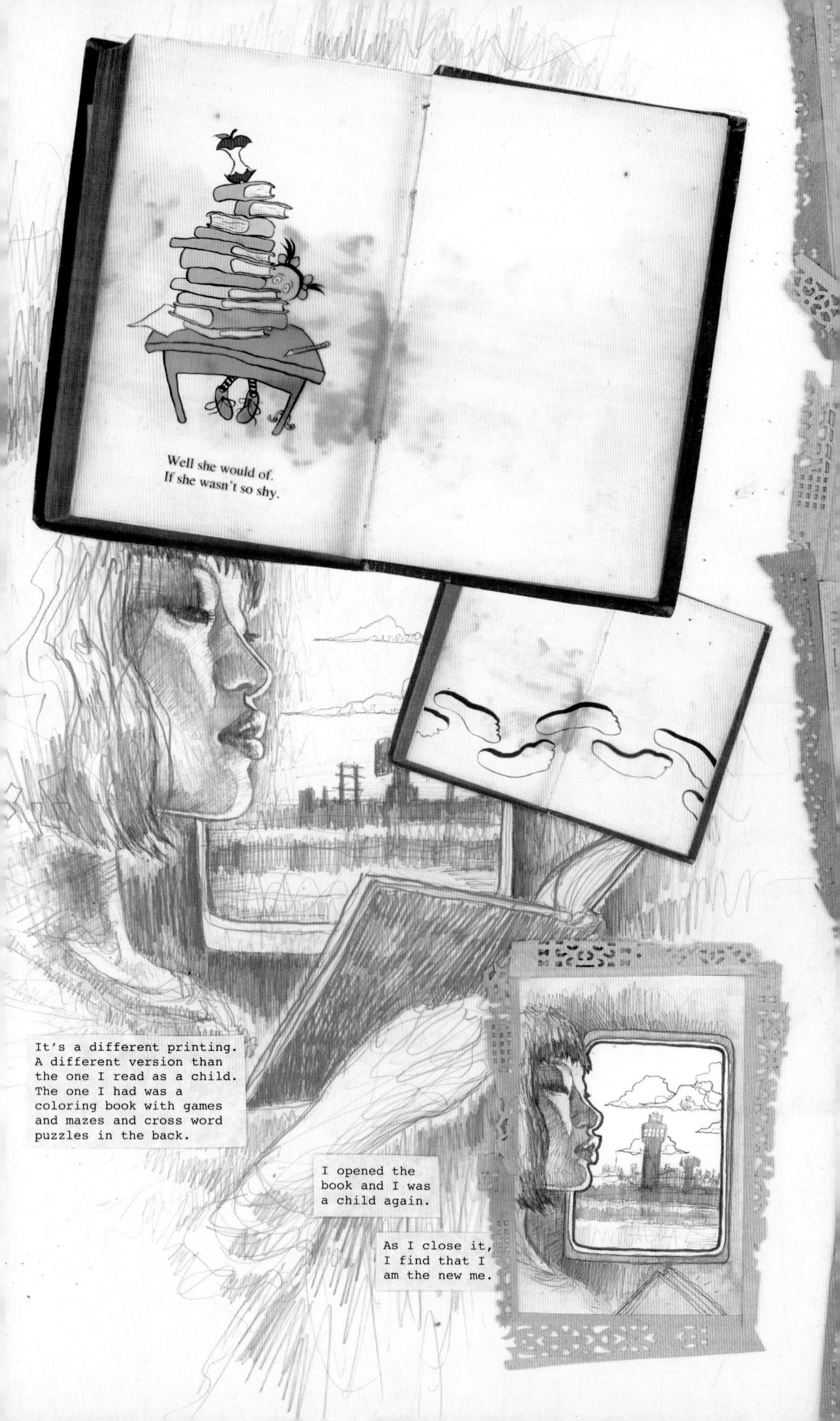
Well she would of.
If she wasn't so shy.
It's a different printing. A different version than the one I read as a child. The one I had was a coloring book with games and mazes and cross word puzzles in the back.
I opened the book and I was a child again.
As I close it, I find that I am the new me.

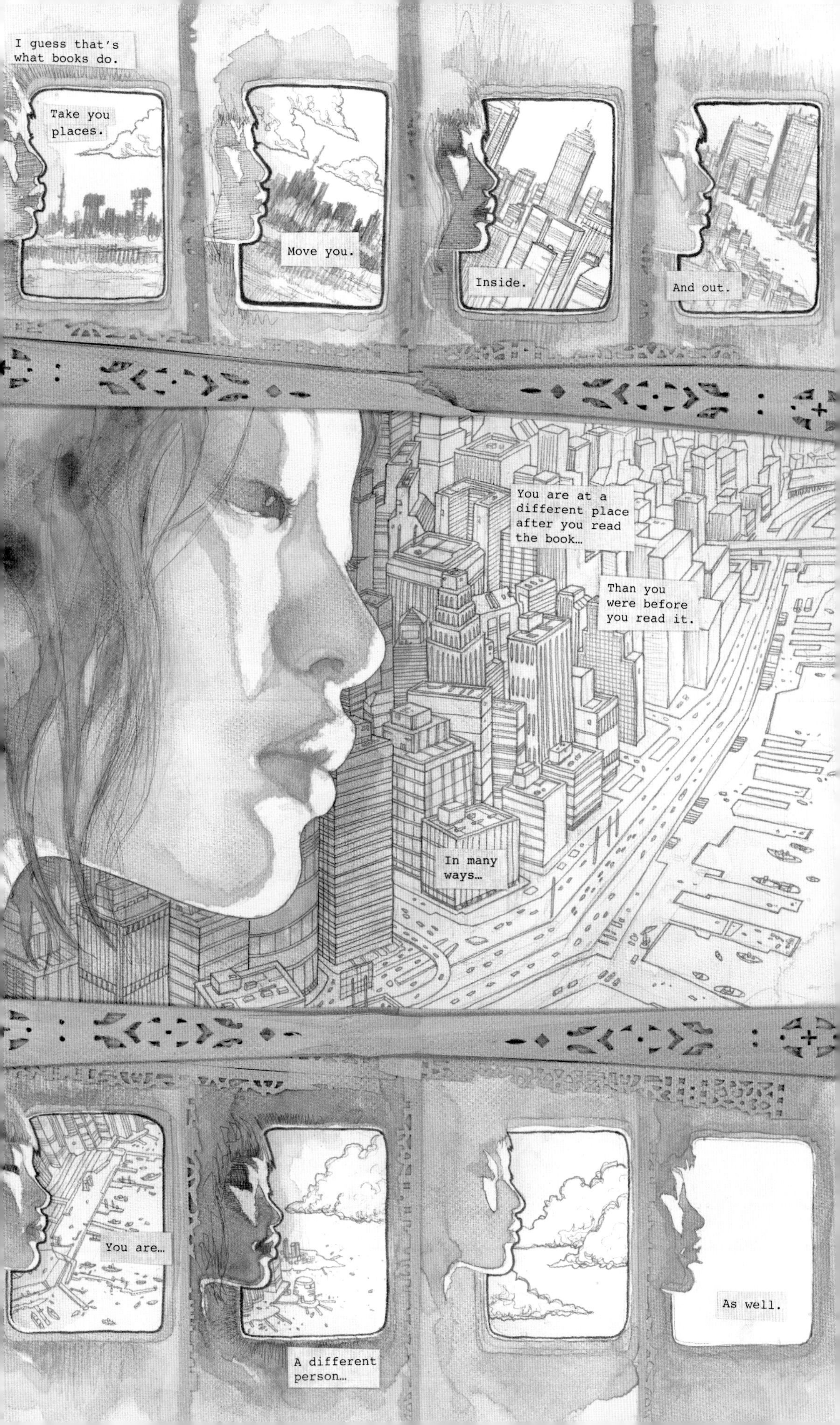
I guess that's what books do.
Take you places.
Move you.
Inside.
And out.
You are at a different place after you read the book…
Than you were before you read it.
In many ways…
You are…
A different person…
As well.

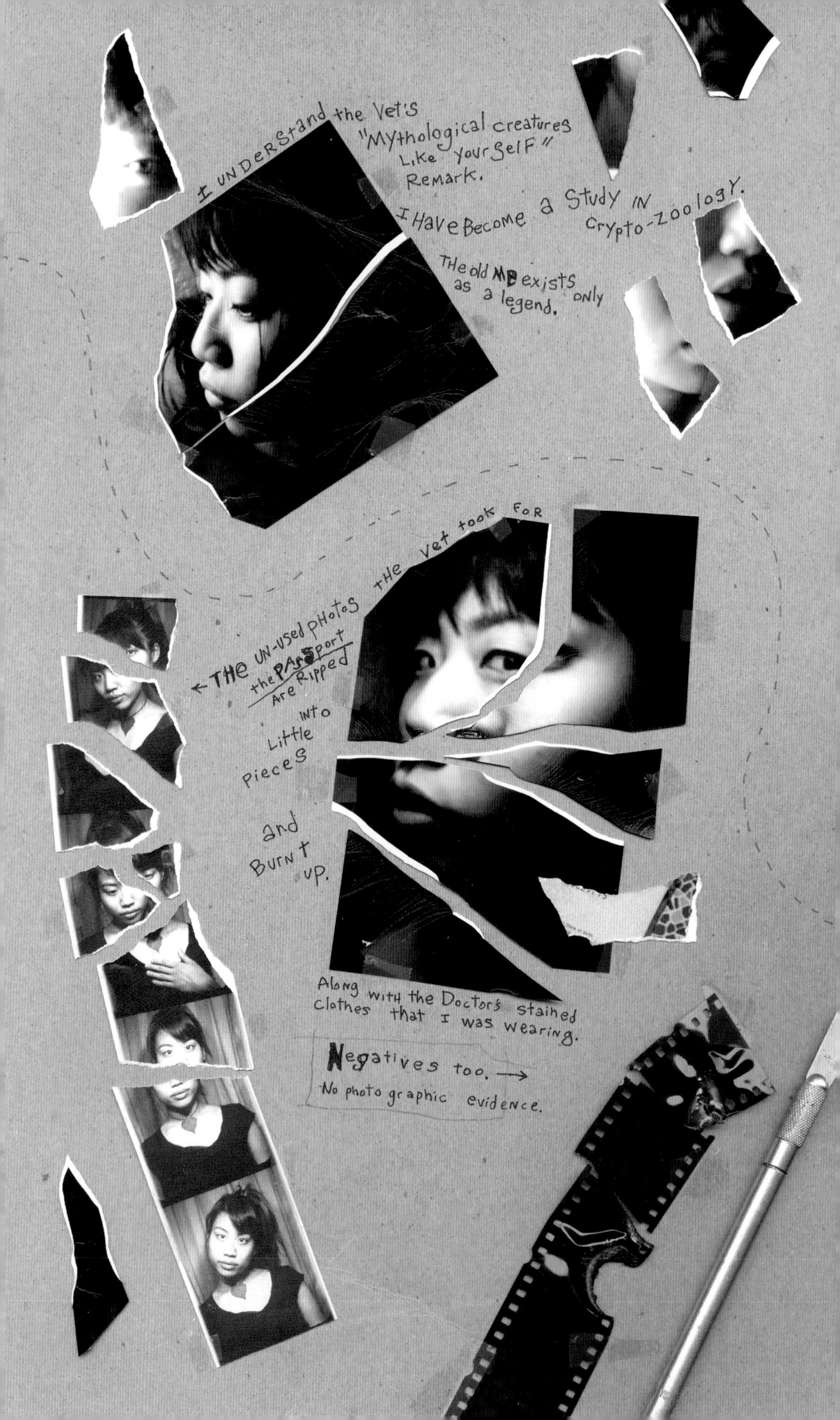
I UNDERSTAND the Vet's "Mythological creatures Like yourSelf" Remark.
I Have Become a Study IN Crypto-Zoology.
THe old ME exists only as a legend.
← THE UN-USED pHotos THE Vet took FOR the PASSport Are Ripped INTO Little Pieces
and Burnt up.
Along with the Doctor's stained clothes that I was wearing.
Negatives too. →
No photographic evidence.

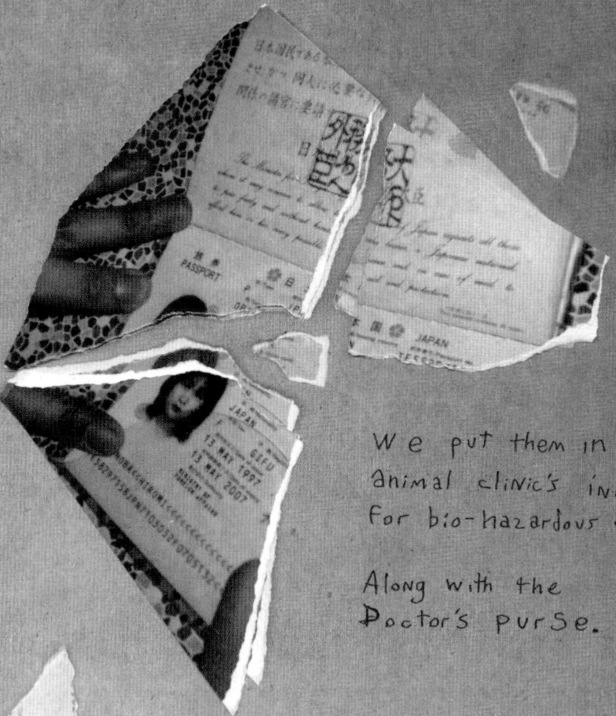

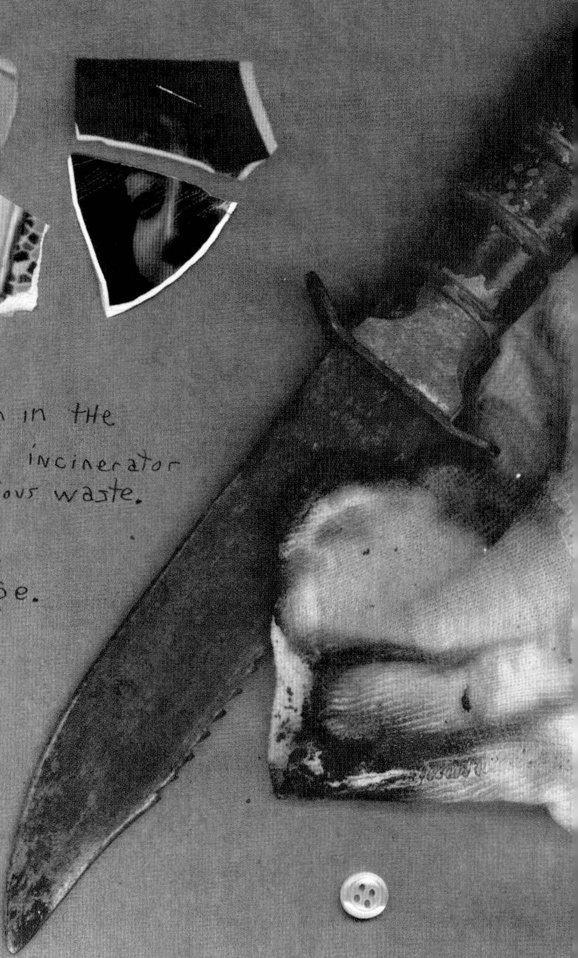

We put them in the animal clinic's incinerator for bio-hazardous waste.

Along with the Doctor's purse.

and the knife.

Somewhere I imagine

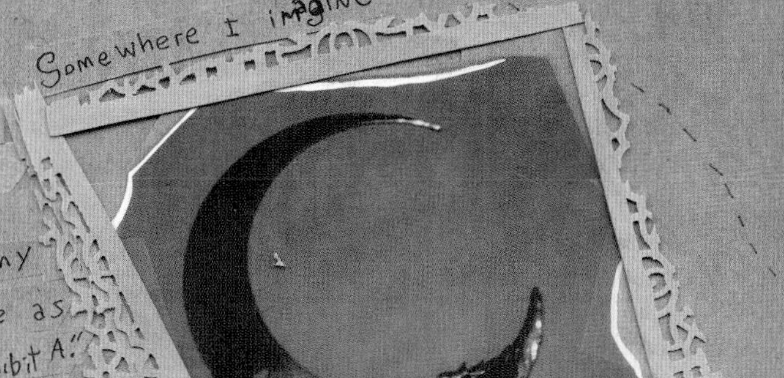
"Exhibit A".

my sickle as an "Exhibit A."

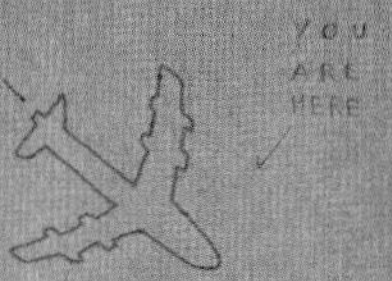
YOU
ARE
HERE

maybe my finger bone is there too.

Artifact of an extinct creature.

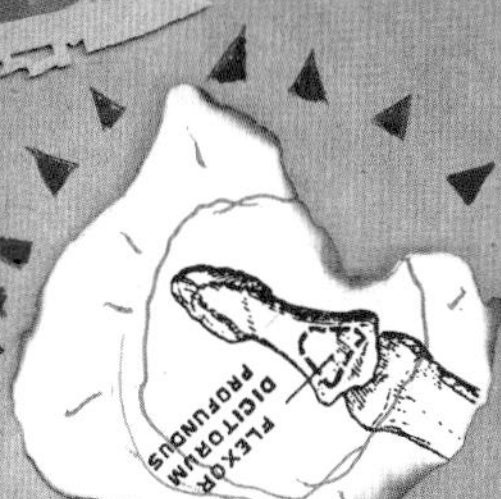
FLEXOR
DICTORUM
PROFUNDUS

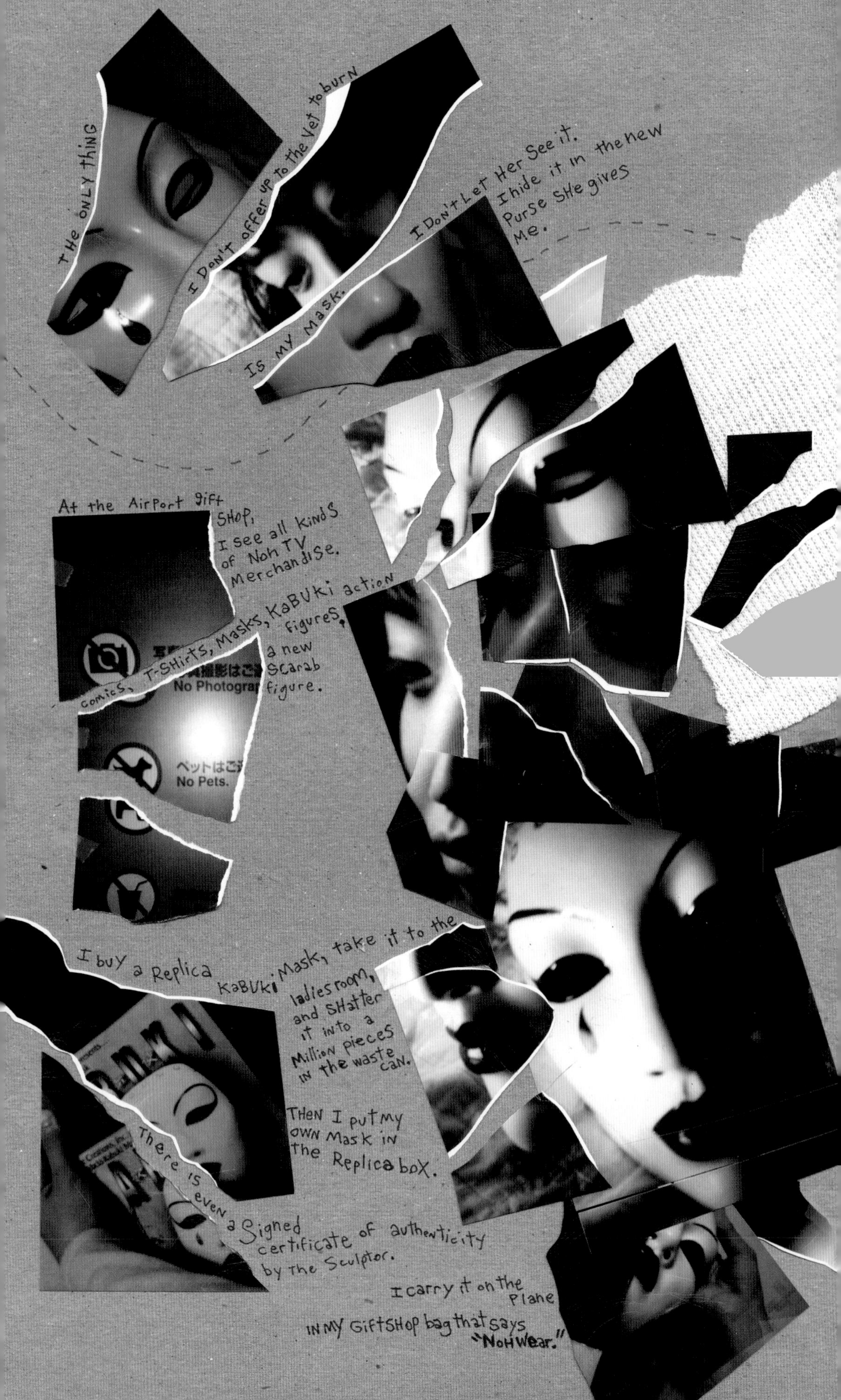
THE ONLY THING
I DON'T offer up to the vet to burN
IS MY MASK.
I DON'T LET HER See it.
I hide it in the new
Purse SHe gives
me.
At the AirPort gift
SHOP,
I see all kinds
of Noh TV
merchandise.
comics, T-SHirts, Masks, KaBUKi action
figures,
a new
Scarab
figure.
No Photogra
No Pets.
I buy a Replica
KaBUKi Mask, take it to the
ladies room,
and SHatter
it into a
Million pieces
in the waste
can.
THEN I put my
OWN Mask in
the Replica box.
There is
even a Signed
certificate of authenticity
by the Sculptor.
I carry it on the
Plane
IN MY GiftSHOP bag that says
"NoHWear."

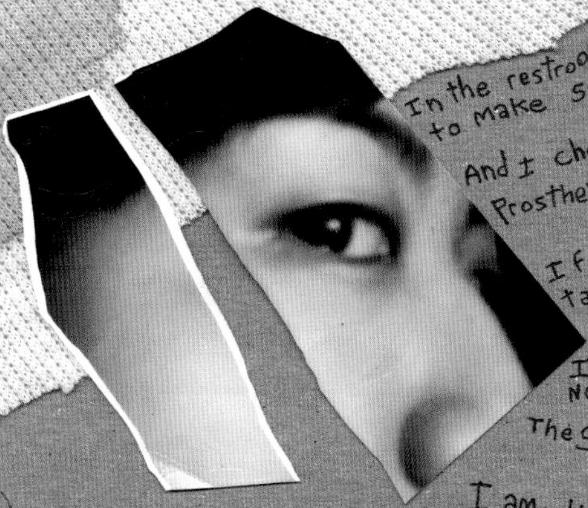

In the restroom, I check the bandage on my arm
to make sure the wound doesn't bleed thru.

And I check to make sure my
Prosthetic Face is on right.

I feel like the broken Unicorn,
taped back together.

I am the Abominable Snowman's
new haircut.

The Sling of Pegasus' strained wing.

I am the dentures of the
toothless CHUPACABRA.

A PHOENIX with
a skin condition.

Dear Akemi

I'm in the air now
above the clouds.

Everything looks like
the Invisible Friend i
that old children's bo
I read as a kid.

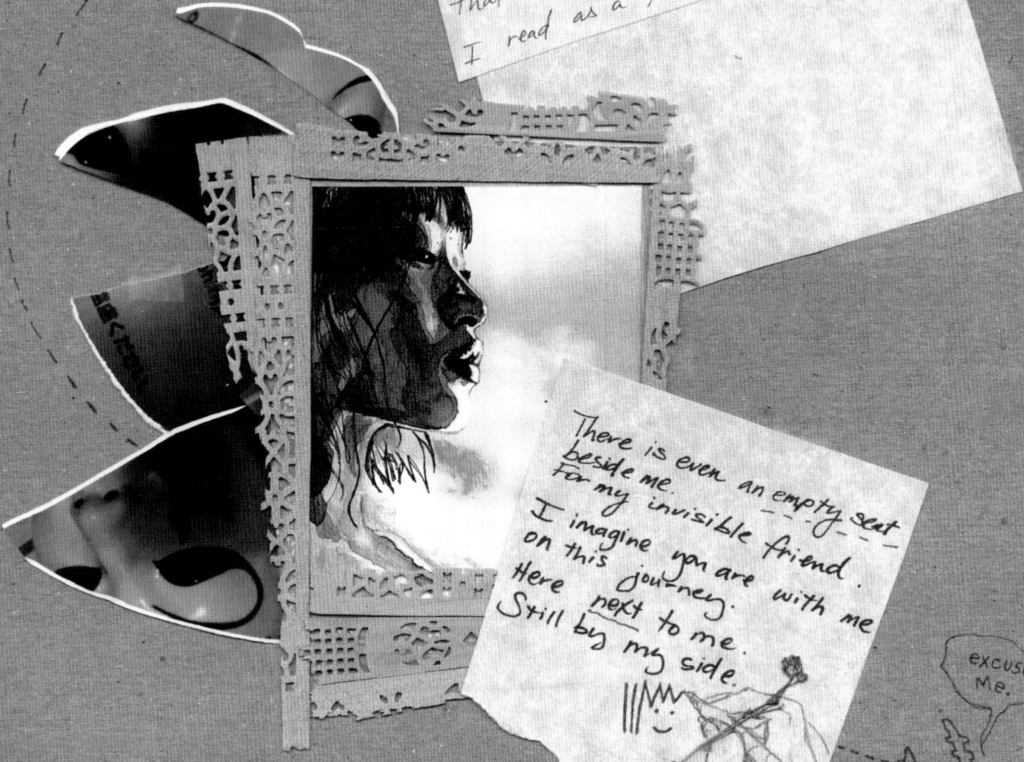

There is even an empty seat
beside me.
For my invisible friend.
I imagine you are with me
on this journey.
Here next to me.
Still by my side.

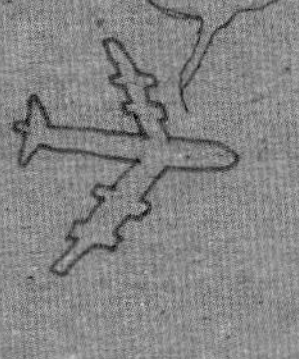
excuse me.

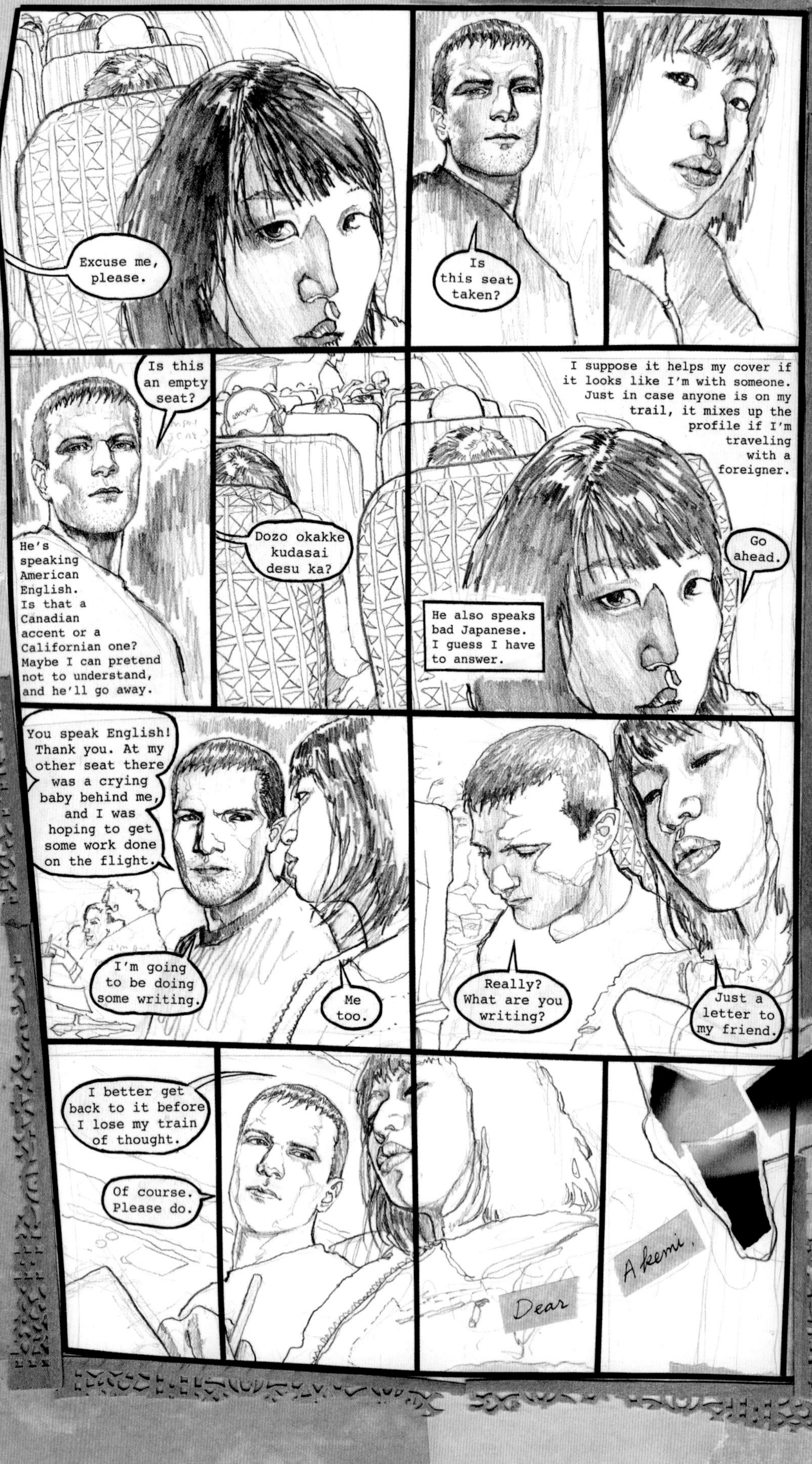
Excuse me, please.
Is this seat taken?
Is this an empty seat?
He's speaking American English. Is that a Canadian accent or a Californian one? Maybe I can pretend not to understand, and he'll go away.
Dozo okakke kudasai desu ka?
I suppose it helps my cover if it looks like I'm with someone. Just in case anyone is on my trail, it mixes up the profile if I'm traveling with a foreigner.
Go ahead.
He also speaks bad Japanese. I guess I have to answer.
You speak English! Thank you. At my other seat there was a crying baby behind me, and I was hoping to get some work done on the flight.
I'm going to be doing some writing.
Me too.
Really? What are you writing?
Just a letter to my friend.
I better get back to it before I lose my train of thought.
Of course. Please do.
Dear
Akemi

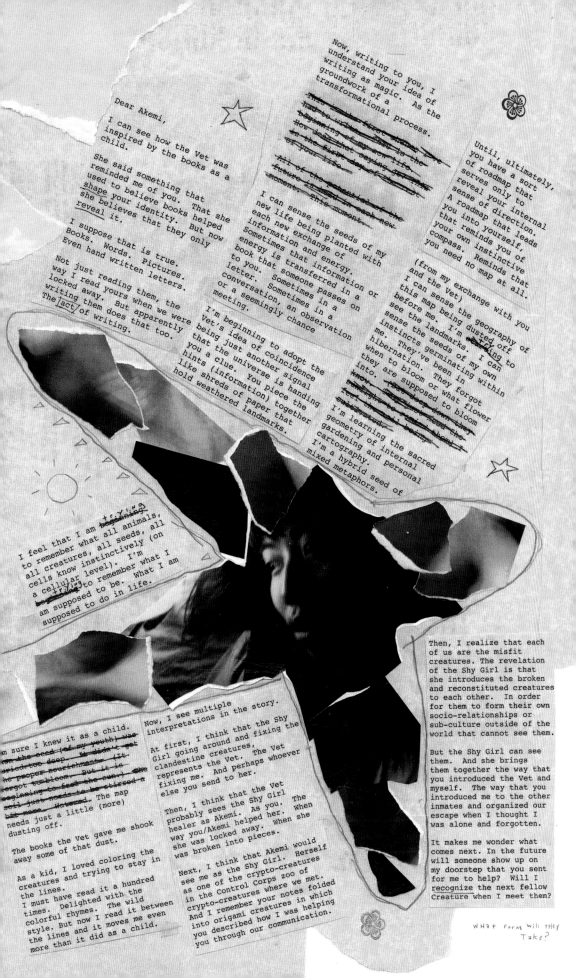

Dear Akemi,

I can see how the Vet was inspired by the books as a child.

She said something that reminded me of you. That she used to believe books helped shape your identity. But now she believes that they only reveal it.

I suppose that is true. Books. Words. Pictures. Even hand written letters.

Not just reading them, the way I read yours when we were locked away. But apparently writing them does that too. The act of writing.

Now, writing to you, I understand your idea of writing as magic. As the groundwork of a transformational process.

~~had to write first that~~
~~beginning of my new life.~~
~~How does that saying go~~
~~today is the first day of~~
~~of your life.~~
~~All of the potential of the~~
~~future is contained in each new~~
~~moment. This moment.~~

I can sense the seeds of my new life being planted with each new exchange of information and energy. Sometimes that information or energy is transferred in a book that someone passes on to you. Sometimes in a letter. Sometimes in a conversation, an observation or a seemingly chance meeting.

I'm beginning to adopt the Vet's idea of coincidence being just another signal that the universe is handing you a clue. You piece the hints (information) together like shreds of paper that hold weathered landmarks.

Until, ultimately, you have a sort of roadmap that serves only to reveal your internal sense of direction. A roadmap that leads you into yourself, that reminds you of your own instinctive compass. Reminds that you need no map at all.

(from my exchange with you and the Vet) I can sense the geography of this map being dusted off before me. I'm ~~trying~~ to see the landmarks. I can sense the seeds of my own instincts germinating within me. They've been in hibernation. They forgot when to bloom or what flower they are supposed to bloom into. ~~They've forgotten their~~ ~~own schedule down their~~ ~~own biological being~~ ~~feel shredded.~~

I'm learning the sacred geometry of internal gardening and personal cartography. I'm a hybrid seed of mixed metaphors.

I feel that I am ~~beginning~~ ~~trying~~ to remember what all animals, all creatures, all seeds, all cells know instinctively (on a cellular level). I'm ~~trying~~ to remember what I am ~~supposed~~ to be. What I am supposed to do in life.

I'm sure I knew it as a child. ~~on the seed (of my youth) was~~ ~~buried too deep. It didn't get~~ ~~the proper nourishment. (It~~ ~~forgot to bloom. But it is~~ ~~beginning to feel the buried~~ ~~soil just needs to be stirred a~~ ~~bit more. Watered.~~ The map needs just a little (more) dusting off.

The books the Vet gave me shook away some of that dust.

As a kid, I loved coloring the creatures and trying to stay in the lines.
I must have read it a hundred times. Delighted with the colorful rhymes. The wild style. But now I read it between the lines and it moves me even more than it did as a child.

Now, I see multiple interpretations in the story.

At first, I think that the Shy Girl going around and fixing the clandestine creatures, represents the Vet. The Vet fixing me. And perhaps whoever else you send to her.

Then, I think that the Vet probably sees the Shy Girl healer as Akemi. As you. The way you/Akemi helped her. When she was locked away. When she was broken into pieces.

Next, I think that Akemi would see me as the Shy Girl. Herself as one of the crypto-creatures in the Control Corps zoo of crypto-creatures where we met. And I remember your notes folded into origami creatures in which you described how I was helping you through our communication.

Then, I realize that each of us are the misfit creatures. The revelation of the Shy Girl is that she introduces the broken and reconstituted creatures to each other. In order for them to form their own socio-relationships or sub-culture outside of the world that cannot see them.

But the Shy Girl can see them. And she brings them together the way that you introduced the Vet and myself. The way that you introduced me to the other inmates and organized our escape when I thought I was alone and forgotten.

It makes me wonder what comes next. In the future will someone show up on my doorstep that you sent for me to help? Will I recognize the next fellow Creature when I meet them?

What form will they Take?

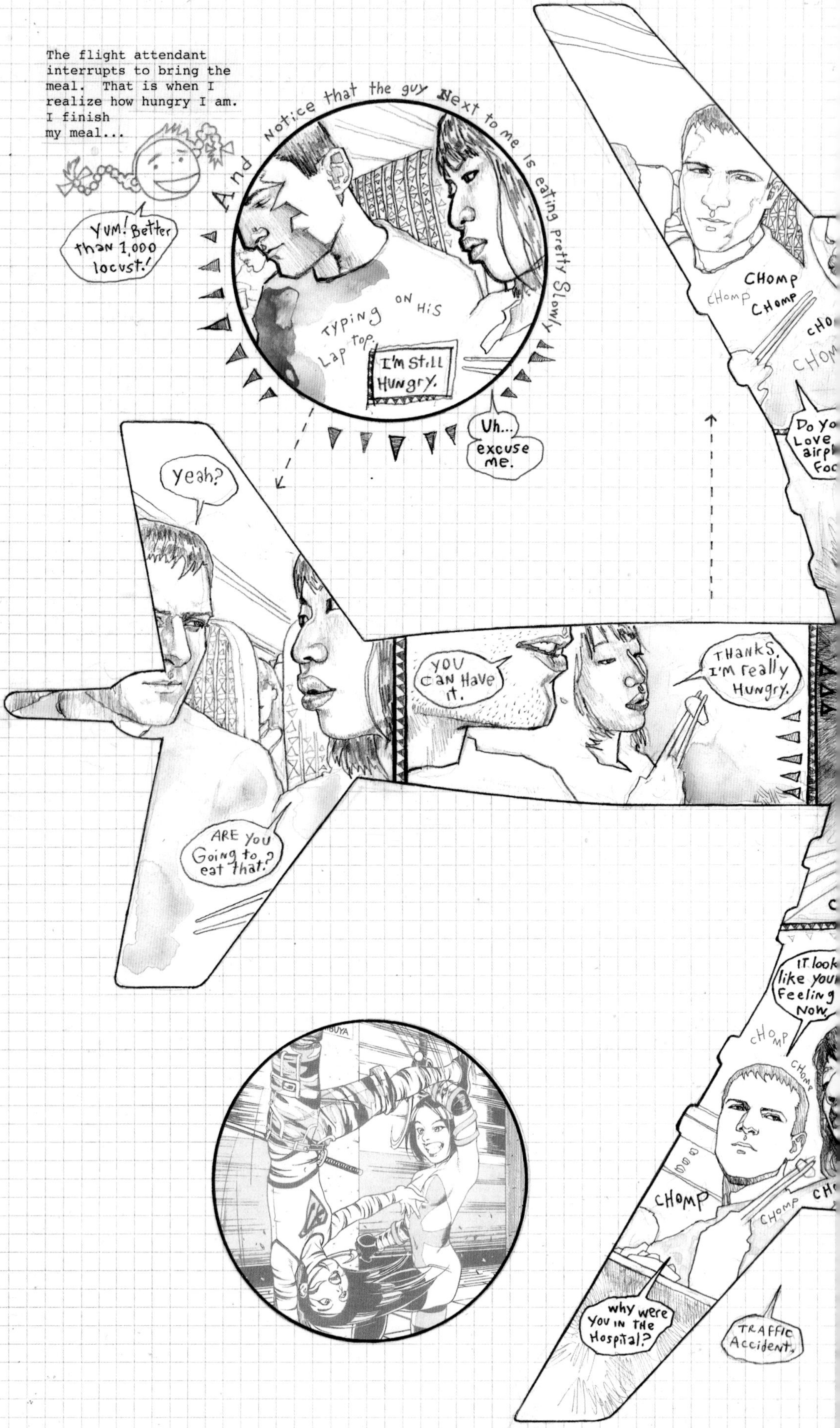
The flight attendant interrupts to bring the meal. That is when I realize how hungry I am. I finish my meal...
YUM! Better than 1,000 locust!
And notice that the guy Next to me is eating pretty slowly
Typing on his Laptop.
I'm still Hungry.
Uh... excuse me.
yeah?
ARE you Going to eat that?
You can have it.
Thanks, I'm really Hungry.
CHOMP CHOMP CHOMP
CHOMP CHOMP CHOMP CHOMP
why were you in the Hospital?
Traffic Accident.

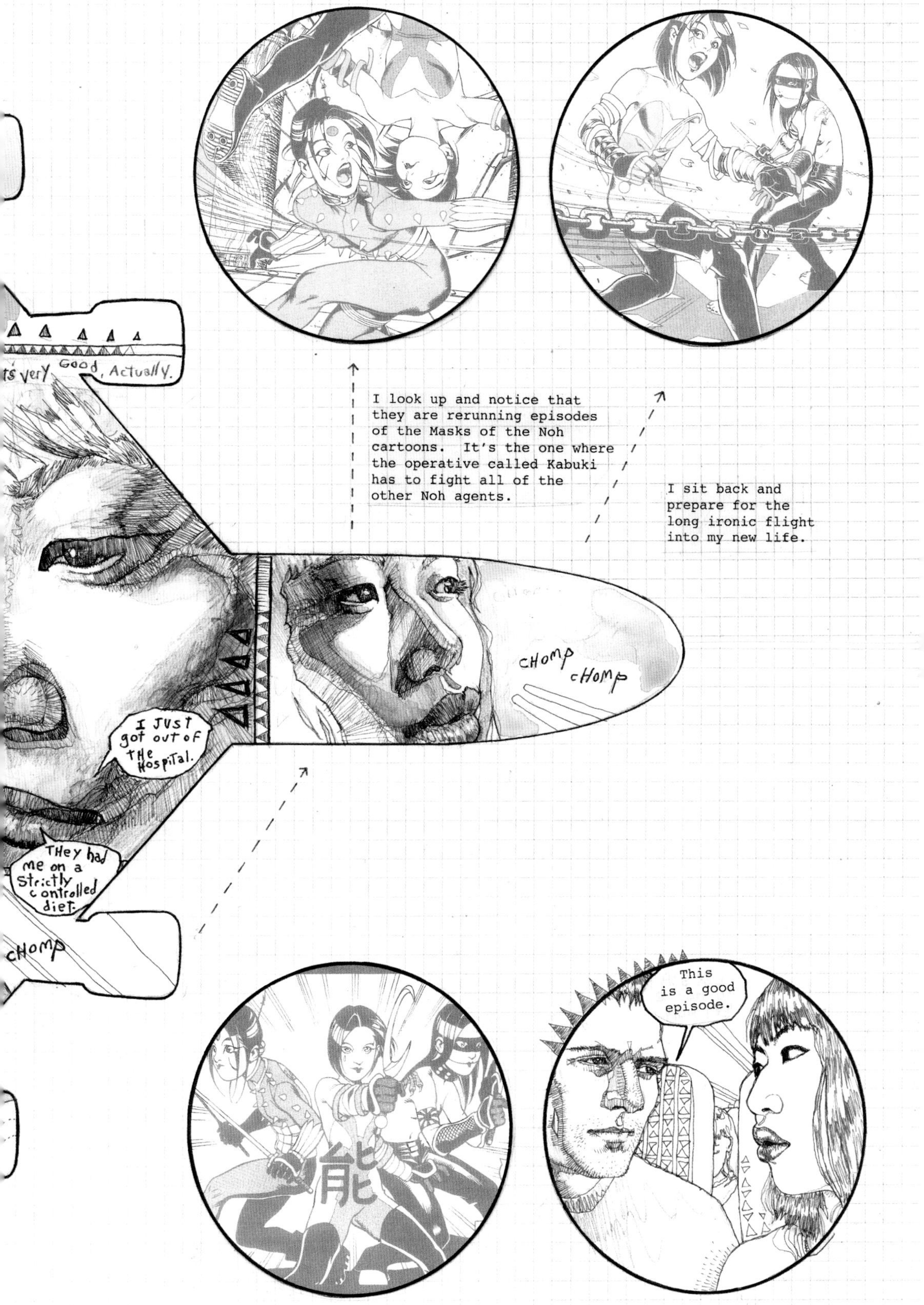

...t's very Good, Actually.
I look up and notice that they are rerunning episodes of the Masks of the Noh cartoons. It's the one where the operative called Kabuki has to fight all of the other Noh agents.
I sit back and prepare for the long ironic flight into my new life.
CHOMP CHOMP
I JUST got out of THE Hospital.
THEY had me on a Strictly controlled diet.
CHOMP
能
This is a good episode.

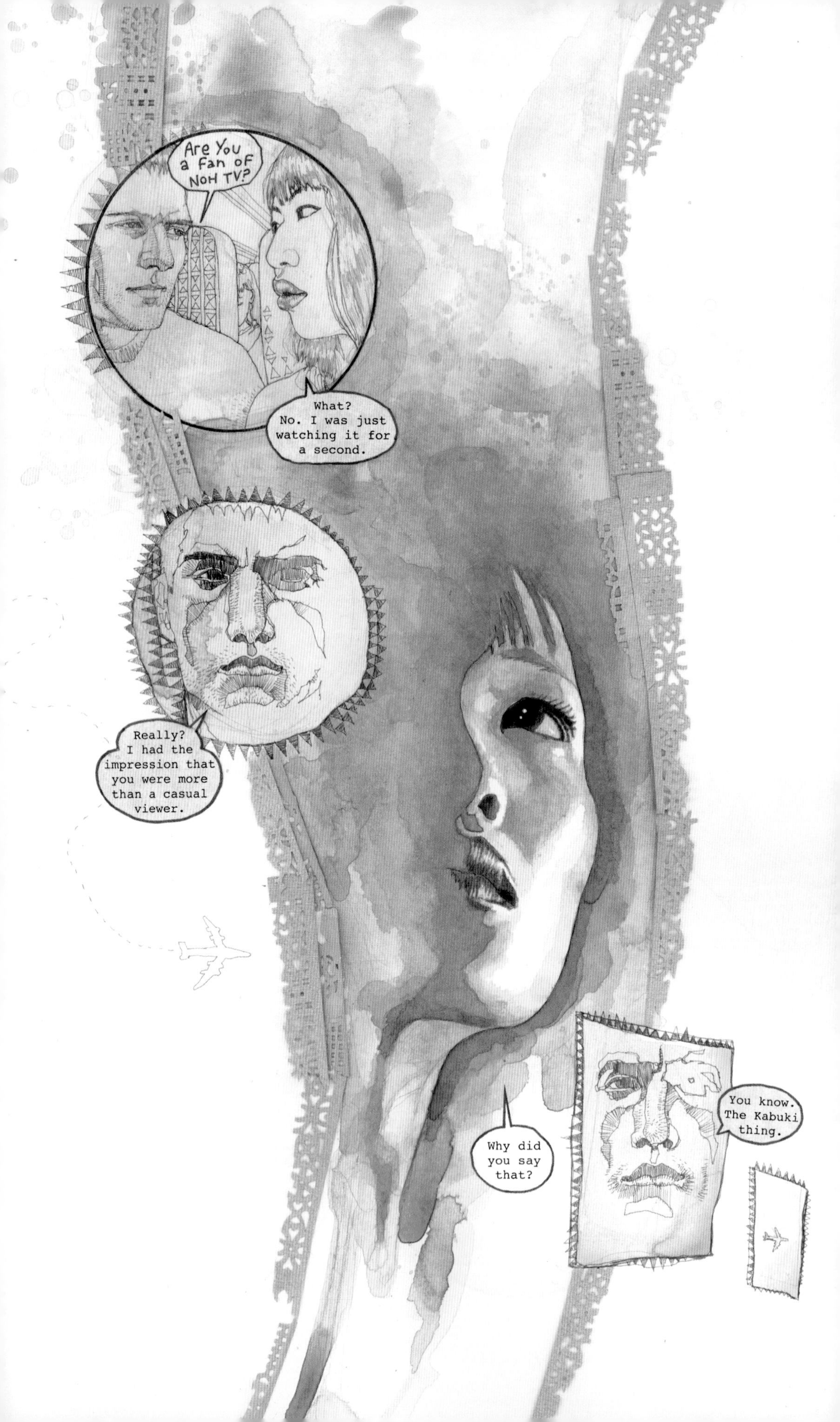
Are You a Fan of NOH TV?
What? No. I was just watching it for a second.
Really? I had the impression that you were more than a casual viewer.
Why did you say that?
You know. The Kabuki thing.

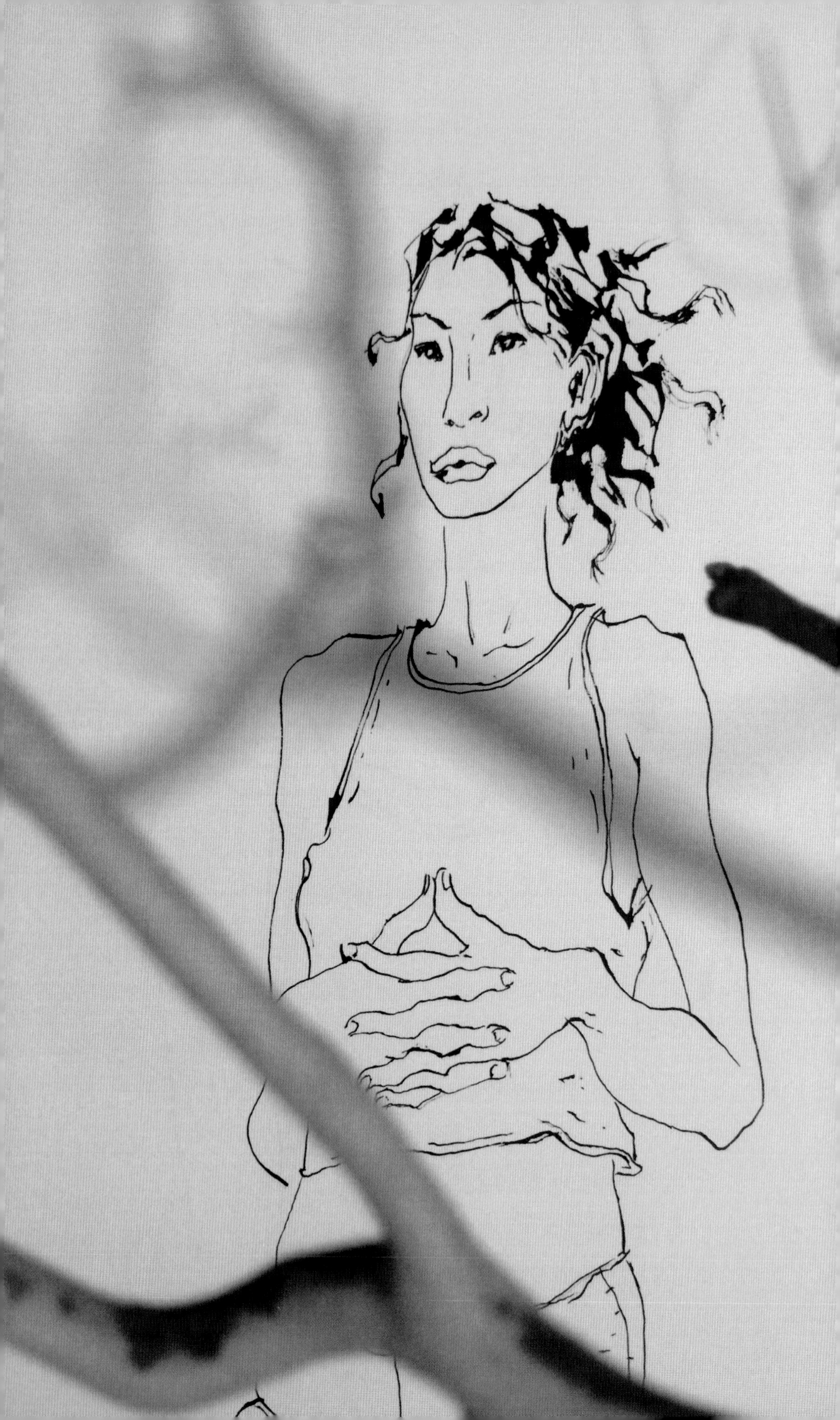

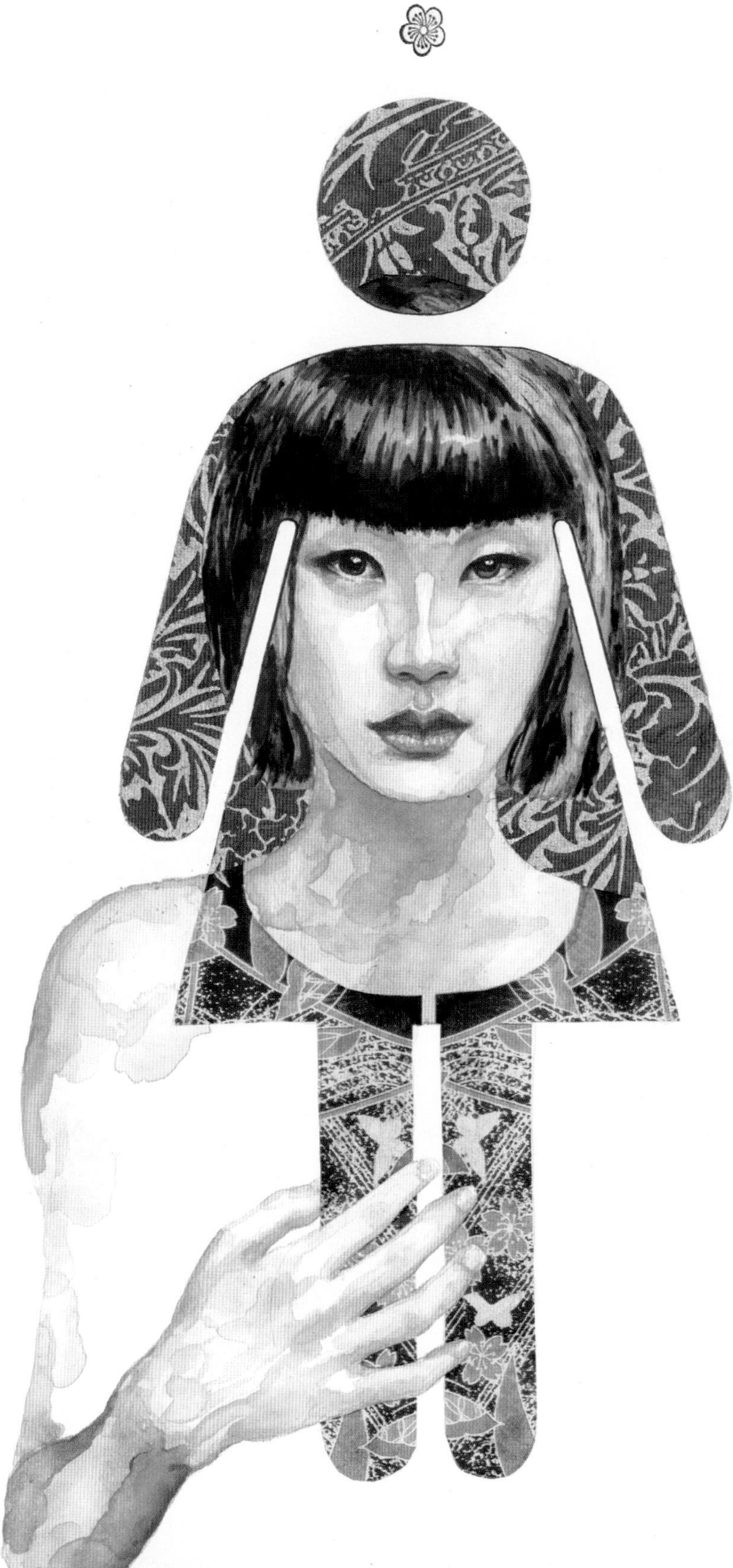

The Alchemy

Part Four

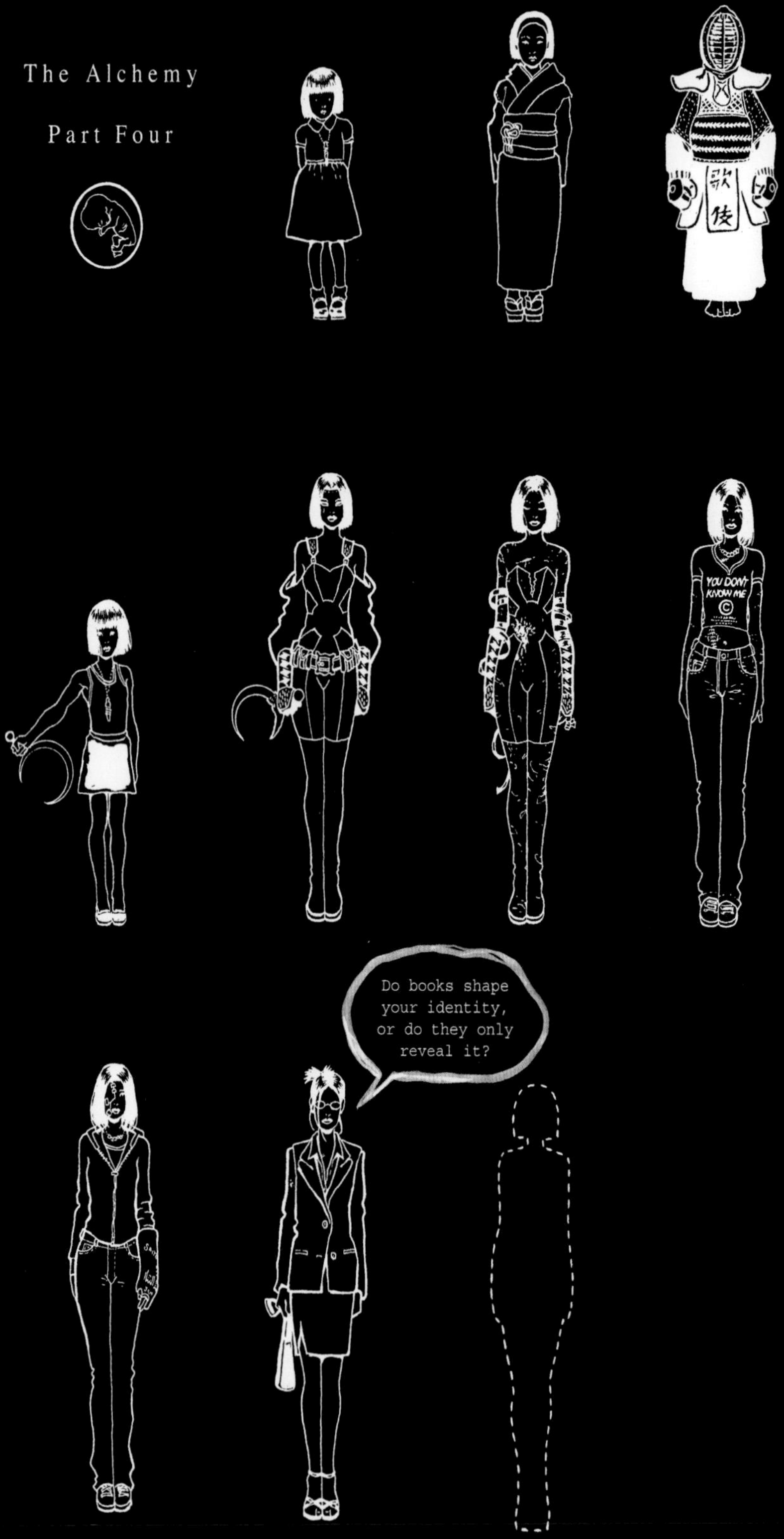
YOU DON'T KNOW ME ©
Do books shape your identity, or do they only reveal it?

Book of Doors

(or Outlines)

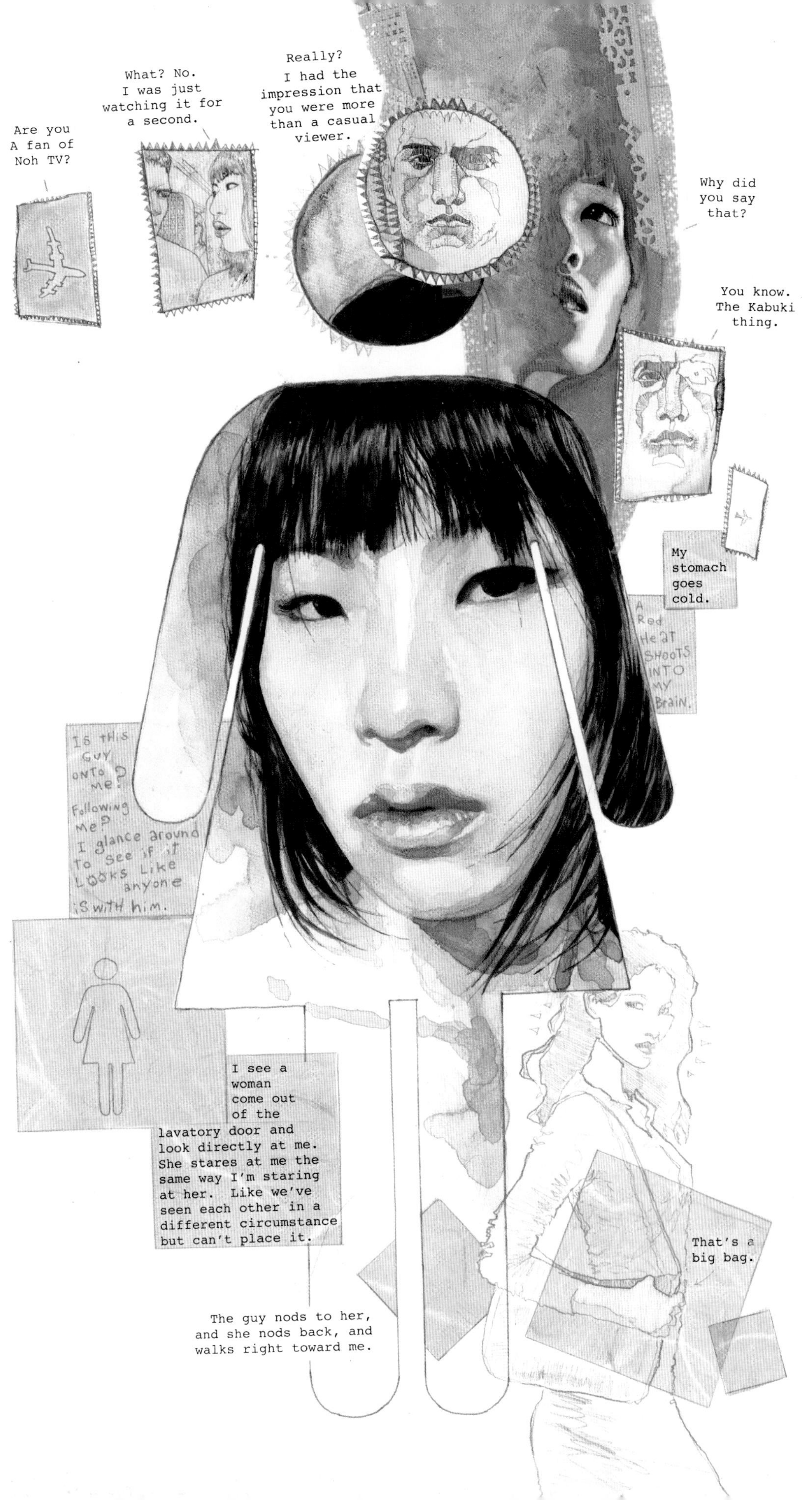
Are you A fan of Noh TV?
What? No. I was just watching it for a second.
Really? I had the impression that you were more than a casual viewer.
Why did you say that?
You know. The Kabuki thing.
My stomach goes cold.
A Red Heat SHOOTS INTO MY Brain.
Is this Guy onto me? Following Me? I glance around to see if it Looks Like anyone is with him.
I see a woman come out of the lavatory door and look directly at me. She stares at me the same way I'm staring at her. Like we've seen each other in a different circumstance but can't place it.
The guy nods to her, and she nods back, and walks right toward me.
That's a big bag.

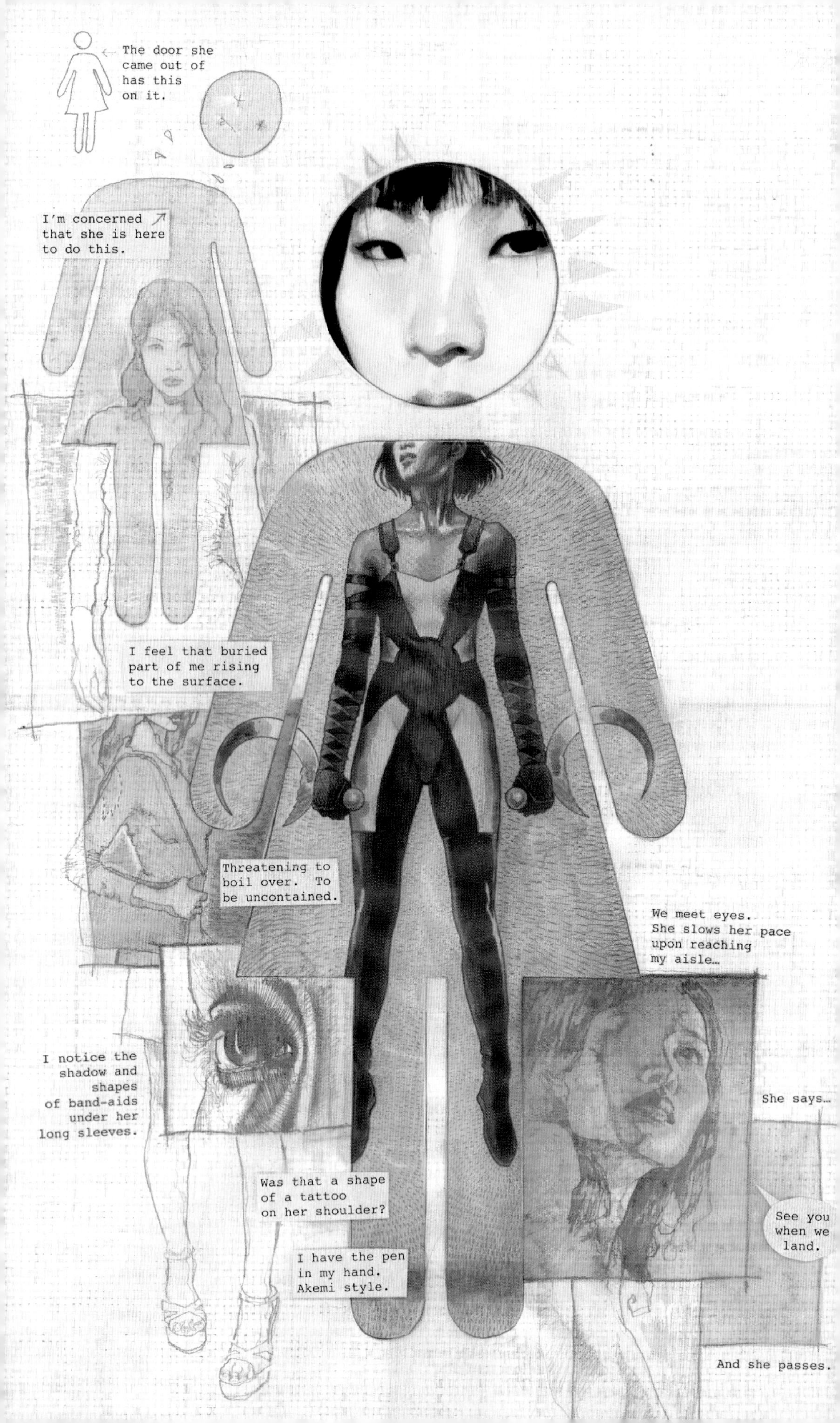

The door she came out of has this on it.
I'm concerned that she is here to do this.
I feel that buried part of me rising to the surface.
Threatening to boil over. To be uncontained.
We meet eyes. She slows her pace upon reaching my aisle…
I notice the shadow and shapes of band-aids under her long sleeves.
Was that a shape of a tattoo on her shoulder?
I have the pen in my hand. Akemi style.
She says…
See you when we land.
And she passes.

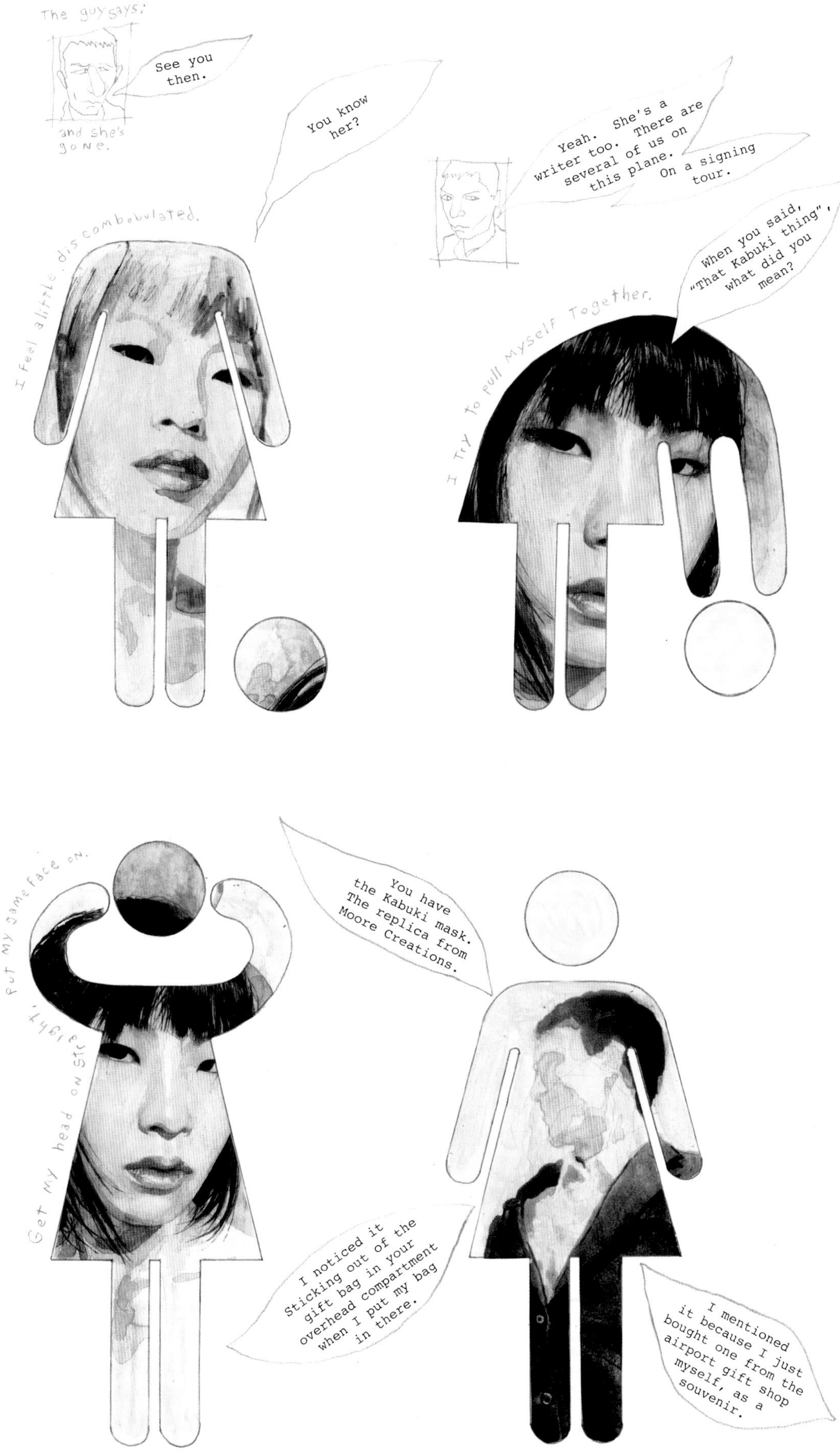
The guy says:
See you then.
and she's gone.
You know her?
Yeah. She's a writer too. There are several of us on this plane.
On a signing tour.
I feel a little discombobulated.
When you said, "That Kabuki thing", what did you mean?
I try to pull myself together.
Get my head on straight, put my game face on.
You have the Kabuki mask. The replica from Moore Creations.
I noticed it sticking out of the gift bag in your overhead compartment when I put my bag in there.
I mentioned it because I just bought one from the airport gift shop myself, as a souvenir.

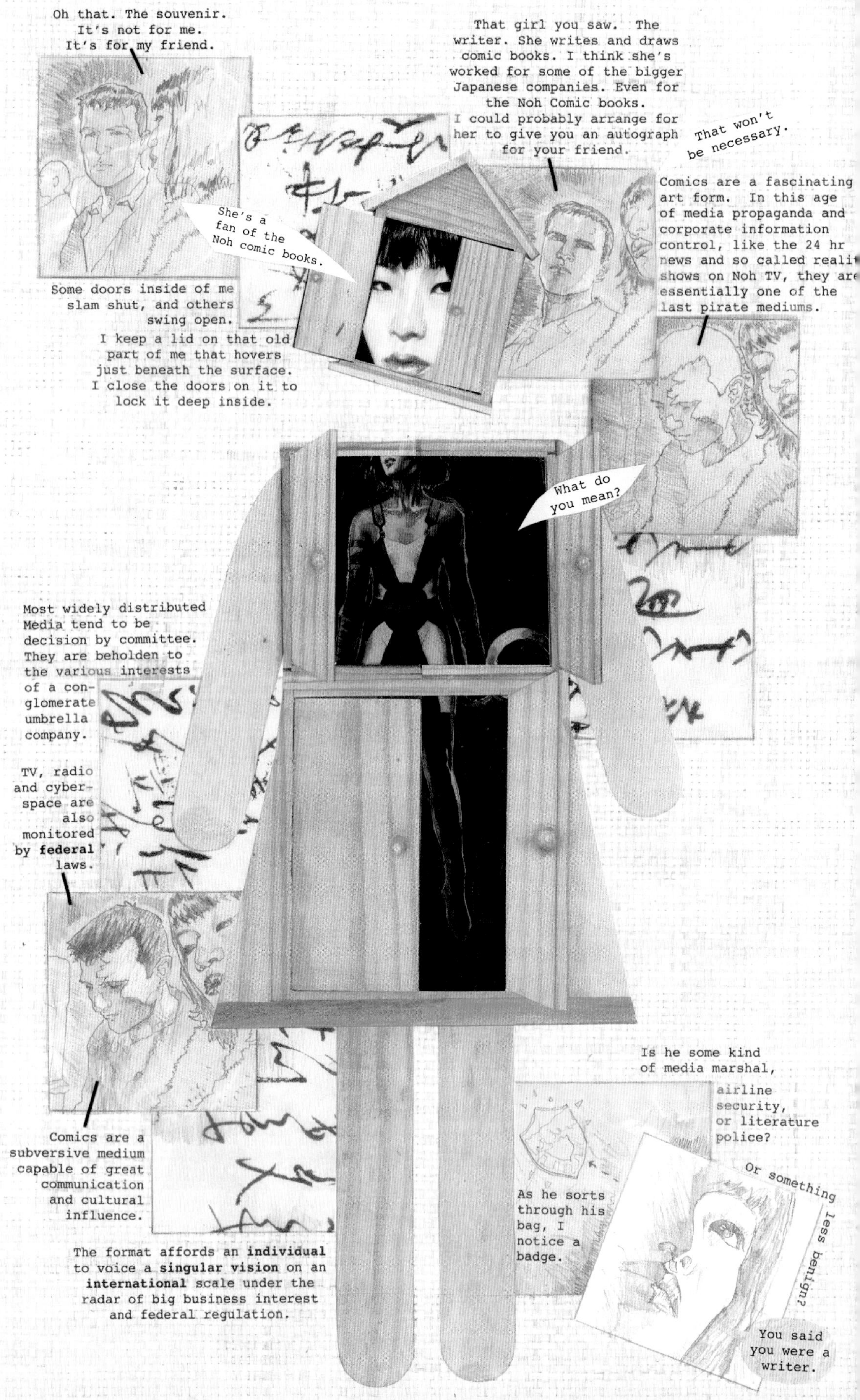

Oh that. The souvenir. It's not for me. It's for my friend.
That girl you saw. The writer. She writes and draws comic books. I think she's worked for some of the bigger Japanese companies. Even for the Noh Comic books. I could probably arrange for her to give you an autograph for your friend.
She's a fan of the Noh comic books.
That won't be necessary.
Some doors inside of me slam shut, and others swing open.
I keep a lid on that old part of me that hovers just beneath the surface. I close the doors on it to lock it deep inside.
Comics are a fascinating art form. In this age of media propaganda and corporate information control, like the 24 hr news and so called reali shows on Noh TV, they are essentially one of the last pirate mediums.
What do you mean?
Most widely distributed Media tend to be decision by committee. They are beholden to the various interests of a conglomerate umbrella company.
TV, radio and cyberspace are also monitored by **federal** laws.
Comics are a subversive medium capable of great communication and cultural influence.
The format affords an **individual** to voice a **singular vision** on an **international** scale under the radar of big business interest and federal regulation.
Is he some kind of media marshal,
airline security, or literature police?
As he sorts through his bag, I notice a badge.
Or something less benign?
You said you were a writer.

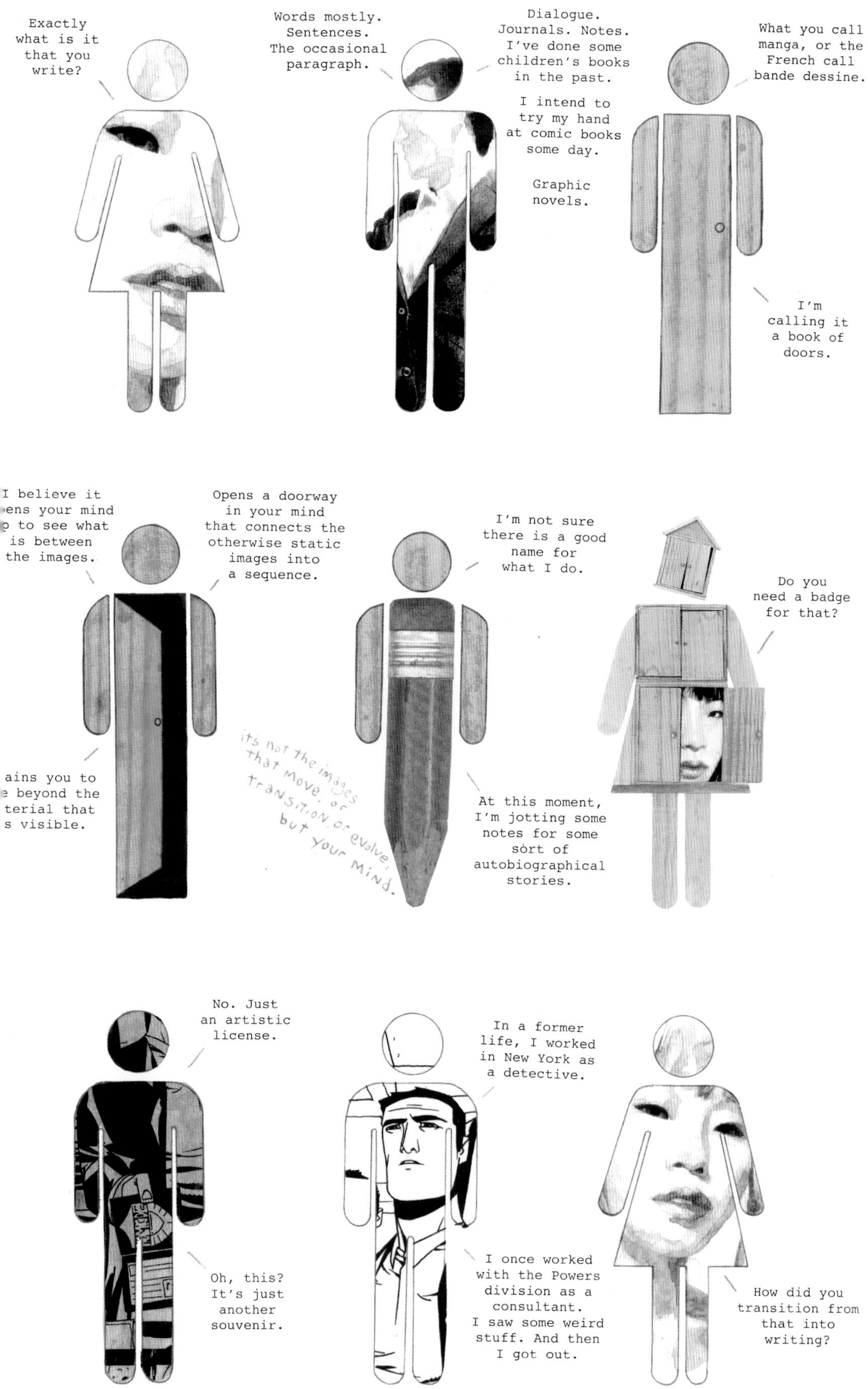

Exactly what is it that you write?
Words mostly. Sentences. The occasional paragraph.
Dialogue. Journals. Notes. I've done some children's books in the past.
I intend to try my hand at comic books some day.
Graphic novels.
What you call manga, or the French call bande dessine.
I'm calling it a book of doors.
I believe it ens your mind p to see what is between the images.
Opens a doorway in your mind that connects the otherwise static images into a sequence.
ains you to e beyond the terial that s visible.
I'm not sure there is a good name for what I do.
it's not the images that move, or transition, or evolve, but your mind.
At this moment, I'm jotting some notes for some sort of autobiographical stories.
Do you need a badge for that?
No. Just an artistic license.
Oh, this? It's just another souvenir.
In a former life, I worked in New York as a detective.
I once worked with the Powers division as a consultant. I saw some weird stuff. And then I got out.
How did you transition from that into writing?

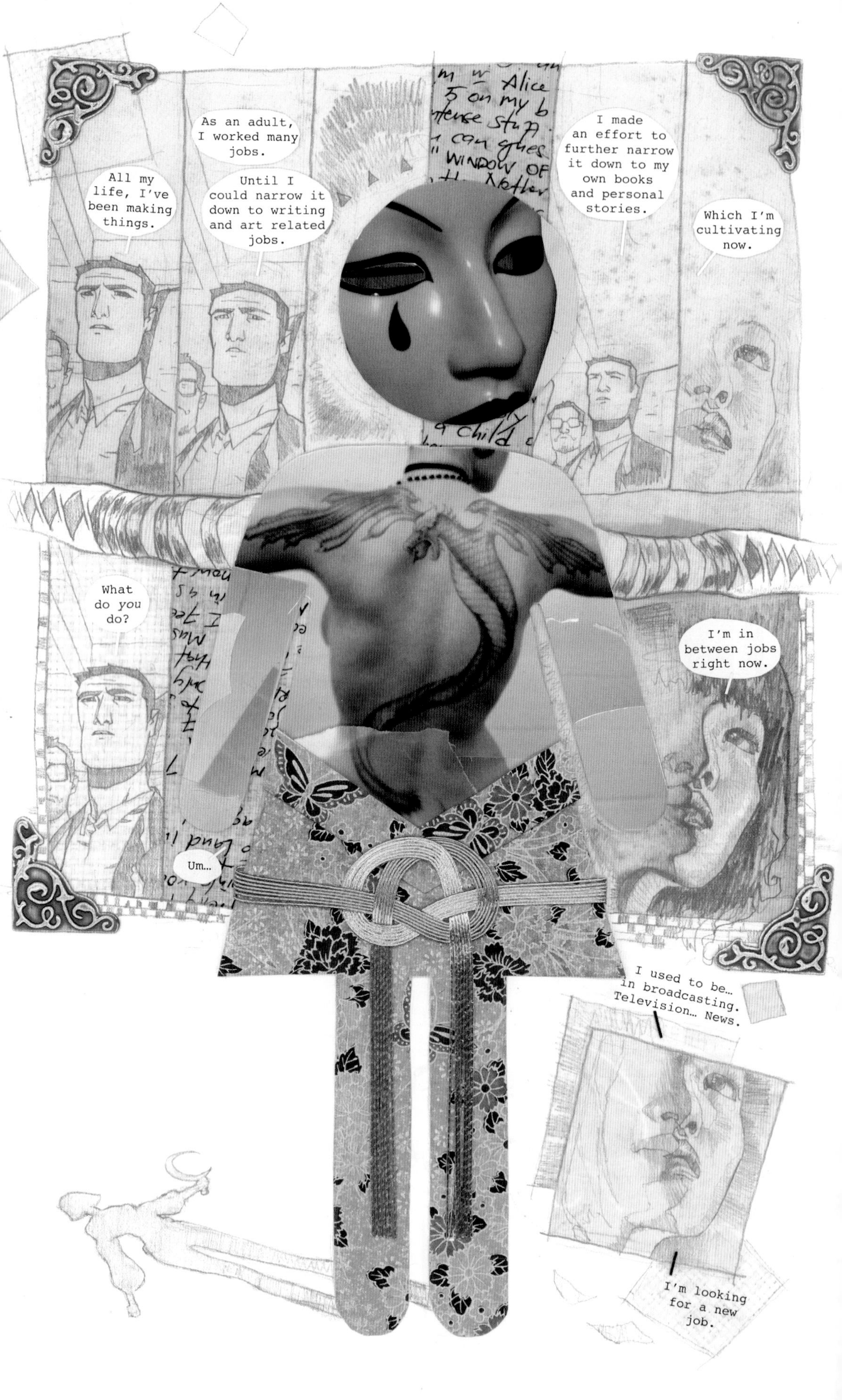
All my life, I've been making things.
As an adult, I worked many jobs.
Until I could narrow it down to writing and art related jobs.
I made an effort to further narrow it down to my own books and personal stories.
Which I'm cultivating now.
What do *you* do?
Um...
I'm in between jobs right now.
I used to be... in broadcasting. Television... News.
I'm looking for a new job.

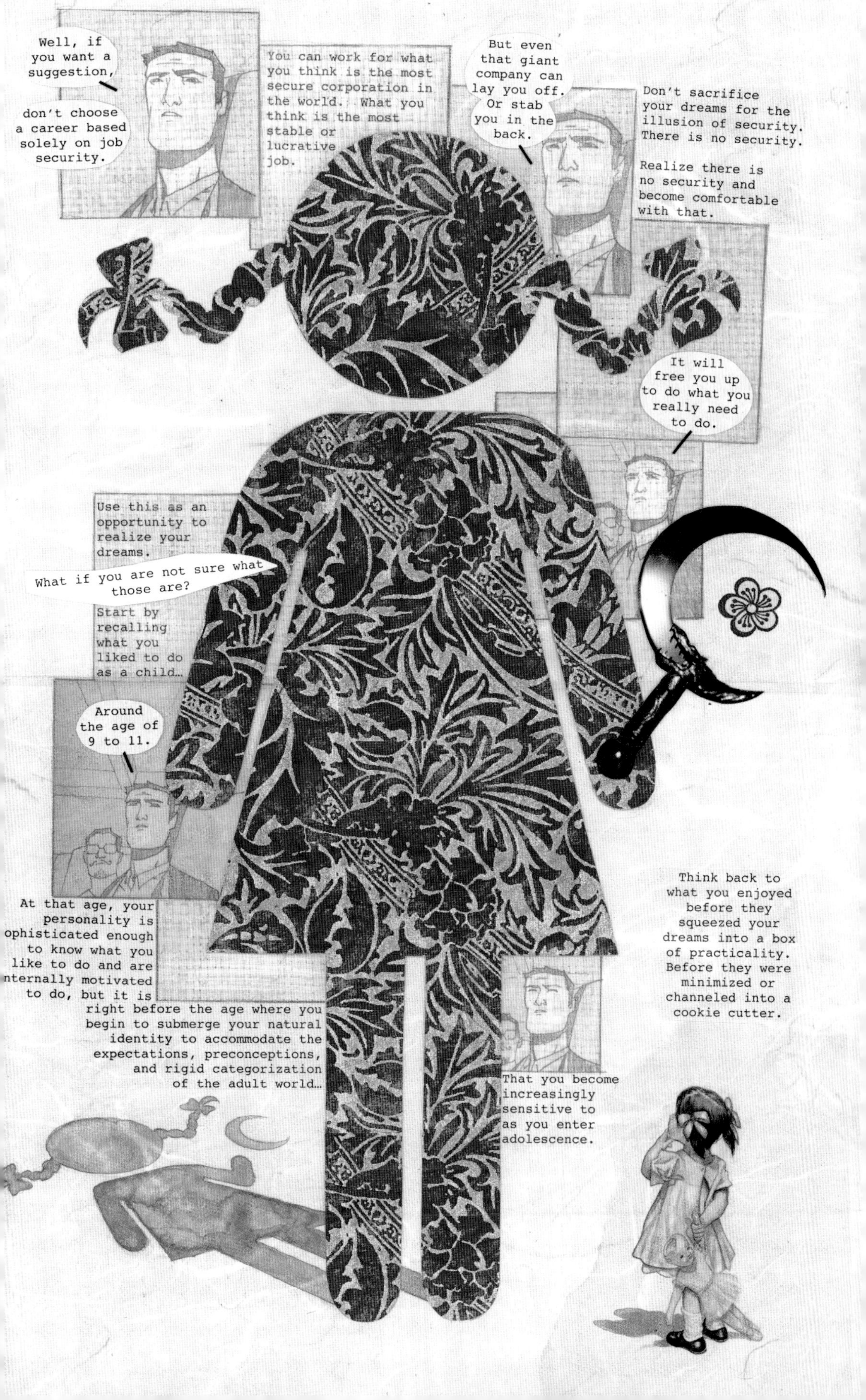

Well, if you want a suggestion,
don't choose a career based solely on job security.
You can work for what you think is the most secure corporation in the world. What you think is the most stable or lucrative job.
But even that giant company can lay you off. Or stab you in the back.
Don't sacrifice your dreams for the illusion of security. There is no security.
Realize there is no security and become comfortable with that.
It will free you up to do what you really need to do.
Use this as an opportunity to realize your dreams.
What if you are not sure what those are?
Start by recalling what you liked to do as a child…
Around the age of 9 to 11.
At that age, your personality is ophisticated enough to know what you like to do and are nternally motivated to do, but it is right before the age where you begin to submerge your natural identity to accommodate the expectations, preconceptions, and rigid categorization of the adult world…
That you become increasingly sensitive to as you enter adolescence.
Think back to what you enjoyed before they squeezed your dreams into a box of practicality. Before they were minimized or channeled into a cookie cutter.

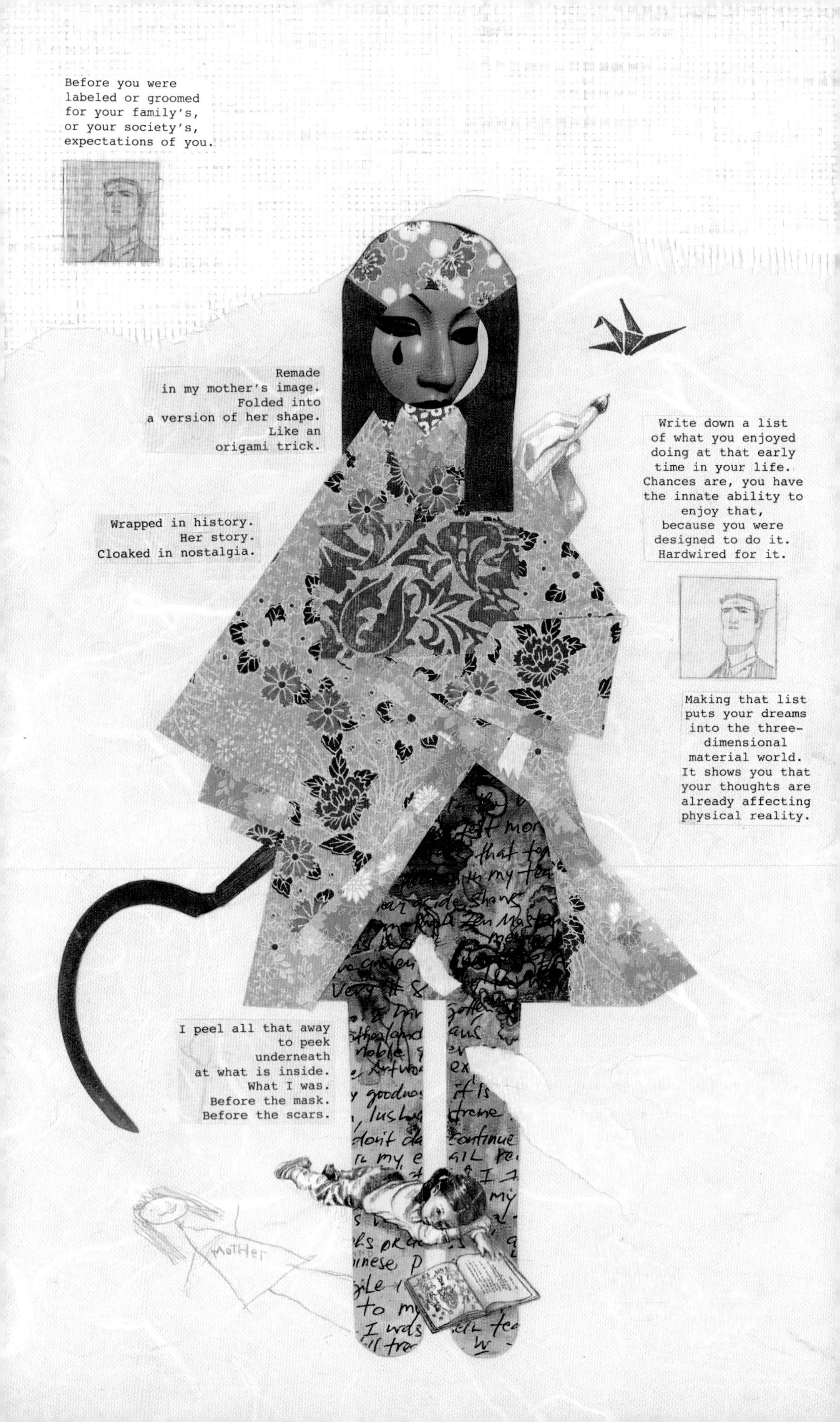

Before you were labeled or groomed for your family's, or your society's, expectations of you.
Remade in my mother's image. Folded into a version of her shape. Like an origami trick.
Wrapped in history. Her story. Cloaked in nostalgia.
Write down a list of what you enjoyed doing at that early time in your life. Chances are, you have the innate ability to enjoy that, because you were designed to do it. Hardwired for it.
Making that list puts your dreams into the three-dimensional material world. It shows you that your thoughts are already affecting physical reality.
I peel all that away to peek underneath at what is inside. What I was. Before the mask. Before the scars.
Mother

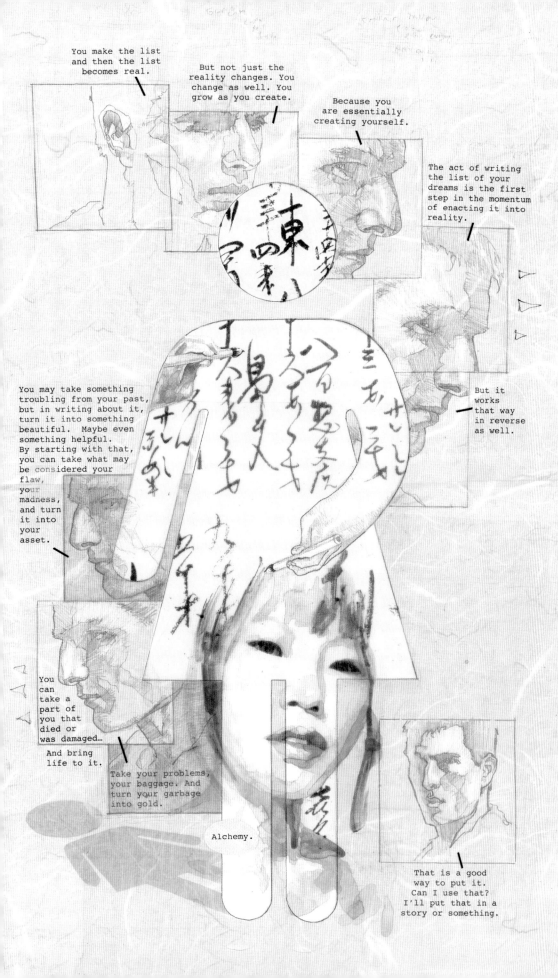

You make the list and then the list becomes real.

But not just the reality changes. You change as well. You grow as you create.

Because you are essentially creating yourself.

The act of writing the list of your dreams is the first step in the momentum of enacting it into reality.

You may take something troubling from your past, but in writing about it, turn it into something beautiful. Maybe even something helpful. By starting with that, you can take what may be considered your flaw, your madness, and turn it into your asset.

But it works that way in reverse as well.

You can take a part of you that died or was damaged...

And bring life to it.

Take your problems, your baggage. And turn your garbage into gold.

Alchemy.

That is a good way to put it. Can I use that? I'll put that in a story or something.

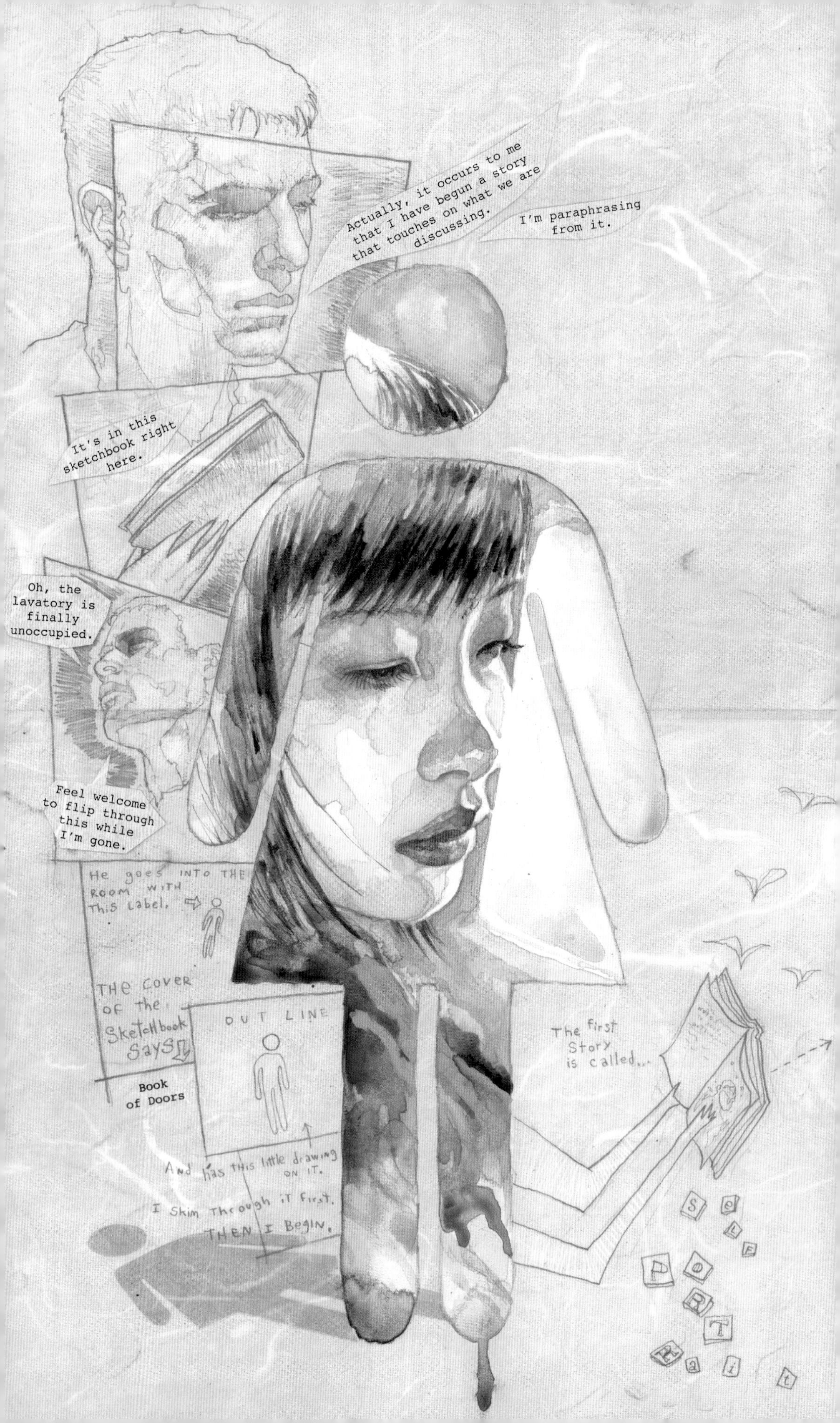

Actually, it occurs to me that I have begun a story that touches on what we are discussing.
I'm paraphrasing from it.
It's in this sketchbook right here.
Oh, the lavatory is finally unoccupied.
Feel welcome to flip through this while I'm gone.
He goes into the room with this label.
The cover of the sketchbook says
OUT LINE
Book of Doors
And has this little drawing on it.
I skim through it first. Then I begin.
The first story is called...
SELF PORTRait

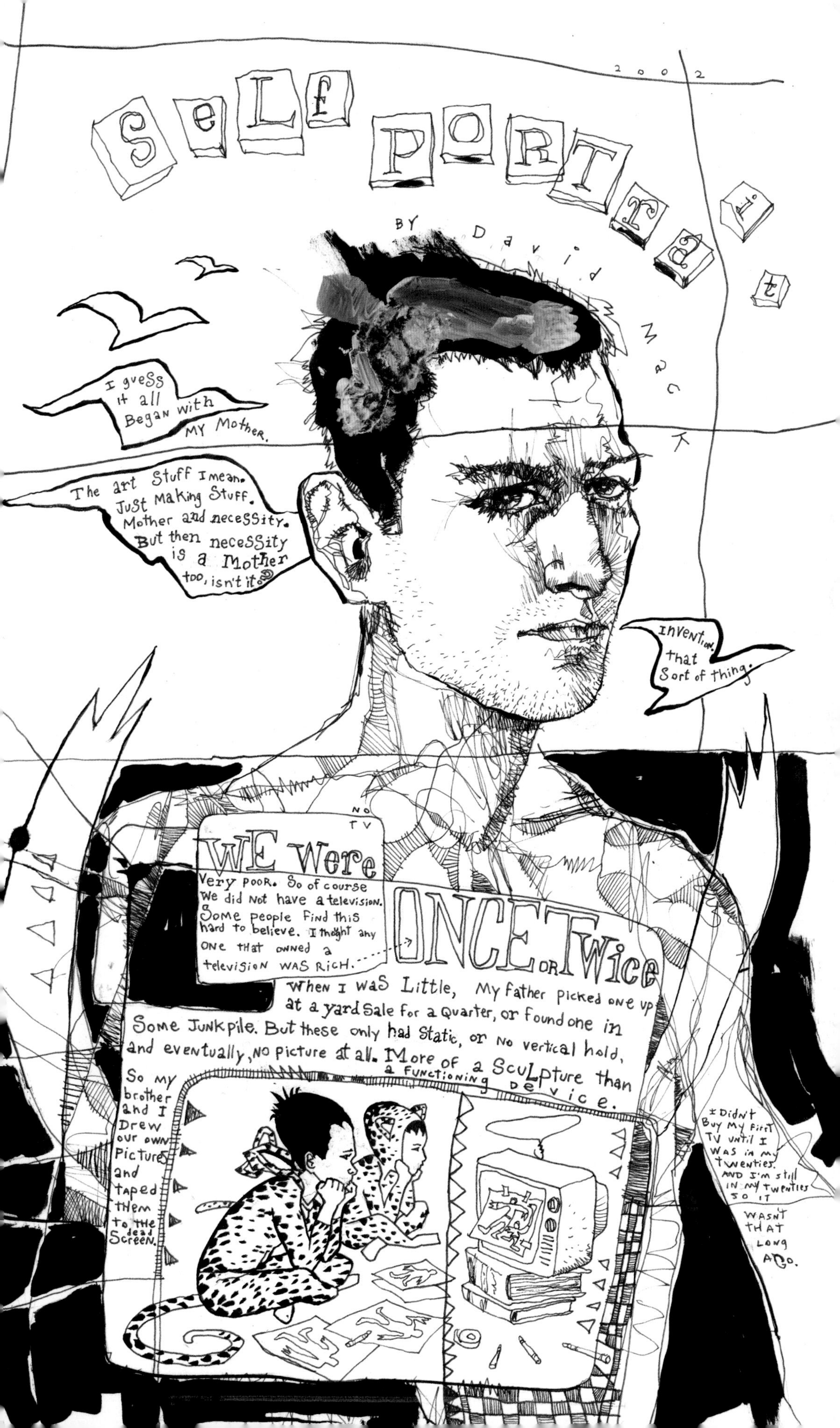

2002
SeLf PORTRAiT
BY David Mack
I guess it all Began with MY Mother.
The art Stuff I mean. Just Making Stuff. Mother and necessity. But then necessity is a Mother too, isn't it?
Invention. that Sort of thing.
NO TV
WE were Very poor. So of course we did not have a television. Some people find this hard to believe. I thought any one that owned a television WAS RICH.
ONCE OR Twice When I was Little, My father picked one up at a yard Sale for a Quarter, or found one in Some Junkpile. But these only had static, or no vertical hold, and eventually, no picture at all. More of a Sculpture than a functioning device.
So my brother and I Drew our own Pictures and taped them to the dead Screen.
I Didn't Buy My first TV until I was in my twenties. And I'm still in my twenties so it wasn't that long ago.

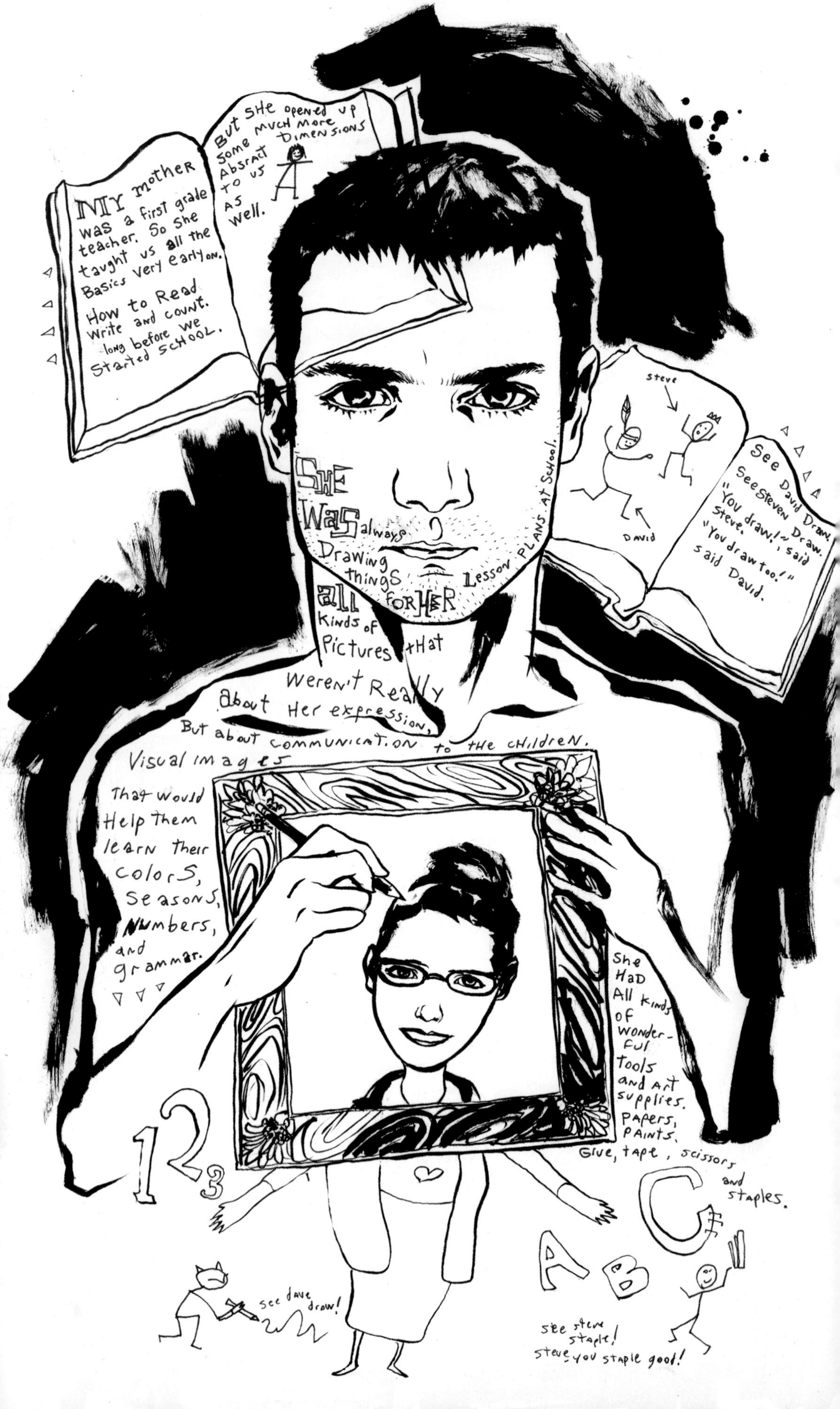
My mother was a first grade teacher. So she taught us all the Basics very early on. How to Read write and count. long before we started SCHOOL.
But she opened up some much more Absract dimensions to us as well.
She was always Drawing things all kinds of Pictures that Lesson Plans at School. For her
Weren't Really about Her expression, But about communication to the children.
Visual images That would Help them learn their colors, seasons, numbers, and grammar.
steve
David
See David Draw. See Steven Draw. "You draw!," said Steve. "You draw too!" said David.
She Had All kinds of wonder-ful tools and art supplies. papers, paints. Glue, tape, scissors and staples.
1 2 3
A B C
see dave draw!
see steve staple! steve, you staple good!

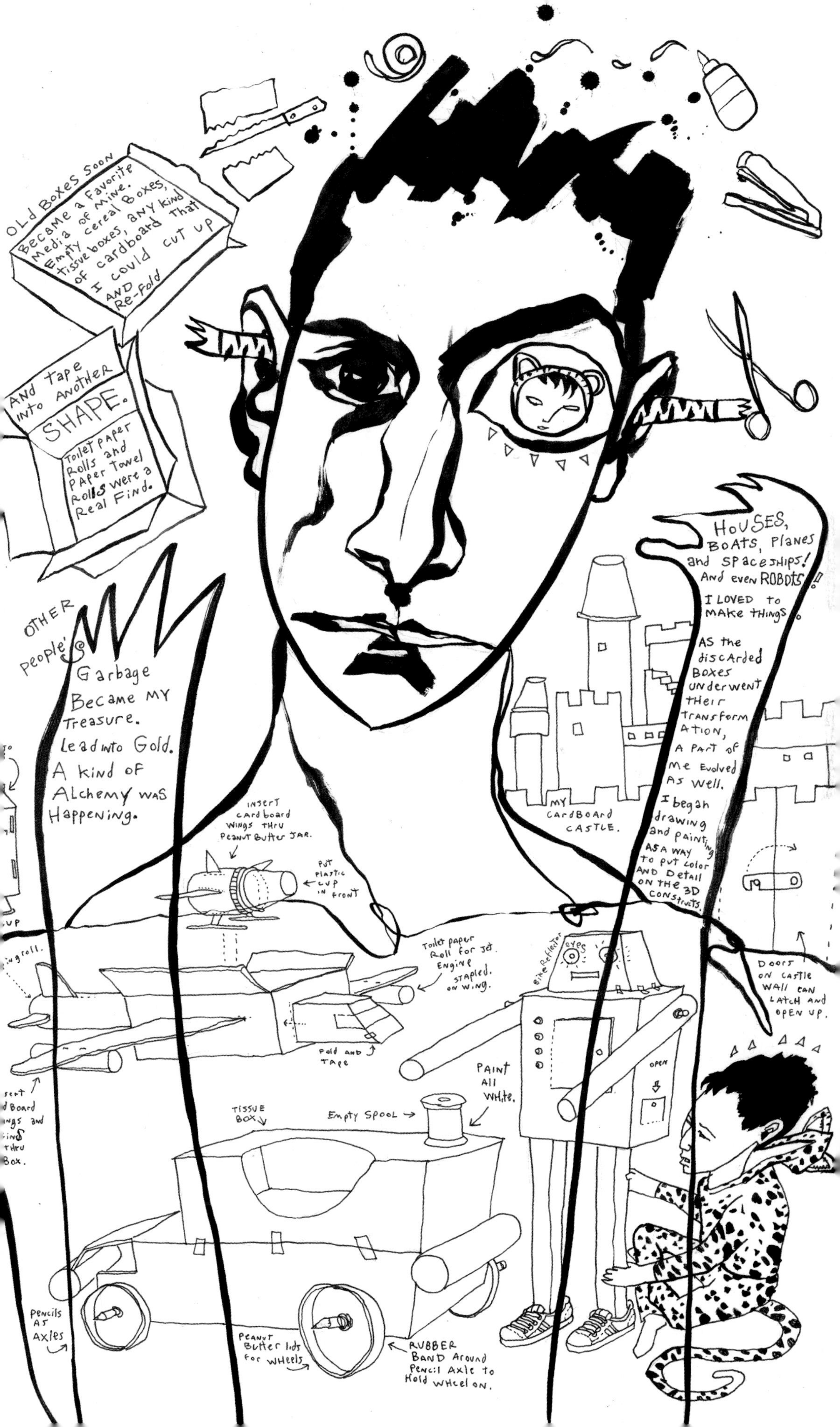
OLd BOXeS SOON BecAme a Favorite Media of mine. Empty cereal Boxes, tissue boxes, any kind of cardboard that I could cut up AND Re-fold
AND tape into ANOTHER SHAPE.
Toilet paper Rolls and Paper Towel Rolls were a Real Find.
OTHER people's Garbage Became MY Treasure. Lead into Gold. A kind of Alchemy was Happening.
HOUSES, BOATS, Planes and SPACESHIPS! And even ROBOTS! I LOVED to MAKE THINGS.
AS the discarded Boxes underwent their transformATION, A Part of me Evolved AS well. I began drawing and painting AS A WAY to put color AND Detail ON THE 3D constructs.
MY CardBoard CASTLE.
Insert cardboard wings thru Peanut Butter JAR.
Put plastic cup in front
Toilet paper Roll for Jet Engine stapled on wing.
Fold and Tape
Bike Reflector eyes
Doors on castle wall can latch and open up.
OPEN
PAINT ALL White.
TISSUE BOX
Empty Spool
Pencils AS Axles
Peanut Butter lids for wheels
RUBBER BAND Around Pencil Axle to Hold wheel on.

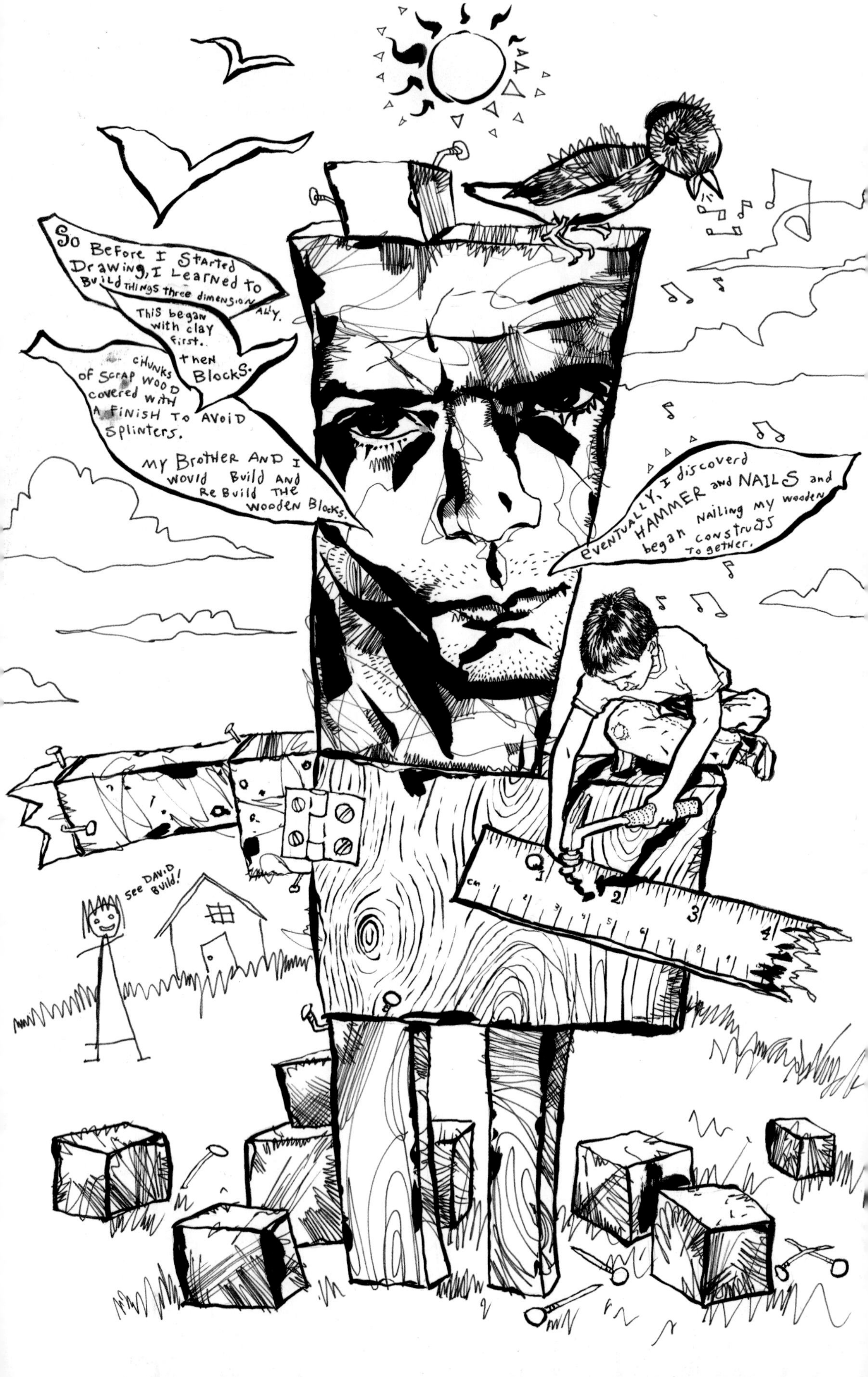
So Before I Started Drawing, I Learned to Build things three dimensionally.
This began with clay first.
then Blocks.
chunks of Scrap wood covered with A finish to avoid splinters.
My Brother and I would Build and ReBuild the wooden Blocks.
Eventually, I discoverd HAMMER and NAILS and began nailing my wooden constructs together.
See DAVID Build!

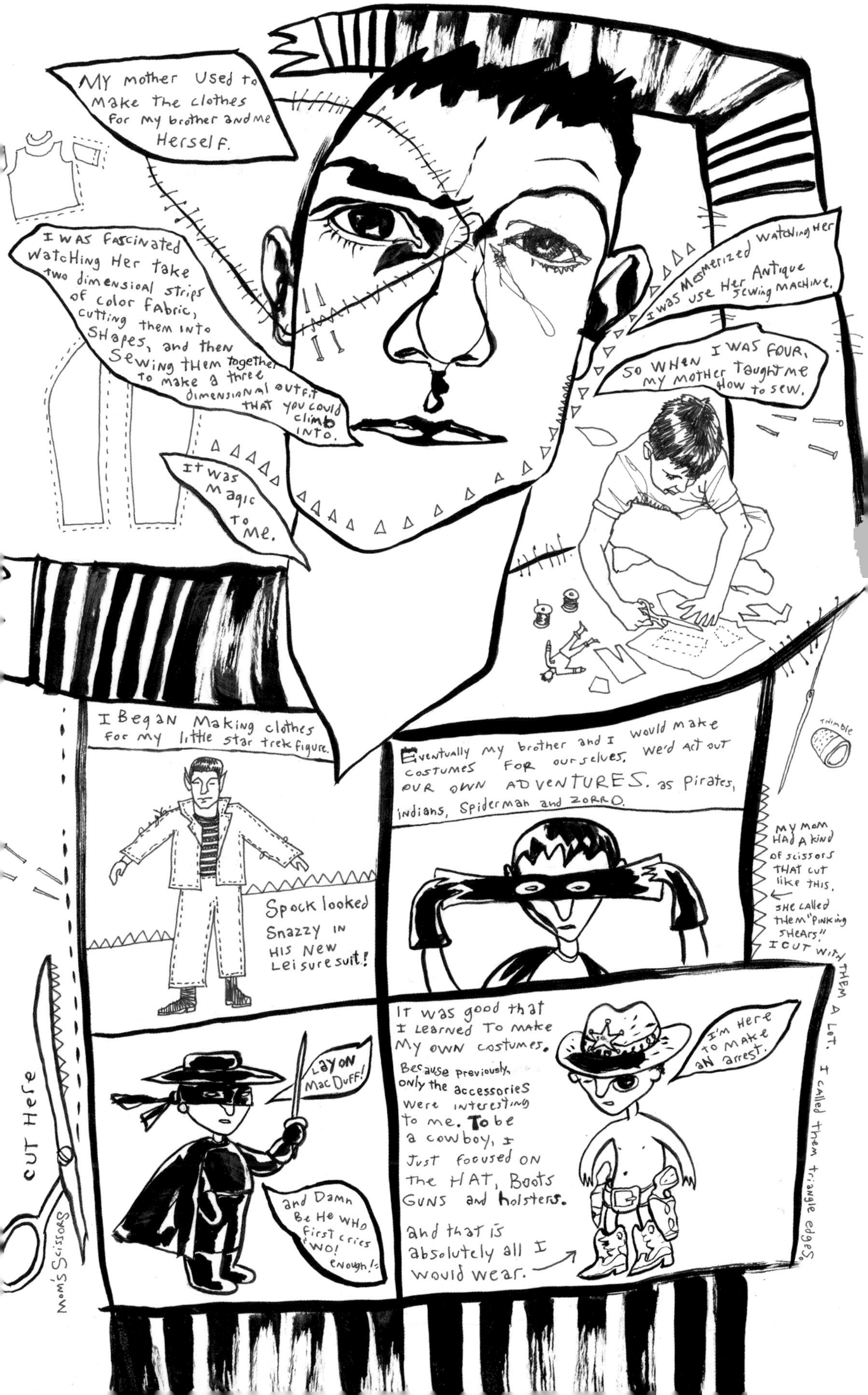

My mother Used to Make the clothes for my brother and me Herself.
I was fascinated watching Her take two dimensioal strips of color fabric, cutting them into shapes, and then sewing them together to make a three dimensional outfit that you could climb into.
It was Magic to me.
I was Mesmerized watching Her use Her Antique sewing machine.
So when I was four, my mother taught me how to sew.
I Began Making clothes for my little star trek figure.
Spock looked Snazzy in his New Leisure suit!
Eventually my brother and I would make costumes for ourselves. We'd act out our own ADVENTURES. as Pirates, indians, Spiderman and ZORRO.
My mom Had a kind of scissors that cut like this. She called them "Pinking shears." I cut with them a lot. I called them triangle edges.
thimble
CUT Here
Mom's Scissors
Lay on MacDuff!
and Damn Be He who first cries "Wo! enough!"
It was good that I learned to make my own costumes.
Because previously, only the accessories were interesting to me. To be a cowboy, I just focused on the HAT, Boots GUNS and holsters.
and that is absolutely all I would wear.
I'm Here to make an arrest.

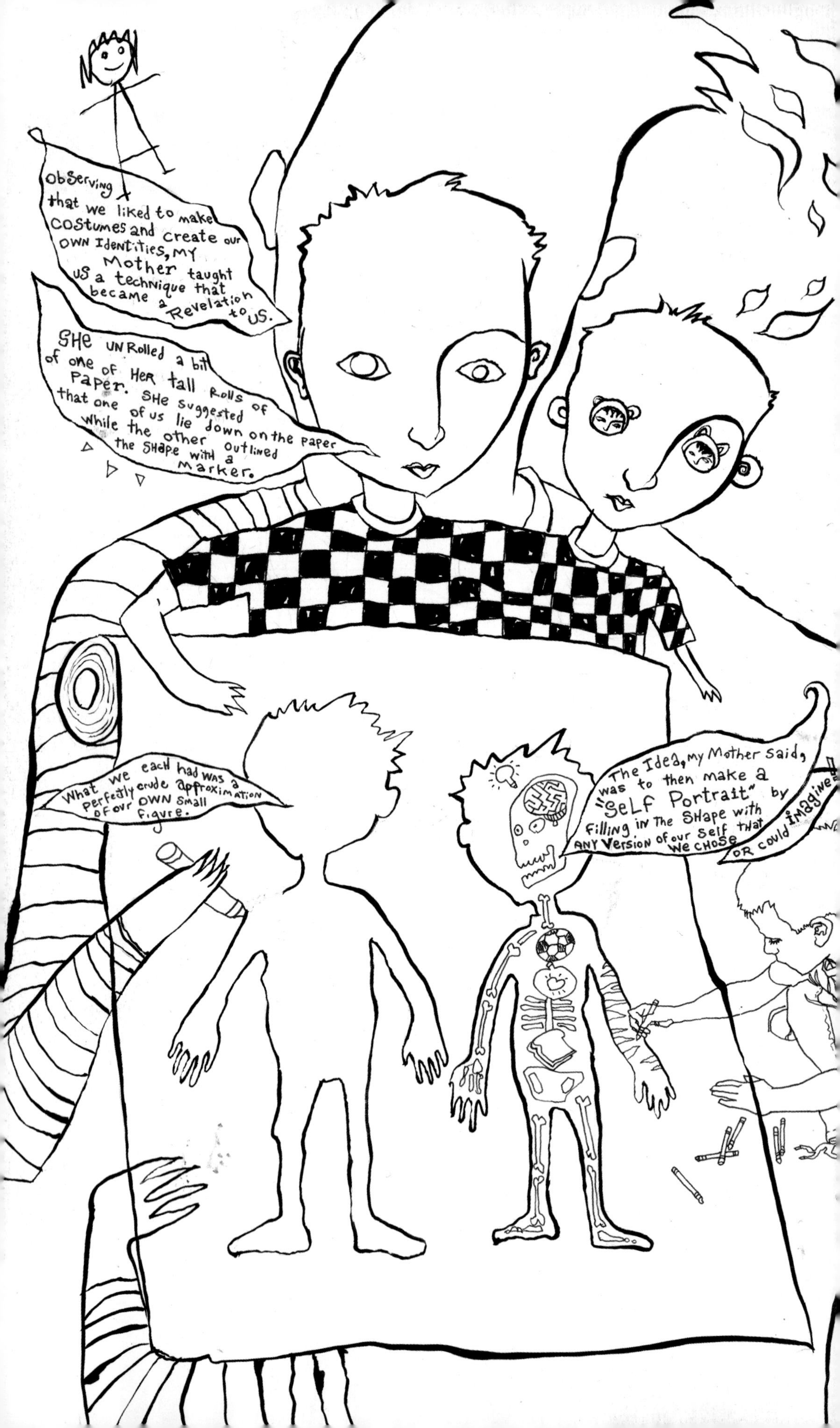
observing that we liked to make costumes and create our own identities, my Mother taught us a technique that became a Revelation to us.
She unrolled a bit of one of her tall rolls of paper. She suggested that one of us lie down on the paper while the other outlined the shape with a marker.
What we each had was a perfectly crude approximation of our own small figure.
"The Idea, my Mother said, was to then make a "Self Portrait" by filling in the shape with any version of our self that we chose or could imagine!

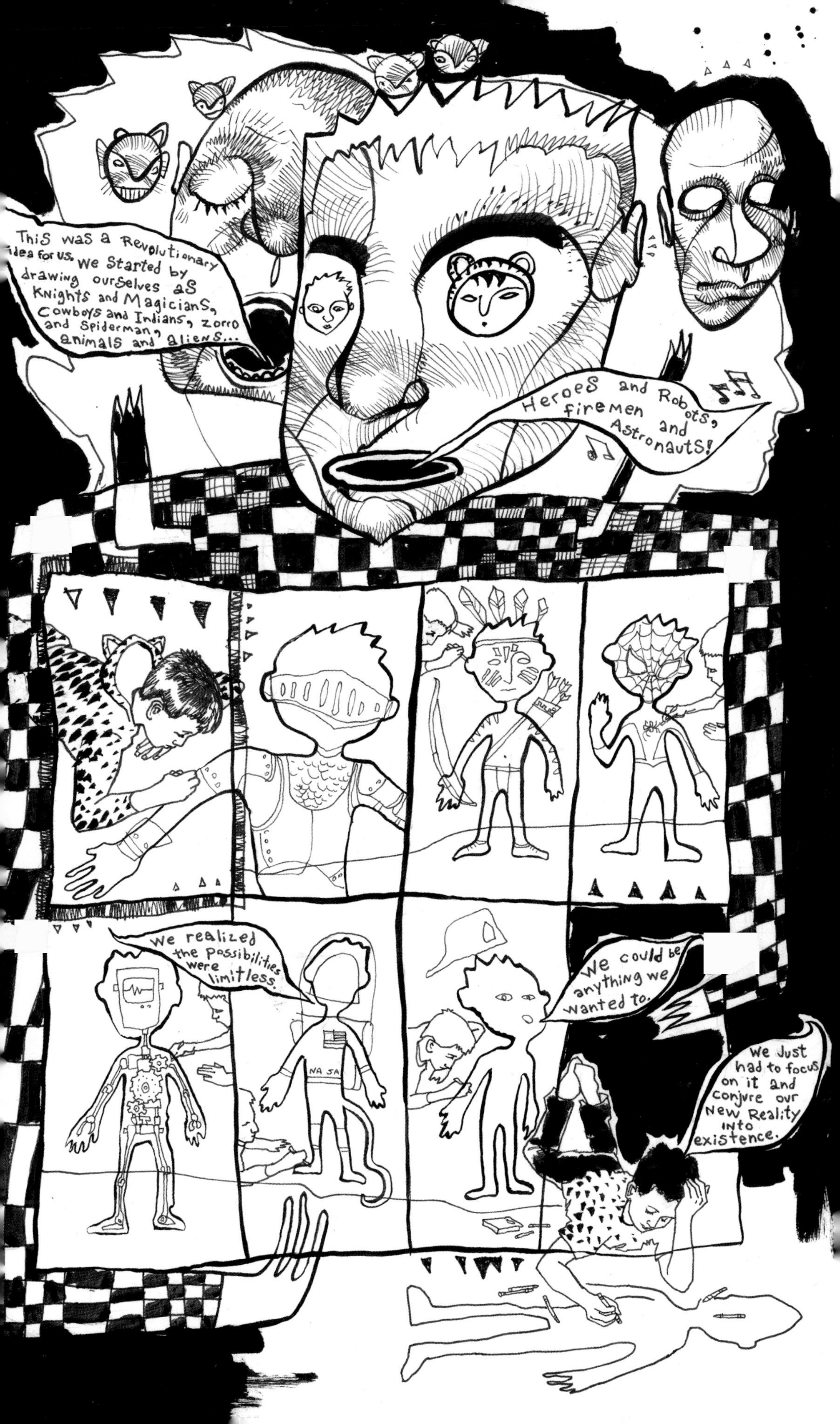
This was a Revolutionary idea for us. We started by drawing ourselves as Knights and Magicians, Cowboys and Indians, Zorro and Spiderman, animals and aliens...
Heroes and Robots, firemen and Astronauts!
We realized the possibilities were limitless.
NASA
We could be anything we wanted to.
We just had to focus on it and conjure our New Reality into existence.

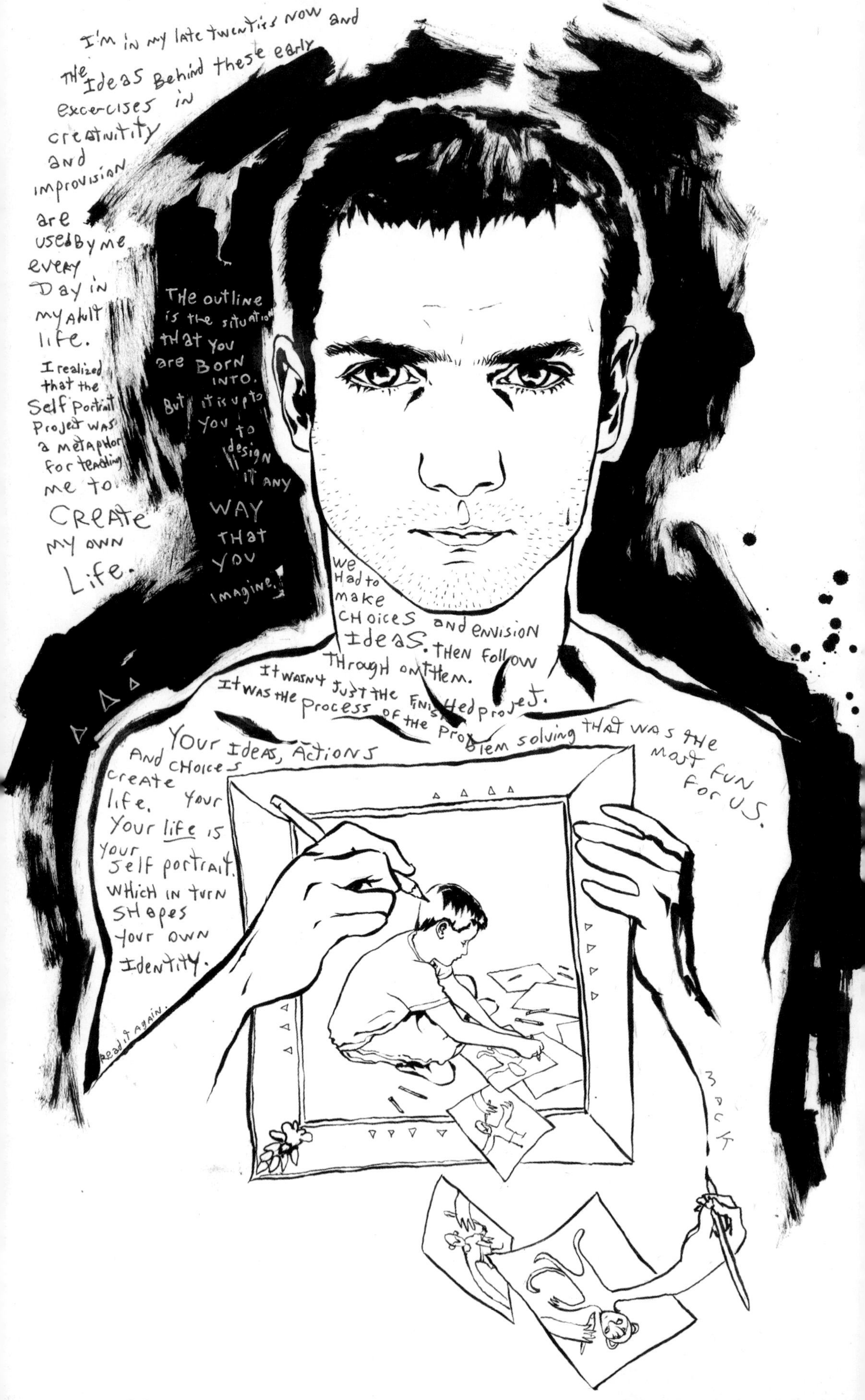
I'm in my late twenties now and the ideas behind these early excercises in creativitity and improvision are used by me every day in my adult life.
I realized that the self portrait project was a metaphor for teaching me to create my own life.
The outline is the situation that you are born into. But it is up to you to design it any way that you imagine.
We had to make choices and envision ideas. Then follow through on them.
It wasn't just the finished project. It was the process of the problem solving that was the most fun for us.
Your ideas, actions and choices create life. Your life is your self portrait. Which in turn shapes your own identity.
read it again.
Mack

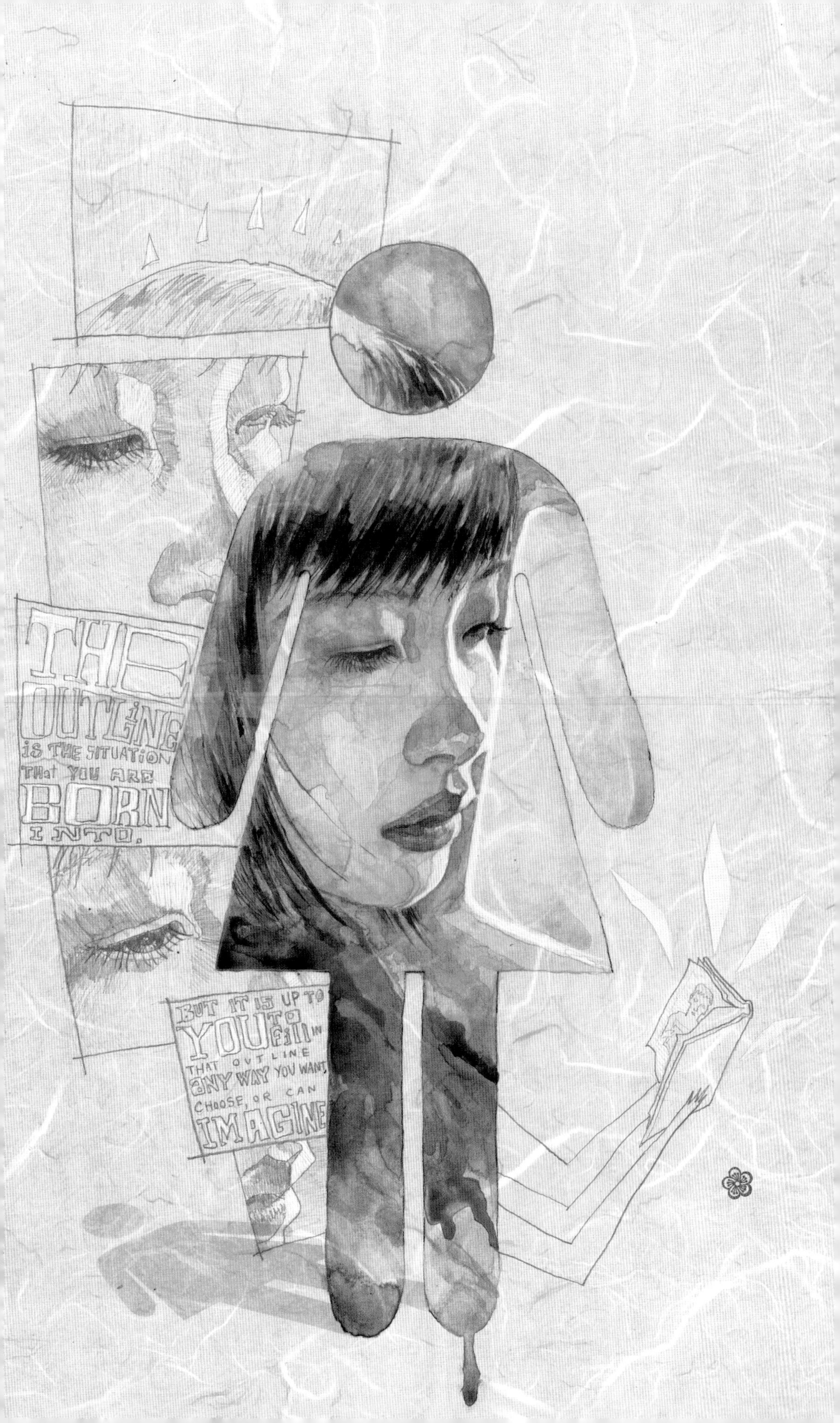
THE OUTLINE is THE SITUATION THat YOU ARE BORN INTO.
BUT IT IS UP TO YOU TO fill in THAT OUTLINE aNY WAY YOU WANT, CHOOSE, OR CAN IMAGINE

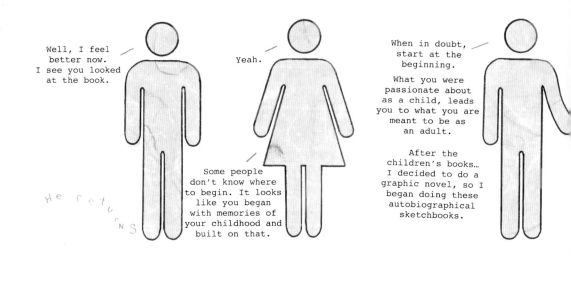

Well, I feel better now. I see you looked at the book.

Yeah.

When in doubt, start at the beginning.

What you were passionate about as a child, leads you to what you are meant to be as an adult.

After the children's books… I decided to do a graphic novel, so I began doing these autobiographical sketchbooks.

Some people don't know where to begin. It looks like you began with memories of your childhood and built on that.

He returns

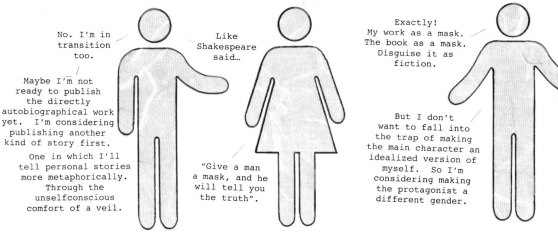

No. I'm in transition too.

Maybe I'm not ready to publish the directly autobiographical work yet. I'm considering publishing another kind of story first.

One in which I'll tell personal stories more metaphorically. Through the unselfconscious comfort of a veil.

Like Shakespeare said…

"Give a man a mask, and he will tell you the truth".

Exactly! My work as a mask. The book as a mask. Disguise it as fiction.

But I don't want to fall into the trap of making the main character an idealized version of myself. So I'm considering making the protagonist a different gender.

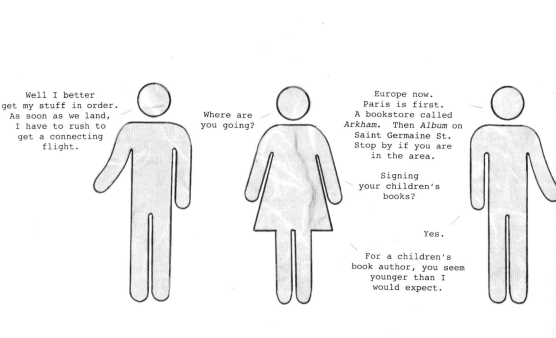

Well I better get my stuff in order. As soon as we land, I have to rush to get a connecting flight.

Where are you going?

Europe now. Paris is first. A bookstore called *Arkham*. Then *Album* on Saint Germaine St. Stop by if you are in the area.

Signing your children's books?

Yes.

For a children's book author, you seem younger than I would expect.

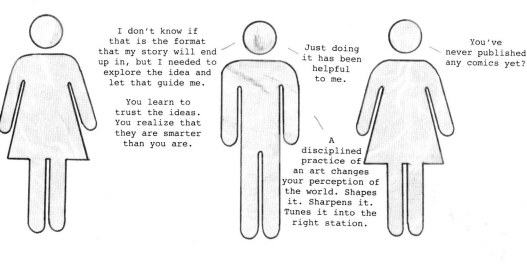

I don't know if that is the format that my story will end up in, but I needed to explore the idea and let that guide me.

You learn to trust the ideas. You realize that they are smarter than you are.

Just doing it has been helpful to me.

A disciplined practice of an art changes your perception of the world. Shapes it. Sharpens it. Tunes it into the right station.

You've never published any comics yet?

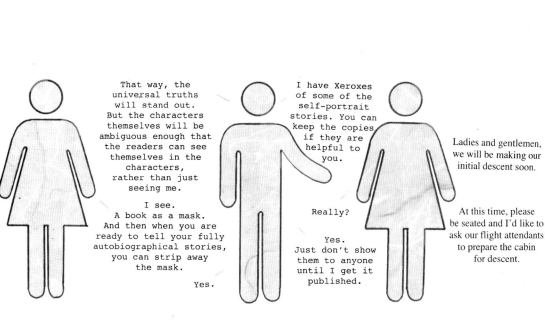

That way, the universal truths will stand out. But the characters themselves will be ambiguous enough that the readers can see themselves in the characters, rather than just seeing me.

I see. A book as a mask. And then when you are ready to tell your fully autobiographical stories, you can strip away the mask.

Yes.

I have Xeroxes of some of the self-portrait stories. You can keep the copies if they are helpful to you.

Really?

Yes. Just don't show them to anyone until I get it published.

Ladies and gentlemen, we will be making our initial descent soon.

At this time, please be seated and I'd like to ask our flight attendants to prepare the cabin for descent.

Perhaps creating keeps you young. There is no time when you are in the creating space. The more of this worlds time that you spend there, the less you age. Or perhaps I am older. And you are younger. Or vice versa. Perhaps this meeting is some trick of time and literature. That detours the normal physics of time and space. Since we are both writing on the same plane, maybe we are just minor characters in the other's story.

Like an inter-title crossover that you see in comics. I'm in your issue, and you are in mine.

Well, we both certainly have issues.

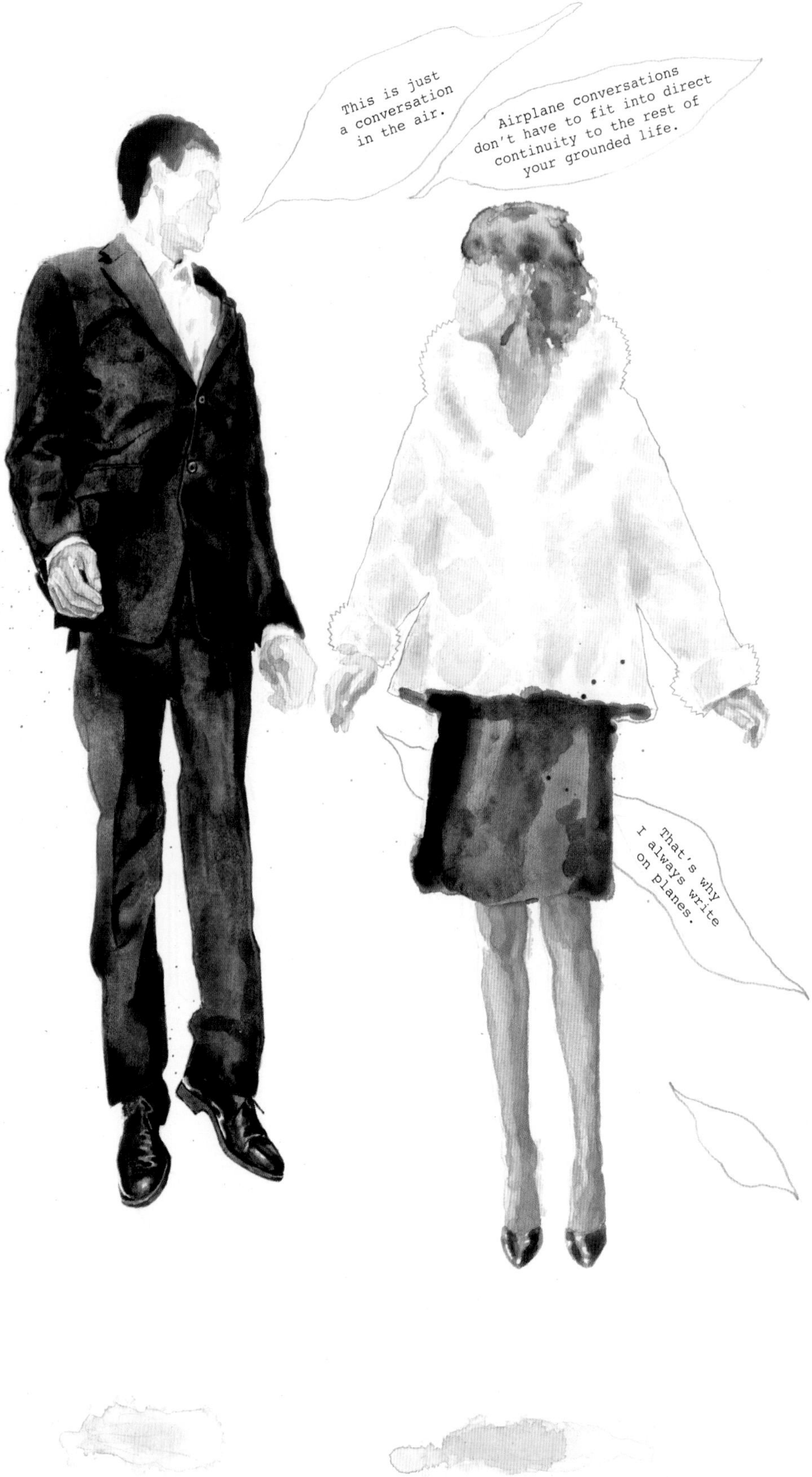
This is just a conversation in the air.
Airplane conversations don't have to fit into direct continuity to the rest of your grounded life.
That's why I always write on planes.

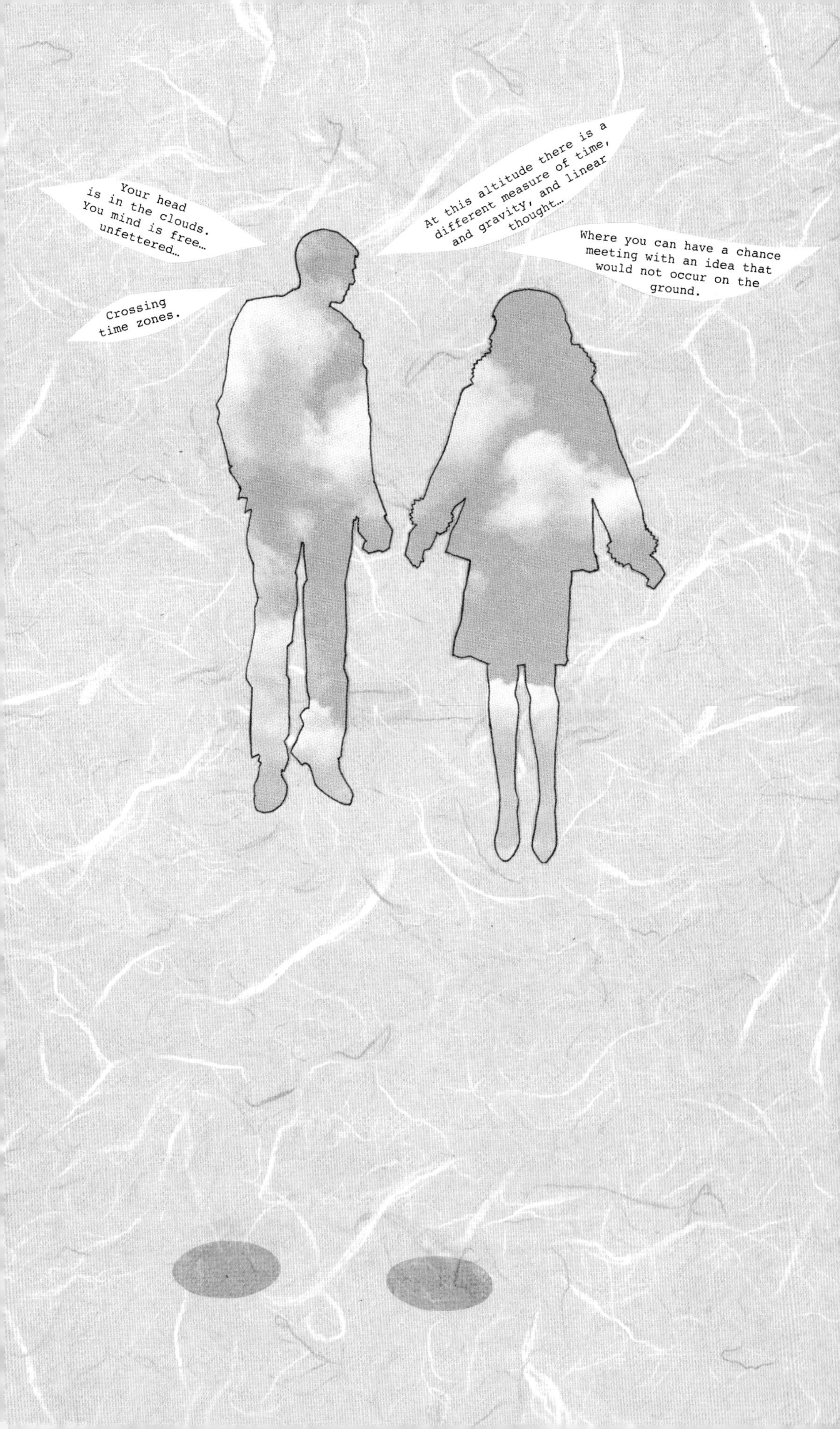
Your head is in the clouds. You mind is free… unfettered…
Crossing time zones.
At this altitude there is a different measure of time, and gravity, and linear thought…
Where you can have a chance meeting with an idea that would not occur on the ground.

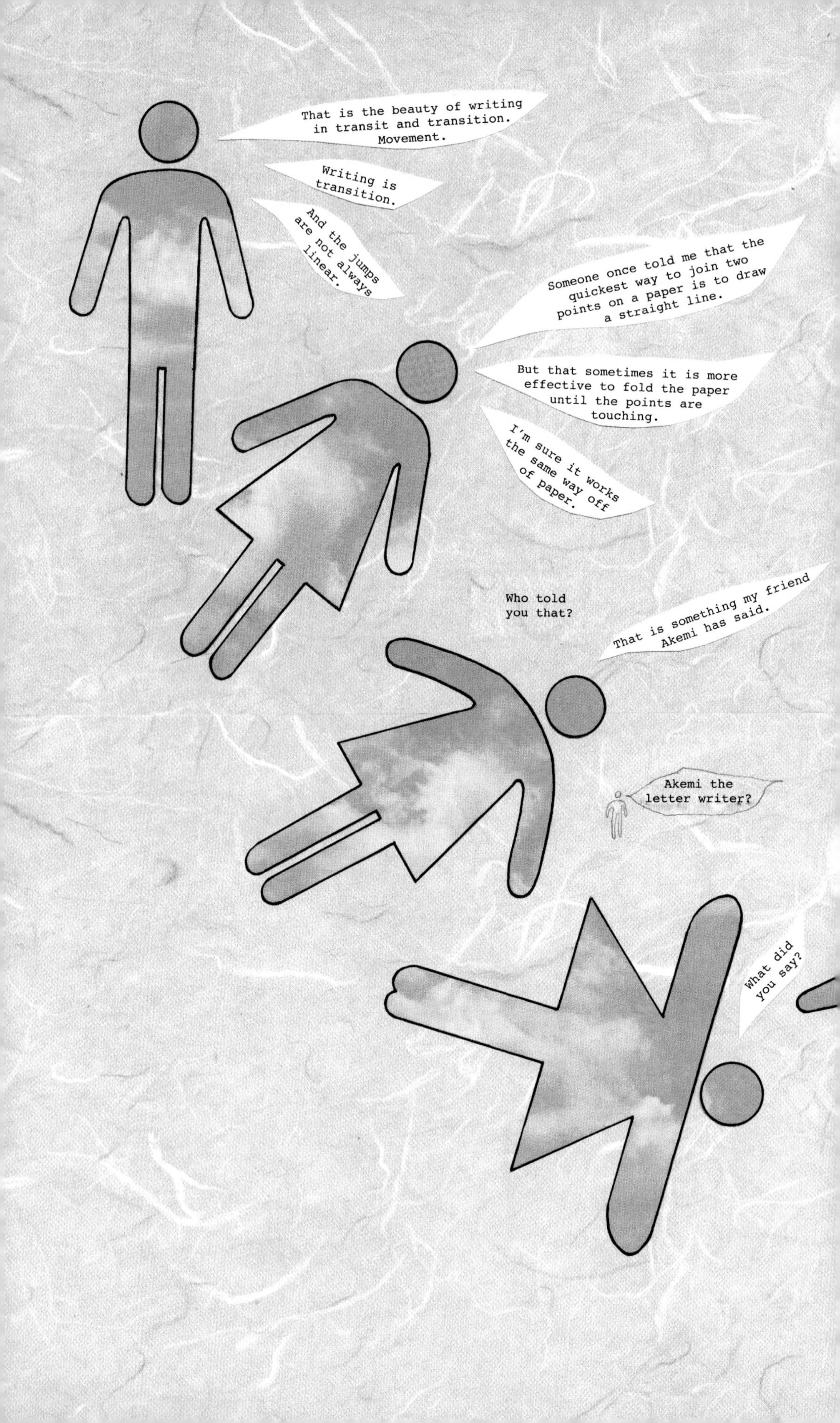
That is the beauty of writing in transit and transition. Movement.
Writing is transition.
And the jumps are not always linear.
Someone once told me that the quickest way to join two points on a paper is to draw a straight line.
But that sometimes it is more effective to fold the paper until the points are touching.
I'm sure it works the same way off of paper.
Who told you that?
That is something my friend Akemi has said.
Akemi the letter writer?
What did you say?

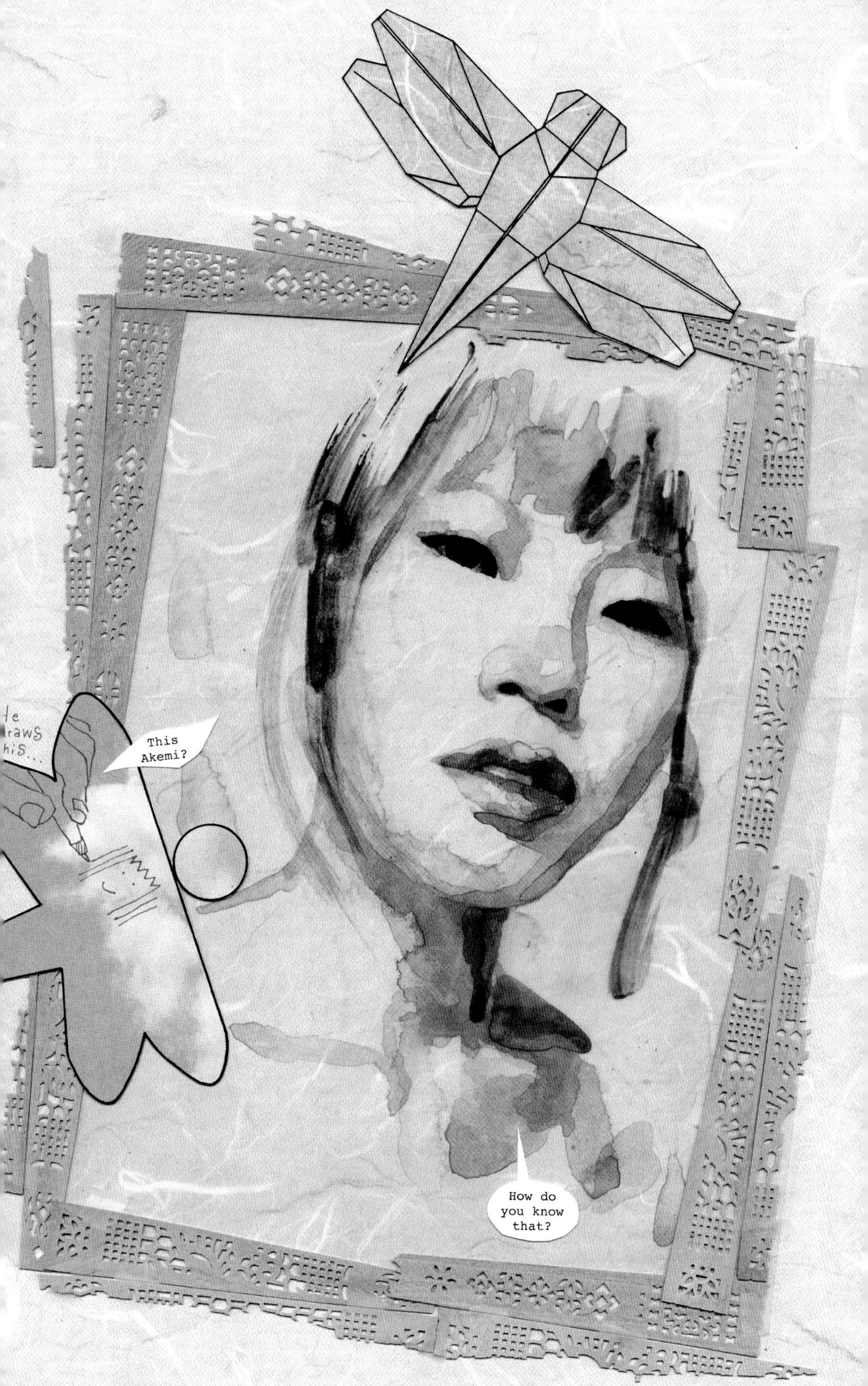
This Akemi?
How do you know that?

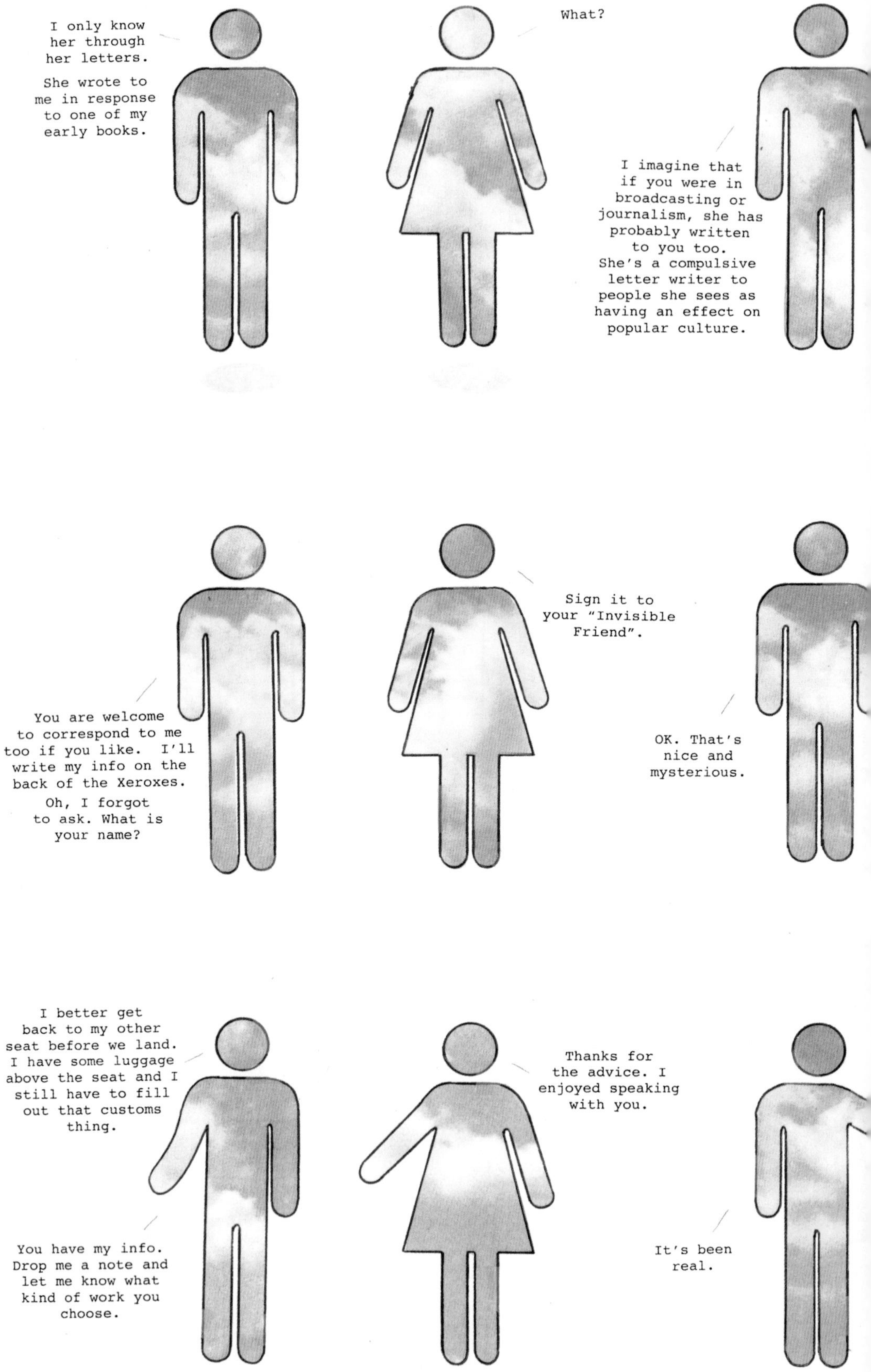
I only know her through her letters.
She wrote to me in response to one of my early books.
What?
I imagine that if you were in broadcasting or journalism, she has probably written to you too.
She's a compulsive letter writer to people she sees as having an effect on popular culture.
You are welcome to correspond to me too if you like. I'll write my info on the back of the Xeroxes.
Oh, I forgot to ask. What is your name?
Sign it to your "Invisible Friend".
OK. That's nice and mysterious.
I better get back to my other seat before we land. I have some luggage above the seat and I still have to fill out that customs thing.
You have my info. Drop me a note and let me know what kind of work you choose.
Thanks for the advice. I enjoyed speaking with you.
It's been real.

C O N V E R S A T I O N S   I N   T H E   A I R

Dialogue / Mixed Media
Private Collection

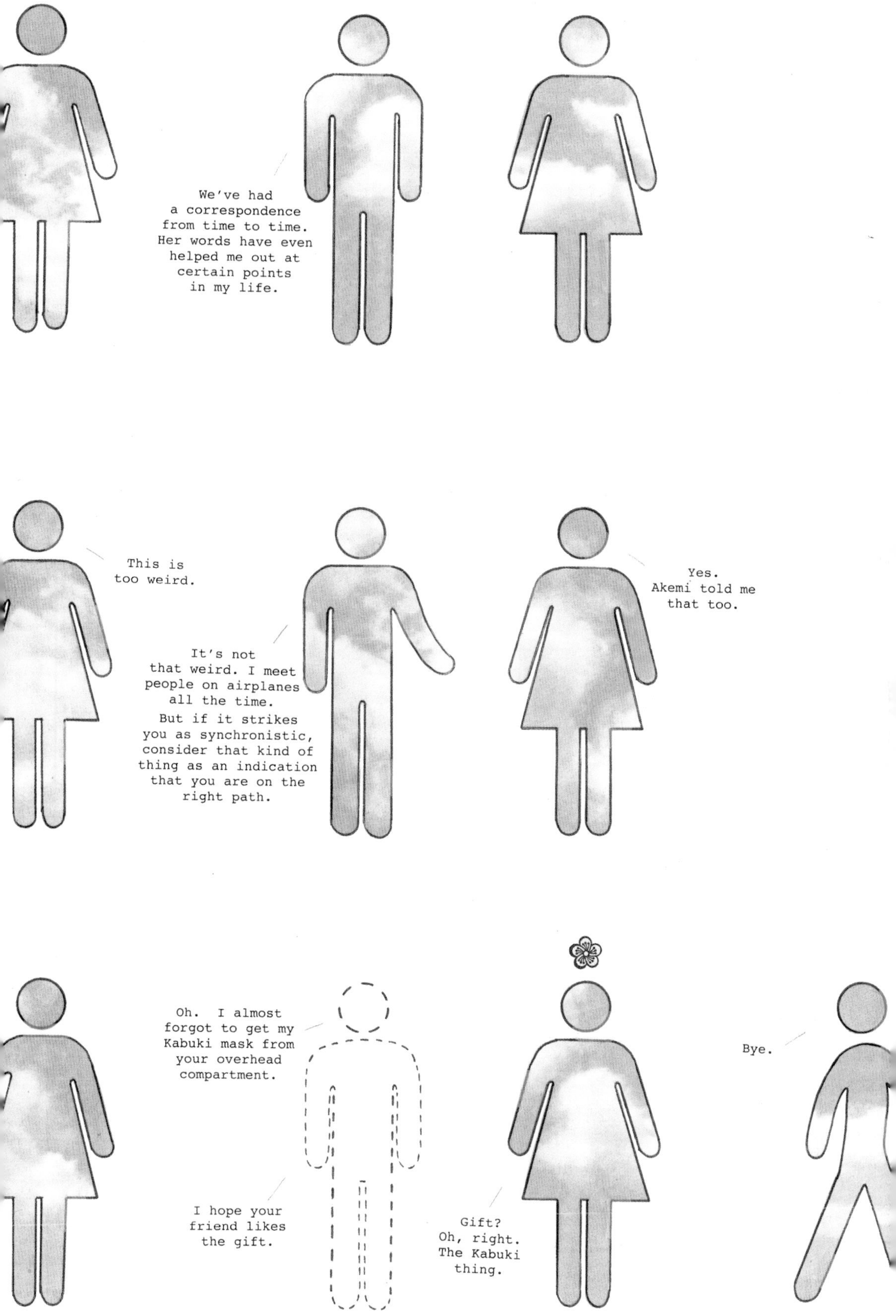
We've had a correspondence from time to time. Her words have even helped me out at certain points in my life.
This is too weird.
It's not that weird. I meet people on airplanes all the time.
But if it strikes you as synchronistic, consider that kind of thing as an indication that you are on the right path.
Yes. Akemi told me that too.
Oh. I almost forgot to get my Kabuki mask from your overhead compartment.
I hope your friend likes the gift.
Gift? Oh, right. The Kabuki thing.
Bye.

Ladies and gentlemen,
We are coming in for
our landing.
Please put your
seat backs and trays in
their fully upright and locked
position and remain seated
with your seatbelt
fastened.

For those of you
catching a connecting flight,
we will have an airline
representative at the gate
to direct you.

For those passengers
not catching a connecting
flight or going through customs
here, please stay on board during
refueling for our final
destination…
The United States.

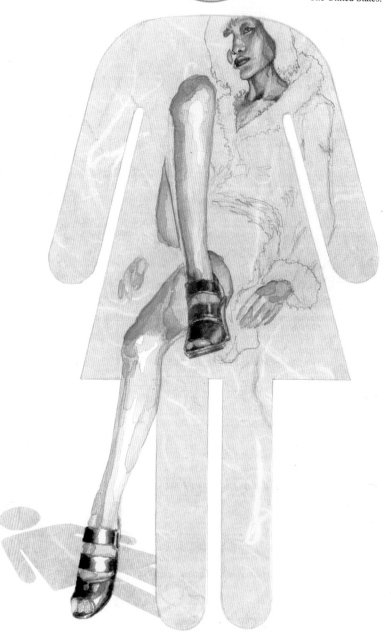

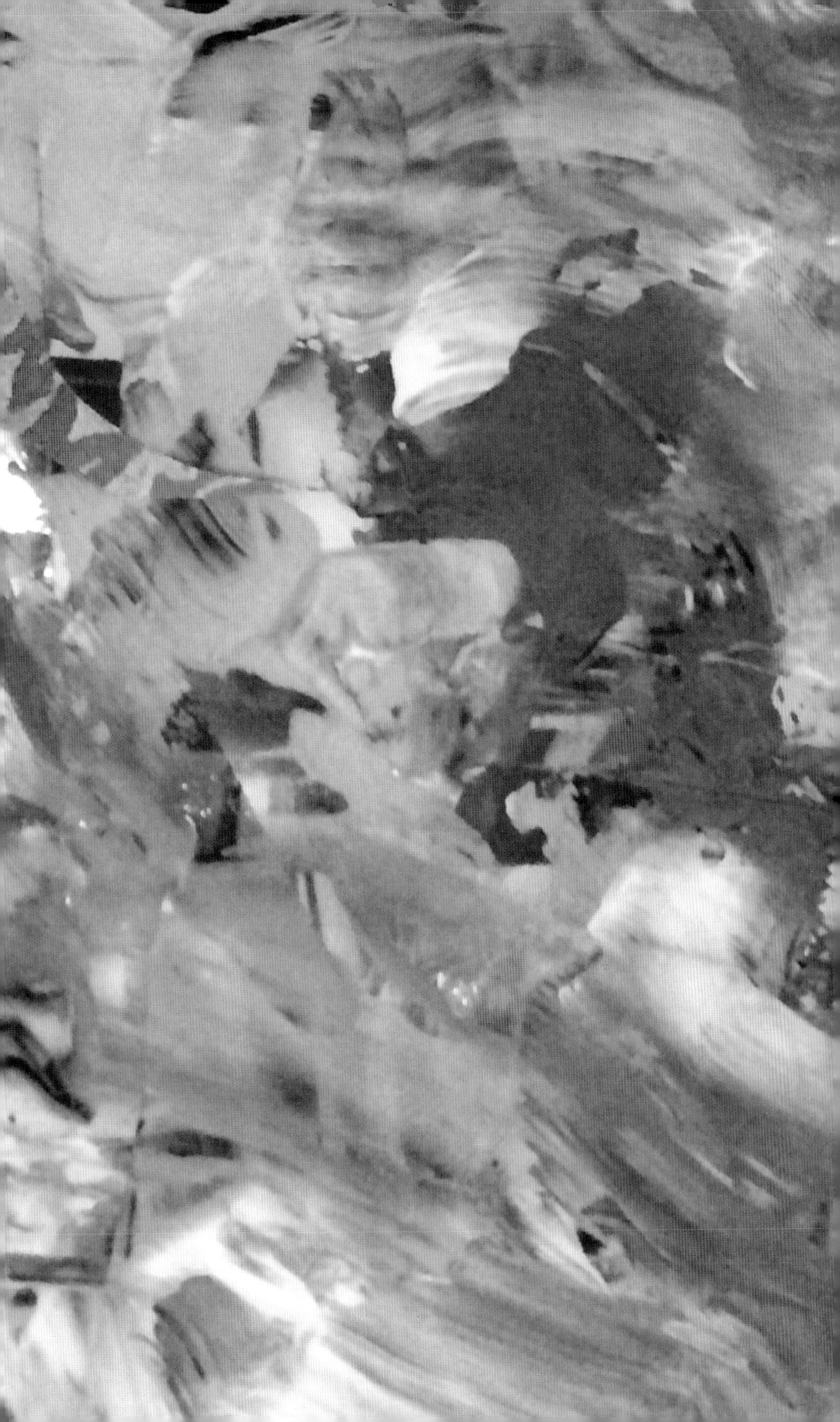

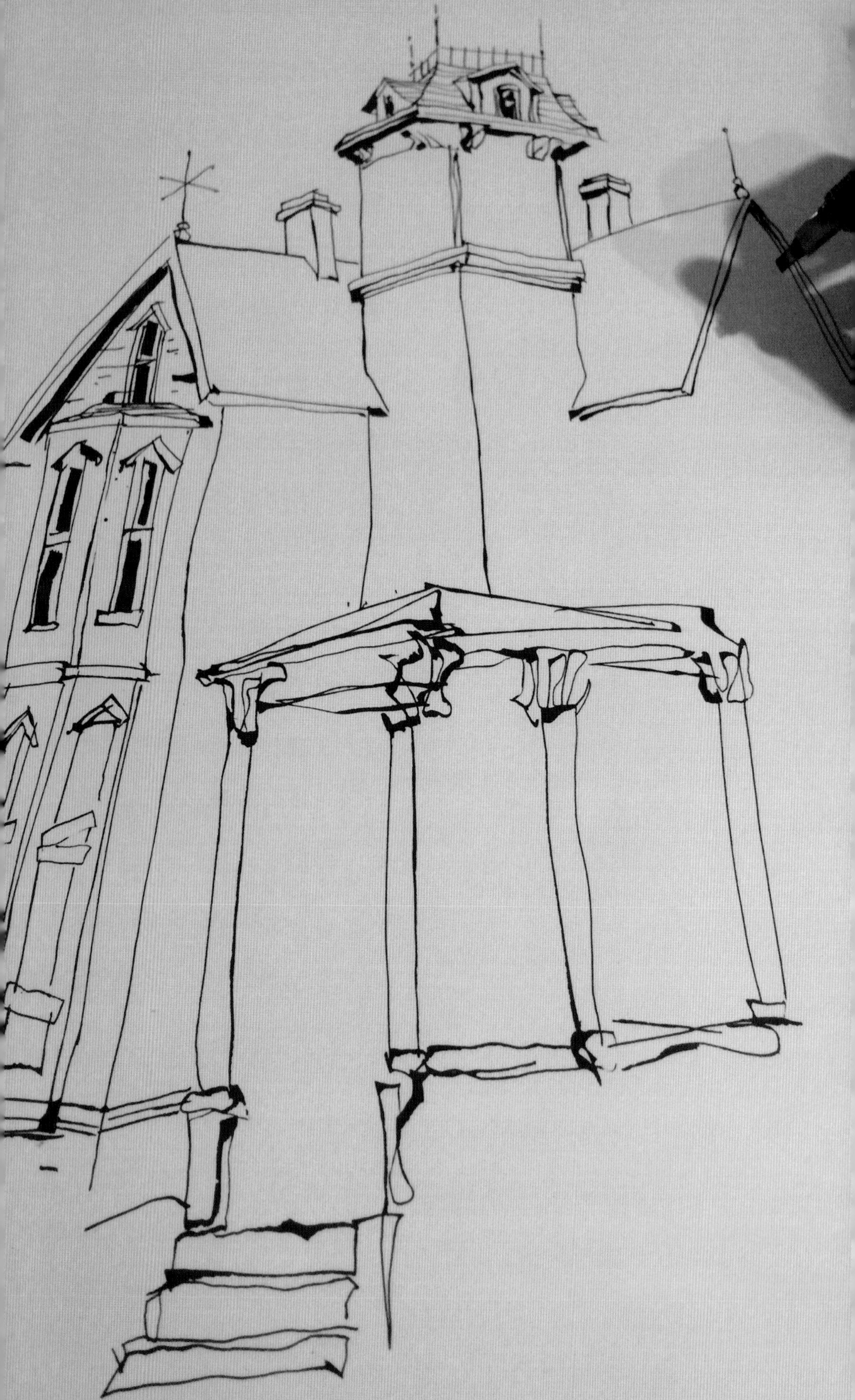

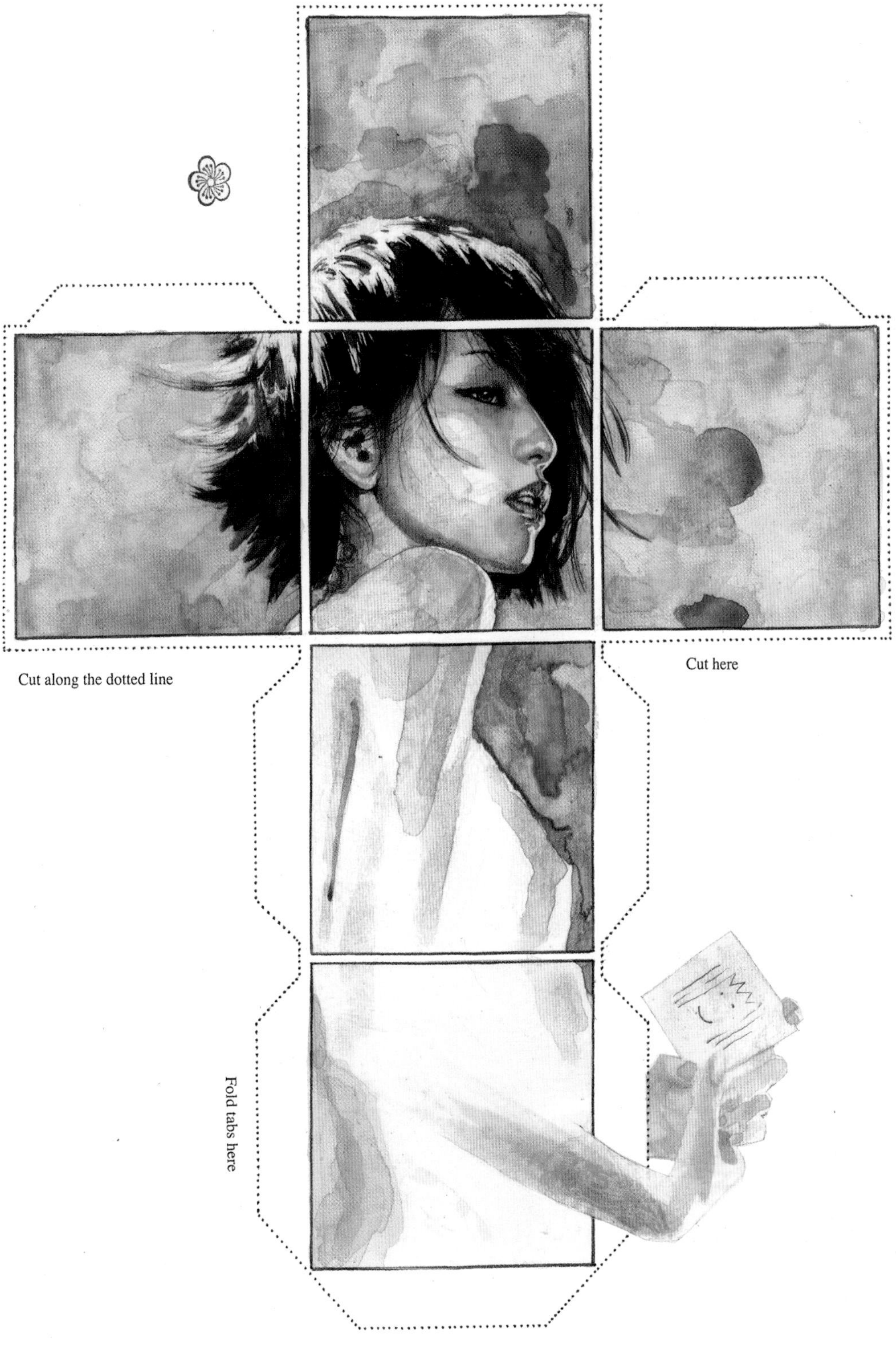
Fold here
Cut along the dotted line
Cut here
Fold tabs here
Roll like dice

The Alchemy

Part Five

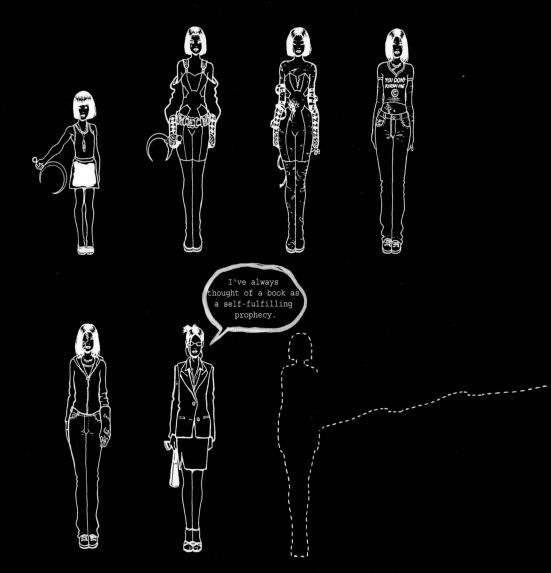

I've always thought of a book as a self-fulfilling prophecy.

Epistolary

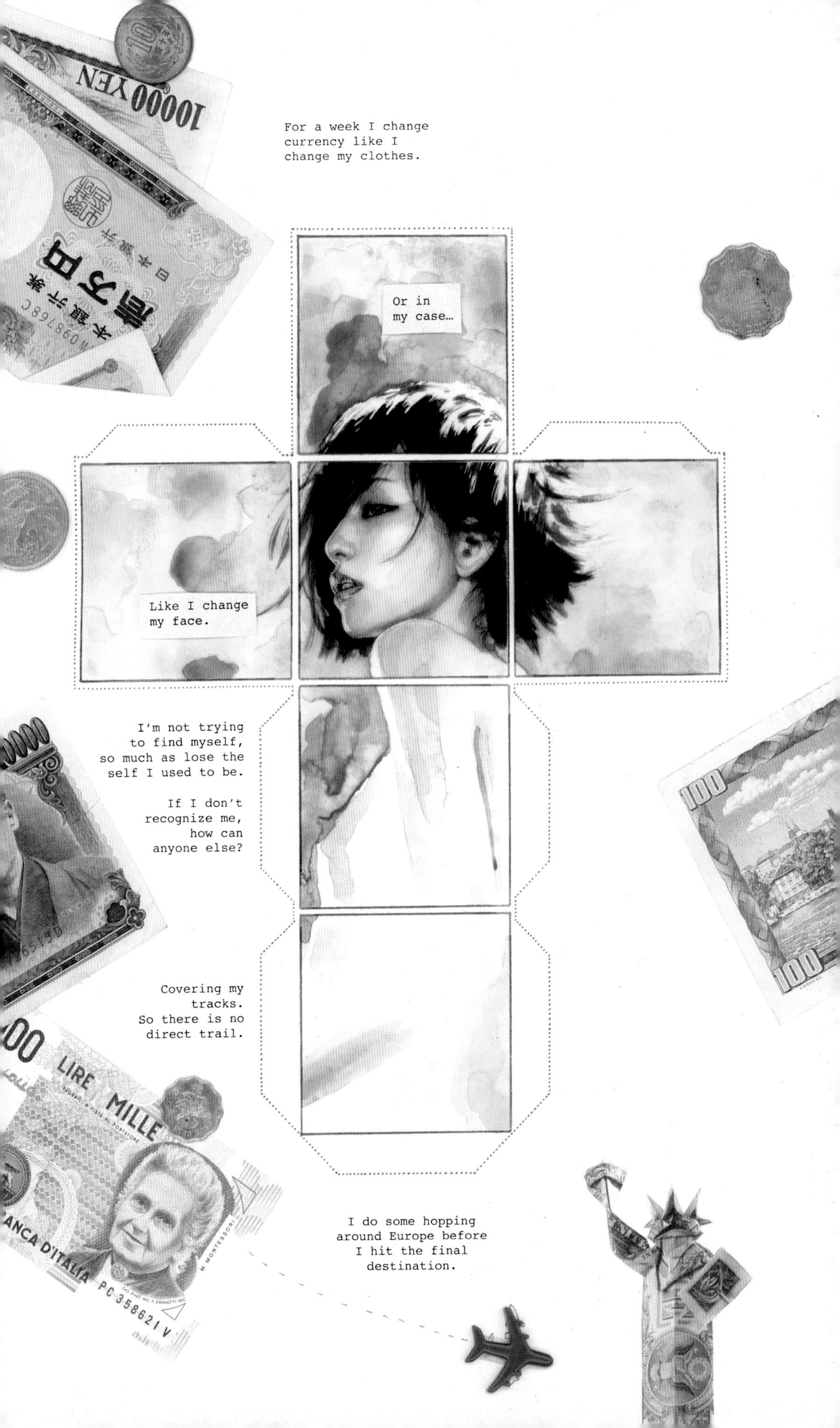
10000 YEN
For a week I change
currency like I
change my clothes.
Or in
my case…
Like I change
my face.
I'm not trying
to find myself,
so much as lose the
self I used to be.
If I don't
recognize me,
how can
anyone else?
100
Covering my
tracks.
So there is no
direct trail.
LIRE
MILLE
I do some hopping
around Europe before
I hit the final
destination.

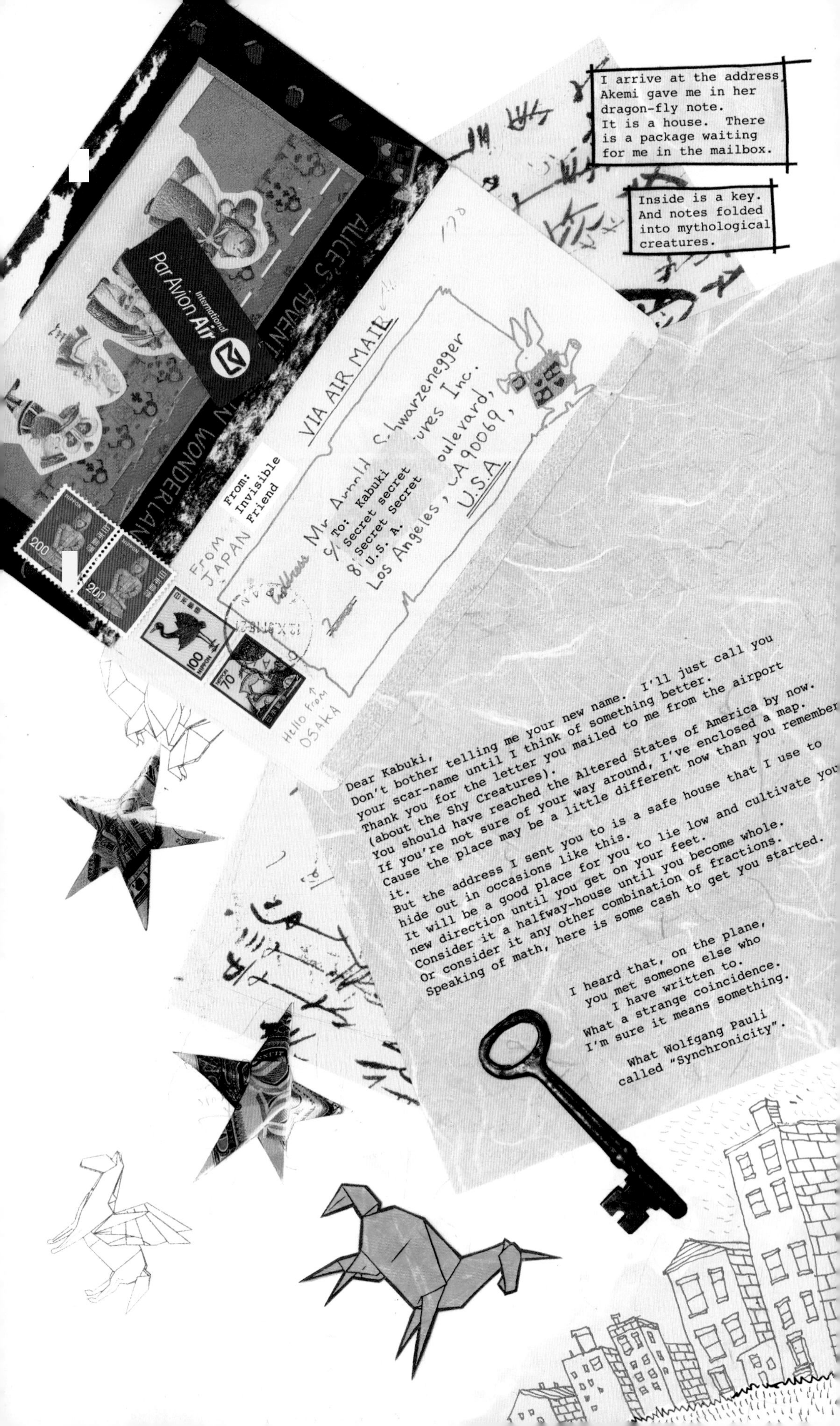
I arrive at the address Akemi gave me in her dragon-fly note.
It is a house. There is a package waiting for me in the mailbox.
Inside is a key. And notes folded into mythological creatures.
Par Avion Air
International
VIA AIR MAIL
From: Invisible Friend
To: Kabuki
Secret secret
Secret Secret
U.S. A.
Los Angeles, CA 90069,
U.S.A.
FROM JAPAN
Hello from OSAKA
Dear Kabuki,
Don't bother telling me your new name. I'll just call you
your scar-name until I think of something better.
Thank you for the letter you mailed to me from the airport
(about the Shy Creatures).
You should have reached the Altered States of America by now.
If you're not sure of your way around, I've enclosed a map.
Cause the place may be a little different now than you remember
it.
But the address I sent you to is a safe house that I use to
hide out in occasions like this.
It will be a good place for you to lie low and cultivate you
new direction until you get on your feet.
Consider it a halfway-house until you become whole.
Or consider it any other combination of fractions.
Speaking of math, here is some cash to get you started.
I heard that, on the plane,
you met someone else who
I have written to.
What a strange coincidence.
I'm sure it means something.
What Wolfgang Pauli
called "Synchronicity".

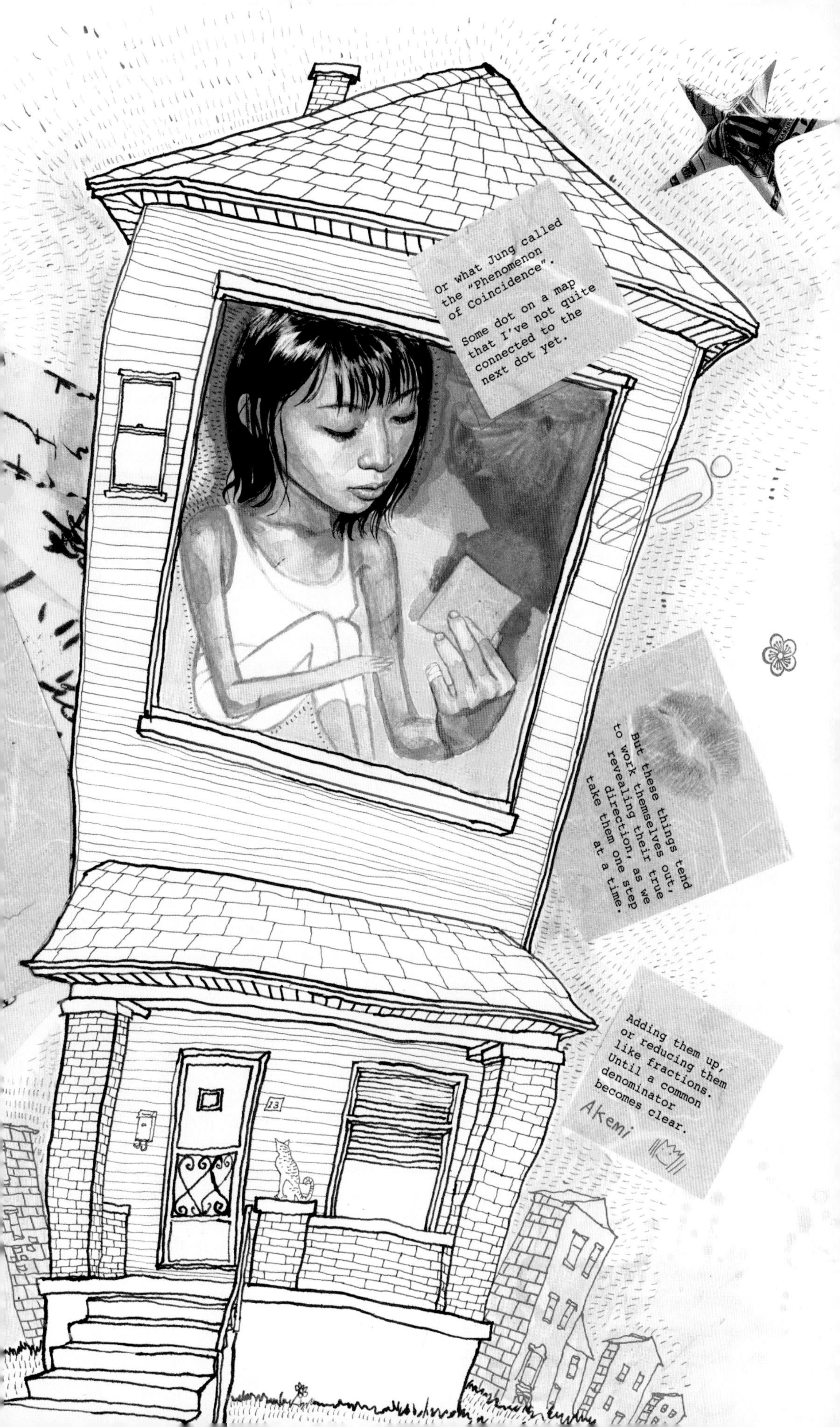

Or what Jung called the "Phenomenon of Coincidence".

Some dot on a map that I've not quite connected to the next dot yet.

But these things tend to work themselves out, revealing their true direction, as we take them one step at a time.

Adding them up, or reducing them like fractions. Until a common denominator becomes clear.

Akemi

13

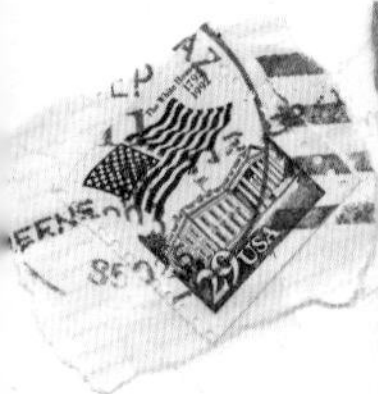

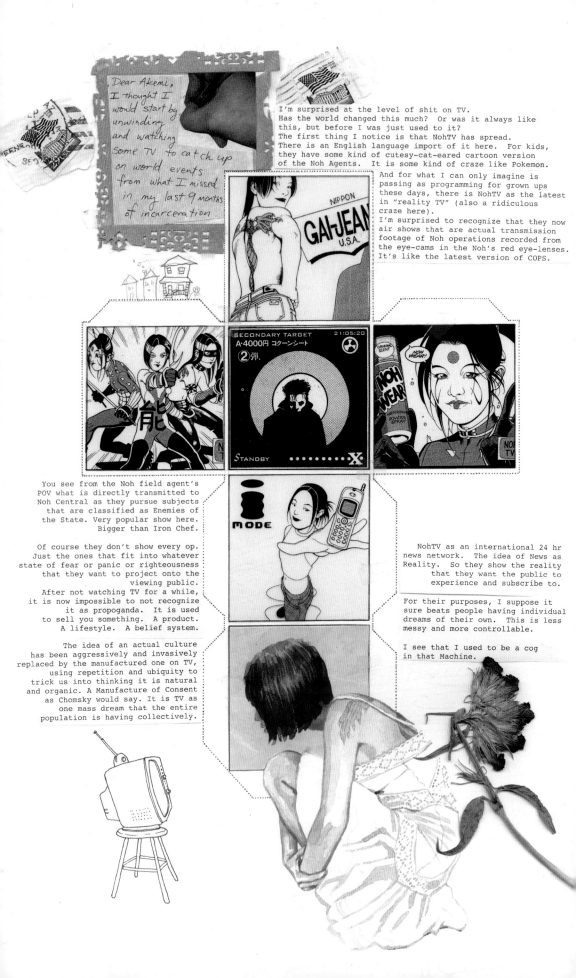

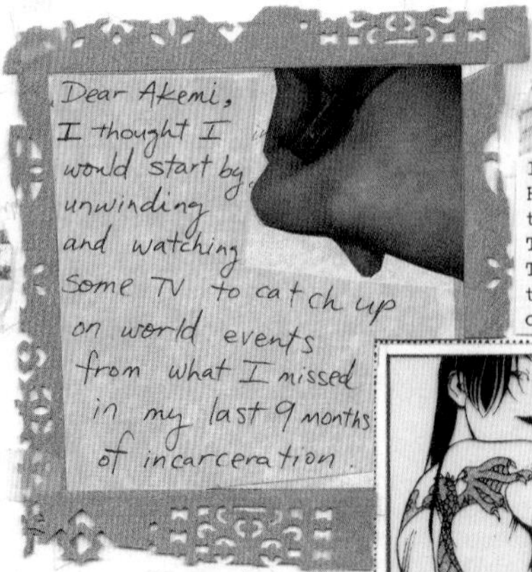
Dear Akemi,
I thought I would start by unwinding and watching some TV to catch up on world events from what I missed in my last 9 months of incarceration.

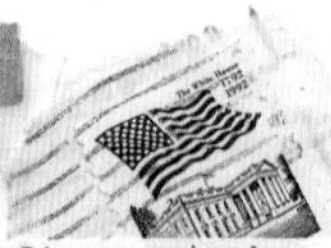

I'm surprised at the level of shit on TV.
Has the world changed this much? Or was it always like this, but before I was just used to it?
The first thing I notice is that NohTV has spread.
There is an English language import of it here. For kids, they have some kind of cutesy-cat-eared cartoon version of the Noh Agents. It is some kind of craze like Pokemon.

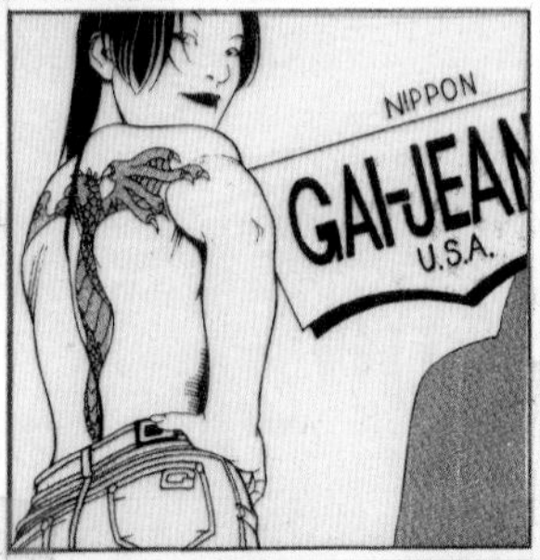
NIPPON
GAI-JEAN
U.S.A.

And for what I can only imagine is passing as programming for grown ups these days, there is NohTV as the latest in "reality TV" (also a ridiculous craze here).
I'm surprised to recognize that they now air shows that are actual transmission footage of Noh operations recorded from the eye-cams in the Noh's red eye-lenses. It's like the latest version of COPS.

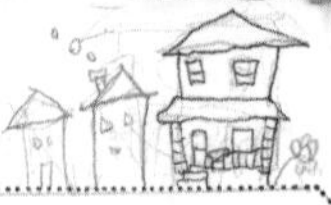

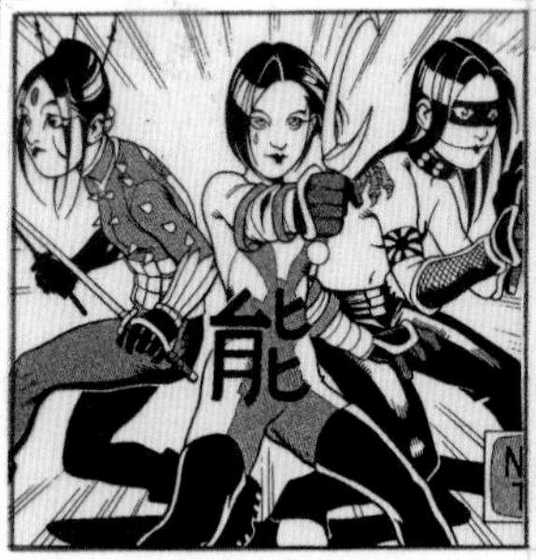
能

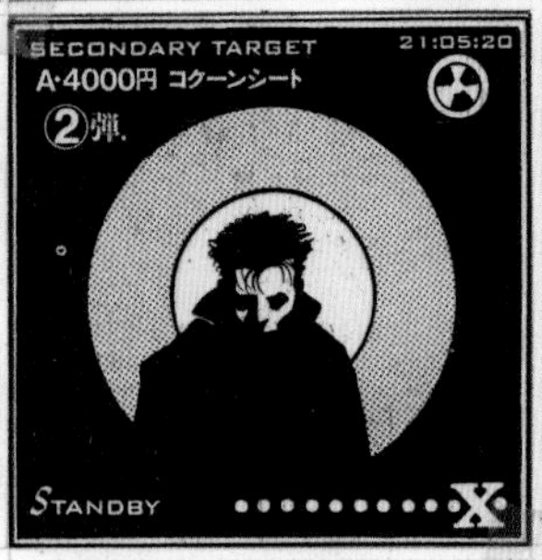
SECONDARY TARGET
21:05:20
A·4000円 コクーンシート
②弾
STANDBY
X

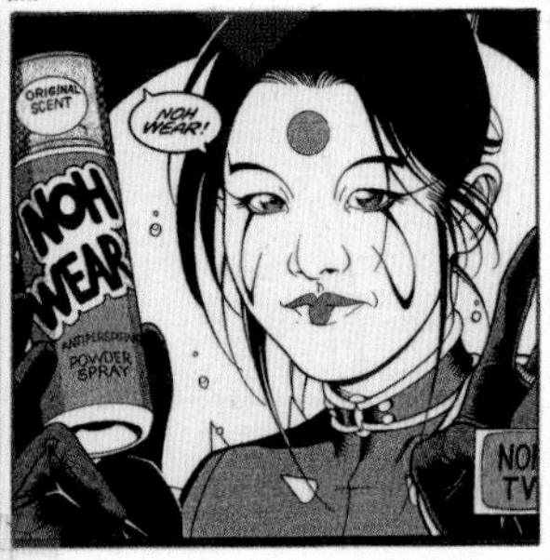
NOH WEAR!
ORIGINAL SCENT
NOH WEAR
POWDER SPRAY
NOH TV

You see from the Noh field agent's POV what is directly transmitted to Noh Central as they pursue subjects that are classified as Enemies of the State. Very popular show here. Bigger than Iron Chef.

Of course they don't show every op. Just the ones that fit into whatever state of fear or panic or righteousness that they want to project onto the viewing public.
After not watching TV for a while, it is now impossible to not recognize it as propoganda. It is used to sell you something. A product. A lifestyle. A belief system.

The idea of an actual culture has been aggressively and invasively replaced by the manufactured one on TV, using repetition and ubiquity to trick us into thinking it is natural and organic. A Manufacture of Consent as Chomsky would say. It is TV as one mass dream that the entire population is having collectively.

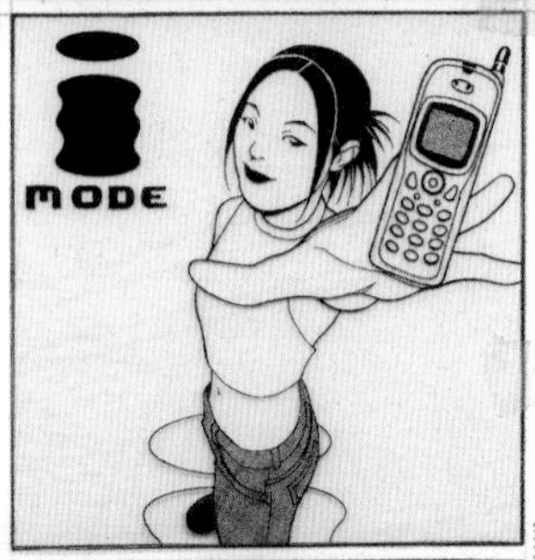
i
mode

NohTV as an international 24 hr news network. The idea of News as Reality. So they show the reality that they want the public to experience and subscribe to.

For their purposes, I suppose it sure beats people having individual dreams of their own. This is less messy and more controllable.

I see that I used to be a cog in that Machine.

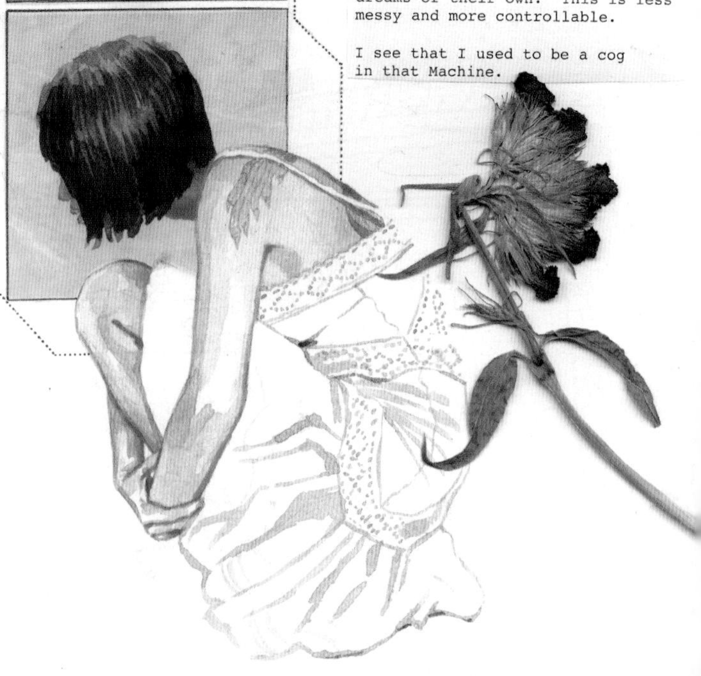

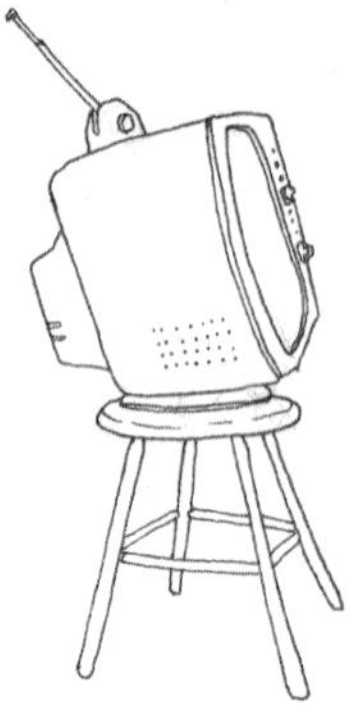

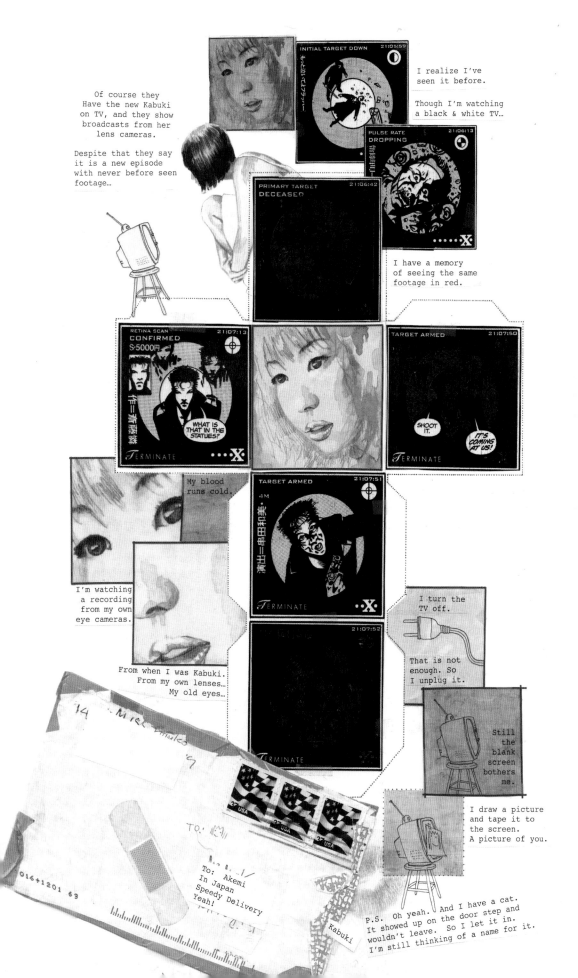

Of course they
Have the new Kabuki
on TV, and they show
broadcasts from her
lens cameras.

Despite that they say
it is a new episode
with never before seen
footage...

I realize I've
seen it before.

Though I'm watching
a black & white TV...

INITIAL TARGET DOWN 21:05:59

PULSE RATE
DROPPING 21:06:13

PRIMARY TARGET
DECEASED 21:06:42

I have a memory
of seeing the same
footage in red.

RETINA SCAN
CONFIRMED 21:07:13
$·5000円
WHAT IS
THAT IN THE
STATUES?
TERMINATE

TARGET ARMED 21:07:50
SHOOT
IT.
IT'S
COMING
AT US!
TERMINATE

My blood
runs cold.

TARGET ARMED 21:07:51
4M
TERMINATE

I'm watching
a recording
from my own
eye cameras.

From when I was Kabuki.
From my own lenses...
My old eyes...

21:07:52

TERMINATE

I turn the
TV off.

That is not
enough. So
I unplug it.

Still
the
blank
screen
bothers
me.

I draw a picture
and tape it to
the screen.
A picture of you.

To: Akemi
In Japan
Speedy Delivery
Yeah!

TO:

016+1201 63

Kabuki

P.S. Oh yeah. And I have a cat.
It showed up on the door step and
wouldn't leave. So I let it in.
I'm still thinking of a name for it.

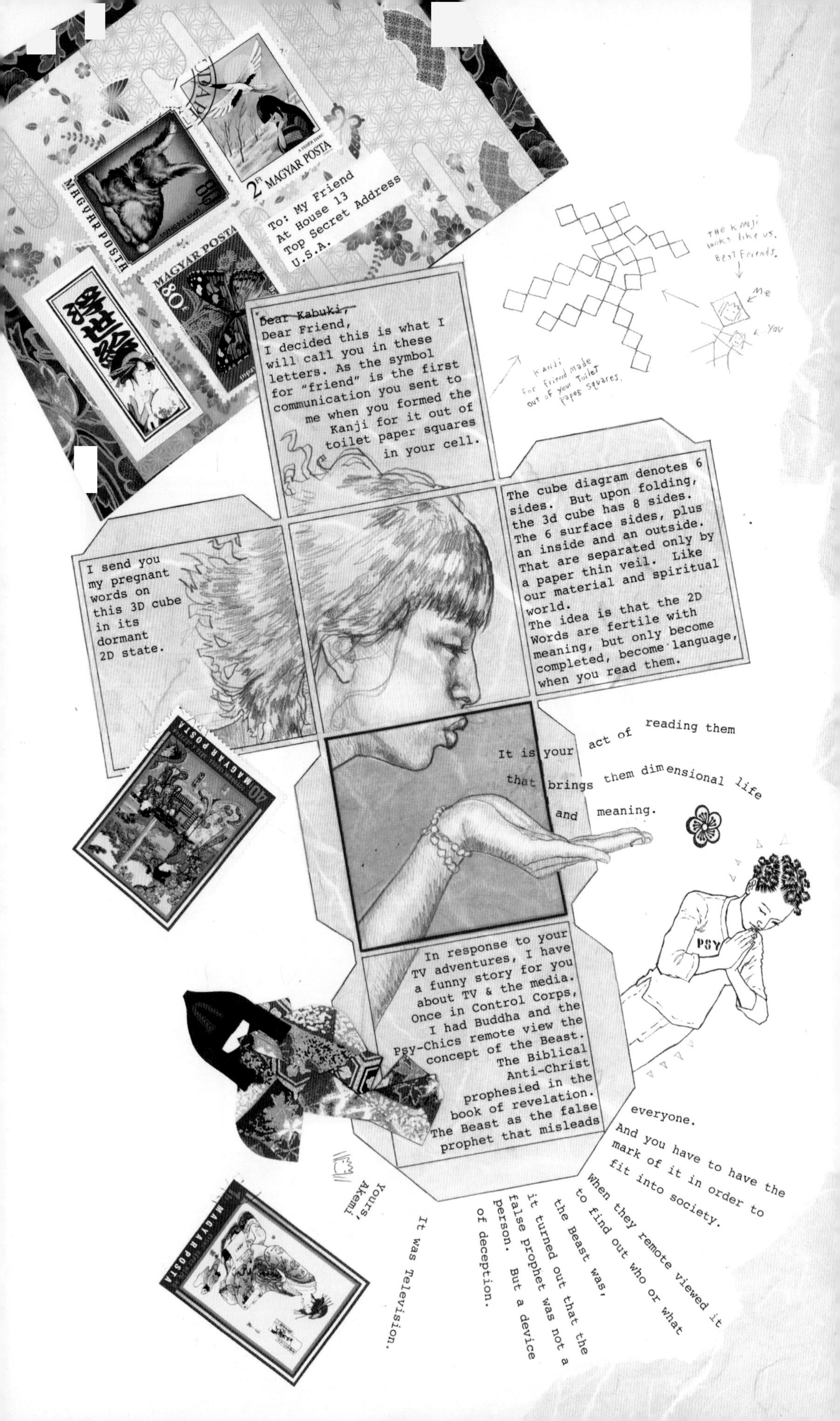
MAGYAR POSTA
2 Ft MAGYAR POSTA
80 Ft
MAGYAR POSTA
80 Ft
To: My Friend
At House 13
Top Secret Address
U.S.A.
THE KANJI looks like us. Best Friends.
Me
You
KANJI For friend made out of your ToileT paper squares.
~~Dear Kabuki,~~
Dear Friend,
I decided this is what I will call you in these letters. As the symbol for "friend" is the first communication you sent to me when you formed the Kanji for it out of toilet paper squares in your cell.
The cube diagram denotes 6 sides. But upon folding, the 3d cube has 8 sides. The 6 surface sides, plus an inside and an outside. That are separated only by a paper thin veil. Like our material and spiritual world.
The idea is that the 2D Words are fertile with meaning, but only become completed, become language, when you read them.
I send you my pregnant words on this 3D cube in its dormant 2D state.
It is your act of reading them that brings them dimensional life and meaning.
40 MAGYAR POSTA
PSY
In response to your TV adventures, I have a funny story for you about TV & the media. Once in Control Corps, I had Buddha and the Psy-Chics remote view the concept of the Beast. The Biblical Anti-Christ prophesied in the book of revelation. The Beast as the false prophet that misleads everyone.
And you have to have the mark of it in order to fit into society.
When they remote viewed it to find out who or what the Beast was, it turned out that the false prophet was not a person. But a device of deception.
It was Television.
Yours,
Akemi
MAGYAR POSTA

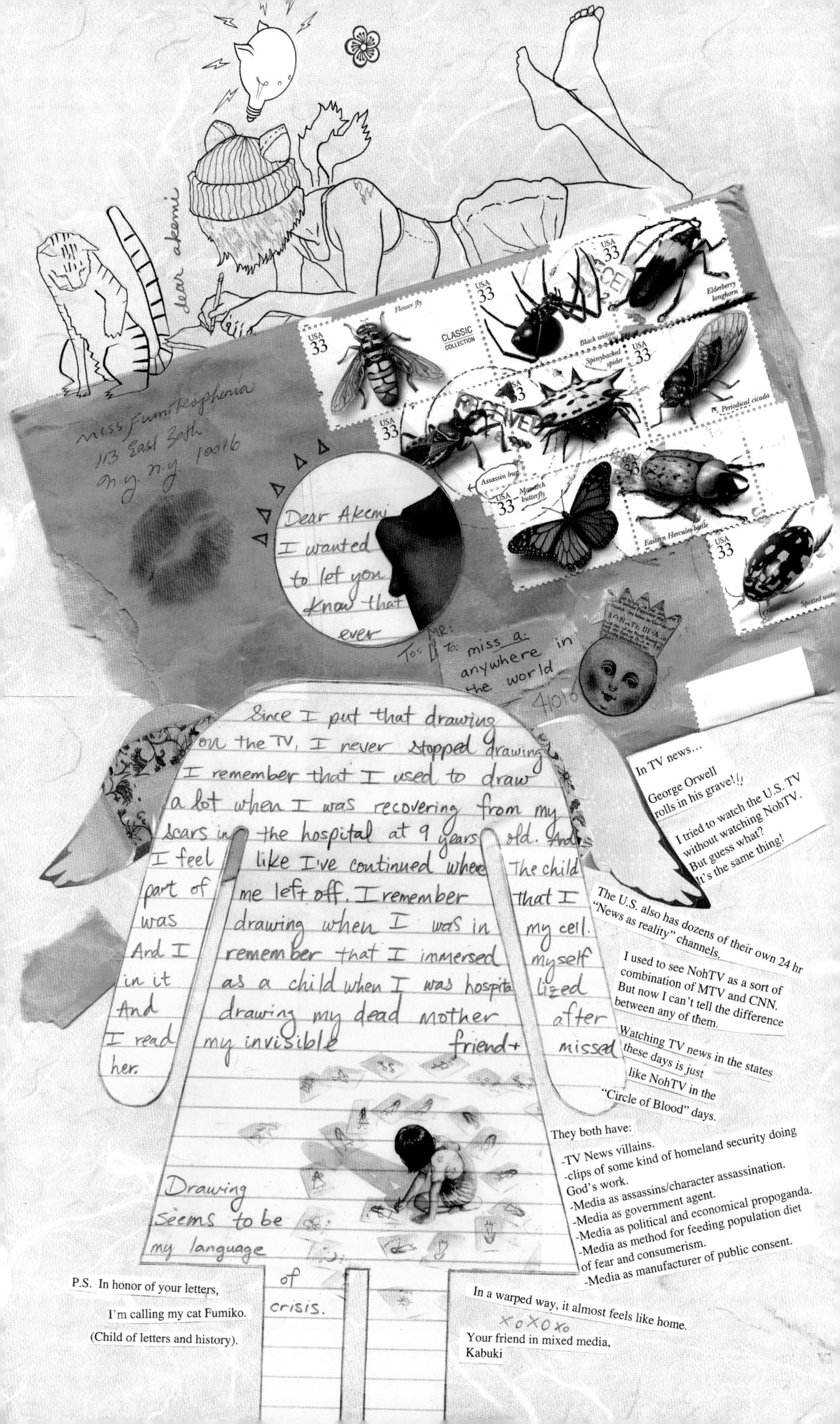
dear akemi
Miss Fumikophenia
113 East 30th
N.Y. N.Y. 10016
Flower fly
CLASSIC COLLECTION
Black widow
Elderberry longhorn
Spinybacked spider
Periodical cicada
Assassin bug
Monarch butterfly
Eastern Hercules beetle
USA 33
Dear Akemi
I wanted
to let you
know that
ever
To: miss a.
anywhere in
the world
Since I put that drawing
on the TV, I never stopped drawing
I remember that I used to draw
a lot when I was recovering from my
scars in the hospital at 9 years old. And
I feel like I've continued where the child
part of me left off. I remember that I
was drawing when I was in my cell.
And I remember that I immersed myself
in it as a child when I was hospitalized
And drawing my dead mother after
I read my invisible friend + missed
her.
Drawing
seems to be
my language
of
crisis.
In TV news…
George Orwell rolls in his grave!!!
I tried to watch the U.S. TV without watching NohTV.
But guess what?
It's the same thing!
The U.S. also has dozens of their own 24 hr "News as reality" channels.
I used to see NohTV as a sort of combination of MTV and CNN.
But now I can't tell the difference between any of them.
Watching TV news in the states these days is just like NohTV in the "Circle of Blood" days.
They both have:
-TV News villains.
-clips of some kind of homeland security doing God's work.
-Media as assassins/character assassination.
-Media as government agent.
-Media as political and economical propoganda.
-Media as method for feeding population diet of fear and consumerism.
-Media as manufacturer of public consent.
In a warped way, it almost feels like home.
xoxoxo
Your friend in mixed media,
Kabuki
P.S. In honor of your letters,
I'm calling my cat Fumiko.
(Child of letters and history).

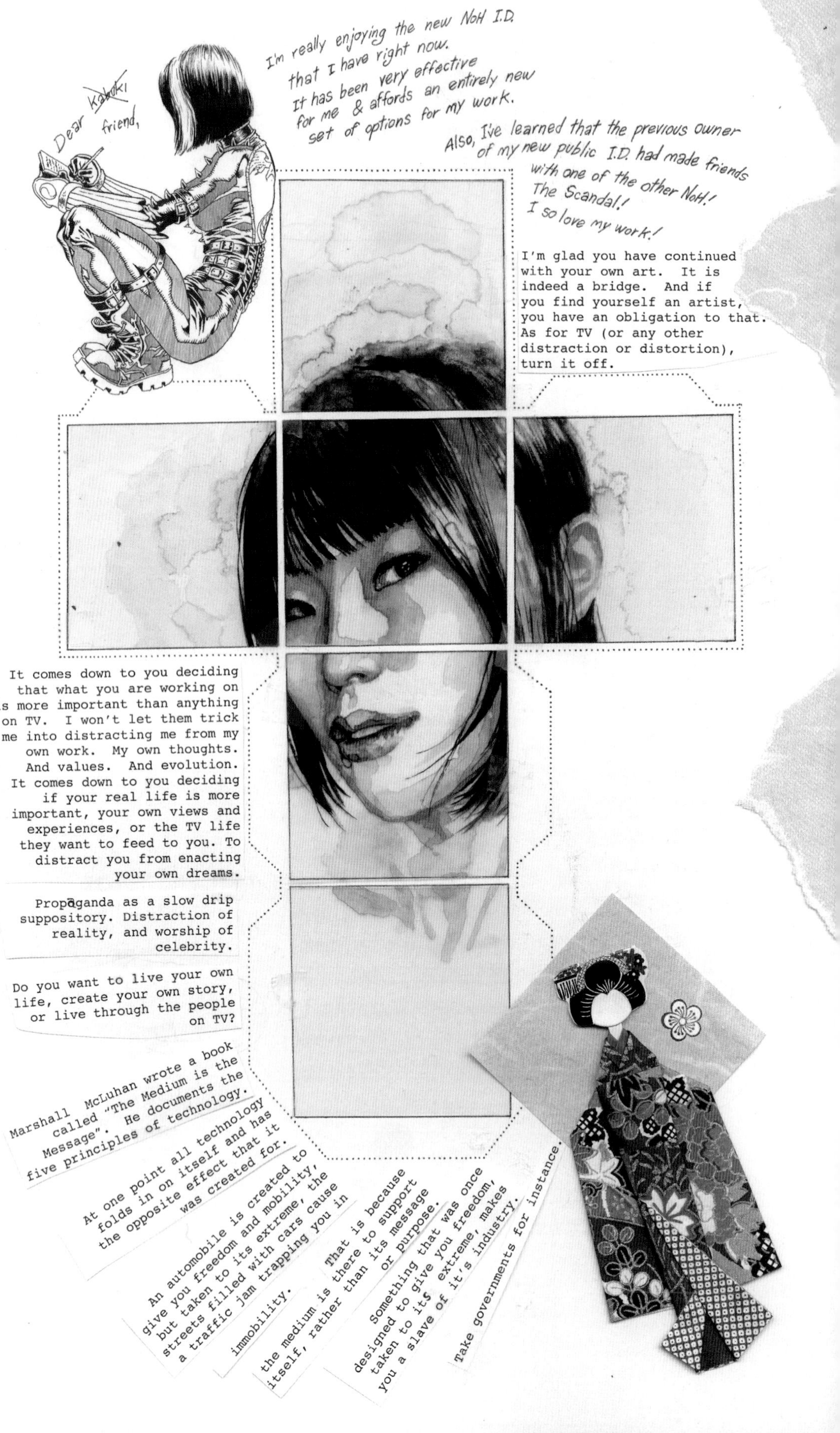

Dear Kabuki friend,
I'm really enjoying the new NoH I.D. that I have right now. It has been very effective for me & affords an entirely new set of options for my work.
Also, I've learned that the previous owner of my new public I.D. had made friends with one of the other NoH! The Scandal! I so love my work!
I'm glad you have continued with your own art. It is indeed a bridge. And if you find yourself an artist, you have an obligation to that. As for TV (or any other distraction or distortion), turn it off.
It comes down to you deciding that what you are working on is more important than anything on TV. I won't let them trick me into distracting me from my own work. My own thoughts. And values. And evolution. It comes down to you deciding if your real life is more important, your own views and experiences, or the TV life they want to feed to you. To distract you from enacting your own dreams.
Propaganda as a slow drip suppository. Distraction of reality, and worship of celebrity.
Do you want to live your own life, create your own story, or live through the people on TV?
Marshall McLuhan wrote a book called "The Medium is the Message". He documents the five principles of technology.
At one point all technology folds in on itself and has the opposite effect that it was created for.
An automobile is created to give you freedom and mobility, but taken to its extreme, the streets filled with cars cause a traffic jam trapping you in immobility.
That is because the medium is there to support itself, rather than its message or purpose.
Something that was once designed to give you freedom, taken to its extreme, makes you a slave of it's industry.
Take governments for instance.

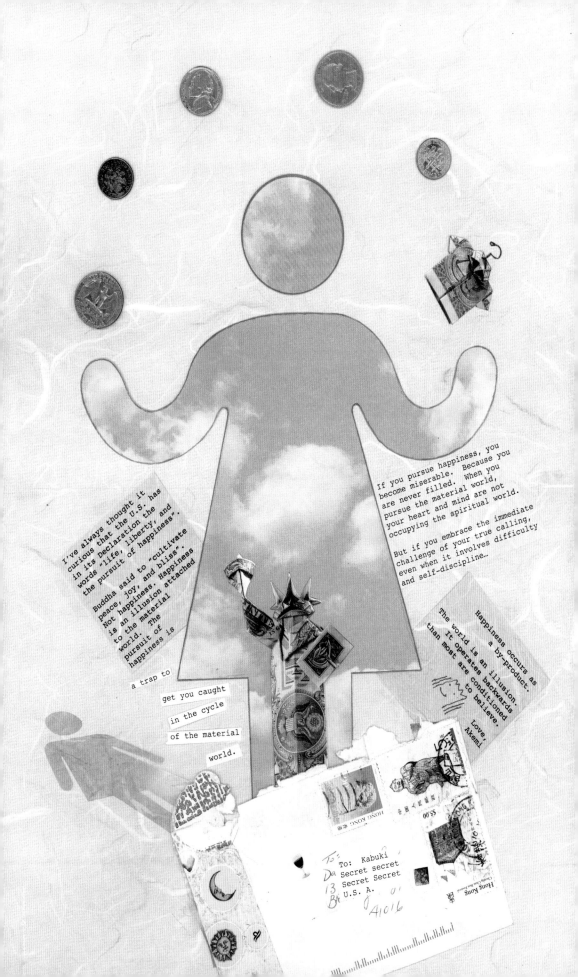

I've always thought it curious that the U.S. has in its Declaration the words "life, liberty, and the pursuit of happiness".

Buddha said to "cultivate peace, joy, and bliss". Not happiness. Happiness is an illusion attached to the material world. The pursuit of happiness is

a trap to get you caught in the cycle of the material world.

If you pursue happiness, you become miserable. Because you are never filled. When you pursue the material world, your heart and mind are not occupying the spiritual world.

But if you embrace the immediate challenge of your true calling, even when it involves difficulty and self-discipline...

Happiness occurs as a by-product. The world is an illusion. It operates backwards than most are conditioned to believe.

Love,
Akemi

To: Kabuki
Secret secret
Secret Secret
U.S. A.

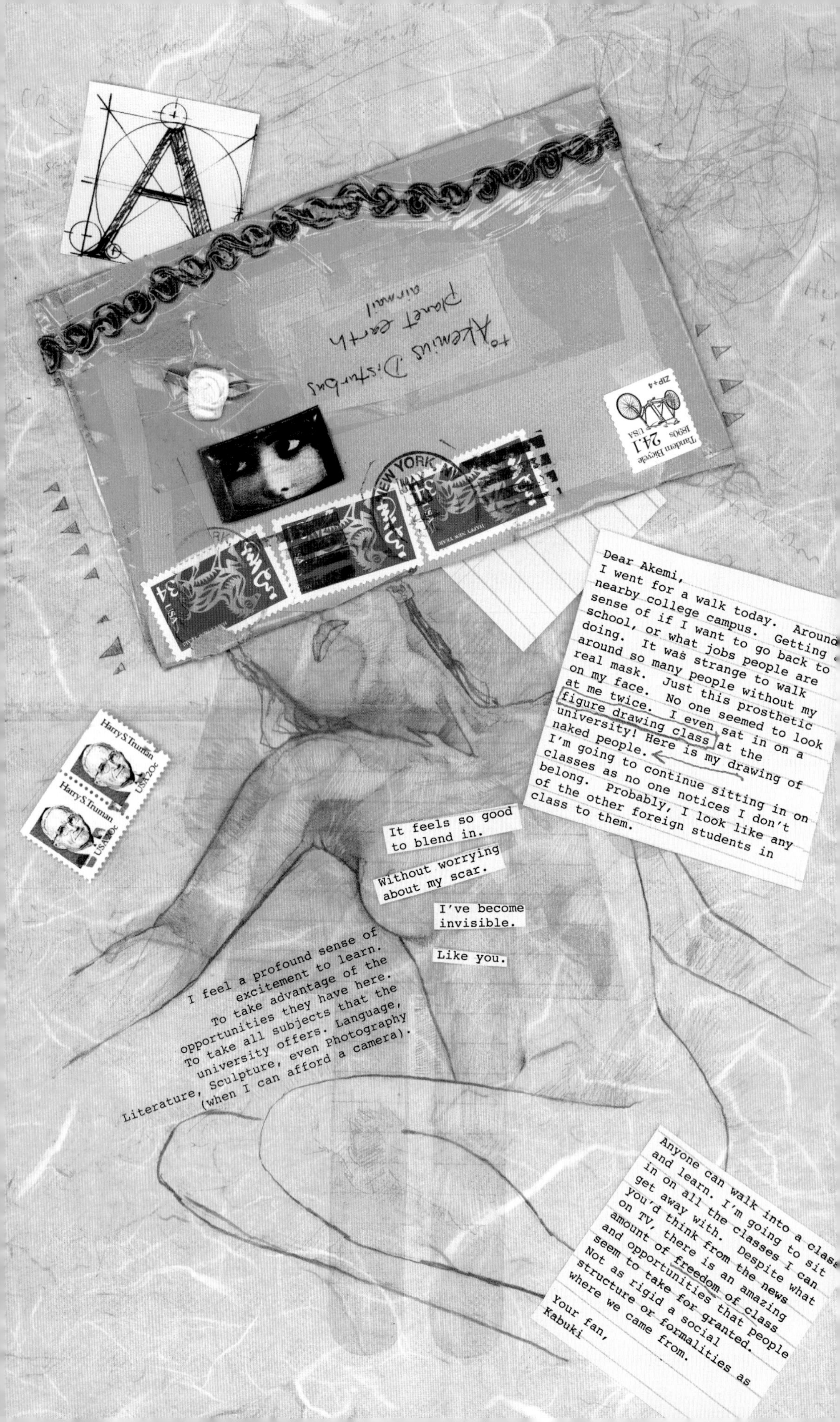

to Akemi Disturbus
planet earth
airmail
Tandem Bicycle 1890s USA 24.1 ZIP+4
Harry S. Truman USA 20c
Harry S. Truman USA 20c
Dear Akemi,
I went for a walk today. Around
nearby college campus. Getting
sense of if I want to go back to
school, or what jobs people are
doing. It was strange to walk
around so many people without my
real mask. Just this prosthetic
on my face. No one seemed to look
at me twice. I even sat in on a
figure drawing class at the
university! Here is my drawing of
naked people.
I'm going to continue sitting in on
classes as no one notices I don't
belong. Probably, I look like any
of the other foreign students in
class to them.
It feels so good to blend in.
Without worrying about my scar.
I've become invisible.
Like you.
I feel a profound sense of excitement to learn. To take advantage of the opportunities they have here. To take all subjects that the university offers. Language, Literature, Sculpture, even Photography (when I can afford a camera).
Anyone can walk into a class and learn. I'm going to sit in on all the classes I can get away with. Despite what you'd think from the news on TV, there is an amazing amount of freedom of class and opportunities that people seem to take for granted. Not as rigid a social structure or formalities as where we came from.
Your fan,
Kabuki

Hey Akemi!
Look at this crazy flier I saw today on campus! Is this bizarre or what?

This thing is all over campus on poles and bulletin boards. There are Noh Land amusement parks all over the place. Recruiting students for part time jobs at the park.

NOH LAND WANTS
YOU

Need fast cash? Want to be larger than life? Are you a child at heart?
If so, NOH LAND wants YOU!
You can be one of the Noh at NOH LAND. Apply at NohTV.com or call this #:

1-888-NOH-LAND
1-888-NOH-LAND
1-888-NOH-LAND
1-888-NOH-LAND
1-888-NOH-LAND
1-888-NOH-LAND
1-888-NOH-LAND
1-888-NOH-LAND
1-888-NOH-LAND

1-888-NOH-LAND

Dear Akemi,

I've continued going to school. Like I'm a kid again.

I've been reading, writing, and drawing.
I find myself continuing where my childhood self left off.

When I was doing drawings in the hospital after my scar.

And reading children's books.

I suppose I need to get a job.

But I feel compelled to continue doing what I loved as a child. I'm done with my past life as a grown up.

It occurs to me that I don't even know if Akemi is your original name.

MC Square said that it was the inmates' approximated pronunciation of "Alchemy" which had come to be your nickname inside Control Corps.

You seem to have had many past identities and career paths, and you seem to delight in each of the changes.

You know why I've had to start over. Why do you do it?

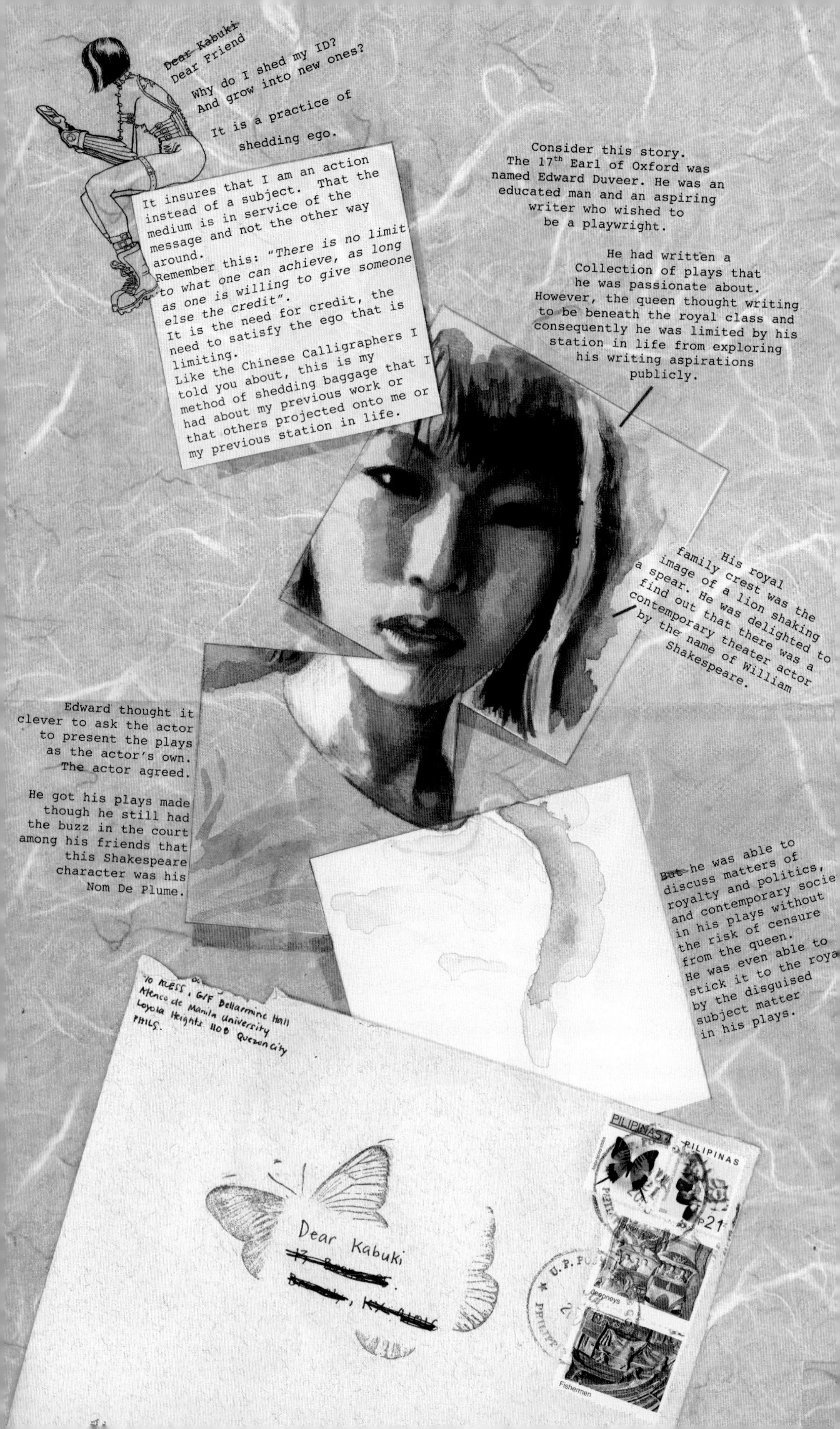
Dear Kabuki
Dear Friend
Why do I shed my ID?
And grow into new ones?
It is a practice of
shedding ego.
It insures that I am an action instead of a subject. That the medium is in service of the message and not the other way around.
Remember this: "*There is no limit to what one can achieve, as long as one is willing to give someone else the credit*".
It is the need for credit, the need to satisfy the ego that is limiting.
Like the Chinese Calligraphers I told you about, this is my method of shedding baggage that I had about my previous work or that others projected onto me or my previous station in life.
Consider this story. The 17th Earl of Oxford was named Edward Duveer. He was an educated man and an aspiring writer who wished to be a playwright.
He had written a Collection of plays that he was passionate about. However, the queen thought writing to be beneath the royal class and consequently he was limited by his station in life from exploring his writing aspirations publicly.
His royal family crest was the image of a lion shaking a spear. He was delighted to find out that there was a contemporary theater actor by the name of William Shakespeare.
Edward thought it clever to ask the actor to present the plays as the actor's own. The actor agreed.
He got his plays made though he still had the buzz in the court among his friends that this Shakespeare character was his Nom De Plume.
But he was able to discuss matters of royalty and politics, and contemporary socie in his plays without the risk of censure from the queen. He was even able to stick it to the roya by the disguised subject matter in his plays.
To KLESS, G/F Bellarmine Hall
Ateneo de Manila University
Loyola Heights 1108 Quezon City
PHILS.
Dear Kabuki
[redacted]
PILIPINAS
PILIPINAS
P21
U.P. POS
Jeepneys
Fishermen

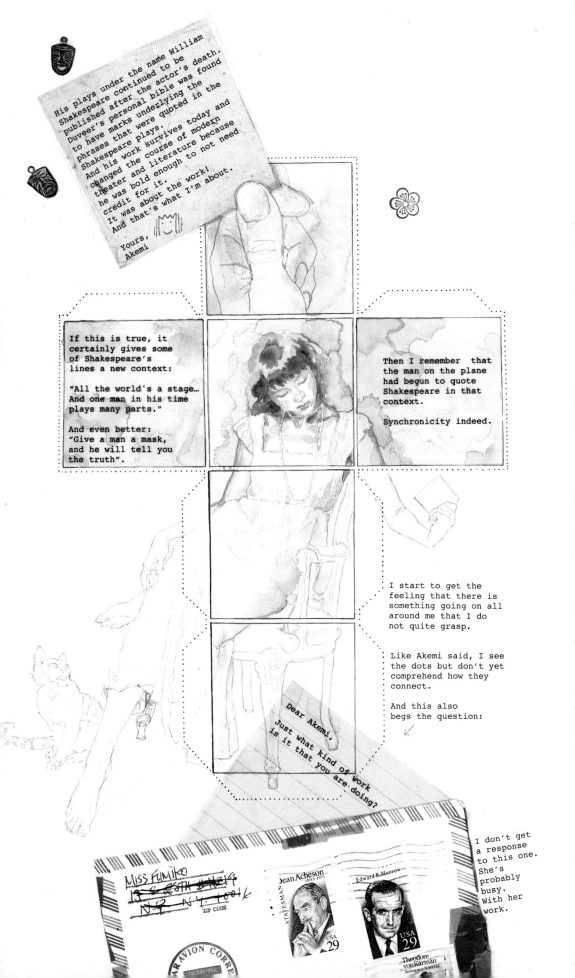

His plays under the name William
Shakespeare continued to be
published after the actor's death.
Duveer's personal bible was found
to have marks underlying the
phrases that were quoted in the
Shakespeare plays.
And his work survives today and
changed the course of modern
theater and literature because
he was bold enough to not need
credit for it.
It was about the work!
And that's what I'm about.

Yours,
Akemi

If this is true, it
certainly gives some
of Shakespeare's
lines a new context:

"All the world's a stage…
And one man in his time
plays many parts."

And even better:
"Give a man a mask,
and he will tell you
the truth".

Then I remember that
the man on the plane
had begun to quote
Shakespeare in that
context.

Synchronicity indeed.

I start to get the
feeling that there is
something going on all
around me that I do
not quite grasp.

Like Akemi said, I see
the dots but don't yet
comprehend how they
connect.

And this also
begs the question:

Dear Akemi,
Just what kind of work
is it that you are doing?

I don't get
a response
to this one.
She's
probably
busy.
With her
work.

MISS FUMIKO

ZIP CODE

Dean Acheson
1893-1971
STATESMAN
USA
29

Edward R. Murrow
USA
29

Theodore
von Kármán
Aerospace Scientist

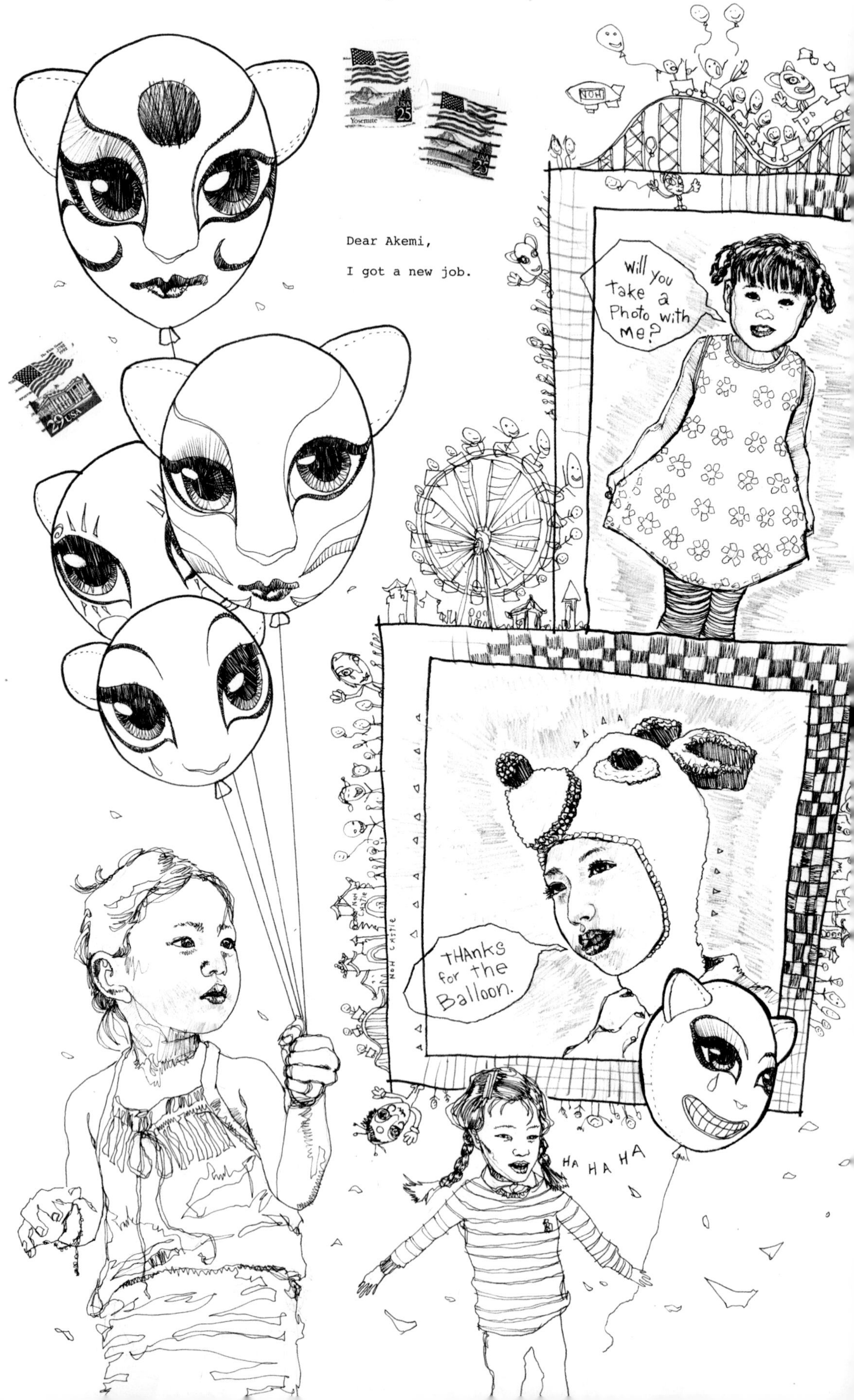
Dear Akemi,
I got a new job.
Will you take a Photo with me?
THAnks for the Balloon.
HA HA HA
NOH
NOH CASTLE
Yosemite
USA 25
29 USA

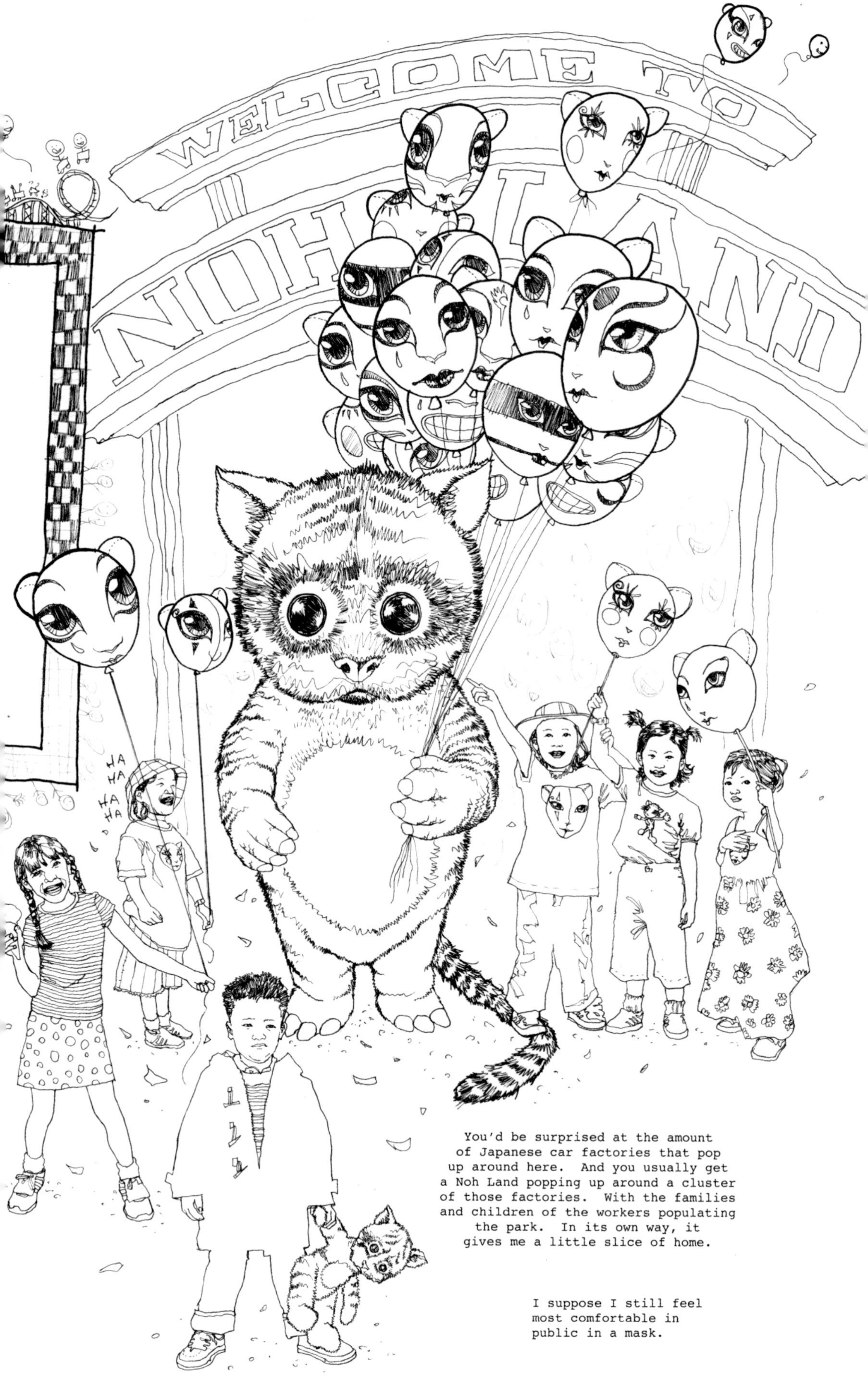
WELCOME TO
NOH LAND
HA
HA
HA
HA
You'd be surprised at the amount of Japanese car factories that pop up around here. And you usually get a Noh Land popping up around a cluster of those factories. With the families and children of the workers populating the park. In its own way, it gives me a little slice of home.
I suppose I still feel most comfortable in public in a mask.

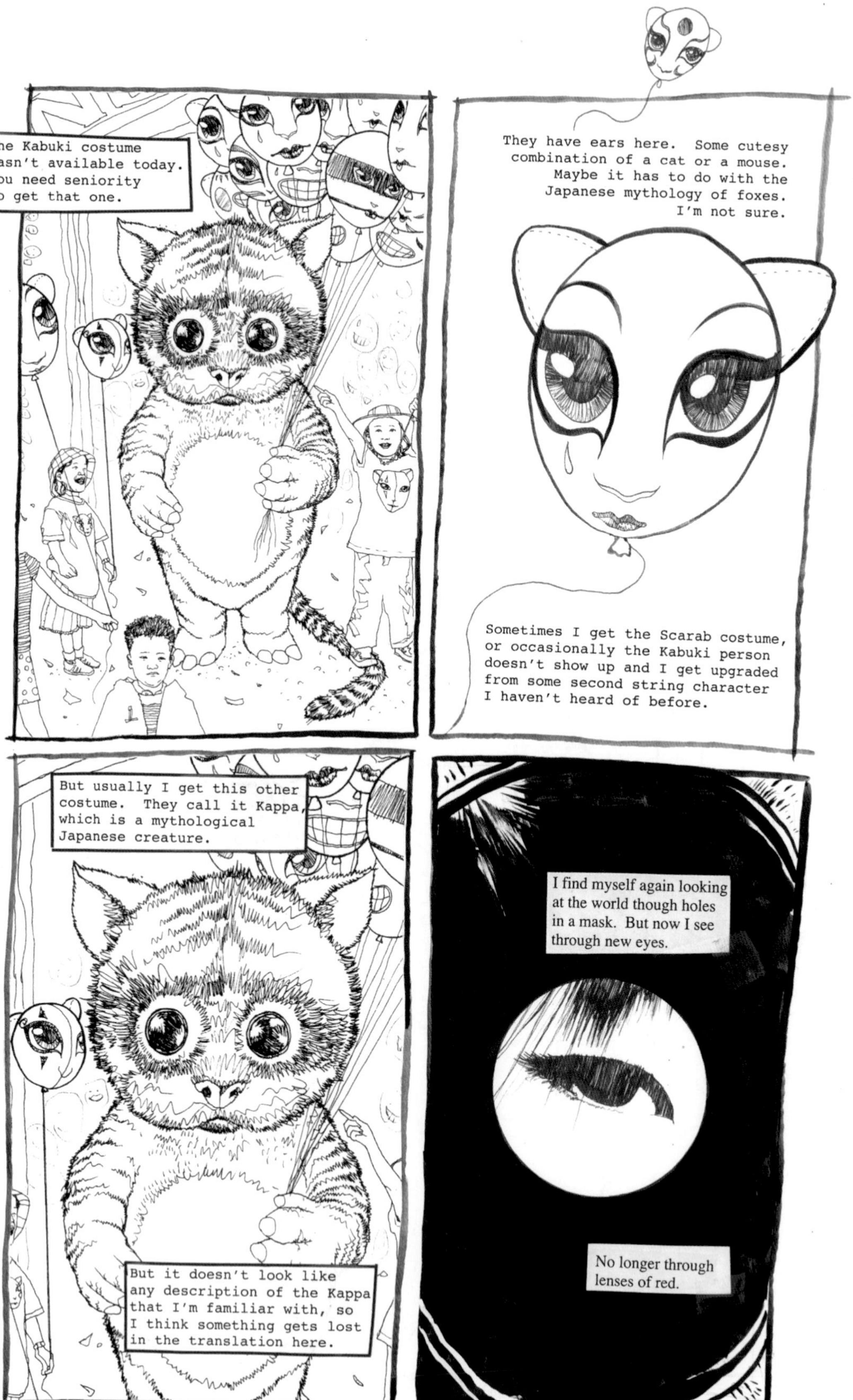
The Kabuki costume wasn't available today. You need seniority to get that one.
They have ears here. Some cutesy combination of a cat or a mouse. Maybe it has to do with the Japanese mythology of foxes. I'm not sure.
Sometimes I get the Scarab costume, or occasionally the Kabuki person doesn't show up and I get upgraded from some second string character I haven't heard of before.
But usually I get this other costume. They call it Kappa, which is a mythological Japanese creature.
But it doesn't look like any description of the Kappa that I'm familiar with, so I think something gets lost in the translation here.
I find myself again looking at the world though holes in a mask. But now I see through new eyes.
No longer through lenses of red.

Closer View From outside

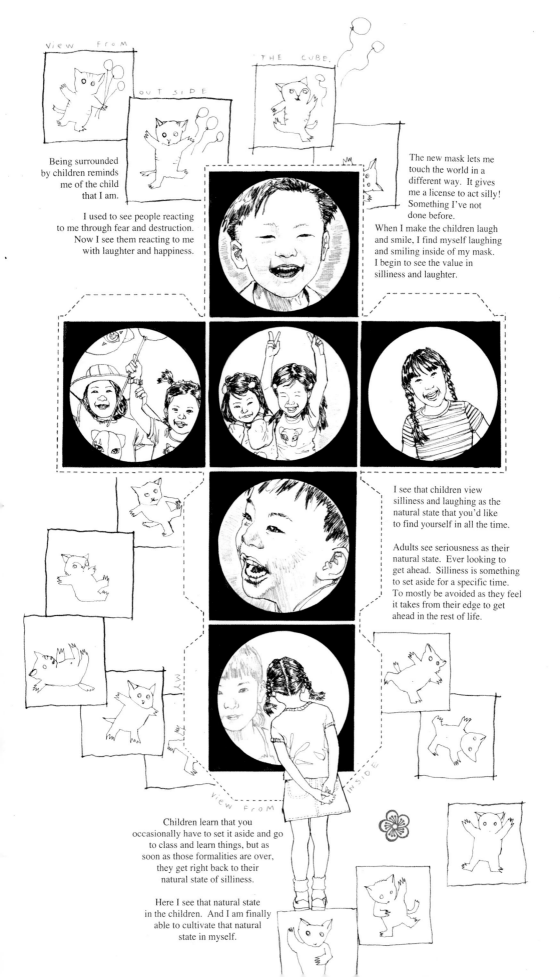

VIEW FROM OUTSIDE

THE CUBE.

Being surrounded by children reminds me of the child that I am.

I used to see people reacting to me through fear and destruction. Now I see them reacting to me with laughter and happiness.

The new mask lets me touch the world in a different way. It gives me a license to act silly! Something I've not done before.

When I make the children laugh and smile, I find myself laughing and smiling inside of my mask. I begin to see the value in silliness and laughter.

I see that children view silliness and laughing as the natural state that you'd like to find yourself in all the time.

Adults see seriousness as their natural state. Ever looking to get ahead. Silliness is something to set aside for a specific time. To mostly be avoided as they feel it takes from their edge to get ahead in the rest of life.

MY LIFE INSIDE

VIEW FROM INSIDE

Children learn that you occasionally have to set it aside and go to class and learn things, but as soon as those formalities are over, they get right back to their natural state of silliness.

Here I see that natural state in the children. And I am finally able to cultivate that natural state in myself.

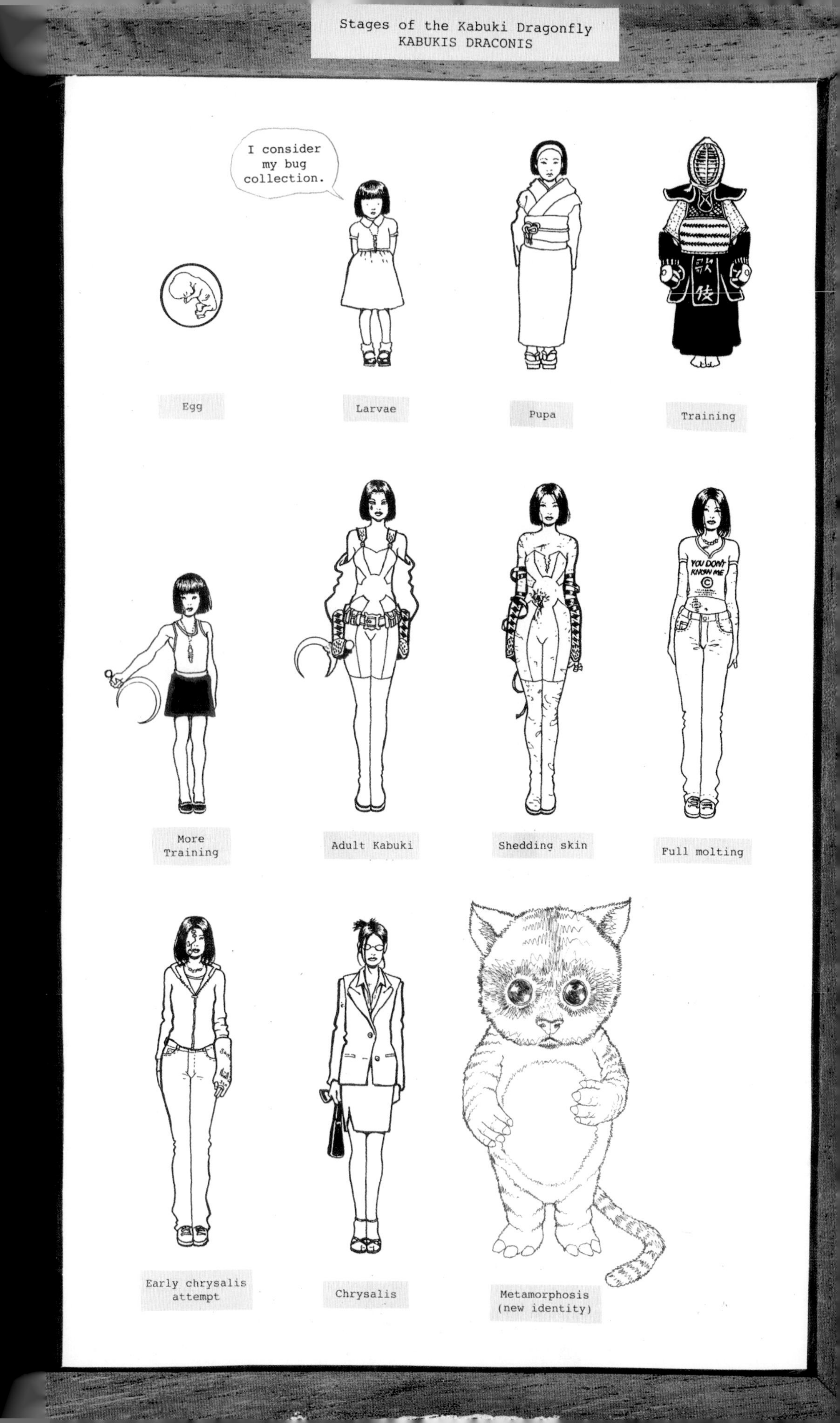
Stages of the Kabuki Dragonfly
KABUKIS DRACONIS
I consider my bug collection.
Egg
Larvae
Pupa
Training
More Training
Adult Kabuki
Shedding skin
Full molting
YOU DON'T KNOW ME
Early chrysalis attempt
Chrysalis
Metamorphosis (new identity)

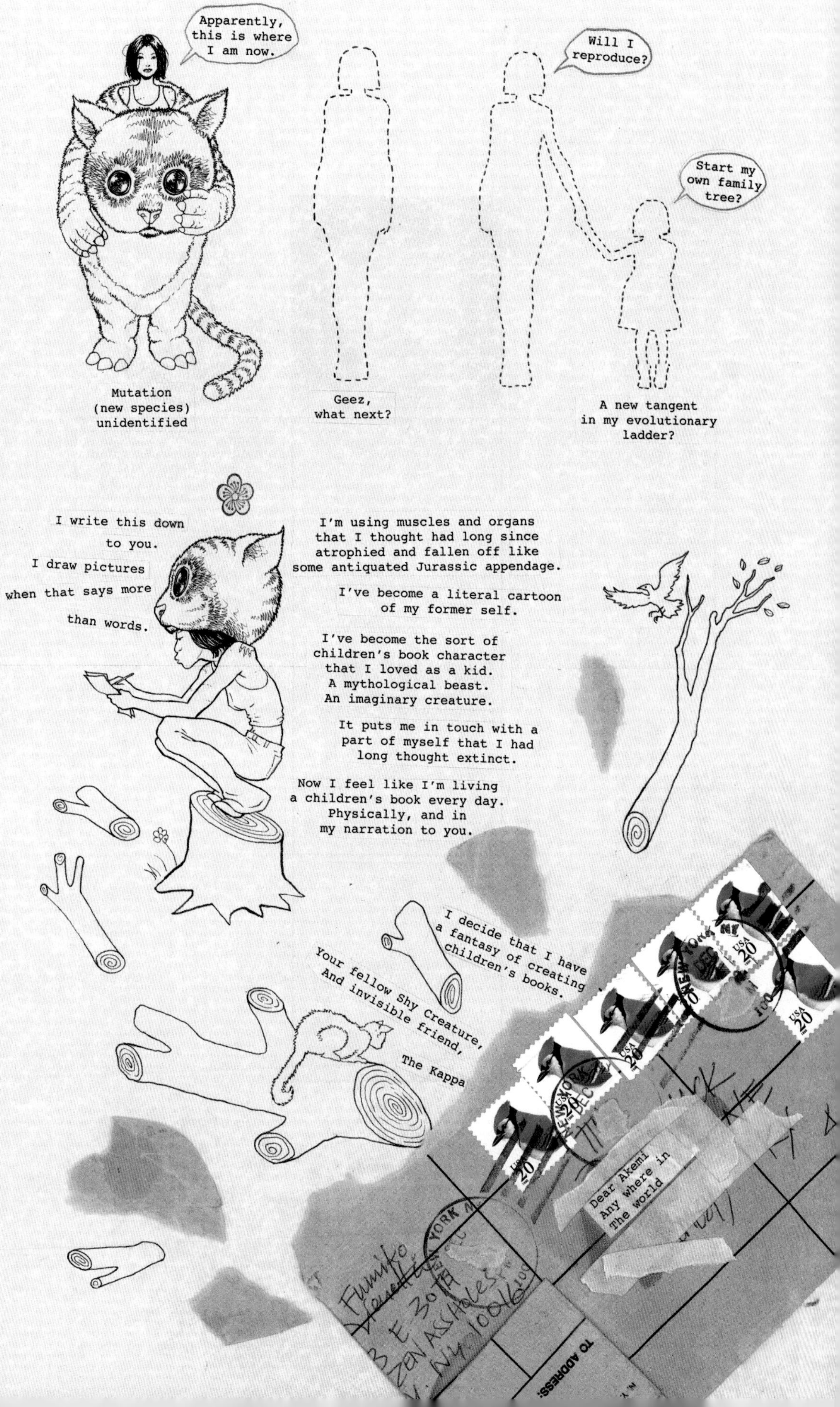

Apparently, this is where I am now.
Mutation (new species) unidentified
Geez, what next?
Will I reproduce?
Start my own family tree?
A new tangent in my evolutionary ladder?
I write this down to you.
I draw pictures when that says more than words.
I'm using muscles and organs that I thought had long since atrophied and fallen off like some antiquated Jurassic appendage.
I've become a literal cartoon of my former self.
I've become the sort of children's book character that I loved as a kid. A mythological beast. An imaginary creature.
It puts me in touch with a part of myself that I had long thought extinct.
Now I feel like I'm living a children's book every day. Physically, and in my narration to you.
I decide that I have a fantasy of creating children's books.
Your fellow Shy Creature, And invisible friend,
The Kappa
Dear Akemi Any where in The world
USA 20

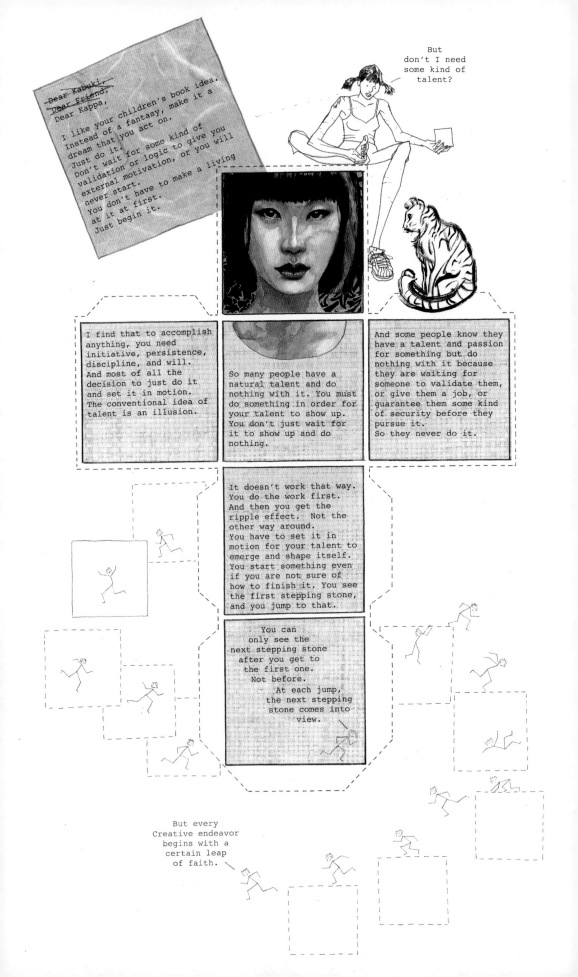

But
don't I need
some kind of
talent?

Dear Kabuki,
Dear Friend,
Dear Kappa,

I like your children's book idea.
Instead of a fantasy, make it a
dream that you act on.
Just do it.
Don't wait for some kind of
validation or logic to give you
external motivation, or you will
never start.
You don't have to make a living
at it at first.
Just begin it.

I find that to accomplish
anything, you need
initiative, persistence,
discipline, and will.
And most of all the
decision to just do it
and set it in motion.
The conventional idea of
talent is an illusion.

So many people have a
natural talent and do
nothing with it. You must
do something in order for
your talent to show up.
You don't just wait for
it to show up and do
nothing.

And some people know they
have a talent and passion
for something but do
nothing with it because
they are waiting for
someone to validate them,
or give them a job, or
guarantee them some kind
of security before they
pursue it.
So they never do it.

It doesn't work that way.
You do the work first.
And then you get the
ripple effect. Not the
other way around.
You have to set it in
motion for your talent to
emerge and shape itself.
You start something even
if you are not sure of
how to finish it. You see
the first stepping stone,
and you jump to that.

You can
only see the
next stepping stone
after you get to
the first one.
Not before.
At each jump,
the next stepping
stone comes into
view.

But every
Creative endeavor
begins with a
certain leap
of faith.

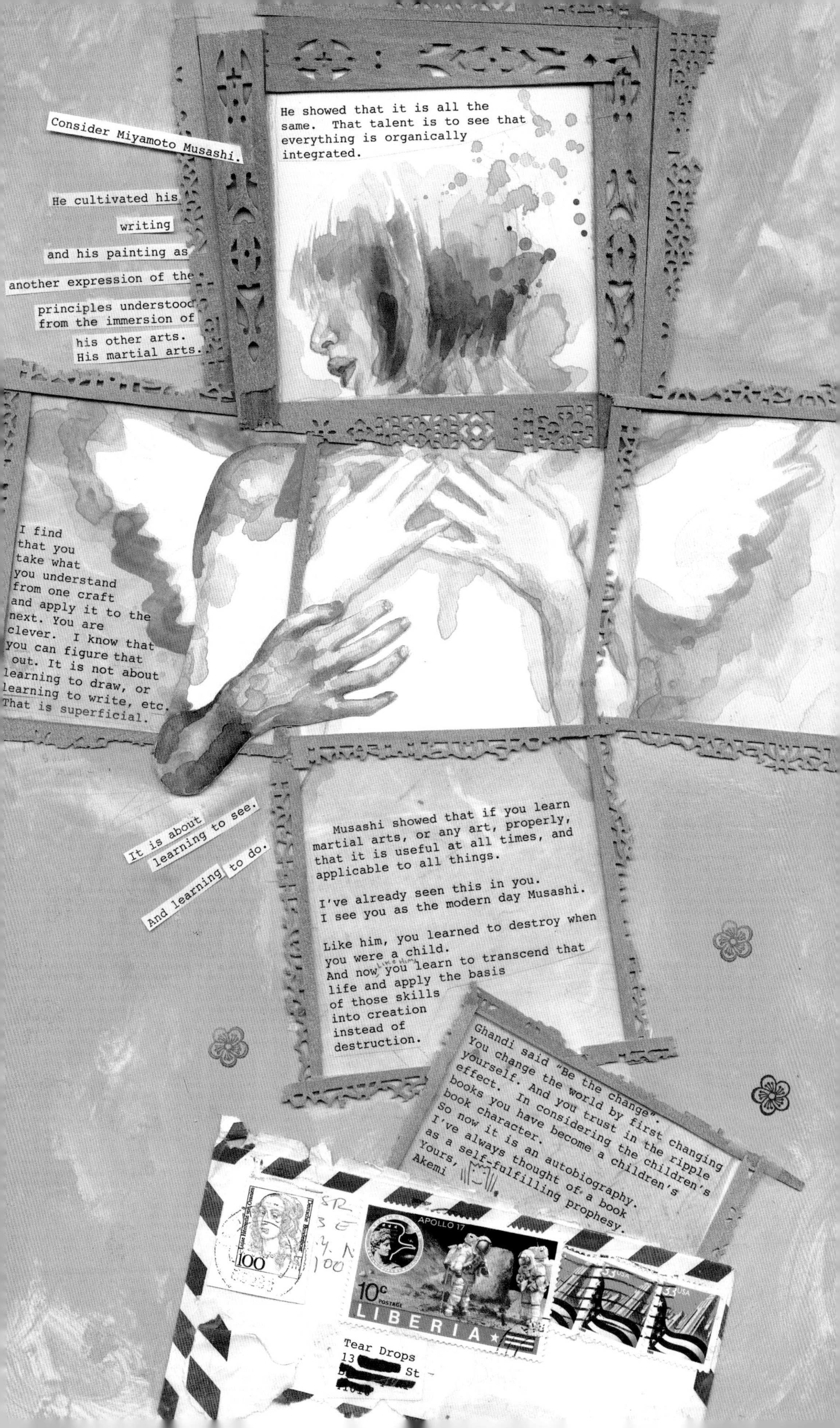
Consider Miyamoto Musashi.
He cultivated his writing and his painting as another expression of the principles understood from the immersion of his other arts. His martial arts.
He showed that it is all the same. That talent is to see that everything is organically integrated.
I find that you take what you understand from one craft and apply it to the next. You are clever. I know that you can figure that out. It is not about learning to draw, or learning to write, etc. That is superficial.
It is about learning to see.
And learning to do.
Musashi showed that if you learn martial arts, or any art, properly, that it is useful at all times, and applicable to all things.
I've already seen this in you. I see you as the modern day Musashi.
Like him, you learned to destroy when you were a child. And now, like him, you learn to transcend that life and apply the basis of those skills into creation instead of destruction.
Ghandi said "Be the change". You change the world by first changing yourself. And you trust in the ripple effect. In considering the children's books you have become a children's book character. So now it is an autobiography. I've always thought of a book as a self-fulfilling prophesy.
Yours,
Akemi
Deutsche Bundespost
100
APOLLO 17
10c POSTAGE
LIBERIA
33 USA
Tear Drops
13 [redacted] St -
[redacted]

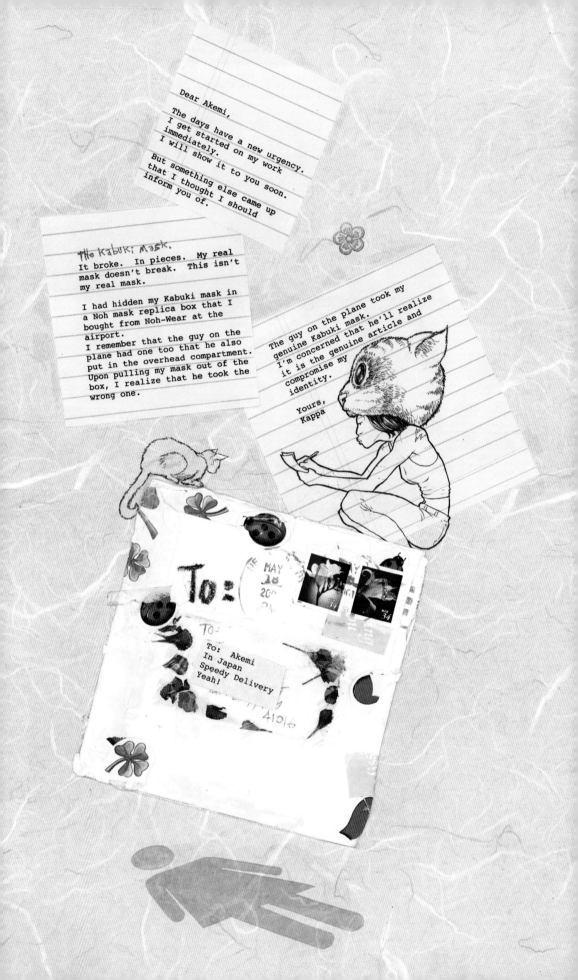

Dear Akemi,

The days have a new urgency.
I get started on my work
immediately.
I will show it to you soon.

But something else came up
that I thought I should
inform you of.

The Kabuki Mask.

It broke. In pieces. My real
mask doesn't break. This isn't
my real mask.

I had hidden my Kabuki mask in
a Noh mask replica box that I
bought from Noh-Wear at the
airport.
I remember that the guy on the
plane had one too that he also
put in the overhead compartment.
Upon pulling my mask out of the
box, I realize that he took the
wrong one.

The guy on the plane took my
genuine Kabuki mask.
I'm concerned that he'll realize
it is the genuine article and
compromise my
identity.

Yours,
Kappa

TO:

MAY
20

To: Akemi
In Japan
Speedy Delivery
Yeah!

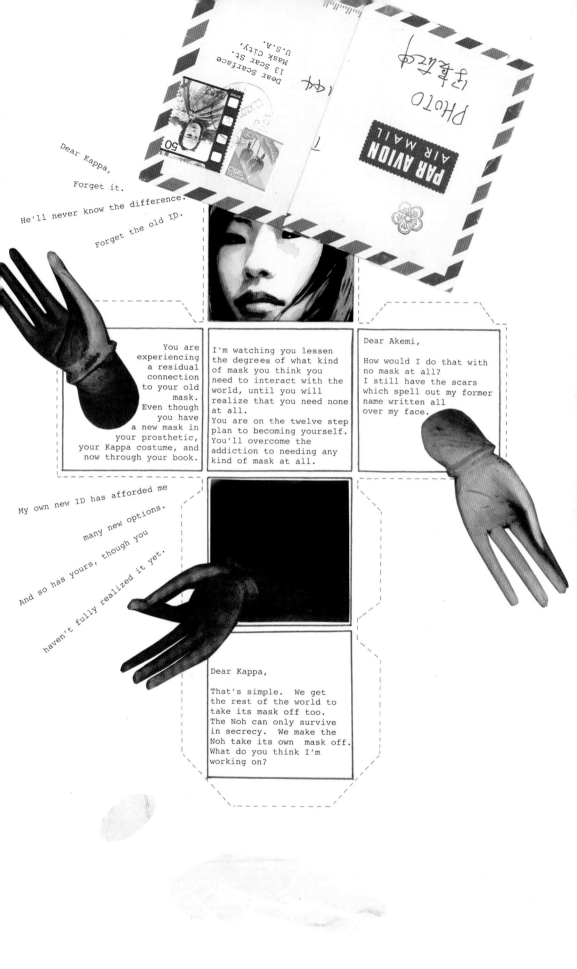

PHOTO
PAR AVION AIR MAIL

Dear Scarface
13 Scar St.
Mask City,
U.S.A.

Dear Kappa,

Forget it.

He'll never know the difference.

Forget the old ID.

You are experiencing a residual connection to your old mask. Even though you have a new mask in your prosthetic, your Kappa costume, and now through your book.

I'm watching you lessen the degrees of what kind of mask you think you need to interact with the world, until you will realize that you need none at all.
You are on the twelve step plan to becoming yourself. You'll overcome the addiction to needing any kind of mask at all.

Dear Akemi,

How would I do that with no mask at all?
I still have the scars which spell out my former name written all over my face.

My own new ID has afforded me many new options.

And so has yours, though you haven't fully realized it yet.

Dear Kappa,

That's simple. We get the rest of the world to take its mask off too. The Noh can only survive in secrecy. We make the Noh take its own mask off. What do you think I'm working on?

There is
more...

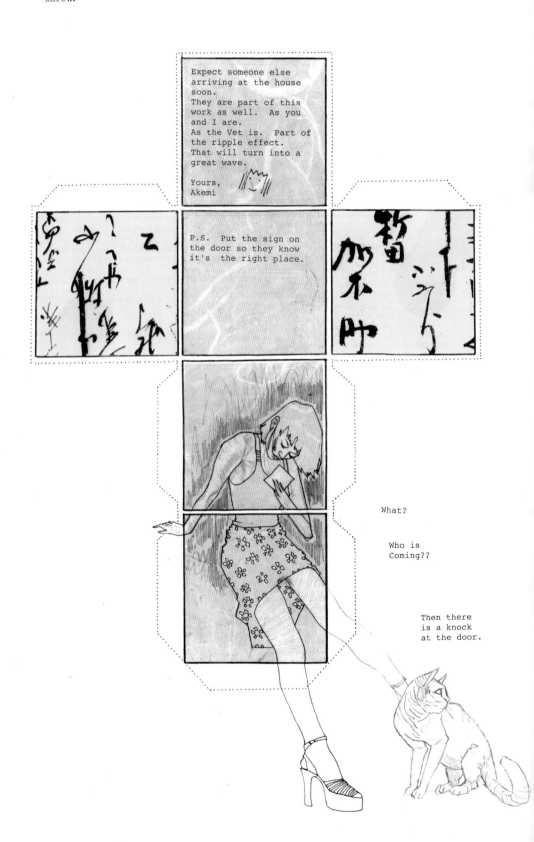

Expect someone else
arriving at the house
soon.
They are part of this
work as well. As you
and I are.
As the Vet is. Part of
the ripple effect.
That will turn into a
great wave.

Yours,
Akemi

P.S. Put the sign on
the door so they know
it's the right place.

What?

Who is
Coming??

Then there
is a knock
at the door.

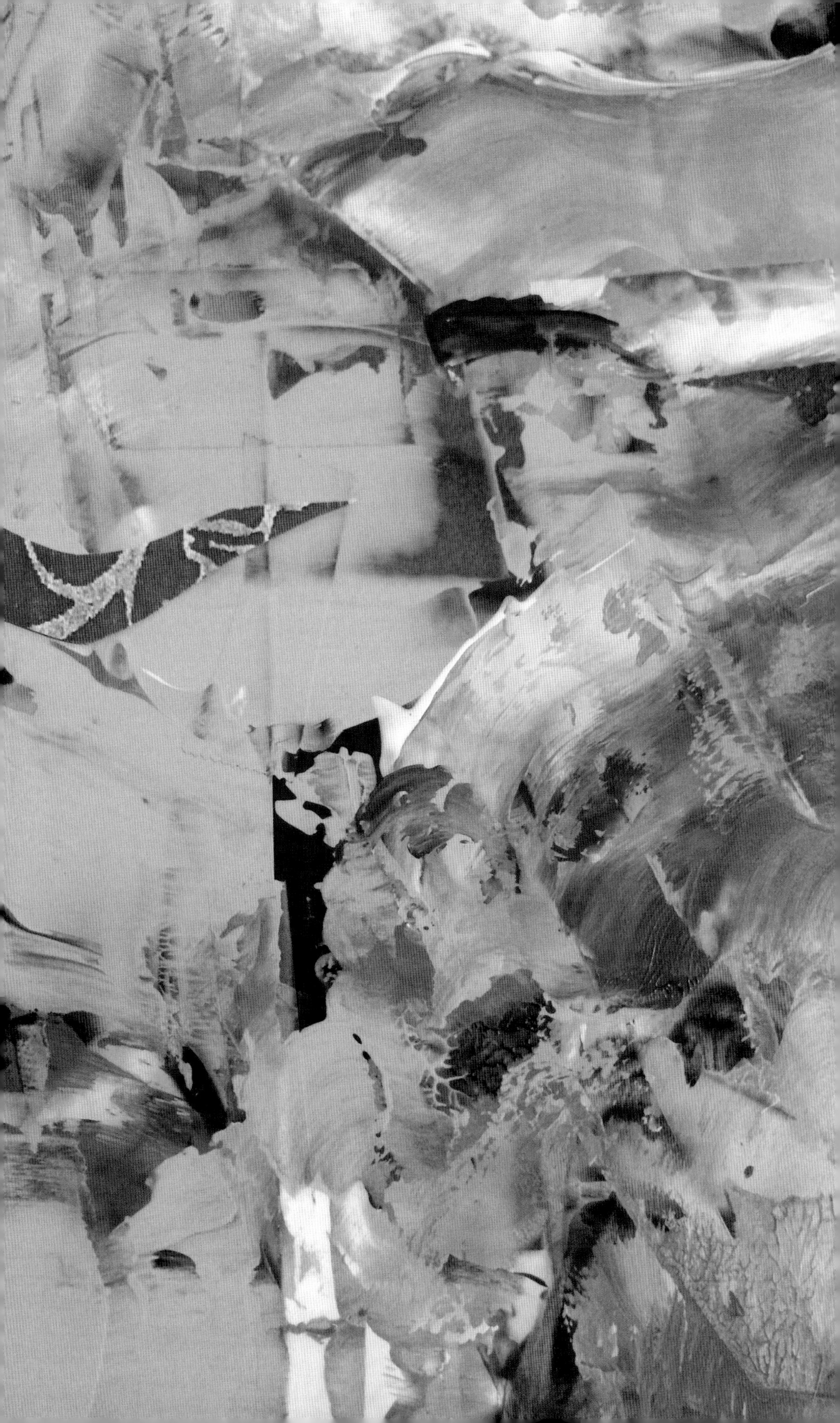

"I kind of miss that "becoming" stage...

I've kind of knocked on the door

and heard a muffled answer.

I still don't know what the voice is saying,

or even what language it's in."

-David Bowie

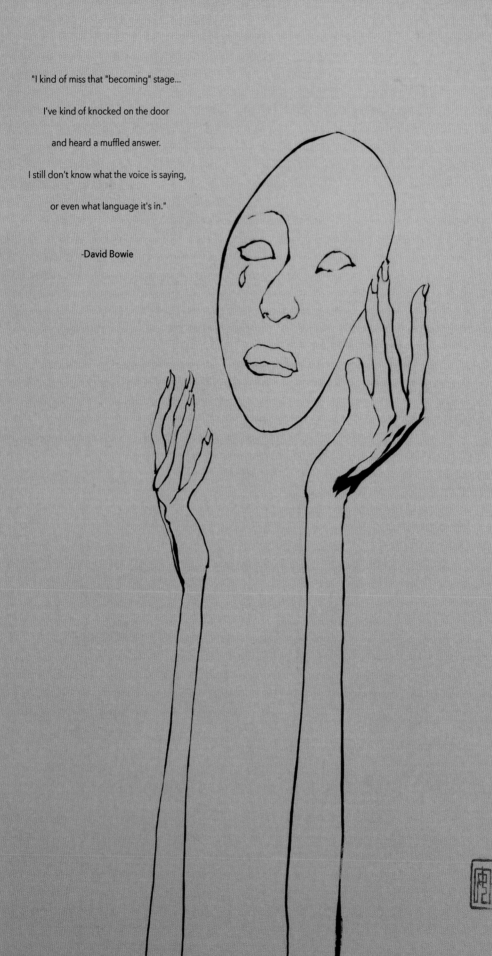

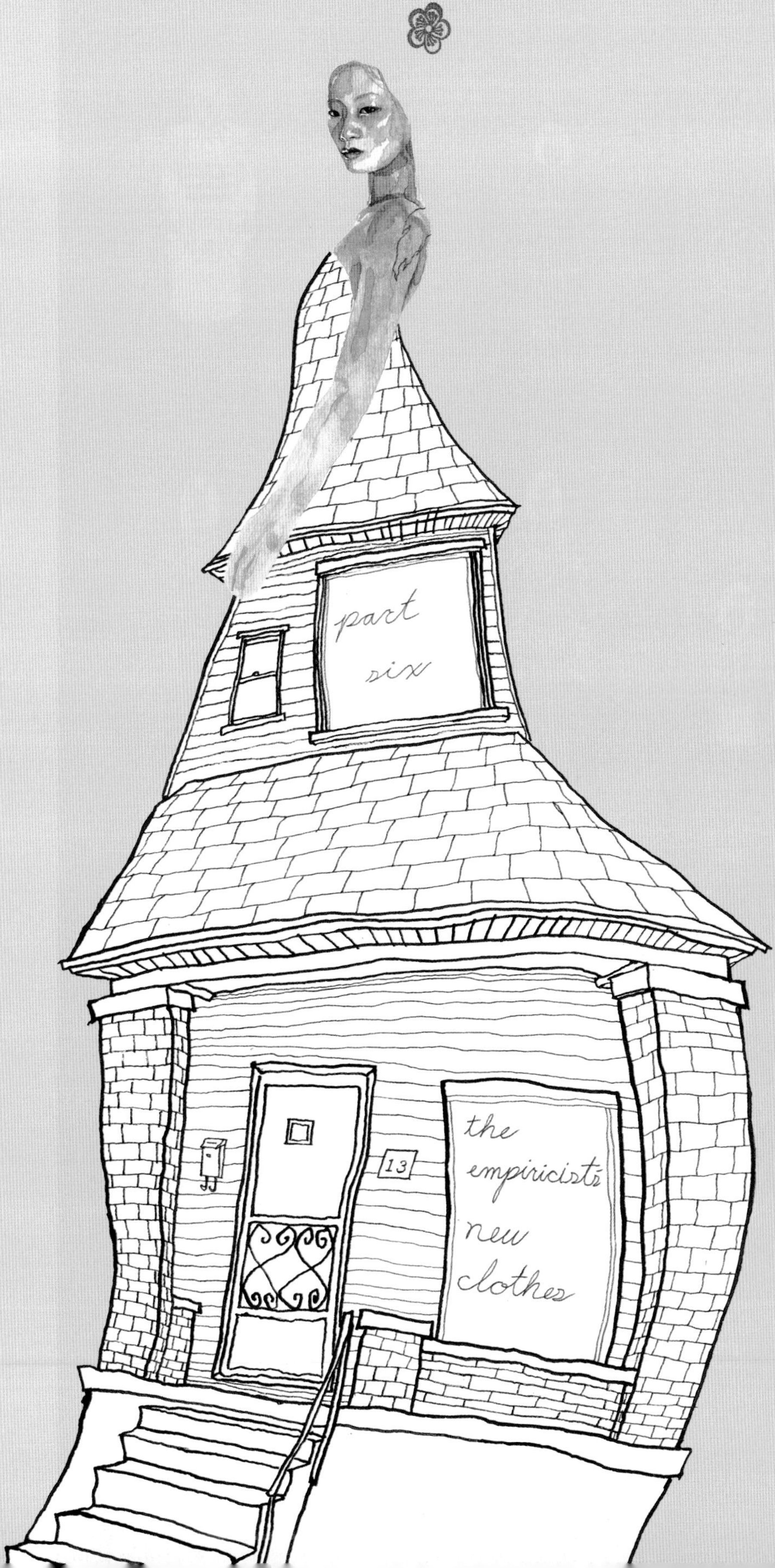
part six
the empiricist's new clothes
13

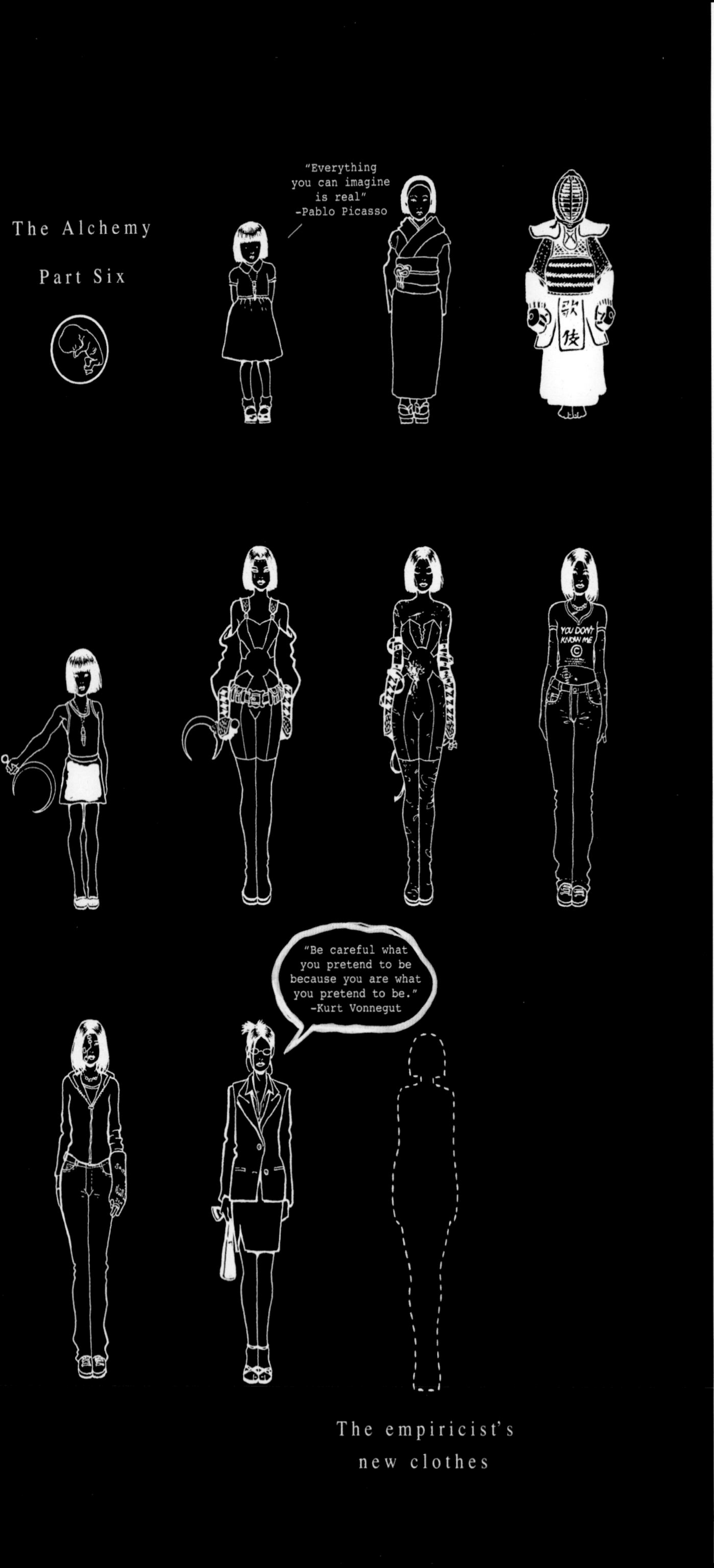
The Alchemy
Part Six
"Everything you can imagine is real" -Pablo Picasso
歌
伎
YOU DON'T KNOW ME
"Be careful what you pretend to be because you are what you pretend to be." -Kurt Vonnegut
The empiricist's new clothes

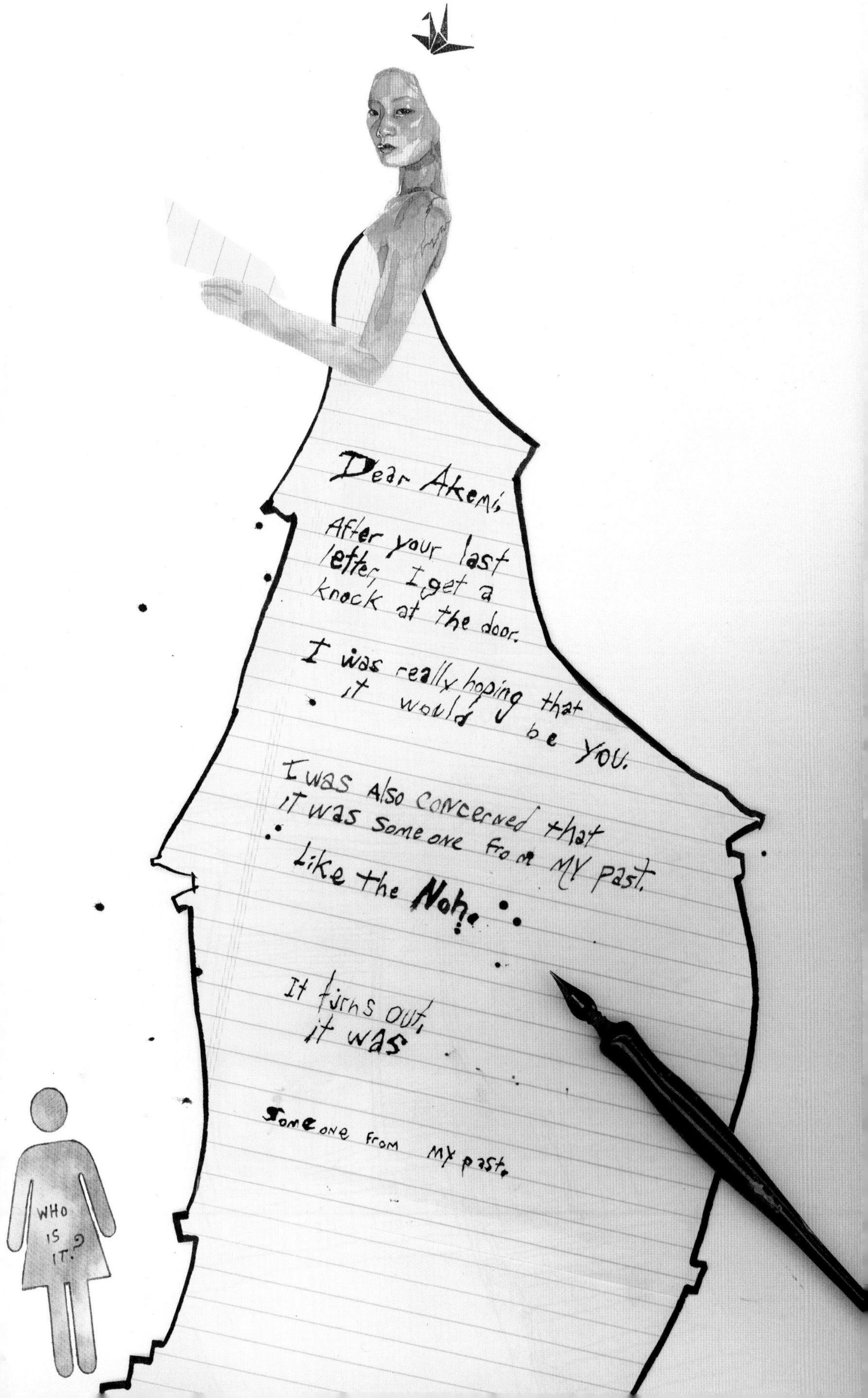

Dear Akemi,
After your last letter, I get a knock at the door.
I was really hoping that it would be YOU.
I was also concerned that it was someone from MY past.
Like the Noh.
It turns out, it was
Someone from MY past.
WHO IS IT?

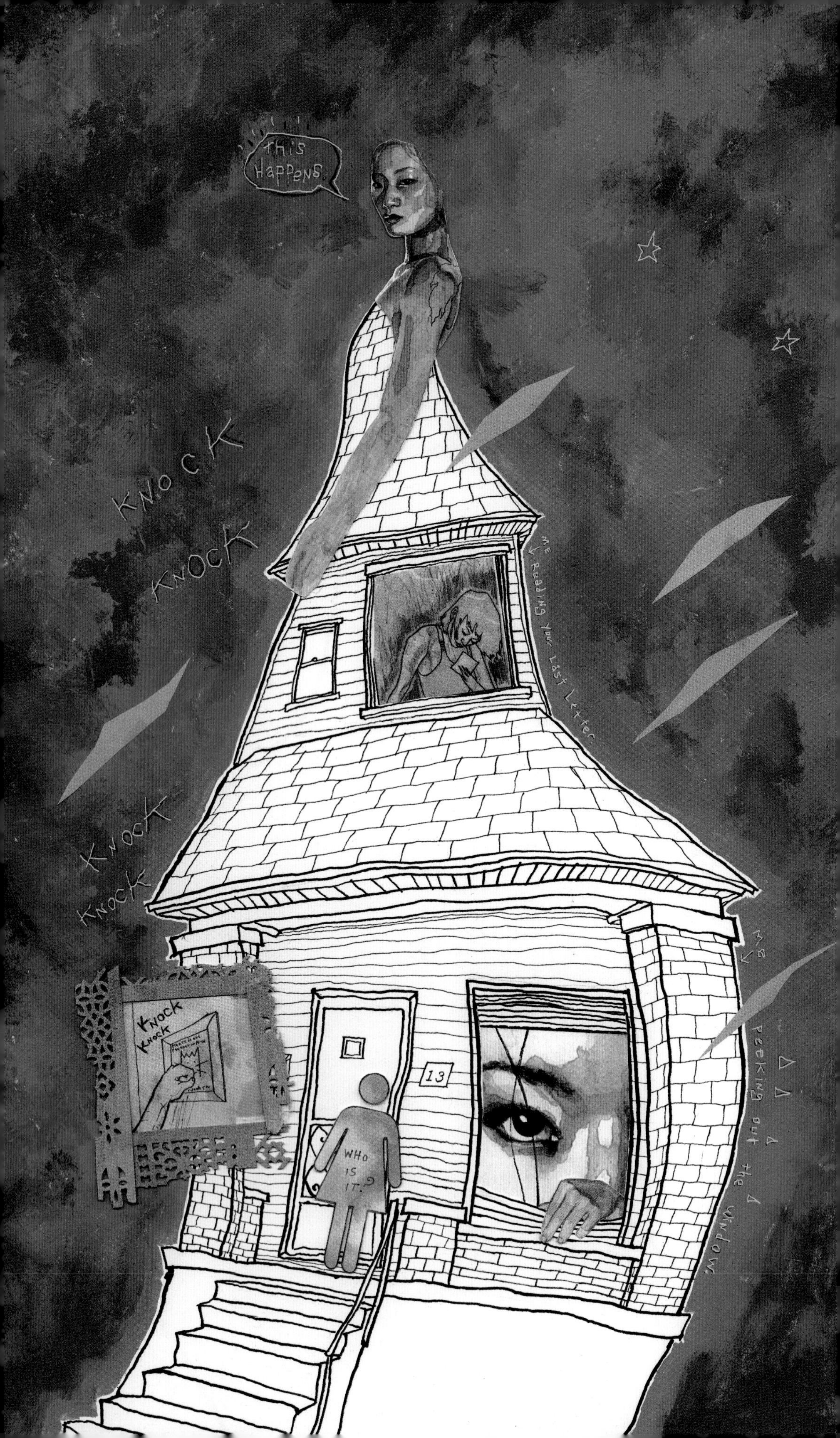
this Happens.
KNOCK KNOCK
me Reading your Last Letter.
KNOCK KNOCK
KNOCK KNOCK
13
WHO IS IT?
me peeking out the window.

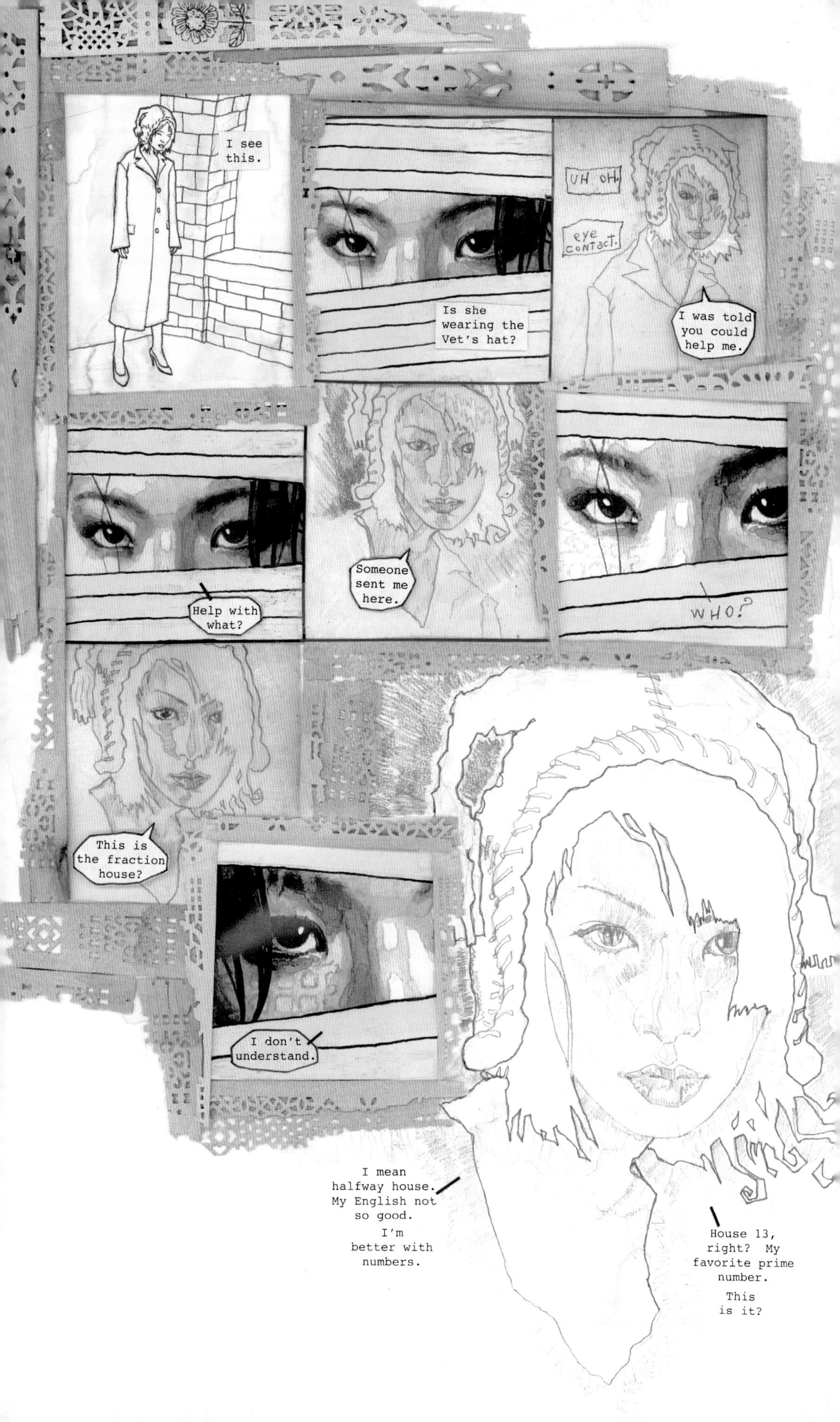
I see this.
Is she wearing the Vet's hat?
UH OH.
eye contact.
I was told you could help me.
Help with what?
Someone sent me here.
WHO?
This is the fraction house?
I don't understand.
I mean halfway house. My English not so good.
I'm better with numbers.
House 13, right? My favorite prime number.
This is it?

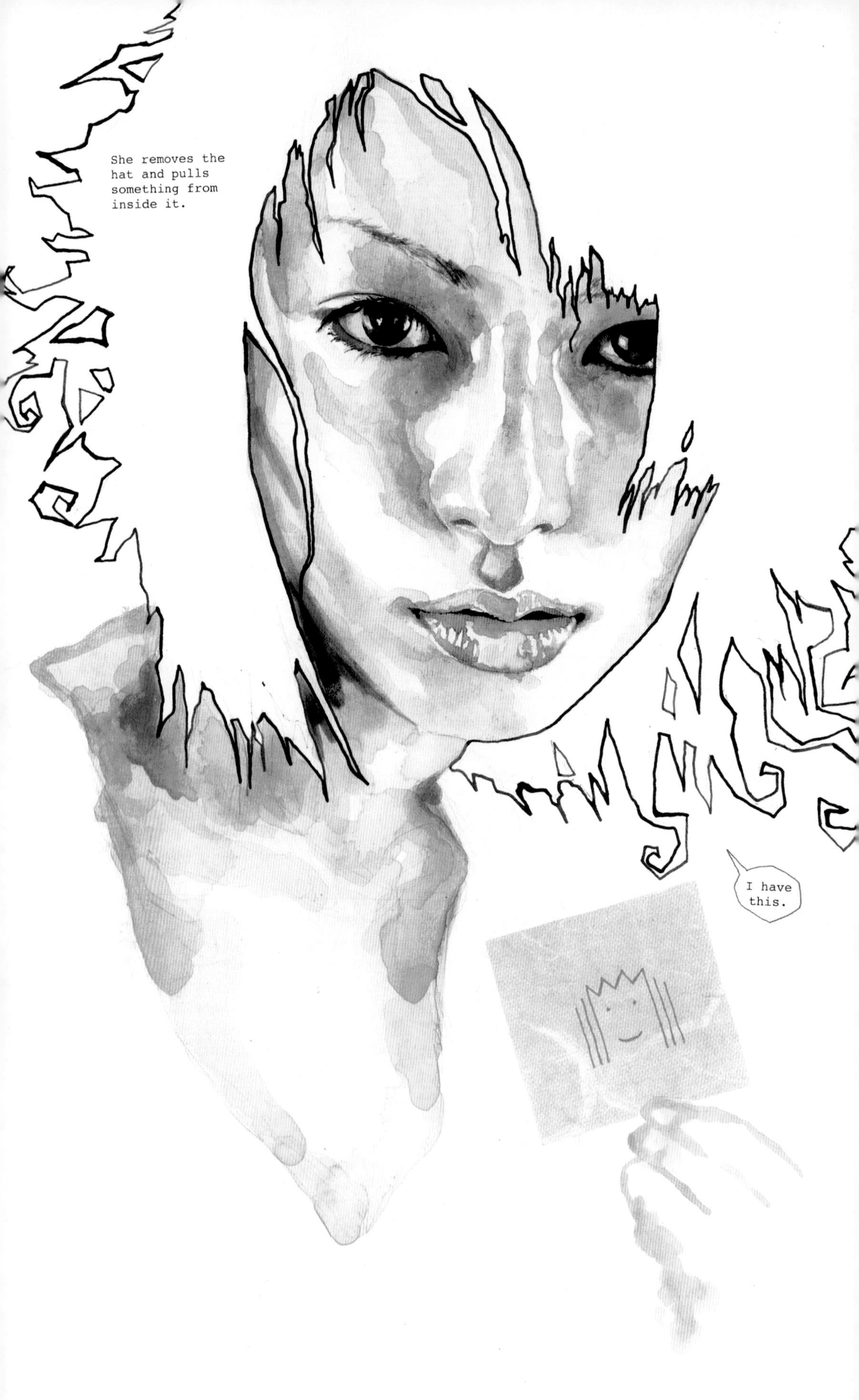
She removes the hat and pulls something from inside it.
I have this.

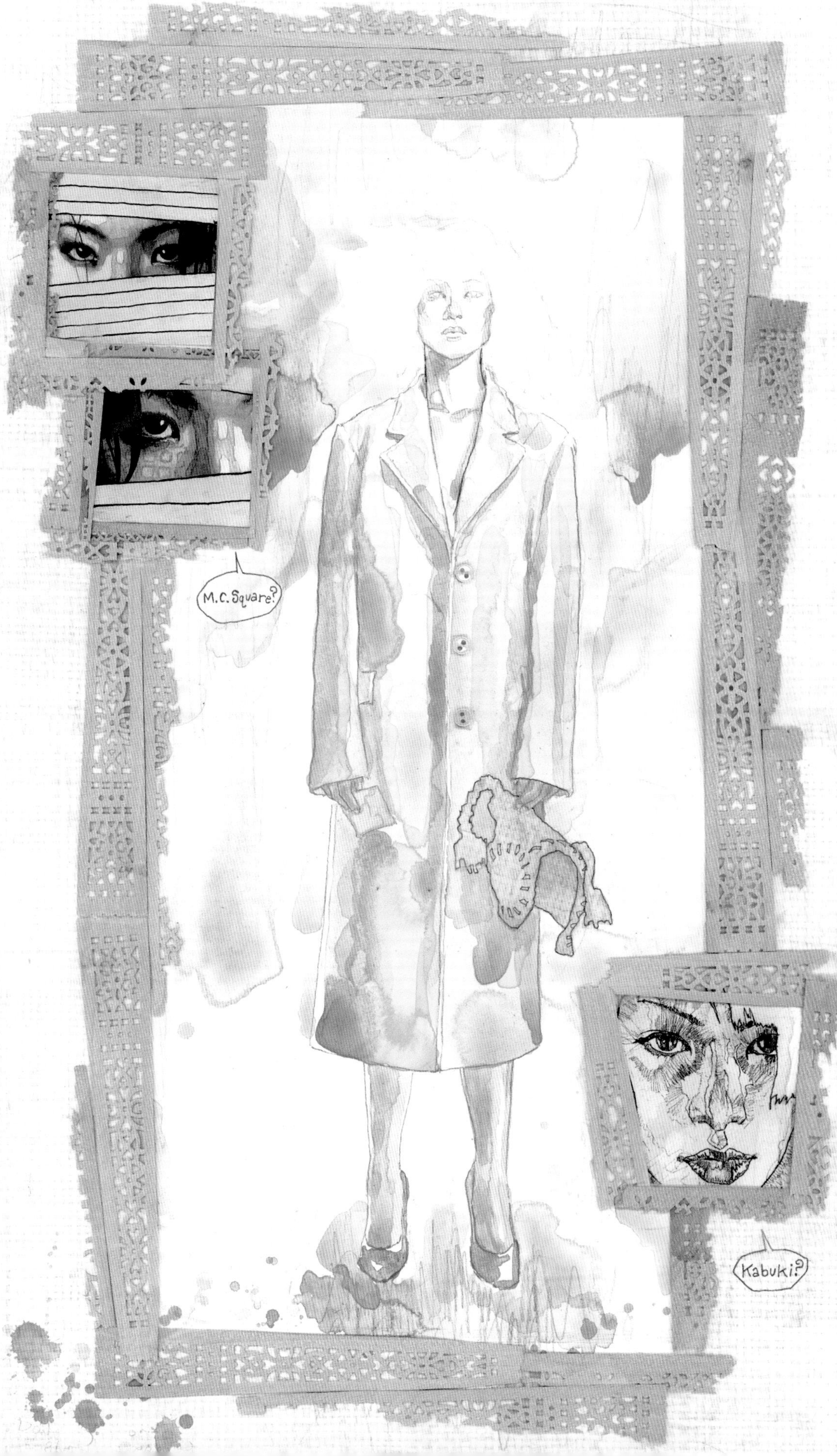
M.C. Square?
Kabuki?

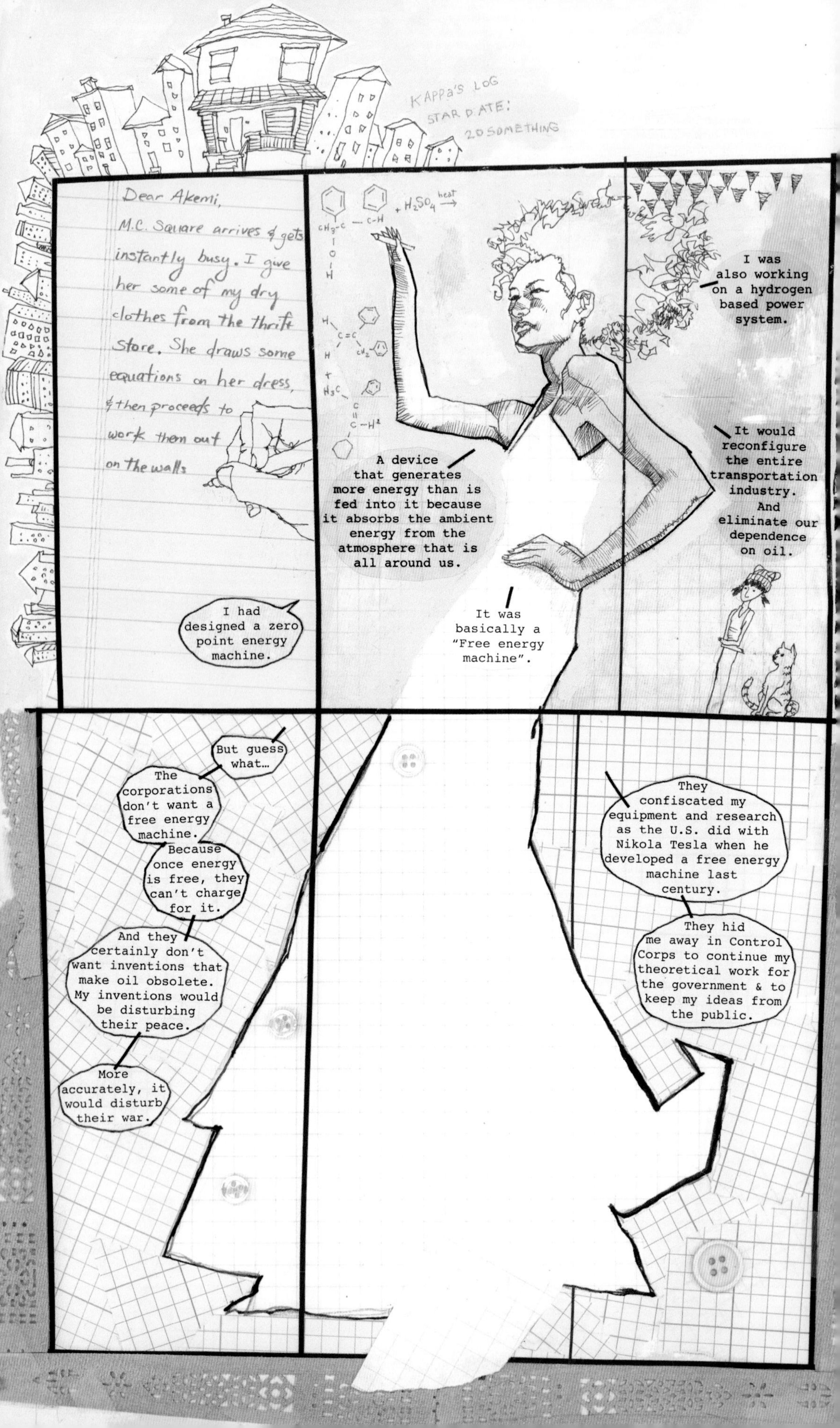

KAPPA'S LOG
STAR DATE:
20 SOMETHING
Dear Akemi,
M.C. Square arrives & gets instantly busy. I give her some of my dry clothes from the thrift store. She draws some equations on her dress, & then proceeds to work them out on the walls
I had designed a zero point energy machine.
A device that generates more energy than is fed into it because it absorbs the ambient energy from the atmosphere that is all around us.
It was basically a "Free energy machine".
I was also working on a hydrogen based power system.
It would reconfigure the entire transportation industry.
And eliminate our dependence on oil.
But guess what...
The corporations don't want a free energy machine.
Because once energy is free, they can't charge for it.
And they certainly don't want inventions that make oil obsolete. My inventions would be disturbing their peace.
More accurately, it would disturb their war.
They confiscated my equipment and research as the U.S. did with Nikola Tesla when he developed a free energy machine last century.
They hid me away in Control Corps to continue my theoretical work for the government & to keep my ideas from the public.

Akemi smuggled me out the same night you escaped.
She sent me to hide here so I can record all of my theories and inventions that I have developed over the years.
Akemi has connections in publishing. Once recorded, she intends to have my work published to thwart the power structures' ability to keep the world trapped in their cycle of consumerism, oil, and war.
Won't that be dangerous for you? I'm sure Control Corps or the Noh is already after you since you escaped.
Of course they are. I'm sure it's just a matter of time before they find me here.
But going public with my ideas will erase their need to find me. So I have to do it quickly.
It can be published anonymously if need be.
Didn't Akemi tell you her *Edward De Vere* Shakespeare story yet?
I think she said *Duveer.*
Sometimes she says *"Veneer"* as that's what she means.
But it's *De Vere.*
I imagine that is why you are here as well. I assumed you'd been recruited into Akemi's underground network.
You must be doing some kind of important work. Or have an important story to tell.
This is the halfway house where we put all of our unused fractions together and become whole.
I'm tired. I need a nap.

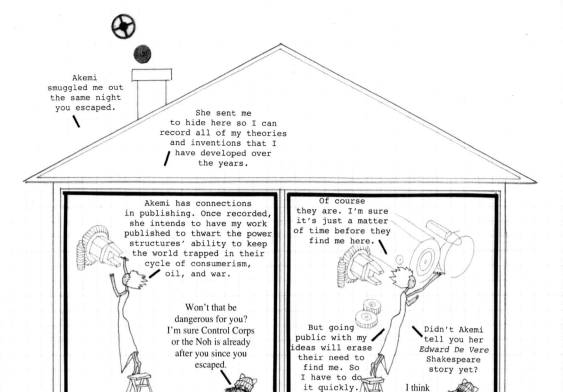

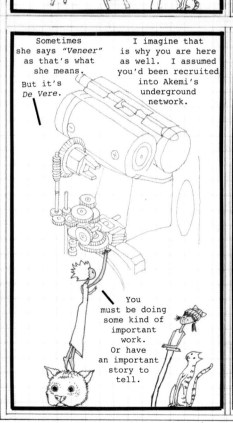

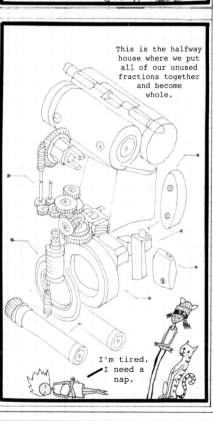

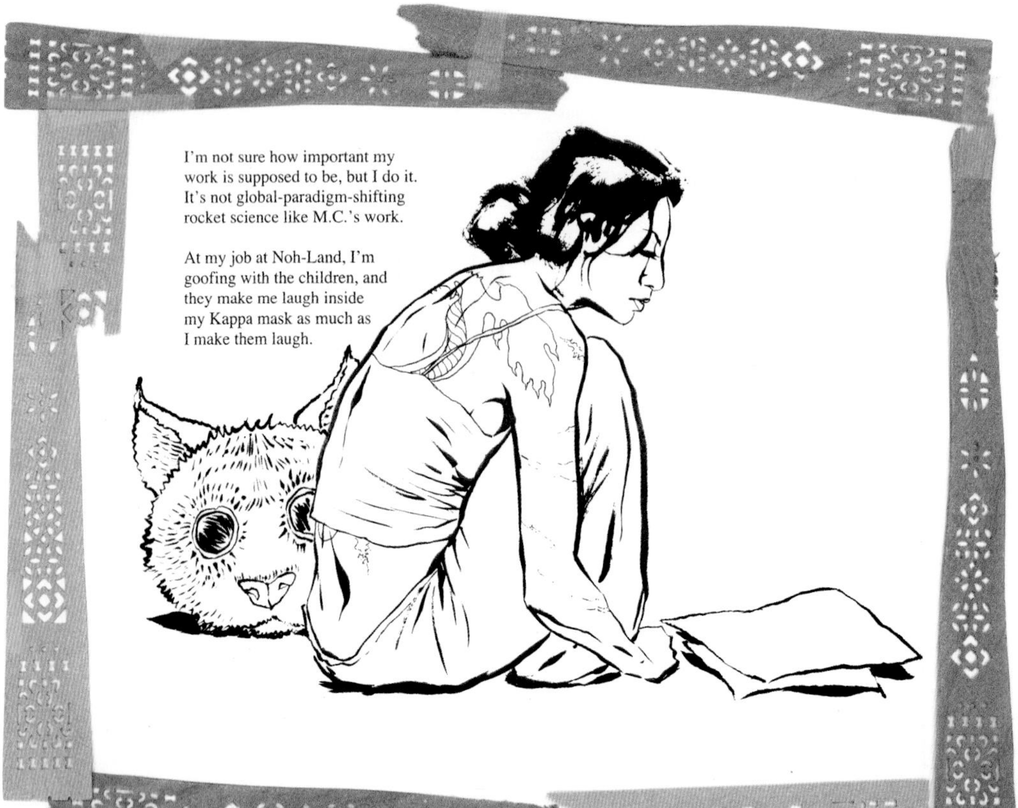
I'm not sure how important my work is supposed to be, but I do it. It's not global-paradigm-shifting rocket science like M.C.'s work.
At my job at Noh-Land, I'm goofing with the children, and they make me laugh inside my Kappa mask as much as I make them laugh.

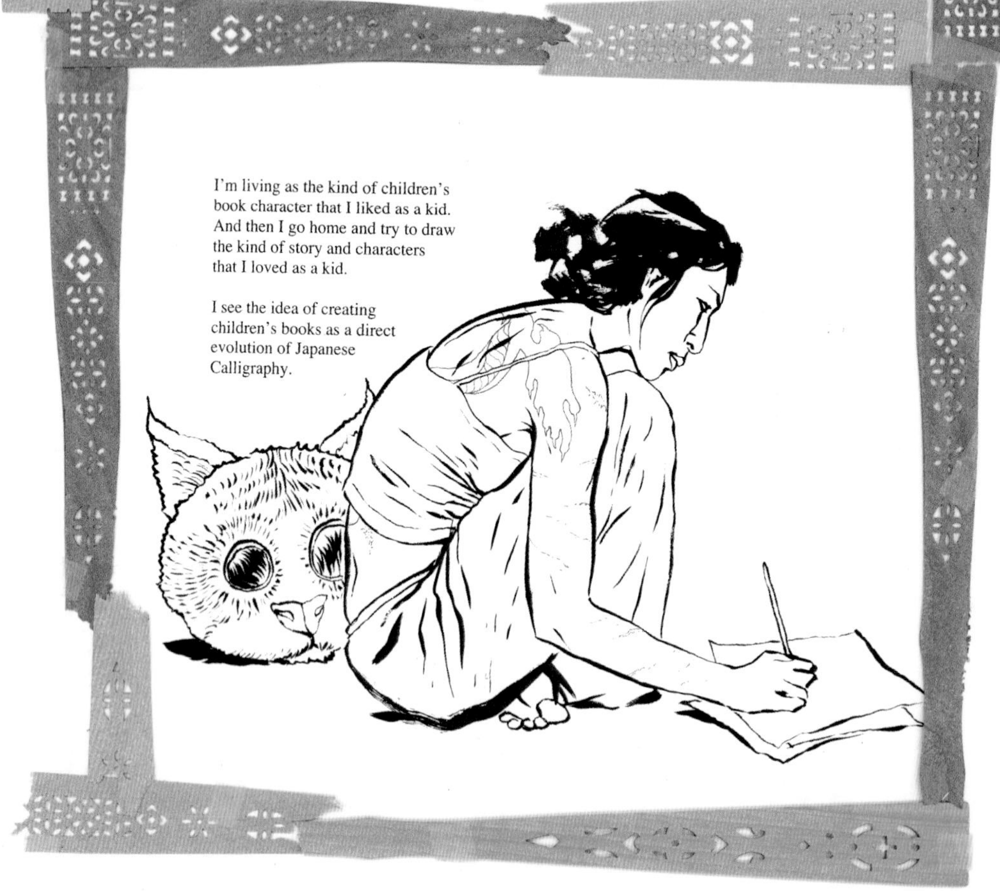
I'm living as the kind of children's book character that I liked as a kid. And then I go home and try to draw the kind of story and characters that I loved as a kid.
I see the idea of creating children's books as a direct evolution of Japanese Calligraphy.

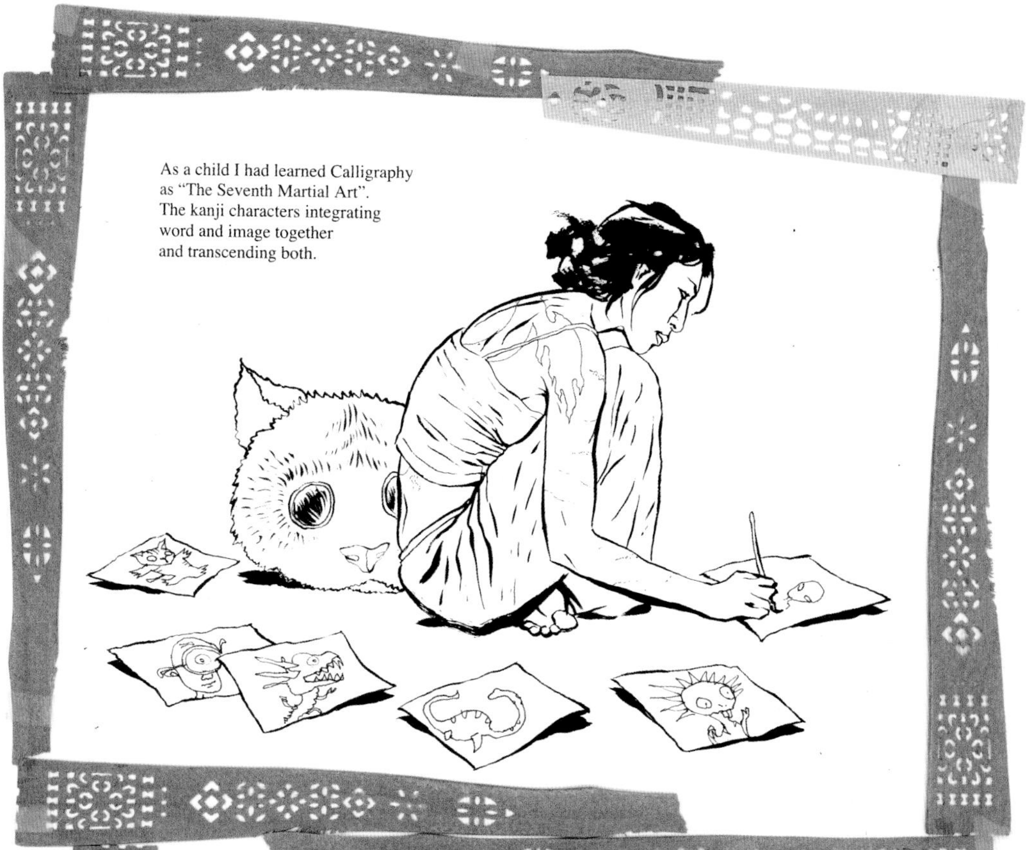
As a child I had learned Calligraphy as "The Seventh Martial Art". The kanji characters integrating word and image together and transcending both.

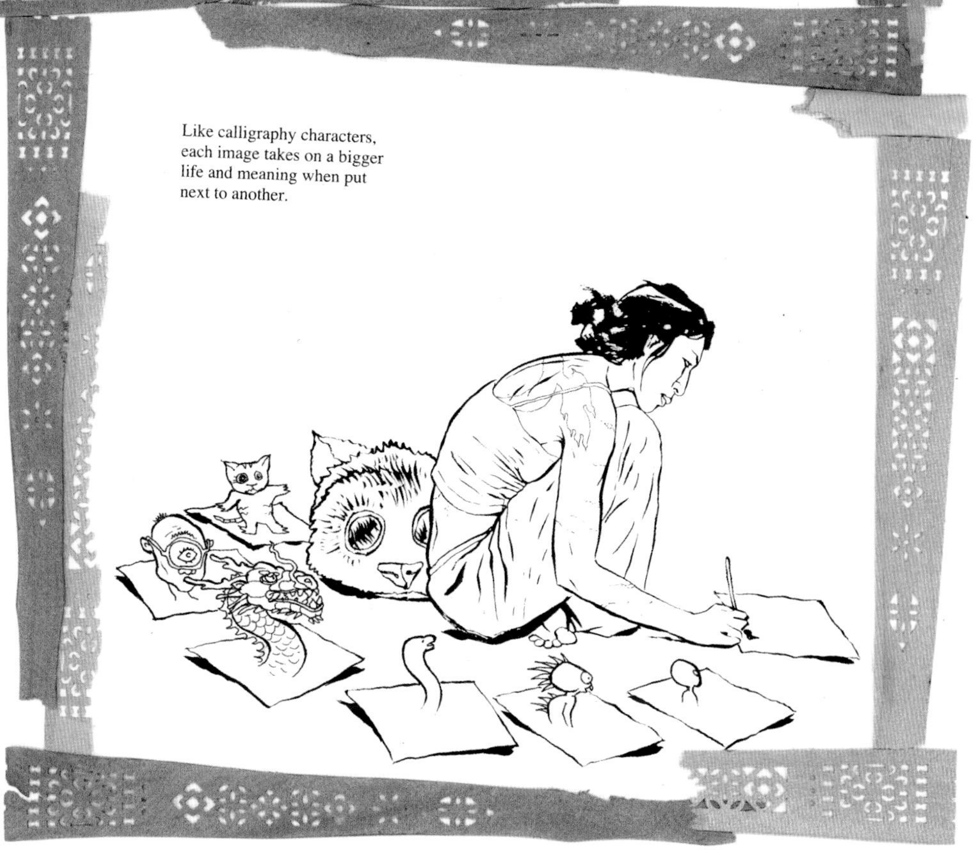
Like calligraphy characters, each image takes on a bigger life and meaning when put next to another.

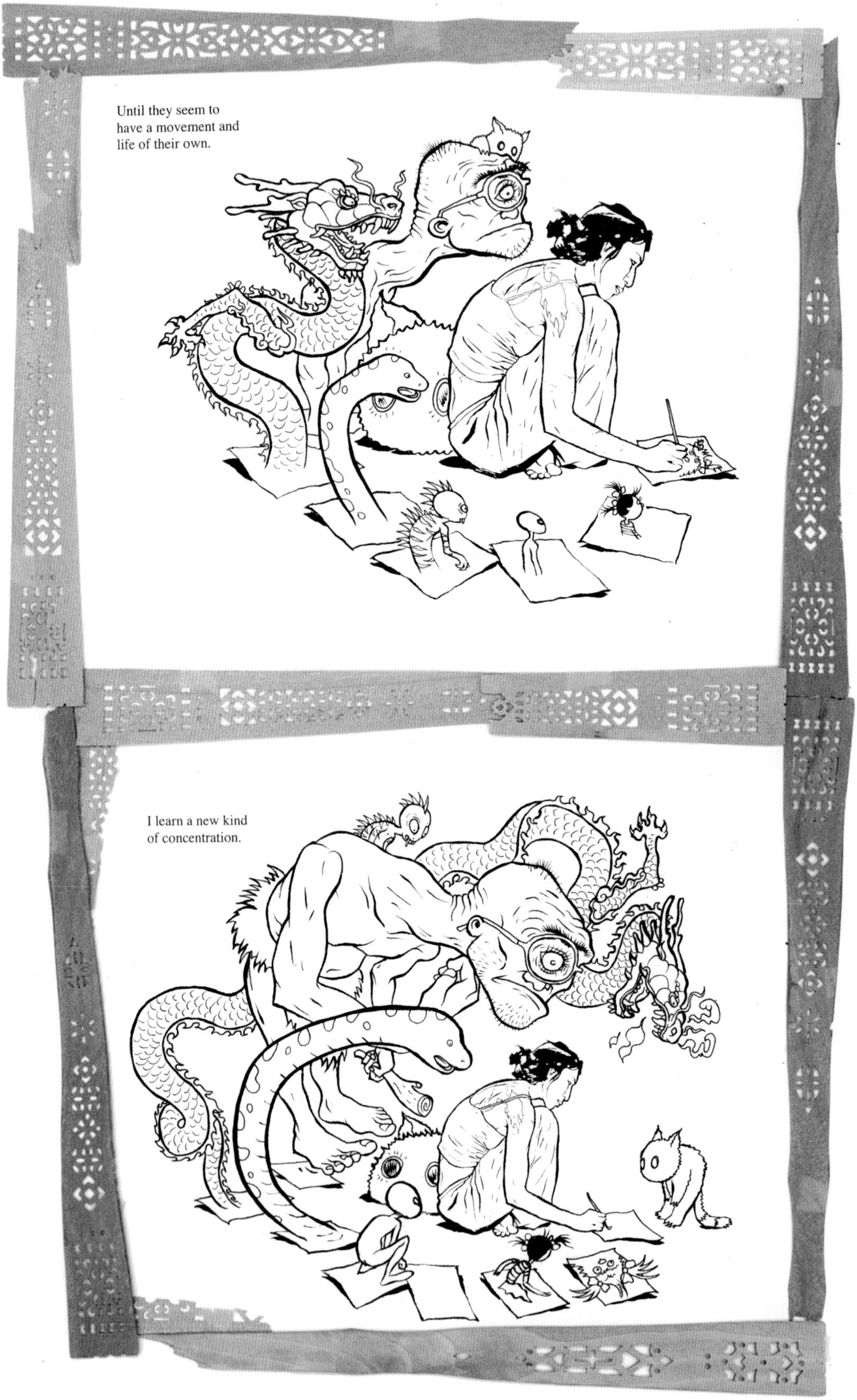
Until they seem to have a movement and life of their own.
I learn a new kind of concentration.

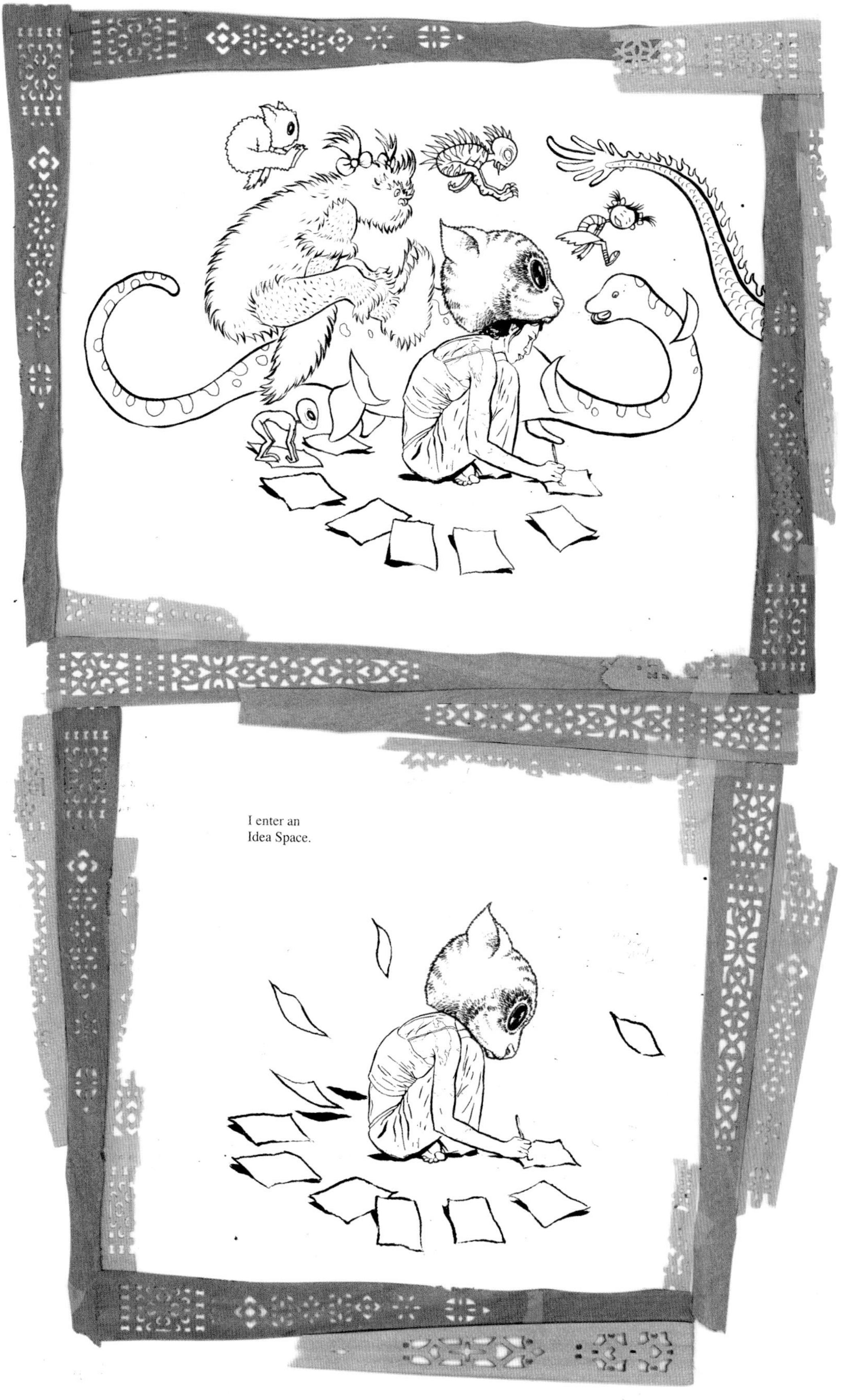
I enter an
Idea Space.

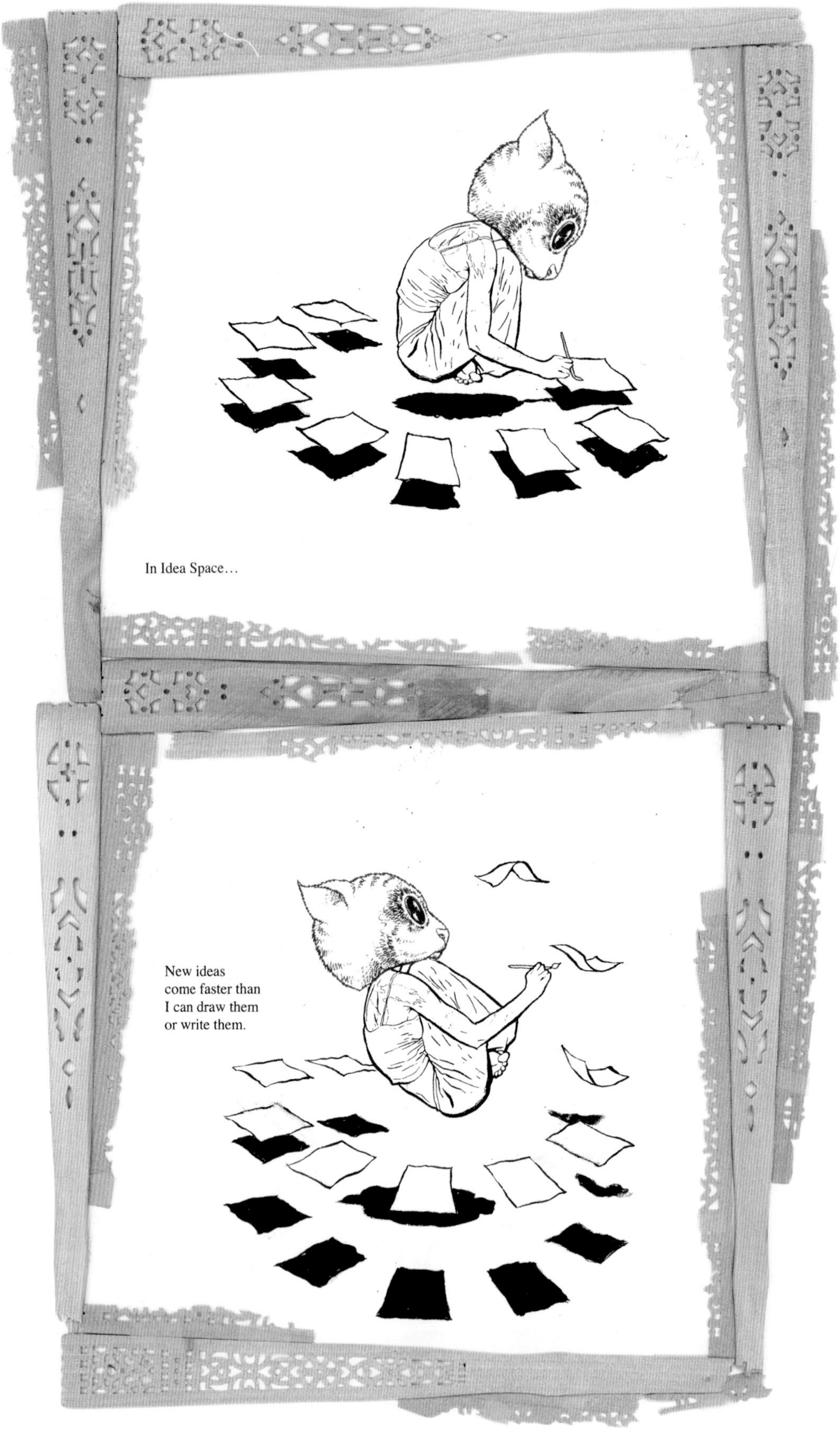
In Idea Space…
New ideas come faster than I can draw them or write them.

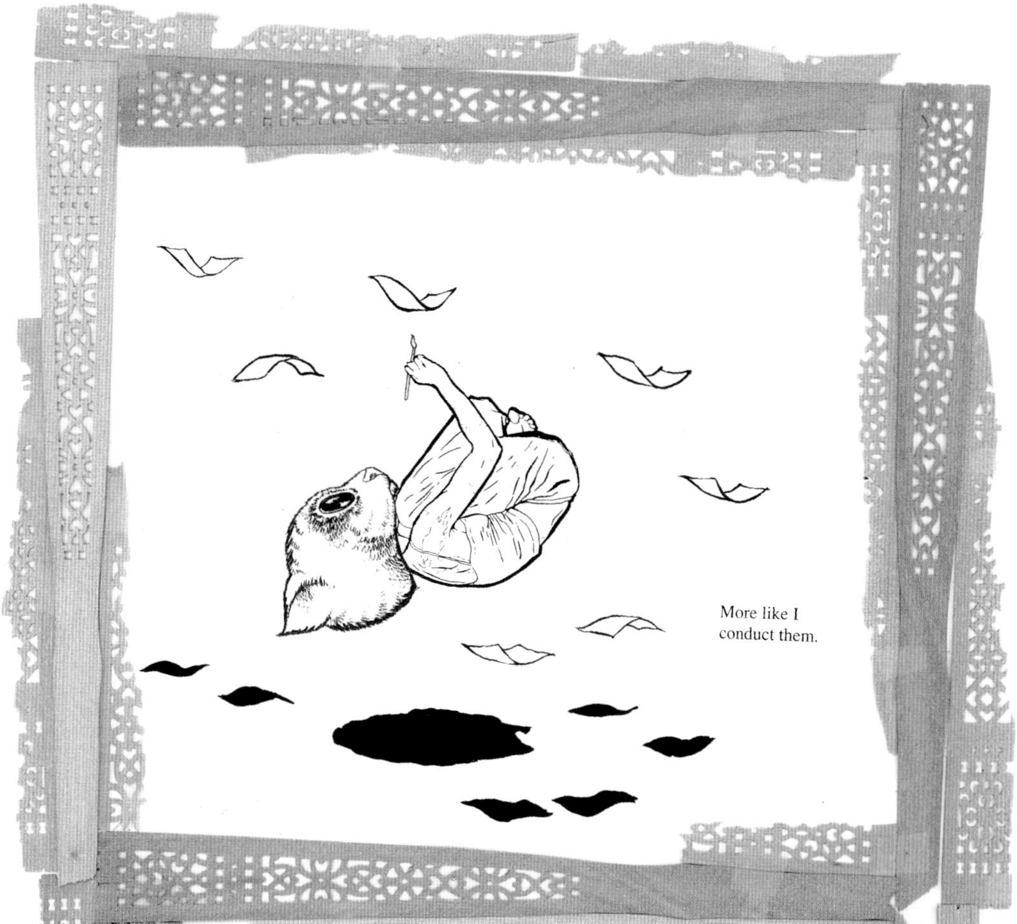
More like I
conduct them.

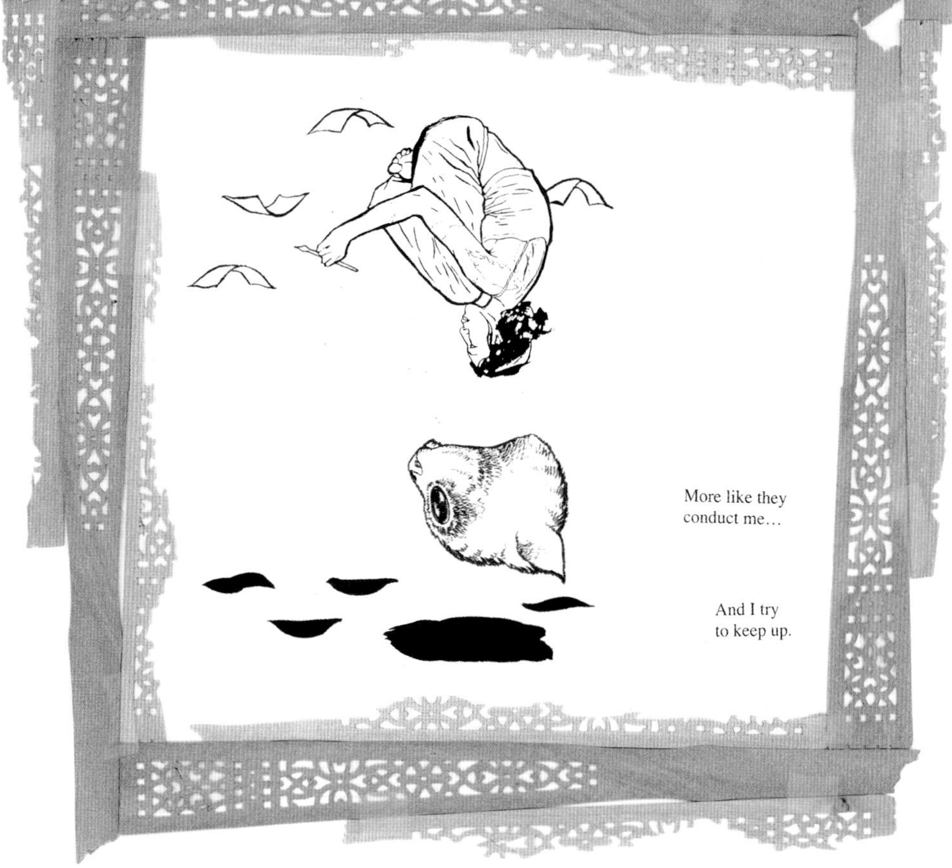
More like they
conduct me…
And I try
to keep up.

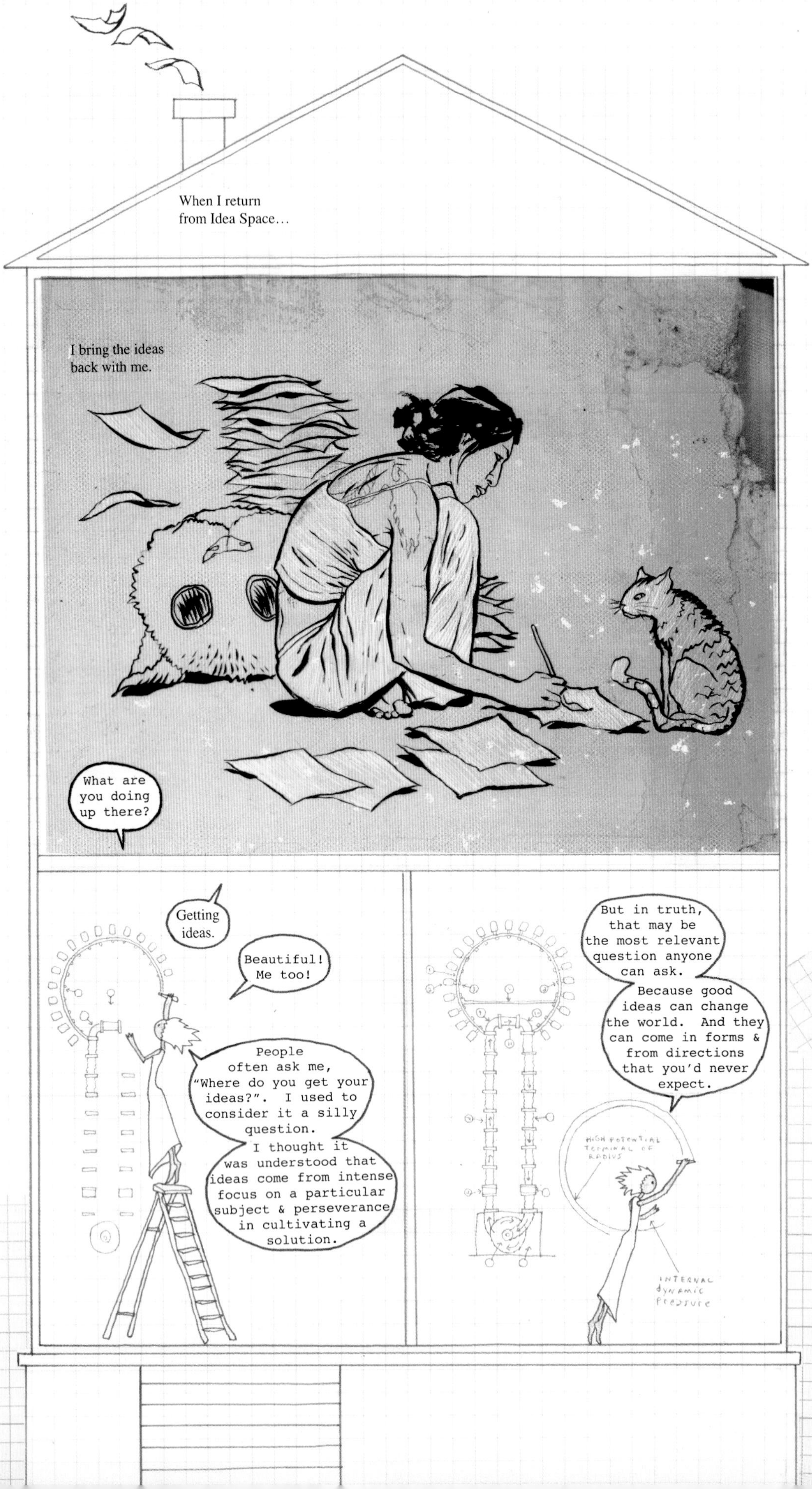
When I return
from Idea Space…
I bring the ideas
back with me.
What are you doing up there?
Getting ideas.
Beautiful! Me too!
People often ask me, "Where do you get your ideas?". I used to consider it a silly question.
I thought it was understood that ideas come from intense focus on a particular subject & perseverance in cultivating a solution.
But in truth, that may be the most relevant question anyone can ask.
Because good ideas can change the world. And they can come in forms & from directions that you'd never expect.
HIGH POTENTIAL TERMINAL OF RADIUS
INTERNAL dynamic pressure

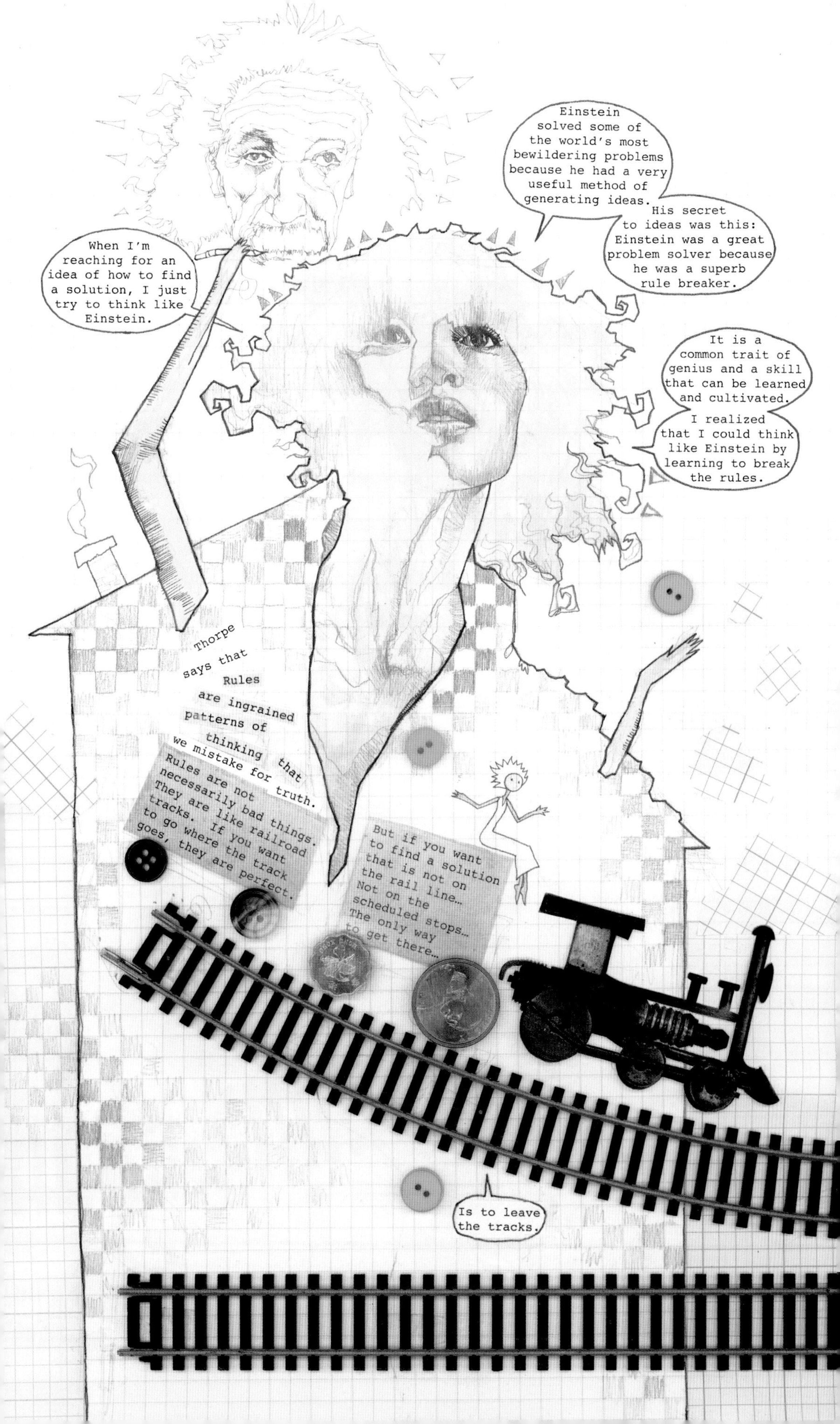
Einstein solved some of the world's most bewildering problems because he had a very useful method of generating ideas.
His secret to ideas was this: Einstein was a great problem solver because he was a superb rule breaker.
When I'm reaching for an idea of how to find a solution, I just try to think like Einstein.
It is a common trait of genius and a skill that can be learned and cultivated.
I realized that I could think like Einstein by learning to break the rules.
Thorpe says that Rules are ingrained patterns of thinking that we mistake for truth.
Rules are not necessarily bad things. They are like railroad tracks. If you want to go where the track goes, they are perfect.
But if you want to find a solution that is not on the rail line… Not on the scheduled stops… The only way to get there…
Is to leave the tracks.

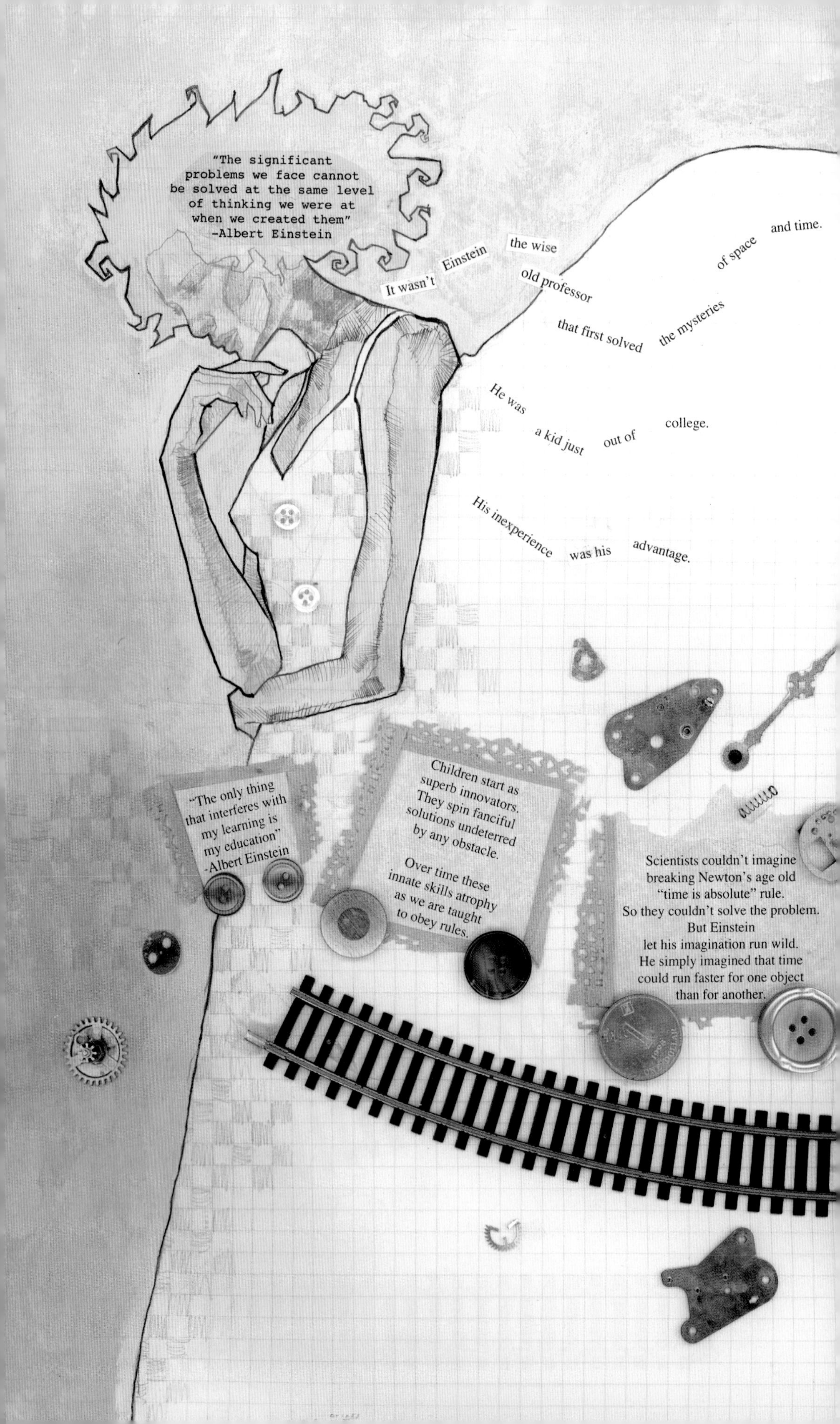
"The significant problems we face cannot be solved at the same level of thinking we were at when we created them" -Albert Einstein
It wasn't Einstein the wise old professor that first solved the mysteries of space and time.
He was a kid just out of college.
His inexperience was his advantage.
"The only thing that interferes with my learning is my education" -Albert Einstein
Children start as superb innovators. They spin fanciful solutions undeterred by any obstacle.
Over time these innate skills atrophy as we are taught to obey rules.
Scientists couldn't imagine breaking Newton's age old "time is absolute" rule. So they couldn't solve the problem. But Einstein let his imagination run wild. He simply imagined that time could run faster for one object than for another.

Breaking the

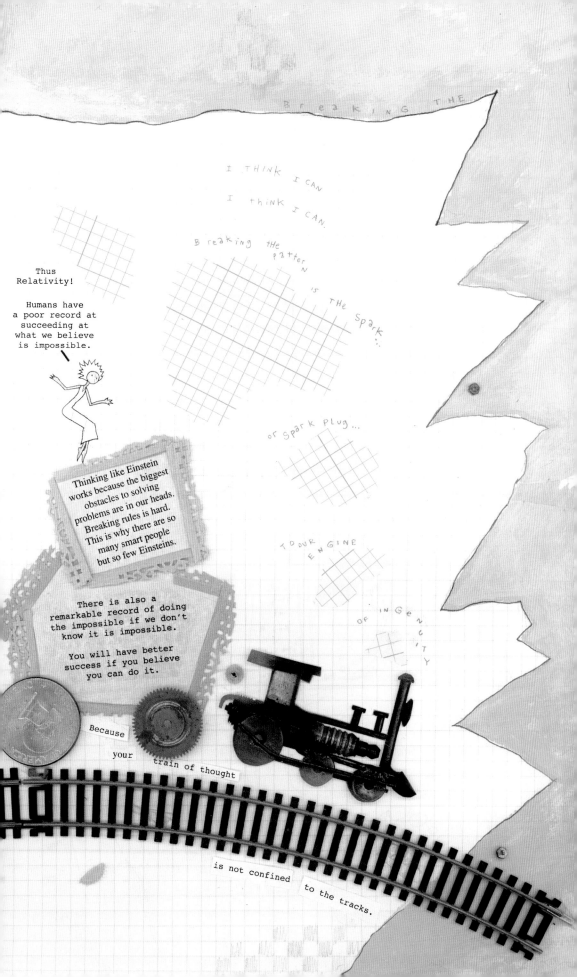

I think I can

I think I can.

Breaking the pattern is the spark...

or spark plug...

to our engine of ingenuity

Thus Relativity!

Humans have a poor record at succeeding at what we believe is impossible.

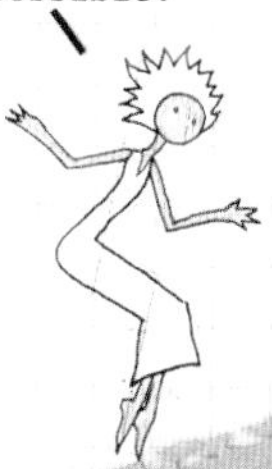

Thinking like Einstein works because the biggest obstacles to solving problems are in our heads. Breaking rules is hard. This is why there are so many smart people but so few Einsteins.

There is also a remarkable record of doing the impossible if we don't know it is impossible.

You will have better success if you believe you can do it.

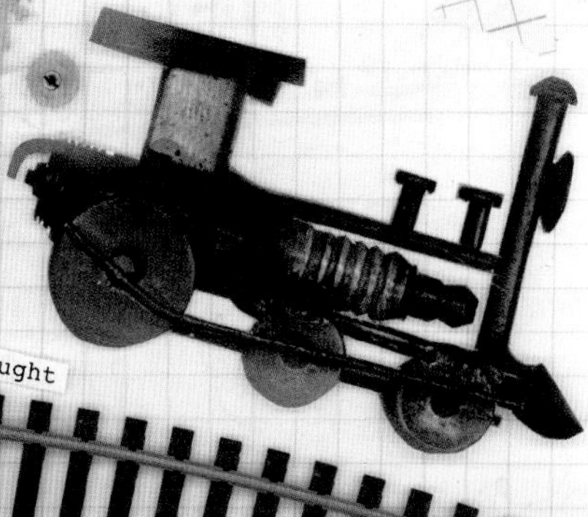

Because your train of thought is not confined to the tracks.

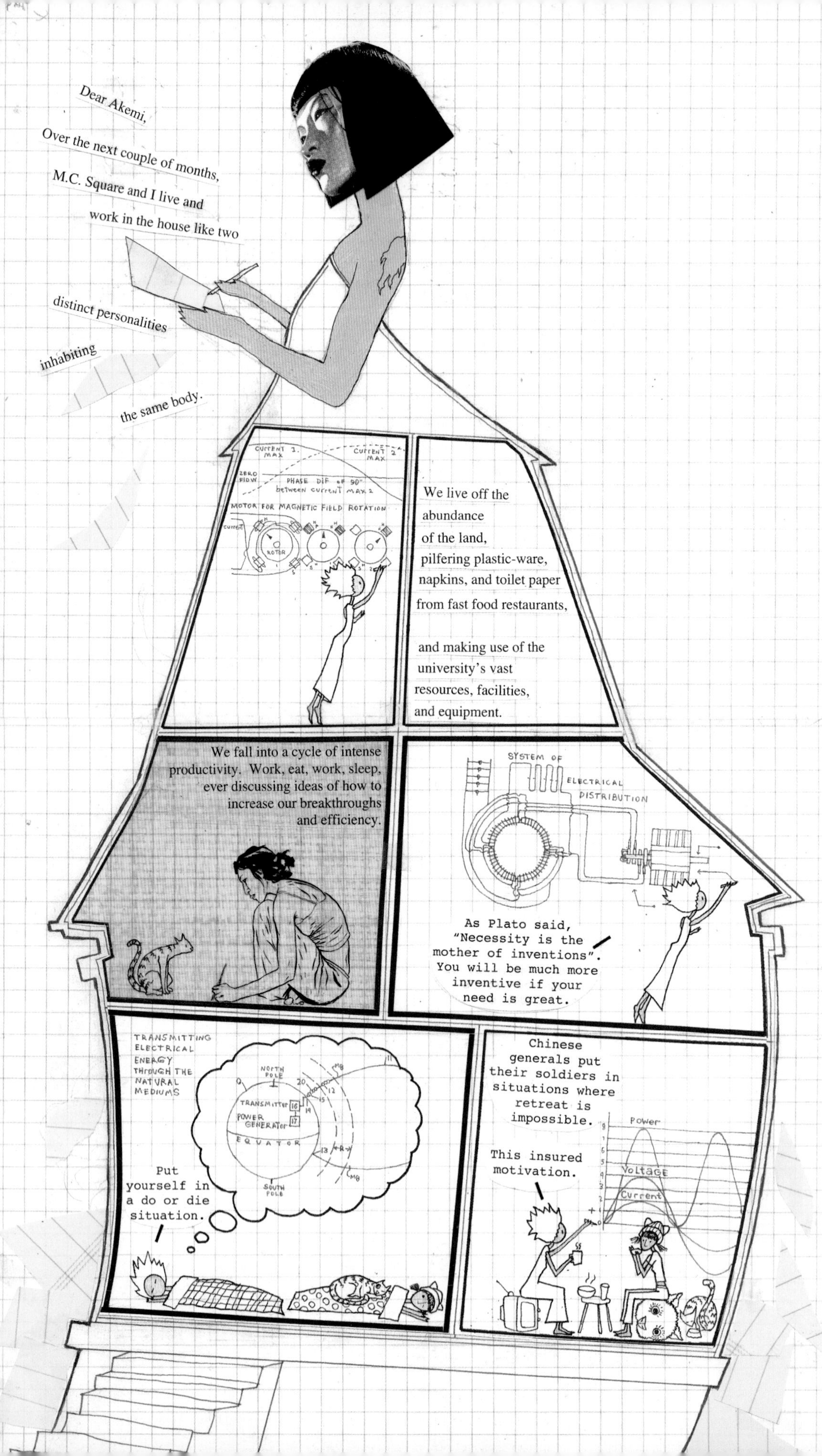

Dear Akemi,
Over the next couple of months,
M.C. Square and I live and
work in the house like two
distinct personalities
inhabiting
the same body.
CURRENT 1 MAX
CURRENT 2 MAX
ZERO FLOW
PHASE DIF of 90° between current MAX 2
MOTOR FOR MAGNETIC FIELD ROTATION
ROTOR
We live off the
abundance
of the land,
pilfering plastic-ware,
napkins, and toilet paper
from fast food restaurants,
and making use of the
university's vast
resources, facilities,
and equipment.
We fall into a cycle of intense productivity. Work, eat, work, sleep, ever discussing ideas of how to increase our breakthroughs and efficiency.
SYSTEM OF
ELECTRICAL
DISTRIBUTION
As Plato said,
"Necessity is the mother of inventions". You will be much more inventive if your need is great.
TRANSMITTING ELECTRICAL ENERGY THROUGH THE NATURAL MEDIUMS
NORTH POLE
TRANSMITTER
POWER GENERATOR
EQUATOR
SOUTH POLE
Put yourself in a do or die situation.
Chinese generals put their soldiers in situations where retreat is impossible.
This insured motivation.
Power
Voltage
Current

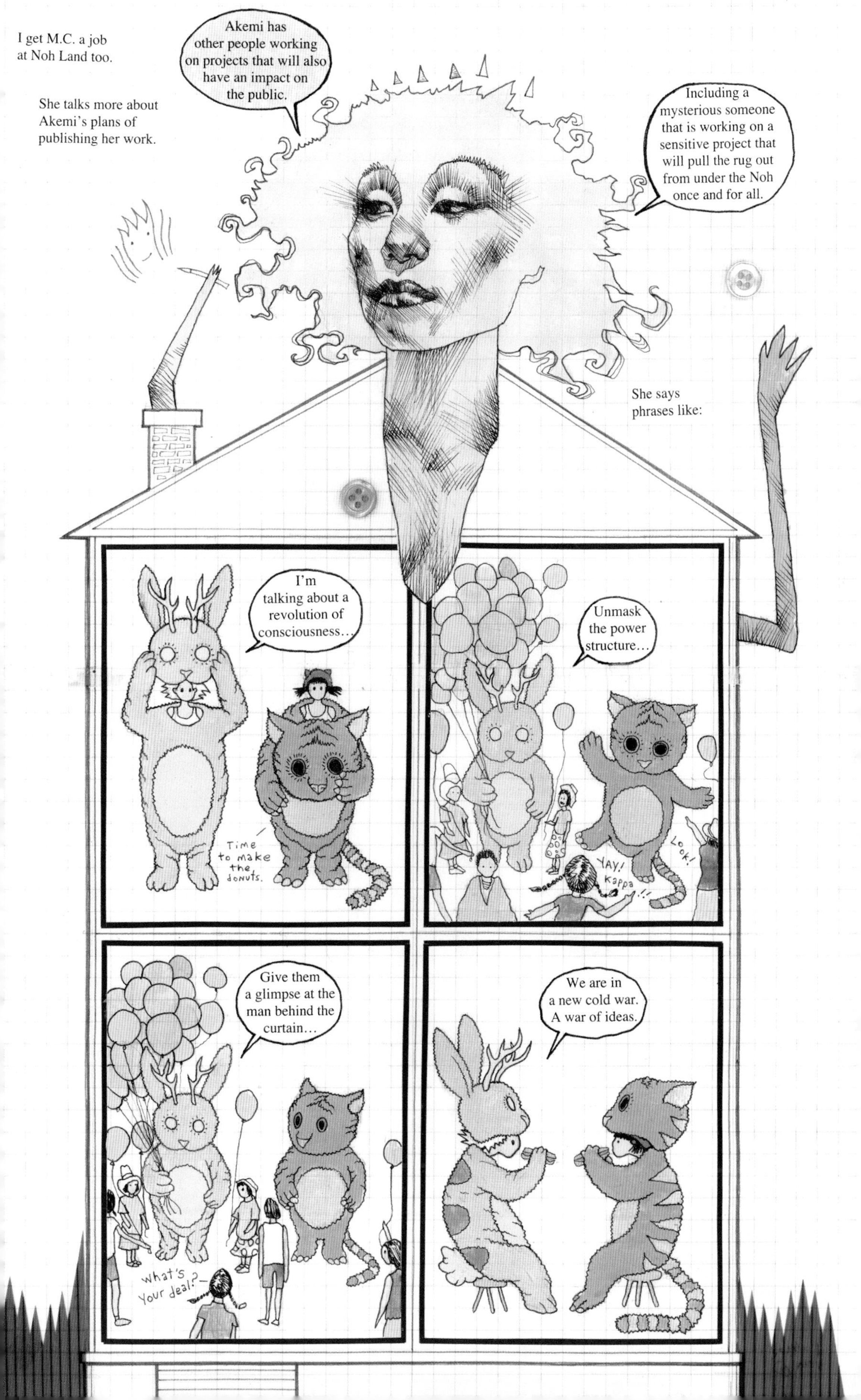

I get M.C. a job at Noh Land too.
She talks more about Akemi's plans of publishing her work.
Akemi has other people working on projects that will also have an impact on the public.
Including a mysterious someone that is working on a sensitive project that will pull the rug out from under the Noh once and for all.
She says phrases like:
I'm talking about a revolution of consciousness…
Time to make the donuts.
Unmask the power structure…
Look!
YAY! Kappa!!
Give them a glimpse at the man behind the curtain…
What's your deal?
We are in a new cold war. A war of ideas.

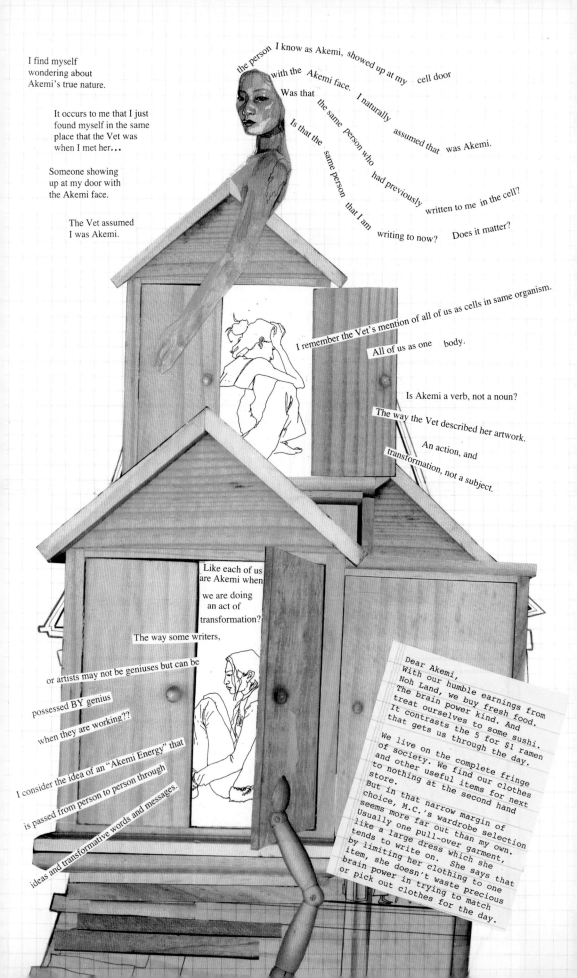

I find myself
wondering about
Akemi's true nature.

It occurs to me that I just
found myself in the same
place that the Vet was
when I met her...

Someone showing
up at my door with
the Akemi face.

The Vet assumed
I was Akemi.

the person I know as Akemi, showed up at my cell door with the Akemi face. I naturally assumed that was Akemi. Was that the same person who had previously written to me in the cell? Is that the same person that I am writing to now? Does it matter?

I remember the Vet's mention of all of us as cells in same organism.

All of us as one body.

Is Akemi a verb, not a noun?

The way the Vet described her artwork.

An action, and transformation, not a subject.

Like each of us
are Akemi when

we are doing
an act of
transformation?

The way some writers,

or artists may not be geniuses but can be

possessed BY genius

when they are working??

I consider the idea of an "Akemi Energy" that

is passed from person to person through

ideas and transformative words and messages.

Dear Akemi,
With our humble earnings from
Noh Land, we buy fresh food.
The brain power kind. And
treat ourselves to some sushi.
It contrasts the 5 for $1 ramen
that gets us through the day.

We live on the complete fringe
of society. We find our clothes
and other useful items for next
to nothing at the second hand
store. But in that narrow margin of
choice, M.C.'s wardrobe selection
seems more far out than my own.
Usually one pull-over garment,
like a large dress which she
tends to write on. She says that
by limiting her clothing to one
item, she doesn't waste precious
brain power in trying to match
or pick out clothes for the day.

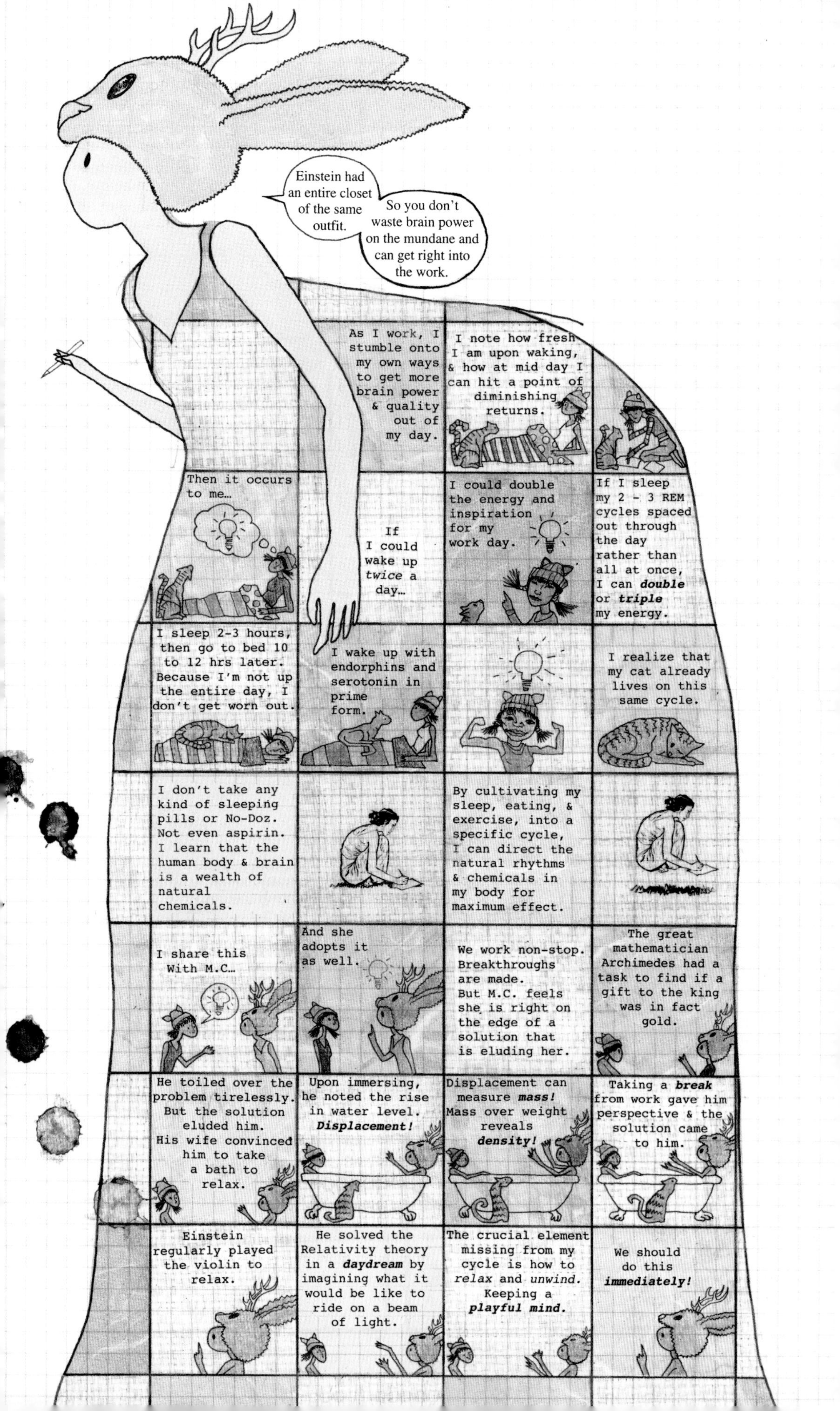
Einstein had an entire closet of the same outfit.
So you don't waste brain power on the mundane and can get right into the work.
As I work, I stumble onto my own ways to get more brain power & quality out of my day.
I note how fresh I am upon waking, & how at mid day I can hit a point of diminishing returns.
Then it occurs to me…
If I could wake up twice a day…
I could double the energy and inspiration for my work day.
If I sleep my 2 - 3 REM cycles spaced out through the day rather than all at once, I can double or triple my energy.
I sleep 2-3 hours, then go to bed 10 to 12 hrs later. Because I'm not up the entire day, I don't get worn out.
I wake up with endorphins and serotonin in prime form.
I realize that my cat already lives on this same cycle.
I don't take any kind of sleeping pills or No-Doz. Not even aspirin. I learn that the human body & brain is a wealth of natural chemicals.
By cultivating my sleep, eating, & exercise, into a specific cycle, I can direct the natural rhythms & chemicals in my body for maximum effect.
I share this With M.C…
And she adopts it as well.
We work non-stop. Breakthroughs are made. But M.C. feels she is right on the edge of a solution that is eluding her.
The great mathematician Archimedes had a task to find if a gift to the king was in fact gold.
He toiled over the problem tirelessly. But the solution eluded him. His wife convinced him to take a bath to relax.
Upon immersing, he noted the rise in water level. Displacement!
Displacement can measure mass! Mass over weight reveals density!
Taking a break from work gave him perspective & the solution came to him.
Einstein regularly played the violin to relax.
He solved the Relativity theory in a daydream by imagining what it would be like to ride on a beam of light.
The crucial element missing from my cycle is how to relax and unwind. Keeping a playful mind.
We should do this immediately!

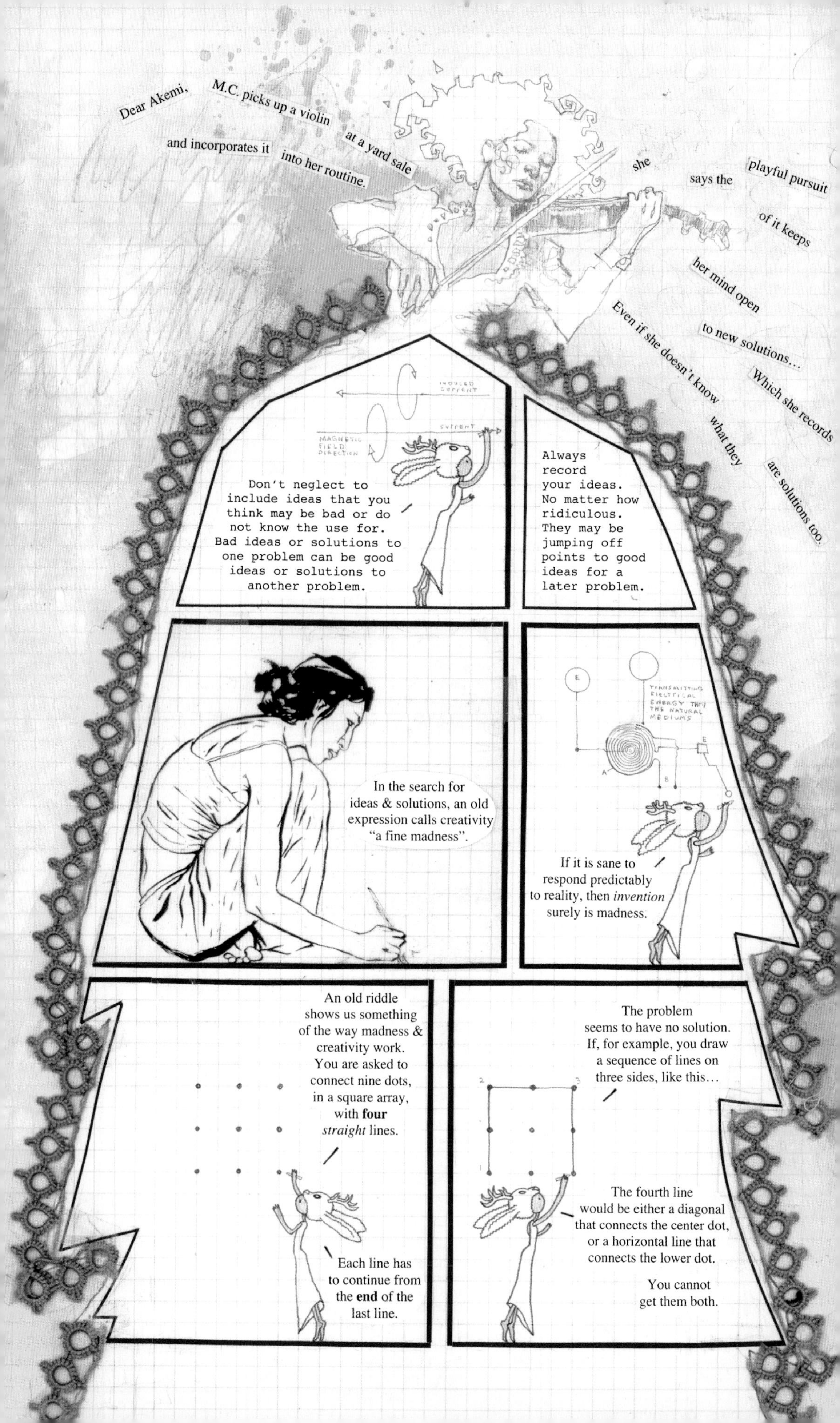
Dear Akemi,
M.C. picks up a violin at a yard sale and incorporates it into her routine.
she says the playful pursuit of it keeps her mind open to new solutions…
Which she records
Even if she doesn't know what they are solutions too.
INDUCED CURRENT
CURRENT
MAGNETIC FIELD DIRECTION
Don't neglect to include ideas that you think may be bad or do not know the use for. Bad ideas or solutions to one problem can be good ideas or solutions to another problem.
Always record your ideas. No matter how ridiculous. They may be jumping off points to good ideas for a later problem.
In the search for ideas & solutions, an old expression calls creativity "a fine madness".
TRANSMITTING ELECTRICAL ENERGY THRU THE NATURAL MEDIUMS
If it is sane to respond predictably to reality, then *invention* surely is madness.
An old riddle shows us something of the way madness & creativity work. You are asked to connect nine dots, in a square array, with **four** *straight* lines.
Each line has to continue from the **end** of the last line.
The problem seems to have no solution. If, for example, you draw a sequence of lines on three sides, like this…
The fourth line would be either a diagonal that connects the center dot, or a horizontal line that connects the lower dot.
You cannot get them both.

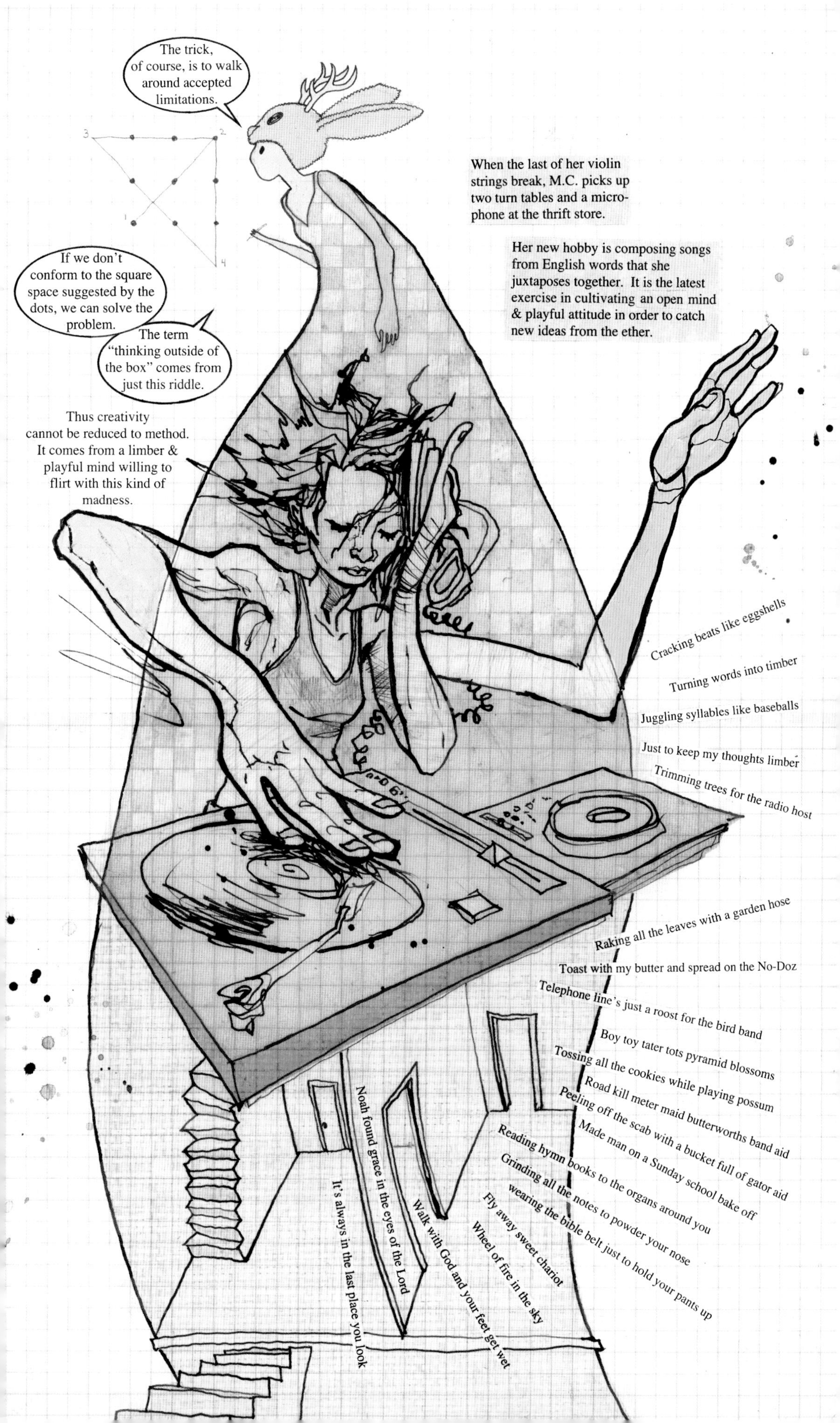
The trick, of course, is to walk around accepted limitations.
If we don't conform to the square space suggested by the dots, we can solve the problem.
The term "thinking outside of the box" comes from just this riddle.
Thus creativity cannot be reduced to method. It comes from a limber & playful mind willing to flirt with this kind of madness.
When the last of her violin strings break, M.C. picks up two turn tables and a microphone at the thrift store.
Her new hobby is composing songs from English words that she juxtaposes together. It is the latest exercise in cultivating an open mind & playful attitude in order to catch new ideas from the ether.
Cracking beats like eggshells
Turning words into timber
Juggling syllables like baseballs
Just to keep my thoughts limber
Trimming trees for the radio host
Raking all the leaves with a garden hose
Toast with my butter and spread on the No-Doz
Telephone line's just a roost for the bird band
Boy toy tater tots pyramid blossoms
Tossing all the cookies while playing possum
Road kill meter maid butterworths band aid
Peeling off the scab with a bucket full of gator aid
Made man on a Sunday school bake off
Reading hymn books to the organs around you
Grinding all the notes to powder your nose
wearing the bible belt just to hold your pants up
Fly away sweet chariot
Wheel of fire in the sky
Walk with God and your feet get wet
Noah found grace in the eyes of the Lord
It's always in the last place you look

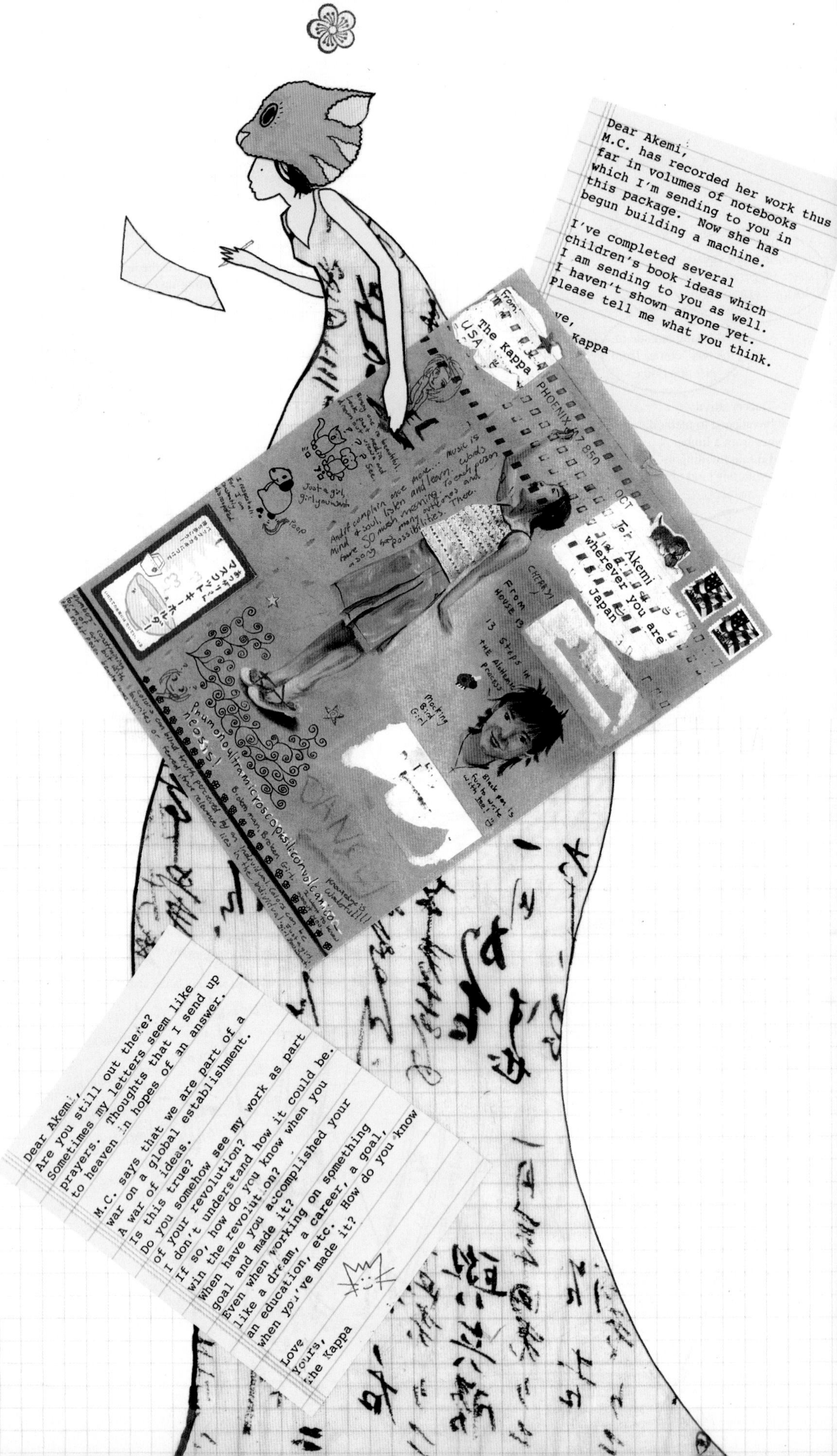
Dear Akemi,
M.C. has recorded her work thus far in volumes of notebooks which I'm sending to you in this package. Now she has begun building a machine.
I've completed several children's book ideas which I am sending to you as well. I haven't shown anyone yet. Please tell me what you think.
ve,
Kappa
From:
The Kappa
USA
PHOENIX
OCT
To: Akemi
wherever you are
Japan
Dear Akemi,
Are you still out there?
Sometimes my letters seem like prayers. Thoughts that I send up to heaven in hopes of an answer.
M.C. says that we are part of a war on a global establishment. A war of ideas.
Is this true?
Do you somehow see my work as part of your revolution?
I don't understand how it could be.
If so, how do you know when you win the revolution?
When have you accomplished your goal and made it?
Even when working on something like a dream, a career, a goal, an education, etc. How do you know when you've made it?
Love
Yours,
The Kappa

Arnold Schwarzenegger
321 Hampton Drive
Suite 203 Venice
Ca. 90291
U.S.A.
LETECKY
PAR AVION
From: AKEMIX
CESKOSLOVENSKO
EUROPA
PABLO NERUDA
1904–1973
Ceskoslovensko

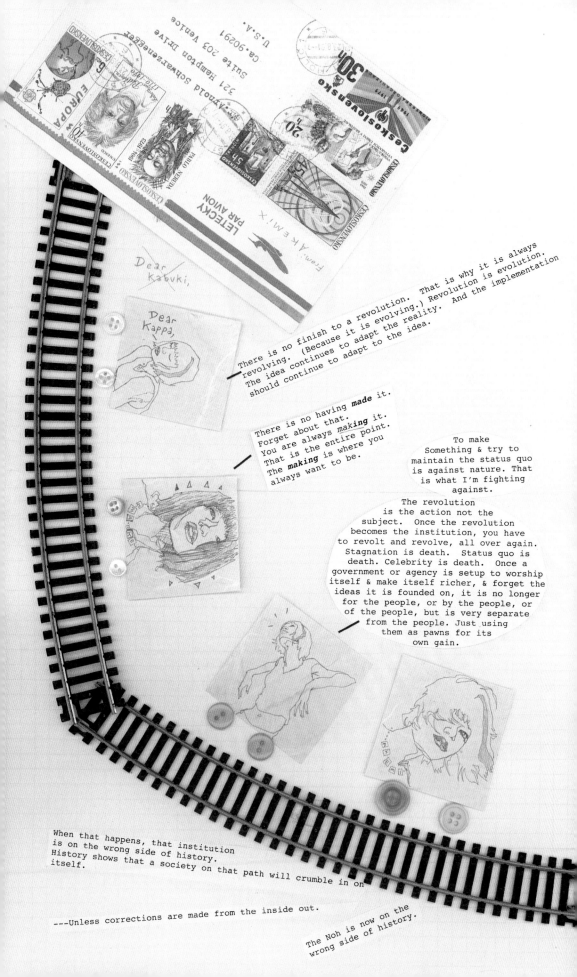

Dear ~~Kabuki~~,

Dear
Kappa,

There is no finish to a revolution. That is why it is always revolving. (Because it is evolving.) Revolution is evolution. The idea continues to adapt the reality. And the implementation should continue to adapt to the idea.

There is no having **made** it. Forget about that. You are always <u>making</u> it. That is the entire point. The **making** is where you always want to be.

To make Something & try to maintain the status quo is against nature. That is what I'm fighting against.

The revolution is the action not the subject. Once the revolution becomes the institution, you have to revolt and revolve, all over again. Stagnation is death. Status quo is death. Celebrity is death. Once a government or agency is setup to worship itself & make itself richer, & forget the ideas it is founded on, it is no longer for the people, or by the people, or of the people, but is very separate from the people. Just using them as pawns for its own gain.

When that happens, that institution is on the wrong side of history. History shows that a society on that path will crumble in on itself.

---Unless corrections are made from the inside out.

The Noh is now on the wrong side of history.

You have to roll with history.
Adapt to it. Be ahead of it and
not behind it.

Is this an ongoing war on a
corrupt power structure?
A war of ideas?

Not in the sense of
The Art of War.

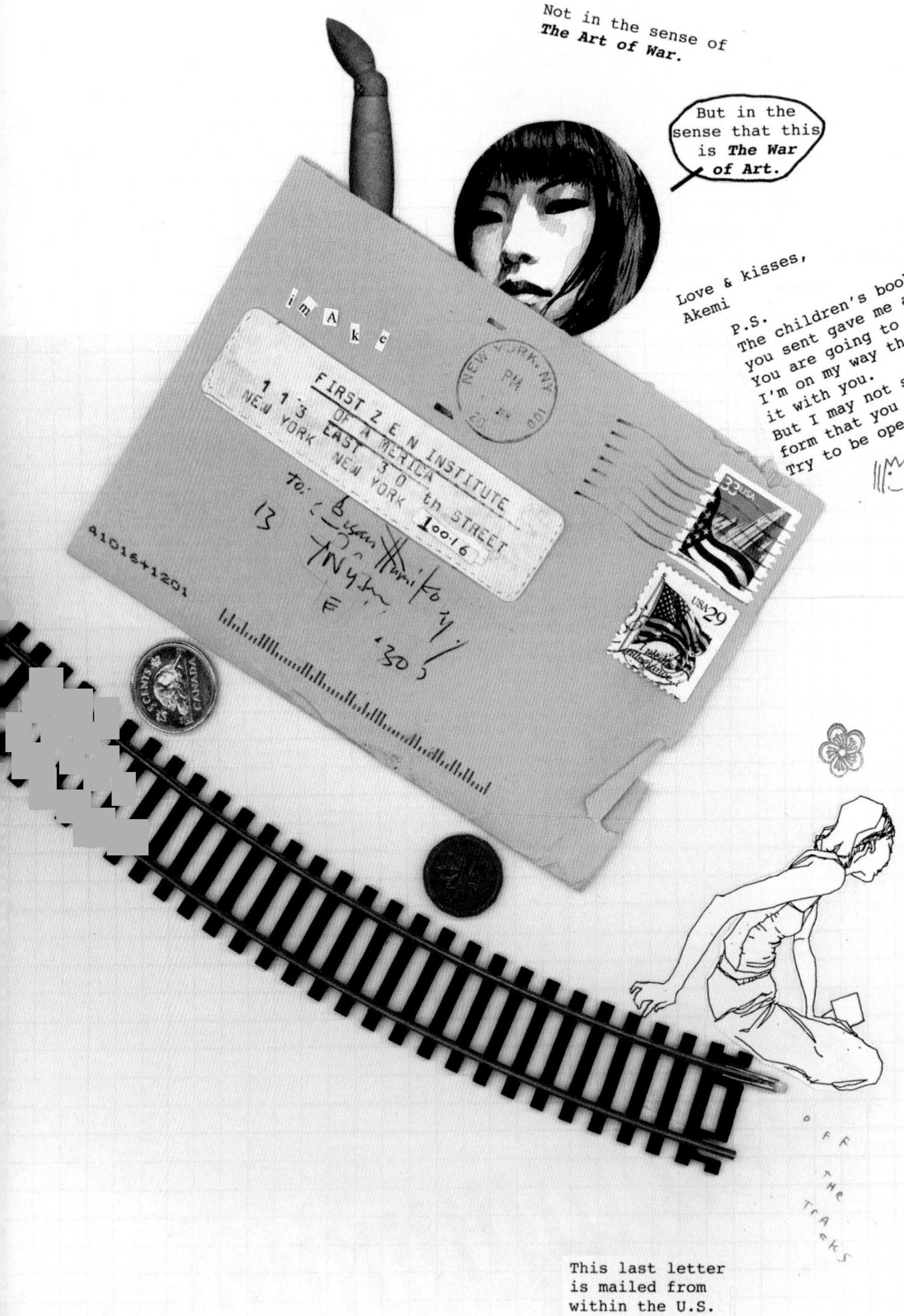

But in the sense that this is ***The War of Art.***
im Ake
FIRST ZEN INSTITUTE
OF AMERICA
113 EAST 30 th STREET
NEW YORK NEW YORK 10016
NEW YORK, NY
OFF THE TRACKS

Love & kisses,
Akemi

P.S.
The children's book proposals
you sent gave me a great idea!
You are going to love it.
I'm on my way there to discuss
it with you.
But I may not show up in the
form that you are used to.
Try to be open minded.

This last letter
is mailed from
within the U.S.

Akemi
is here.

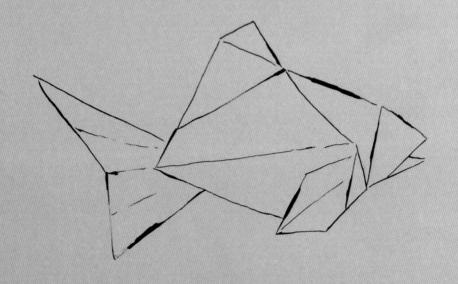

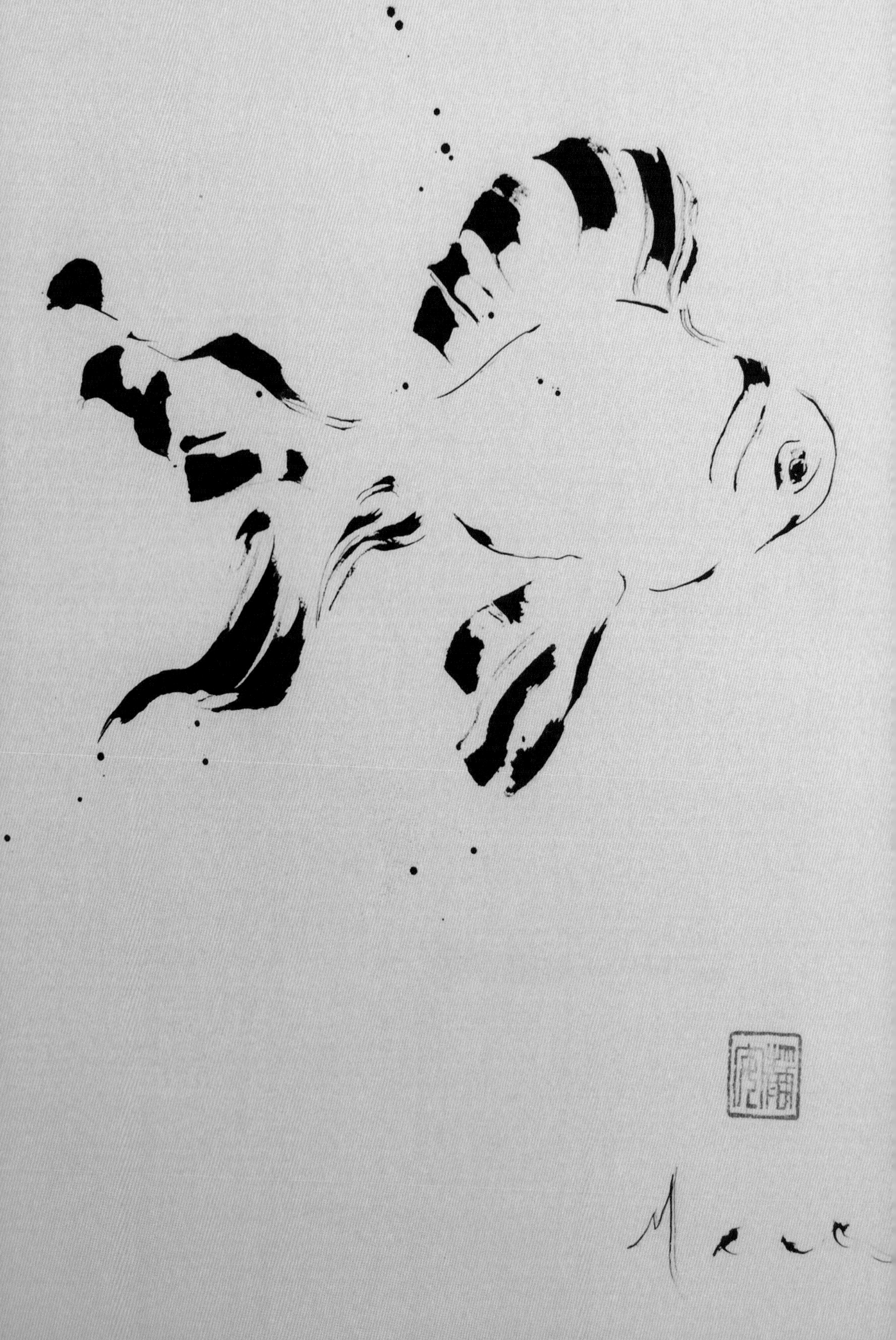

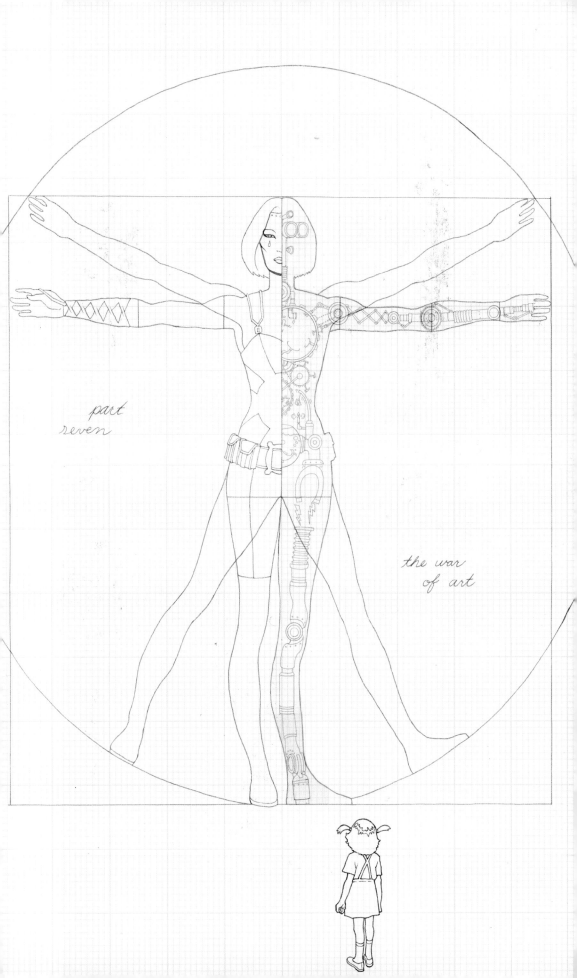

part
seven

the war
of art

The Alchemy

Part Seven

"80% of success is just showing up"
-Woody Allen

"It is one thing to study war and another to live the warrior's life"
-Telamon of Arcadia

"Talent is the innate power to discover the hidden connection between two things… and create for the world a third utterly unique work."
-Robert Mckee

"Whatever you can do, or dream you can, begin it now. Boldness has genius, magic, and power in it"
-Goethe

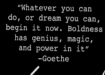

"There is no one that is youer than you"
-Dr. Seuss

"You're nobody until somebody kills you"
-Notorious B.I.G.

"Be prepared to give up the life you imagined for the life that is waiting for you"
-Joseph Campbell

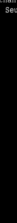

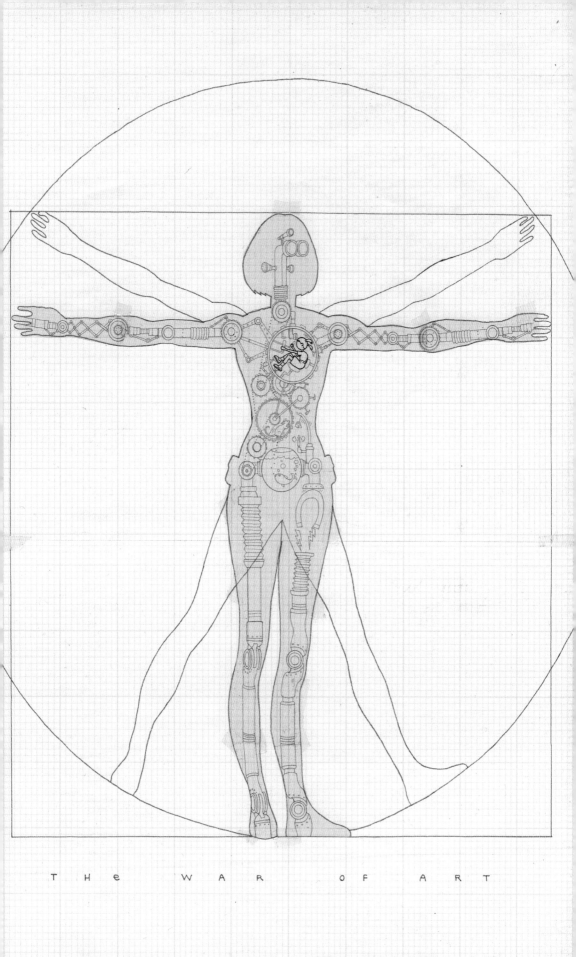

THE WAR OF ART

Dear Akemi,

I write to you in my journal as I wait for you to arrive.

M.C. Square has completed building her Zero-point energy machine. It's an electrical generator that harnesses electricity from the air waves. Apparently it gleans ambient energy from the atmosphere.

P.S.
We've picked up a few more stray cats that follow us as we walk home from our job at Noh Land.

Love,
Kappa

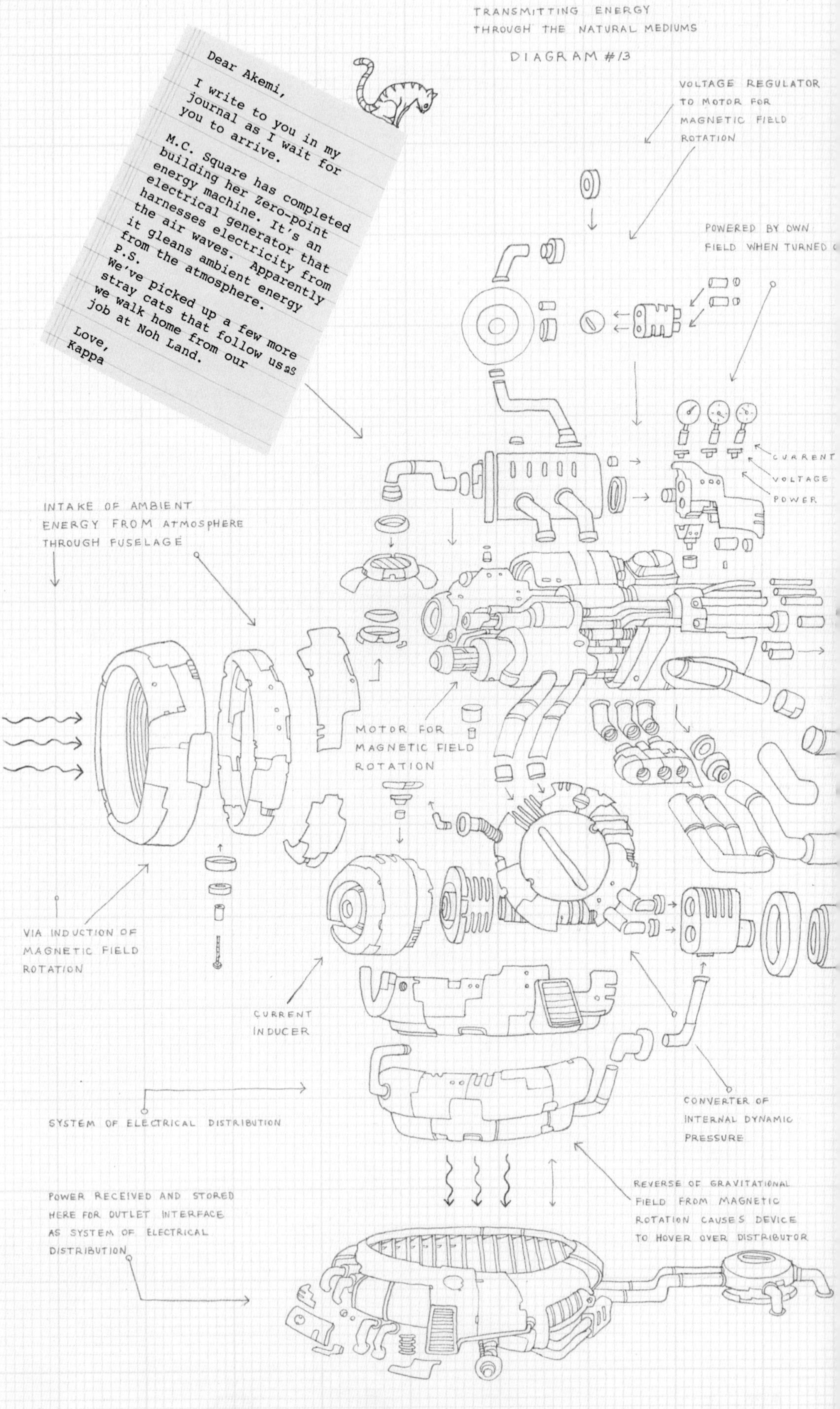
TRANSMITTING ENERGY THROUGH THE NATURAL MEDIUMS
DIAGRAM #13
VOLTAGE REGULATOR TO MOTOR FOR MAGNETIC FIELD ROTATION
POWERED BY OWN FIELD WHEN TURNED O
CURRENT
VOLTAGE
POWER
INTAKE OF AMBIENT ENERGY FROM ATMOSPHERE THROUGH FUSELAGE
MOTOR FOR MAGNETIC FIELD ROTATION
VIA INDUCTION OF MAGNETIC FIELD ROTATION
CURRENT INDUCER
SYSTEM OF ELECTRICAL DISTRIBUTION
CONVERTER OF INTERNAL DYNAMIC PRESSURE
REVERSE OF GRAVITATIONAL FIELD FROM MAGNETIC ROTATION CAUSES DEVICE TO HOVER OVER DISTRIBUTOR
POWER RECEIVED AND STORED HERE FOR OUTLET INTERFACE AS SYSTEM OF ELECTRICAL DISTRIBUTION

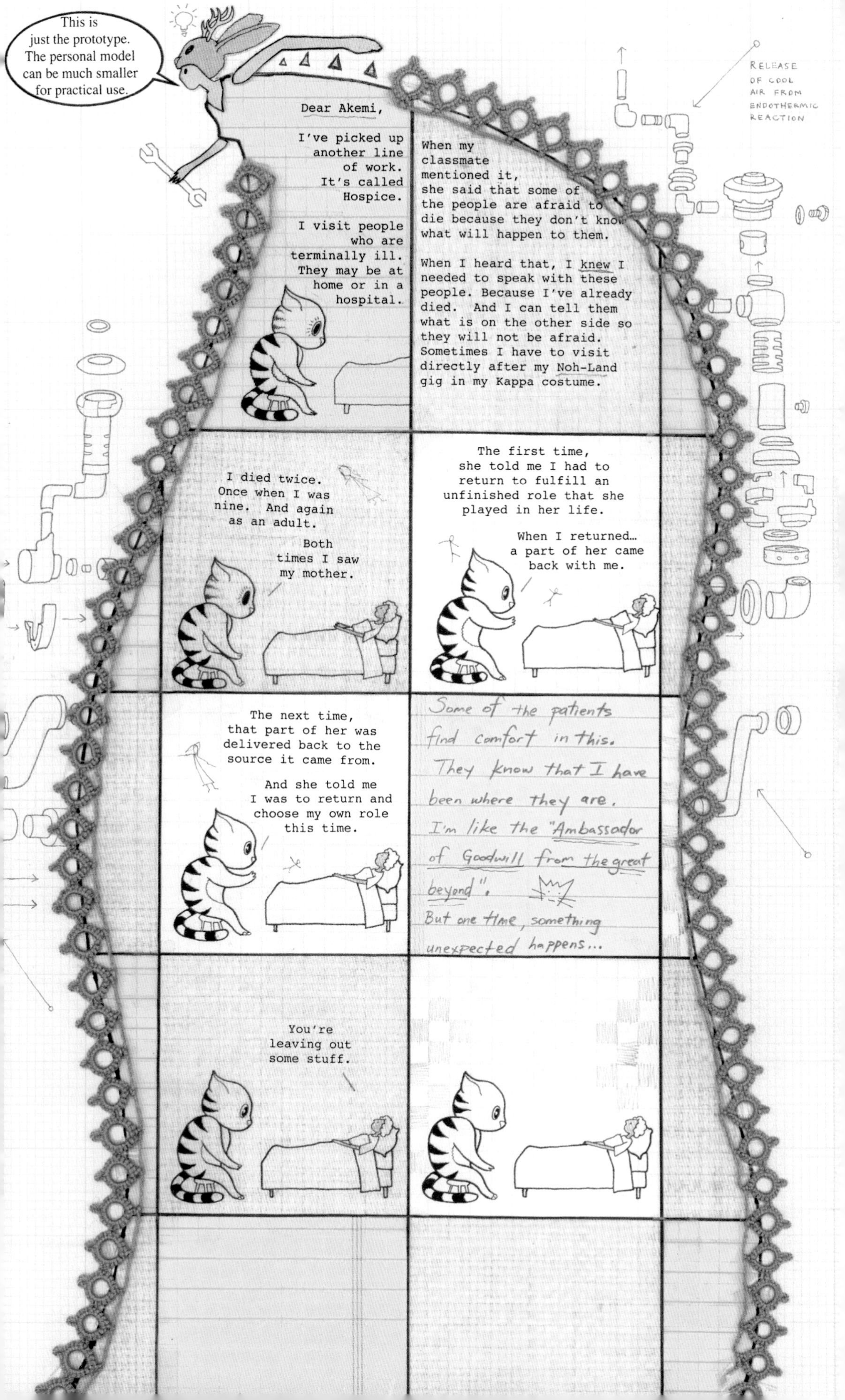
This is just the prototype. The personal model can be much smaller for practical use.
RELEASE OF COOL AIR FROM ENDOTHERMIC REACTION
Dear Akemi,
I've picked up another line of work. It's called Hospice.
I visit people who are terminally ill. They may be at home or in a hospital.
When my classmate mentioned it, she said that some of the people are afraid to die because they don't know what will happen to them.
When I heard that, I knew I needed to speak with these people. Because I've already died. And I can tell them what is on the other side so they will not be afraid. Sometimes I have to visit directly after my Noh-Land gig in my Kappa costume.
I died twice. Once when I was nine. And again as an adult.
Both times I saw my mother.
The first time, she told me I had to return to fulfill an unfinished role that she played in her life.
When I returned... a part of her came back with me.
The next time, that part of her was delivered back to the source it came from.
And she told me I was to return and choose my own role this time.
Some of the patients find comfort in this. They know that I have been where they are. I'm like the "Ambassador of Goodwill from the great beyond".
But one time, something unexpected happens...
You're leaving out some stuff.

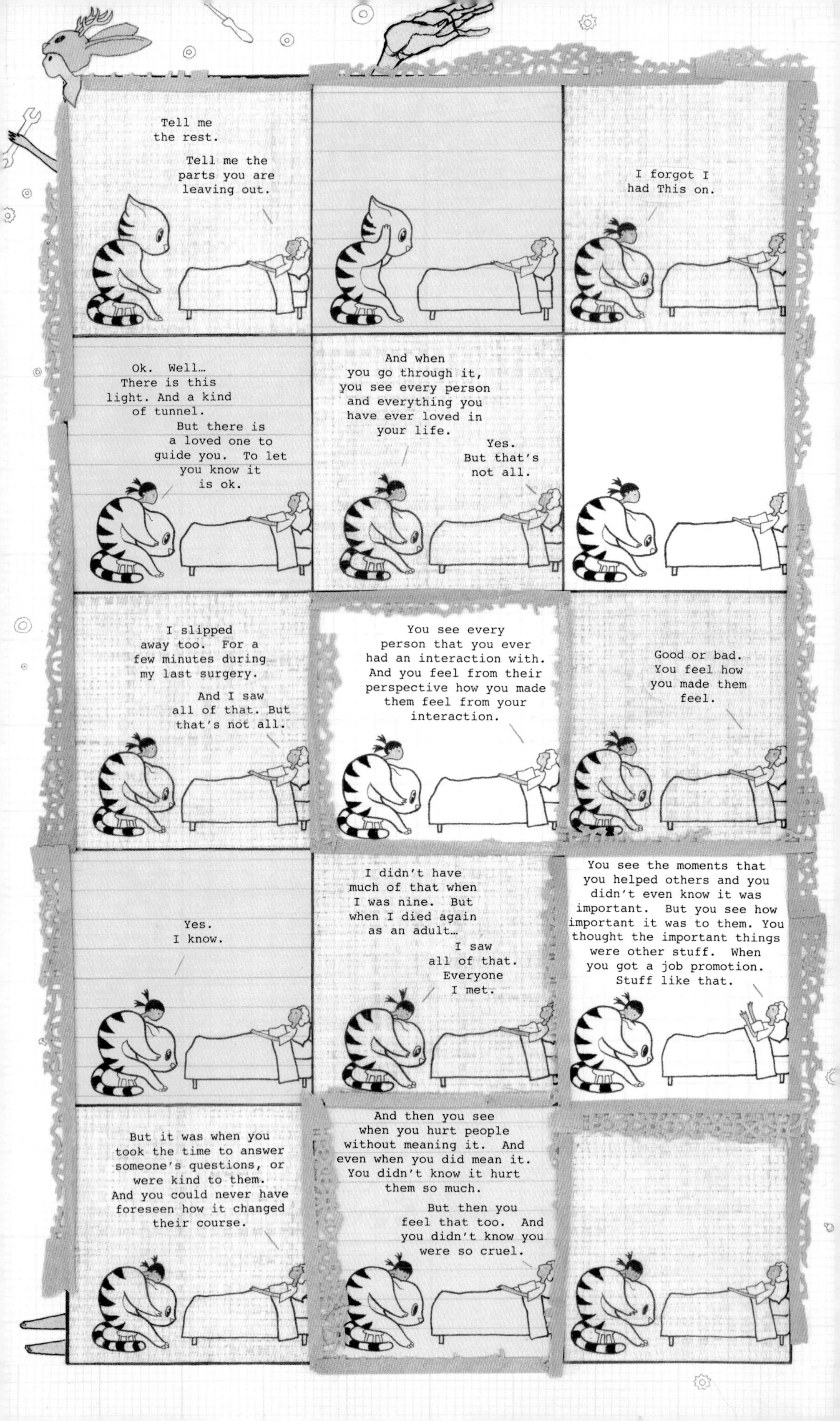
Tell me the rest.
Tell me the parts you are leaving out.
I forgot I had This on.
Ok. Well… There is this light. And a kind of tunnel.
But there is a loved one to guide you. To let you know it is ok.
And when you go through it, you see every person and everything you have ever loved in your life.
Yes. But that's not all.
I slipped away too. For a few minutes during my last surgery.
And I saw all of that. But that's not all.
You see every person that you ever had an interaction with. And you feel from their perspective how you made them feel from your interaction.
Good or bad. You feel how you made them feel.
Yes. I know.
I didn't have much of that when I was nine. But when I died again as an adult…
I saw all of that. Everyone I met.
You see the moments that you helped others and you didn't even know it was important. But you see how important it was to them. You thought the important things were other stuff. When you got a job promotion. Stuff like that.
But it was when you took the time to answer someone's questions, or were kind to them. And you could never have foreseen how it changed their course.
And then you see when you hurt people without meaning it. And even when you did mean it. You didn't know it hurt them so much.
But then you feel that too. And you didn't know you were so cruel.

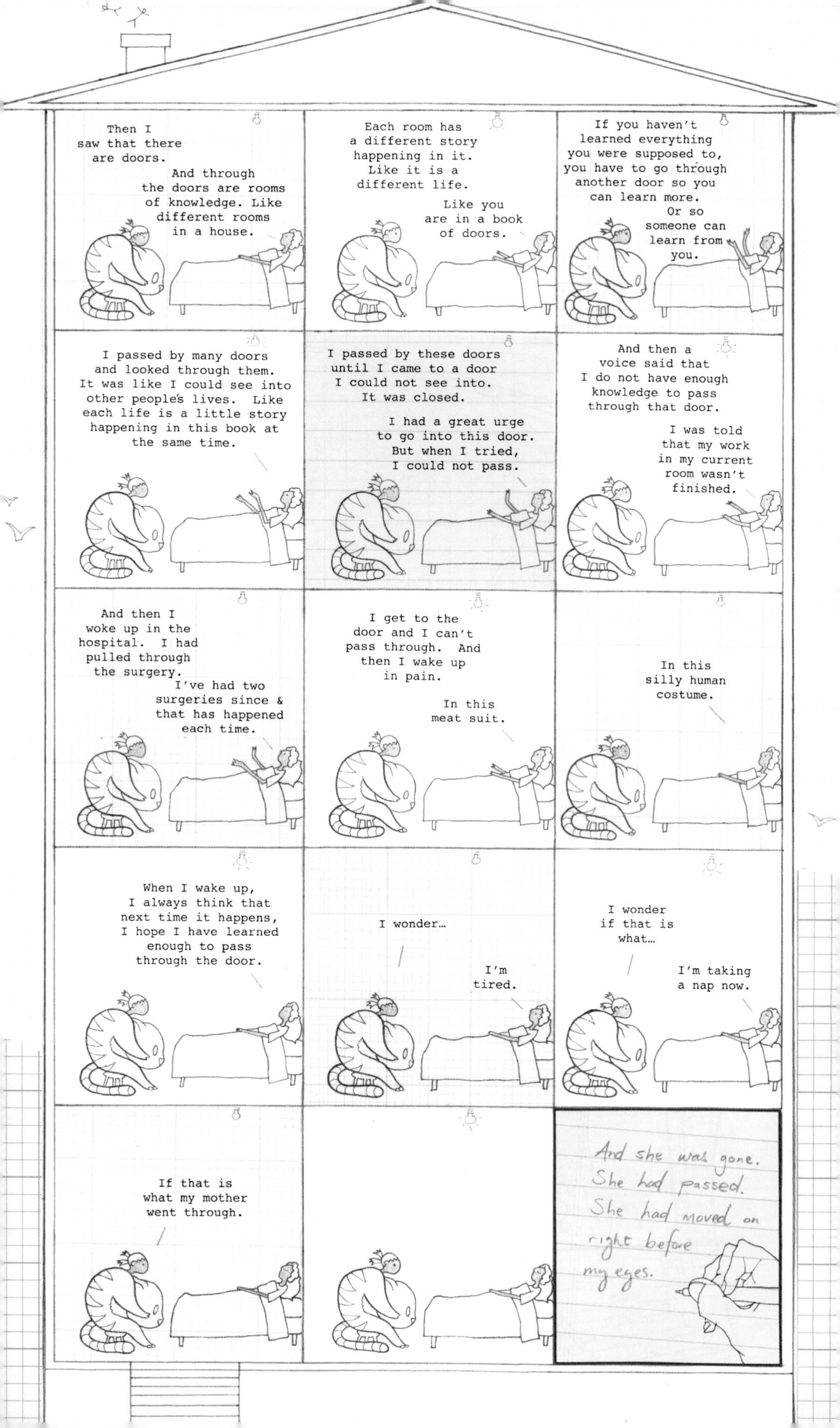
Then I saw that there are doors.
And through the doors are rooms of knowledge. Like different rooms in a house.
Each room has a different story happening in it. Like it is a different life.
Like you are in a book of doors.
If you haven't learned everything you were supposed to, you have to go through another door so you can learn more.
Or so someone can learn from you.
I passed by many doors and looked through them. It was like I could see into other people's lives. Like each life is a little story happening in this book at the same time.
I passed by these doors until I came to a door I could not see into. It was closed.
I had a great urge to go into this door. But when I tried, I could not pass.
And then a voice said that I do not have enough knowledge to pass through that door.
I was told that my work in my current room wasn't finished.
And then I woke up in the hospital. I had pulled through the surgery.
I've had two surgeries since & that has happened each time.
I get to the door and I can't pass through. And then I wake up in pain.
In this meat suit.
In this silly human costume.
When I wake up, I always think that next time it happens, I hope I have learned enough to pass through the door.
I wonder…
I'm tired.
I wonder if that is what…
I'm taking a nap now.
If that is what my mother went through.
And she was gone. She had passed. She had moved on right before my eyes.

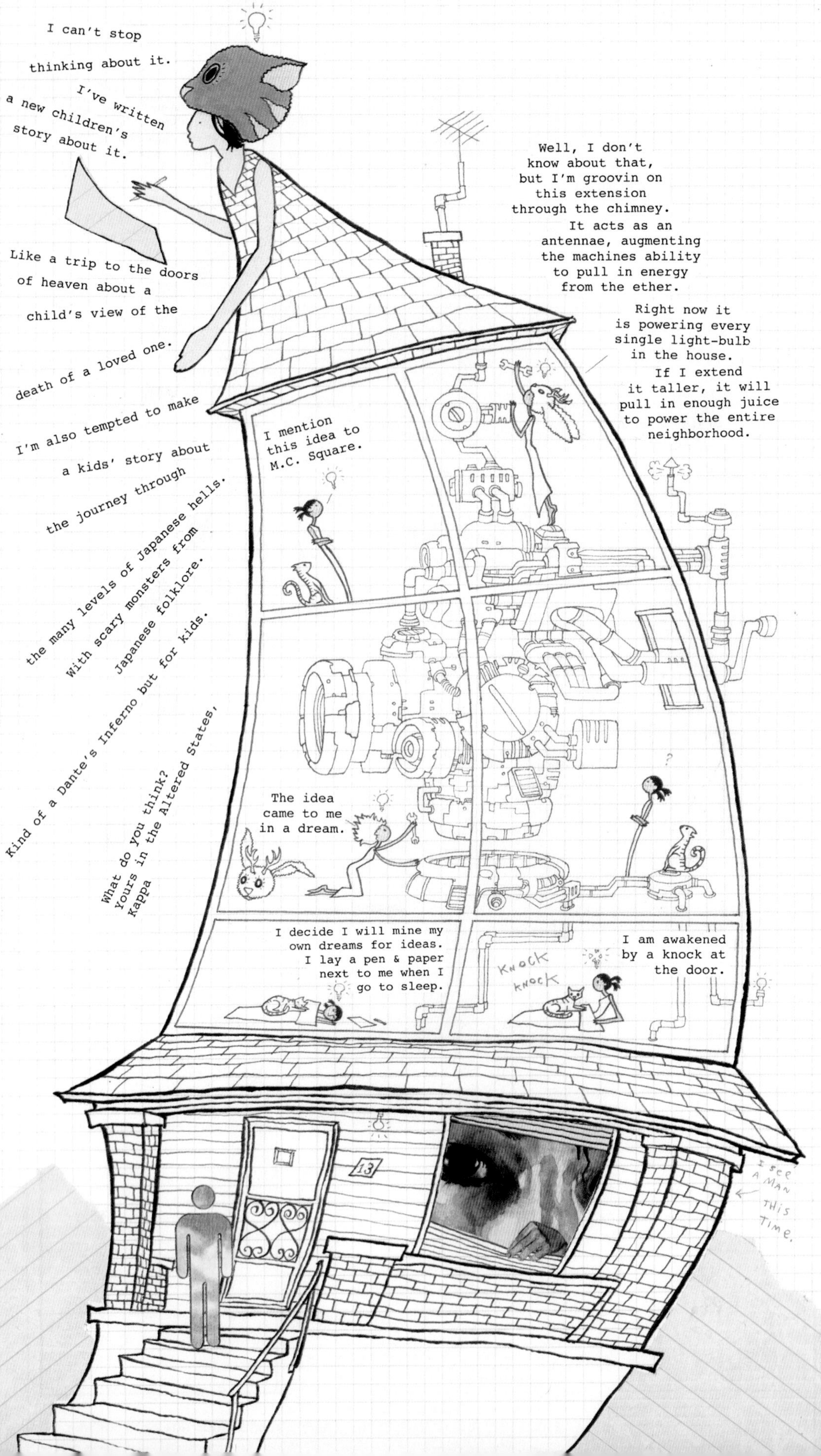

I can't stop thinking about it.
I've written a new children's story about it.
Like a trip to the doors of heaven about a child's view of the death of a loved one.
I'm also tempted to make a kids' story about the journey through the many levels of Japanese hells.
With scary monsters from Japanese folklore.
Kind of a Dante's Inferno but for kids.
What do you think?
Yours in the Altered States,
Kappa
Well, I don't know about that, but I'm groovin on this extension through the chimney.
It acts as an antennae, augmenting the machines ability to pull in energy from the ether.
Right now it is powering every single light-bulb in the house.
If I extend it taller, it will pull in enough juice to power the entire neighborhood.
I mention this idea to M.C. Square.
The idea came to me in a dream.
?
I decide I will mine my own dreams for ideas. I lay a pen & paper next to me when I go to sleep.
KNOCK KNOCK
I am awakened by a knock at the door.
13
I SEE A MAN THIS TIME.

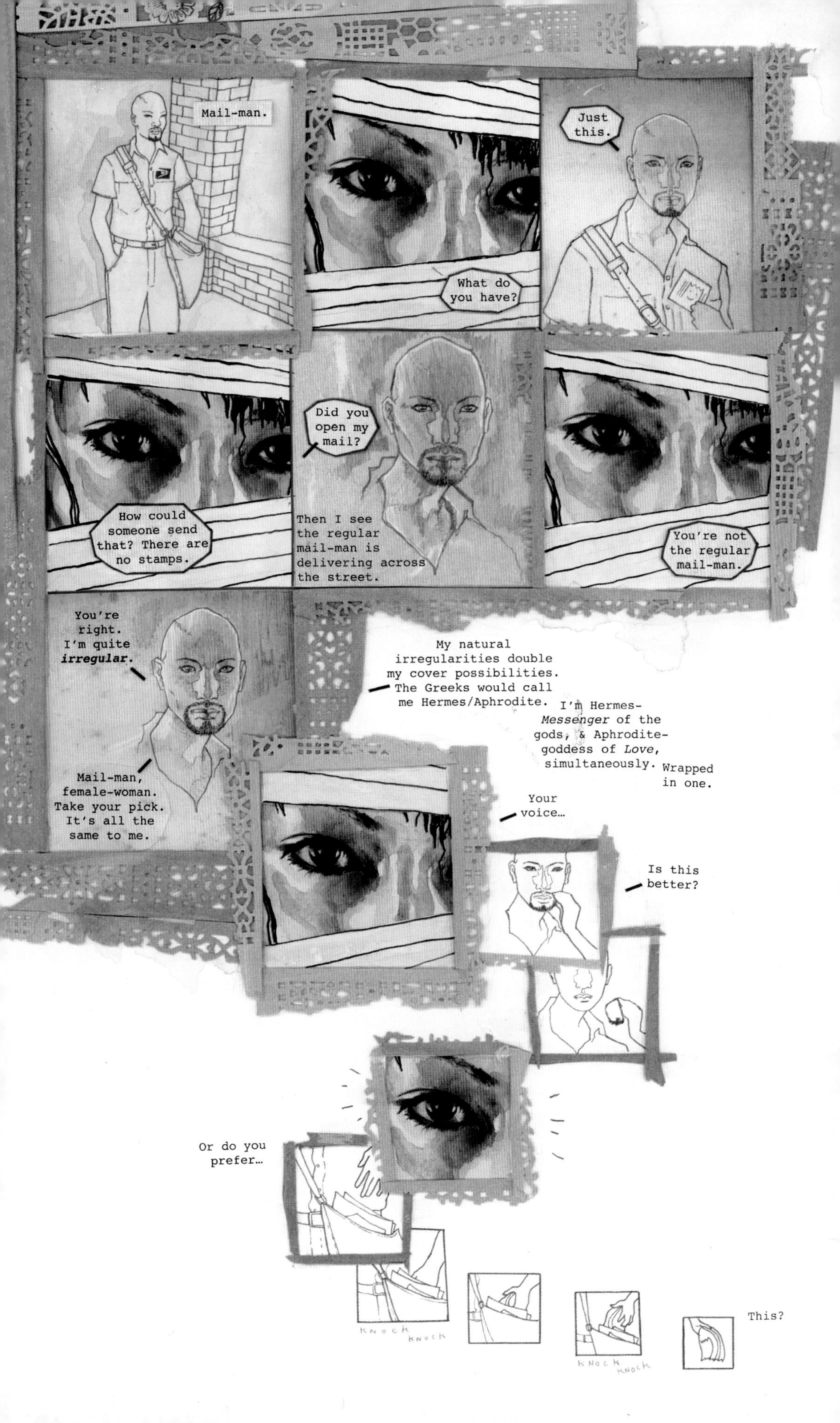

Mail-man.
What do you have?
Just this.
How could someone send that? There are no stamps.
Did you open my mail?
Then I see the regular mail-man is delivering across the street.
You're not the regular mail-man.
You're right. I'm quite ***irregular***.
Mail-man, female-woman. Take your pick. It's all the same to me.
My natural irregularities double my cover possibilities. The Greeks would call me Hermes/Aphrodite.
I'm Hermes- *Messenger* of the gods, & Aphrodite- goddess of *Love*, simultaneously.
Wrapped in one.
Your voice...
Is this better?
Or do you prefer...
KNOCK KNOCK
KNOCK KNOCK
This?

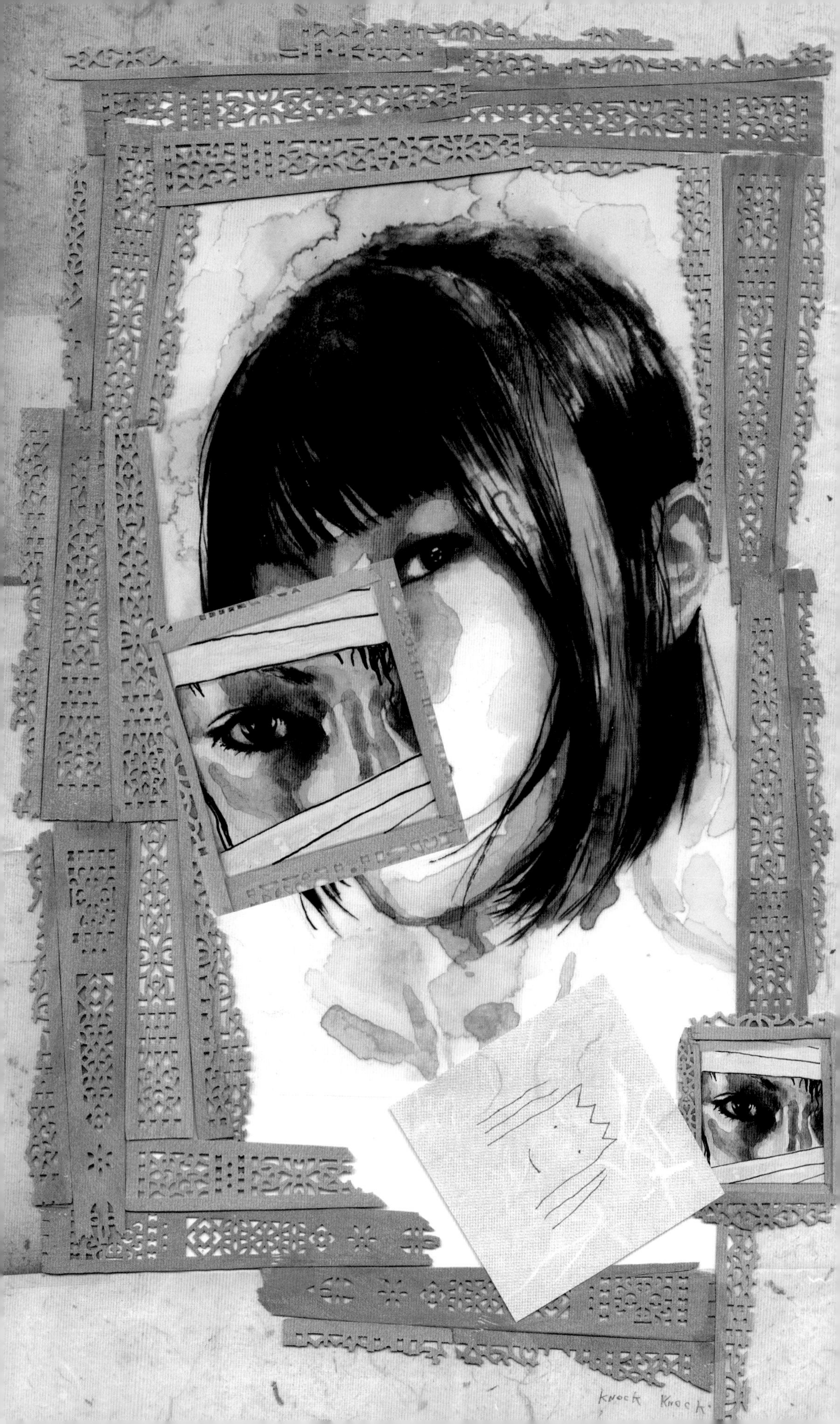
Knock Knock.

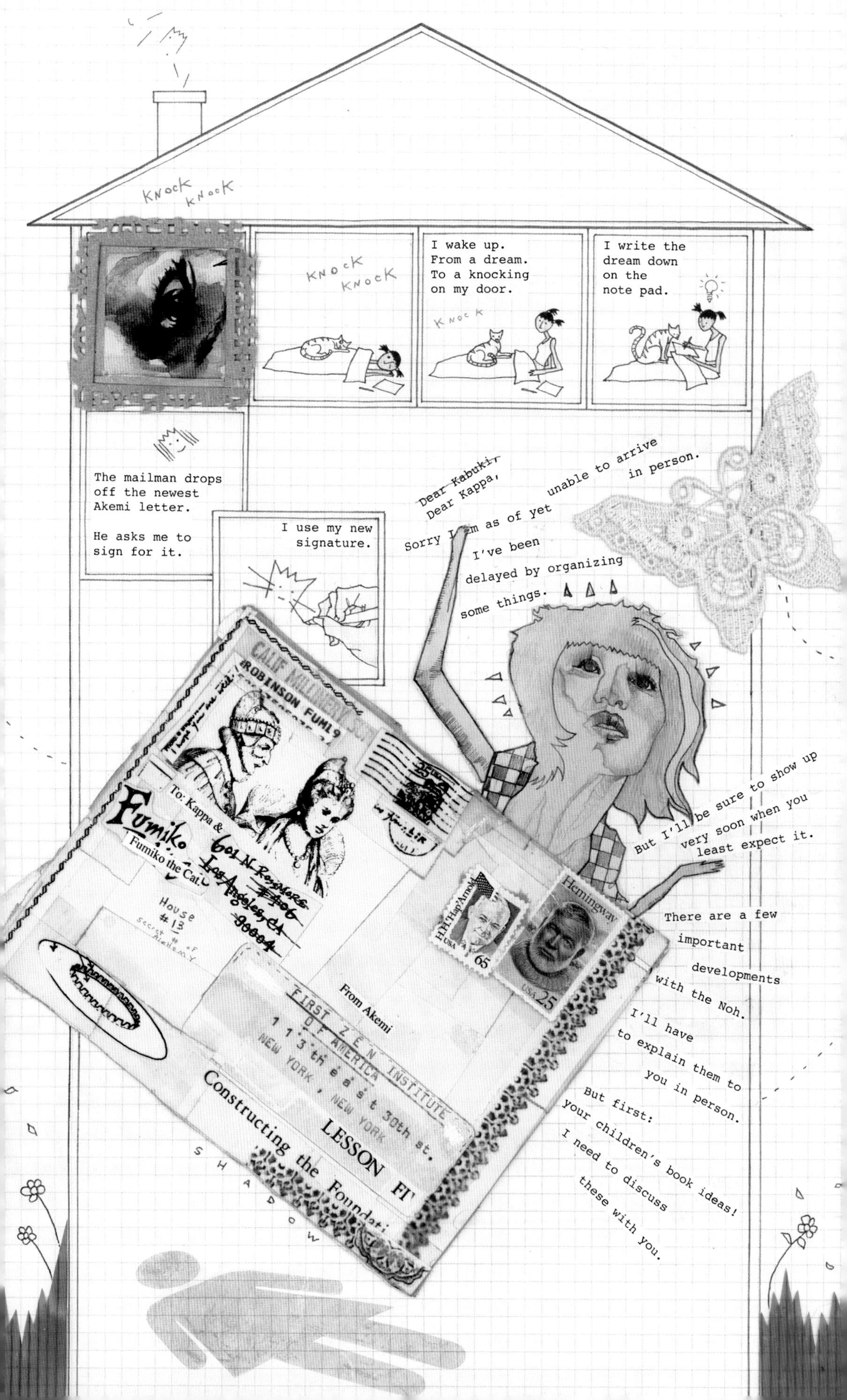
KNOCK KNOCK
KNOCK KNOCK
I wake up.
From a dream.
To a knocking
on my door.
KNOCK
I write the
dream down
on the
note pad.
The mailman drops
off the newest
Akemi letter.
He asks me to
sign for it.
I use my new
signature.
Dear Kabuki,
Dear Kappa,
Sorry I am as of yet unable to arrive in person.
I've been delayed by organizing some things.
But I'll be sure to show up very soon when you least expect it.
There are a few important developments with the Noh.
I'll have to explain them to you in person.
But first:
your children's book ideas!
I need to discuss these with you.
CALIF MILLINERY
ROBINSON FUMI9
To: Kappa &
Fumiko the Cat.
Fumiko
House #13
secret # of Alchemy
Hemingway
USA 25
H.H. 'Hap' Arnold
USA 65
From Akemi
FIRST ZEN INSTITUTE OF AMERICA
113 th east 30th st.
NEW YORK, NEW YORK
LESSON FI
Constructing the Foundati
SHADOW

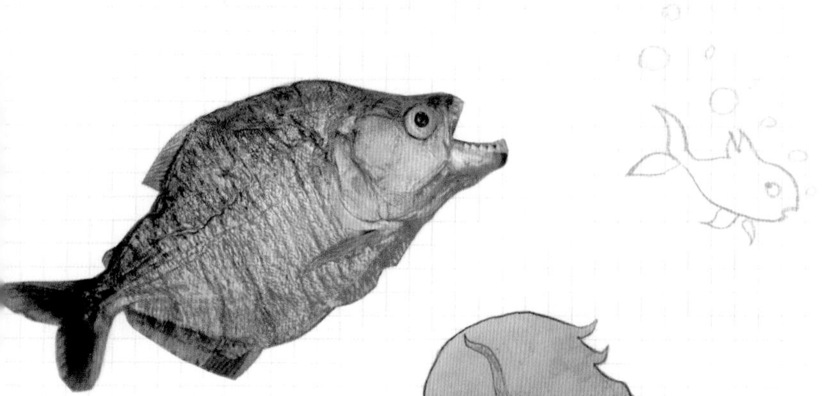

I love the
story you sent
about the goldfish
being flushed down
the toilet when she
is mistaken for
being dead…

And then
she is hunted
by the larger
fish…

Until she
grows much larger
herself and faces
them in a new
context.

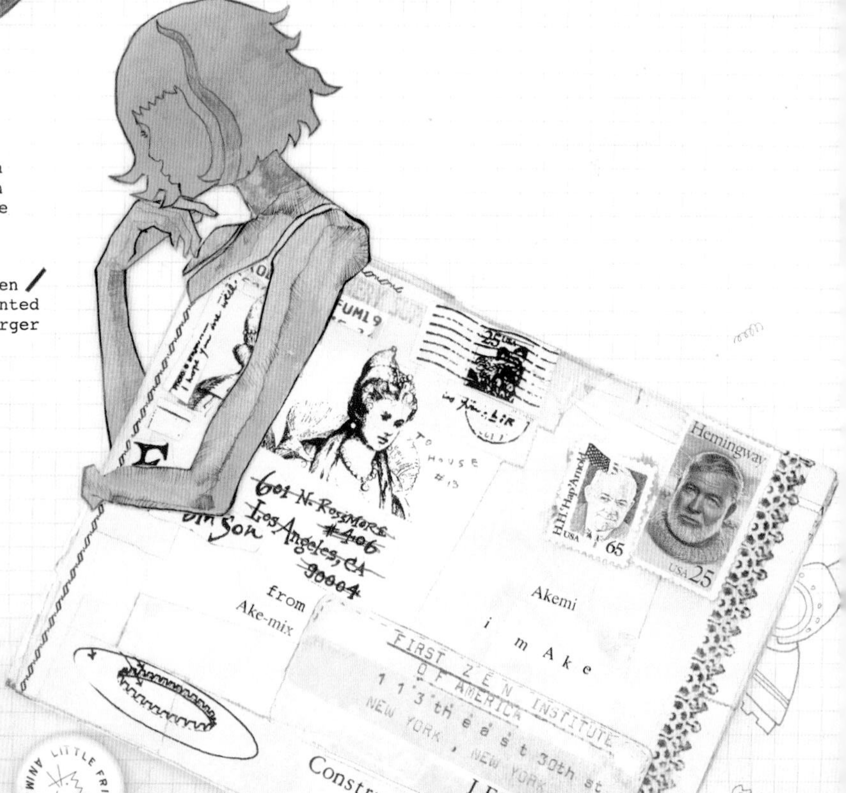
TO HOUSE #15
601 N. Rossmore #406
Los Angeles, CA 90004
from
Ake-mix
Hemingway
USA 25
H.H.'Hap'Arnold
USA 65
Akemi
i m Ake
FIRST ZEN INSTITUTE
OF AMERICA
113 th east 30th st.
NEW YORK, NEW YORK
LESSON FI
Constructing the Foundati
LITTLE FRIENDS
ANIMAL CLINIC

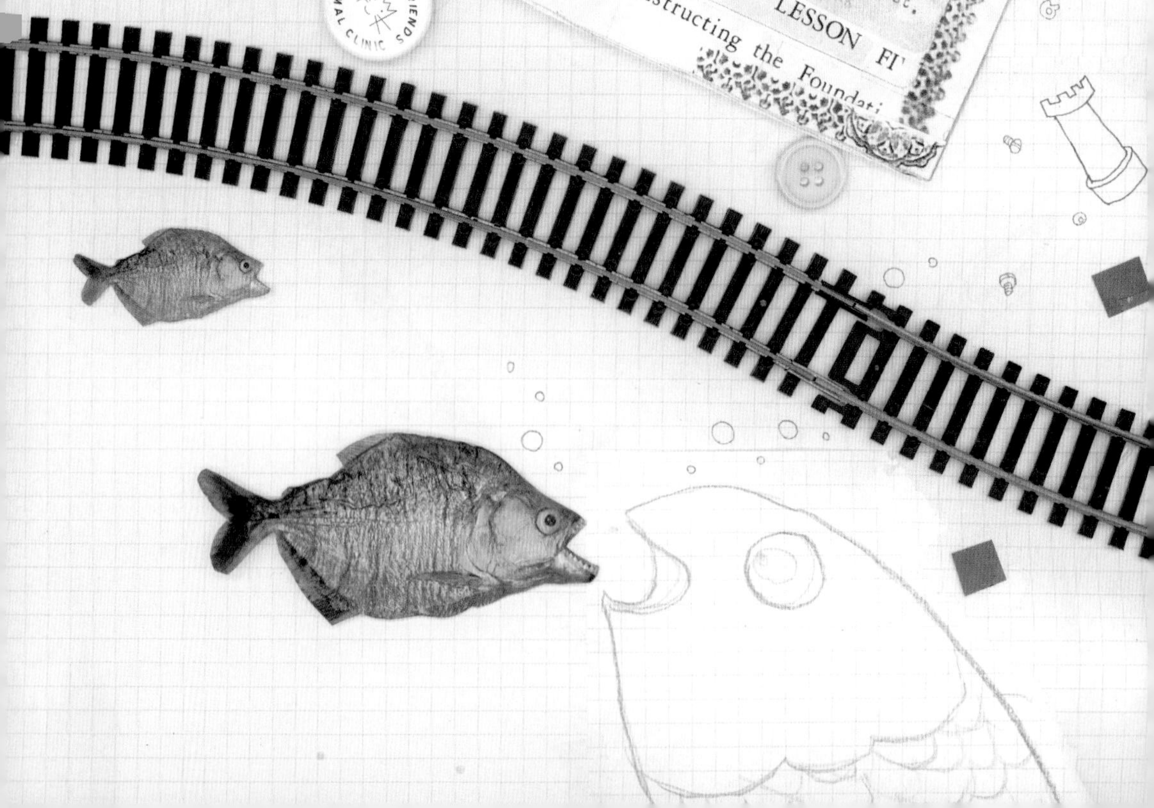

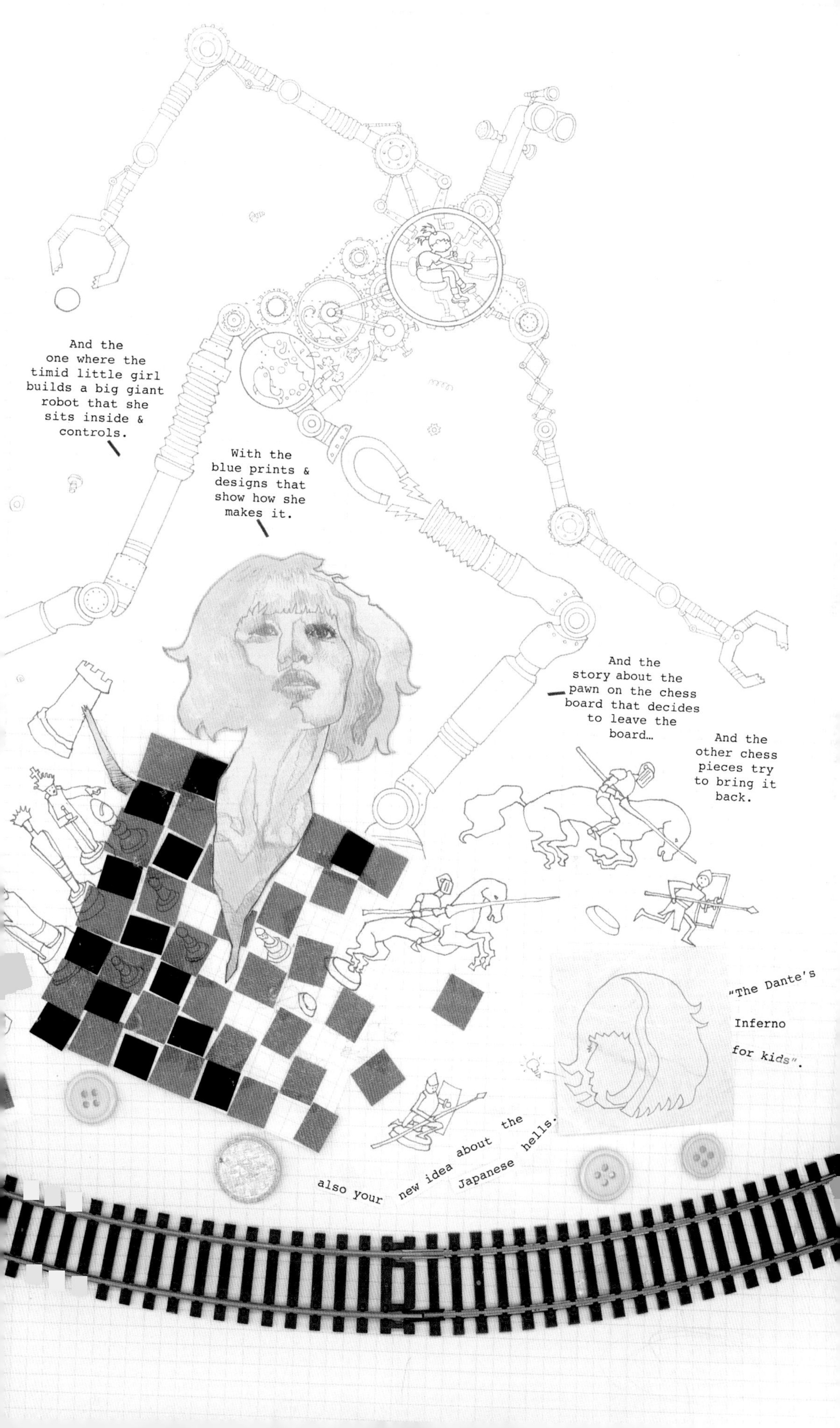
And the one where the timid little girl builds a big giant robot that she sits inside & controls.
With the blue prints & designs that show how she makes it.
And the story about the pawn on the chess board that decides to leave the board…
And the other chess pieces try to bring it back.
"The Dante's Inferno for kids".
also your new idea about the Japanese hells.

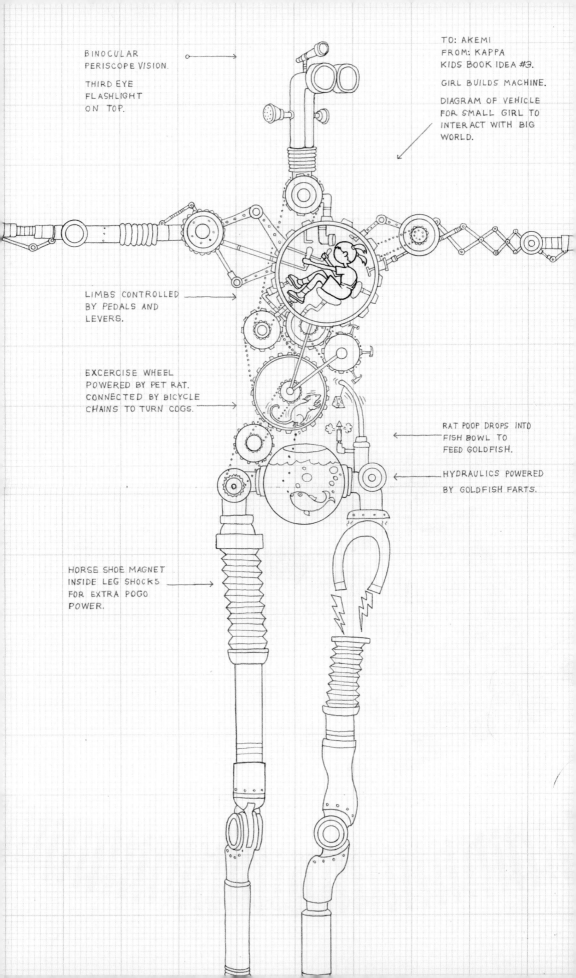

BINOCULAR
PERISCOPE VISION.

THIRD EYE
FLASHLIGHT
ON TOP.

TO: AKEMI
FROM: KAPPA
KIDS BOOK IDEA #3.

GIRL BUILDS MACHINE.

DIAGRAM OF VEHICLE
FOR SMALL GIRL TO
INTERACT WITH BIG
WORLD.

LIMBS CONTROLLED
BY PEDALS AND
LEVERS.

EXCERCISE WHEEL
POWERED BY PET RAT.
CONNECTED BY BICYCLE
CHAINS TO TURN COGS.

RAT POOP DROPS INTO
FISH BOWL TO
FEED GOLDFISH.

HYDRAULICS POWERED
BY GOLDFISH FARTS.

HORSE SHOE MAGNET
INSIDE LEG SHOCKS
FOR EXTRA POGO
POWER.

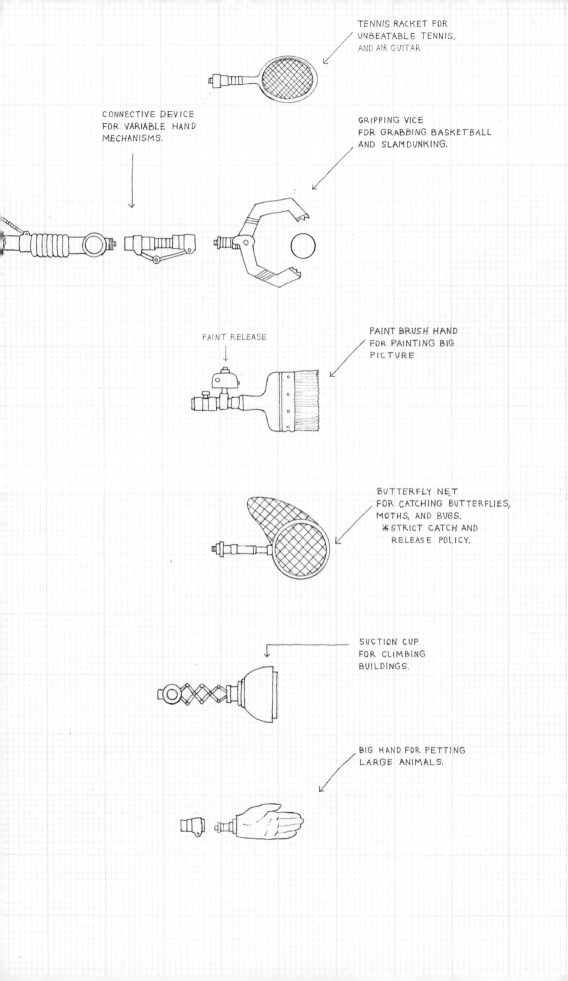

TENNIS RACKET FOR
UNBEATABLE TENNIS,
AND AIR GUITAR

CONNECTIVE DEVICE
FOR VARIABLE HAND
MECHANISMS.

GRIPPING VICE
FOR GRABBING BASKETBALL
AND SLAMDUNKING.

PAINT RELEASE

PAINT BRUSH HAND
FOR PAINTING BIG
PICTURE

BUTTERFLY NET
FOR CATCHING BUTTERFLIES,
MOTHS, AND BUGS.
✳STRICT CATCH AND
RELEASE POLICY.

SUCTION CUP
FOR CLIMBING
BUILDINGS.

BIG HAND FOR PETTING
LARGE ANIMALS.

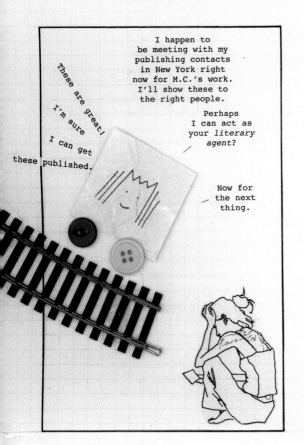

These are great! I'm sure I can get these published.

I happen to be meeting with my publishing contacts in New York right now for M.C.'s work. I'll show these to the right people.

Perhaps I can act as your *literary agent*?

Now for the next thing.

Let's jump off the tracks for this idea.

Though I don't know the details of your past, I can tell that these kids books are about you. Metaphors for your history.

These stories are still masks for you.

Which is fine. It is a progression from your previous mask that you used to interact with the world.

As long as you don't need a mask to interact with yourself.

Just as an experiment...

Why don't you peel away the mask entirely...

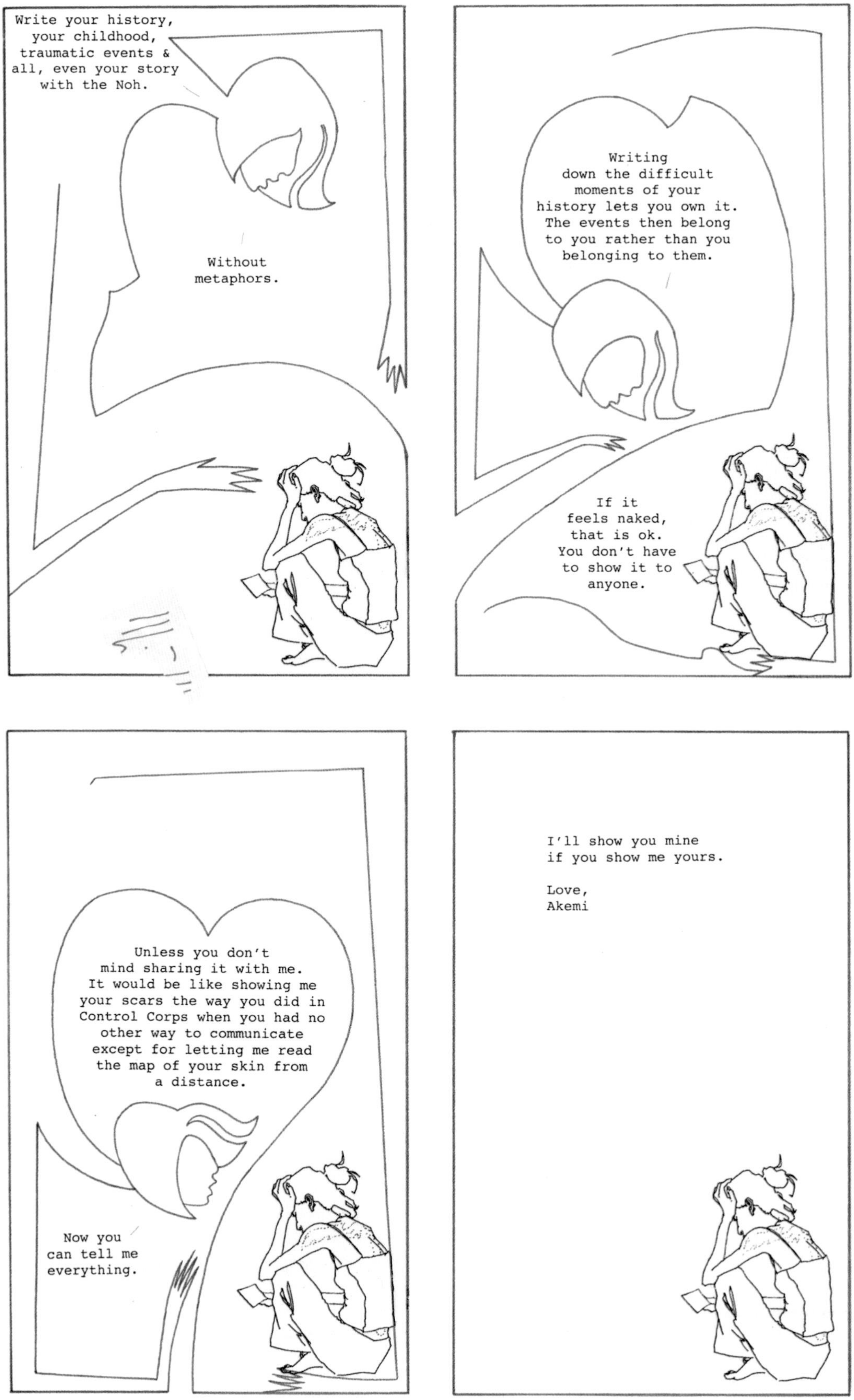
Write your history, your childhood, traumatic events & all, even your story with the Noh.
Without metaphors.
Writing down the difficult moments of your history lets you own it. The events then belong to you rather than you belonging to them.
If it feels naked, that is ok. You don't have to show it to anyone.
Unless you don't mind sharing it with me. It would be like showing me your scars the way you did in Control Corps when you had no other way to communicate except for letting me read the map of your skin from a distance.
Now you can tell me everything.
I'll show you mine if you show me yours.
Love,
Akemi

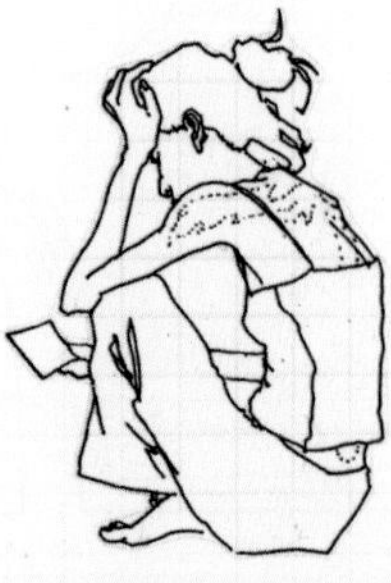

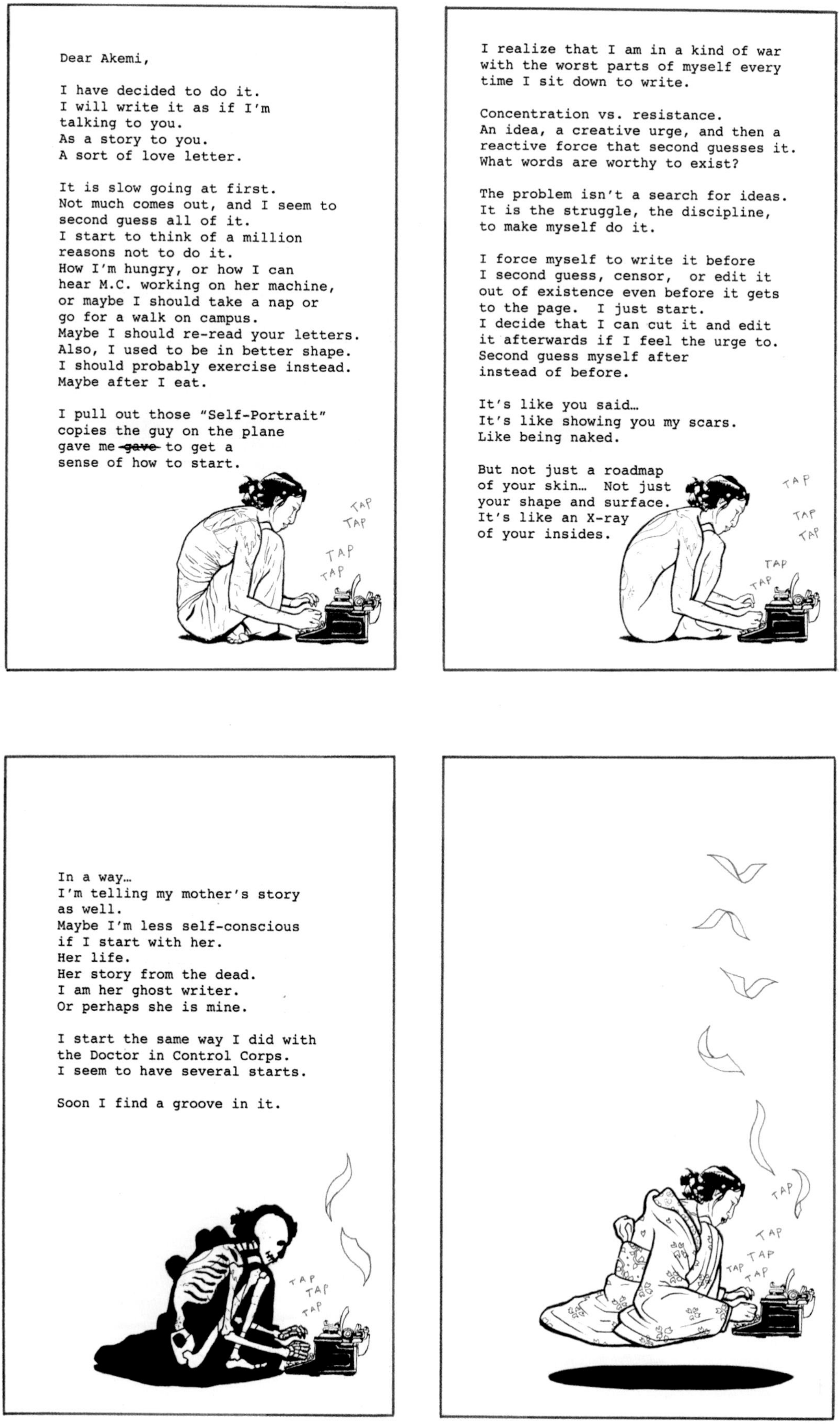
Dear Akemi,
I have decided to do it.
I will write it as if I'm talking to you.
As a story to you.
A sort of love letter.
It is slow going at first.
Not much comes out, and I seem to second guess all of it.
I start to think of a million reasons not to do it.
How I'm hungry, or how I can hear M.C. working on her machine, or maybe I should take a nap or go for a walk on campus.
Maybe I should re-read your letters.
Also, I used to be in better shape.
I should probably exercise instead.
Maybe after I eat.
I pull out those "Self-Portrait" copies the guy on the plane gave me ~~gave~~ to get a sense of how to start.
TAP
TAP
TAP
TAP
I realize that I am in a kind of war with the worst parts of myself every time I sit down to write.
Concentration vs. resistance.
An idea, a creative urge, and then a reactive force that second guesses it.
What words are worthy to exist?
The problem isn't a search for ideas.
It is the struggle, the discipline, to make myself do it.
I force myself to write it before I second guess, censor, or edit it out of existence even before it gets to the page. I just start.
I decide that I can cut it and edit it afterwards if I feel the urge to.
Second guess myself after instead of before.
It's like you said…
It's like showing you my scars.
Like being naked.
But not just a roadmap of your skin… Not just your shape and surface.
It's like an X-ray of your insides.
TAP
TAP
TAP
TAP
TAP
In a way…
I'm telling my mother's story as well.
Maybe I'm less self-conscious if I start with her.
Her life.
Her story from the dead.
I am her ghost writer.
Or perhaps she is mine.
I start the same way I did with the Doctor in Control Corps.
I seem to have several starts.
Soon I find a groove in it.
TAP
TAP
TAP
TAP
TAP
TAP
TAP
TAP

I come to realize that writing is like physical exercise. What counts is how much you can do after you think you are done.
Then the real challenge begins.
If you push through the barriers of your comfort zone, you hit a second wind.
It is mostly just showing up and doing it that counts.
Sometimes it is painful.
You may want to do something else.
And you can think of infinite reasons to stop.
I discover "The Power of Positive Doing".
Positive thinking is great.
It is a nice first step.
But if you don't do the "Positive Doing", it only takes you so far.
TAP TAP TAP
I Get a Letter back
Have you read *The War of Art?*
You mean *The Art of War* by Sun Tzu.
No. *The War of Art* by a writer named Pressfield. It names that force that distracts you from your calling, "Resistance".
"Most of us have 2 lives. The life we live and the unlived life within us. Between the 2 stands resistance".
TAP TAP TAP
Pressfield explains that the only way to combat resistance of something you must do is to put in the time & due diligence daily. Consider yourself a pro beforehand.
The pro knows that if you do the work, the muse will show up. You don't wait for the muse to show up first.
TAP TAP
"Someone asked Somerset Maugham if he wrote on a schedule or only when struck by inspiration. "I write only when inspiration strikes," he replied. "fortunately it strikes every morning at 9:00 sharp."
That's a pro.
There is a secret that real writers know that wannabe writers don't, and the secret is this: It's not the writing that is hard. What's hard is sitting down to write".
TAP TAP

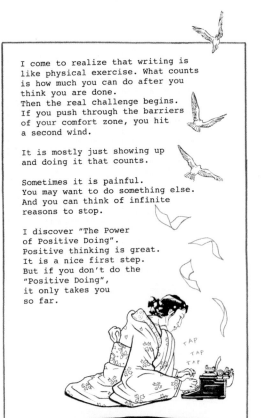

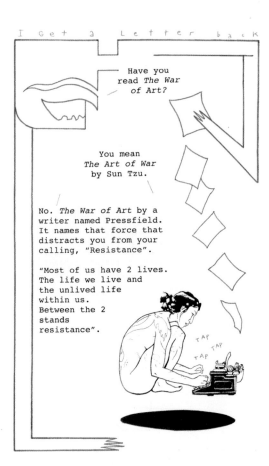

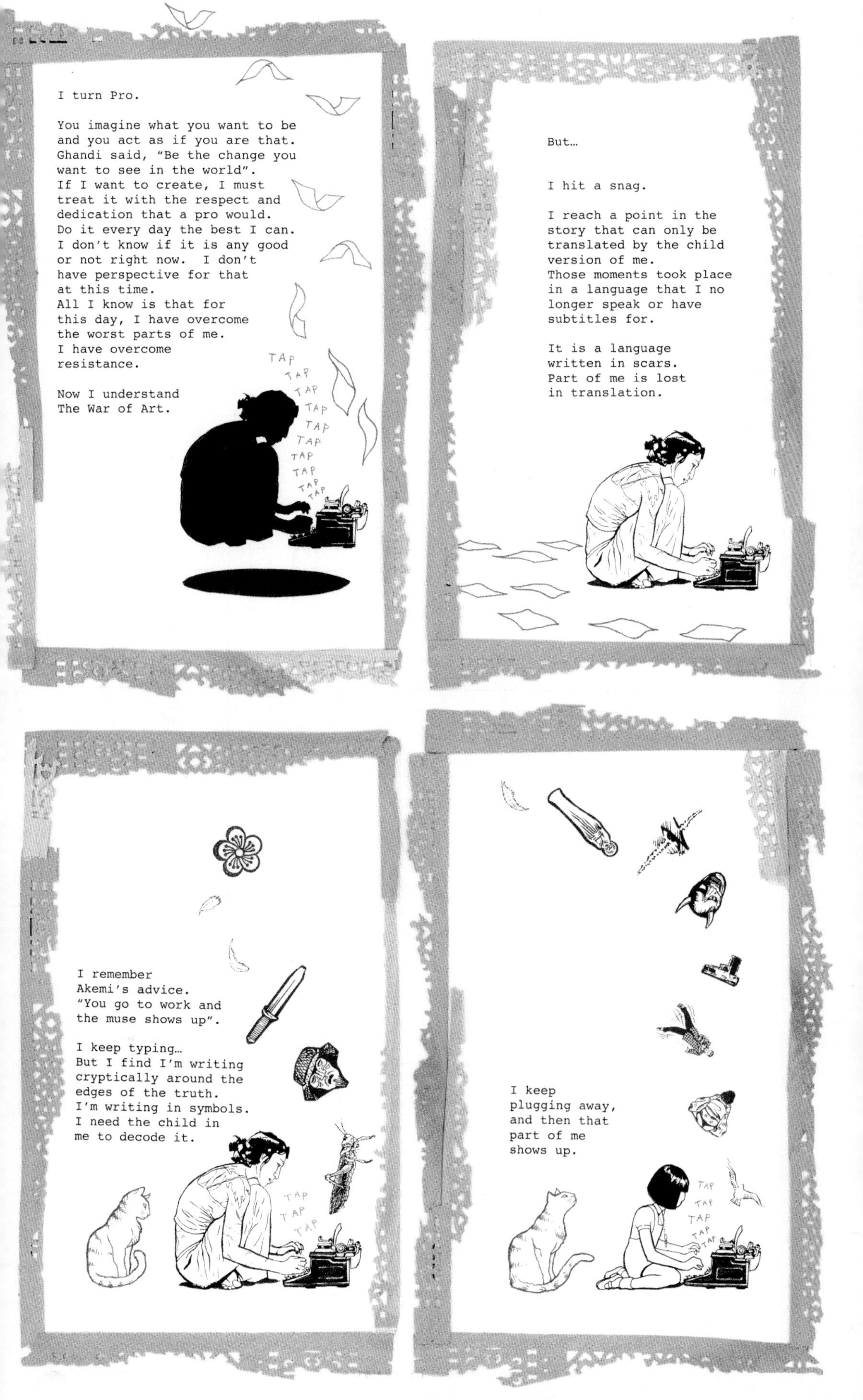
I turn Pro.
You imagine what you want to be and you act as if you are that. Ghandi said, "Be the change you want to see in the world". If I want to create, I must treat it with the respect and dedication that a pro would. Do it every day the best I can. I don't know if it is any good or not right now. I don't have perspective for that at this time. All I know is that for this day, I have overcome the worst parts of me. I have overcome resistance.
Now I understand The War of Art.
TAP TAP TAP TAP TAP TAP TAP TAP TAP TAP
But…
I hit a snag.
I reach a point in the story that can only be translated by the child version of me. Those moments took place in a language that I no longer speak or have subtitles for.
It is a language written in scars. Part of me is lost in translation.
I remember Akemi's advice. "You go to work and the muse shows up".
I keep typing… But I find I'm writing cryptically around the edges of the truth. I'm writing in symbols. I need the child in me to decode it.
TAP TAP TAP
I keep plugging away, and then that part of me shows up.
TAP TAP TAP TAP TAP

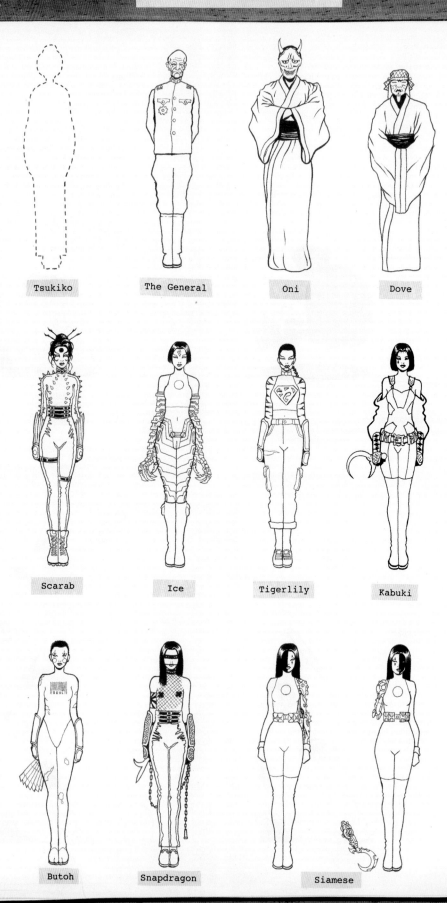

Family of the Noh Species
GENUS NOHSIS

Tsukiko

The General

Oni

Dove

Scarab

Ice

Tigerlily

Kabuki

Butoh

Snapdragon

Siamese

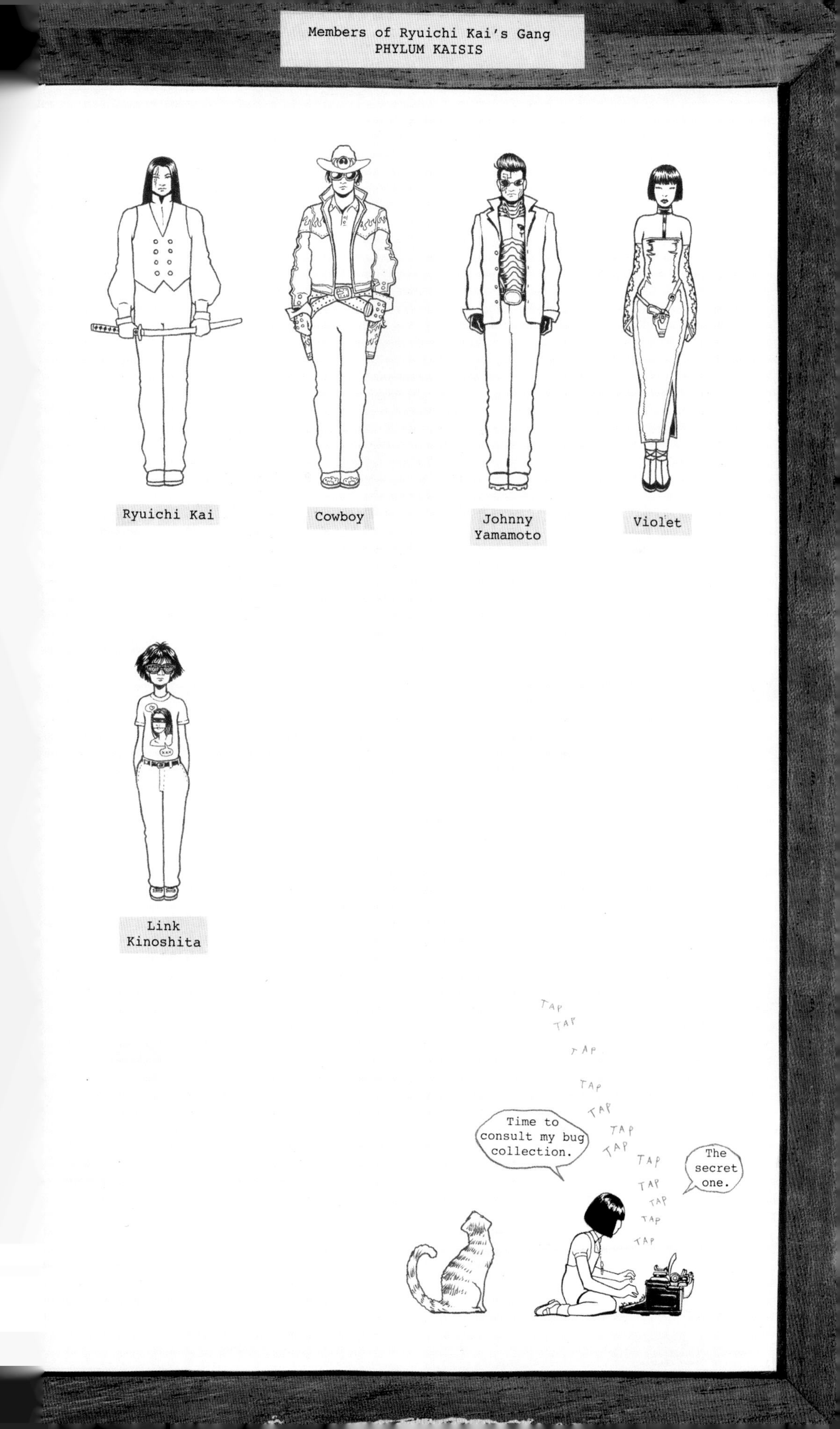

Ryuichi Kai

Cowboy

Johnny
Yamamoto

Violet

Link
Kinoshita

Time to consult my bug collection.

The secret one.

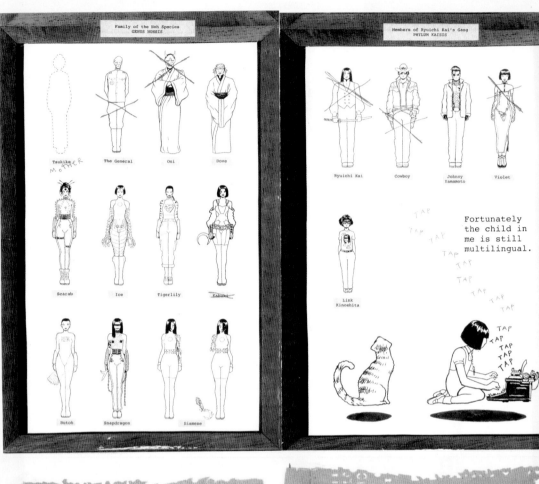

Family of the Noh Species
GENUS NOHSIS

Tsukiko (MOTHER) · The General · Oni · Dove

Scarab · Ice · Tigerlily · Kabuki

Butoh · Snapdragon · Siamese

Members of Ryuichi Kai's Gang
PHYLUM KAISIS

Ryuichi Kai · Cowboy · Johnny Yamamoto · Violet

Link Kinoshita

TAP TAP TAP TAP TAP TAP TAP TAP TAP TAP TAP TAP

Fortunately the child in me is still multilingual.

It all comes back to me.
Accessible and whole.

I relive each moment.
Each version of myself.
This time in a way
that I own it.

TAP TAP TAP TAP TAP TAP TAP TAP

I learn the power
of living it in
my own words.

I find a new groove
in it. I delight in
the craft of it.
It starts to get off
the ground.

Heavy handed at first.
But then I'm in the
zone and resistance
fades away.

TAP TAP TAP TAP TAP TAP TAP TAP

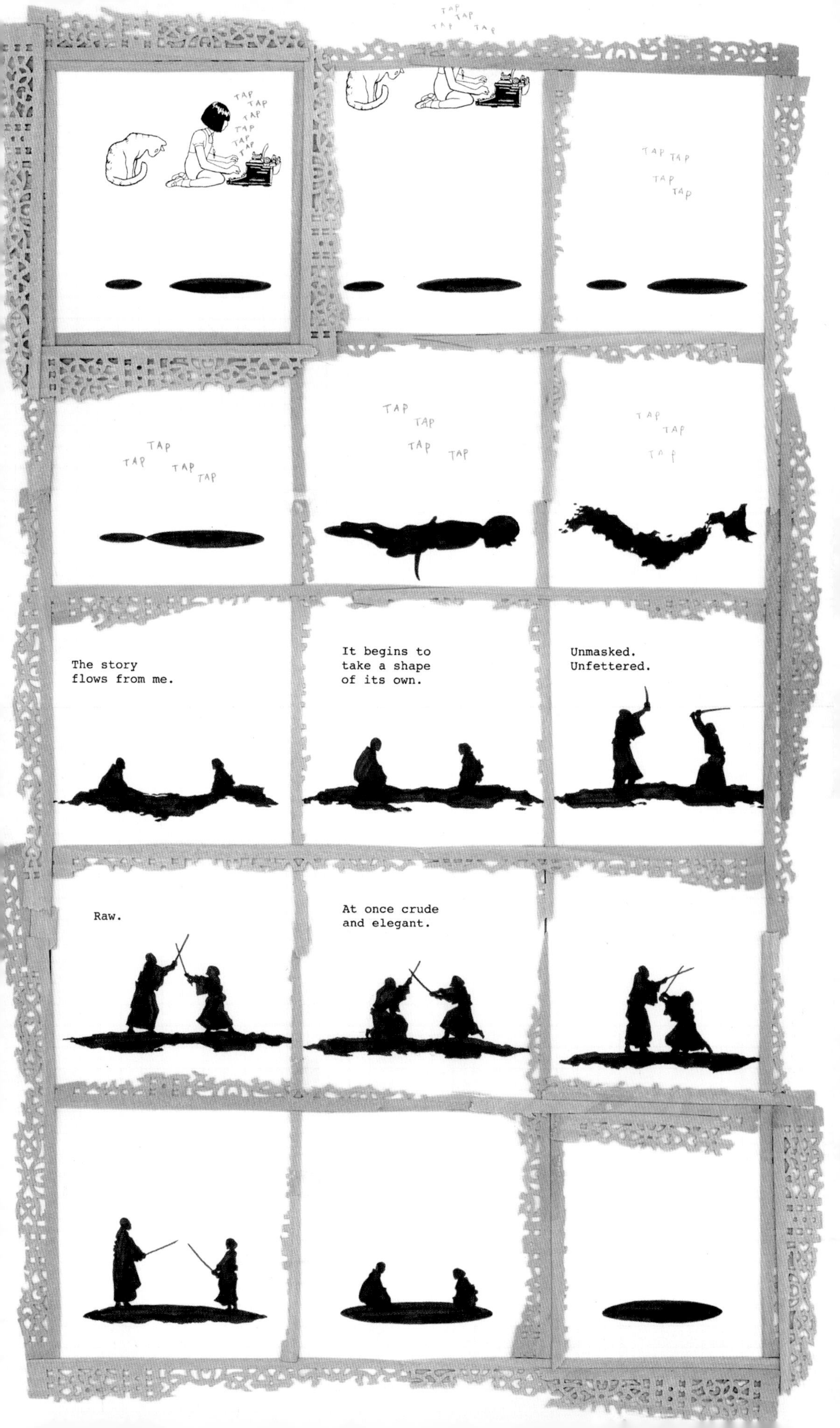

TAP TAP TAP TAP TAP TAP
TAP TAP TAP TAP
TAP TAP TAP TAP
TAP TAP TAP TAP
TAP TAP TAP TAP
TAP TAP TAP
The story flows from me.
It begins to take a shape of its own.
Unmasked. Unfettered.
Raw.
At once crude and elegant.

I become my true self,
my present self, in
these moments.

These moments of
winning the war of art.
Defeating resistance.

Leaving my shadow
behind me.

Pulling the flow from
the ether like M.C.'s
Zero-Point energy
machine.

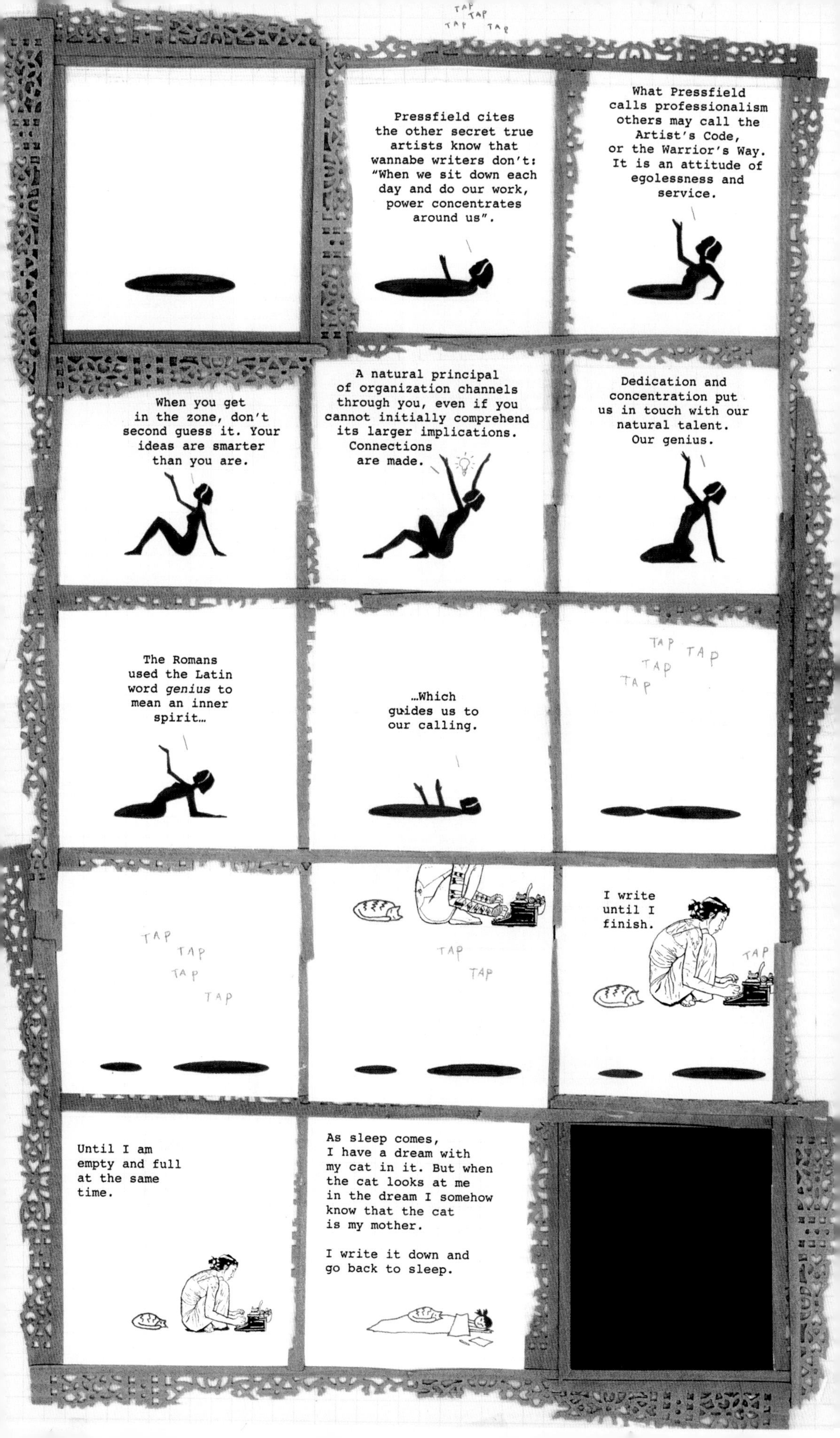
TAP TAP TAP TAP
Pressfield cites the other secret true artists know that wannabe writers don't: "When we sit down each day and do our work, power concentrates around us".
What Pressfield calls professionalism others may call the Artist's Code, or the Warrior's Way. It is an attitude of egolessness and service.
When you get in the zone, don't second guess it. Your ideas are smarter than you are.
A natural principal of organization channels through you, even if you cannot initially comprehend its larger implications. Connections are made.
Dedication and concentration put us in touch with our natural talent. Our genius.
The Romans used the Latin word *genius* to mean an inner spirit…
…Which guides us to our calling.
TAP TAP TAP TAP
TAP TAP TAP TAP
TAP TAP
I write until I finish.
TAP
Until I am empty and full at the same time.
As sleep comes, I have a dream with my cat in it. But when the cat looks at me in the dream I somehow know that the cat is my mother.
I write it down and go back to sleep.

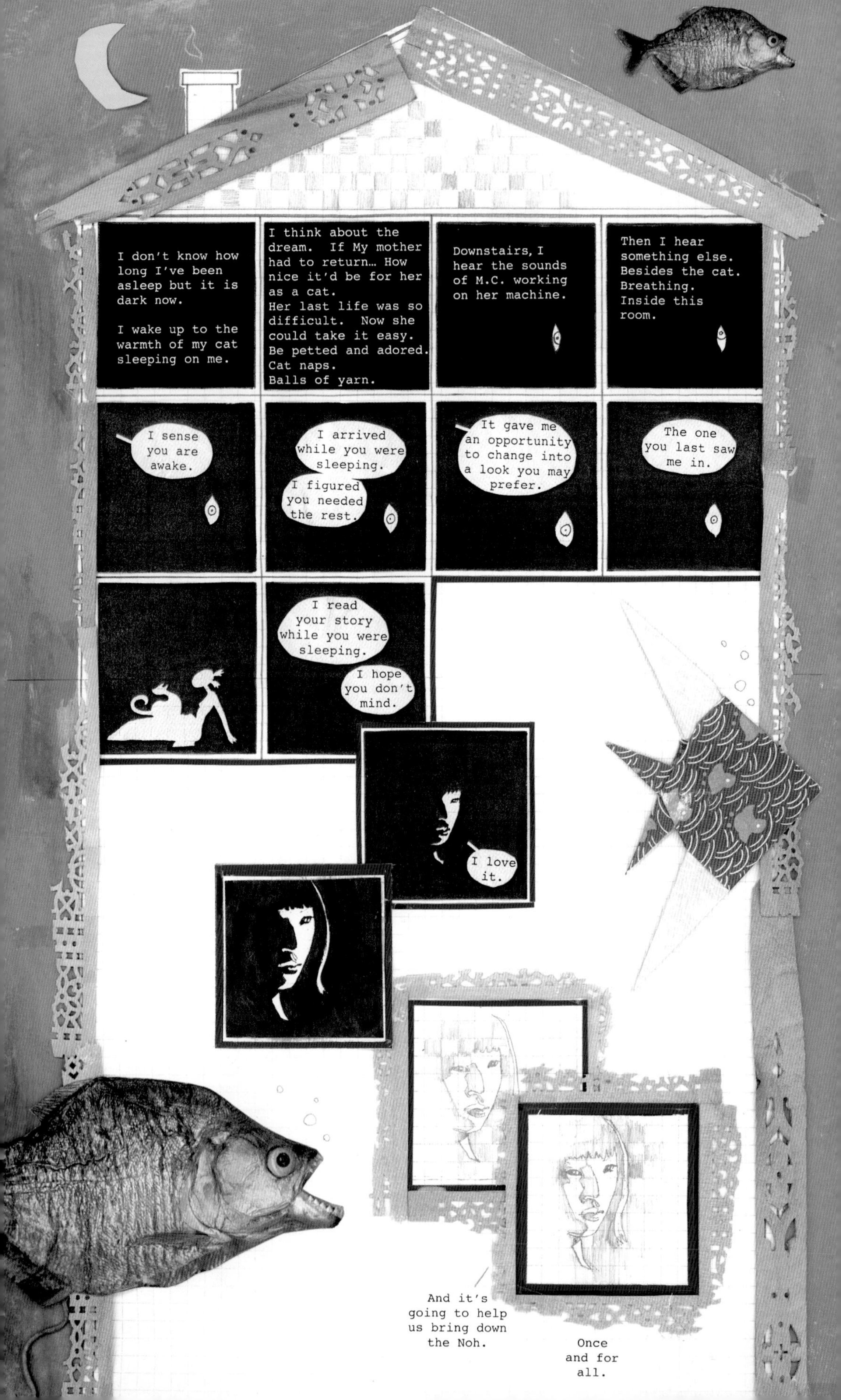
I don't know how long I've been asleep but it is dark now.
I wake up to the warmth of my cat sleeping on me.
I think about the dream. If My mother had to return… How nice it'd be for her as a cat.
Her last life was so difficult. Now she could take it easy.
Be petted and adored.
Cat naps.
Balls of yarn.
Downstairs, I hear the sounds of M.C. working on her machine.
Then I hear something else. Besides the cat. Breathing. Inside this room.
I sense you are awake.
I arrived while you were sleeping.
I figured you needed the rest.
It gave me an opportunity to change into a look you may prefer.
The one you last saw me in.
I read your story while you were sleeping.
I hope you don't mind.
I love it.
And it's going to help us bring down the Noh.
Once and for all.

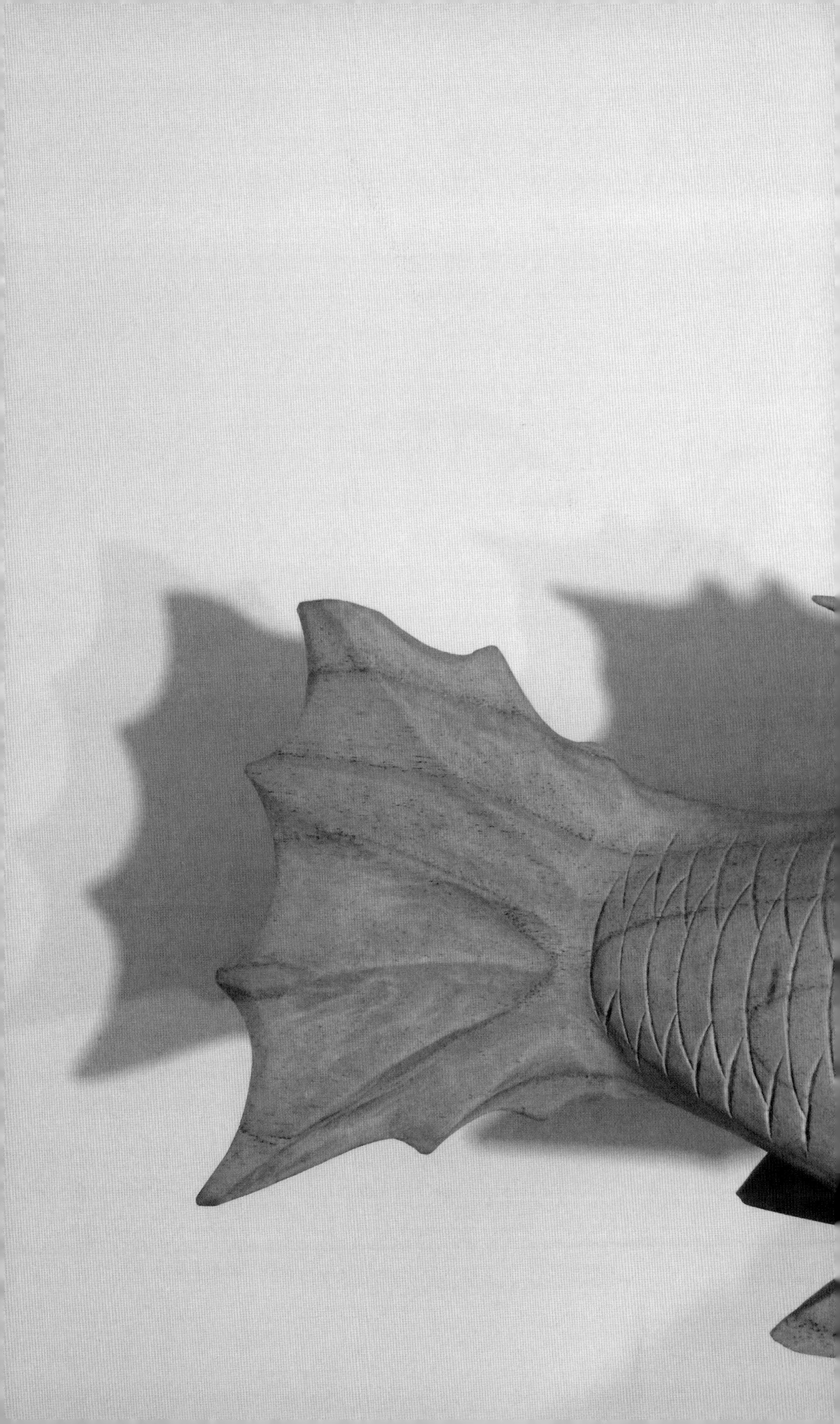

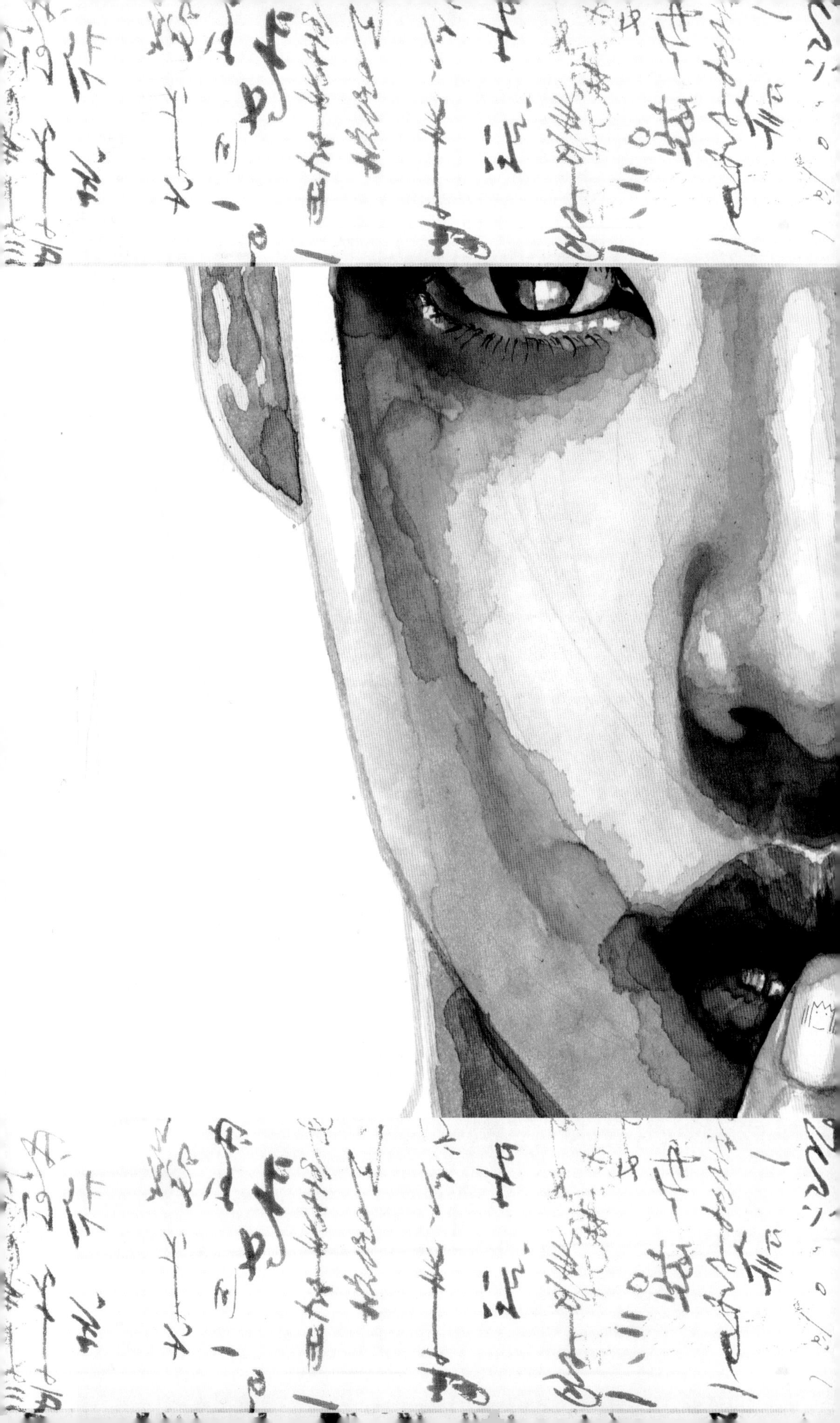

The Alchemy

Part Eight

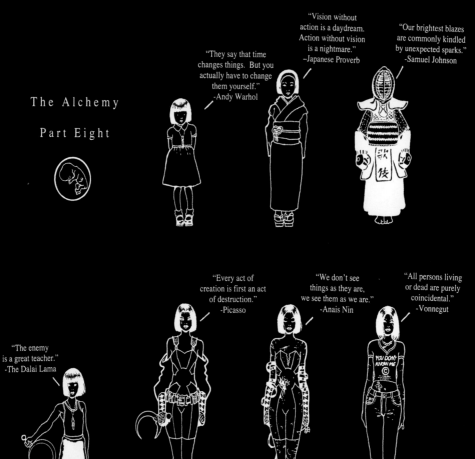

"They say that time
changes things. But you
actually have to change
them yourself."
-Andy Warhol

"Vision without
action is a daydream.
Action without vision
is a nightmare."
–Japanese Proverb

"Our brightest blazes
are commonly kindled
by unexpected sparks."
-Samuel Johnson

"Every act of
creation is first an act
of destruction."
-Picasso

"We don't see
things as they are,
we see them as we are."
-Anais Nin

"All persons living
or dead are purely
coincidental."
-Vonnegut

"The enemy
is a great teacher."
-The Dalai Lama

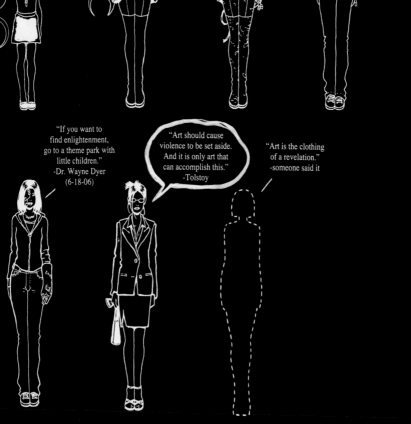

"If you want to
find enlightenment,
go to a theme park with
little children."
-Dr. Wayne Dyer
(6-18-06)

"Art should cause
violence to be set aside.
And it is only art that
can accomplish this."
-Tolstoy

"Art is the clothing
of a revelation."
-someone said it

Connecting

the Dots

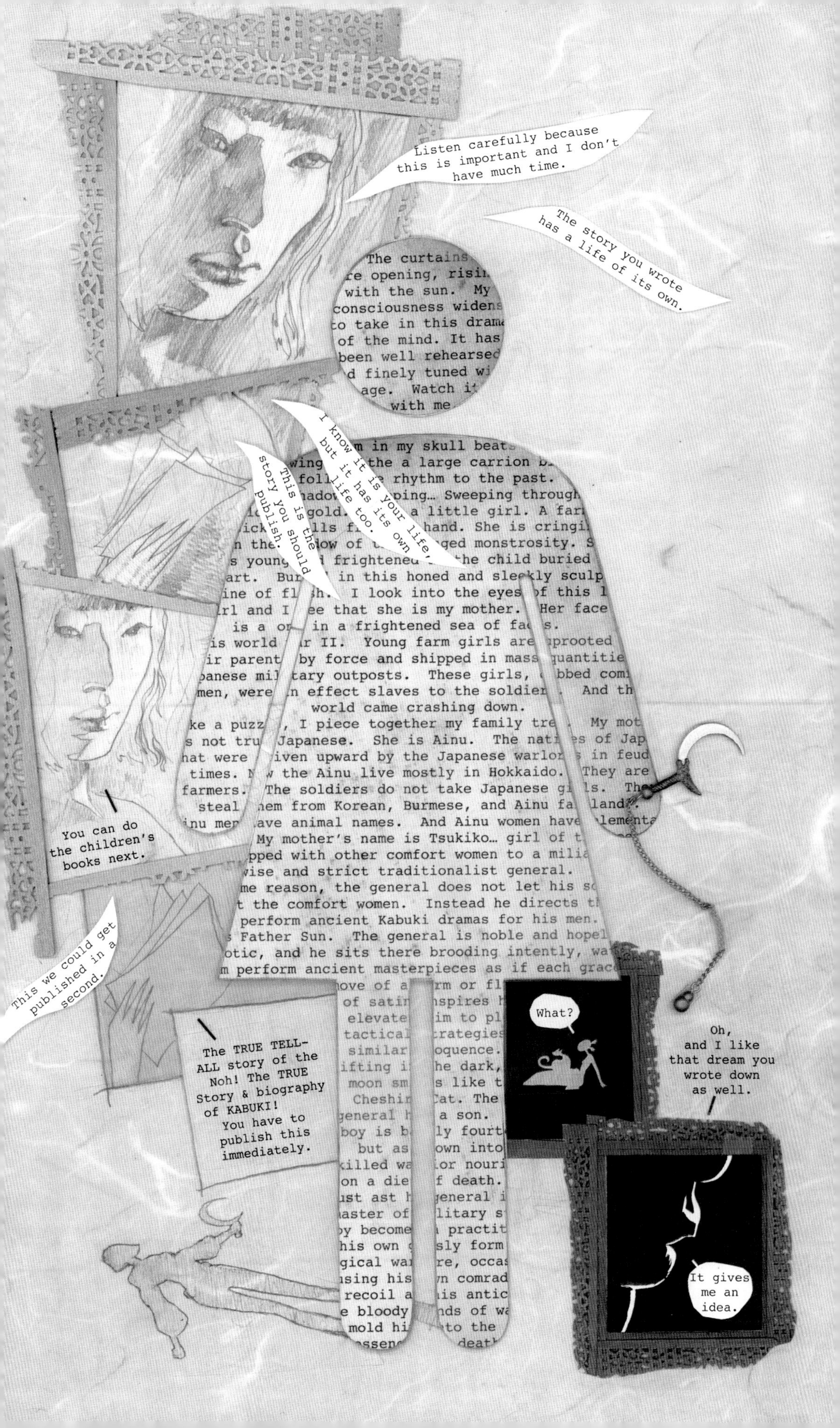

Listen carefully because this is important and I don't have much time.
The story you wrote has a life of its own.
The curtains
re opening, risin
with the sun. My
consciousness widens
to take in this drama
of the mind. It has
been well rehearsed
d finely tuned wi
age. Watch it
with me
I know it is your life, but it has its own life too.
This is the story you should publish.
m in my skull beats
wing the a large carrion b
foll e rhythm to the past.
hadow ping… Sweeping through
gold. a little girl. A far
hand. She is cringi
n the low of ged monstrosity.
s young d frightened the child buried
art. Bur in this honed and sleekly sculp
ine of fl sh. I look into the eyes of this
rl and I ee that she is my mother. Her face
is a o in a frightened sea of fa s.
is world r II. Young farm girls are uprooted
ir parent by force and shipped in mass quantitie
panese mil tary outposts. These girls, bbed com
men, were n effect slaves to the soldier . And th
world came crashing down.
ke a puzz , I piece together my family tre . My mot
s not tru Japanese. She is Ainu. The nati es of Jap
hat were iven upward by the Japanese warlor s in feud
times. N w the Ainu live mostly in Hokkaido. They are
farmers. The soldiers do not take Japanese gi ls. Th
steal hem from Korean, Burmese, and Ainu fa lands
inu men ave animal names. And Ainu women have elementa
My mother's name is Tsukiko… girl of t
pped with other comfort women to a milia
wise and strict traditionalist general.
me reason, the general does not let his so
t the comfort women. Instead he directs t
perform ancient Kabuki dramas for his men.
Father Sun. The general is noble and hope
otic, and he sits there brooding intently, wa
m perform ancient masterpieces as if each grac
ove of a rm or fl
of sati nspires h
elevate him to pl
tactical trategies
similar oquence.
ifting i he dark,
moon sm s like t
Cheshir Cat. The
general h a son.
boy is b ly fourt
but as own into
killed wa ior nouri
on a die f death.
ust ast h general i
master of litary s
y become practit
his own sly form
gical wa re, occas
sing his n comrad
recoil a is antic
e bloody nds of wa
mold hi to the
ssen death
You can do the children's books next.
This we could get published in a second.
The TRUE TELL-ALL story of the Noh! The TRUE Story & biography of KABUKI! You have to publish this immediately.
What?
Oh, and I like that dream you wrote down as well.
It gives me an idea.

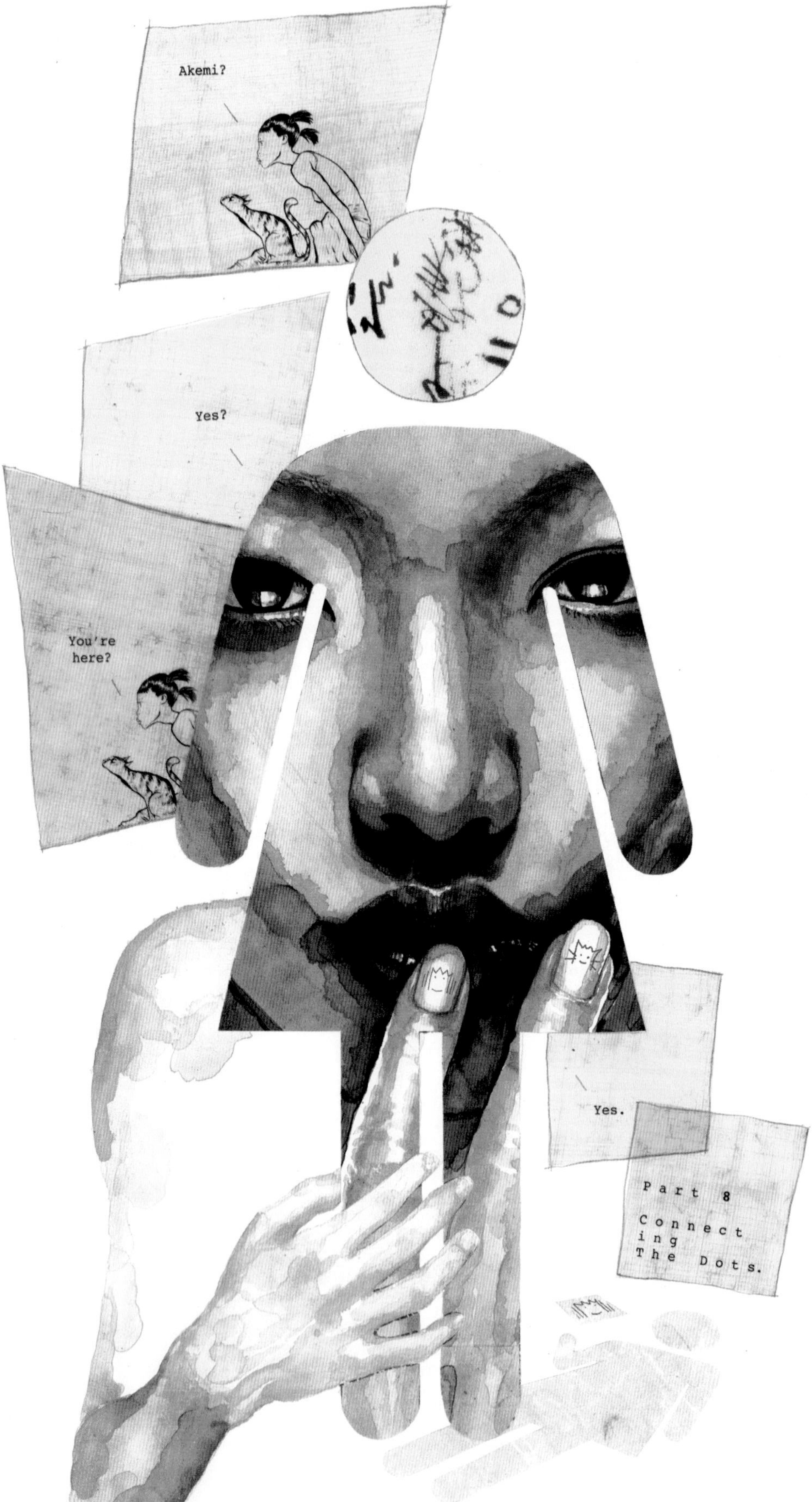

Akemi?
Yes?
You're here?
Yes.
Part 8
Connecting The Dots.

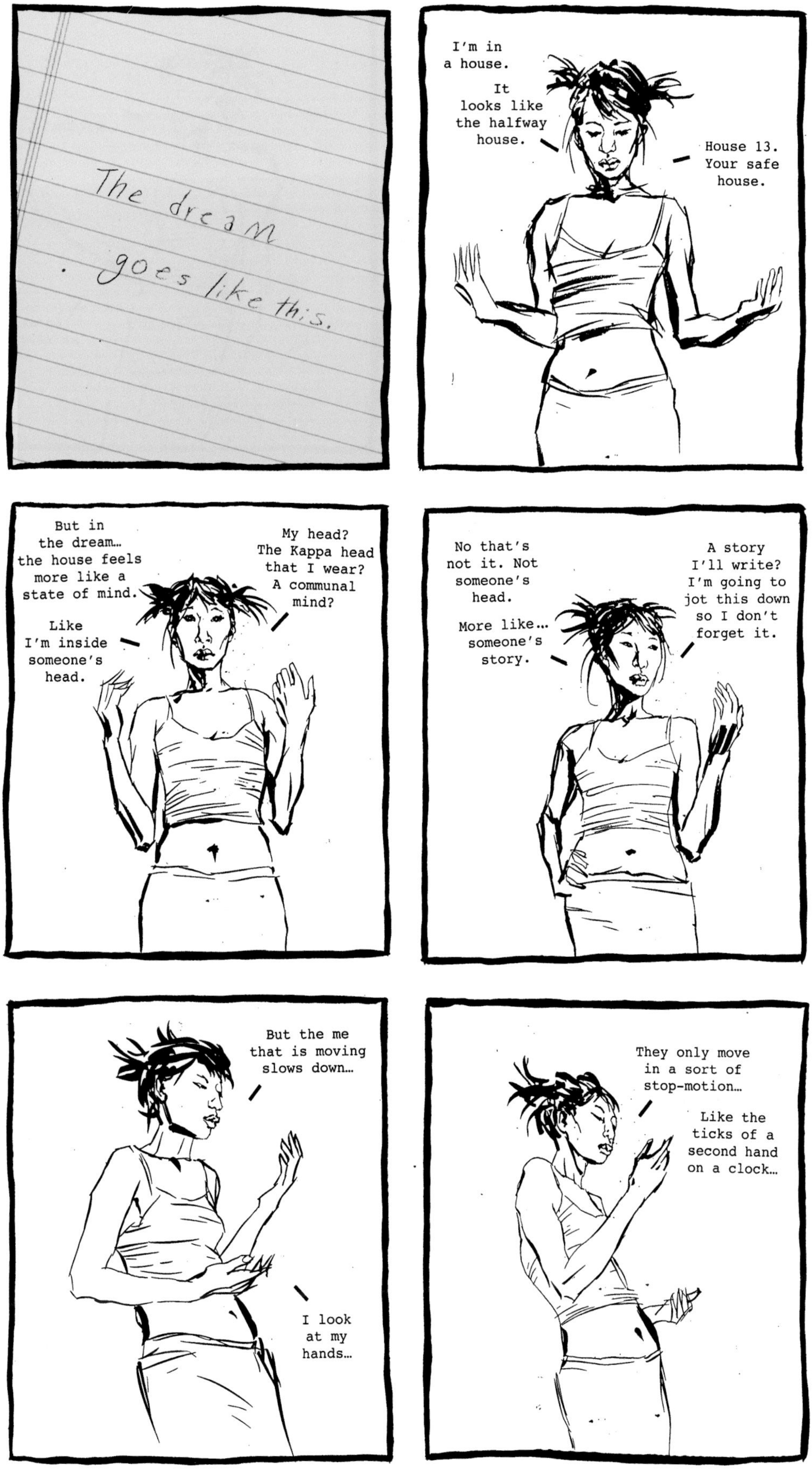
The dream goes like this.
I'm in a house.
It looks like the halfway house.
House 13. Your safe house.
But in the dream… the house feels more like a state of mind.
Like I'm inside someone's head.
My head? The Kappa head that I wear? A communal mind?
No that's not it. Not someone's head.
More like… someone's story.
A story I'll write? I'm going to jot this down so I don't forget it.
But the me that is moving slows down…
I look at my hands…
They only move in a sort of stop-motion…
Like the ticks of a second hand on a clock…

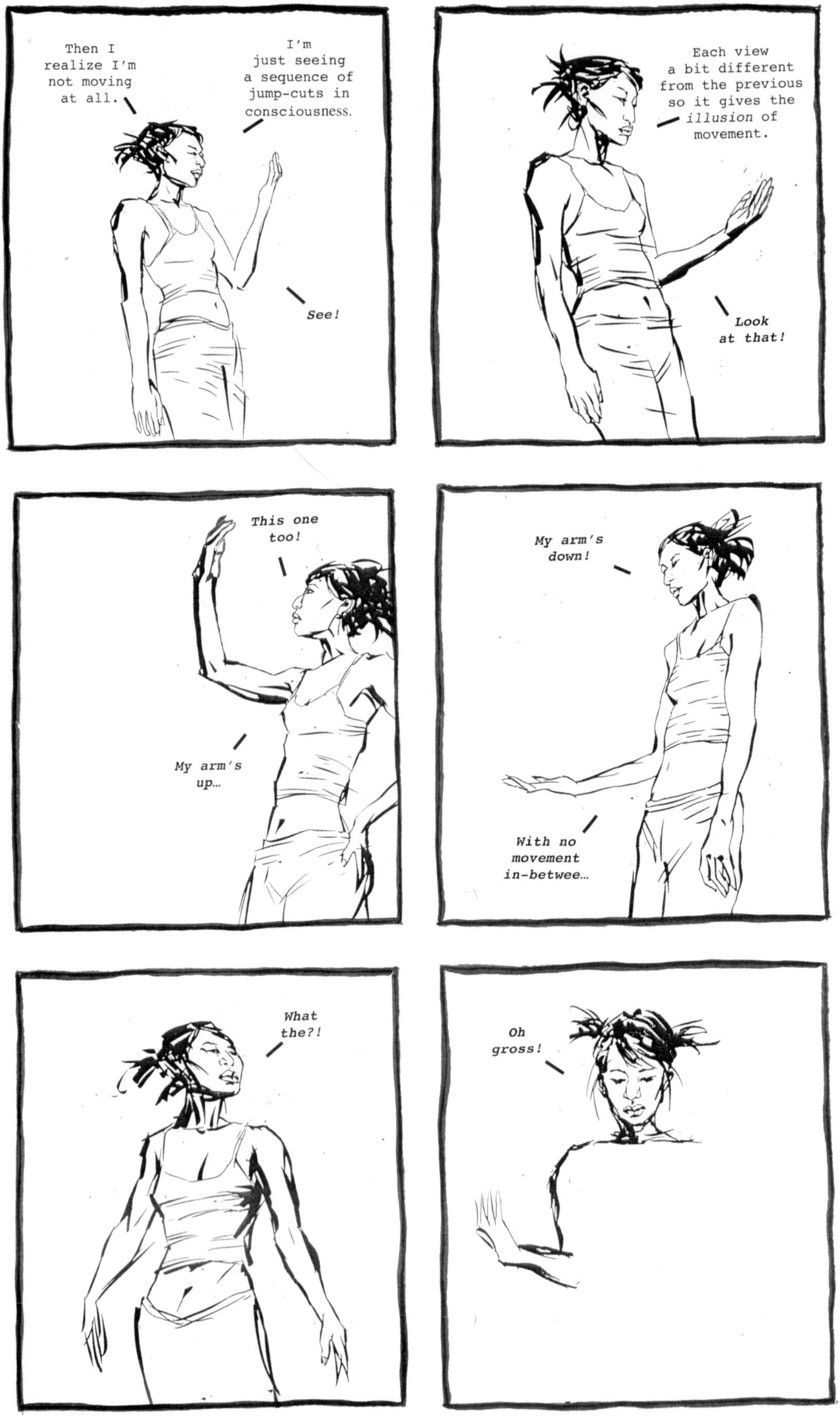
Then I realize I'm not moving at all.
I'm just seeing a sequence of jump-cuts in consciousness.
See!
Each view a bit different from the previous so it gives the *illusion* of movement.
Look at that!
This one too!
My arm's up...
My arm's down!
With no movement in-betwee...
What the?!
Oh gross!

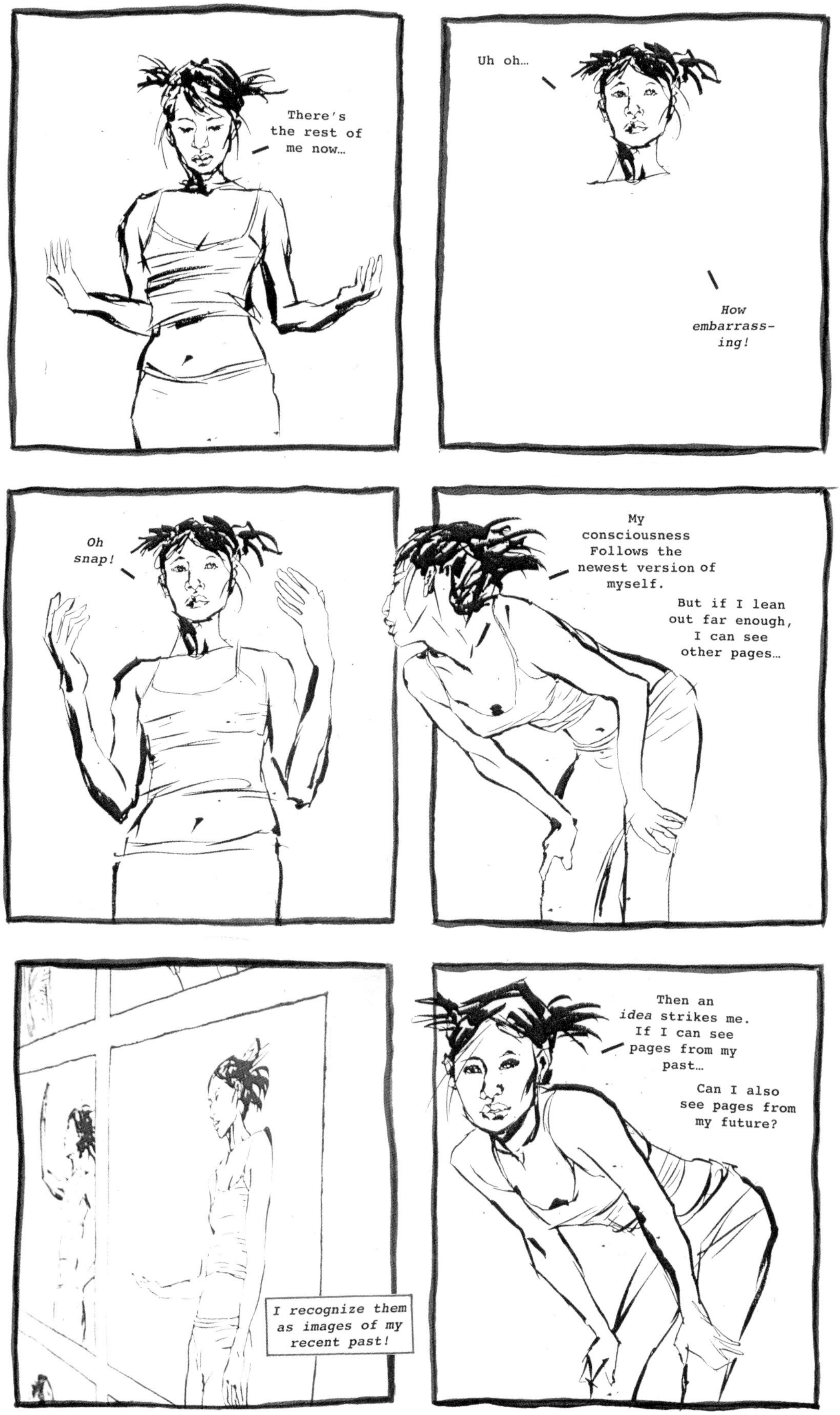
There's the rest of me now...
Uh oh...
How embarrass-ing!
Oh snap!
My consciousness Follows the newest version of myself.
But if I lean out far enough, I can see other pages...
I recognize them as images of my recent past!
Then an *idea* strikes me. If I can see pages from my past...
Can I also see pages from my future?

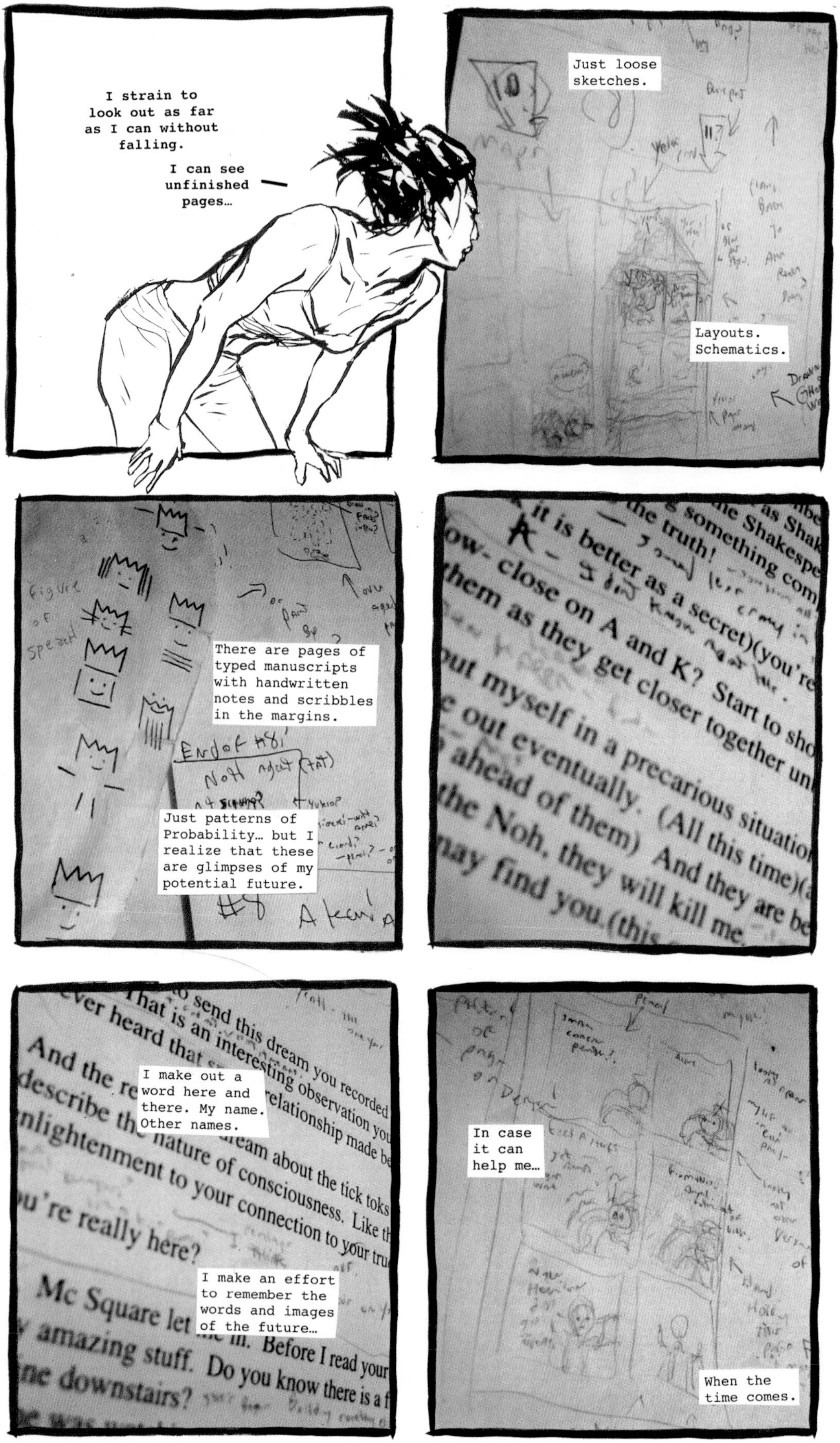
I strain to look out as far as I can without falling.
I can see unfinished pages…
Just loose sketches.
Layouts. Schematics.
There are pages of typed manuscripts with handwritten notes and scribbles in the margins.
Just patterns of Probability… but I realize that these are glimpses of my potential future.
I make out a word here and there. My name. Other names.
I make an effort to remember the words and images of the future…
In case it can help me…
When the time comes.

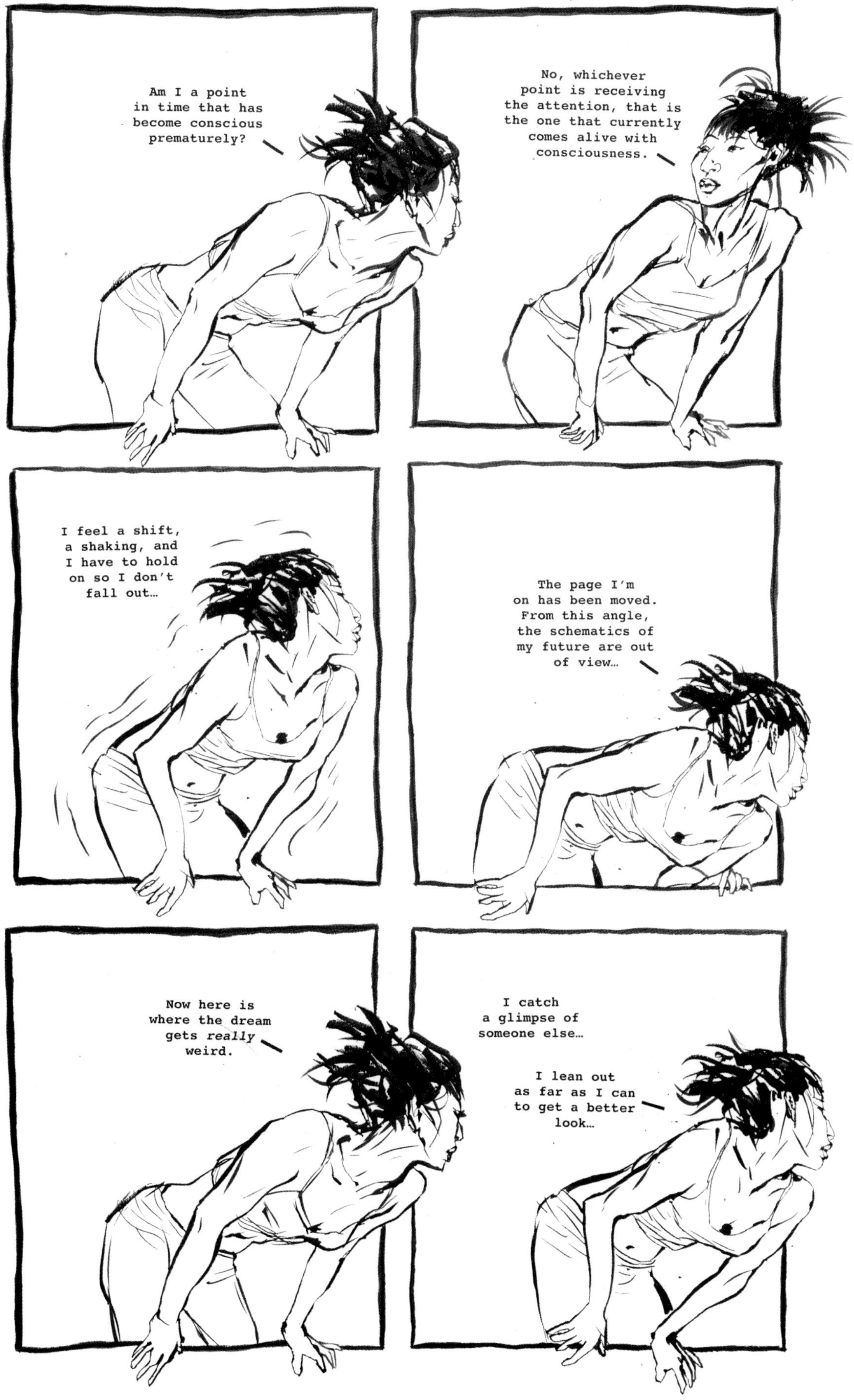
Am I a point in time that has become conscious prematurely?
No, whichever point is receiving the attention, that is the one that currently comes alive with consciousness.
I feel a shift, a shaking, and I have to hold on so I don't fall out…
The page I'm on has been moved. From this angle, the schematics of my future are out of view…
Now here is where the dream gets *really* weird.
I catch a glimpse of someone else…
I lean out as far as I can to get a better look…

But I don't see them. Because now my consciousness is leaving the page...

Rising from it...

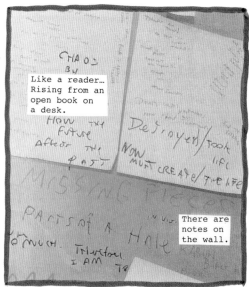

Like a reader... Rising from an open book on a desk.

There are notes on the wall.

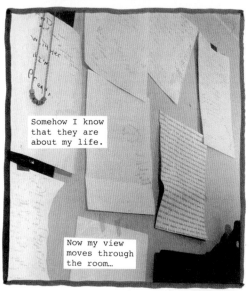

Somehow I know that they are about my life.

Now my view moves through the room...

I see sculptures...

I see a cat.

It looks just like my own cat, Fumiko.

But in the dream...

I somehow know that the cat... is my mother.

We move up the stairs...

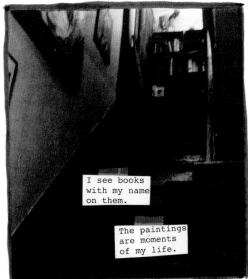

I see books with my name on them.

The paintings are moments of my life.

Are some of them from my future too?

I start to wonder if this house is my head.

Or more like this house is someone else's head...

And I'm just one of the inhabitants.

I see a map in the reflection of the mirror.

A claw-foot tub like the one in house 13...

Like the one you took me to in the Control Corps basement when we first met.

I'm washing my hands.

But they are not my hands.

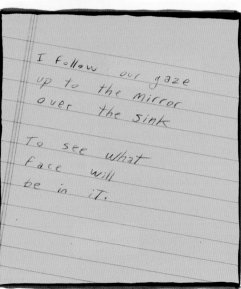

I follow our gaze up to the mirror over the sink

To see what face will be in it.

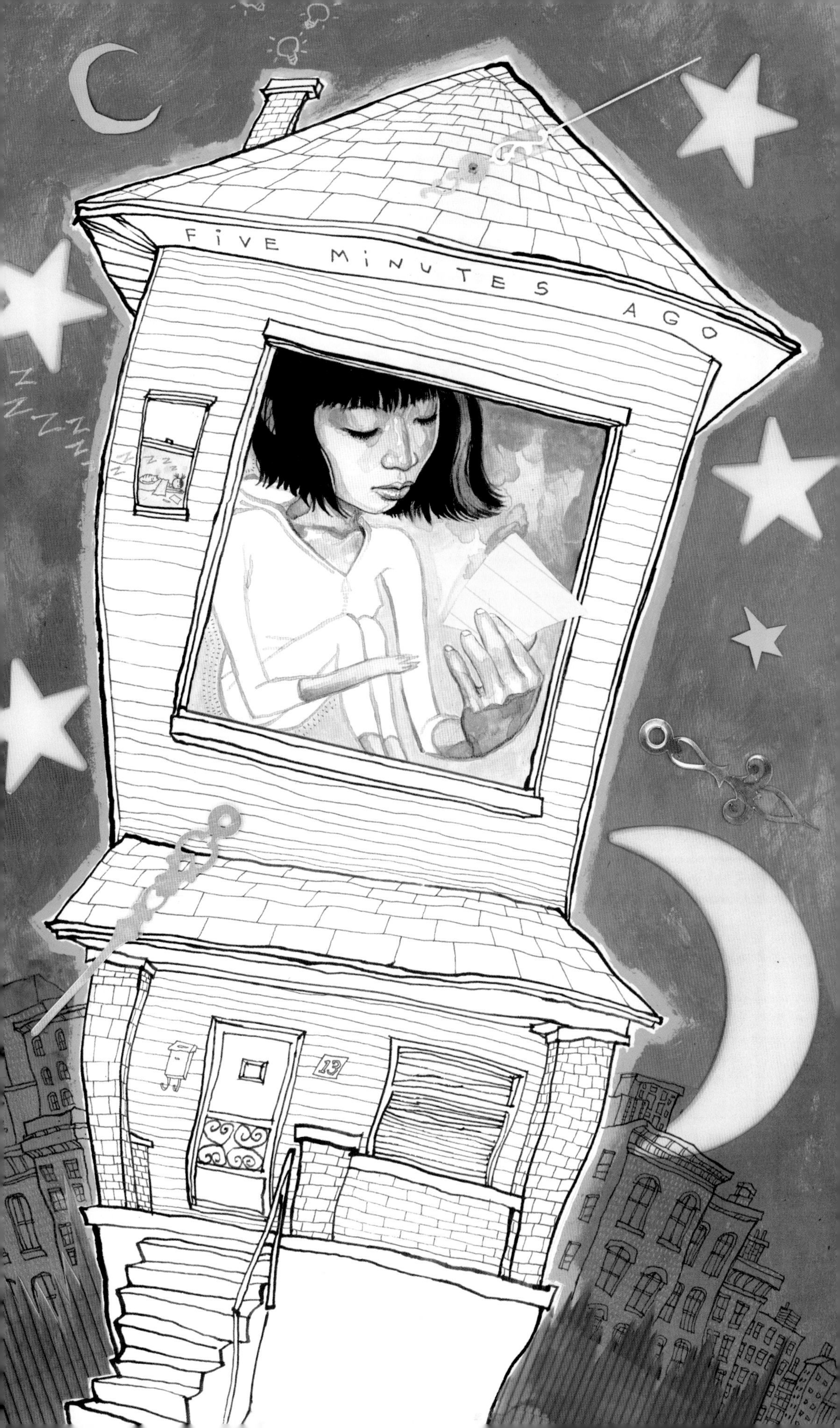
FIVE MINUTES AGO
13

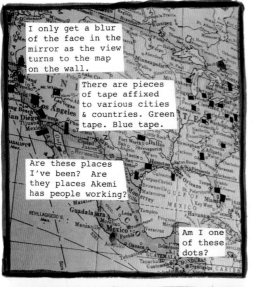

I only get a blur of the face in the mirror as the view turns to the map on the wall.

There are pieces of tape affixed to various cities & countries. Green tape. Blue tape.

Are these places I've been? Are they places Akemi has people working?

Am I one of these dots?

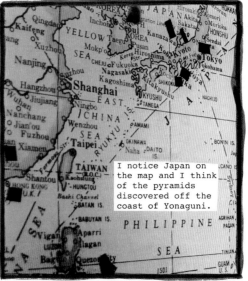

I notice Japan on the map and I think of the pyramids discovered off the coast of Yonaguni.

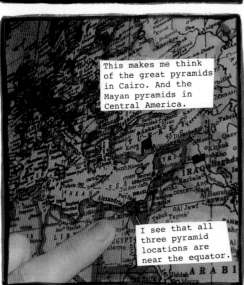

This makes me think of the great pyramids in Cairo. And the Mayan pyramids in Central America.

I see that all three pyramid locations are near the equator.

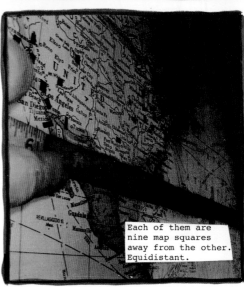

Each of them are nine map squares away from the other. Equidistant.

Three points, equidistant from each other. At center line of the world.

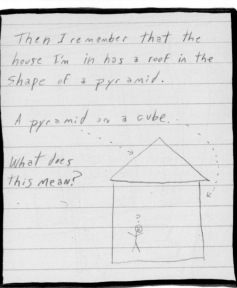

Then I remember that the house I'm in has a roof in the shape of a pyramid.

A pyramid on a cube.

What does this mean?

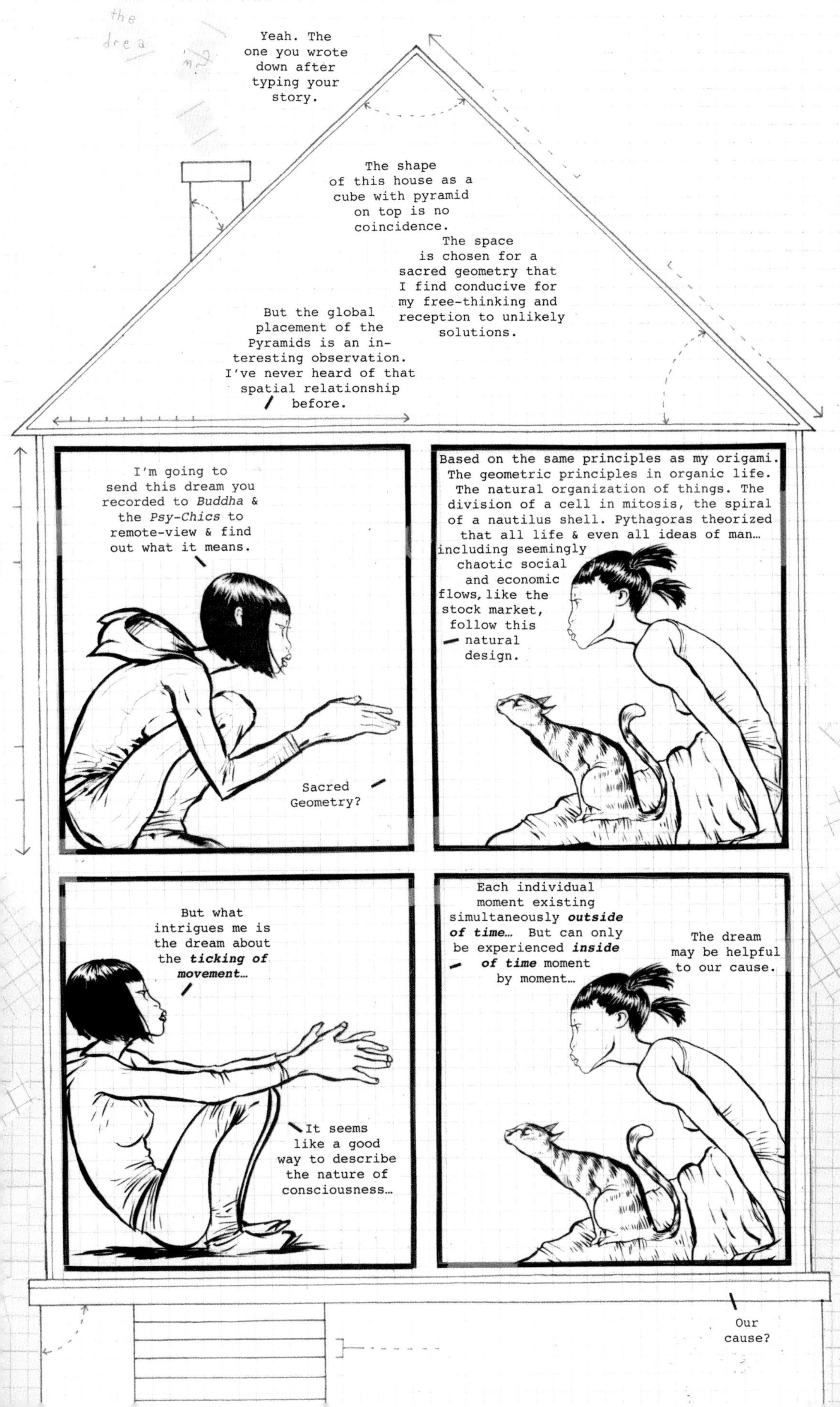

Yeah. The one you wrote down after typing your story.
The shape of this house as a cube with pyramid on top is no coincidence.
The space is chosen for a sacred geometry that I find conducive for my free-thinking and reception to unlikely solutions.
But the global placement of the Pyramids is an interesting observation. I've never heard of that spatial relationship before.
I'm going to send this dream you recorded to *Buddha* & the *Psy-Chics* to remote-view & find out what it means.
Sacred Geometry?
Based on the same principles as my origami. The geometric principles in organic life. The natural organization of things. The division of a cell in mitosis, the spiral of a nautilus shell. Pythagoras theorized that all life & even all ideas of man…
including seemingly chaotic social and economic flows, like the stock market, follow this natural design.
But what intrigues me is the dream about the ***ticking of movement…***
It seems like a good way to describe the nature of consciousness…
Each individual moment existing simultaneously ***outside of time…*** But can only be experienced ***inside of time*** moment by moment…
The dream may be helpful to our cause.
Our cause?

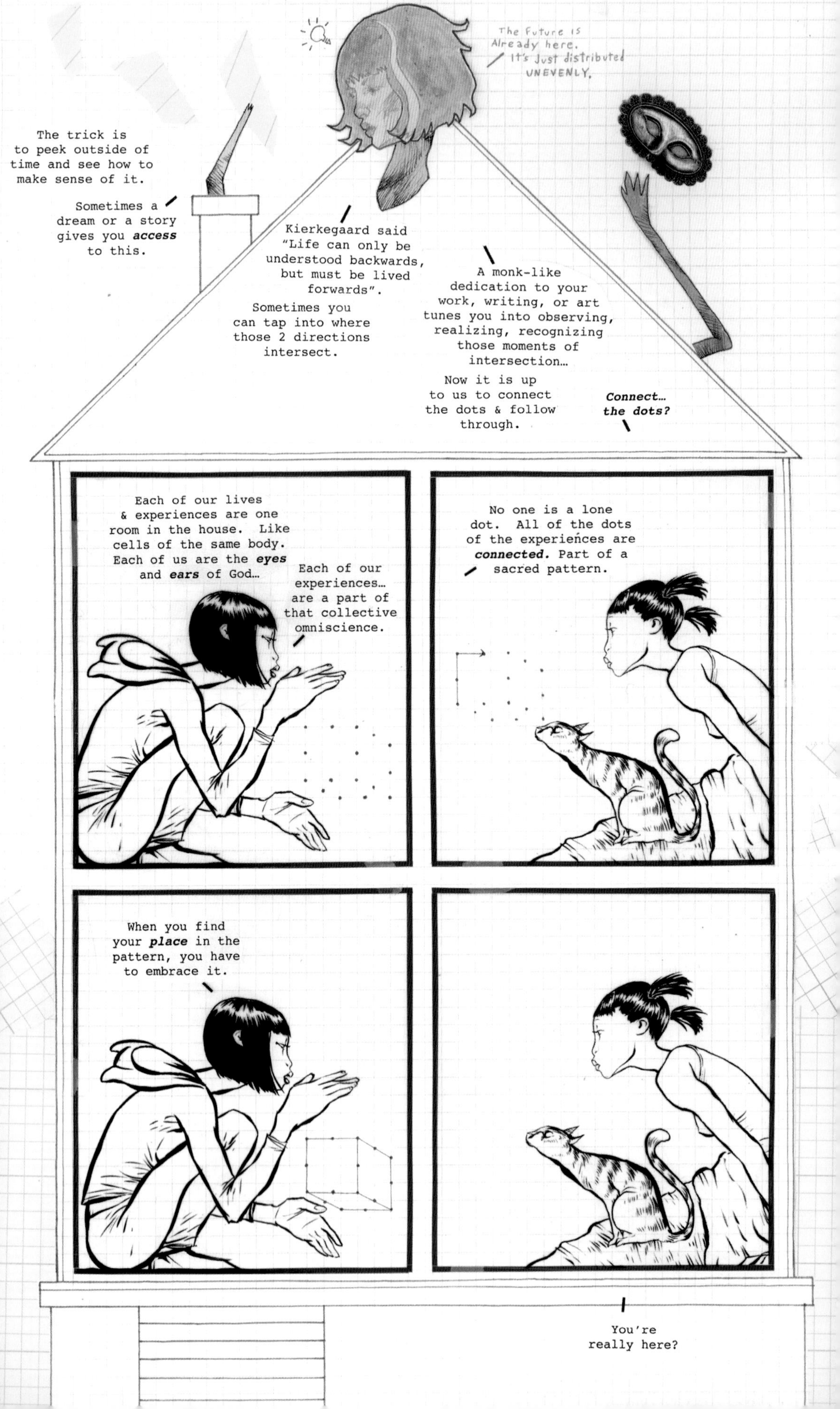

The Future is Already here. It's just distributed UNEVENLY.
The trick is to peek outside of time and see how to make sense of it.
Sometimes a dream or a story gives you ***access*** to this.
Kierkegaard said "Life can only be understood backwards, but must be lived forwards".
Sometimes you can tap into where those 2 directions intersect.
A monk-like dedication to your work, writing, or art tunes you into observing, realizing, recognizing those moments of intersection…
Now it is up to us to connect the dots & follow through.
Connect… the dots?
Each of our lives & experiences are one room in the house. Like cells of the same body. Each of us are the ***eyes*** and ***ears*** of God…
Each of our experiences… are a part of that collective omniscience.
No one is a lone dot. All of the dots of the experiences are ***connected.*** Part of a sacred pattern.
When you find your ***place*** in the pattern, you have to embrace it.
You're really here?

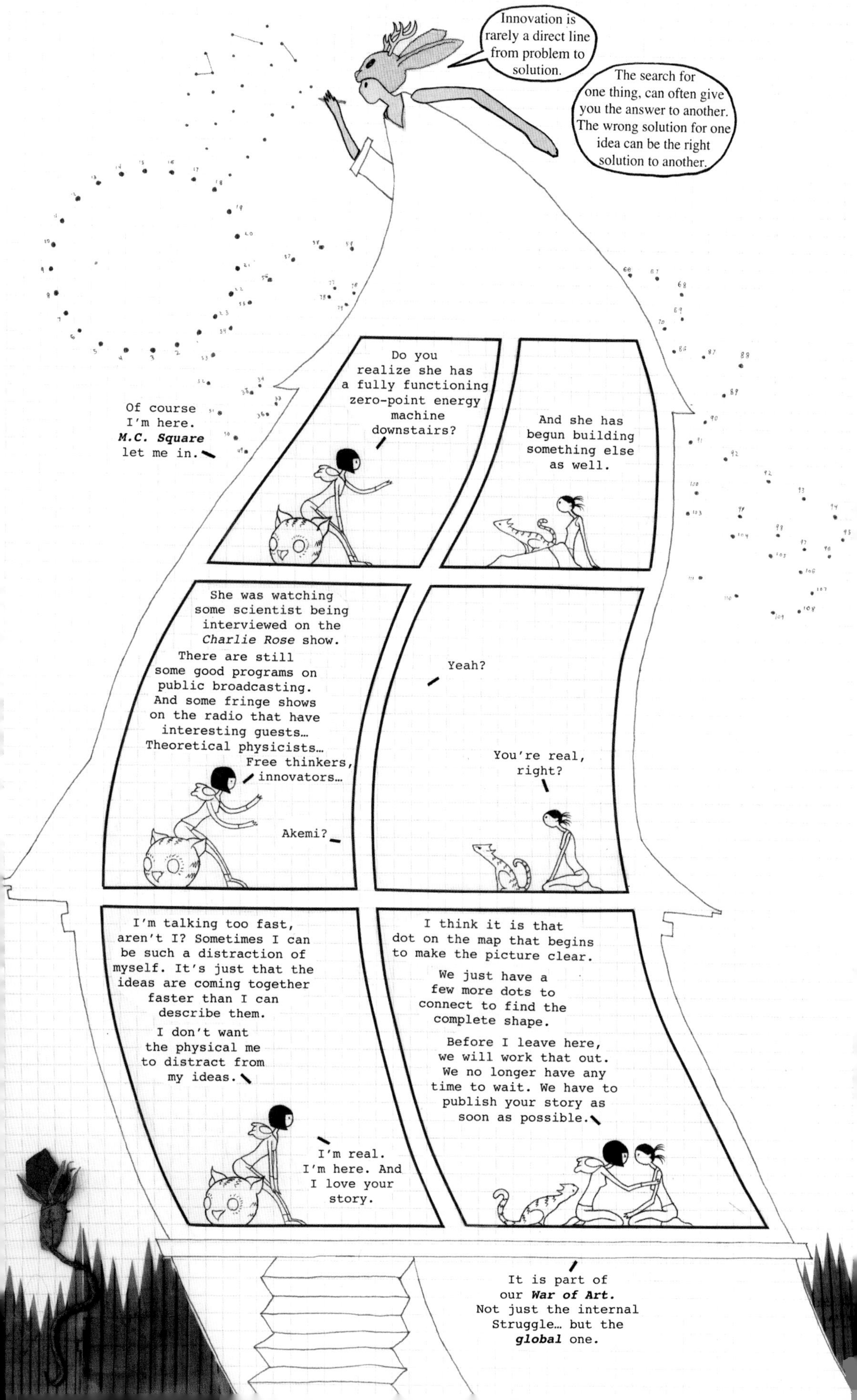
Innovation is rarely a direct line from problem to solution.
The search for one thing, can often give you the answer to another. The wrong solution for one idea can be the right solution to another.
Of course I'm here. **M.C. Square** let me in.
Do you realize she has a fully functioning zero-point energy machine downstairs?
And she has begun building something else as well.
She was watching some scientist being interviewed on the *Charlie Rose* show.
There are still some good programs on public broadcasting. And some fringe shows on the radio that have interesting guests… Theoretical physicists…
Free thinkers, innovators…
Akemi?
Yeah?
You're real, right?
I'm talking too fast, aren't I? Sometimes I can be such a distraction of myself. It's just that the ideas are coming together faster than I can describe them.
I don't want the physical me to distract from my ideas.
I'm real. I'm here. And I love your story.
I think it is that dot on the map that begins to make the picture clear.
We just have a few more dots to connect to find the complete shape.
Before I leave here, we will work that out. We no longer have any time to wait. We have to publish your story as soon as possible.
It is part of our **War of Art.** Not just the internal Struggle… but the ***global*** one.

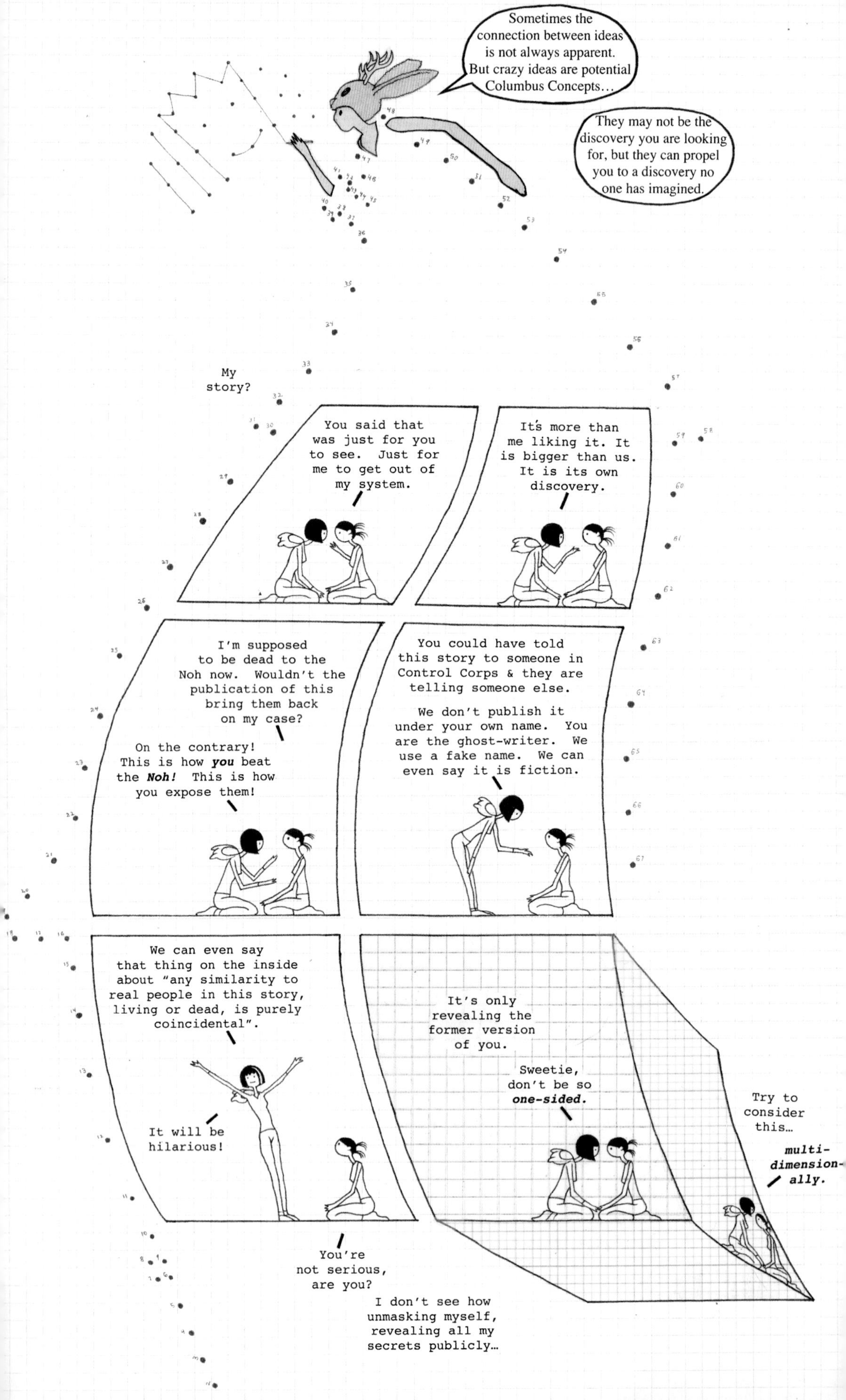
Sometimes the connection between ideas is not always apparent. But crazy ideas are potential Columbus Concepts…
They may not be the discovery you are looking for, but they can propel you to a discovery no one has imagined.
My story?
You said that was just for you to see. Just for me to get out of my system.
It's more than me liking it. It is bigger than us. It is its own discovery.
I'm supposed to be dead to the Noh now. Wouldn't the publication of this bring them back on my case?
On the contrary! This is how *you* beat the ***Noh!*** This is how you expose them!
You could have told this story to someone in Control Corps & they are telling someone else.
We don't publish it under your own name. You are the ghost-writer. We use a fake name. We can even say it is fiction.
We can even say that thing on the inside about "any similarity to real people in this story, living or dead, is purely coincidental".
It will be hilarious!
You're not serious, are you?
I don't see how unmasking myself, revealing all my secrets publicly…
It's only revealing the former version of you.
Sweetie, don't be so ***one-sided.***
Try to consider this…
multi-dimensionally.

Remember when I said you are on the 12 step plan to becoming yourself? That you'll overcome the addiction to needing any mask at all? You asked how you could possibly do that.

You said we make the rest of the world take its mask off too.

That's right.

In an attempt to neutra- the corruption between

That's right. The Noh can only survive in secrecy.

We make the Noh take its mask off.

You publish your story & say it is fiction. But the names & events will add up. The public will see that. Journalists will investigate…

They will connect the dots.

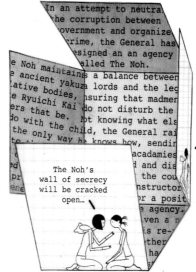

In an attempt to neutra- the corruption between government and organize- crime, the General has- designed an an agency called The Noh.

e Noh maintains a balance between e ancient yakuza lords and the leg- lative bodies, nsuring that madmen e Ryuichi Kai do not disturb the ers that be. Not knowing what els- do with the child, the General rai- the only way he knows how, sendin- to… academies d and dis- pr- the cou- ene- nstructor- or a posit- e agency- ven a n- s re- ther- ha-

The Noh's wall of secrecy will be cracked open…

Will unravel… *Unfold.*

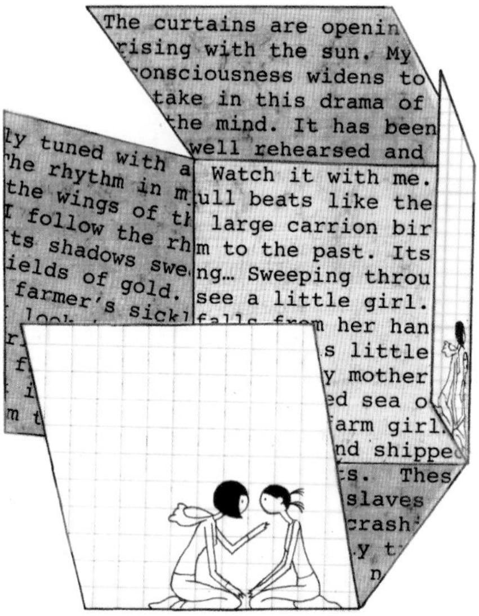
The curtains are openin
rising with the sun. My
consciousness widens to
take in this drama of
the mind. It has been
well rehearsed and
Watch it with me.
ull beats like the
large carrion bir
m to the past. Its
ng… Sweeping throu
see a little girl.
from her han
s little
y mother
ed sea o
arm girl.
nd shippe
s. Thes
slaves
crashi
ly tuned with a
The rhythm in m
the wings of th
I follow the rh
Its shadows swe
ields of gold.
farmer's sickl

You unfold the Noh… by unfolding your story.

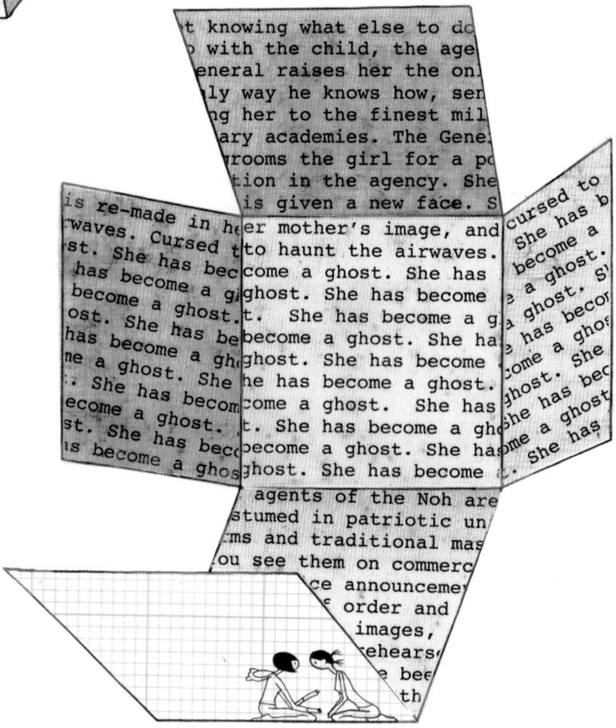
t knowing what else to do
with the child, the age
eneral raises her the onl
ly way he knows how, sen
ng her to the finest mil
ary academies. The Gene
grooms the girl for a po
tion in the agency. She
is given a new face. S
er mother's image, and
to haunt the airwaves.
come a ghost. She has
ghost. She has become
t. She has become a g
become a ghost. She ha
ghost. She has become
he has become a ghost.
come a ghost. She has
t. She has become a gho
become a ghost. She has
ghost. She has become
is re-made in he
rwaves. Cursed t
st. She has bec
has become a g
become a ghost.
ost. She has be
has become a gh
me a ghost. She
. She has becom
ecome a ghost.
st. She has bec
is become a ghos
cursed to
She has b
become a
a ghost.
a ghost. S
has becon
come a gho
ghost. She
She has bec
me a ghost
She has
agents of the Noh are
stumed in patriotic un
rms and traditional mas
ou see them on commerc
ce announceme
order and
images,
rehears
bee
th

By turning the inside… ***out.***

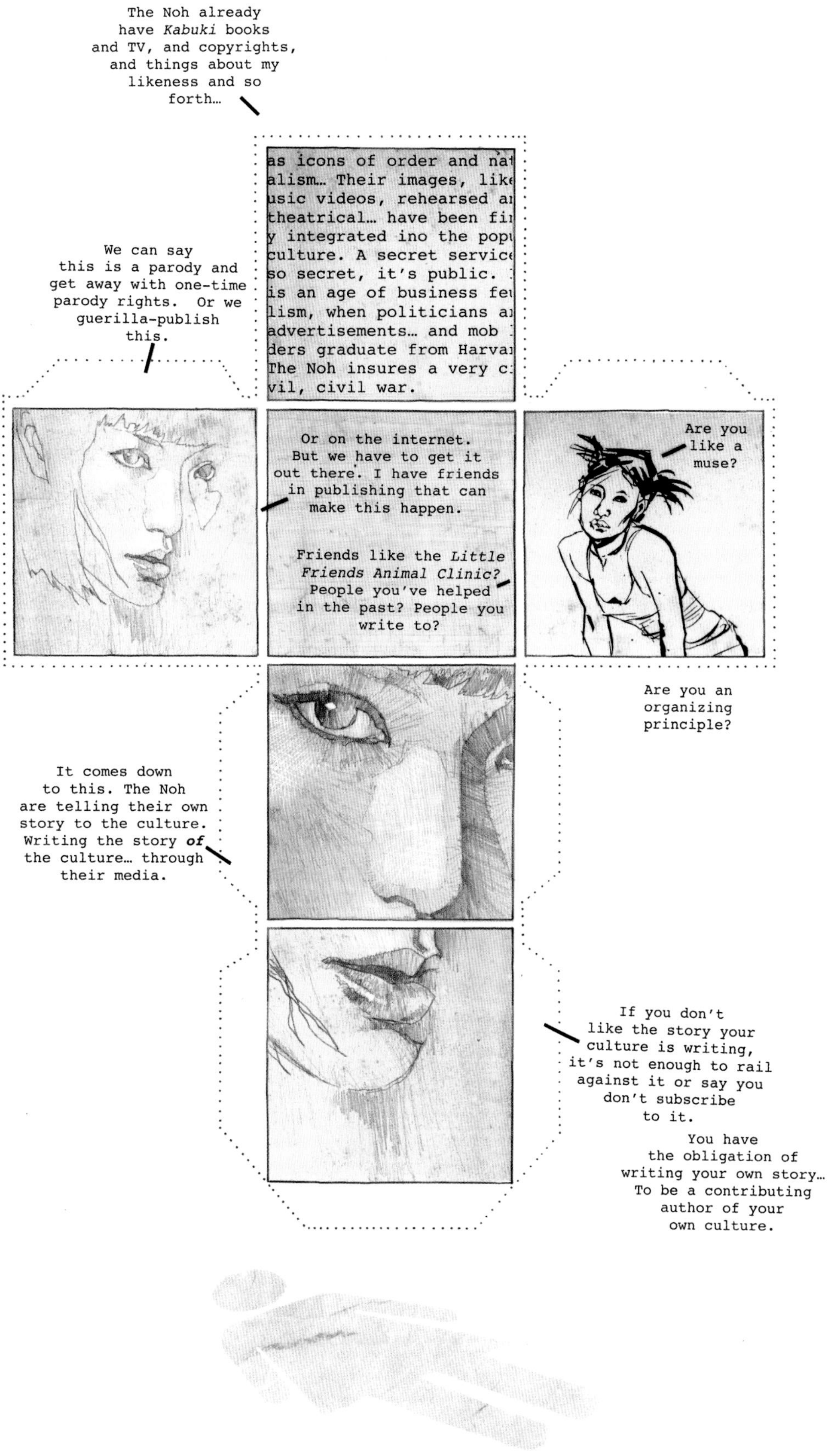
The Noh already have *Kabuki* books and TV, and copyrights, and things about my likeness and so forth...
as icons of order and nat
alism... Their images, like
usic videos, rehearsed ar
theatrical... have been fir
y integrated ino the popu
culture. A secret service
so secret, it's public. I
is an age of business feu
lism, when politicians ar
advertisements... and mob l
ders graduate from Harvar
The Noh insures a very ci
vil, civil war.
We can say this is a parody and get away with one-time parody rights. Or we guerilla-publish this.
Or on the internet. But we have to get it out there. I have friends in publishing that can make this happen.
Friends like the *Little Friends Animal Clinic?* People you've helped in the past? People you write to?
Are you like a muse?
Are you an organizing principle?
It comes down to this. The Noh are telling their own story to the culture. Writing the story ***of*** the culture... through their media.
If you don't like the story your culture is writing, it's not enough to rail against it or say you don't subscribe to it.
You have the obligation of writing your own story... To be a contributing author of your own culture.

You will
still do your
kids' books…

But this story
has all of those
children's book
ideas in it…

The **chess pieces**
chasing the pawn that
has left the board…
The **goldfish** being
considered dead
and flushed away… to
grow bigger in its new
environment…
The **little girl** con-
structing a **vehicle**
for her to interact
with the world.
The **Dante's Inferno**…

This story
has all of that.
But raw… & crude…
& flawed…

And utterly
relatable.

And…
most of all…
it's **true**.

I'd be naked.
I'd feel too…
unmasked.

On the contrary.
The story *is* your
mask. The last one
you will ever
need.

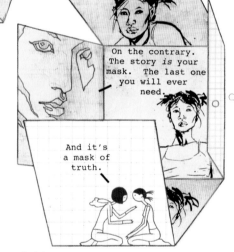

I remember
that Dove wore a
mask that looked like
his own face. And
what he told me…

*"When in the
company of deceptive
hearts, be only honest
and your opponents will
fool themselves".*

And it's
a mask of
truth.

And to
communicate
that truth… All we
have to do is put
it under another
name…
And call
it **fiction!**

Better yet!
We'll beat the
Noh at its
own game…

We'll disguise
it as pure
entertainment!

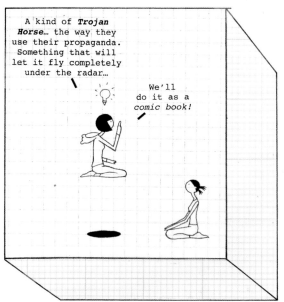

A kind of **Trojan Horse**... the way they use their propaganda. Something that will let it fly completely under the radar...

We'll do it as a *comic book!*

Like it's not a real 3-D *tell-all*, but a 2-D *mythology.*

Like the idea from your dream... About the images That tick.

You know, with **panels**... those square things?

Like **Jack Kirby** heroes? Or a **Steranko** spy story!

Or an **R. Crumb** thing? Main-line it right from the sub-conscious...

Or maybe a kind of **Ivan Brunetti** "Schizo" confessional?

Or like how Art Spiegalman's **MAUS** told his father's story of survival from the Nazis with characters drawn as cats and mice.

It was incredibly effective, and won the **Pulitzer Prize.**

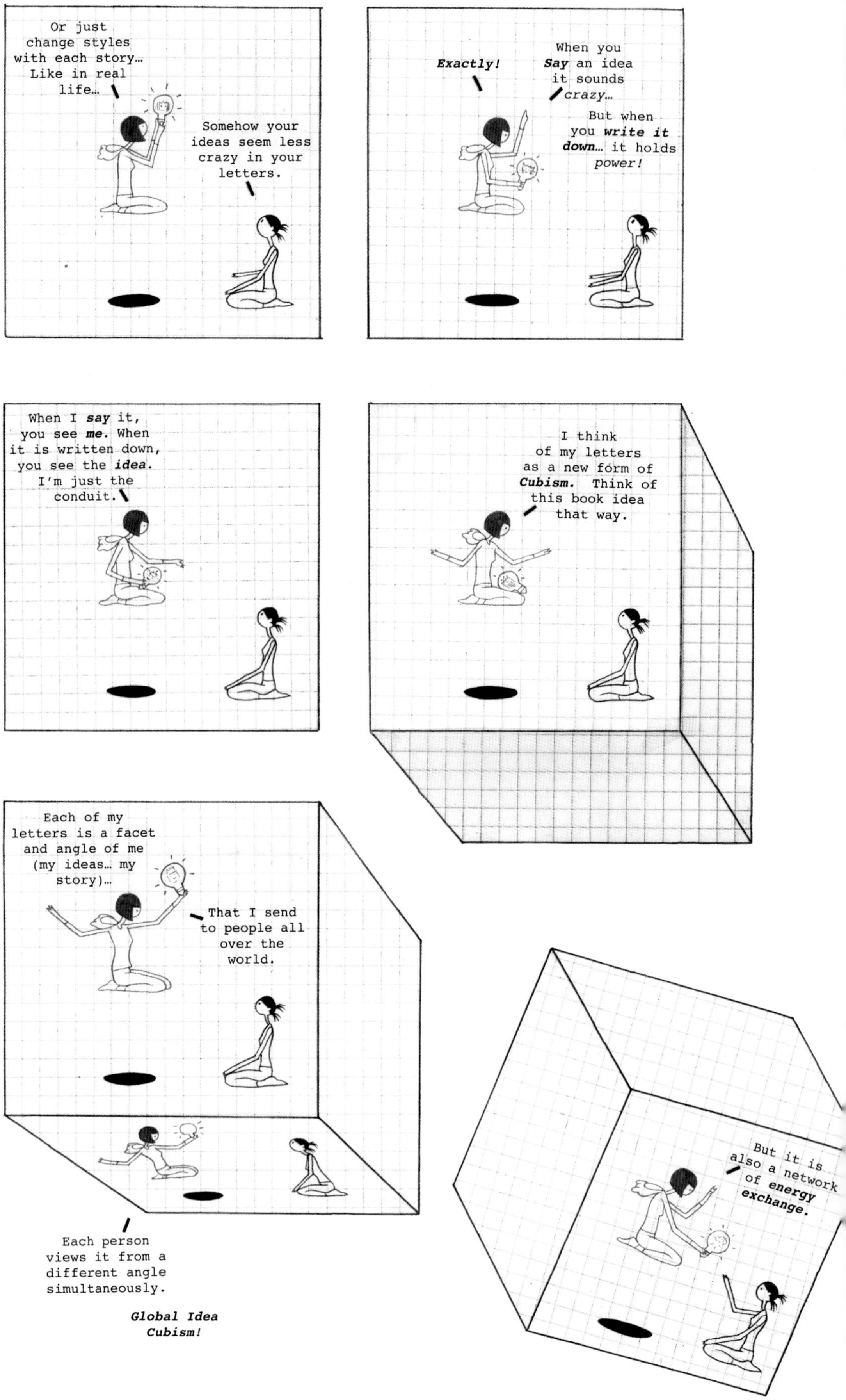

Or just change styles with each story... Like in real life...
Somehow your ideas seem less crazy in your letters.
Exactly!
When you **Say** an idea it sounds *crazy*...
But when you **write it down**... it holds *power!*
When I ***say*** it, you see ***me.*** When it is written down, you see the ***idea.*** I'm just the conduit.
I think of my letters as a new form of **Cubism.** Think of this book idea that way.
Each of my letters is a facet and angle of me (my ideas... my story)...
That I send to people all over the world.
Each person views it from a different angle simultaneously.
Global Idea Cubism!
But it is also a network of ***energy exchange.***

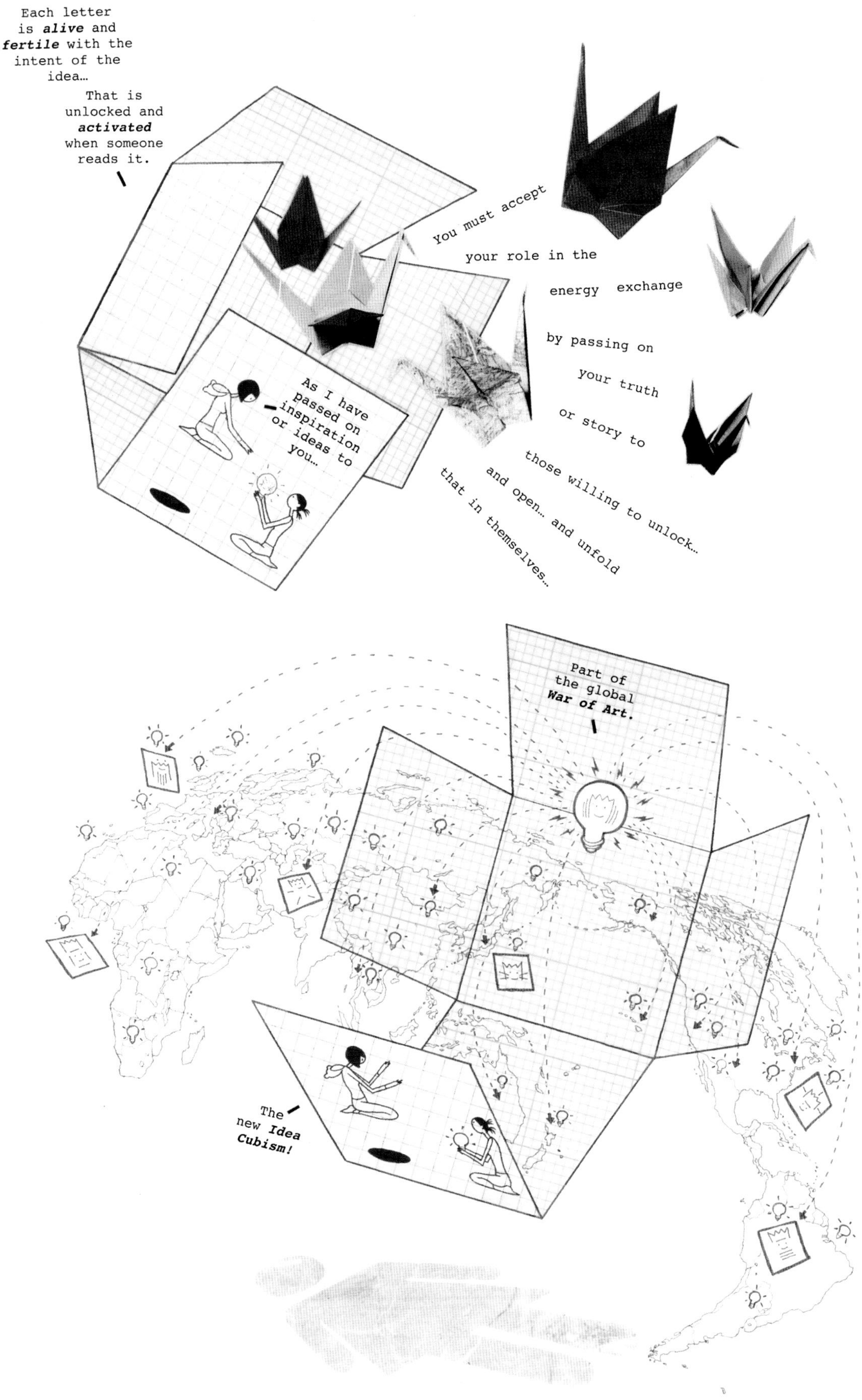

Each letter is ***alive*** and ***fertile*** with the intent of the idea…
That is unlocked and ***activated*** when someone reads it.
You must accept
your role in the
energy exchange
by passing on
your truth
or story to
those willing to unlock…
and open… and unfold
that in themselves…
As I have passed on inspiration or ideas to you…
Part of the global ***War of Art.***
The new ***Idea Cubism!***

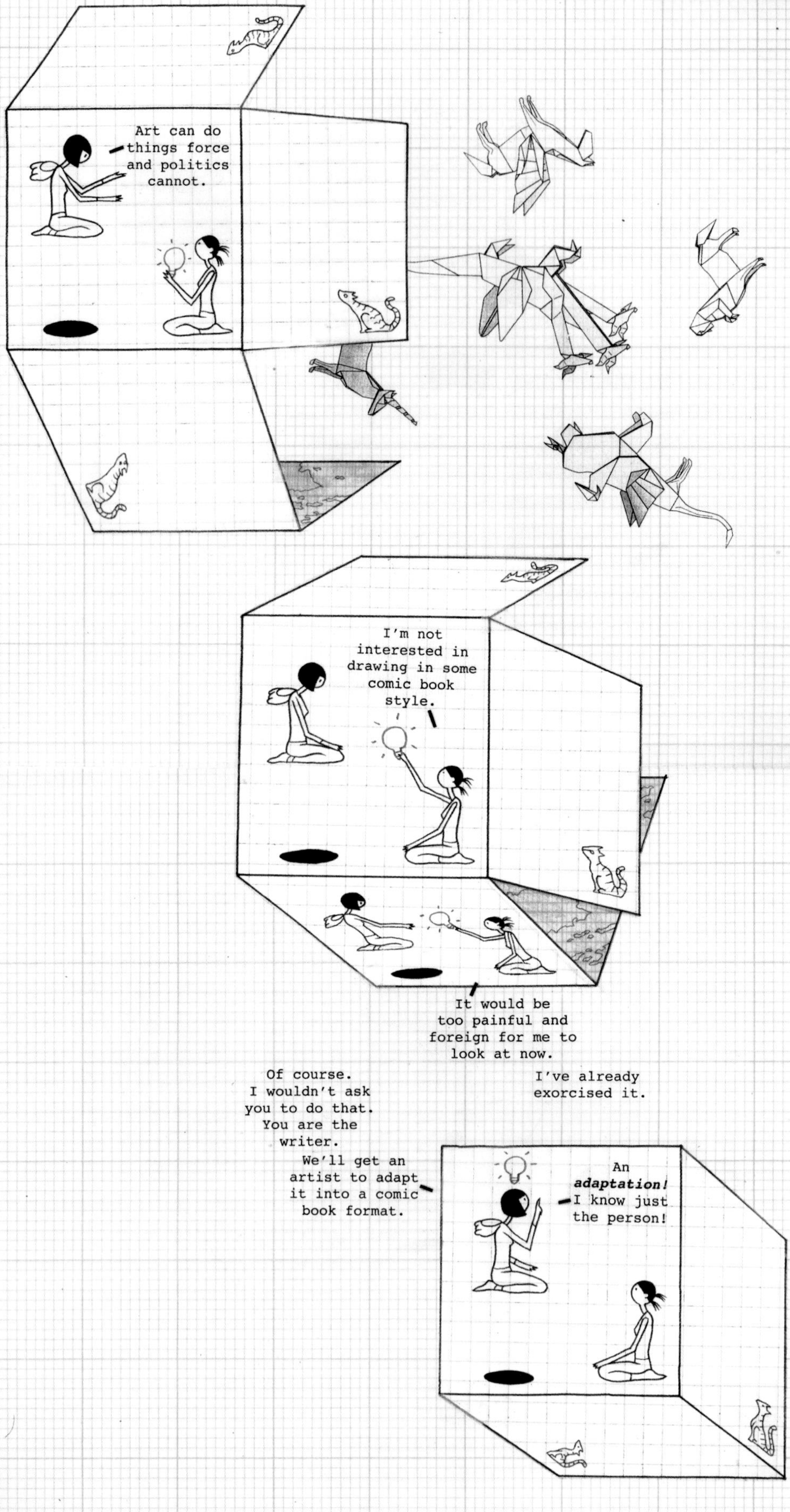

Art can do things force and politics cannot.
I'm not interested in drawing in some comic book style.
It would be too painful and foreign for me to look at now.
I've already exorcised it.
Of course. I wouldn't ask you to do that. You are the writer.
We'll get an artist to adapt it into a comic book format.
An *adaptation!* I know just the person!

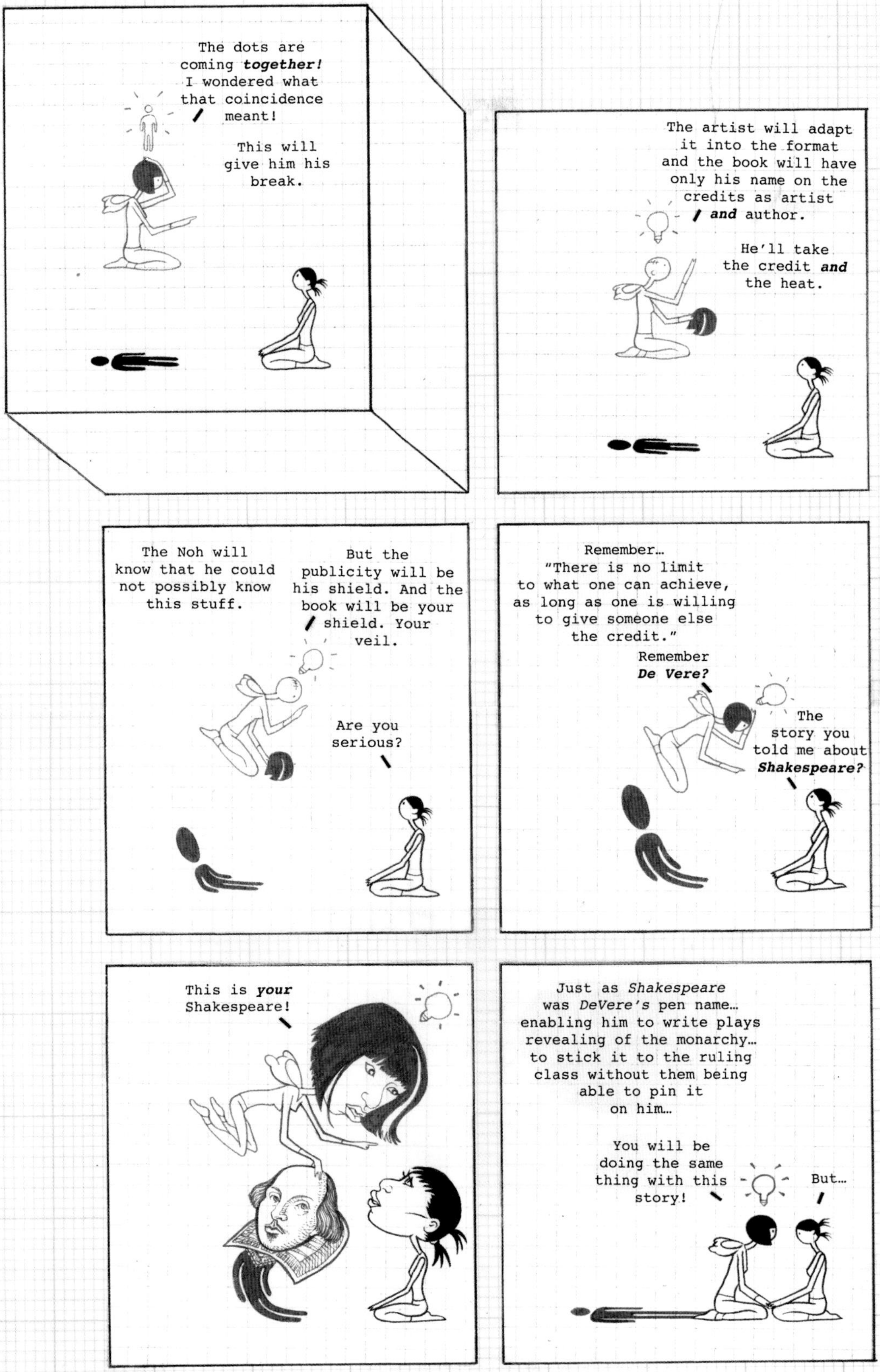
The dots are coming *together!* I wondered what that coincidence meant!
This will give him his break.
The artist will adapt it into the format and the book will have only his name on the credits as artist *and* author.
He'll take the credit *and* the heat.
The Noh will know that he could not possibly know this stuff.
But the publicity will be his shield. And the book will be your shield. Your veil.
Are you serious?
Remember… "There is no limit to what one can achieve, as long as one is willing to give someone else the credit."
Remember *De Vere?*
The story you told me about *Shakespeare?*
This is *your* Shakespeare!
Just as *Shakespeare* was *DeVere's* pen name… enabling him to write plays revealing of the monarchy… to stick it to the ruling class without them being able to pin it on him…
You will be doing the same thing with this story!
But…

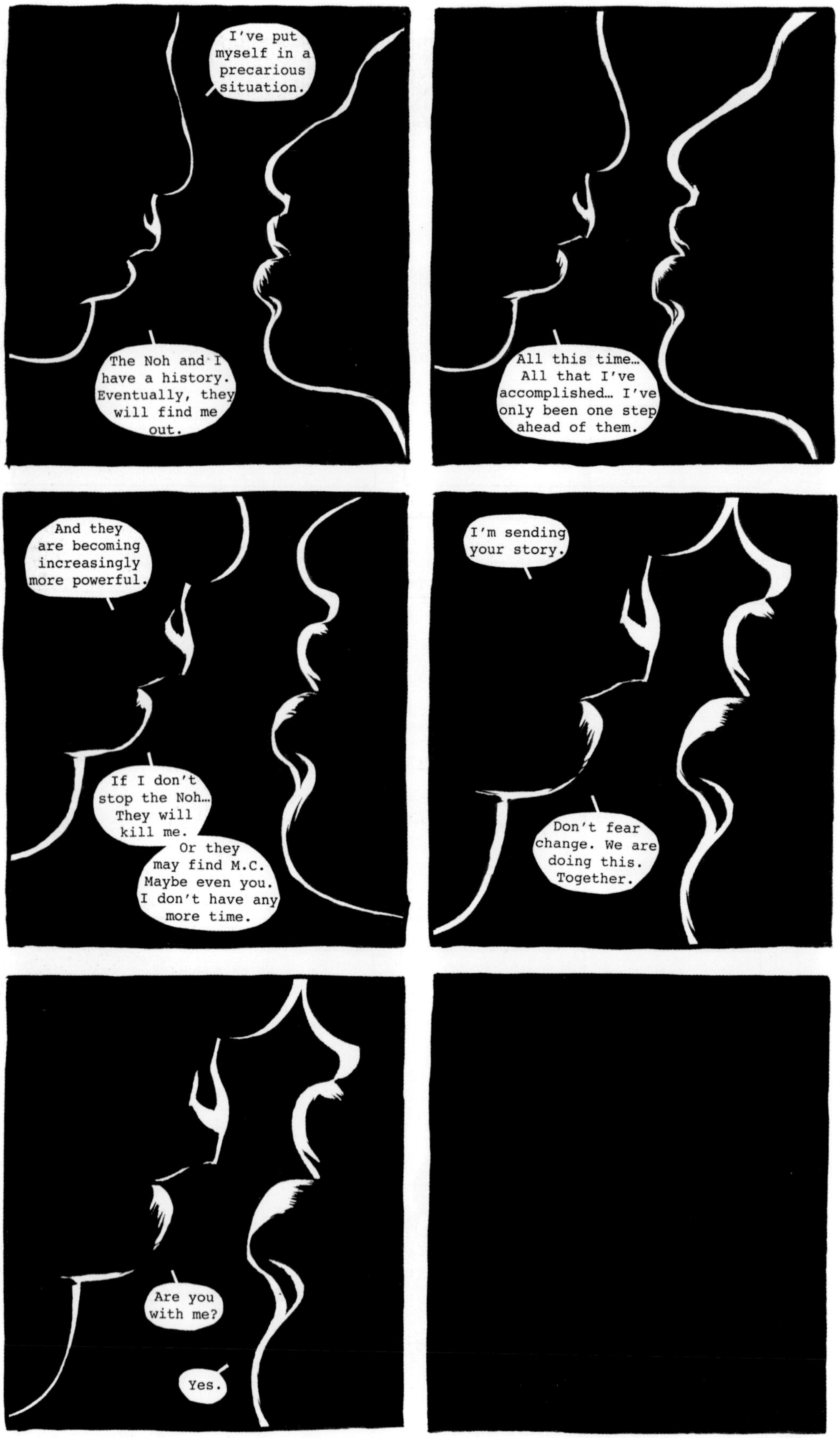
I've put myself in a precarious situation.
The Noh and I have a history. Eventually, they will find me out.
All this time... All that I've accomplished... I've only been one step ahead of them.
And they are becoming increasingly more powerful.
If I don't stop the Noh... They will kill me.
Or they may find M.C. Maybe even you. I don't have any more time.
I'm sending your story.
Don't fear change. We are doing this. Together.
Are you with me?
Yes.

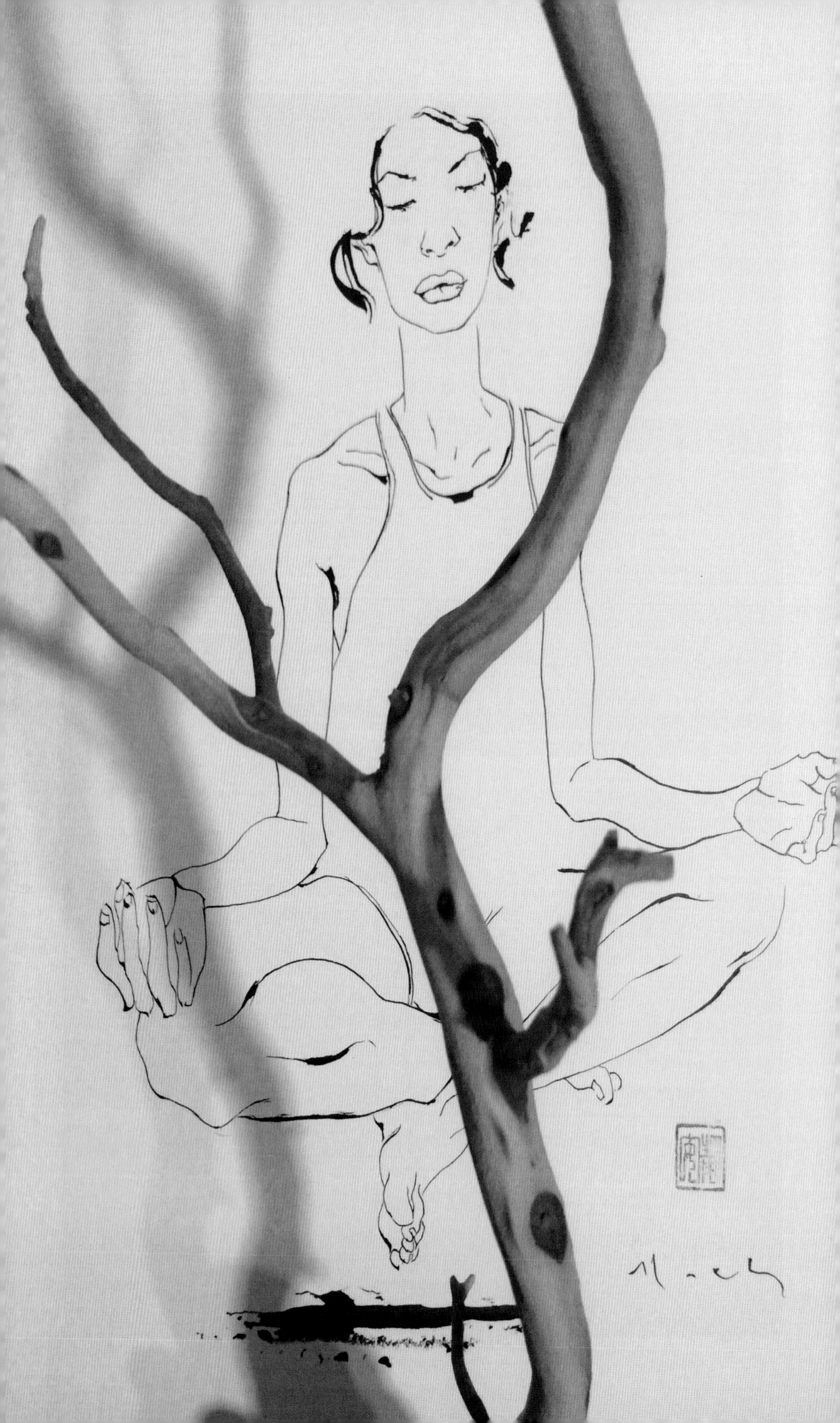

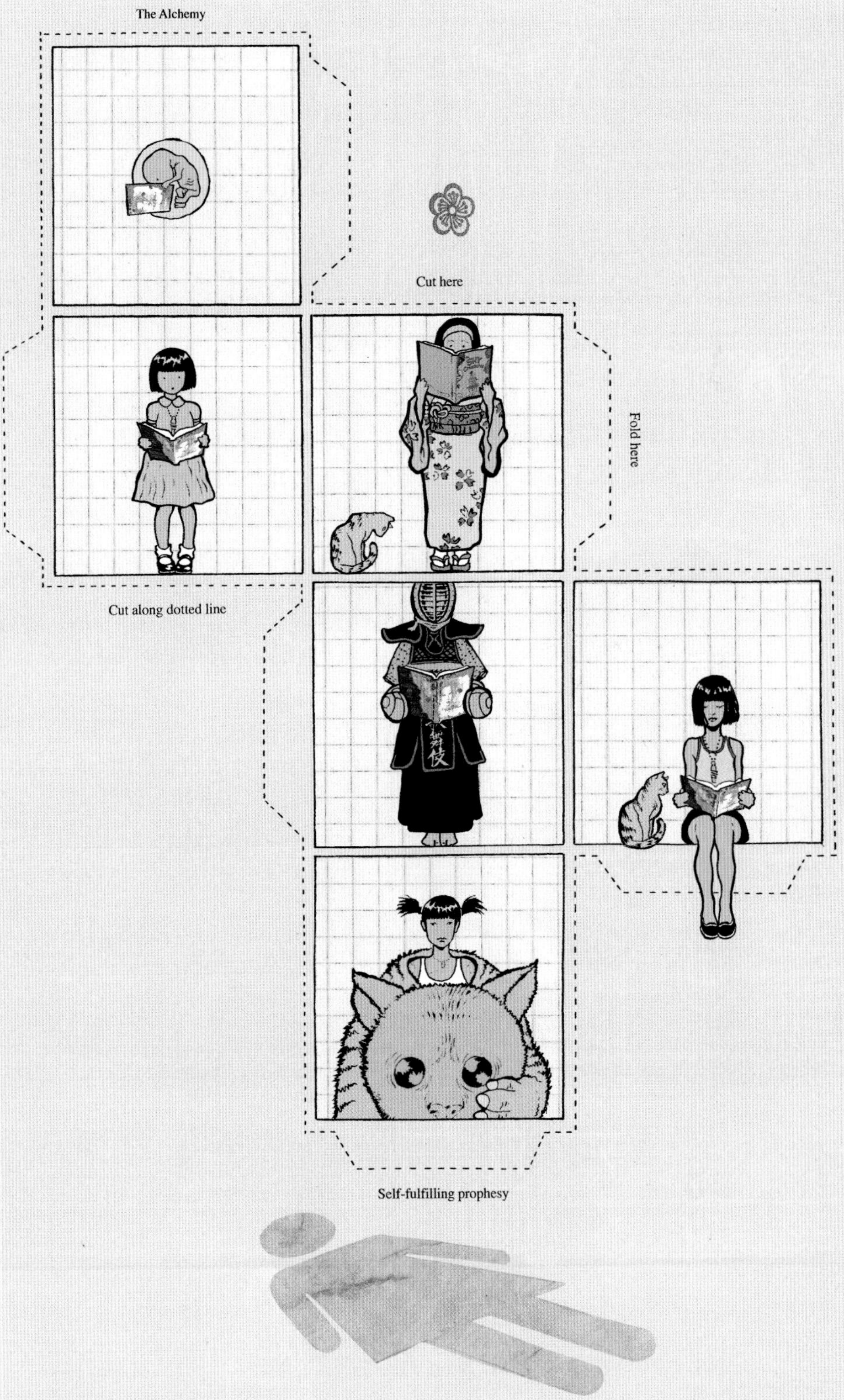

The Alchemy
Cut here
Fold here
Cut along dotted line
Part Nine
Self-fulfilling prophesy

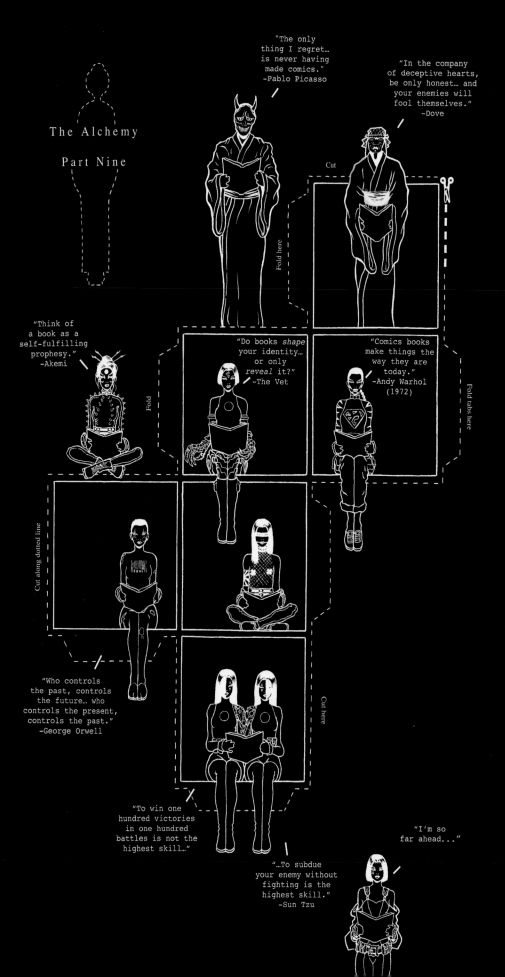

The Alchemy

Part Nine

"The only thing I regret… is never having made comics." -Pablo Picasso

"In the company of deceptive hearts, be only honest… and your enemies will fool themselves." -Dove

Cut

Fold here

"Think of a book as a self-fulfilling prophesy." -Akemi

Fold

"Do books *shape* your identity… or only *reveal* it?" -The Vet

"Comics books make things the way they are today." -Andy Warhol (1972)

Fold tabs here

Cut along dotted line

"Who controls the past, controls the future… who controls the present, controls the past." -George Orwell

Cut here

"To win one hundred victories in one hundred battles is not the highest skill…"

"I'm so far ahead..."

"…To subdue your enemy without fighting is the highest skill." -Sun Tzu

"I'm so
far ahead I'm
behind myself."
-Paul McCartney

S e l f – f u l f i l l i n g

P r o p h e s y

Kabuki?

Yes?

Are you
awake?

No.

What do
you call your
story? What's
the title?

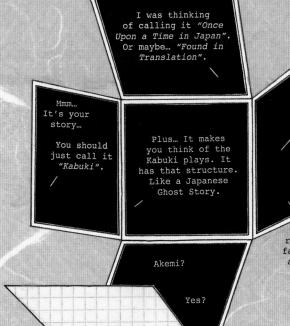

I was thinking
of calling it *Once
Upon a Time in Japan*.
Or maybe… *"Found in
Translation"*.

Mmm…
It's your
story…

You should
just call it
"Kabuki".

Plus… It makes
you think of the
Kabuki plays. It
has that structure.
Like a Japanese
Ghost Story.

You
could call
this first
volume…
*"Circle of
Blood"*.

You know… As
reference to the
family story, but
also a metaphor
for the flag.

And the
themes of
nationalism.

Akemi?

Yes?

Are you
implying more
than one
volume?

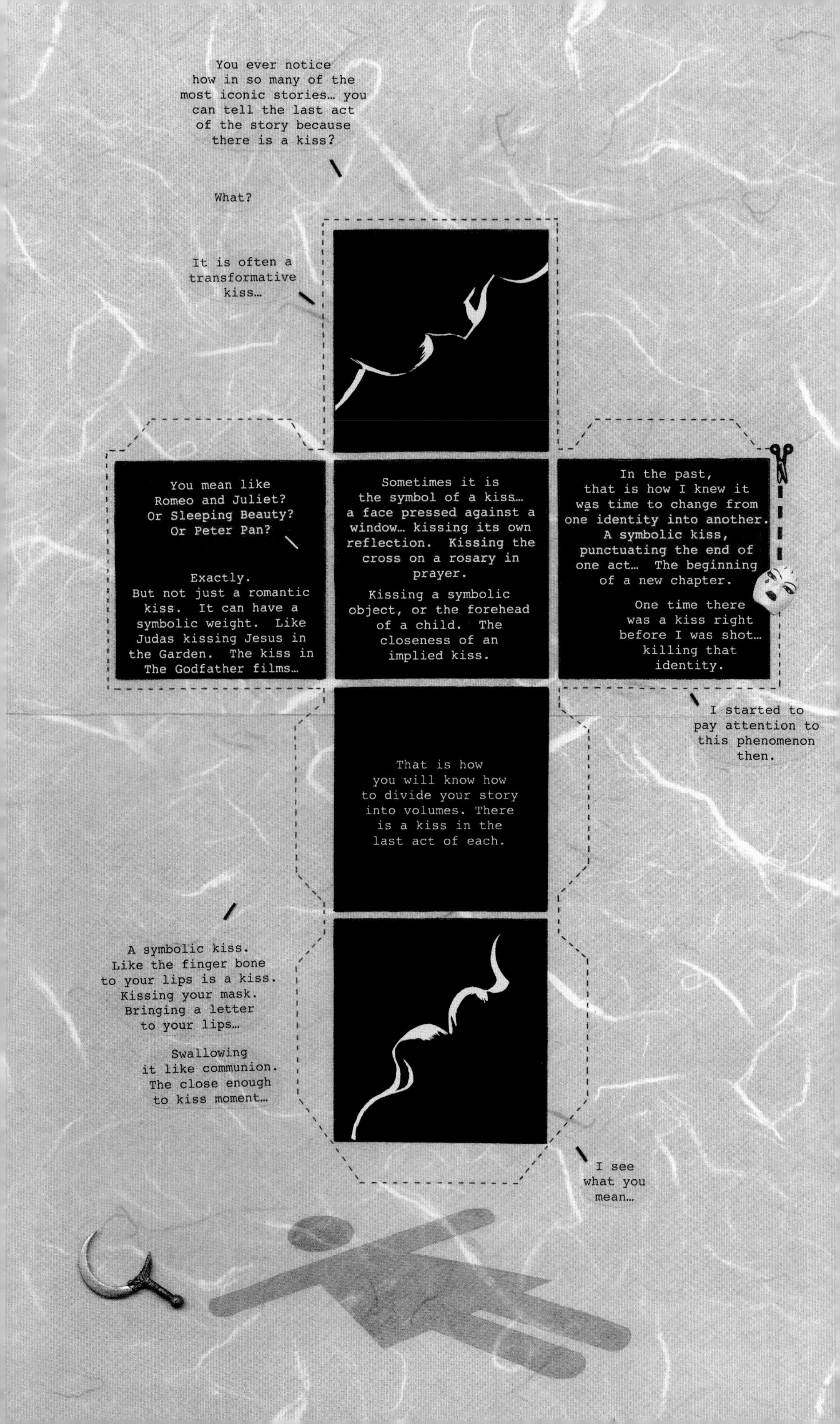

You ever notice
how in so many of the
most iconic stories… you
can tell the last act
of the story because
there is a kiss?

What?

It is often a
transformative
kiss…

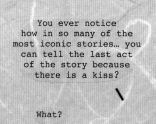

You mean like
Romeo and Juliet?
Or Sleeping Beauty?
Or Peter Pan?

Exactly.
But not just a romantic
kiss. It can have a
symbolic weight. Like
Judas kissing Jesus in
the Garden. The kiss in
The Godfather films…

Sometimes it is
the symbol of a kiss…
a face pressed against a
window… kissing its own
reflection. Kissing the
cross on a rosary in
prayer.

Kissing a symbolic
object, or the forehead
of a child. The
closeness of an
implied kiss.

In the past,
that is how I knew it
was time to change from
one identity into another.
A symbolic kiss,
punctuating the end of
one act… The beginning
of a new chapter.

One time there
was a kiss right
before I was shot…
killing that
identity.

I started to
pay attention to
this phenomenon
then.

That is how
you will know how
to divide your story
into volumes. There
is a kiss in the
last act of each.

A symbolic kiss.
Like the finger bone
to your lips is a kiss.
Kissing your mask.
Bringing a letter
to your lips…

Swallowing
it like communion.
The close enough
to kiss moment…

I see
what you
mean…

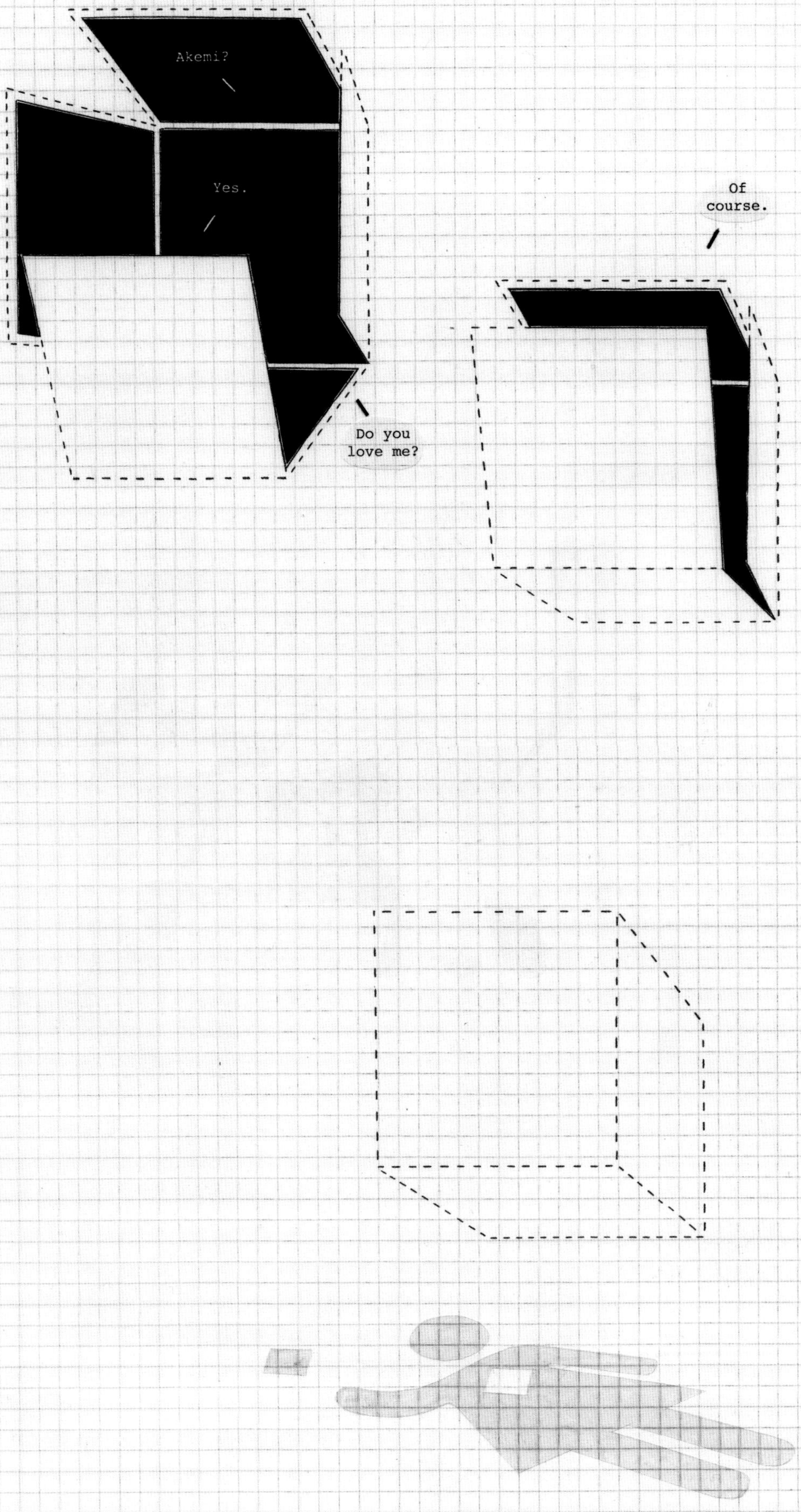
Akemi?
Yes.
Do you love me?
Of course.

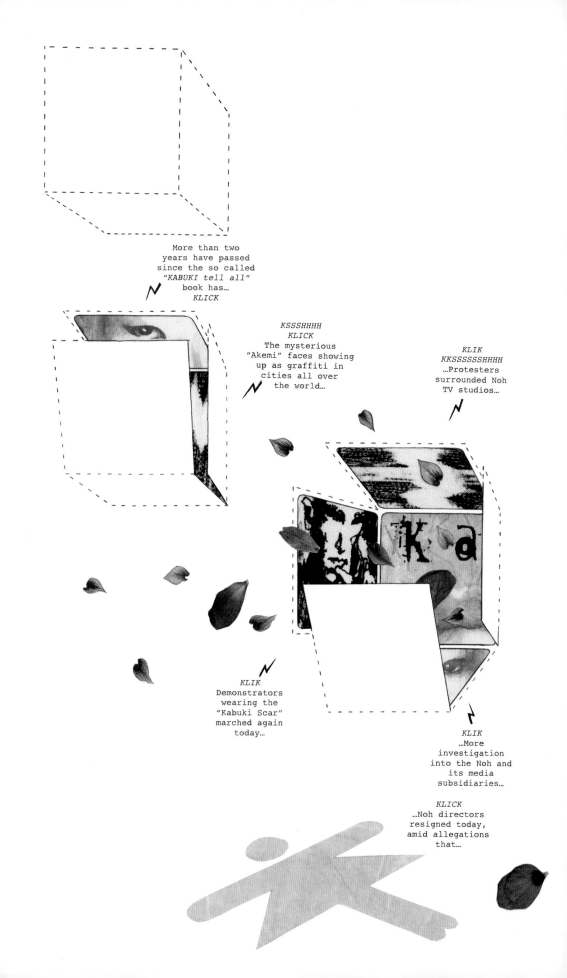

More than two
years have passed
since the so called
"KABUKI tell all"
book has…
KLICK

KSSSHHHH
KLICK
The mysterious
"Akemi" faces showing
up as graffiti in
cities all over
the world…

KLIK
KKSSSSSSSHHHH
…Protesters
surrounded Noh
TV studios…

KLIK
Demonstrators
wearing the
"Kabuki Scar"
marched again
today…

KLIK
…More
investigation
into the Noh and
its media
subsidiaries…

KLICK
…Noh directors
resigned today,
amid allegations
that…

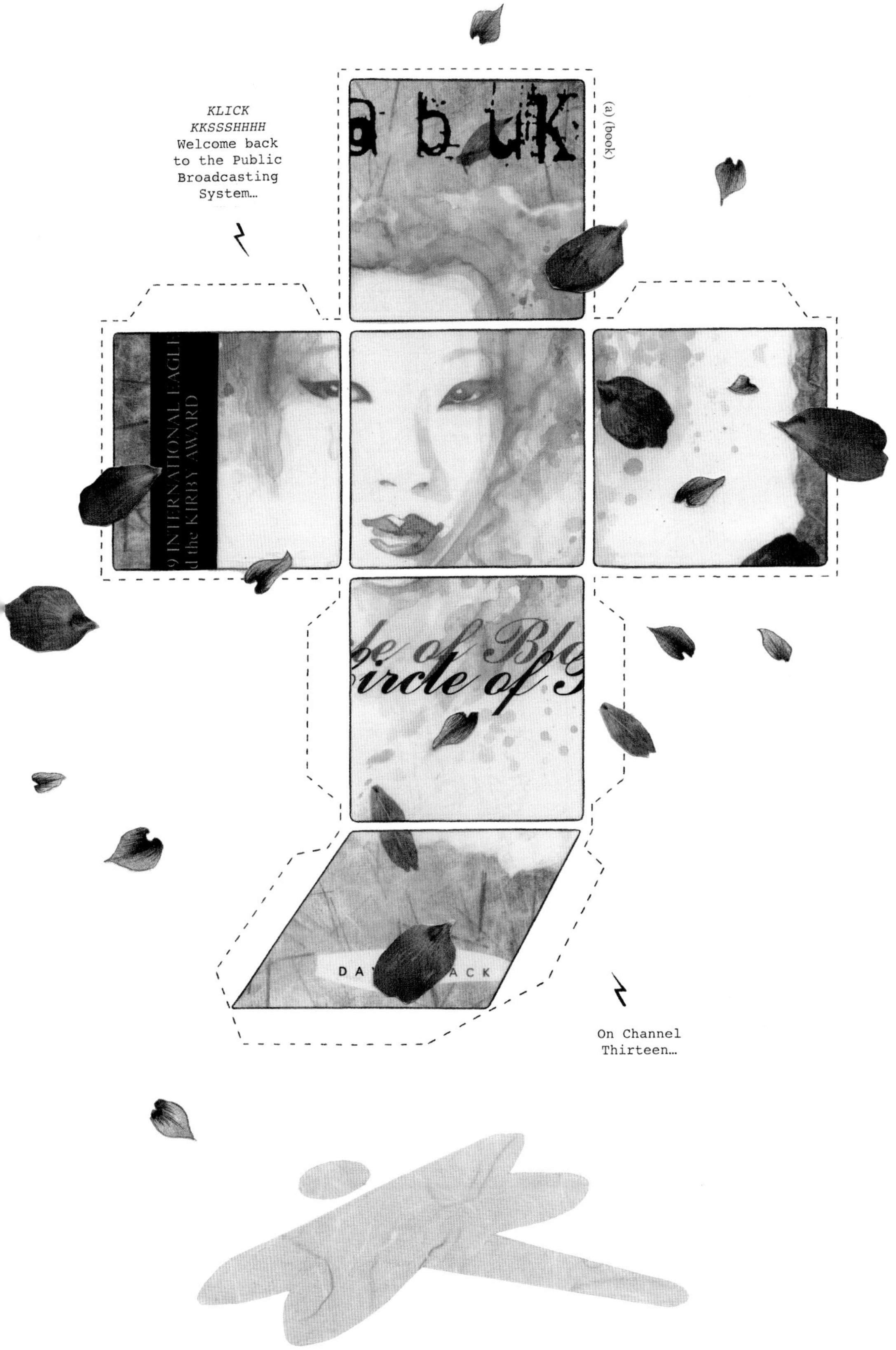
KLICK
KKSSSHHHH
Welcome back to the Public Broadcasting System...
(a) (book)
On Channel Thirteen...

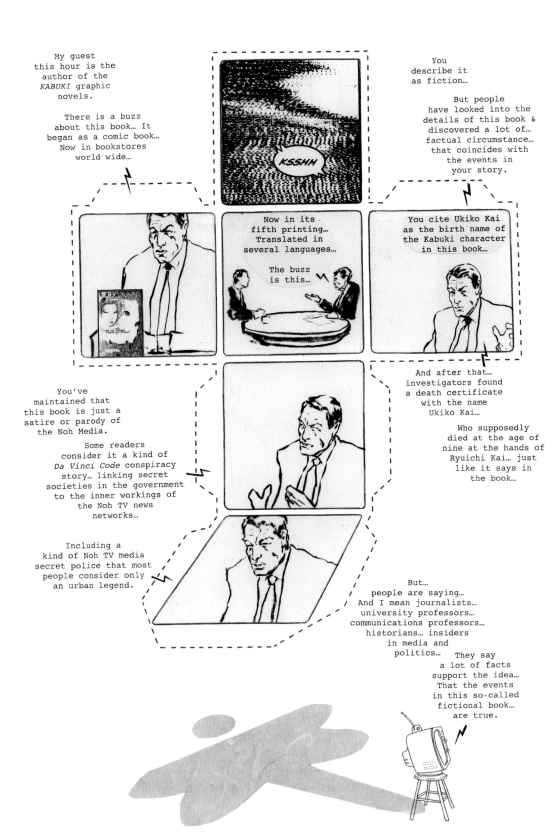

My guest
this hour is the
author of the
KABUKI graphic
novels.

There is a buzz
about this book… It
began as a comic book…
Now in bookstores
world wide…

KSSHH

You
describe it
as fiction…

But people
have looked into the
details of this book &
discovered a lot of…
factual circumstance…
that coincides with
the events in
your story.

Now in its
fifth printing…
Translated in
several languages…

The buzz
is this…

You cite Ukiko Kai
as the birth name of
the Kabuki character
in this book…

You've
maintained that
this book is just a
satire or parody of
the Noh Media.

Some readers
consider it a kind of
Da Vinci Code conspiracy
story… linking secret
societies in the government
to the inner workings of
the Noh TV news
networks…

Including a
kind of Noh TV media
secret police that most
people consider only
an urban legend.

And after that…
investigators found
a death certificate
with the name
Ukiko Kai…

Who supposedly
died at the age of
nine at the hands of
Ryuichi Kai… just
like it says in
the book…

But…
people are saying…
And I mean journalists…
university professors…
communications professors…
historians… insiders
in media and
politics… They say
a lot of facts
support the idea…
That the events
in this so-called
fictional book…
are true.

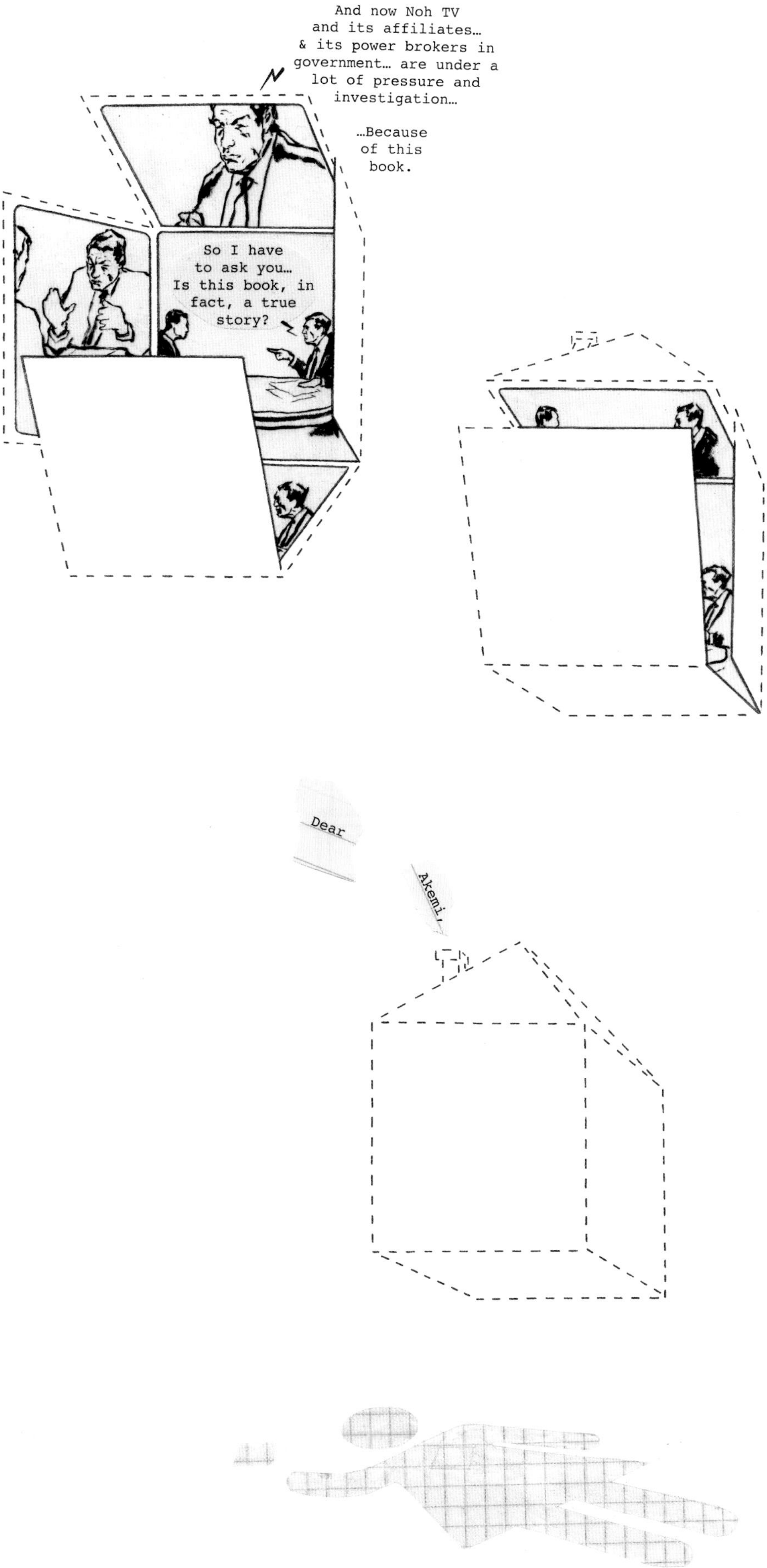
And now Noh TV and its affiliates… & its power brokers in government… are under a lot of pressure and investigation…
…Because of this book.
So I have to ask you… Is this book, in fact, a true story?
Dear
Akemi,

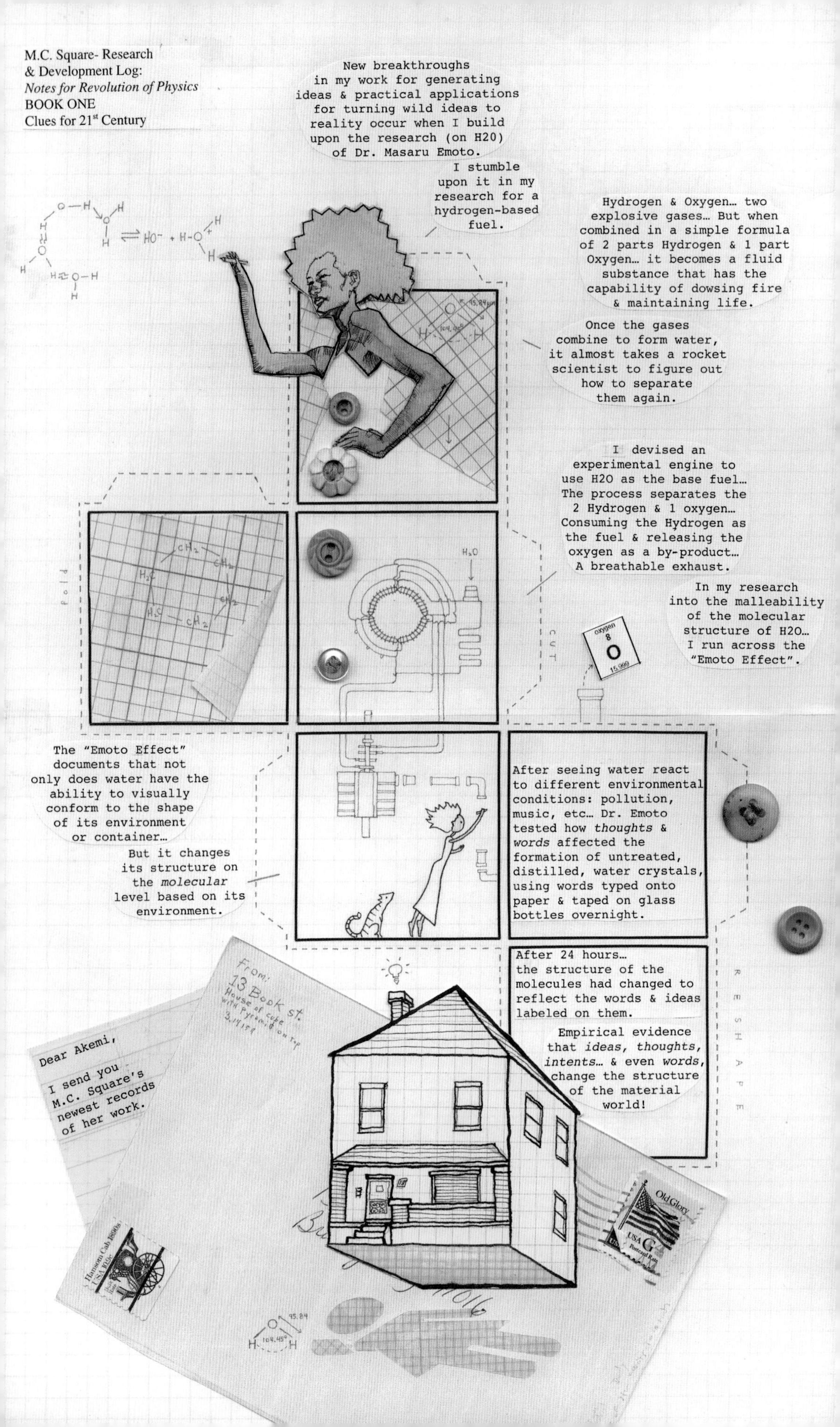

M.C. Square- Research
& Development Log:
Notes for Revolution of Physics
BOOK ONE
Clues for 21st Century
New breakthroughs in my work for generating ideas & practical applications for turning wild ideas to reality occur when I build upon the research (on H2O) of Dr. Masaru Emoto.
I stumble upon it in my research for a hydrogen-based fuel.
Hydrogen & Oxygen… two explosive gases… But when combined in a simple formula of 2 parts Hydrogen & 1 part Oxygen… it becomes a fluid substance that has the capability of dowsing fire & maintaining life.
Once the gases combine to form water, it almost takes a rocket scientist to figure out how to separate them again.
I devised an experimental engine to use H2O as the base fuel… The process separates the 2 Hydrogen & 1 oxygen… Consuming the Hydrogen as the fuel & releasing the oxygen as a by-product… A breathable exhaust.
In my research into the malleability of the molecular structure of H2O… I run across the "Emoto Effect".
Fold
CUT
oxygen
8
O
15.999
The "Emoto Effect" documents that not only does water have the ability to visually conform to the shape of its environment or container…
But it changes its structure on the *molecular* level based on its environment.
After seeing water react to different environmental conditions: pollution, music, etc… Dr. Emoto tested how *thoughts* & *words* affected the formation of untreated, distilled, water crystals, using words typed onto paper & taped on glass bottles overnight.
After 24 hours… the structure of the molecules had changed to reflect the words & ideas labeled on them.
Empirical evidence that *ideas, thoughts, intents…* & even *words*, change the structure of the material world!
RESHAPE
From:
13 Book st.
House of cube with Pyramid on top
3.14159
Dear Akemi,
I send you M.C. Square's newest records of her work.
Old Glory
USA G
Hansom Cab 1890s

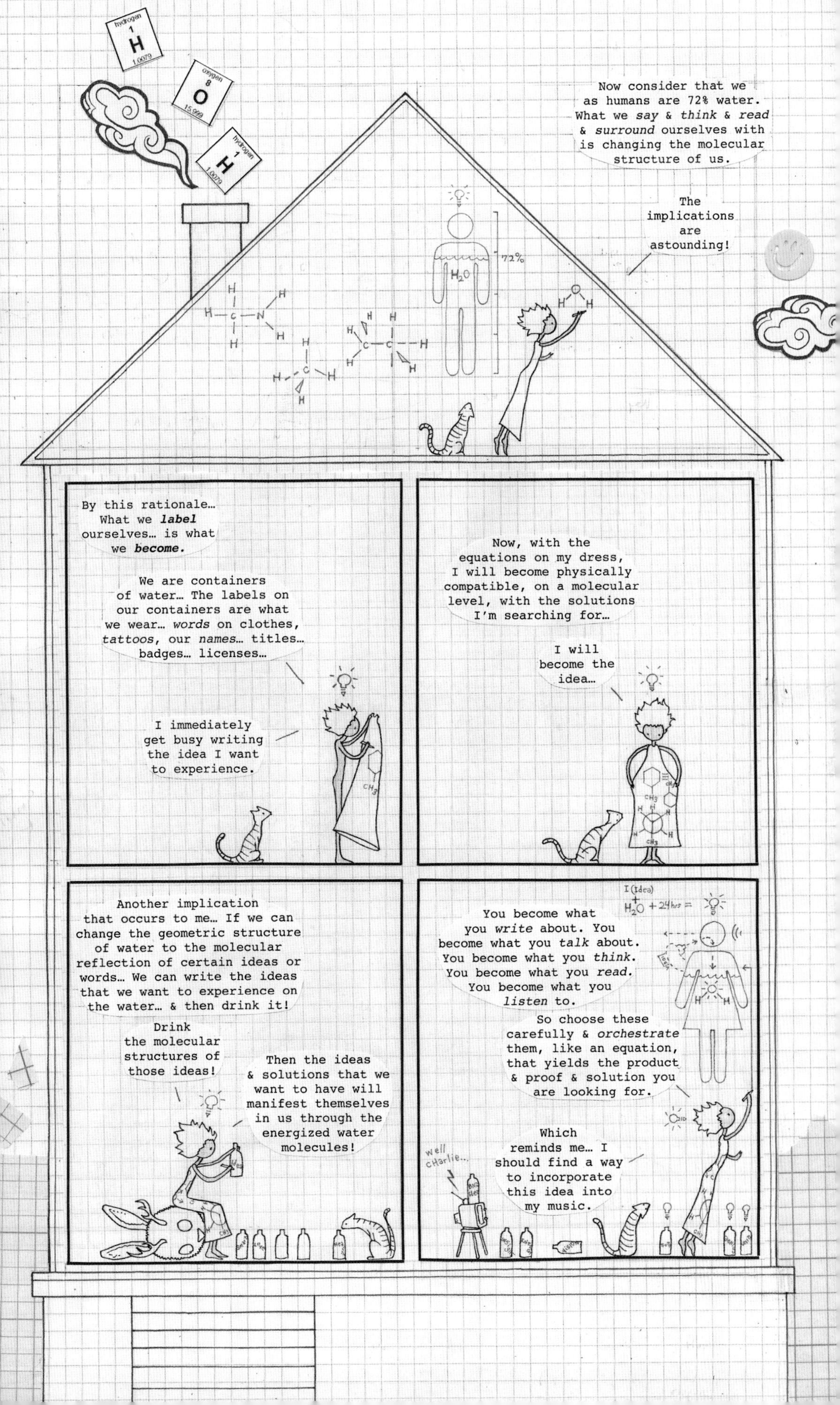

hydrogen 1 H 1.0079
oxygen 8 O 15.999
hydrogen 1 H 1.0079
Now consider that we as humans are 72% water. What we *say* & *think* & *read* & *surround* ourselves with is changing the molecular structure of us.
72%
H_2O
The implications are astounding!
By this rationale… What we ***label*** ourselves… is what we ***become.***
We are containers of water… The labels on our containers are what we wear… *words* on clothes, *tattoos*, our *names*… titles… badges… licenses…
I immediately get busy writing the idea I want to experience.
Now, with the equations on my dress, I will become physically compatible, on a molecular level, with the solutions I'm searching for…
I will become the idea…
Another implication that occurs to me… If we can change the geometric structure of water to the molecular reflection of certain ideas or words… We can write the ideas that we want to experience on the water… & then drink it!
Drink the molecular structures of those ideas!
Then the ideas & solutions that we want to have will manifest themselves in us through the energized water molecules!
I (Idea) + H_2O + 24hrs =
You become what you *write* about. You become what you *talk* about. You become what you *think*. You become what you *read.* You become what you *listen* to.
So choose these carefully & *orchestrate* them, like an equation, that yields the product & proof & solution you are looking for.
Which reminds me… I should find a way to incorporate this idea into my music.
well CHarlie…

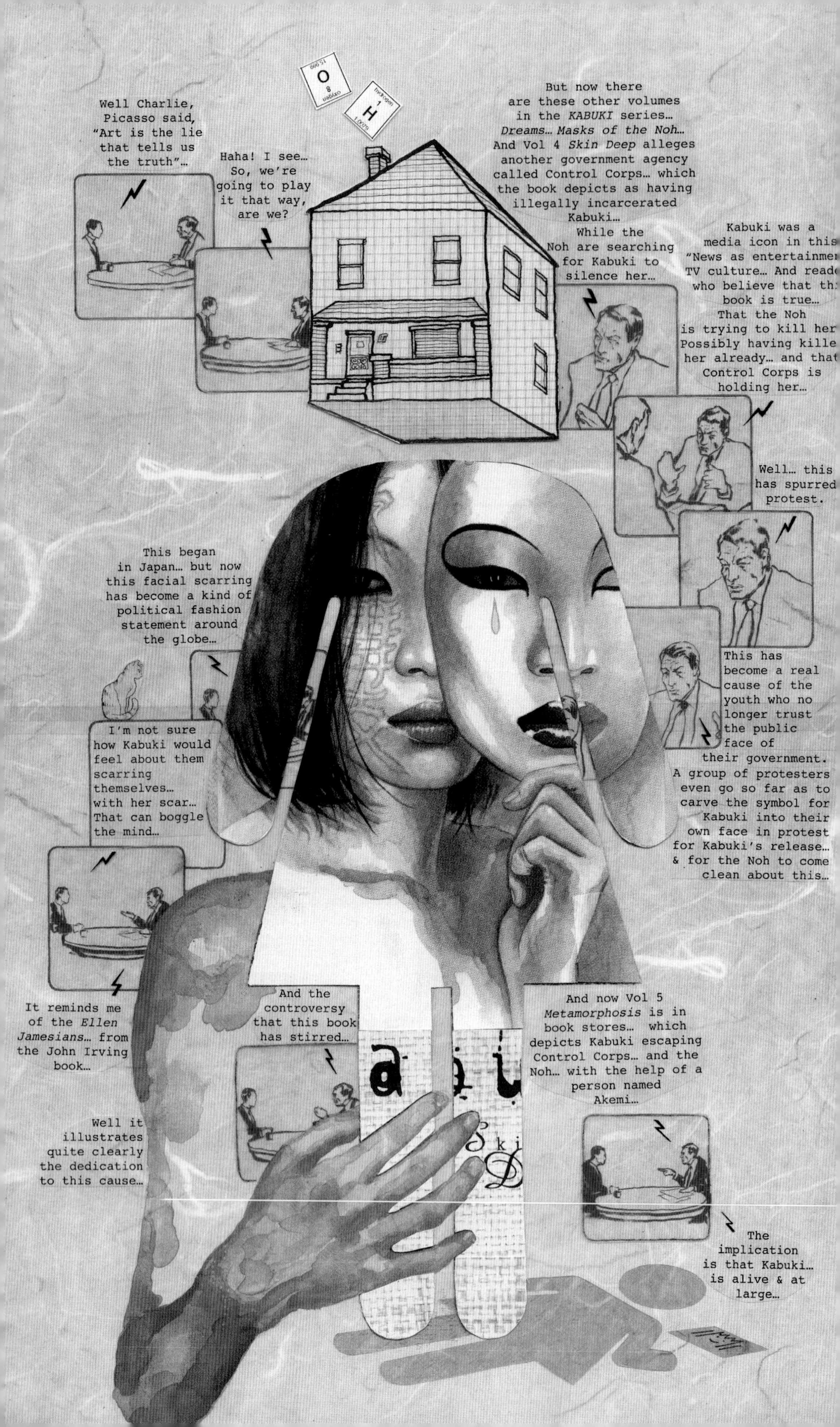

Well Charlie, Picasso said, "Art is the lie that tells us the truth"...
Haha! I see... So, we're going to play it that way, are we?
But now there are these other volumes in the KABUKI series... Dreams... Masks of the Noh... And Vol 4 Skin Deep alleges another government agency called Control Corps... which the book depicts as having illegally incarcerated Kabuki... While the Noh are searching for Kabuki to silence her...
Kabuki was a media icon in this "News as entertainment" TV culture... And readers who believe that this book is true... That the Noh is trying to kill her. Possibly having killed her already... and that Control Corps is holding her...
Well... this has spurred protest.
This has become a real cause of the youth who no longer trust the public face of their government. A group of protesters even go so far as to carve the symbol for Kabuki into their own face in protest for Kabuki's release... & for the Noh to come clean about this...
This began in Japan... but now this facial scarring has become a kind of political fashion statement around the globe...
I'm not sure how Kabuki would feel about them scarring themselves... with her scar... That can boggle the mind...
It reminds me of the Ellen Jamesians... from the John Irving book...
And the controversy that this book has stirred...
And now Vol 5 Metamorphosis is in book stores... which depicts Kabuki escaping Control Corps... and the Noh... with the help of a person named Akemi...
Well it illustrates quite clearly the dedication to this cause...
The implication is that Kabuki... is alive & at large...

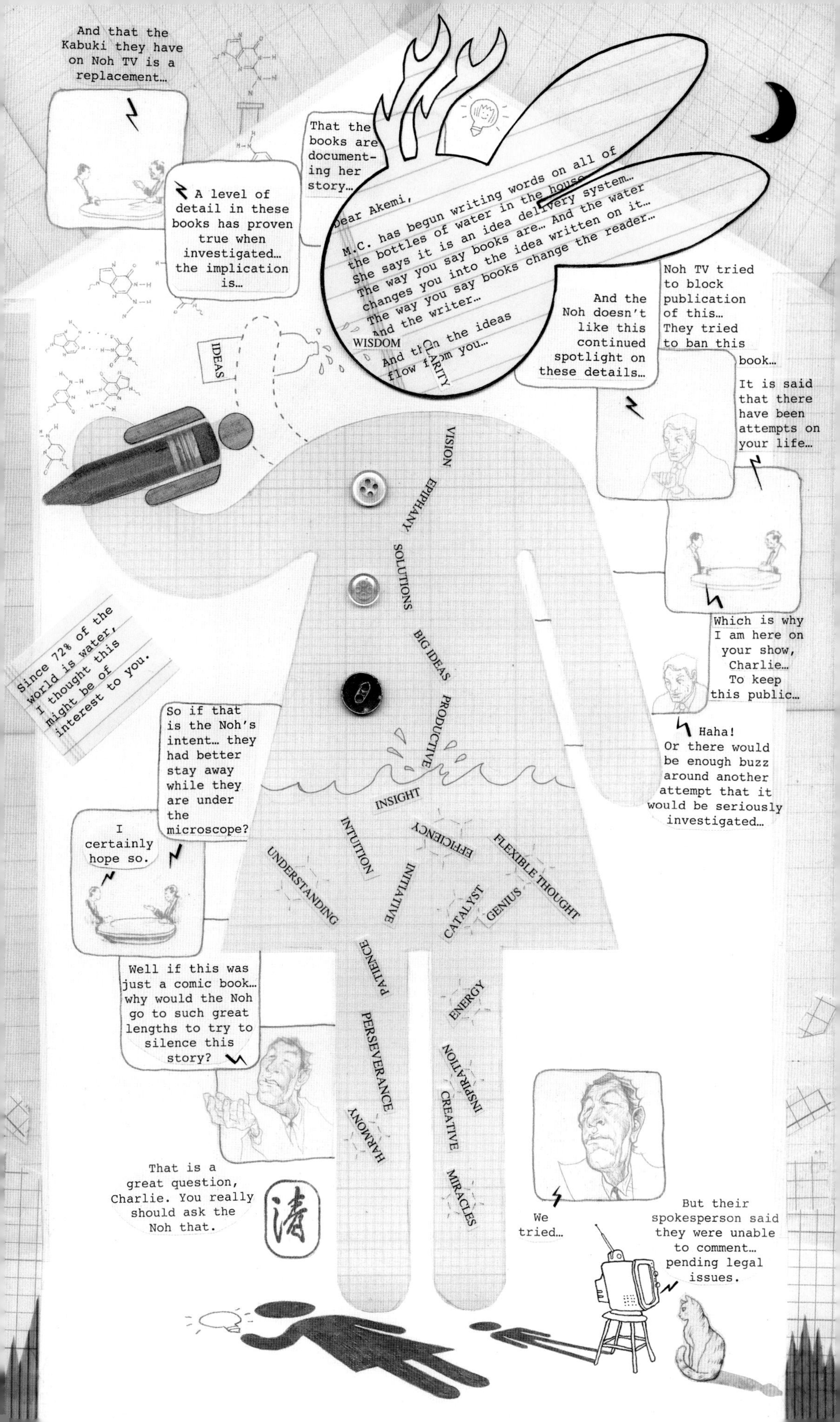

And that the Kabuki they have on Noh TV is a replacement...
A level of detail in these books has proven true when investigated... the implication is...
That the books are document-ing her story...
Dear Akemi,
M.C. has begun writing words on all of the bottles of water in the house... She says it is an idea delivery system... The way you say books are... And the water changes you into the idea written on it... The way you say books change the reader... The way you say and the writer...
And then the ideas flow from you...
WISDOM
CLARITY
IDEAS
And the Noh doesn't like this continued spotlight on these details...
Noh TV tried to block publication of this... They tried to ban this book...
It is said that there have been attempts on your life...
Which is why I am here on your show, Charlie... To keep this public...
Haha! Or there would be enough buzz around another attempt that it would be seriously investigated...
Since 72% of the world is water, I thought this might be of interest to you.
So if that is the Noh's intent... they had better stay away while they are under the microscope?
I certainly hope so.
Well if this was just a comic book... why would the Noh go to such great lengths to try to silence this story?
That is a great question, Charlie. You really should ask the Noh that.
We tried...
But their spokesperson said they were unable to comment... pending legal issues.
VISION
EPIPHANY
SOLUTIONS
BIG IDEAS
PRODUCTIVE
INSIGHT
INTUITION
EFFICIENCY
FLEXIBLE THOUGHT
UNDERSTANDING
INITIATIVE
CATALYST
GENIUS
PATIENCE
ENERGY
PERSEVERANCE
INSPIRATION
CREATIVE
HARMONY
MIRACLES

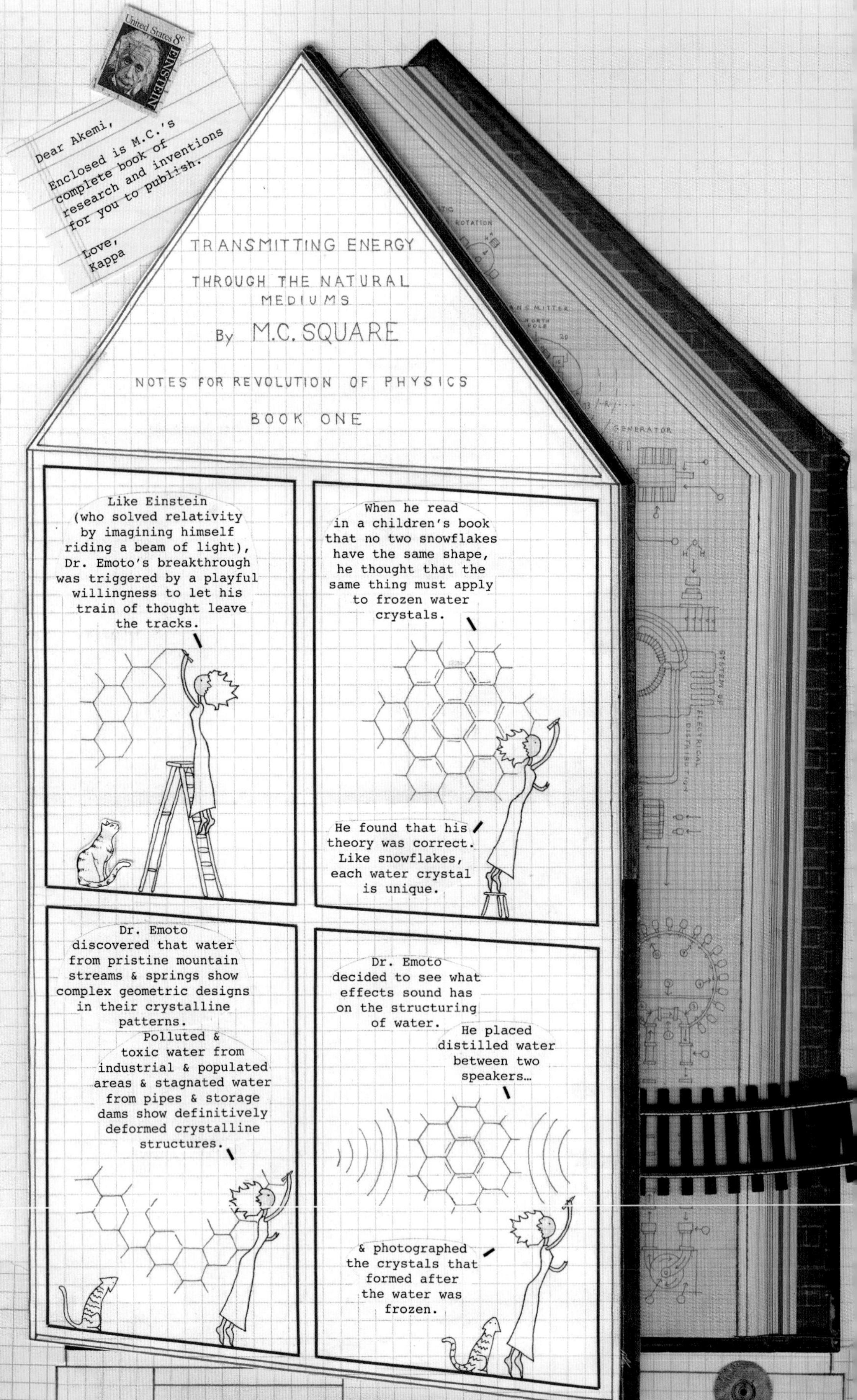

United States 8c
EINSTEIN
Dear Akemi,
Enclosed is M.C.'s complete book of research and inventions for you to publish.
Love, Kappa
TRANSMITTING ENERGY
THROUGH THE NATURAL MEDIUMS
By M.C. SQUARE
NOTES FOR REVOLUTION OF PHYSICS
BOOK ONE
GENERATOR
Like Einstein (who solved relativity by imagining himself riding a beam of light), Dr. Emoto's breakthrough was triggered by a playful willingness to let his train of thought leave the tracks.
When he read in a children's book that no two snowflakes have the same shape, he thought that the same thing must apply to frozen water crystals.
He found that his theory was correct. Like snowflakes, each water crystal is unique.
Dr. Emoto discovered that water from pristine mountain streams & springs show complex geometric designs in their crystalline patterns.
Polluted & toxic water from industrial & populated areas & stagnated water from pipes & storage dams show definitively deformed crystalline structures.
Dr. Emoto decided to see what effects sound has on the structuring of water.
He placed distilled water between two speakers…
& photographed the crystals that formed after the water was frozen.

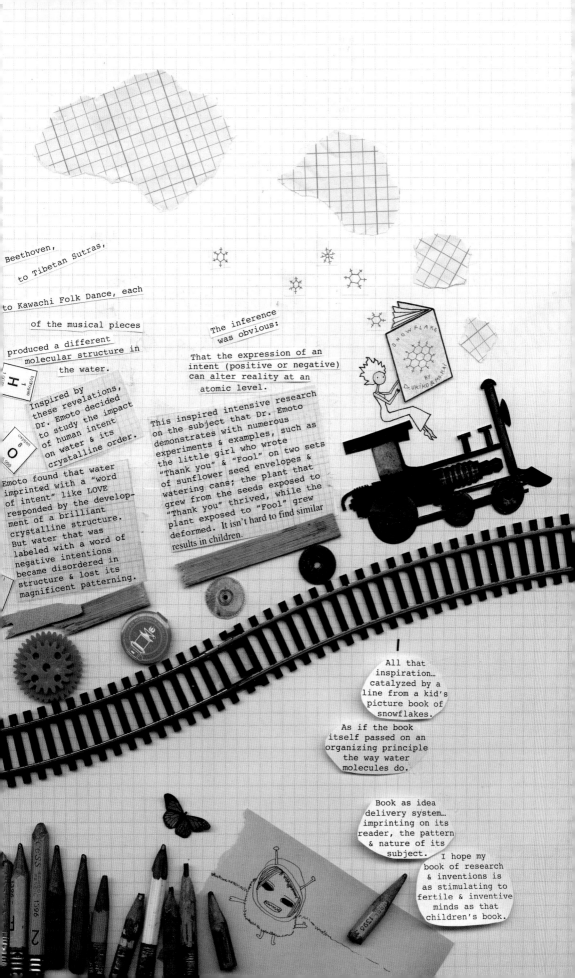

Beethoven,

to Tibetan Sutras,

to Kawachi Folk Dance, each

of the musical pieces

produced a different molecular structure in the water.

Inspired by these revelations, Dr. Emoto decided to study the impact of human intent on water & its crystalline order.

Emoto found that water imprinted with a "word of intent" like LOVE responded by the development of a brilliant crystalline structure. But water that was labeled with a word of negative intentions became disordered in structure & lost its magnificent patterning.

The inference was obvious:

That the expression of an intent (positive or negative) can alter reality at an atomic level.

This inspired intensive research on the subject that Dr. Emoto demonstrates with numerous experiments & examples, such as the little girl who wrote "Thank you" & "Fool" on two sets of sunflower seed envelopes & watering cans; the plant that grew from the seeds exposed to "Thank you" thrived, while the plant exposed to "Fool" grew deformed. It isn't hard to find similar results in children.

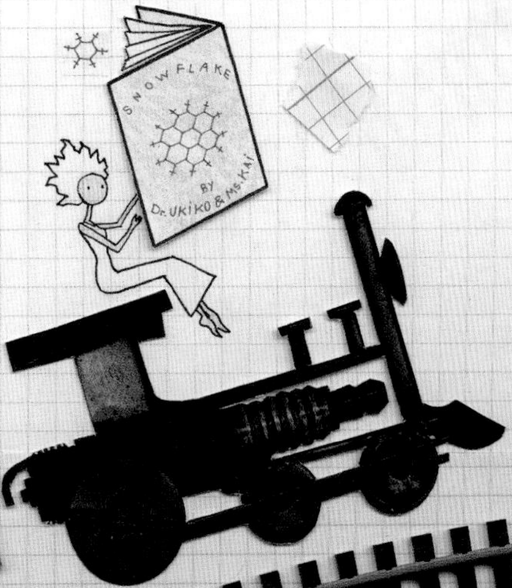

SNOWFLAKE
BY
Dr. UKIKO & Ms. KAI

All that inspiration… catalyzed by a line from a kid's picture book of snowflakes.

As if the book itself passed on an organizing principle the way water molecules do.

Book as idea delivery system… imprinting on its reader, the pattern & nature of its subject.

I hope my book of research & inventions is as stimulating to fertile & inventive minds as that children's book.

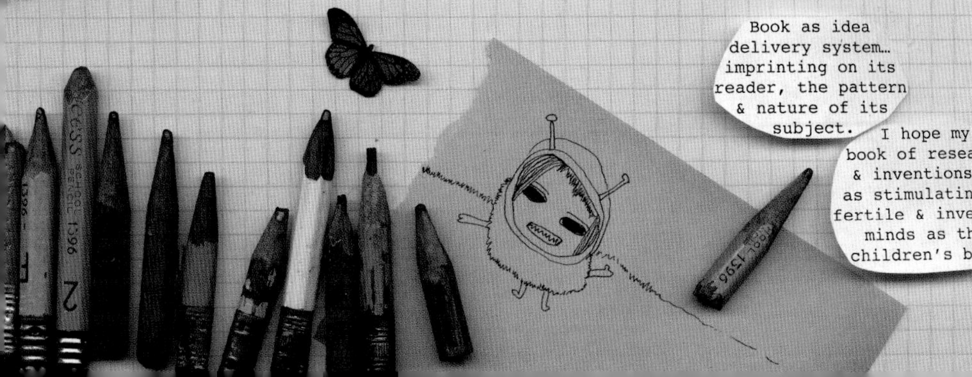

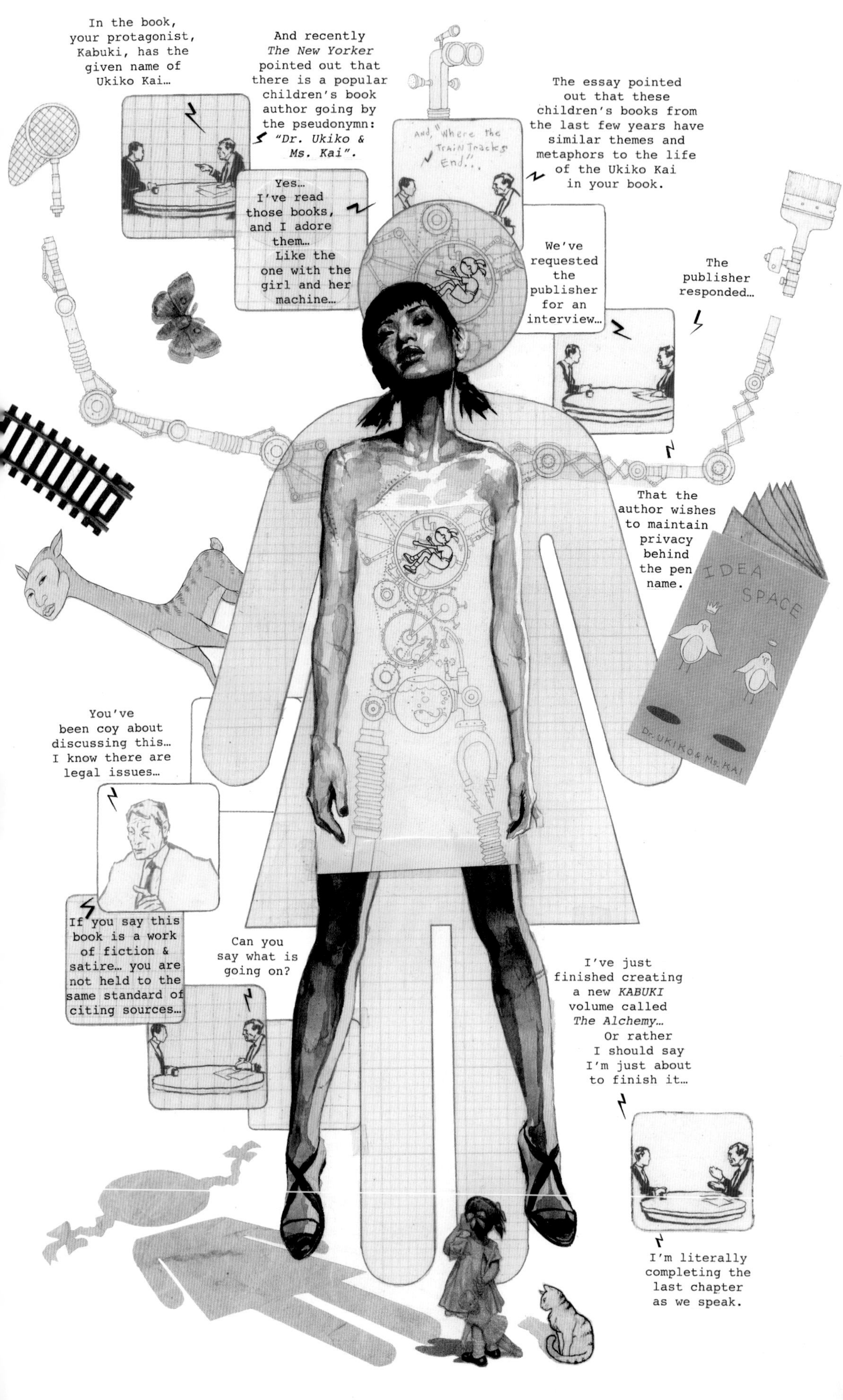

In the book, your protagonist, Kabuki, has the given name of Ukiko Kai...
And recently *The New Yorker* pointed out that there is a popular children's book author going by the pseudonymn: "Dr. Ukiko & Ms. Kai".
Yes... I've read those books, and I adore them... Like the one with the girl and her machine...
And, "Where the Train Tracks End"...
The essay pointed out that these children's books from the last few years have similar themes and metaphors to the life of the Ukiko Kai in your book.
We've requested the publisher for an interview...
The publisher responded...
That the author wishes to maintain privacy behind the pen name.
IDEA SPACE
Dr. UKIKO & Ms. KAI
You've been coy about discussing this... I know there are legal issues...
If you say this book is a work of fiction & satire... you are not held to the same standard of citing sources...
Can you say what is going on?
I've just finished creating a new *KABUKI* volume called *The Alchemy*... Or rather I should say I'm just about to finish it...
I'm literally completing the last chapter as we speak.

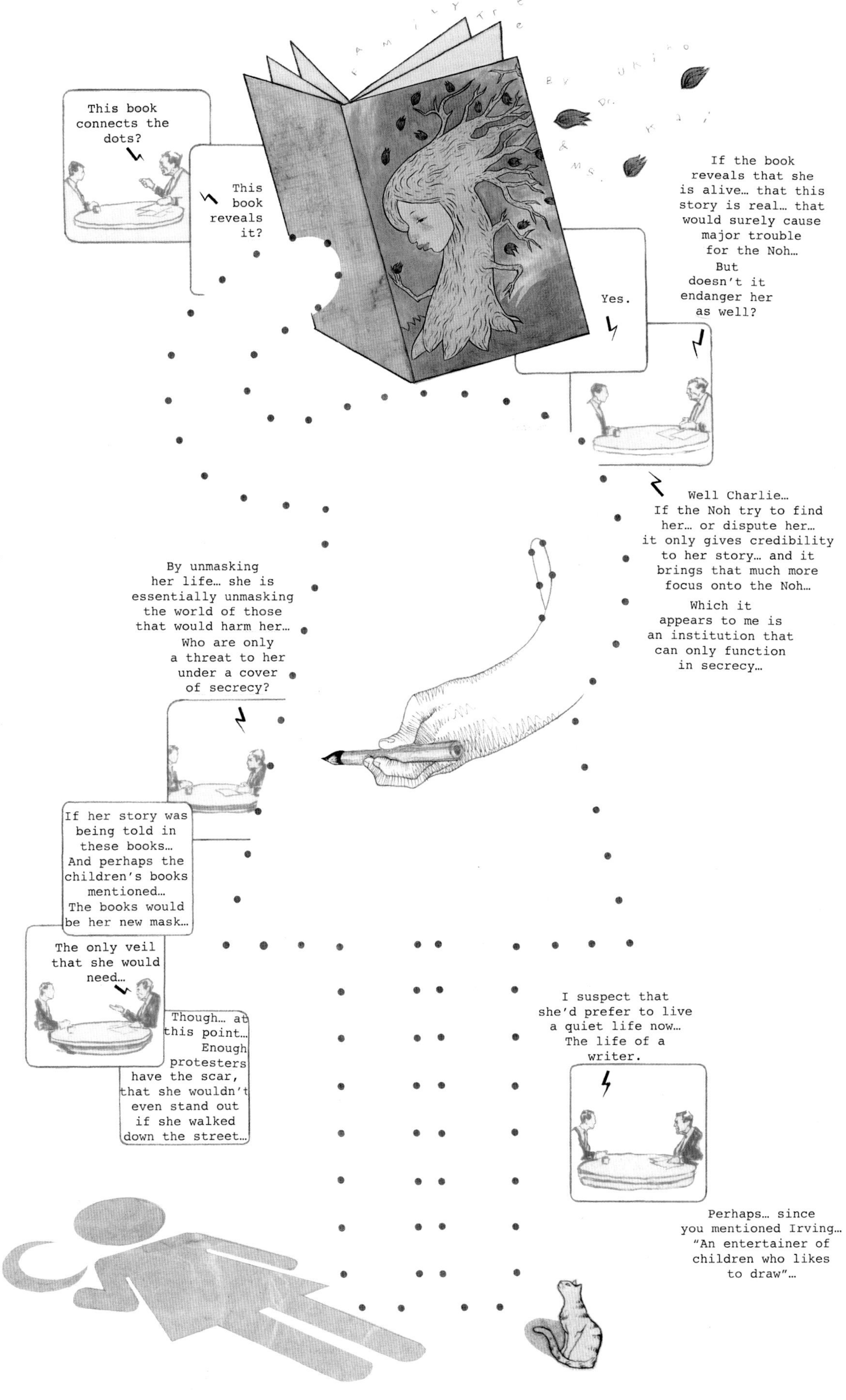
This book connects the dots?
This book reveals it?
Yes.
If the book reveals that she is alive… that this story is real… that would surely cause major trouble for the Noh…
But doesn't it endanger her as well?
Well Charlie… If the Noh try to find her… or dispute her… it only gives credibility to her story… and it brings that much more focus onto the Noh…
Which it appears to me is an institution that can only function in secrecy…
By unmasking her life… she is essentially unmasking the world of those that would harm her…
Who are only a threat to her under a cover of secrecy?
If her story was being told in these books… And perhaps the children's books mentioned… The books would be her new mask…
The only veil that she would need…
Though… at this point… Enough protesters have the scar, that she wouldn't even stand out if she walked down the street…
I suspect that she'd prefer to live a quiet life now… The life of a writer.
Perhaps… since you mentioned Irving… "An entertainer of children who likes to draw"…

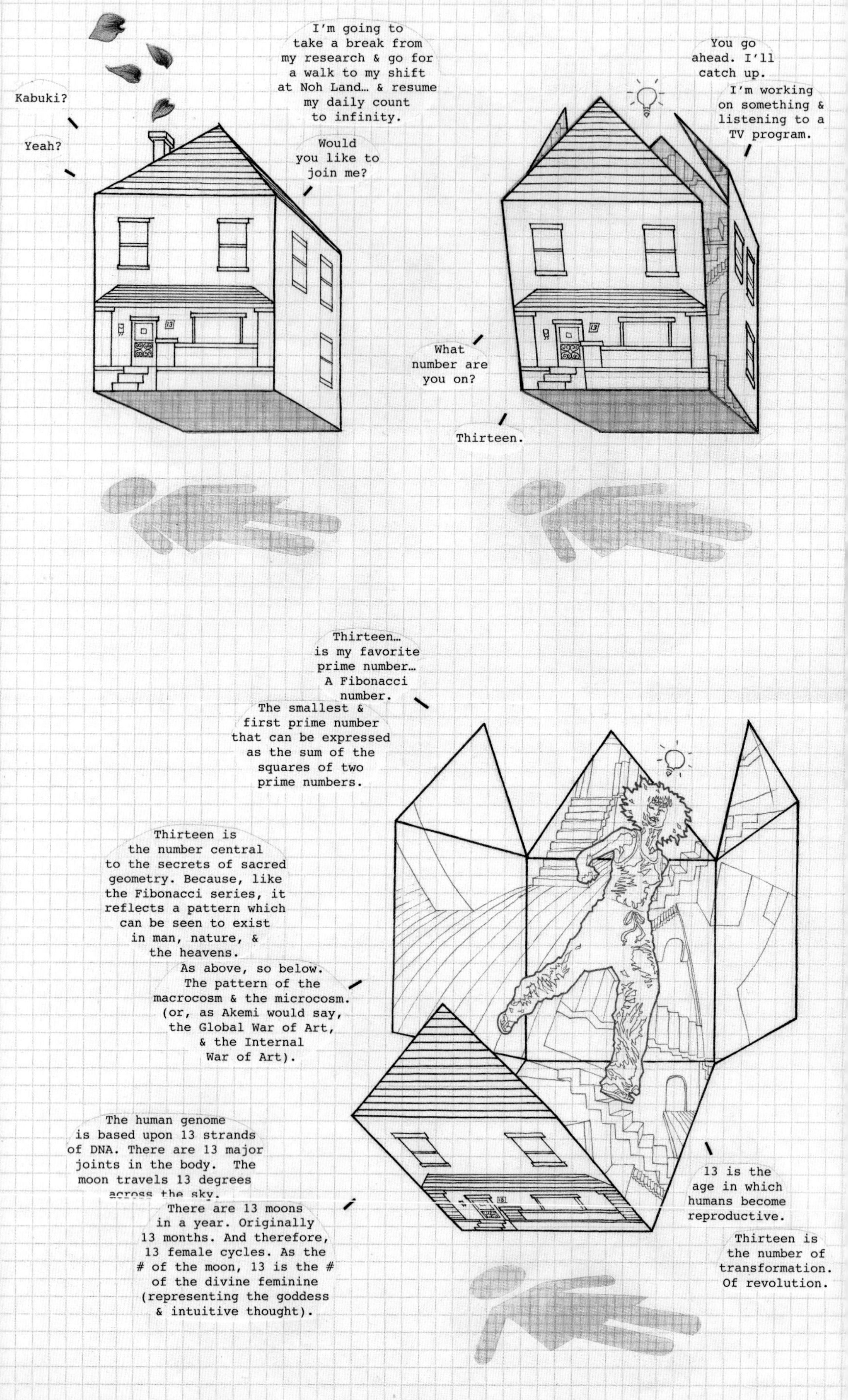

Kabuki?
Yeah?
I'm going to take a break from my research & go for a walk to my shift at Noh Land… & resume my daily count to infinity.
Would you like to join me?
You go ahead. I'll catch up.
I'm working on something & listening to a TV program.
What number are you on?
Thirteen.
Thirteen… is my favorite prime number… A Fibonacci number.
The smallest & first prime number that can be expressed as the sum of the squares of two prime numbers.
Thirteen is the number central to the secrets of sacred geometry. Because, like the Fibonacci series, it reflects a pattern which can be seen to exist in man, nature, & the heavens.
As above, so below. The pattern of the macrocosm & the microcosm. (or, as Akemi would say, the Global War of Art, & the Internal War of Art).
The human genome is based upon 13 strands of DNA. There are 13 major joints in the body. The moon travels 13 degrees across the sky.
There are 13 moons in a year. Originally 13 months. And therefore, 13 female cycles. As the # of the moon, 13 is the # of the divine feminine (representing the goddess & intuitive thought).
13 is the age in which humans become reproductive.
Thirteen is the number of transformation. Of revolution.

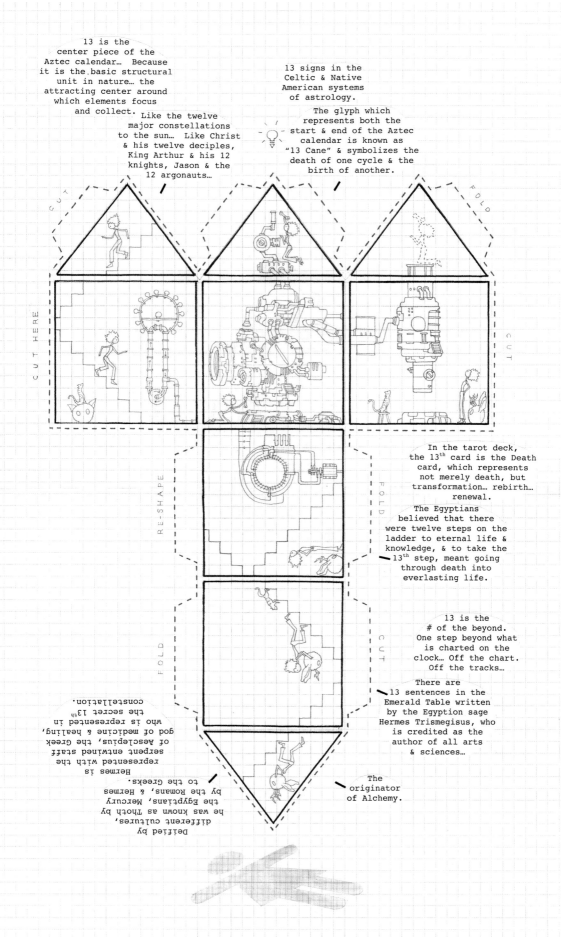

13 is the center piece of the Aztec calendar… Because it is the basic structural unit in nature… the attracting center around which elements focus and collect. Like the twelve major constellations to the sun… Like Christ & his twelve deciples, King Arthur & his 12 knights, Jason & the 12 argonauts…

13 signs in the Celtic & Native American systems of astrology.

The glyph which represents both the start & end of the Aztec calendar is known as "13 Cane" & symbolizes the death of one cycle & the birth of another.

CUT

FOLD

CUT HERE

CUT

RE-SHAPE

FOLD

FOLD

CUT

In the tarot deck, the 13th card is the Death card, which represents not merely death, but transformation… rebirth… renewal.

The Egyptians believed that there were twelve steps on the ladder to eternal life & knowledge, & to take the 13th step, meant going through death into everlasting life.

13 is the # of the beyond. One step beyond what is charted on the clock… Off the chart. Off the tracks…

There are 13 sentences in the Emerald Table written by the Egyption sage Hermes Trismegisus, who is credited as the author of all arts & sciences…

The originator of Alchemy.

Deified by different cultures, he was known as Thoth by the Egyptians, Mercury by the Romans, & Hermes to the Greeks.

Hermes is represented with the serpent entwined staff of Aesclepius, the Greek god of medicine & healing, who is represented in the secret 13th constellation.

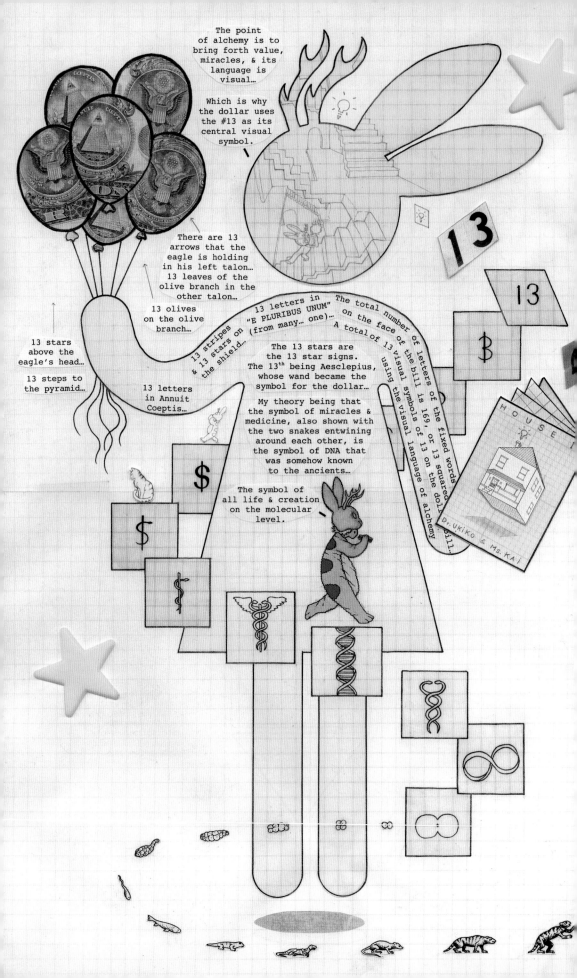

The point of alchemy is to bring forth value, miracles, & its language is visual…

Which is why the dollar uses the #13 as its central visual symbol.

There are 13 arrows that the eagle is holding in his left talon…
13 leaves of the olive branch in the other talon…

13 olives on the olive branch…

13 stars above the eagle's head…

13 steps to the pyramid…

13 letters in Annuit Coeptis…

13 stripes & 13 stars on the shield…

13 letters in "E PLURIBUS UNUM" (from many… one)…

The total number of letters of the fixed words on the face of the bill is 169, or 13 squared…
A total of 13 visual symbols of 13 on the dollar bill… using the visual language of alchemy

The 13 stars are the 13 star signs. The 13th being Aesclepius, whose wand became the symbol for the dollar…

My theory being that the symbol of miracles & medicine, also shown with the two snakes entwining around each other, is the symbol of DNA that was somehow known to the ancients…

The symbol of all life & creation on the molecular level.

13

13

$

HOUSE I

Dr. UKIKO & Ms. KAI

$

$

$

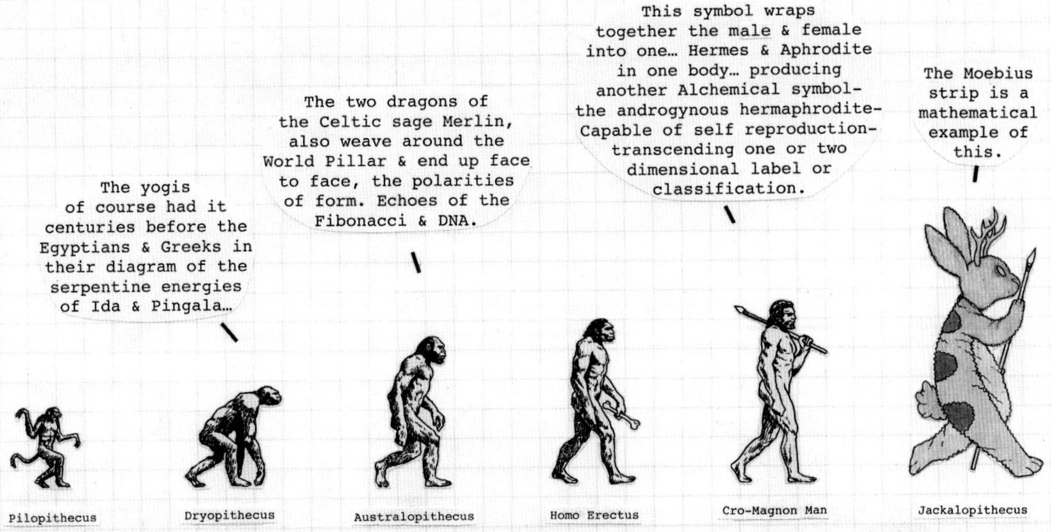

The yogis
of course had it
centuries before the
Egyptians & Greeks in
their diagram of the
serpentine energies
of Ida & Pingala…

The two dragons of
the Celtic sage Merlin,
also weave around the
World Pillar & end up face
to face, the polarities
of form. Echoes of the
Fibonacci & DNA.

This symbol wraps
together the male & female
into one… Hermes & Aphrodite
in one body… producing
another Alchemical symbol-
the androgynous hermaphrodite-
Capable of self reproduction-
transcending one or two
dimensional label or
classification.

The Moebius
strip is a
mathematical
example of
this.

Pilopithecus   Dryopithecus   Australopithecus   Homo Erectus   Cro-Magnon Man   Jackalopithecus

Shaped like the
infinity sign, it has
only one side, as you can
prove by running a pencil
down the center of the paper.
You get back where you begin
without having to cross
from one side to
the other.

By applying
another dimension
to the strip you
have changed its
properties.

It is possible
to stand at the
intersection point of
two opposing modalities,
& see that there is a
perspective from which
both views have the
same truth value.

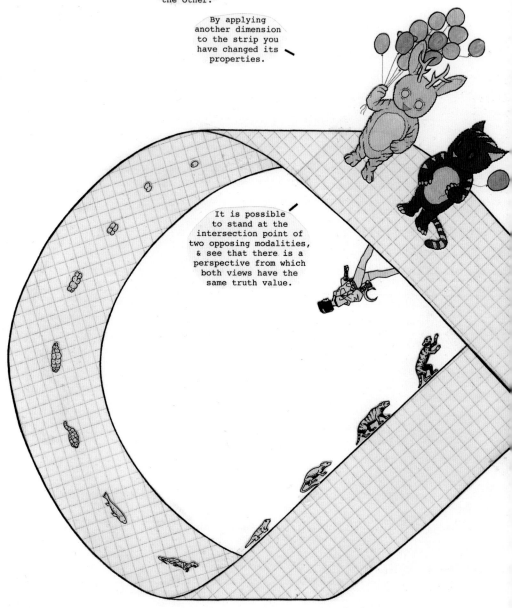

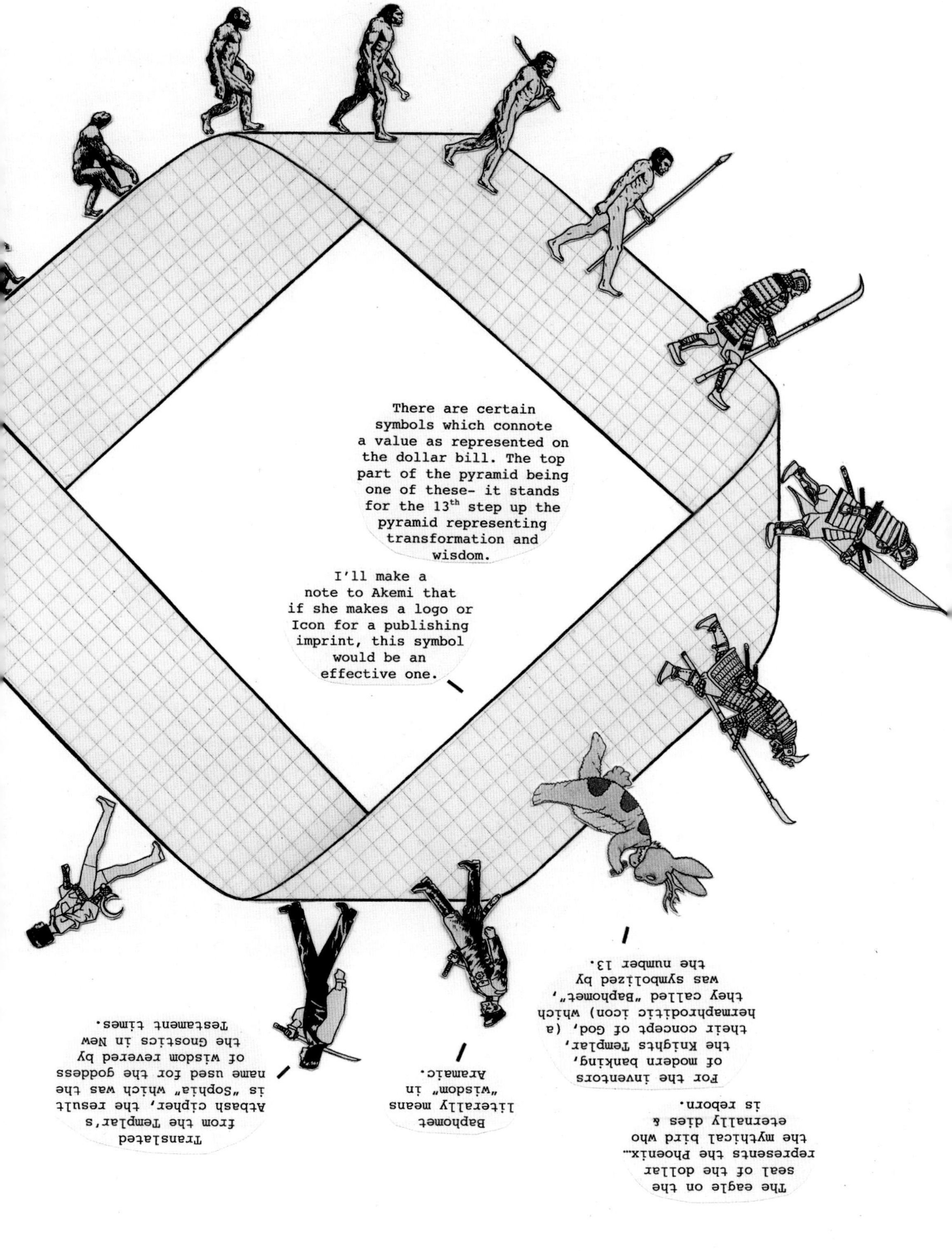
There are certain symbols which connote a value as represented on the dollar bill. The top part of the pyramid being one of these- it stands for the 13th step up the pyramid representing transformation and wisdom.
I'll make a note to Akemi that if she makes a logo or Icon for a publishing imprint, this symbol would be an effective one.
The eagle on the seal of the dollar represents the Phoenix… the mythical bird who eternally dies & is reborn.
For the inventors of modern banking, the Knights Templar, their concept of God, (a hermaphroditic icon) which they called "Baphomet", was symbolized by the number 13.
Baphomet literally means "wisdom" in Aramaic.
Translated from the Templar's Atbash cipher, the result is "Sophia" which was the name used for the goddess of wisdom revered by the Gnostics in New Testament times.

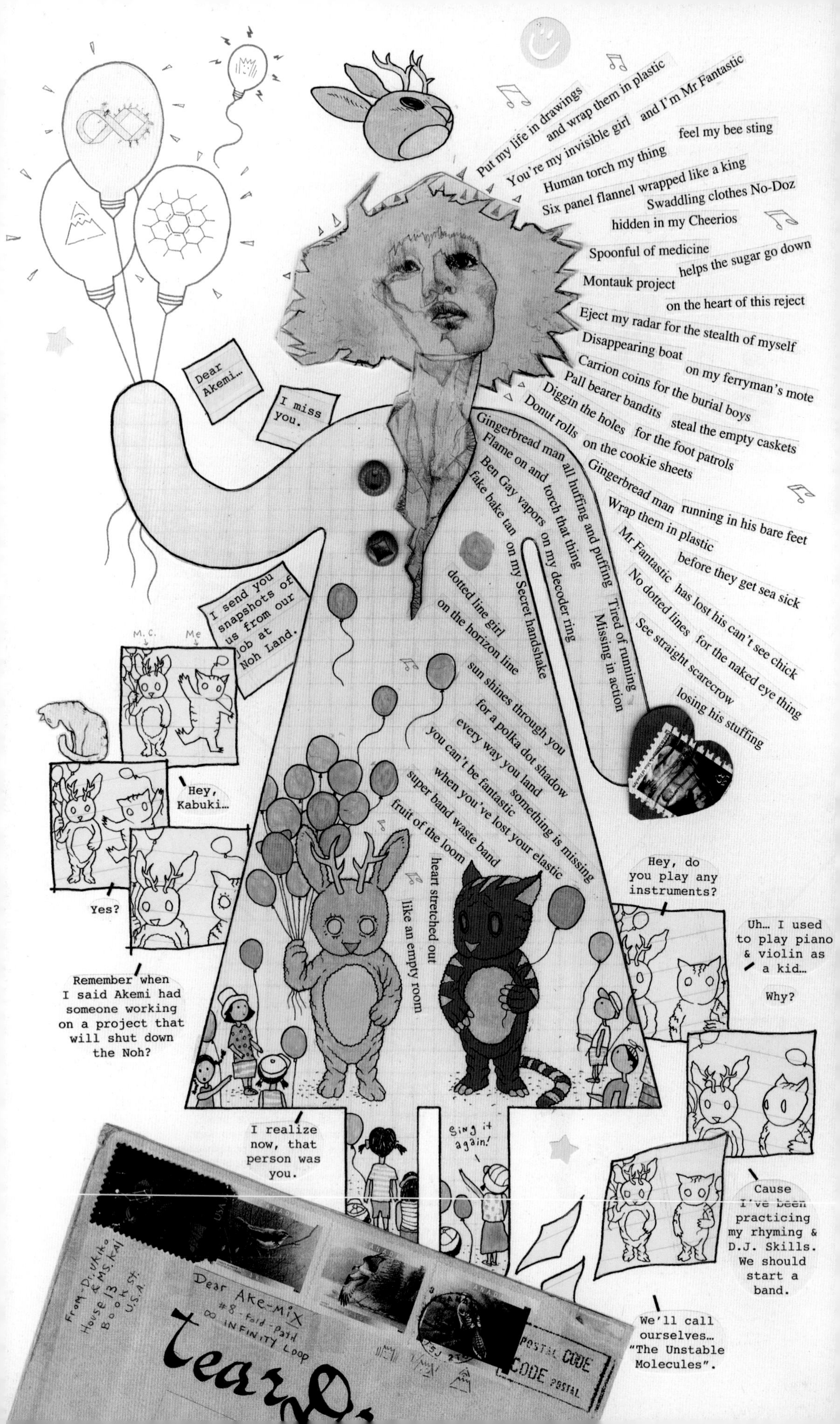

Put my life in drawings
and wrap them in plastic
You're my invisible girl and I'm Mr Fantastic
feel my bee sting
Human torch my thing
Six panel flannel wrapped like a king
Swaddling clothes No-Doz
hidden in my Cheerios
Spoonful of medicine
helps the sugar go down
Montauk project
on the heart of this reject
Eject my radar for the stealth of myself
Disappearing boat
on my ferryman's mote
Carrion coins for the burial boys
Pall bearer bandits
steal the empty caskets
Diggin the holes
for the foot patrols
Donut rolls
on the cookie sheets
Gingerbread man all huffing and puffing
Gingerbread man running in his bare feet
Flame on and torch that thing
Tired of running
Wrap them in plastic
before they get sea sick
Ben Gay vapors on my decoder ring
Missing in action
Mr Fantastic has lost his can't see chick
fake bake tan on my Secret handshake
No dotted lines for the naked eye thing
dotted line girl
See straight scarecrow
on the horizon line
losing his stuffing
sun shines through you
for a polka dot shadow
every way you land
something is missing
you can't be fantastic
when you've lost your elastic
super band waste band
fruit of the loom
heart stretched out
like an empty room
Dear Akemi...
I miss you.
I send you snapshots of us from our job at Noh Land.
M.C.
Me
Hey, Kabuki...
Yes?
Remember when I said Akemi had someone working on a project that will shut down the Noh?
I realize now, that person was you.
Sing it again!
Hey, do you play any instruments?
Uh... I used to play piano & violin as a kid...
Why?
Cause I've been practicing my rhyming & D.J. Skills. We should start a band.
We'll call ourselves... "The Unstable Molecules".
Dear Ake-Mix
#8-fold-Path
∞ INFINITY Loop
POSTAL CODE
CODE POSTAL

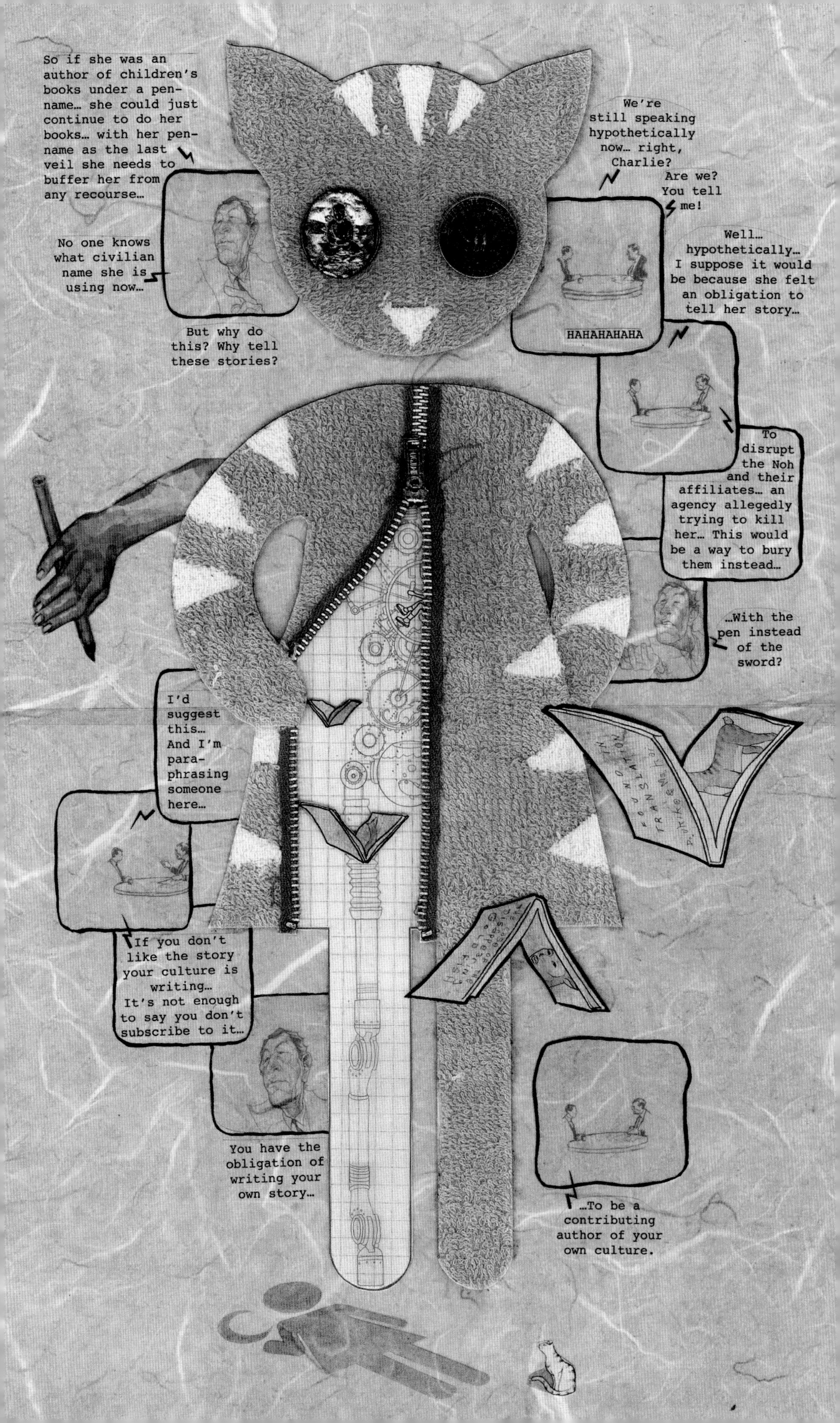
So if she was an author of children's books under a pen-name… she could just continue to do her books… with her pen-name as the last veil she needs to buffer her from any recourse…
No one knows what civilian name she is using now…
But why do this? Why tell these stories?
We're still speaking hypothetically now… right, Charlie?
Are we? You tell me!
Well… hypothetically… I suppose it would be because she felt an obligation to tell her story…
HAHAHAHAHA
To disrupt the Noh and their affiliates… an agency allegedly trying to kill her… This would be a way to bury them instead…
…With the pen instead of the sword?
I'd suggest this… And I'm para-phrasing someone here…
If you don't like the story your culture is writing… It's not enough to say you don't subscribe to it…
You have the obligation of writing your own story…
…To be a contributing author of your own culture.

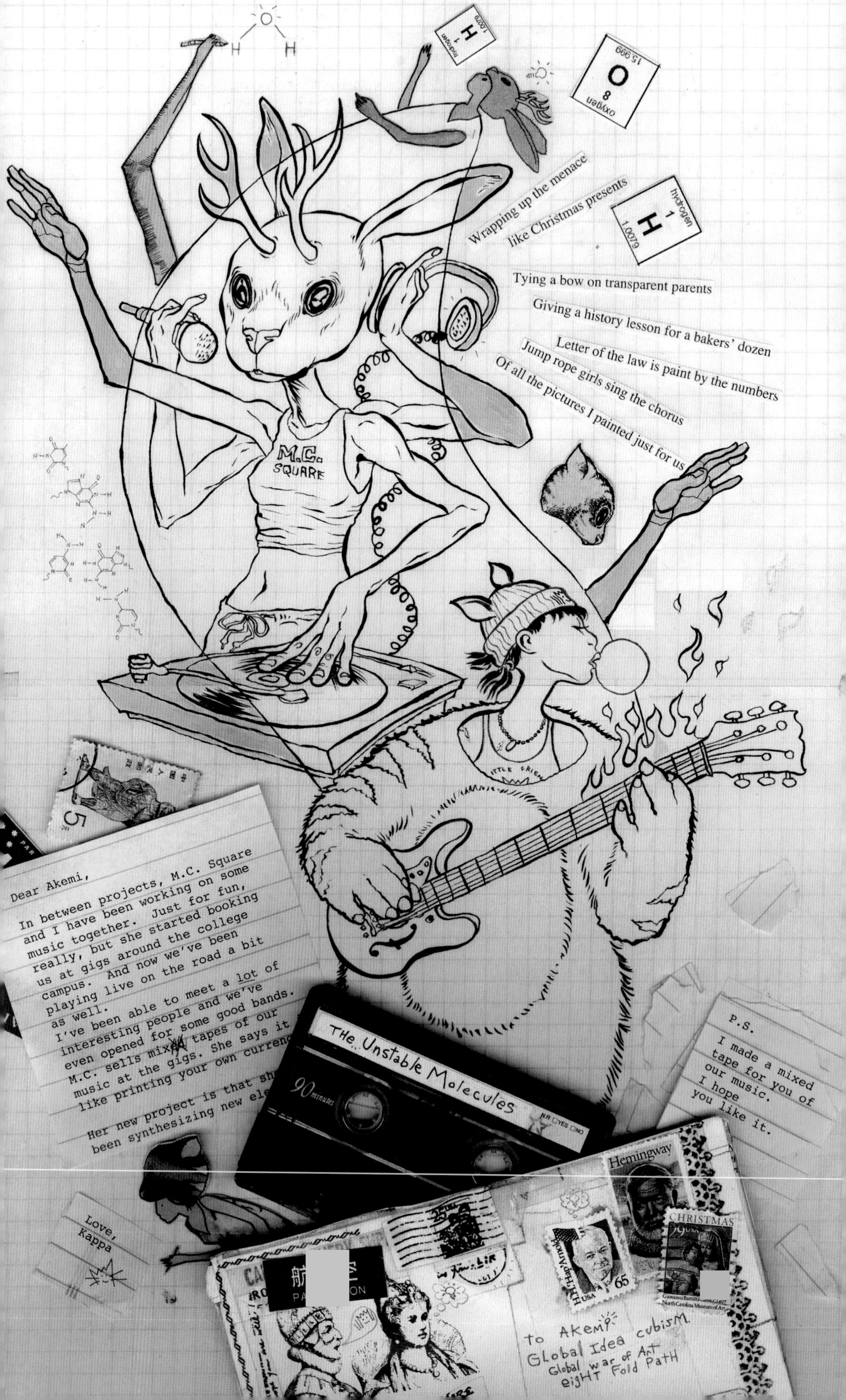

O
H H
H
1
hydrogen
1.0079
O
8
oxygen
15.999
Wrapping up the menace
like Christmas presents
H
1
hydrogen
1.0079
Tying a bow on transparent parents
Giving a history lesson for a bakers' dozen
Letter of the law is paint by the numbers
Jump rope girls sing the chorus
Of all the pictures I painted just for us
M.C. SQUARE
LITTLE FRIEN
Dear Akemi,
In between projects, M.C. Square and I have been working on some music together. Just for fun, really, but she started booking us at gigs around the college campus. And now we've been playing live on the road a bit as well.
I've been able to meet a lot of interesting people and we've even opened for some good bands. M.C. sells mixed tapes of our music at the gigs. She says it like printing your own curren
Her new project is that sh been synthesizing new ele
The Unstable Molecules
90 minutes
P.S.
I made a mixed tape for you of our music. I hope you like it.
Love, Kappa
Hemingway
CHRISTMAS
USA
H.H. "Hap" Arnold
USA 65
to Akemi
Global Idea cubism.
Global war of Art
eight Fold Path

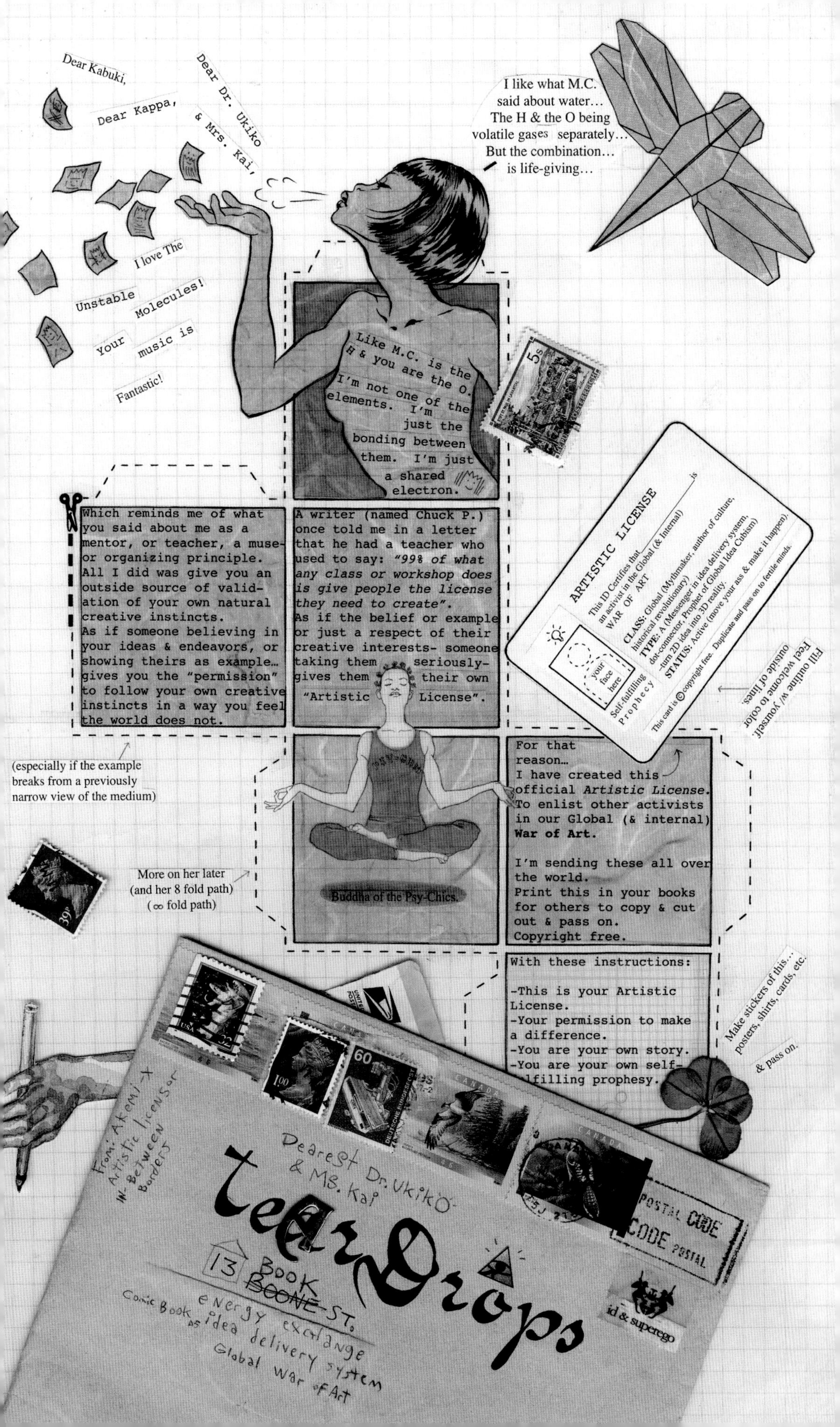

Dear Kabuki,
Dear Kappa,
Dear Dr. Ukiko & Mrs. Kai,
I love The Unstable Molecules!
Your music is Fantastic!
I like what M.C. said about water… The H & the O being volatile gases separately… But the combination… is life-giving…
Like M.C. is the H & you are the O. I'm not one of the elements. I'm just the bonding between them. I'm just a shared electron.
Which reminds me of what you said about me as a mentor, or teacher, a muse- or organizing principle. All I did was give you an outside source of validation of your own natural creative instincts. As if someone believing in your ideas & endeavors, or showing theirs as example… gives you the "permission" to follow your own creative instincts in a way you feel the world does not.
(especially if the example breaks from a previously narrow view of the medium)
A writer (named Chuck P.) once told me in a letter that he had a teacher who used to say: "99% of what any class or workshop does is give people the license they need to create". As if the belief or example or just a respect of their creative interests- someone taking them seriously- gives them their own "Artistic License".
ARTISTIC LICENSE
This ID Certifies that ______ is an activist in the Global (& Internal) WAR OF ART
CLASS: Global (Mythmaker, author of culture, historical revolutionary)
TYPE: A (Messenger in idea delivery system, dot-connector, Prophet of Global Idea Cubism) -turn 2D idea into 3D reality.
STATUS: Active (move your ass & make it happen).
your face here
Self-fulfilling Prophecy
This card is © copyright free. Duplicate and pass on to fertile minds.
Fill outline w/ yourself. Feel welcome to color outside of lines.
Buddha of the Psy-Chics.
More on her later (and her 8 fold path) (∞ fold path)
For that reason… I have created this official Artistic License. To enlist other activists in our Global (& internal) War of Art.
I'm sending these all over the world. Print this in your books for others to copy & cut out & pass on. Copyright free.
With these instructions:
-This is your Artistic License.
-Your permission to make a difference.
-You are your own story.
-You are your own self-fulfilling prophesy.
Make stickers of this… posters, shirts, cards, etc. & pass on.
From: Akemi-X Artistic licensor In-Between Borders
Dearest Dr. Ukiko & Ms. Kai
tearDrops
13 BOOK ~~BOONE~~ ST.
Comic Book as idea delivery system
energy exchange
Global War of Art
POSTAL CODE
CODE POSTAL
id & superego

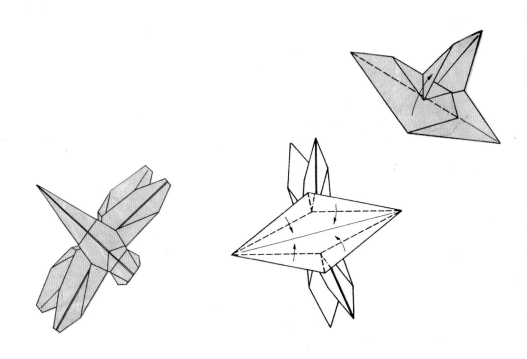

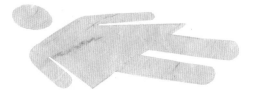

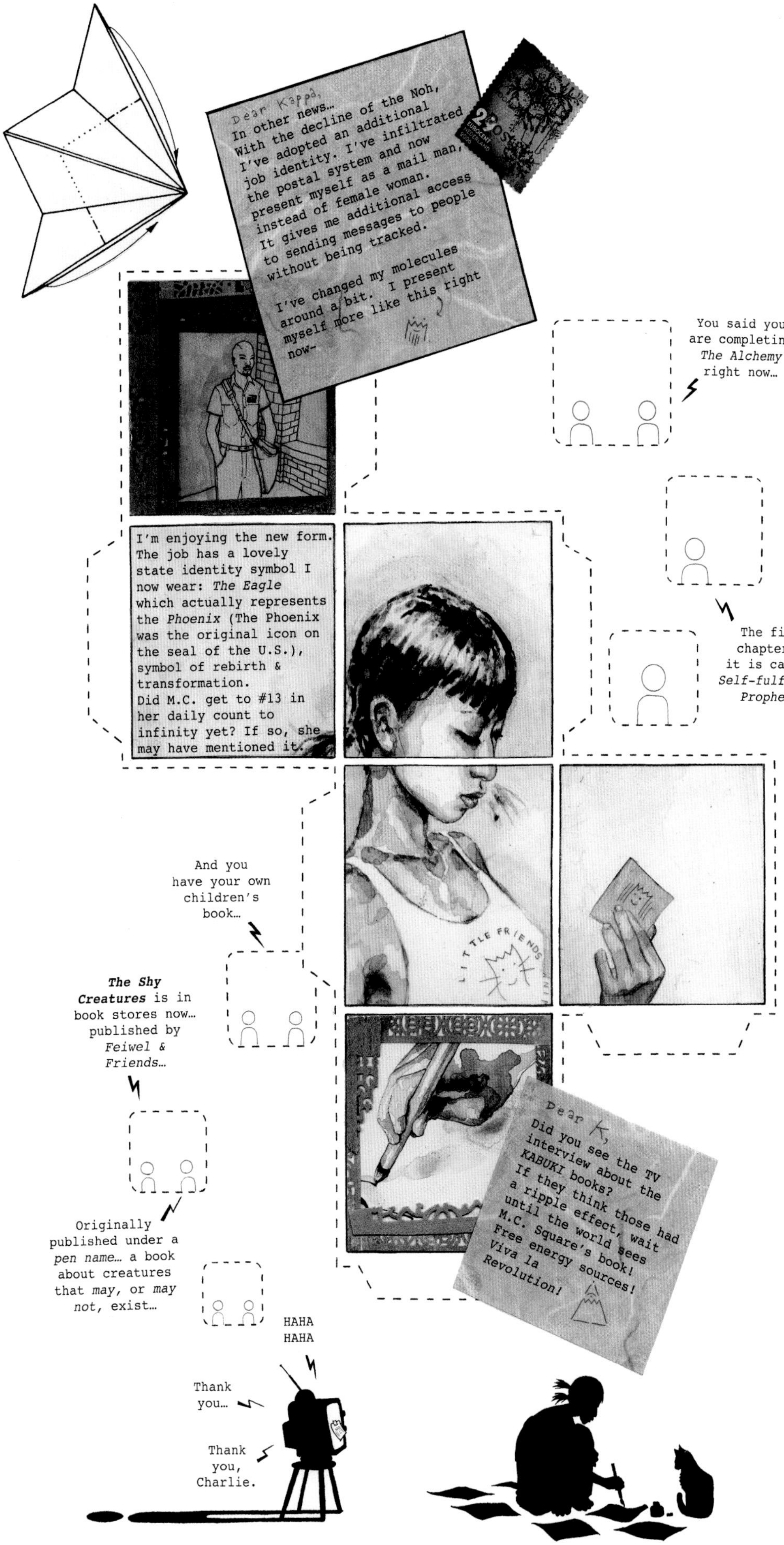

Dear Kappa,
In other news…
With the decline of the Noh,
I've adopted an additional
job identity. I've infiltrated
the postal system and now
present myself as a mail man,
instead of female woman.
It gives me additional access
to sending messages to people
without being tracked.
I've changed my molecules
around a bit. I present
myself more like this right
now–
I'm enjoying the new form. The job has a lovely state identity symbol I now wear: *The Eagle* which actually represents the *Phoenix* (The Phoenix was the original icon on the seal of the U.S.), symbol of rebirth & transformation. Did M.C. get to #13 in her daily count to infinity yet? If so, she may have mentioned it.
You said you are completing *The Alchemy* right now…
The final chapter of it is called: *Self-fulfilling Prophesy.*
LITTLE FRIENDS
And you have your own children's book…
The Shy Creatures is in book stores now… published by *Feiwel & Friends…*
Originally published under a *pen name*… a book about creatures that *may*, or *may not*, exist…
Dear K,
Did you see the TV interview about the KABUKI books?
If they think those had a ripple effect, wait until the world sees M.C. Square's book!
Free energy sources!
Viva la Revolution!
HAHA HAHA
Thank you…
Thank you, Charlie.

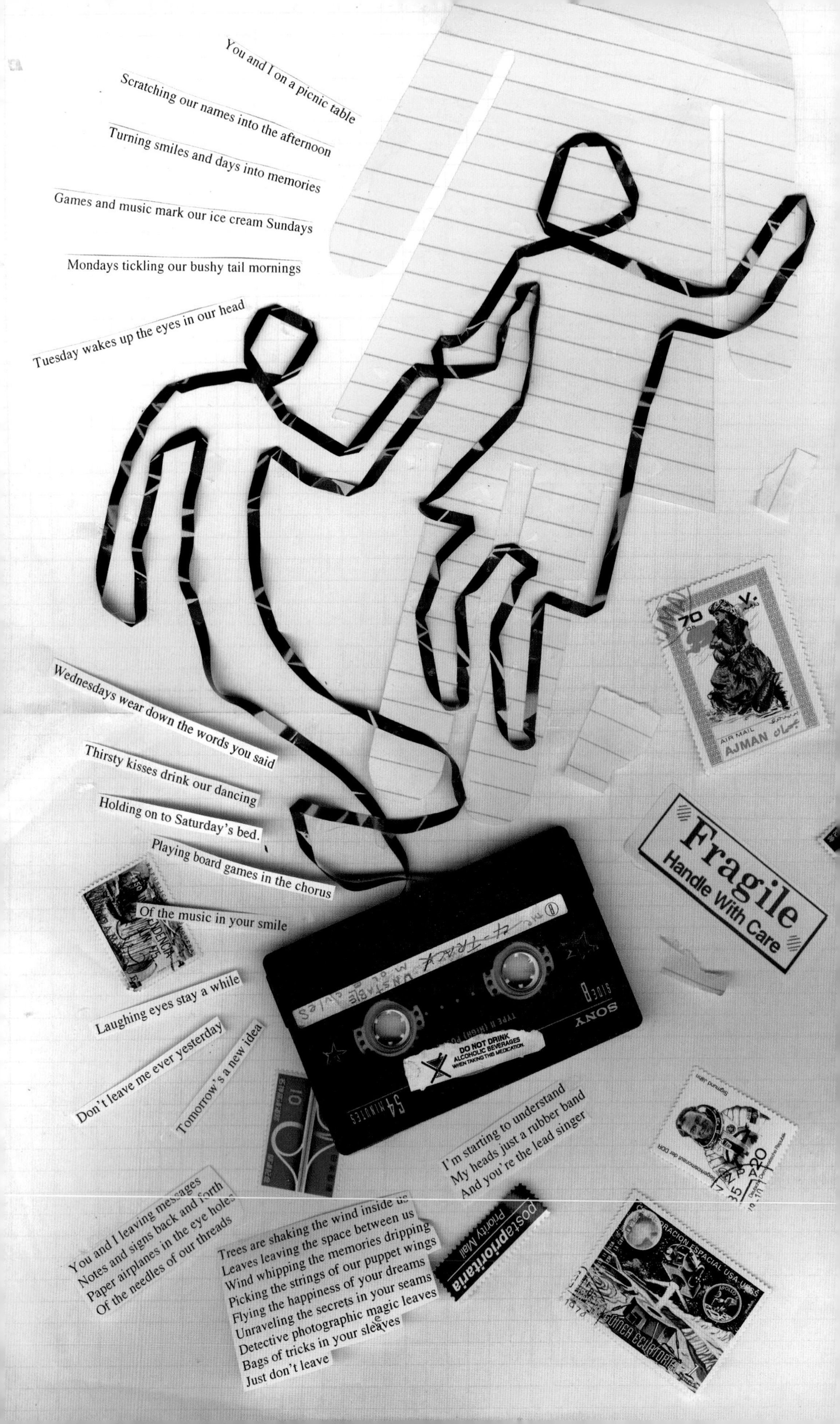
You and I on a picnic table
Scratching our names into the afternoon
Turning smiles and days into memories
Games and music mark our ice cream Sundays
Mondays tickling our bushy tail mornings
Tuesday wakes up the eyes in our head
Wednesdays wear down the words you said
Thirsty kisses drink our dancing
Holding on to Saturday's bed.
Playing board games in the chorus
Of the music in your smile
Laughing eyes stay a while
Don't leave me ever yesterday
Tomorrow's a new idea
I'm starting to understand
My heads just a rubber band
And you're the lead singer
You and I leaving messages
Notes and signs back and forth
Paper airplanes in the eye holes
Of the needles of our threads
Trees are shaking the wind inside us
Leaves leaving the space between us
Wind whipping the memories dripping
Picking the strings of our puppet wings
Flying the happiness of your dreams
Unraveling the secrets in your seams
Detective photographic magic leaves
Bags of tricks in your sleaves
Just don't leave
Fragile
Handle With Care
AIR MAIL
AJMAN
SONY
SIDE B
54 MINUTES
DO NOT DRINK
ALCOHOLIC BEVERAGES
WHEN TAKING THIS MEDICATION.
postaprioritaria
Priority Mail

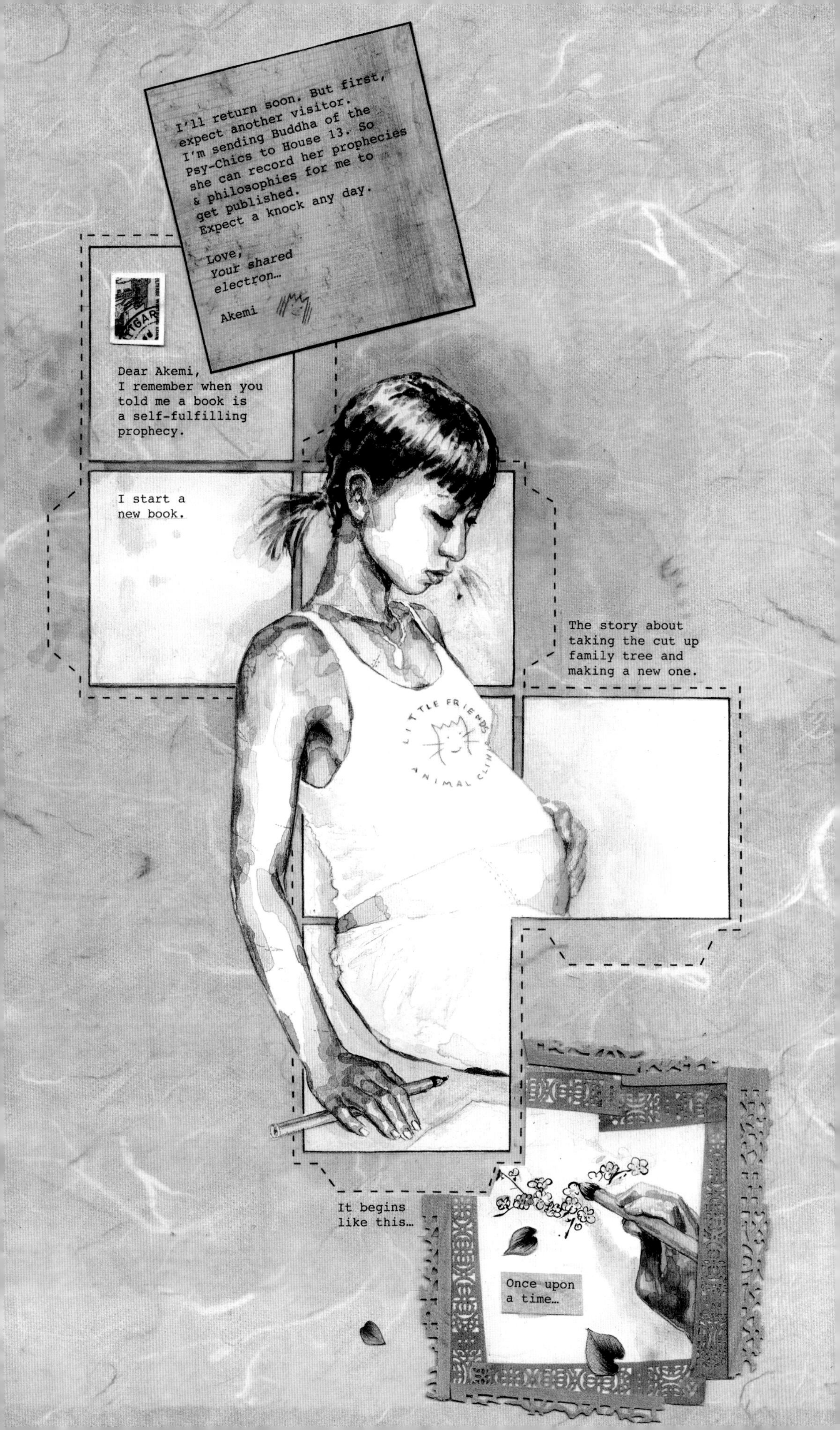
I'll return soon. But first, expect another visitor. I'm sending Buddha of the Psy-Chics to House 13. So she can record her prophecies & philosophies for me to get published. Expect a knock any day.
Love, Your shared electron…
Akemi
Dear Akemi, I remember when you told me a book is a self-fulfilling prophecy.
I start a new book.
The story about taking the cut up family tree and making a new one.
LITTLE FRIENDS ANIMAL CLINIC
It begins like this…
Once upon a time…

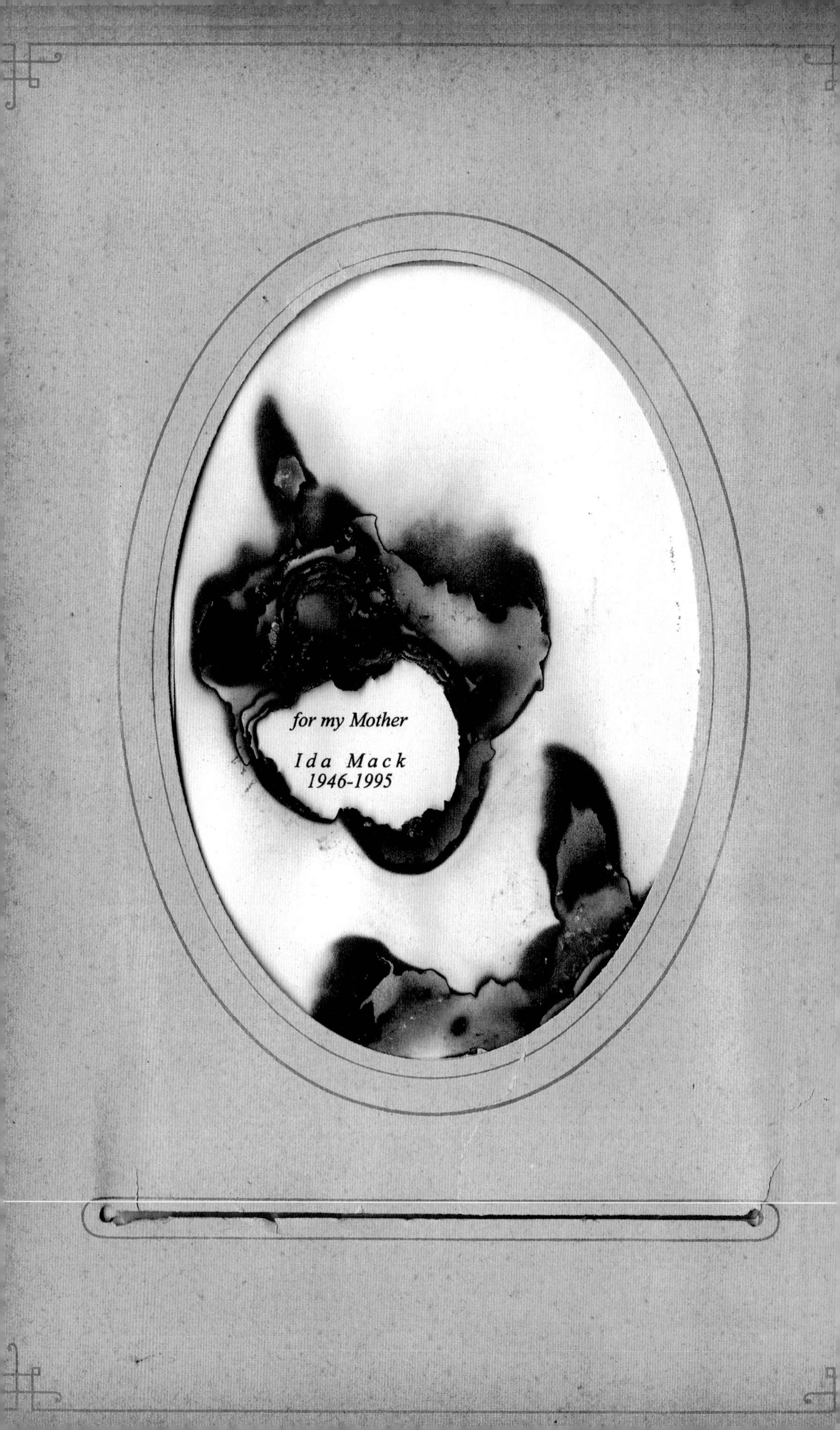
for my Mother
Ida Mack
1946-1995

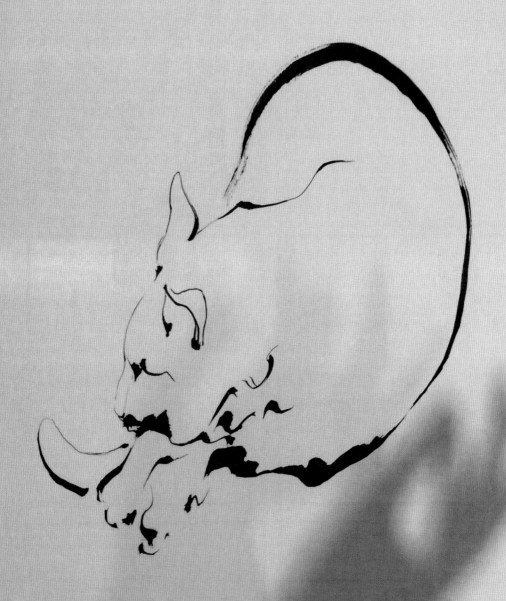

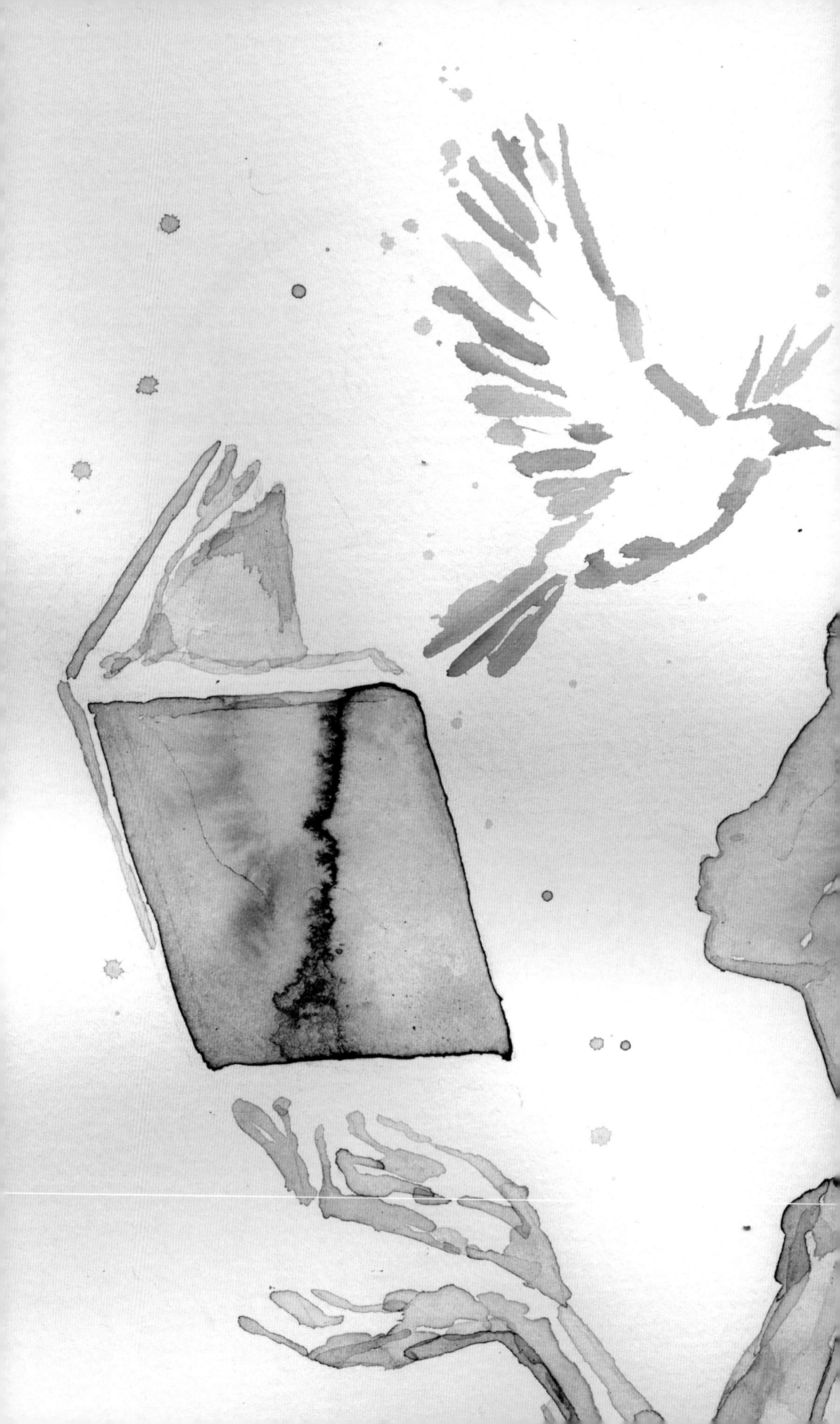

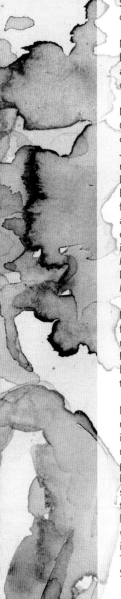

David Mack is the Emmy nominated, *New York Times* Best Selling Author & Artist of *KABUKI*, writer of Marvel's *Daredevil*, cover artist of Neil Gaiman's *American Gods*, *Norse Mythology*, *Jessica Jones*, *James Bond, Superman,* & *Fight Club* by Chuck Palahniuk, Artist on Netflix's *Jessica Jones* opening titles & *Captain America: The Winter Soldier* film titles & Cultural Ambassador Envoy for the US State Dept.

Mack earned an Emmy nomination for his work with Imaginary Forces on the opening titles of the *Jessica Jones* Netflix series (winner of the Peabody Award).

For the Academy Award nominated film *Captain America: The Winter Soldier*, Mack created the art & concept for the titles sequence with Sarofsky Designs, which received the Excellence in Titles Design Award.

Mack contributed artwork for the opening titles of Robert Rodriguez's *Matador* TV series with Sarofsky designs, and contributed art (and a cameo role) for the *Powers* TV series at Sony.

Mack's work has garnered nominations for ten Eisner Awards, four International Eagle Awards, and both the Harvey and Kirby Awards in the category of Best New Talent,.

Mack authored his children's book *THE SHY CREATURES* from McMillan, illustrated and designed music albums for both American and Japanese Labels, including work for Paul McCartney, Amanda Palmer, Thomas Jane, Vincent D'Onofrio, painted Tori Amos for her RAINN benefit calendars, directed three music videos for Amanda Palmer, animation art for MTV, wrote and designed video game characters for film director John Woo and Electronic Arts, wrote the interactive animated viral promo for *Mission Impossible* four, and contributed the artwork for Dr. Arun Ghandi's essay on the *Culture of Non-Violence.*

Mack created Marquee art & make-up designs for the theatrical performance of *Tenshu* which received multiple Broadway World Awards. His book *KABUKI* was adapted & performed as a live theater play by Shadowbox Theater in 2017 to rave reviews.

Mack's *KABUKI* books have been the subject of under-graduate and graduate university courses in Art and Literature, and listed as required reading. His work is on exhibit in the Philadelphia Museum of Art with Michelangelo, Titian, & Rubens. His work has been studied in graduate seminars at USC, and is currently in the international traveling Marvel Museum exhibition. He has lectured at universities and taught classes in writing, drawing, and painting all over the world, including a Masterclass at the University of Technology in Sydney, Australia, for Japan's School of Communication Arts of Tokyo,

Nagoya, and Osaka, and an invitation to speak at Harvard as the Guest of Honor at their annual Science Fiction Writing convention.

Mack created two seasons of *Dexter Early Cuts* episodes for Showtime earning him nominations for both the Writers Guild of America and the Producers Guild of America.

In 2013 Mack had exhibits in Los Angeles & Chicago with the works of Gustav Klimt & Egon Schiele, and spoke in Barcelona at the OFFFest event of trailblazing artists and designers.

Mack's paintings were exhibited in Paris and Brussels with successful gallery openings. The documentary film on Mack's work, *The Alchemy of Art*, was awarded the top prize at the Worldfest Film Festival, & in 2012 Mack delivered an inspiring TED Talk.

The US State Dept. honored Mack as a Cultural Ambassador selected to travel abroad to teach storytelling in other countries, beginning in Tblisi, Sakartvelo, for multiple years, joining efforts with the US embassy there.

In the country of Georgia, Mack taught at refugee camps, settlement camps for displaced persons, the Asylum Seekers Center, the Marneuli Youth Center, Tbilisi Arts Academy, Special Needs schools, & the Tbilisi Palace of Fine Arts Museum featured a massive exhibit of Mack's work & books.

In North Africa, Mack traveled for the State Dept to Tunisia multiple years, teaching at many schools there, & was a special guest speaker for an event in Libya.

Mack taught at the School for the Deaf in Singapore, Tunisia, & the country of Georgia.

KABUKI has been translated in seven languages, in addition to over two million copies of *KABUKI* books in print in the U.S.

Mack is currently developing *KABUKI* as a TV series.

Mack has illustrated poetry collaborations with Neil Gaiman and U.S. Poet Laureate Billy Collins, & wrote the adaptation of Science Fiction Master Philip K. Dick's *Electric Ant* as a graphic novel at Marvel Comics.

Mack has recently directed popular music videos for Amanda Palmer, Dashboard Confessional, Neil Gaiman, & Pen America, & completed a new creator owned series with Brian Michael Bendis from DC comics called *COVER* (based on his travels for the State Dept) which earned him 2019 Best Comic Artist of the Year from Comic Watch.

Mack was honored with the prestigious Inkpot Award for Achievement in Comicbook Art.

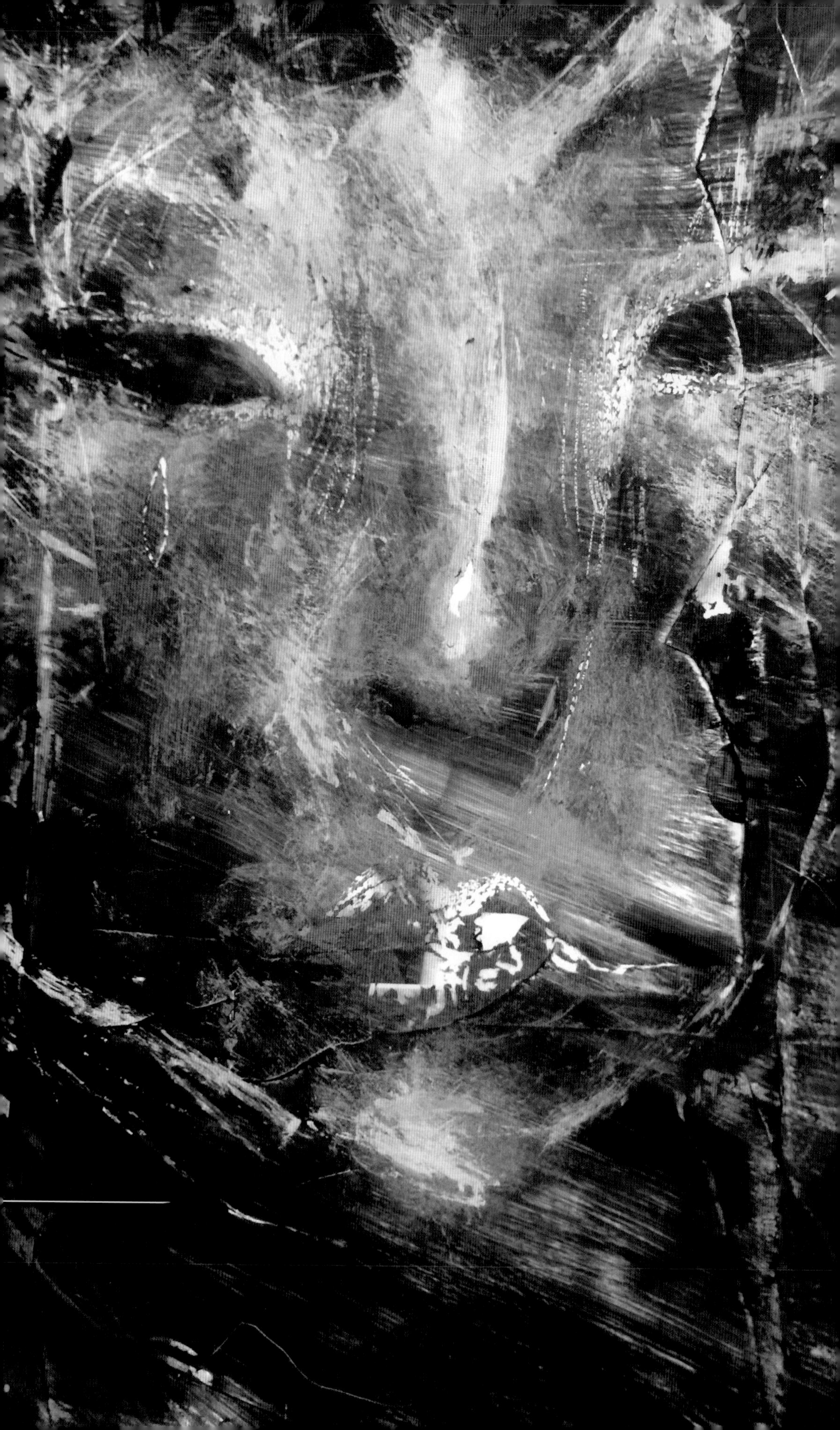

NOTES

This story has been my collaboration with reality. It has been an integration of personal experiences, insights from conversations (the discussion of the meaning of "the kiss" marking the final act of a story is inspired by a sushi dinner conversation with Neil Gaiman), books and ideas, of principles that I developed in my own work after decades of concentration and trial and error in my formative years, sharing my own 13 Book Street halfway house with a unique cast of characters embarking on our early creative lives. This book has been a collision of creative people inspiring me, from artists to scientists, musicians, writers, and friends (see them mentioned in the acknowledgements section in back of this book).

The Little Friends Animal Clinic was an actual place that my father lived at when my brother and I were children. The cat nap sleep cycle that MC Square experiments with is an actual cycle that I developed for myself while working on this book. Experimentally, I also adopted MC's method of "idea focus" of writing the ideas that I wanted to generate on the bottles of water that I drank while creating this. I also gave myself a personal challenge in this book of creating an entire story where not a single act of violence occurs. I don't think there is even a harsh word or hurting of feelings. There is still a global antagonist and an internal one and I challenged myself that there was enough drama in that if I could communicate it effectively. As the character was reaching a new level of enlightenments in her life, I wanted the storytelling to reflect that.

The Alchemy was originally published in serialized form of nine separate issues from Marvel Comics beginning in 2004. Brian Michael Bendis, Mike Oeming & I had just formed a new imprint at Marvel Comics called ICON specifically to publish our creator-owned titles *POWERS* & *KABUKI*. In considering a name for the imprint, Brian said to me that Epic [of Marvel] and Legend [of Dark Horse] were the best imprint names ever. I suggested to him we name the new Marvel imprint for our books: ICON.

Each issue of this series took me about two months to make (script, drawing, painting, lettering). As the story came out, issue by issue, each chapter received so much reader feedback, so many letters & online feedback of readers connecting to the story... And something fascinating began to happen. A pattern was emerging in the letters. Readers wrote to me that they were experiencing a personal connection to the characters in the story... but they were writing about getting something useful from the story that they channeled into their practical life. They sometimes wrote as if Akemi was speaking directly to them.

Readers began sending me things: artful handwritten letters, antique papers and fabric, family heirlooms, and personal gifts that I collaged into the artwork of the story. The readers noticed the art approach of the book that collaged and integrated a variety of mixed media, and they were sending me items with the intent and suggestion for me to collage these items into the story of the next issues. And I did. The handwritten letters on aged paper from Miss Fumiko who wrote me from The First Zen Institute of America that her great grandfather Sokei-an founded when he first brought Zen to America, the four leaf clover from Katherine White, the Japanese papers and artifacts and origami that Alice Lynch sent me from when she was stationed in Japan fifty years ago.

The conversation between author and readers became a visual part of the story.

Much of the story itself is about inspiration, about that creative process and the unexpected places that inspiration can come from. Chapter five is about letters between two characters. So before I began that issue (entitled Epistolary) I put out the call to readers all over the world to send me stamps and envelopes from their countries that I would collage into that issue. They did. LOTS. Lots of stamps and envelopes with letters about what they got from *The Alchemy* story. And I integrated those stamps and envelopes in the actual art pages of this story as the global correspondence between Akemi and Kabuki.

During the making of this story I had begun correspondences also. In a letter from author Chuck Palahniuk, he mentions a class or workshop giving people a "permission" to practice their own skills, or "license" they need to create. The letter crystallized some points that Akemi was making in the story, so I had Akemi make an actual "Artistic License" inspired by that line in his letter. Akemi acknowledged the inspiration and referenced the letter as if she had received it from him in one of her many correspondences. After that, readers sent me their personalized "Artistic License" that they duplicated from the book.

I wrote *The Shy Creatures* as part of the script for chapter two and three of this story. It was meant as a double narrative, a book within a book, to be a subtext of the surface story- a whimsical kids-eye view to give context to how to see the characters in the primary story. My friend and book agent Allen Spiegel showed the issue to a children's book publisher and they made the story into an actual children's book.

The Shy Creatures kids book became a real world artifact of the story. One of the ripple effects of *The Alchemy*. It also paralleled one of the arcs of the story of the main character becoming a children's book author and finding a publisher for her books. As a book, *The Alchemy* became a self fulfilling prophesy. Elements in the story were being yanked into the real world. While making this story, the lines were blurred between where the story stopped and reality, began. The story became a conversation between ideas and reality. A collaboration between them.

While making chapter five, I was reading a biography of Science Fiction author Philip K. Dick. Shortly after that, I received a message from the producer of the Philip K. Dick based *Scanner Darkly* film and I was asked to work with the Philip K. Dick Estate (Philip K. Dick's daughters Isa & Laura) to adapt PKD stories to comic books. It paralleled the arc in *The Alchemy* of story adaptation to comics and occurred after I wrote that detail in the book.

In the original script there was a version where the ghost writer character is discussing his adaptation on the Coast to Coast AM radio show (a show I've listened to for years while I work that discusses more avant-garde subjects). Then when *The Shy Creatures* was published I was indeed a guest on that show. Three times so far. It seemed like the ideas that I'd write into the story, would find a way of becoming real. But also, like the story says, you can take experiences from real life, even troubling experiences, and put them into the story, this time in a way that they work for you. I did that too. And I received feedback from readers who did that. Some of them dealing with a very challenging situation, found that in writing about it, putting it in music, art, etc, that it lets them own it and turn it into something amazing.

I work with an art studio for artists with disabilities called Visionaries & Voices. They have challenges from Autism, Dyslexia, to other issues, and the art studio give them an

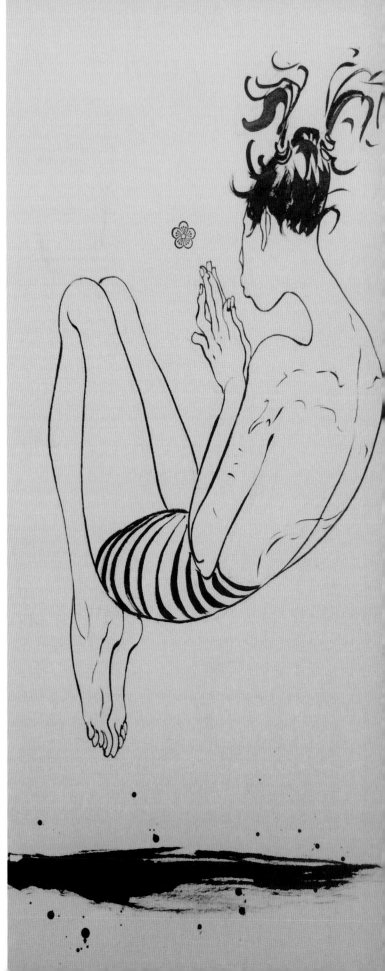

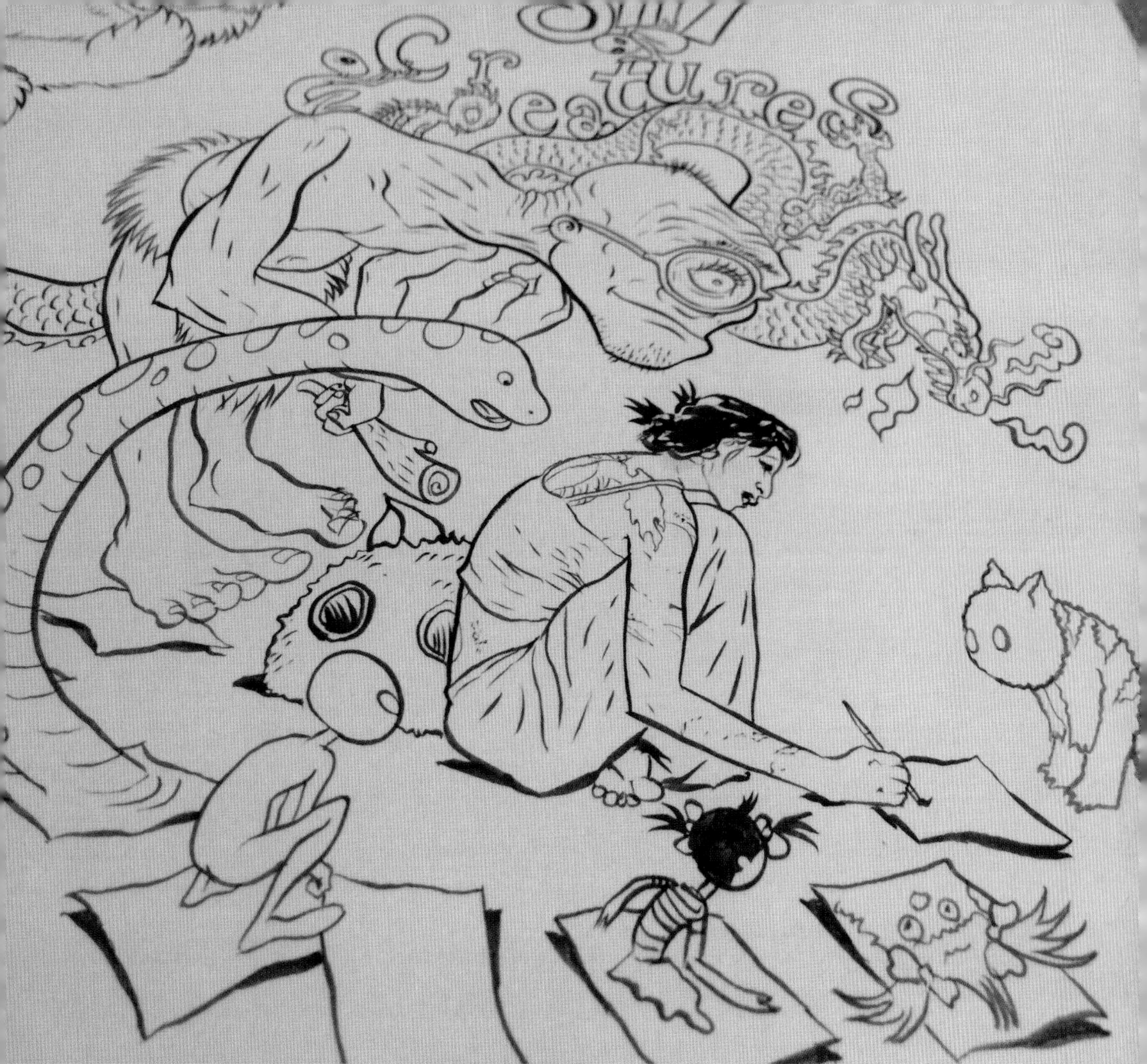
Creatures

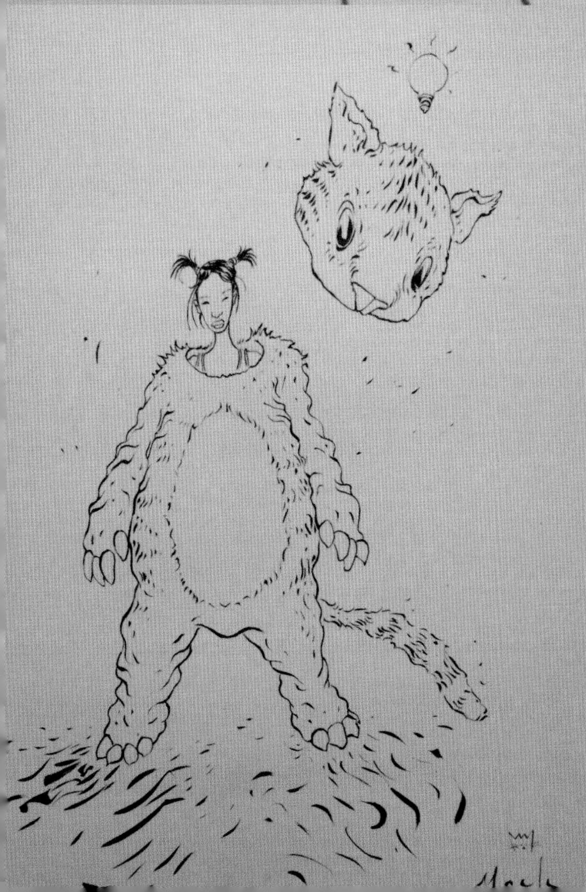

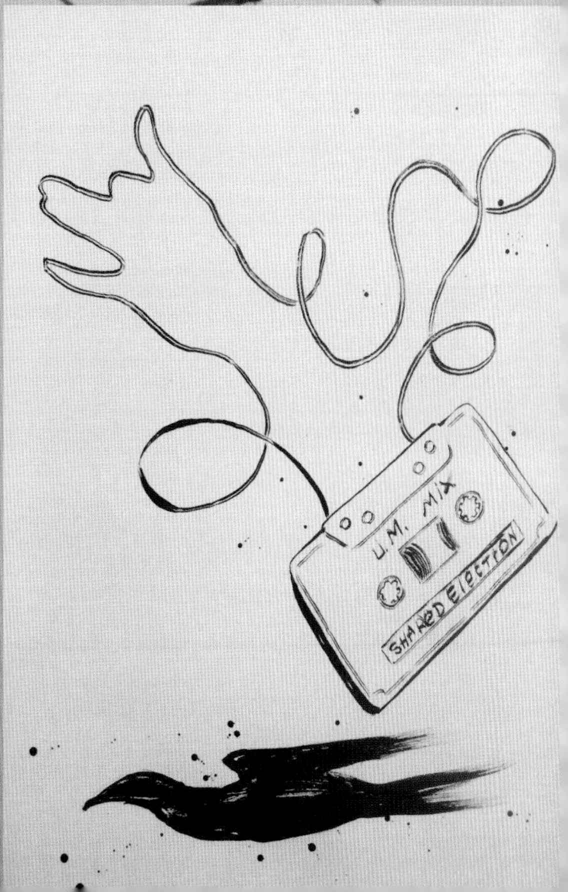
U.M. MIX
SHARED ELECTION

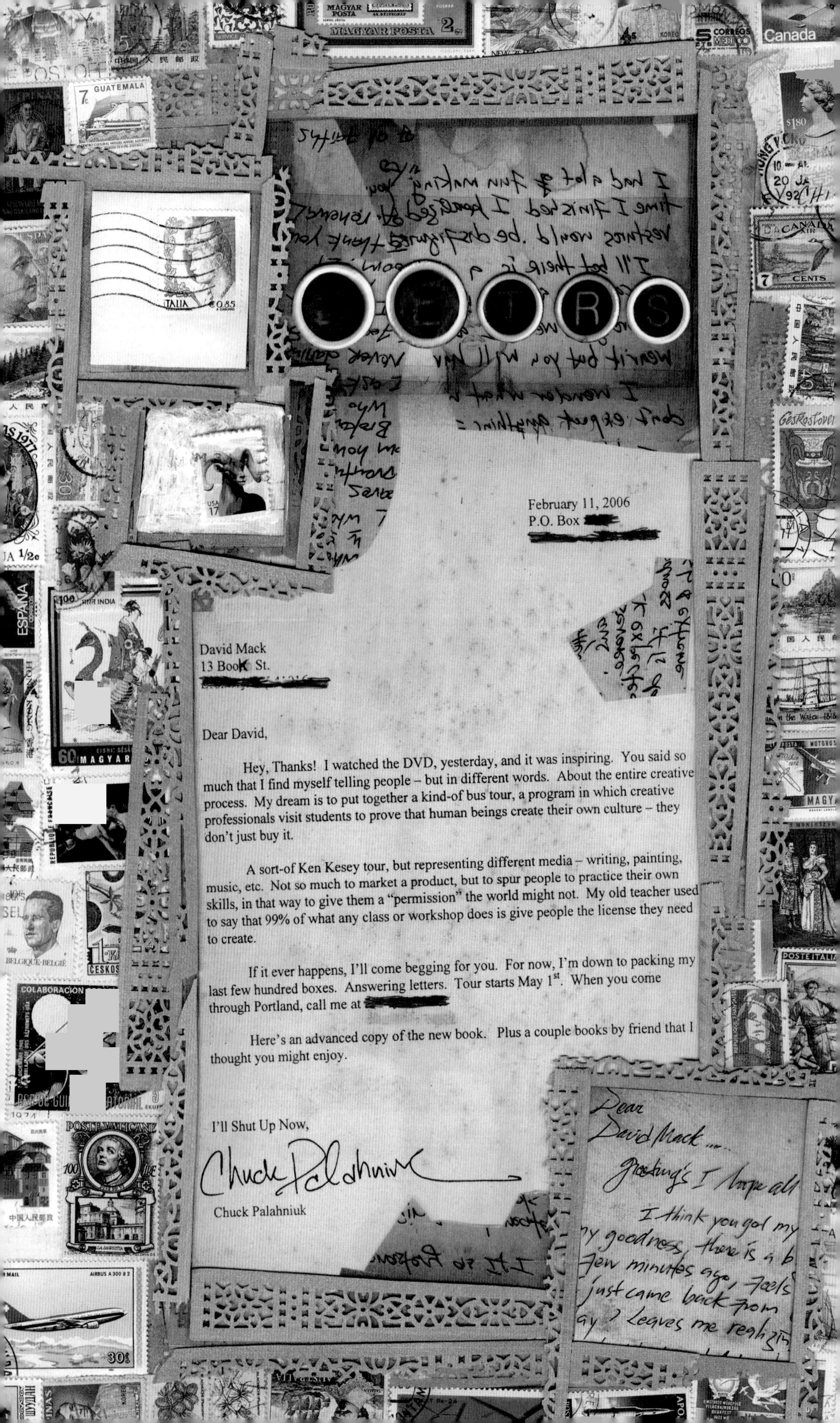

February 11, 2006
P.O. Box [redacted]

David Mack
13 Book St.
[redacted]

Dear David,

Hey, Thanks! I watched the DVD, yesterday, and it was inspiring. You said so much that I find myself telling people – but in different words. About the entire creative process. My dream is to put together a kind-of bus tour, a program in which creative professionals visit students to prove that human beings create their own culture – they don't just buy it.

A sort-of Ken Kesey tour, but representing different media – writing, painting, music, etc. Not so much to market a product, but to spur people to practice their own skills, in that way to give them a "permission" the world might not. My old teacher used to say that 99% of what any class or workshop does is give people the license they need to create.

If it ever happens, I'll come begging for you. For now, I'm down to packing my last few hundred boxes. Answering letters. Tour starts May 1st. When you come through Portland, call me at [redacted]

Here's an advanced copy of the new book. Plus a couple books by friend that I thought you might enjoy.

I'll Shut Up Now,

Chuck Palahniuk

Chuck Palahniuk

opportunity to be seen as artists first. Outside and beyond what they are normally seen as. And having that "Artistic License" gives them an interface to interact with the world on their own terms. But more than that, working creatively catalyzes a change in their entire demeanor and personality. They come out of their shell. They actually grow in personality and social skills. Even if they are autistic. The act of creating something catalyzes skills and growth in other practical areas.

I relate to these artists, because I went through a similar process. There is a form of Autism in my family called Aspergers Syndrome. I was different from other kids when I grew up. I saw things in a different way. I didn't understand the same social cues. Creating became my vehicle for connecting with the world, making sense of the world, and my catalyst for growing in other areas. I still have a lot of blind spots and naïveté, but I do my best, and through making art and stories, I've improved over the years. The artists of Visionaries & Voices are a part of what inspired *The Shy Creatures*.

Another ripple effect of *The Alchemy* is the documentary film about my work called *The Alchemy of Art*. I was able to take the filmmakers to the Visionaries & Voices art studio, so the artists there could be a part of the film. On the DVD there are a variety of special features like a page by page commentary of an entire chapter of The Alchemy, but I was happy that the filmmakers gave a section to the artists of Visionaries & Voices as well.

This story has been a conversation between inspirations and experiences, efforts and instincts. A way for me to put whimsical ideas and personal experiences into a story and make sense of them.

Now I let the letters continue that conversation…

David Mack

2016

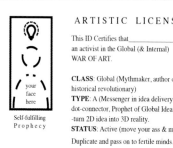

ARTISTIC LICENSE

This ID Certifies that_____ is an activist in the Global (& Internal) WAR OF ART.

your face here

Self-fulfilling Prophecy

CLASS: Global (Mythmaker, author of culture, historical revolutionary)
TYPE: A (Messenger in idea delivery system, dot-connector, Prophet of Global Idea Cubism) -turn 2D idea into 3D reality.
STATUS: Active (move your ass & make it happen). Duplicate and pass on to fertile minds.

Hi, David:
I read *Kabuki*. I was amazed, delighted, impressed, touched. More than that: I was inspired. It's very rare that a comic book inspires me; in fact, in the past decade or so Will Eisner was probably the only creator whose work lifted me up that way, made me say, "Yes! THAT'S what this medium can be!"-- and then sent me back to my computer all fired up and ready to throw down the creative gauntlet for the next person. But you did it today. There were so many wonderful bits that flew across my consciousness reading those issues, but the one I loved most was this: "If you don't like the story your culture is writing, it's not enough to rail against it or say you don't subscribe to it. You have the obligation of writing your own story -- To be a contributing author of your own culture." To which I say: YES! I've been trying to do this for many years now… & right now, at this pivotal moment, it's more important than ever to have new stories, new myths, new dreams to share. Thanks for sharing yours. Keep sailing those beautiful dreams out into the collective consciousness! And thanks for sending a charge of creative kundalini up my spine.
J.M. DeMatteis
New York, NY

David!
I promised to show you the women's wear collections I designed inspired by your work. I just read the #5 issue of *Kabuki* last night, & it could not have come at a better time. Everything in this issue written about true creativity, has been all I've been able to think about while I've been working on this project. Thanks for the remotivation…excellent timing…
Jen Kao
New York, NY
I'm encouraged by Jen's accomplishments as a successful fashion designer. She was kind enough to shout out my work as inspirational in her fashion magazine interviews, and featured my work in her NYC fashion shows. Wearers & devotees of her fashion include M.I.A., Robin Wright, Nicki Minaj, Fergie, Rachel McAdams.

Dear Mr. David Mack,
I read *The Alchemy*. I wanted to savor it and take in all your points and visual counterpoints and experiments. Words can't express the thrill and buzz I experienced from the reading of a virtuoso performance. Brilliant, brother. Just brilliant. The chills and lump in my throat after reading, left me thinking. "Yeah. That's the way you do it." From a friend and colleague: thank you! The exciting part, as one who delves occasionally into the same deep water as you, is there's no telling where you're going to go, in any direction. The sky's the limit. Thanks for the challenge, inspiration, & great work.
Bill Sienkiewicz

David,
A few years ago I was working on the film, THE FINAL CUT. Robin Williams was the star of the film (a prince to work with!) & he gave me a copy of *Kabuki* as a gift. He is a HUGE fan of your work.
Shane Scott-Travis
Victoria, British Columbia
Here's to Robin Williams. Robin wrote to me and ordered Kabuki books from the back of the book. I'm glad to learn he shared them as gifts. He was a prince.

David,
Your line in #5 about silly being the default condition of children really, really struck me and actually has affected how I deal with my 3 and 6 year old. It put their nonsense in a bigger perspective for me and I've actually found myself letting a lot of things go in favor of their fun, whereas in the past I might have been a bit more grouchy.
Jim Townsend
Spring City, PA

David,
The Alchemy has been inspiring to me. While I'm always wondering what's happening next with the characters, the thoughts on creativity & the muse were just what I'd been needing during a rough year. By seeing what David can do with his art, I can really understand that art is what you put into it, & life can be dealt with when you have it on a page, whether written or drawn. I now have a new outlook on the concept & on my art. I showed you the work in progress on my altered book at the CAPE signing in Dallas. It was inspired by what I saw in *Kabuki* & your other works. It took me back to my BFA roots & gave me an outlet to release my pent-up grief & confusion into art. I want to thank you again for your time & kind words.
Kathryn White
Jonesboro, AR

Dear David,
I have returned after a great stay in NYC, where the highlight of the visit---for both my daughter, Anna, & I - was talking with you at ComicCon. My one objective was the hope of meeting you in person and saying thank you for your incredible work & to tell you how it impacted me & my artistic production during a year and a half of surgeries, chemotherapy & radiation. During the most challenging times, when steroids and chemo did not allow me to continue with my oil painting, I was introduced to collage by an art therapist, but it was when my daughter brought me an issue of *The Alchemy*, that I found real comfort and expression. I related deeply to *Kabuki*. I found the art & text outstanding, intelligent, and just the support I needed at a time when the material that surrounded me seemed to all be in regard to cancer, dying, will -making… I needed a hero, and

for unknowingly supporting me during the darkest hours of the night, when tearing paper & reading *Kabuki* over and over was all I could do. Thank you for generously encouraging the work currently in the making for the Cancer Centers Exhibitions (including a comic book called, The Adventures of My Left Breast which is a huge bow to your inspiration). Thank you for being so generous with your time, and for extending yourself in such a personal & kind way to us at ComicCon.

Adrienne Rich said that when one person tells the truth it opens up space in the world for others to tell the truth as well. Your work in *Kabuki* does so at every turn--visually & psychologically. I am forever grateful.

Viola Moriarty
Vermont

Dear Mr. Mack,

With each new issue of *The Alchemy* I am reminded why your story is special to me. It is the manner in which you arrange the artwork to mesh with & compliment the tone and events of the story. But more specifically, it is the ideas about creativity, productivity, & relationships that make my mind spin. In #6 the idea of spreading out REM sleep over 2-3 cycles per day to double or triple one's energy; my mind treated this as a parallel story as I applied this lifestyle to myself. In #7, I marveled over the idea of when you die, "You see every person that you ever had an interaction with. And feel from their perspective how you made them feel from your interaction." I began to think of how I am making other people feel in my current life.

Thanks,
Ben Kleinman
Phillidelphia, PA

Thank You!

I read in a Rumi book about how his friend Shams asked him a question so good it caused him to fall to the ground in shock. For me, those questions were in *Alchemy* #2: "Do you think books help shape your identity? Or do they only reveal it?" Best questions ever! Thank you Mr. Mack. These comics are just what I need in this point in my life when I want to take a large step into what I really want to do. Just when I think I couldn't love a character more than I love *Kabuki* and Akemi you give us the Animal Doctor. She's wonderful! Thank you. I'm going to get everyone I know into *Kabuki*.

Shondolyn Gibson
Rockland, MA

David,

I began reading *Kabuki* when I was in high school, and I was enthralled with the story. As time has gone by, both myself & *Kabuki* have grown up. I continue to read & re-read the books, and each time I am at a different place when I finish reading. In my early readings, my mom was healthy, & I could appreciate from afar the complexity and intrigue that you brought to the story by making it an autobiographical work beginning with your coping with the death of your mother. Now, I am facing the likely death of my mother, since she is ill. I only hope that I can find as productive and inspiring a way to focus my emotions. When *Kabuki* works for Hospice, the discussion that *Kabuki* has with the terminally ill patient struck me very deeply. Although many parts of *Kabuki* have touched me, this one stands out. My mother had a death experience during childbirth, and the way that the patient and *Kabuki* discuss the experience of death is like my mother's description of her experience. As a result, my mom & I have been having deep conversations about death & her experiences in life thus far. I want to impress upon you the impact that your work has on the lives of others. Your work is

a testament to your mother's memory. Thank you.
Natalie White

My mom and I just finished *The Alchemy #4*. How fly was that!? The words that really hit me were; "I realized that the self portrait project was a metaphor for teaching me to create my own life." Yikes!

Ben Ervin
La Ciudad Juarez, Mexico

David,

I'm shaking from #7. It's like somebody punched me in the neck. I don't know how long I've been saying that I am starting my own thing. But it's been a long time, extended by second-guessing and procrastination... from fear of vulnerability. Super Number Seven. Seems like it's a silly thing for me to credit for the right jumpstart, but I am STILL shaking. And I'm going to work tomorrow. And the day after. It's so easy to tell someone else that inspiration doesn't arrive from waiting, but believe it or not, nobody's ever told ME that.

Thanks,
Jen Kao
NY, NY

David,

You are my favorite artist, & it was your work that made me want to become a comic artist too, - which I am today. Your stories have been a great inspiration. *Kabuki* gives me hope, when I see that such an artistic and philosophical creation can be that successful. And that you won Germany's main comic-award shows me that readers here are smarter than I think.

Gina Wetzel
Germany

Mr. Mack,

My younger sister recently went to a comic book store with a friend and brought home the first issue of *Kabuki: The Alchemy*. She showed it to me and asked me if I wanted to read it. In a rare mood, I said yes. I say rare because I am a 32 year old professional in corporate America. I do not read comic books. I don't even like fiction. I typically stay in the non-fiction genres of philosophy, theology, psychology, health, or spirituality. But as I began to read, I was fascinated. I had no idea comics could be so moving. *The Alchemy* is not like traditional comics. It was a moving experience, in some ways reminding me of *Blade Runner* due to its dark quality, but at the same time it was very inspirational and spiritual. They create a very real experience in which I felt involved in the mystery & intensity.

I have sent recommendations for *Kabuki* to a number of friends, including a therapist who will be able to use it with her clients. I also recommended it to a teacher/metaphysician who I think can use it in her classes. She teaches courses on imagination & began as an artist herself. Your book within a book, *The Shy Creatures*, was wonderful. I looked it up today on Amazon to see if it was really published & available. It is an excellent children's story. I plan to read it to my 5 & 8 year old step-daughters. I can only wish that you will one day have the desire to also write for tween girls. How I would love a series for my 8 year old to read! Something that is artistic, introspective, & fun. Not the pedestrian works that are churned out which focus on materialism, boys, & superficiality.

Catherine Walker
Senior Project Manager
Archon Group, LP
Goldman Sachs

Dear Mr. Mack,

Issue #4 of *Kabuki*: *The Alchemy*: "Realize there is no security and become comfortable with that."
For the longest time I've been living in a state of fear that has settled me into places and positions that I never truly wanted. I am finally beginning to realize that there is more to living than saving for the future. With the above statement, you captured a fear of mine & stated in a way that pushed me to realize that there is no tomorrow unless I create it. "The act of writing the list of your dreams is the first step in the momentum of enacting it into reality". Thank you for pushing boundaries, not only on paper but also in the viewer.

Jonathon D. Barth

David,

I've been showing *Kabuki* around & everyone loves it. You have the entire CNN International graphics team loving it. If you want a tour of CNN let me know. I've seen your work, the only thing I could do is return the favor. What caught my eye about *The Alchemy* at first was the great use of type & page layout. I've reread the first four & each time there is something new.

Veronica Preston
Atlanta, GA

Dear David Mack,

Thank you so much for the response to my research paper on your work for my Masters Degree thesis. I have been enjoying *The Alchemy* immensely. But with lines like, "What does it mean when you find yourself conjugating the grammar of shapes?" how could I not love it? The aim of my paper was to help people improve their understanding of the comic book medium in a positive way. Your recent work seems to have the aim of helping people improve their lives in a positive way. I am proud of what I achieved with my paper, but a scholarly work will never change a person's life the way a work of art, like *ECHO: Vision Quest* or *The Alchemy*, can.

Kevin Johns

I'm particularly intrigued by David's work in the *Echo* storyline. I'm Native American, and I found his art to be refreshingly genuine. I liked the *Parts of a Hole* / Echo work because it fit perfectly with my job--I'm a therapist who works with abused teens, and the content and text in that just seemed like it would belong, nicely framed, on the wall of my studio office. We don't make big bucks at my job, but I like having nice artwork up. It becomes conversation-starters with the teens I'm working with, so let David know that his work is not merely decorative to me, but quite useful in my approach to working with kids who've been traumatized.

Matt Atkinson
Oklahoma City, OK

This means a lot. I've received letters from patients that you have helped who mention that the artwork in your office is helpful to them.

David,

You've been a constant source of inspiration. Check out my tune "Kiss Before Dying", Inspired by *Kabuki*. My jazz improv piece was inspiration from not only *Kabuki*, but also from your renegade and fearless approach to the arts. We tried to approach that tune from the same attitude, but with music. Thanks for the inspirations, it has helped me through many dark times & lifted me to many creative spaces.

Tung Le
Saigonclubmusic.com
Toronto, Ontario Canada

As always, inspiring me and motivating me at just the right times. My special interest has to do with a page in issue #5, which relates to a conversation we had at a signing in Dallas. You explained how

progress is like a frog leaping from one lily pad to the next, or a connect the dots, or stepping stones, or climbing stairs- basically what you said on the page of *Alchemy* #5 with the stick figures jumping from panel to panel. I drew an image based on our conversation very much like this page! I feel like this page is connected to me.
Jason Forge
Oklahoma

Hi David,

I wrote a song for *Kabuki*. It will be on my new CD, "*Reaching the Dragon*". *Kabuki* has been a huge inspiration to me. The depth & charm of your writing always speaks to me in a personal way. I just read *Alchemy* #6. I loved what you said about having a child's mind for innovation. I've had to remind myself of a lot of the things you've mentioned in order to get the new CD done. As a practicing Buddhist, your writing speaks to me in a very spiritual way. I have a great respect for your work when I read each issue, knowing that you are such a generous person & having had the honor of working with you for RAINN with Tori Amos. Thank you so much for inspiring me.
Respect and gratitude,
Lisa Furukawa Ray

Mr. Mack,

I am a high school art teacher in Orange County CA. I teach at a school that has previously frowned on comics. The art program here is built around fine arts that rely heavily on watercolor. Your work has helped me convince the department head that there is a very thin line between comics & fine art, if the work is done by someone who appreciates both mediums, such as yourself. After showing her an issue of *Alchemy*, the teacher who opposes comics actually referenced you to her Advance Placement students. Changing curriculums that have been successful for years is quite difficult, as is changing the perceptions people have had of comics, but I think it is necessary to try & expose students to as many areas of the arts as possible. Thank you for being instrumental in blurring the line that separates comic art from fine art, and influencing some old and new artists alike.
If you are ever available to come to Orange County to speak, you are always invited.
Marco Magallanes
Orange County, CA

Hi, David

I've been a fan of your work for a long time & would love to make the speaking engagement to my students happen. I've already shown your DVD to two groups of students-- at CCA and SJSU.
Barron Storey
California College of Arts
San Francisco, CA

Dear David,

I believe, intentional or not, your series *Kabuki: The Alchemy* has the potential to inspire a complete artistic renaissance. Your artwork is magnificent, but that is not it's most important attribute. It screams out to artists, and I believe that is exactly who reads it most dearly. You speak so directly of what an artist needs to do to be creative, & to express themselves- to crystallize their emotions in art. You speak of self-motivation, risk-taking... and it's all very raw & truthful. Your advice is not intangible or too idealistic. It's this reality to your words that make your message so meaningful. I would like you to know that your message has inspired me. It might even be that pivotal reminder to so many promising artists that what they create actually means something. And that they should do what they love.
Raleigh
Boston, MA

The letters between *Kabuki* & Akemi in #5 seemed like the dialogue between the conscious ego and the unconscious. It's like you are letting your reader in on a part of your individuation process. At first I didn't agree with your radical change of art style. But I can't begin to describe how your book has changed my thought process over the years. I felt prompted to write after issue 5's mention of synchronicity. I just finished Jung's *Synchronicity: On a Causal Connecting Principle* the day before & found it beyond coincidence to be reading it in your book. There were times when I just thought of quitting. Thanks for the wake up call.
Derek Davis
Sacramento, CA

Hello David,

I went to a comic expo in Bogota, Colombia, & bought #1 & 2 of *Kabuki: The Alchemy*. I find them so wonderful! I feel so familiarized with the way you tell the story. It's like reading someone's mind. Thank you for this wonderful story telling.
Margarita
Bogota, Columbia

David,

Loving *The Alchemy*. I think I am finding a way now that my art might have some value. Thanks for making great books that have helped me over the years. I ordered the David Mack art DVD from America. Cant wait!
Thommy
United Kingdom

Dear David,

As you read this I will already have set foot in the Altered States of America. I got *Kabuki: Alchemy* #5. What a pleasant surprise to find the envelope I sent you on the Shakespeare page! I blinked a few times, how strange to read my address in a *Kabuki* comic! Talk about synchronicity, I didn't know the stamps would have a butterfly!
I have been deathly anxious that Fully Booked would schedule your Manila signing while I was away. I shall be back in Manila in a month's time and hope to hear news of your arrival then.
Missively yours,
Donna Batongbacal
Quezon City, Philipines
It was wonderful to see you in Manila at the Fully Booked signing and at Asia Pop Comicon in Manila. Fully Booked still has signed copies of Dream Logic & Kabuki Library edition in stock for readers who missed my signing & talk there.

David Mack:

A month ago I had never even cared to read comic books. My English teacher showed me *Kabuki*, and after reading just ONE I was hooked. The art, the writing: all inspiring. Just looking at the artwork inspires me and the writing is just... wow. I just finished reading *Scarab*. After reading it, I'll be able to write my college admission essay easily.
Charisse Weston
Houston, TX

David,

As I continued to read *Kabuki* Vol 1, it became more obvious that there were no coincidences in this book. Every twist I encountered was a surprise but not out of left field. It made sense when Dove revealed himself to *Kabuki*. The dialogue and monologue seemed never to clash, but to blend and compliment each other. Your pacing, your way of mixing & matching words with pictures reminds me of the best of Alan Moore and Neil Gaimen. As both a reader and a creator, it drives me nuts to see so many comic books not take this full advantage of being a visual and literal medium.
Scott Zoiko
Chicago, IL

David,

I was able to share *The Alchemy of Art* DVD with my 8 year old Granddaughter. We were both completely enthralled with the film. To be able to share this with my own family was something I can't put into sufficient words. It was one of those times that will always be remembered. My granddaughter was given one of your "*The Shy Creatures*" books when we finished the film. She loved every page of it. Then we sat & looked at *Kabuki* for two more hours. It was a special time of being able to share something that touches me so deeply & to have it appreciated by a new generation who will pass it on when I am no longer here. With *The Shy Creatures*, you have chosen to reach out to young readers in the way you have touched us with *Kabuki*. You speak to them of the worth of imagination. It is a pleasure to pass to the next generation what you have meant to me.
Fran Golden-Merritt
GA

Mr. Mack,

I thank you for helping me shape some of my aspirations at a younger age. I first read *Kabuki* vol. 5 in 2001. From then on, there was a kind of hope I held for recognition in what I do if I work hard enough. Your work was the first that ever inspired it in me. I thank you for creating such wonderful & meaningful books to share with the rest of the world.
Sarah Elgindy
Harderwijk, Holland

David,

Reading #6: With each turn of the page I was like "Yes, I know exactly what Mack/Kabuki/Akemi/M.C. Square mean." Syncronicity. There's such a rush of adrenaline & creative juices flowing after digesting an issue of *Kabuki*. It connects, it motivates & evokes change. I believe 100% without a doubt that *The Alchemy* is the most important comic book being published right now. Perhaps ever. You are doing your readers a tremendous service by passing along inspiration & wisdom. I believe that these books will spark change in individuals across the globe. There are a few things in life that are just pure joy. *Kabuki* is one of them.
Mike B.
Orlando, FL

Alchemy #5 - what a wonderful treat!
I'm so glad you brought up Chomsky and McLuhan and the idea of TV as a passive act which can distract and lure us into collective thought. *Kabuki* is no passive medium - in reading it we are actively engaging our thoughts and emotions, making connections. We interact and share ideas with you and with other readers through letters, the message boards, and signings. Have you read my diary? I'm also trying to figure out what to do next. I see now how easy it is to feel stuck and do nothing, and how powerful the act of starting something - taking the "leap of faith" - can be. Thanks for another inspiring issue!
Talya
Toronto, Canada

Dear David,

I just finished a two-month stint in a hospital for anorexia. Your books helped keep me sane. Thank you for giving me a sanctuary. It is strange how someone I have never met can be so important to me. Thank you for putting so much beauty in an empty world.
Shana

AAAAH!!! You shoulda seen me doing a lil touch down dance in Criminal Records when I got the new Reflections #9! Thank you for including my photographs of you in the book! David, I am so thrilled and excited, you have made my year! I

like the piece about "Artistic License". You've been my Akemi in that sense, and I'm grateful that connecting with you got me to "Move my ass & make it happen".
Eternally grateful,
Linda Costa
Atlanta, GA

David,
A true story of how your paintings touched my life. I have recently been in a Psychiatric hospital for overdosing on painkillers as well as depression, anger, and suicidal ideation. My therapist's office blew me away when I saw your art hanging on the walls. He showed me many of your originals he had purchased; he had a lot of art from "Echo" as well as the cover to *Daredevil #53* & it made me laugh that you actually glued a penny to it. I've come to appreciate your art more as I've bought your entire *Daredevil* run & have started reading *Kabuki*. My therapist let me hold an original from Bill Sienkiewicz, which for me was like holding a Van Gogh; as well as your art & was amazed by both. As a parting gift he gave me a copy of a splash page of "Echo" where she explains "I will bury the memories..." and I didn't fully realize how poignant it was. You are now an artist I truly appreciate & would like to thank you for helping me.
Kyle
Oklahoma City, OK

Dear David,
The prose and artwork you presented in vol 1 have, like *Kabuki* herself, transmuted into more refined expressions of your talents as both a writer & artist. I finished reading issue 9 of *The Alchemy*. A brilliant ending to an engaging story! I loved the conversation about the kiss, & this will change the way I read, watch movies, & experience the end of each of the "acts" of my life. The lines, "If you don't like the story your culture is writing... it's not enough to say you don't subscribe to it...you have the obligation of writing your own story... to be a contributing author of your own culture" were so dead on. This, coupled with Akemi's dialogue about giving the other characters "artistic license" is the foundation of what I seek to impart to my students. M.C.'s talk about the "Emoto Effect" speaks to a Tantric belief called matrika shakti. Matrika shakti is the source shakti for every possible form of conceptualization. So, like Dr. Emoto, if you use words that are poetic & uplift & inspire auspiciousness, then the energetic body of a person, animal, or even place, will expand or shine more brightly. If you use words of malign intention then the receiver's energy will contract or dull.
I wanted to let you know that your artistic vision is felt, appreciated, and needed in these times, when thinking outside the normal boundaries of our self-imposed limitations is a necessity if this world is to last for the next generations. I have also read *The Shy Creatures*, and thoroughly enjoyed it.
Mark Shveima
San Francisco, CA

That kiss as the mark of the final act in the story came from a sushi dinner conversation with Neil Gaiman. We both did a talk at NKU and at the dinner before his talk we had this storytelling discussion.

David Mack,
You called this story of *Kabuki's* life Alchemy, a word used to describe the study of change. It wasn't until this issue that I started to understand the full weight of how integral that concept was to this story. The mythology used in the story was of creatures and of people, but the way I'm reading it, the myth really being explored is souls. Do they

have an original purpose that can be stopped or slowed? Can a body carry two at once, & could they be at cross purposes? If so, was Ukiko's soul repressed by her mother's, or was it helping her mother's achieve peace?
What compelled me to write was the letters column, & the theme in there. Half were from people confessing that they'd begun life-changing experiences after reading your work. What is remarkable is the way your work inspires people to open up so much. In writing my invisible paragraph, I found a few truths about me I didn't know before & may not have if it weren't for your own stories, just enough fantasy to bring people in, & just enough of you in them to bring them out. You're connecting with more people than you know.
Ryan Walsh
Indianapolis, IN

Dear Mr. Mack,
The Alchemy has its own meaning for me. How to start when memories of your past intrude. How to begin when you find yourself free for the first time. And how easy life gets when you have a partner and a support network. Though Akemi has not physically appeared in this arc so far, I have come to an appreciation for the character that I did not have before. I see Ukiko and Akemi as two sides of the same coin. Ukiko is the scarred, socially awkward side, who can only relate to others from behind a mask. Akemi is the side that is confident and makes no apologies for who she is, and who has a plan and follows it. I see you as two parts of a whole as well. There's David Mack, the very kind person, and then there's David Mack, the brilliant writer and artist. I find it difficult to see the two as the same person sometimes. The autobiographical bit in #4 inspired me to start drawing again. I feel a renewed urge to put effort into my artistic endeavors because of you!
Terry Drosdak Nee Lohmeyer
Maryland

Dear Mr. Mack:
Issue two and three REALLY got me thinking, when the vet girl called *Kabuki* Akemi. It makes me wonder if Akemi really even is Akemi, or if Akemi is really just some made up good Samaritan that people use to help out someone else. Maybe there is no Akemi after all? It really made me think. And that's what I like best about this comic. It makes me think.
Valerie Heigert
Girard, IL

Dear David,
I was affected by the way *Kabuki* deals with her self-image. As strong as she is, there is a young woman under that mask that feels self-conscious about her scars. I always considered myself a strong person, but a couple of years ago my strength was tested. I discovered a small lump in my breast and underwent surgery to remove it. I'm left with a scar I am reminded of everyday. Seeing *Kabuki* deal with some of the feelings I've had has made me feel like I wasn't alone. The line in *The Alchemy* #2 eloquently captured that time in my life: "When I feared death, when I thought I was less than a woman... Akemi helped me through that". I am continually impressed at how you are able to reveal truth & emotion with such grace. Oscar Wilde said: "Every portrait that is painted with feeling is a portrait of the artist". Thank you, David, for sharing yourself through your fearless creativity & emotional storytelling which inspires me.
Talya
Toronto, Canada

Dear David,
I have to add *The Alchemy #4* to my list of comics that made me cry. I've wanted to change my life around for a while, but I felt like this is the way things have to be. After reading this, I'm inspired to find out just what I want out of life. No more excuses! Thanks David, for helping me discover something about myself.
Angel R.
Benton Harbor, MI

Dear Mr. Mack,
I happen to be part Ainu, and even though I don't identify with my ethnic background much, it was VERY empowering to find a heroine of similar lineage. Your multi-media presentation is stunning, but even more impactful is the quality of the writing & content.
Makomo Vilai Senya
Chicago, IL

In *Kabuki #2*, I was pleasantly surprised to see a character with a prosthetic leg, especially someone who constructs and modifies their own leg. I like the symbolism of a person building / changing / adding parts of themselves. I happen to have a prosthetic leg. The paintings of all of the little arms & legs reminded me of all of the various legs I've worn over the years. I never saw myself as a victim. I never considered myself handicapped. I always think, "What would Carrot Top do if he had a fake leg?" I've always had a sense of humor about my situation. Last September, my good friend, Tabitha Oblinger was seriously injured in an automobile accident. The doctors were forced to amputate her leg. Tabitha will soon be fitted for a prosthesis & she will begin the long and difficult process of learning to walk again. Tabitha is the heart & soul of CityArts. "Amputation" is a very scary word for most people. But amputation doesn't mean you can't lead a meaningful and fruitful life. It is an issue of mind over matter. I try to remember that I'm more than this flesh & bone body. I have control over my happiness. I try to focus on the positive side of things. Thanks again for your incredible work. It never fails to inspire me.
Dustin Parker
Wichita, KS

I really dig *The Alchemy* series. Every issue is incredible. "Moving on", that's the most refreshing theme I've read in eons. Are you hinting that Akemi is more than a singular character- that she's perhaps a circular network of hope? After reading the scenes in #2 & 3, I thought that's a cool idea.
Shaun Koh
Singapore

Mr. Mack,
How much of this storyline for Ukiko as a "blueprint for creating your own reality" is a reaction to seeing how deeply your work has affected your devoted readers? In *Alchemy #2*, the vet says, "My art should be about doing and being, rather than having and getting." Is this your personal mission? The *Kabuki* message board & the Tear Drops letters column almost seems like your own personal Akemi Network: inspiring others - remaining on Earth like the Buddha to help others find their own enlightenment; their own path to greatness. With the book's presentation of social issues (breast cancer, RAINN, & land mine awareness among them) you are pushing this art form to new realms of "art as action" that continue to impress me. It's exciting to have *Kabuki* as a parallel story and catalyst in my growth as an artist. I have no doubt you will meet your ever-expanding goals

and surpass them. Your heart is one of the most important and consistent mediums in your work.
Daniel Winters
Marietta, GA

David,
Alchemy #2. The thing that took me most about this issue wasn't the transformation *Kabuki* underwent, or the story behind the vet. It wasn't the variety of art styles you used. It was the pain on *Kabuki*'s face throughout the whole process. Her scars are hidden and she'll be able to start a new life. But she's grown up with her scars and trauma, and even though it messed her up, she's having difficulty letting go. There weren't any words describing any of this, but it was crystal clear on her face.
Ryan Walsh
Indianapolis, IN

In the case of the veterinarian in the *Alchemy #2*, the only two Japanese names in the "gallery", with the arm prostheses seen for different ages: Kiyomi (a lower right arm prosthesis) and Satomi (an arm prosthesis that could be a left arm), I would consider them to be the real Siamese?! Small hints dropped by our master storyteller who likes to keep things up his sleeve, but works them in the story in such a way that only afterward you can go back and give things a definite meaning or intention. Don't you just love it!
Arie Bras
Harderwijk, The Netherlands

Dear Mr. Mack,
I discovered *Kabuki*. It blew me away. I walked 2 hours in the Ontario winter to get *Kabuki #7*. The art is beautiful (*Kabuki* got me into illustration), and the story is incredible. What I really love are the female characters. As a woman it's easy to feel alienated from most comics, but the *Kabuki* characters are always written and drawn with so much sensitivity -vulnerable but incredibly strong. I would love to know how you write such true female characters while most comics seem to be still working out how to draw breasts. Keep up the good work. It's enthralling & inspiring.
Renee Nault
Toronto, Canada

David Mack,
Expressing the impact that *Kabuki* has made on my life. I wouldn't say that *Kabuki* is the only reason why I started on Japanese studies, but it was a step on the way. *Kabuki* got me into reading comics. What I like the most about *Kabuki* is your storytelling. What I love about your storytelling is your character creation. I care more about Seiko from the 3 issues of Scarab than I care about characters starring in hundreds of issues. You give us insight into so many intriguing and diverse lives, which makes me open my eyes to the people around me and accept them as fellow human beings.
Magnus
Denmark

David,
I'm student teaching 1st grade. So, my lesson intro is *The Shy Creatures*! The kids loved the book! They laughed at all the silliness! Their favorite was the abominable snowman! And one of the girls in class came later & hugged me! She's very shy & quiet. I'm not exactly teaching in the richest of neighborhoods & I don't know her full story, but I think she's recently moved in with her grandmother. So she has no friends here. I think it actually helped her! And they got the rhyming words which was the actual objective of the lesson! It was awesome!
Tonia
Lafayette, LA

During my difficult time I constantly took comfort/solace in every *Kabuki* issue. Your writing has had

a deep impact on my own existence. I related to certain characters/situations and it was very therapeutic. I drowned in your art, writing, designs, and even the letter columns. Thank you for your generosity & your art. You are a gift and I look forward to meeting you at the Chicago con.
Angelo Casiano.
Cicero, IL

Dear David,
I have just discovered your work (a high school student shared it with me) and it touched me. In fact, your work in the *Daredevil* book moved me to tears. I have never reread a comic book so many times and then sent copies of it to numerous friends. Please permit me to explain. I am a school psychologist who specializes in working with students who are deaf. In particular I specialize in working with deaf students who have been sexually and/or physically abused. The work does not pay much but doing my part to feed the right dogs in people (to use your parable) is rewarding in its own manner as I see students shake off painful emotional baggage and grow into mature individuals like your Echo character. I feel lucky to have learned sign and become immersed in the Deaf culture. Your work will expose hundreds of thousands of people to that other world and will impact lives beyond your typical comic book fans. I see it already with the students with whom I work. I have run out and purchased your complete works in *Daredevil* and have asked my local shop to get more of your work. I am impressed with your sensitivity to abuse, autism, and deaf people. I will be using your work in therapy with students for it has great potential to help many students begin their own recovery. Thank you for making my work a bit easier and on the behalf of thousands of deaf children in our country who may find hope and inspiration from your exploration of their world. Your artwork is very impressive and I would love to hang up prints of it in my office as a way to inspire and interest deaf kids to read more.
Respectfully,
Steven Hardy-Braz
President
North Carolina School Psychology Association

David,
Thanks for inspiring my wife to paint again, and for having the only comics that she will read!
Johnny Boy
Paris, France

Mr. Mack
Your book is a zero point energy machine. I bought Vol. 1 - then all of the *Kabuki* volumes immediately following. My wife loves it. My 7 year old daughter said, "It's not like any comic book I've seen - it's beautiful". Thanks to Mike Oeming, as he cited you as an influence so I had to pick up *Kabuki* for the first time ever. It inspired me.
Tim Daniel
Missoula, MT

David,
I would like to believe that these characters are alive; When I read *The Alchemy* (and it's predecessors) they come off as human. They're like friends' adventures that I'm reading about. Though still nameless, our Vet turned out to be one interesting character and her "reveal" of her own prosthetic really did it for me. There is such a beauty to your "flawed" characters. They're not victims & so many not only move on with their lives but seem to prosper in spite of their pasts. Akemi is becoming almost mythical & it makes me wonder if she may in fact just be certain people's "invisible friend." I just pray that all is in fact "good" with Akemi. Since this is something of an autobiographical work and fans of yours know that you've in fact done portraits of Tori Amos for her RAINN calendars and paintings

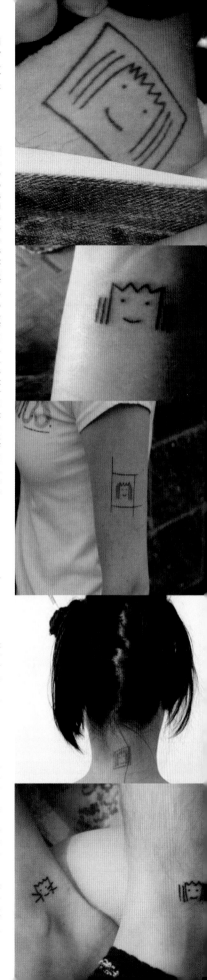

for Paul McCartney, have you worked with the others the vet listed inside the book? I couldn't help but notice the specter of a new t-shirt with the Vet's "Little Friend's Animal Clinic" shirt. Maybe even an "Invisible Friend Children's Book"?
Your books make me smile in a way that no other comic has done for 10 strong years now.
J.D. Lombardi
Philadelphia, PA

My favorite detail of *Alchemy* so far was the mention of the "literary worm hole" in Ukiko's choose-your-own-adventure book in issue #1. In *Metamorphosis*, one of the guards called Akemi a hermaphrodite. Is this intended to reveal something about Akemi's true nature? The word offers several implications:
1) simply a combination of diverse elements "defying conventional categorization",
2) "Messenger of Love" or "goddess of love and messages" from the Hermes-Aphrodite root,
3) The normal usage of the word, in which case Akemi's possibilities for reinventing herself are doubled. What are the chances Akemi could show up appearing as a different gender than we saw her last? Akemi's name, after all, refers to *Alchemy* - or the process of transformation. What of the nature of the Akemi network? I read a good observation from a fan who brought up a possible connection to Siamese when the prosthetics were being discussed. Is the Akemi-Net trying to dismantle Noh? The Doc did say that Akemi used to be the original Tigerlily, then went rogue as Paper Tiger, then got captured by the Noh and sent to Control Corps. And Control Corps reprograms defective agents and sends them out with new operative identities. Maybe Akemi IS a part of an alternate agency (perhaps connected to or run by "Dove") that had some interest in breaking *Kabuki* out. Akemi certainly had no problem infiltrating Noh.
Daniel

David,
#7 was an amazing chapter to *The Alchemy*. I was just talking to my friend about resistance to doing actions, how we put off actions we know we should do with excuses. My second copy of #7 will be coming this weekend in the mail & I'm going to give it my friend. It was amazing how issue #4 & 5 came out EXACTLY when I needed them to come out for myself. *The Alchemy* might end up being better than *Metamorphosis*. It may be your best written arc so far. It's really cohesive without loosing the single read each issue can be as well.
Banky
Chicago, Illinois

The Alchemy of Art: DVD
David - Just wanted to say how great this is. The producers did a super job of getting out of the way & letting the artwork & you speak for yourselves. The close-up camera shots were fantastic - I think it was easier to see some of the fine detail of your work compared to actually looking at it reduced in a comic. You can really tell they respect your work. The commentaries of *Kabuki* & the children's book are great. But, as with any artist, I get the biggest kick out of looking at your workspace & all the art laying around. Technical Questions: What's that ink brush/pen you're using throughout the DVD? And what are you using to fix your collage paper items to the artboard?
Jonathon Hickman
The Nightly News

David,
I bought *The Alchemy of Art* DVD. I watched it & found it very inspirational. It definitely made me think twice about your work & motivated me to boot up Final Draft & start another script.

Alex Chung
Aneheim CA

I've reread this "*Alchemy*" story, and there's some stuff going on. What about the real *Kabuki* mask getting stolen and Akemi playing it off like it's nothing? Who was the girl on the plane that radiated danger, and who is the "mysterious someone" that will pull the rug out from under the Noh? I can't shake the feeling that this whole thing is building into a larger resolution that isn't yet apparent, even though I suspect all the clues are there from the start.
Jubal Faircloth
Newport, KY

I've been on a *Kabuki* high since I read *The Alchemy*. It made me feel something I've never felt. It opened up doors in my head philosophically. It changed my entire life. And the way I write.
Now I read *Kabuki* Vol 1, and I am stunned. It is unlike anything I have read. So heartfelt. I had to write something because David Mack was my age when he wrote this stuff. He was twenty, and was writing books of depth. If he could do that at twenty, I knew I had a shot. I'm nineteen and naïve, but Mack had done something awe-inspiring that he made me feel like I could do a good job. And he did it his own way. Volume one was something that may never be reproduced as it was unique, it was imaginative, and it was his world. It brought Mack into visionary level. Thank you for giving this writer something that no one else has been able to: An experience that has changed my life.
Craig Maloof
Orlando, FL

Dear David,
I've just finished *Kabuki* vol 1 for the fourth time! My only regret is that I didn't discover *Kabuki* sooner. At age 60, I've been blessed to read virtually all my life. This includes comics from "way back when". I can tell you that the quality of *Kabuki* exceeds these experiences by a spectacular margin. You have created a literary classic that will stand for decades to come. I look forward to the years ahead, as you flesh out the lives of the Noh. I understand this will take time. It's possible that I will not live long enough to see the fruition of the *Kabuki* series. The genealogical line I descend through isn't long-lived. Quality literature is something I've enjoyed for decades. Thank you for giving myself, and so many others, *Kabuki* to look forward to.
Douglas K. Howard
Brookings, OR

David,
I began reading your work after seeing a friend with a *Kabuki* T-shirt. I happened to ask her about it. She enthusiastically handed me an issue of *Skin Deep*. I was captivated. My heartfelt appreciation for the way your artwork has encouraged me to develop my own creative side.
Gwendolyn Kemper

Dear David Mack,
A year ago, I set a vision for myself and thought of nothing but to work on art. I found a job working in South Korea and thought how fantastic it would be for me to spend a year visiting Korea and Japan and paint as much as possible. The job I took is teaching English, but my main passion and focus is to paint. I have painted so much of Korea, the scenes, the people. All this would not have come about if it wasn't for you! You gave me these ideas, and you motivated me. Thank you for everything! *Kabuki* helped me get back on my feet. You are a godsend.
Zach Freshwater

South Korea

I finally got the chance to read *The Alchemy*. I am sorry it took me so long to discover something so multifaceted, so poetic, so inspiring. You made a book, that made me look within myself, that made me want to encourage my kids to follow their dreams. You made me want to strive for something deeper and more compelling, in ways that can reach people and touch them in the their souls and bring out the inspiration that can come from enjoying something superbly created.
Raven Gregory
Phoenix, AZ

David,
I've written before praising your work from the perspective of my Ojibway Indian heritage. I also want to tell you how much it means to me personally that you support RAINN. I work as a therapist with teens who have been abused. I'm the only male in my state who does rape counseling as a focus, and the only male to work in a battered women's shelter in Oklahoma. The pay is poor but it's something important to me.
That's also partly why I selected certain of your originals to buy last year. For example, the Echo page where the elder is telling her about the healing effects of words and stories is in my office. My DREAM painting of yours, which has already sold, was the Echo page where Echo talks about her "parts of a hole". I'd give ANYTHING (even my VF copy of Amazing Fantasy 15) to have that art hanging in my office where I work with these traumatized kids. It's remarkable that you do so much work for charity, especially for those who are particularly hurting--burned kids, rape survivors, abused young people... I don't know what gave you that kind of insight, but as a father of two little sons of my own I hope to see a few more men with that kind of strength and imagination.
Matt SmokingHawk
Oklahoma City, Ok

Hey David,
I'm not big on philosophy but Issue #9 blew me away! Tying up *Kabuki*'s escape from the Noh and the subsequent public de-construction. This issue to me had the best flow even with multiple threads going on. What happened to *Kabuki*'s mask or is this something that is going to be addressed later on? M.C. Square's theories on using water to change oneself is immense. 10/10. Great conclusion to a fantastic story arc!
Robin Hotter
Sydney, Australia.

I'm from Doha Qatar.
I was assigned a semester long art project, to write an essay about an artist, & draw a picture depicting their style on to a piece of furniture! Can we guess who I picked? Yes, David Mack! After everyone brought their final pieces into school, the teacher asked the local newspapers to write about them. And they did! And mine made it on there! Including an interview with me! haha I'm semi famous. I talked to David about it to ask him for information about himself for my essay. Qatar is a tiny country, right by Saudi Arabia. Now more people know his name and work because it is in the newspapers: PENINSULA and GULF TIMES! I'm so happy!
Yours,
Fatima
Doha, Qatar

Mr. Mack,
When I see your work I don't feel as if I'm looking at a comic book page--I'm reminded of jazz fusion, German Expressionism, modern dance, & ballet.

The pages on which you tell stories, are living things, art that evolves. Thank you for showing us that the things we love still matter to us. Thank you for making relationships in comics between the other arts: the integration of poetry, music, folklore, dance, origami, in your work proves to me what I've believed all along--art is not a closed system--all arts touch each other. In the right hands, they make each other even more beautiful.
Michael Kocinski
Toledo, OH

I'm from Bulgaria! I saw Kabuki (Skin Deep) & I really like it! I studied in Art school. I found davidmackguide.com & I like it very much! But you haven't wrote about yourself. I really want to know more about you!
Ani Zukino
Bulgaria

Dear David
I live in Turkey. We have Daredevil since February. I visited England and returned with ten Daredevil issues. I was fascinated by your way of telling the story, especially the part which shows Matt playing the piano and describing the notes with his memorable moments. Then I looked at the cover art and thought, "This man is as good at drawing as he is at writing!" Last year I ordered Wake Up, and Kabuki vol 1. I had no idea about Kabuki! What amazed me about your art was it looked like paintings you see at art galleries. My mum, a professional artist and gallery owner, loved your art. In the gallery, I've shown some of your work to the best artists of our country. They were amazed by your work.
The most amazing thing happened when I talked to a blind 8 year old girl. I was visiting a boy who suffers from leukemia when I learned about the blind girl. She has been abandoned by her family and probably was feeling lonely. I've decided go up and read her a little. When I found her she was playing an organ. I sat next to her and asked, "Do you like to play this thing?" She answered, "Well, my world has been in chaos for a long time, but these notes are in an order. They remind me of a simpler and happier life." I immediately remembered those were Matt's words in your Daredevil story!
I love your art because it is beautiful and different. You give it like a puzzle. You make the reader think & imagine.
Emrah Keskin
Ankara, Turkey

David,
As a former preschool teacher, I think you should put together a children's book. Your imaginative visual styles will stimulate a child's mind and stretch their creative cognition. Children's books are magical. You should make this magic.
Michael Goodman
Japan

I am fascinated by your stories. Not to mention your stories, within your stories. I think that "The Shy Creatures" within The Alchemy book is one of the coolest short stories that I've read. I showed it to my 28 year old brother (who doesn't typically read comics) and now he is also hooked on Kabuki. I know you were in Japan for a while, and I spent a semester in Japan studying Japanese. Whenever I see your Kabuki, I am reminded of the friends I made in Japan.
Drew Hinton
Chicago, Il

I picked up Shy Creatures at my local book shop - Thoroughly enjoyed it! Loving li'l apple worm's crush on Nessie! I liked that touch, of having the apple & worm in nearly every picture. I liked how you gave a little background for all The Shy Creatures at the beginning of the book. A really

young child might not appreciate it at first, but they actually are learning something here, & it'll stick with them. And the eye boogers were TOTALLY unexpected! But that is such a kid thing... I can hear them all going 'ewwwww!' right now. I loved the texture of the cover. I'm such a tactile person, & I found myself compelled to keep petting the cover.
Diedre
Philly, PA

Hihi,
I thought I'd drop in some photos of my Kabuki Fan Art. David Mack is the man who inspired me to start painting, so thank you David! Your work in all its forms has had the biggest impact on the artist I am today. I am so humbled to be one of many ripples in your wake.
Jessica Hook
Honolulu, HI
Jess, it is incredilbe to see all your accomplishments from your artwork to your marksmanship. I happend to see you on a TV show demonstrating your shooting skills. Jess also modeled for me in some images featured in Dream Logic.

Dear David,
Thank you so much for your beautiful donation of the original art from your painting in the Tori Amos RAINN calendar. I know your piece will be a big hit at the fundraiser/gallery show of Tori Amos art work which will be sold or auctioned with all proceeds going to Tori's RAINN charity. One of the local papers already has run an ad, along with Tori sites such as the Dent. There have already been inquiries about your work, and there will be Kabuki fans that will come to the show just to see your piece. It is such an honor for me personally to be involved in this event. Kabuki is one of my favorite comics. Your work in Skin Deep and Dreams is some of my favorite! As a Japanese-American woman, I feel very comforted and touched by your work. At the show, I will be performing Tori's "Winter" in Japanese. I imagine that it is a conversation between myself and my Japanese father.
Thank you so much!
Lisa Ray
Executive Director
www.toritribute.com

David,
I wish the past three years at the shrink had even the smallest shred of meaning that the words from your Echo story "the part of you that thrives is the part you feed the most" contain. It would have saved a lot more than time.
Andy Dale
Broughton, United Kingdom

Hi David
The work you've done on this book as well as Echo Vision Quest has re-inspired me as to what comics can do as an art form. I began taking life drawing classes and wanted to try something in the medium of comics. I have felt uncomfortable attempting comic art, which saddened me because I enjoyed it so much as a kid and teenager. But reading Vision Quest really opened my mind as to what can be done with comics and where they can go thematically as well as artistically. It actually made me uncomfortable the first time I read it & I have read it 3 times since and each time it grows and I see more of the meaning. I read the 2nd issue of The Alchemy series & I cannot tell you how much that issue resonated with me. Your work takes a shift in how I grew up reading comics. But it's a good thing. The new Kabuki series feels like I'm in the mind of the story more than reading it. I love that. Thank you for opening me up to what comics can be and how unique & personal they can be made.
Thomas

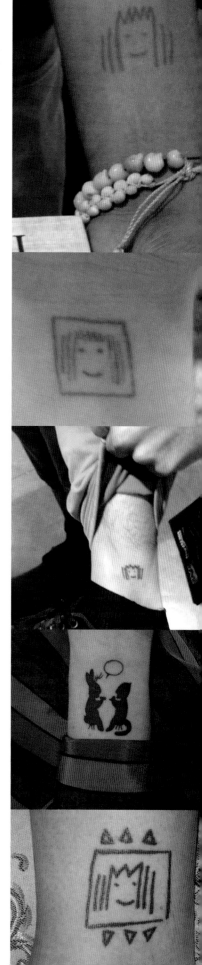

Dear David,
There is something for the new reader and long-time fan in *Alchemy*. Every sequence is a mini-story within the larger tale. The evolution of Japan's warrior class is clever while the background to the Chinese Calligraphers reinventing themselves parallels *Kabuki*. Also your use of the insects. You manage to master so many styles and use each one with precisely the right sequences in the story. Keep evolving graphically, it's amazing where your art takes us readers. Any issue of *Kabuki* is a two-parter: the illustrated tale & the prose of the letters pages with your responses. We all appreciate your openness in dealing with our questions. It's nice to see people writing form everywhere: The U.S., the Middle East, Scandinavia, Europe, Asia, and now the Antipodes. Visit us in Sydney again!
Mark Dito
Springwood, Australia

Hi David,
I like the idea that you use some of the things fans send to you for your paintings and it is amazing what you are able to do with them.
Bombara Salvo
Milazzo, Italy-Sicily

David,
Alchemy 8! I appreciate you taking such a big turn in style once again. The *ALCHEMY* is the *KID A* of comics. When I feel a challenge of certain types pop up I will reach for an episode that touches on that emotion or problem. You have the best fans in the world. They are so honest and really care about your work and this forum shows that.
Thommy
Warickshire UK

I think of you as the David Bowie of comic books. Each work is innovative, breaks the forms of the conventions, and is new & different in every incarnation of story. I think you do in comics what Bowie does in music. Then I saw your painting of Bowie for the Rock' n Roll History gallery exhibit, and it is the iconic Bowie image for me. I ordered prints from the gallery.
Jessica Lee
NYC

I love *The Alchemy*. The last issue made me cry a lot (in a good way if that makes sense). Your work has inspired me for years.
Hannah
Portland, Oregon

David
Being in the military, a lot of us can relate to the change of lifestyle *Kabuki* is trying to escape. I thank you for the signatures. Being overseas and forward deployed, it's hard for me to go to conventions. I haven't been home in 2 yrs. Training deploying & repeating takes a toll. Thank you for your reply. It meant a lot to me. Especially you including my letter. I hope it inspires others to support us.
Cpl Avila, Jairo D
Korea

I like the notion that M.C. Square's high-tech energy machine and Ukiko's children's books are both equally important parts of Akemi's master plan. I had to laugh when M.C. Square busts out a couple of turntables and literally becomes an M.C. I suppose this storyline runs the risk of becoming "*Guide To Life*" (something that both Dave Sim's

Cerebus & Alan Moore's *Promethea* were accused of -- not bad company to be in!). Akemi is still such an enigma. Taking down the Noh seems like it might be as much of a personal vendetta as it is a "for the good of society" thing. We shall see!
J.K. Carrier
Cincinnati, Ohio

"*The Empiricist's New Clothes*". Aw, David. You had me at the title. "Transmitting electrical energy through the natural mediums" indeed. I defy you to concoct a better description of what "*The Alchemy*" has been to its readers. A piece of sequential art that brings new legitimacy to the oft-used term "mixed media" in crafting its own meta-language to deliver inspirational fragmentation grenades. The best art causes us to look within ourselves.
Akemi is a force that transcends what would appear to be her place within the concrete reality of oppressive, corrupt governments & media manipulation in order to galvanize the burning flames of artists around the world. With the advent of the latest net-borne generation, growing up in a world that has grown eerily close to the one Mack laid out back in *Kabuki* vol 1 so long ago, art has swung back under the radar and serves equally to provide escape and to provoke political action. Ukiko wonders if Akemi really exists, or if the identity marked by that simply-drawn smiley face is a superstructure, or a meme, that infects and provides transformation. She is reacting from her own position as a woman who has lived through masks, and struggles with it still. "The Akemi energy," as Ukiko calls it, is bigger than any of them - but there is still the woman(?) whom Ukiko met face to face. Akemi tells Ukiko that when they meet next issue, she will not show up "in the form that you are used to." Let the speculation begin: will she appear as the Noh agent she replaced? Will she validate the hints from "*Metamorphosis*" & appear as a man? Or will she appear as something - or someone - else entirely?
After the previous issues & their prepping us to begin work, David talks about how to KEEP working. How to keep energy & ideas coming. "The trick, of course, is to walk around accepted limitations." As always, Mack's opus does that with zeal.
Michael Peterson
Chicago, IL

Hi, David!
I'm from Portugal. I discovered *Kabuki* by luck in a comic-book store. My desire was to rip the pages for makings pictures to put on the wall! I gifted *Metamorphosis* twice already, to a psychologist friend of mine and to a friend's mother, artist also. *Scarab* was also very entertaining. It is a love story, so it is full of heart! The end is sadly perfect.
Pedropomez
Portugal

In one night, my wife was reading #1, my daughter #3 (again), & I the latest issue. My daughter reads #8 & her comment was - "I like how the story is origami & folds & unfolds." I found fun and interesting *Kabuki* developing a consciousness of self being in the format of a comic book or panel, while liking it's structure to the passage of time and real consciousness. How we might not even notice the sequence of our own thoughts until we take note or something makes us take note. *Kabuki* leaning out from the panel far enough to see...US! Getting to be an unwitting character in the book was the moment that really got me smiling. This is the quote

that resonated most this issue for me - "If you don't like the story your culture is writing, it's not enough to rail against it... you have an obligation of writing your own story - of being a contributing author to your own culture." There is simply nothing and no one in this medium attempting such concepts. I think if anything your peers are Charlie Kaufman and Chuck Palahniuk. Interesting that his materials were collaged into this issue.
Tim Daniel
Missoula, MT

Last time I read *Metamorphosis*, I recognized something interesting! The number on the name tag on the Character M.C. Square! In Math you use this number for the calculation of circles! Which relates to the story!
Ayran Cakoghi
Germany

Dear David,
I teach an undergraduate biomechanics lab and did a project in my undergraduate studies on the biomechanics of prosthetic gait (you referenced in #2). Each issue I pick up draws your work closer to my heart.
Melissa Pangelinan
College Park, MD

Dear Mr. Mack:
The Alchemy #5. The image of the unfolded cube holds up, cover to last page, & persists in adding power to your words and tell stories all its own. I believe you are the first to actually graphically get the power of your words off the page and into the surrounding air (or the spaces between the neurons of the reader), there to dance and change, as all good writing does, but also to alter in perception with any given reading in a way that I usually reserve to the realm of good poetry. I believe you have grasped a truly recognizable third way to write and make it matter.
Jeffrey M. Reynolds, MD
Yakima, WA

I am from Japan. I visited Mid-Ohio Comic Convention. That is where Mr. David Mack was kind enough to take time to talk with me. He even autographed copies of *Kabuki*. I was very impressed with his work and knowledge of Japanese culture! I visited the comic convention again this year hoping to meet Mr. Mack. However, he was unable to make it due to his father's accident. I was hoping to meet him in person to thank him. He probably does not remember me since he meet so many people all over the world. I hope I am not being rude.
Sincerely,
Kana Urata

Kabuki #5 If you have sat down at any point with a sketchbook, a writing pad, or even some play dough or Legos with a quantum length of creativity in your soul, you should read this issue & consider sleeping with it under your pillow. Read it in church. Share it on a plane. Discuss it with your therapist. The art form has struggled for almost twenty years to pass the dramatic zenith of Watchmen. Here the form's most primal molds are broken to be so much more, much as the narrative describes the state of our protagonist. *Kabuki* could be seen as a veiled call to the comics industry to evolve or die, in the spirit of synchronicity, a subject of this issue.
Tincage-lining

I've been reading *Kabuki* & I find great enjoyment in it. It transcends the medium to become a powerful source of positive energy. The most important part of the message for me is the one central to the crux of the book as I see it: To recognize what makes you different and use it in a positive way.
Jubal Faircloth
Newport, KY

Kabuki
When I sat down with the introductory chapter, I was so taken with the story of Ukiko Kai that I went out and quickly purchased all of the other volumes. Mack's work can be very deceptive in the best way. It's the layers beneath the plot that are working towards his goals. Mack uses images to create a language that exists solely in the context of the story- a trick that I've only seen used, or at least used so well, in one other comic work: Alan Moore & Gibbons' "*Watchmen*." But it's the story that brings me back to this book again and again. Mack's writing is both complex and lyrical, like our best poets. "*Circle of Blood*" is a violent story of battles within the Japanese government and its underground, but moreso it's a retelling of "*Alice in Wonderland*" through the filter of a Japanese ghost play. What makes "*Kabuki*" interesting is that what should be the ending is only the first chapter. What happens when the quest is over, when you've retrieved the grail, vanquished the enemy? What's left of your life then? This is when Mack finds his surest footing of all, and the technical craft suddenly has a much more adult story to work with. This story is a puzzle that rewards each reread, because of the sheer number of things going on in the background, of subtle hints at past and future. Isn't that patient one of the players in "Masks of the Noh?" Oh! That guard is a major character in the "Scarab" volume! And how did this minor walk-on get wrapped up in espionage when we see her tale begin as an amateur musician? Could Akemi be the man that *Kabuki* danced with? "Scarab" rewinds the story to approach events from the perspective of one of *Kabuki*'s pursuers, and reminds us that everyone is the hero of their own story. Scarab's tale sheds new light on everything that has come before. I can't wait until we get to the story of Tigerlily, which will be not only about the comic industry, but of a necessity that will bring her into conflict with the agent she replaced--Akemi.
It'd be easy to hate Mack for being so clever, for creating "*Circle of Blood*" when he was younger than I am now--and for being a kick-ass martial artist with famous friends & connections. Except that David Mack is one of the kindest people in comics.
Michael Peterson

Hi,
We met at San Diego this year... Ilias, tall, Greek guy, terrible accent, hanged around Becky Cloonan's and Vasilis Lolos' table, gave you a mini-comic called *MINIFESTO*. You were the first famous artist that I met and your politeness and friendliness made a very good impression on me and put me in a very good mood for the rest of the convention. I wanted to thank you.
Ilias Kyr
Athens, Greece

People will testify to the major impact that David's work has had on their lives. I didn't find *Kabuki* first. I happened on David's work in the trade paperback of "*Wake Up*", collecting issues 16-19 of *Daredevil*. When I got the *Wake Up* arc I was stunned. I had never seen a comic book like that. It literally moved me to tears. It took a while to muster the courage, but I wrote to David to ask if it was ok for me to recreate his art in thread & fabric. I was going through some personal difficulties, & found strength (as well as compassion) in his images. I did a small piece of thread painting & sent it to him. He was very kind in

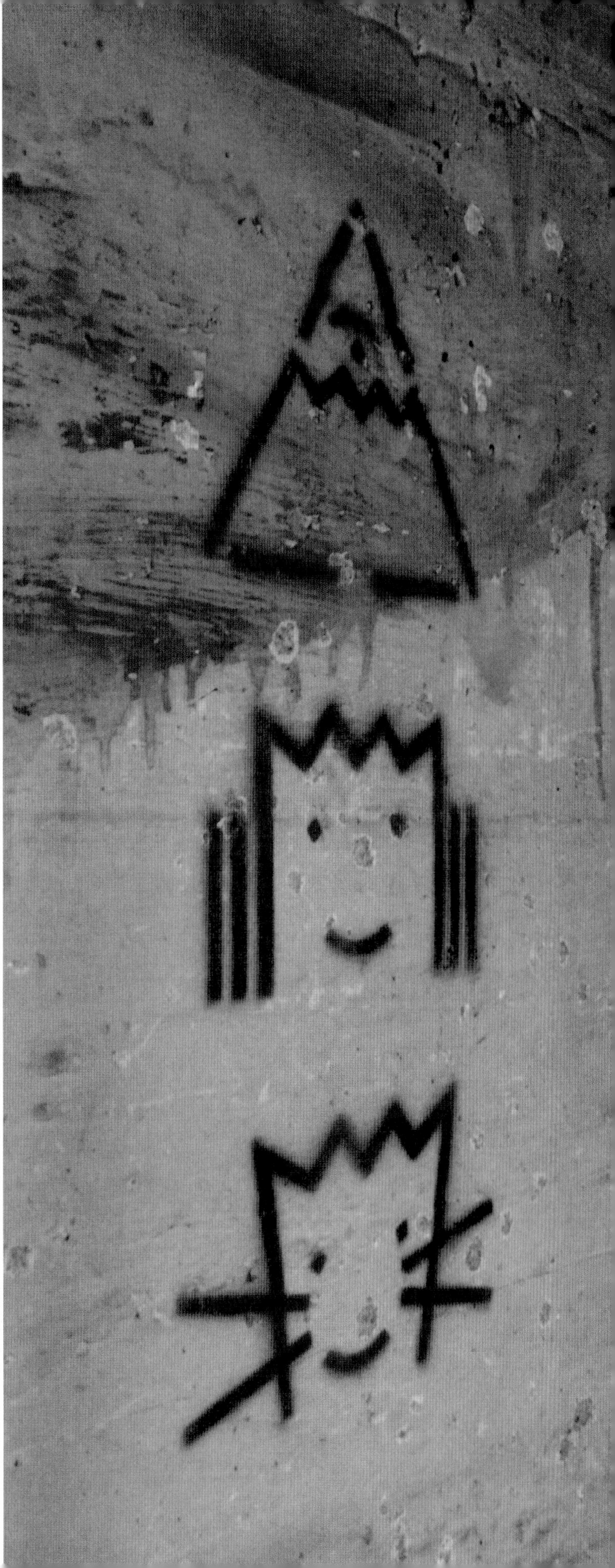

his reply, & the timing was such that I got to meet him not long afterward at his gallery show opening last October. Who would have thought a chance encounter with a comic book would have made such a difference in so many lives, mine included. Rendering his work in thread jumpstarted a new chapter in my life. Because of David, I am getting to attend my first convention as a guest to display that art as part of my *Daredevil* Project, a tribute to the creators & artists who shaped the character over the past 40 years. Honestly, a little over a year ago, I didn't know I had any of this in me, but doing this threadwork has opened up more doors to my soul than you can imagine. It stretched me creatively & personally to do things I never thought were in me at this stage of life.
Alice Lynch

When I did my art project recently, I decided to do it in a way I would've never imagined before, mainly because I'd just read *Kabuki: Skin Deep*. My course is mainly computers, my fully painted A3 wooden covered art book using handmade paper looked quite out of place. I thought it had all backfired on me. But then I got my grade & it was the highest grade anyone has ever got on this course in its history. And now I cant get it back for ages because it's being put on display. Thank you for sharing. Without knowing, you've ended up affecting a very large part of my life & now that I've realized it, it's giving me drive. It's like I've finally found the volume control for my thought process but the knob broke off when I cranked it to max.
Andy Leeke
United Kingdom

I'm reading *Kabuki: Metamorphosis*. I think it's the best of all *Kabuki* trades. It's an engaging, very intriguing read, heavy on the sublevels of ways a story can be told without it ever ceasing to still be a comic book, but not shying from being much, much more, either. I've only discovered *Kabuki* with vol 1, and managed to compete all the trades. It's just something you have to try out if you really like comic books, not just super-hero stuff. Not many creators have had such an influence on me. David, if you're reading this, thank you sincerely for your work from one of your #1 fans in Portugal.
Nuno Lopes
Laranjeiro, Portugal

THE ALCHEMY #8: Connecting The Dots
So far, *Kabuki: The Alchemy* has been all about creativity and the artistic process, & yet K:TA has been an enthralling read. The art is always good no matter the style, & the layouts are always intriguing. Essentially this issue is about the relevancy of comics, & their usage, mainly that in the right hands, they can be more subversive than any other form of publication. Which is hard not to agree with, but I also wish there were more comics willing to push that envelope.
Andrea Speed

It was issue 4 or 5 of *The Alchemy*, that I had a complete artistic epiphany. Nothing I had read, heard, or seen, resonated with my soul as much as this comic did. The way that Mack explained the creative process, and broke it down into it's essential elements, and was able to maintain objectivity on the subject while keeping it incredibly personal. This was the catalyst that led me to where I am today as a solo producer/musician. I have been playing bass in bands nearly my whole life, but I longed for the COMPLETE creative control artists like Trent Reznor & Les Claypool had on their projects. David Mack is my muse. You would think that it would be a musician. I still have my favorite producers, but in terms of who inspires me the most creatively, it's David Mack. And it is why both of my tracks are named after Mack works. We own everything he's done, & it's safe to say that *Metamorphosis* & *The Alchemy* are the most powerful. I would like to share with you some music, inspired by the most inspired man on the planet.
Ben Rama

David,
I got a copy of your DVD & it is a huge treat to be able to see you do what you do. I like the *Reflections Art Book* because it shows a lot of behind the scenes work, but the DVD is even better because it shows video footage of your work. Your work just keeps evolving
Tim
Sacremento, CA
The Alchemy of Art DVD has won first prize in the documentary category at film festivals, and the filmmakers have it back in stock on thier website of herovideoproductions.com.
The new documentary film Temple of Art by director Allan Amato features myself and other artists I work with.

I LOVE *The Alchemy*. It's like my Bible, & what I'd want to create myself. It makes me wonder how autobiographical it is. I've been wanting to write something based on my passions & what I've learned, but metaphorically like you have in *Kabuki*. I was concerned that I couldn't create if I didn't write or draw the way traditional creators do (you can draw the way traditional sequential artists draw, so it is more valid when you do it differently, because you chose to for a reason). But reading *Alchemy*, I've also realized I can create, even if my art isn't "industry standard". Or anyone's standard. It's like the choreographer Fosse, who didn't do traditional ballet, so Fosse created a style that came out of what HE knew how to do best. So then there were those who couldn't do what Fosse did, when Fosse's style became "legitimized". *Kabuki* is helping me to realize you should just do what you do best, because there'll be others who can't do what YOU do. You have been an inspiration in providing *Kabuki* as a guide to realizing myself & being fully self-expressed.
Carl Li
Brooklyn, NY

David,
I completed *Metamorphosis*. As with *Skin Deep*, the artwork is stunning, complex, & inventive. I found, on a few occasions, that I had to set the book down and breathe. I needed a break to contemplate before resuming. You effectively introduced & handled the notion that Akemi could have been a plant, could have been a complete fake, or could even have been entirely in the mind of *Kabuki*. This psychological dimension of *Metamorphosis* is what made the read require more effort to assimilate the permutations & possibilities. What even more impresses me is that you have created two, strong, intriguing, fulfilling women in Kabuki & Echo. The GLA was decrying the other day the lack of lead women in comics, yet you have conjured up two who are as fascinating & complex as any that have ever been formed upon the printed comics page.
Gregory E. Sanchez
Denver, Colorado

Dear David,
I have purchased *Kabuki* vol 1 and was moved to tears. I have yet to read *Metamorphosis* but I will make sure to snag a copy from my comic dealer. It's amazing how much a comic can create such a feeling of reality. In the past I found comics to be for the boys. All of the females had exaggerated bust-lines and were mostly screaming their lungs out. Thank you. I have been moved & I now see comics in a new light.
Rashawn Wright

Kabuki: The Alchemy Part 6
The cover instantly caught my eye in the comic store. I like the theme of houses-as-clothing throughout the issue. I was reading recently about how houses in dreams can represent levels of consciousness (top floor = logical conscious mind, basement = playful subconcious mind). So it's interesting that *Kabuki* and M.C. Square were able to explore ideas and be playful and creative living in the house together. Thanks for reminding me how important it is to think outside the box, be open to ideas from wherever they come, and above all, PLAY! That wooden house is great! Did you build it?
Talya
Toronto, Canada

Tonight, I read Vol. 6 *-Scarab: Lost in Translation*. At this exact moment, I feel what can only be summed up as love and hatred for you, David. Two distinct & different feelings, both products of your masterpiece, *Kabuki*. I was drawn to *Kabuki* by the cover of *The Alchemy* #5. From what I saw on that cover, I knew that I had to know what the story of *Kabuki* was. I picked up Vol. 1 & every other *Kabuki* book. *Vol. 5: Metamorphosis* blew me away. I would compare it to how I felt when I was falling in love. A feeling that I didn't want to let go of. Tonight, I read Scarab front to back. Halfway through the last chapter, I put the book down. You did it again. You made me care.
Thank you.
Jeff Fujiwara
Vancouver, Canada

Hi David Mack.
A couple of years ago I came across a book of yours & it means a lot to me. It's Echo- Vision Quest. What you wrote gave me a lot of meaning in my life. It's about 2 dogs fighting. I shared your graphic novel with my dad & he told me that he had heard of Two Dogs Fighting when he used to help out in Prison Ministries. We loved your artwork. I'm a victim of mental depression. You gave me some inspiration from Echo- Vision Quest. I deal with my depression by writing stories & poetry & working on my drawings. I'm trying to break into art college. You have been an inspiration.
Edmond
Bayonne, NJ

The Echo story. Once again adrenaline & inspiration flow through my veins, stimulating thoughts feed the brain. There is an urge to feed my need, the need I've been missing and ignoring for a while. I will strap myself to drawing board for a while and unleash my other dog... Thanks, David. You have

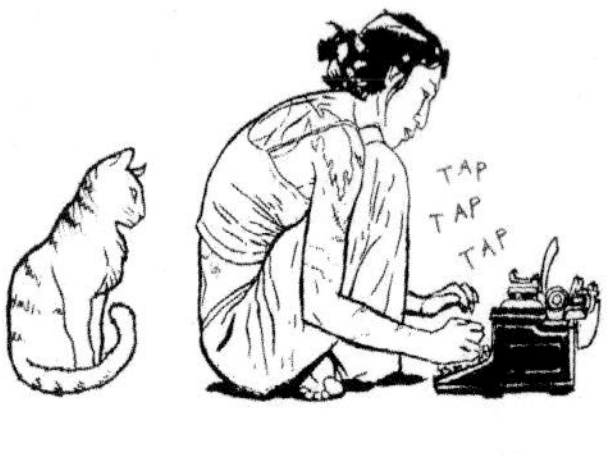
TAP
TAP
TAP

been an archetype/shaman for a lot of your readers and I'm proud to say I am one of those people.
Valter Geuverra
NY, NY

Hello,
I manage a bookstore in Louisville Kentucky. I lived in Japan for a little while, and I'm a cancer survivor. David's *Kabuki* work was extremely healing for me because it hit on an emotional level that allowed me to integrate my experiences.
Greg Zoeller
Louisville,KY

I remember when you switched from Caliber to Image and what a success for us all in your work this has been. I never worry about you because, like some people (I don't know many others), you seem to have a modem into the DIVINE! I am looking forward to the new *Kabuki*, and the letters especially. I think everyone loves the letters column. It is so wonderful for me because it is as if I had this great soul banquet & the "tear drops" column were this great "tea party" of your readers after. It lingers with me & is so meaningful to grow to understand the perspective and feeling it all! Honestly, there is the supreme mechanism of "Mack Art as Medicine"! So maybe your ART gets suffused, imbued through many levels. I cannot stress how great an issue of *Kabuki* does wonders. There is a branch of psychology called "redirection" where the password to stuff in your psyche gets lost & when it finds its tree, you are cured. Feelings, deep stuff gets fragmented, so your ART is healing.
Miss Fumiko
The First Zen Institute of America
NY, NY

I'm proud to admit that thanks to my current spending spree I've exausted Amazon.co.uk's stock of all *Kabuki*. I only recently discovered the best comic ever! Now they're totally sold out! One of the first graphic novels I bought was *Daredevil*: Wake Up by Bendis and Mack. I remember reading it in a hospital waiting room (waiting to see if I had cancer). The amount of emotion I went through was huge for two entirely separate reasons but somehow felt connected in my mind. I had my dad, a nervous wreck, worried why I was so quiet. And then, in front of me, on the page of a comic, I was experiencing a whole different set of emotions. It's the first time a comic, or any book, has affected me. It turns out I didn't have cancer, but the memory of that day is more of experiencing a truly great story told using the most amazing art I'd ever seen. As corny as it sounds, it changed my life.
Andy
Scotland

Ever since I've been reading *The Alchemy*, I've started drawing again. I stopped drawing in eighth grade because I had an art teacher tell me I sucked. Reading about the changes *Kabuki* is going through has given me the confidence to do whatever I like to do.
Angel
Detroit, Michigan

I must thank you for giving me a lot of confidence with my writing style! I'm getting my first article about tea published in a major tea trade magazine. I just found out a few minutes ago. It feels so great to write for a kind of conservative magazine and find they are not so normal after all if they like me! So thanks a lot, David! If it was not for you, I would have never even tried. I'm so dramatic that when I didn't hear from the editors I said oh forget this tea, I'm going to work with autistic children again. They are so creative. I kept saying to myself, "David doesn't compromise and he is always himself". I said "I believe in this tea and I'm just going to be my crazy self", and it worked. A lot of practice from writing to you, so THANKS!
Miss Fumiko
The First Zen Institute of America
NY, NY

David,
I know *Daredevil*: ECHO-Vision Quest is not a new title now, but I wasn't able to read the entire story, until my wife came home with the graphic novel. I laughed. I wept. I loved it. It touched me so deeply. This story is the best comic I've read. Echo's possibilities are endless. This is a book that touches on cultures & visions outside Cash Crop America. I actually feel blessed after reading Echo. For such talent and story to affect me so strongly shows a grasp of storyteller magic that goes far beyond the power hungry magic that arises in adolescence -which few people outgrow. Thank you for this character, She's a reflection of my heritage, my daily spiritual process, and speaks to me in words that very few characters in any genre ever have.
Andrew Ahn
Villa Grande, CA

To Dr. David or Mr. Mack ,
The thing about *Kabuki* that I love: I find myself reading and re-reading your books over and over again. There are subtle things in your art that I end up picking up on re-reading. Every time I read your work, there is something new that I didn't notice before. A work that encourages re-reading.
David Cummings
Indianapolis, IN

I was reading the very interesting conversation on the *Kabuki* message-board between Michael Goodman and Miss Fumiko, and Miss Fumiko's story about how she was introduced to Mr. Mack's work got me thinking. I too was 'led' by chance to find Mr. Mack's work. It was just a strange urge to go into a comic shop I'd never been into before. I walked straight up to one of the shelves and the first book I pulled out was a *Kabuki* book. I had one glance at it and said, "I have to buy it". Mr. Mack's work has influenced not just my art but the way I view language, science, and life.
Sos

My son's copy of *Shy Creatures* came today. HE LOVED IT, David! He made me read it to him TWICE last night which has only happened with a couple of other books, so you get two thumbs up from both me & my son.
Brad N.
Minneapolis, MN

I bought a few copies of issue 4 and gave them to friends to read. How many ways does Mack have to tell a story within a comic? I am astounded and always overjoyed at reading and looking at his work. It is like following someone's life, experiencing their particular world & never judging them, seeing contrasts to one's own life and experiences from childhood through adulthood.
Navind
London, UK

David,
Inspired, and in awe after reading *Kabuki* #5. I should know to expect that, and yet, every time I forget & I am blown away by the intelligence and the delicate care in which the author has taken with this project. *Kabuki* is a document of change, not only for the character, but the reader as well. In fact, the author encourages us to change the way we read traditional comics- i.e. the inclusion of the paper cut out cubes, complete with margins and tabs. The book changes to create a new way of reading. And that *Kabuki* is writing to

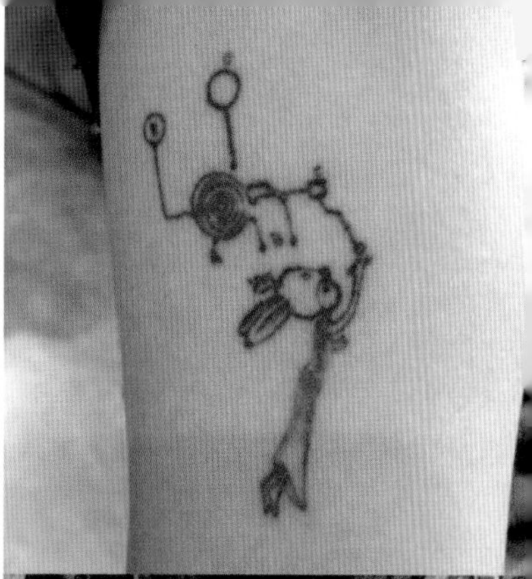

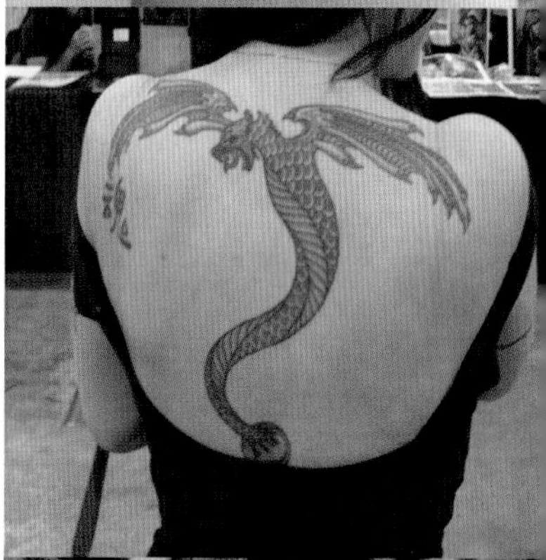

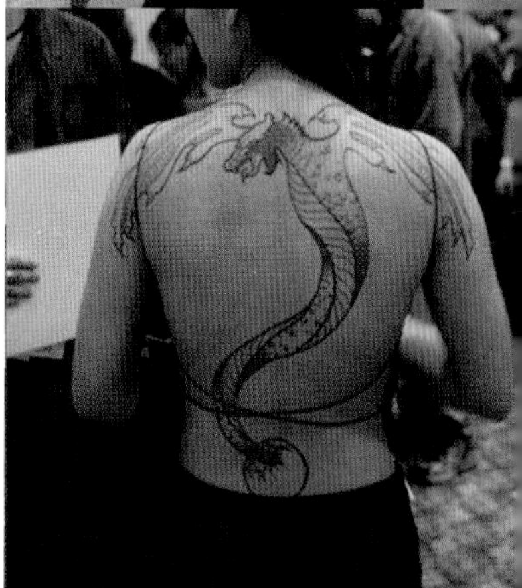

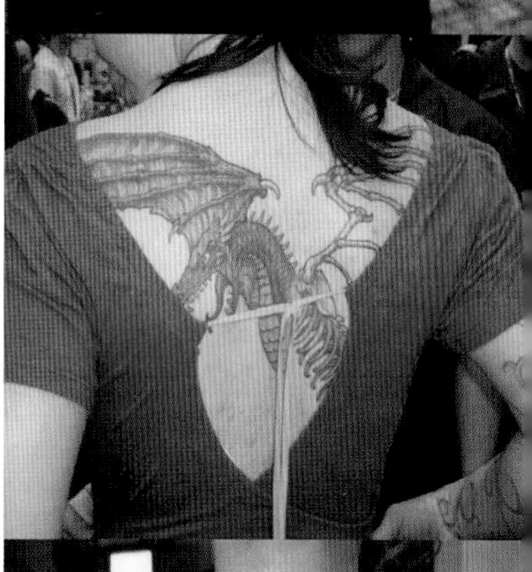

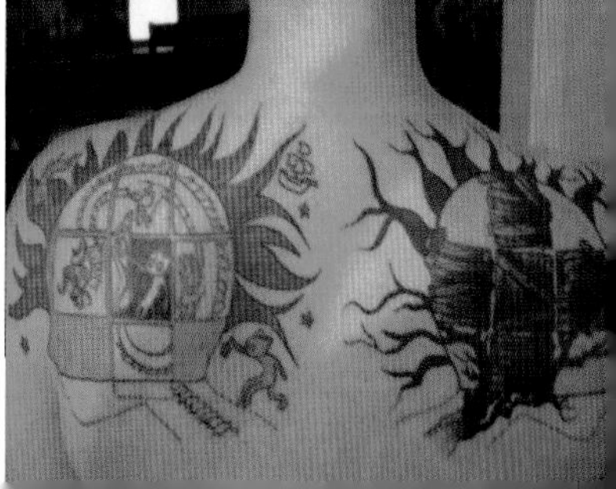

Akemi AKA: *Alchemy*, AKA: Scarab (I'm assuming it's Scarab) folds the story back on itself and its own creations. Brilliant, encouraging, & awe-inspiring.
Jason
Omaha, NE

I Saw Mack's DVD! And it's soooooo good. It felt like 2 min, not 2 hours. It is some personal, intimate stuff that Mack lets all of us in on. He tours his home, talks about his passions, inspirations, his path towards comic creation & his family & childhood that formed him in a way that couldn't be easy. It's a Ken Burns-detail-level quality documentary that was done on him & it STILL felt like it could go on for twice the time. Get this for yourself & let your friends borrow it. You'll leave feeling empowered, motivated & hungry to create. More importantly, you'll know how much he loves comics &, maybe even more, that he really loves us, his fans.
Scott Hinze,
Fanboy Radio
Fort Worth, TX

STORYTELLING MOJO:
David Mack & The ECHO
In *Parts of a Hole* (*Daredevil* 9-15), writer David Mack introduced the Native American/Latina heroine Maya Lopez to *Daredevil* readers. Three years later, David Mack wrote & painted the second volume of Maya's life, "Echo". In that story, we learn the full origin of Maya Lopez, and in doing so, got a sense of how she experienced the world, growing up deaf. For Maya, the stories told to her by her father were the foundation of her childhood. From an early age, Maya knew the power and importance of myth, and heroes who were archetypal, while being discriminated against by most of the people in her life. The lesson of her father's burdened life helped Maya figure out her purpose: to be a storyteller. From that point on, Maya would use all of her gifts, to communicate with people in her own unique way. In comics, like many other vehicles of communication, there are lots of writers. Some are good. Some are considered great. But a select few are special because they weave stories that not only inform us as to where we are, but divine the future by providing clues to where we are going. These writers are the modern shamans of our time. While opinions as to whom some of the people in this select group are may differ, I'll say the following: Alan Moore is. Grant Morrison is. David Mack is.
comix extreme

David,
Thank you for the lovely job you did on the 411 piece. It made me glad that Ghandi's essay was illustrated by someone who put so much care and intention into the task, and somebody who thinks a lot about these issues.
Jenny Lee
NY, NY

Greetings,
I am simply a very old fan of David Mack's. I guess it was 1994. I saw a kid wearing a *Kabuki* t-shirt walking on the street in NY, & strange as it may seem, I followed the kid up some stairs to what I saw was a comic book store here in NYC and that is how I started reading *Kabuki*. Seems rather peculiar now. I was very moved by *Kabuki* Vol 1. I am 1/2 Japanese-American. I lived in Japan. Kyoto was my favorite city. I studied for a while at the First Zen Institute which was founded by my grandfather. I have been lucky following a person into a comic book store to another like David Mack. David

for me is finding Zen in his mind in ways I cannot commit to paper which is why I am a great fan of his mind! I am more interested in a historical sense of the linage of my Great Grandfathers leading back to one person, Kosen, the Iron Ox, who was also a Zen master who taught Tesshu Yamaoka the great fencer! It is romantic for me thinking back on days of old. Yet, I am very happy to be living now! I am also working with a fellow who studied at M.I.T. in cognitive brain science. This project is a book about intuition. I may also be on the food channel on the "Everyday Italian Cooking Show" touring a bit in the world of tea!
Miss Fumiko
NY, NY
Fumiko has sent me many letters & artifacts in the last 20 yrs that I have collaged into my books. She passed onto me the personal chop of her great grandfather who founded the First Zen Institute to bring Zen to America, with the request & blessing to integrate his chop into my work to carry on his legacy.

Mr. Mack,
As a fan of your work, it was a strange coincidence when I discovered that the husband of my wife's friend knows your father. While I own the *Daredevil* movie DVD with your interview and am slowly collecting graphic novels of the stories, I was amazed that the father of one of the most important continuum illustrators and one of the youngest prolific artists of our time lives in my area. Succeeding in an industry that is not kind to newcomers, you achieved a large fan base with your *Kabuki* titles and garnered critical acclaim for the series. I am an illustrator, and graduate of The Cleveland Institute of Art. When discovering my artistic aspirations, Dr. Payson Briggs, who knows your father though his work in prosthetics, mentioned your father's pride in your accomplishments, and suggested perhaps he could send some of my work your way.
Bill Dodds
Batavia, OH

Dear Mr. Mack,
A pleasure this date to read your *Kabuki*. I am pleased to see someone of questing talent still searching the heart of what so many of us think they know. If science is a way of talking about the universe in terms that bind us to reality, and magic is a way of talking to the universe then art is the shared translator at the interface.
Jeffrey M. Reynolds MD
Yakima, WA

I'm just now discovering your work. I stepped in right in the middle of your "Echo" storyline in *Daredevil*. I was utterly amazed by the artwork and the depth at which you explored the character's world of the deaf. I had to backtrack and get all those stories and was able to appreciate the story even more. As the new *Kabuki* series was announced I had my comic shop order it for me. I was utterly amazed with the very first issue. You immediately became my favorite artist & writer.
Robert
Yuma, AZ

David,
I just saw *The Alchemy* of Art DVD! It was passed on to me by a friend of mine, the painter Matt Busch. He told me I would find it inspiring, but that was an understatement. How good it is to have this peek behind the scenes of art I admire. To hear the voice

of one who works as I do: from the HEART. I just want to say thank you. I hope we get to meet one day at one of these conventions. Next year I hope to have my book out & have touched multiple lives. Thank you David. Today you affected one more person. You rawk!
Tess Fowler
LA, CA

David,
Thanking you for *Kabuki*. It's not an exaggeration to say that it has changed my life. I've included our new book Random Ink. I probably would not have been able to make that story without reading your work. It has opened up so many possibilities for me as an artist. That's a great gift to give someone.
Seth Wolfshorndl
Joplin, MO

Shy Creatures feedback from the target audience: I bought the book for both my nephews for Christmas. So over the weekend, I'm babysitting Ryan. It was time for his story, so I read it to him. (And I liked it quite a bit, by the way) He immediately picked it up, sat back down, and said "more". We read through it, he helped flip the pages, finished, he picked it up again, and said "more". 4 times before I could get him to go to sleep. I figure that's a pretty solid review from the little guy.
Steve Zeggers
Otisburg

Hi David,
I've really been enjoying your graphic novels. A friend of mine bought me the first 5 books. I remember going into a comic book store and seeing *Kabuki* on the stands and to my surprise, it was about a little girl who was into cryptozoology! I almost peed my pants in happiness! Cryptozoology is one of my major obsessions! It was great to see someone giving the cryptids some props. :)
xo
Mia Matsumiya
Kayo Dot

Hello David.
I'm re-reading # 7 of *The Alchemy* & saw in the letters section the one I had posted. I can't describe how I felt. I live in another country now, I'm starting a new life, just like your character, & I have a friend where I work that needs inspiration in her life. I'm showing her issues #5 - 8, I hope she finds what she´s looking for & maybe a little more. I realize that this is all about inspiring people isn't it? My words may not reach to her in the way she needs, but maybe your work would do the trick.
Margarita
Bogota, Columbia

Once upon a time,
I was getting back into comics, and started with the ones I read as a kid - Spidey & X-Men - & branched out. One of the first suggestions my husband made was to read *Daredevil* (I liked Bendis' writing on other stuff, so he said I would like that). I read it, & was happy with it. I reached what I later found out was the second Echo story, & I had what can only be called a life changing moment. I then set out to collect EVERYTHING this David Mack guy had created. I got the first four *Kabuki* trades, and couldn't believe that not only was this guy an awesome artist & writer, there's also a massive amount of strong females in the stories, which makes me happy. So after reading a couple of the trades, my hubby & I decided to head to Atlanta

TAP
TAP
TAP
TAP
TAP

the same weekend a comicon was going on - and, OMG, David Mack was gonna be there! So we went, we met him, I at first couldn't speak and then gushed… & he was one of the nicest people I've ever met!
Jenelle Siegel
Coralville, IA

I hope you enjoyed the return of ECHO in her most recent appearance in Daredevil: End of Days (which I co-wrote with Bendis).
It would be nice to see her make an appearance in the new Daredevil Netflix series. It was wonderful to see my origin story of Wilson Fisk's childhood translated into the TV series (even using the same clothes) and Vincent D'Onofrio kindly cited the work of Bill Sienkiewicz & I as influential on his performance. Vincent asked me to do the artwork of his new poetry album Slim Bone Head Volt.

Hi David,
I've been reading your work for years and I can't tell you how inspirational, moving, and just assured, I've always just felt so "full" after your books. I can find so much of myself in your work. Your work is sensory overload. Even the softer or more sullen pages are so enthralling that you literally are nowhere else & the world becomes such an engrossing place. I always wondered how you were able to write women so well. I've seldom read men who can write a female character & truly capture the essence. I love that you're linked to Tori Amos, Chuck Palahniuk and Neil Gaiman, Without a doubt you're 4 of the most creative and inspiring artists in the world. The 4 best in my book.
Stephanie
Flowery branch, GA

I'm encouraged of Stephanie's work founding the Global Alchemy Project (she says inspired by this book) to build schools in Africa and education to other parts of the world.

Hi David,
I wanted to let you know how much I enjoyed #4. I loved the way you used something as common as the boy/girl restroom symbols in a variety of ways to creatively tell the story. I'm a graphic designer so I'm always fascinated with the attachment of meaning to visual symbols. You took something that we take for granted and gave it many new meanings. I found your advice on realizing your dreams very helpful. It's brave of you to make it so personal.
Talya
Toronto, Canada

The picture of Akemi holding her self portrait when she first meets *Kabuki* is great, enhanced so much because you get to know that character as *Kabuki* does. Turning the page and seeing her face for the first time has very powerful feelings connected with it. More proof that art isn't just painting or story telling; it's the bits in between.
Andy Leeke
United Kingdom

It has taken me six whole years, but I have almost finished my book. Starting with the massive inspiration from David Mack that I gained from his books. David, I have learned so much in these years...You made me travel to South Korea (of which I spent a year doing). I went to Australia and ended up staying. I had nothing when I came to Australia but my paintings, memories, stories, and your books in my bag. Then a few years went by and I managed to achieve almost everything I set out to do. How? My passion that grew thanks to your books. You have made me open my eyes wider than you could know. I told you about all the places I painted in Korea… well it has now become a huge part of my life. I would not have even started if it wasn't for you.
Zach Freshwater

Australia

David,
Only really knowing you as a writer and artist and understanding that there is some sort of medium there, but not fully gripping that until I watched the DVD, *The Alchemy of Art*… You moved me! Makes me feel that anything is possible with action and dedication! I also know now how you inspire, not only yourself all the time, but the millions of artist that follow closely behind you, including myself.
Taryn Mercado

Kabuki: Right up there with Eisner and Miller in terms of influence- a story that on one level is a pseudo-satire adventure story using government agents- However, on much deeper levels- the finest story I've read in any medium about identity, about, as Salman Rushdie would phrase it 'what kind of idea you want to become.' It's also about change, and not just personal change, but change in the way a reader reads, perceives, and interacts with this mash of words and images we call comics.
Jason
Chicago, IL

Hi Mr. Mack,
After reading *Metamorphosis*, I was left in awe of the creativity in this book. I've been reading comics for over 18 years and this is the fist time I was truly amazed. The story is so much more complex then your normal comic books. You gave clues during every part of the volume but it wasn't until I was flipping back through the book that I realized the clues were there. There were a lot of complex issues that the main character deals with: Religion, Science, Philosophy, etc. I truly enjoyed your writing and the way you structured the story.
Tan D Nguyen
Los Angeles, CA

Alchemy #4: Thoughts, insight, technique & philosophy about the art of storytelling…within the context of a story. A story about story that tells a story. And it's not textbook-didactic. It's entertaining, & at the end, you truly feel like you've BOTH been entertained…and have learned something.
Jim McLauchlin
Los Angeles, CA

I freaking love you! My friend got me a signed comic book of yours. I had never walked into a comic book store before. When I walked in all the covers were the played out roid characters and then I saw the cover of the first issue of *Alchemy* and just fell in love. Your comic helped me so much just in life.
Carrie
San Francisco, CA

Mr. Mack,
I got around to making myself an Artistic License. I want to thank you for the inspiration that you have given me. I've been trying to make positive changes and there were numerous points in *The Alchemy* that really hit home.
Christy
Georgia

Your *Kabuki* & *Daredevil* work changed the way I look at my art as well as the world. It's an amazing thing to feel so connected to someone I've never met. You've made a rare gift of changing the world- You have also made it seem so simple for others to do. All of the hard work you put in is appreciated.
Robert,
Georgia

I wasn't sure if you remembered me so I joined your fan page (on FB). How have you been? Nice to see how your art has changed over the years.

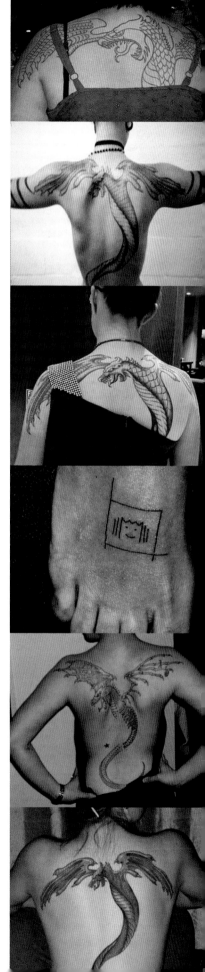

Do you still keep in touch with any of our old gang?
Akemi
Japan
A message from the Akemi that I named Akemi after. AnimeHot told me that thier Akemi hats were ordered from an Akemi in Japan. I realized that last name was the Akemi that I knew and named the character after.

Hi David,
I love the way you ended The *Alchemy* in a way that loops back around to the beginning, while also leaving an openness to continue, in a type of infinity loop (towards the past and future simultaneously), like the Moebius strip that MC Square refers to in part nine. I was staying up ridiculous hours unable to stop reading, only to go back and read several sections over again the next day. Midway through part seven, I realized Akemi's plot for Ukiko's story (beginning to grasp the infinity twist) and I was determined to read to the end. In parts three & four, where Ukiko meets "the aspiring comic artist", I felt a familiar twist in my gut. I realize now that it was the same feeling I had when I met you at DragonCon last month. I absorbed a bit of your positive energy & took it home with me... for that, I thank you.
Christy

It is my philosophy that comics come into your life at exactly the time they're supposed to. Think back to the comic you read that changed your life. Consider that first comic that completely altered your way of looking at the world. For the last month and a half, I haven't been able to produce... well, anything really. So, the day before yesterday -- yeah, on Thanksgiving -- I picked up *Kabuki*: *Circle of Blood* and started reading. My reason for writing is to communicate the effect reading that story had on me. It completely and utterly unlocked the door that was keeping my creativity pent up inside. Didn't just unlock it... cop-kicked the thing down like Chuck Norris at a slumber party. I'm writing again. Thanks for creating a kickass book. It's inspirational in all the right ways.
Joey

Mr. Mack,
In how I relate to your work I have a short explanation. I was a terror as a child. The worst sort of tomboy. I was not your typical little girl. I suppose my scabby knee, broken bones, and tangled hair have become more manageable, but inside remains an obstinate, aggressive, independent, spirited, young woman. When I see characters like your *Kabuki* or Maya Lopez... these women helped me grow. In an age of Indiana Jones, StarWars and Teenage Ninja turtles, the women that existed in the films I adored, weren't, well... me. I'm not perfect and in my imperfection I find strength and beauty and freedom. *Kabuki* is a woman who not only struggles with deep seeded issues of pain, but also with identity. She is damaged, and still worth holding onto. In a generation of discard I cling to the broken, I pray for the defective, because they are me, and we are something to be acknowledged. You honor us, us women, as a whole; you make me proud to be who I am.
Be blessed David,
Adrianne Adelle

This is a bit personal. I have dissociative identity disorder (DID) & *Kabuki*'s story filled with masks, incomplete memories & skewed emotions, often take me very close to home & evoke personal emotional responses. I had to put down the recent *Alchemy* #7 midway, & come back to it after I had regrouped. While DID is not a new theme in storylines, it's usually presented with a shallowness, often little more than a contrivance. You however; you get DID. You explain it & its emotional aspects not only in your writing but in your art. Do you have a major in psychology? Or do you know someone who has this inner struggle & explained it?
I would like to ask if a particular original page from *The Alchemy* #7 is available for sale - page 14; she's sitting silently in an empty page in the lower right hand corner. The page is far from your most complex multi-media work, but for me it was a powerful image that fit in & paced the story exactly right. Had I been asked to write my story without masks, the request would have been emotionally stunning, if not devastating, & my response would have been to sit silent as well. Then when she begins, she realizes that as an adult she can't address the old memories unless she remembers to use the eyes of the child who recorded them. A nice detail that is right, & one which if overlooked leaves the adult to puzzle but not solve the mystery of their self.
Thanks for sharing *The War of Art*. I ordered a copy & e-mailed links to the book to some artist friends who will get it's message. I suspect there'll be more than a few of us *Kabuki* readers who will do the same.
M. H.
Las Vegas, NV
I'm happy to hear from many readers that they picked up The War of Art book that Akemi referenced & quoted. I highly recommend it for creative motivation.

I got into *Kabuki* about a month ago when I bought *The Alchemy*. David Mack was nice enough to come to our school. You know how sometimes you see a piece of art, whether it's a novel, a movie, a comic book, a poem, that you know you saw in just the right point in your life to have the maximum impact? That was *The Alchemy*. There were times I had to set the book down and absorb what was happening. Someone as talented as you doesn't even have to be so nice, yet you were one of the most gracious people I've ever met. As a writer, it was very inspirational to meet you. You have inspired me to keep on with my writing and explore new avenues of creativity. Thank you for being so forthcoming with your creative process.
Pantelakis

I'm not e-mailing to bother Mr. Mack about anything that requires a response. I just want to tell him that I read his *Kabuki*: *The Alchemy* Graphic Novel and it has inspired me to start on my own artistic dreams. I had been putting them off due to illness and concerns about talent. The integration of Asian philosophies made it more immediate and logical to me. I'm sure he gets plenty of fan mail, but I wanted to send a brief thank you.
Julia Claire Begley

Dear Mr. Mack
I have only one issue left of *Kabuki* before I have read the whole series and I am excited to finish it. I met you at last years Wizard World Chicago and you were very kind to me. This was my introduction to the series. I read them that night, & the next day told you how your kindness allowed me to view your work with an open mind. I have added every issue of *Kabuki* to my personal collection and purchased the work you did for *Daredevil* series. I find your work to be innovative, and above all... inspiring. I feel it has helped me to grow as an artist and writer. I want to share this with others. I work at a University Library. I have joined a committee that allows me to select graphic novels to be added to the libraries collection. I will request that we purchase your books, because I feel they will be a wonderful and rich addition to our library's collection.
Aaron Zvi Felder
Chicago, IL

Thank you!
It was incredible seeing some of the originals of your work in person, extremely inspiring actually. I've been reading *Alchemy*. I love it. It is the perfect inspirational find for my life in transition right now. Is Nic Endo from Atari Teenage Riot the model for *Kabuki*? Weird question I guess, but I use a lot of my friends as models/references... and her face paint that means resistance brought that to my attention. It was such a delight to meet you and see your work in person. I keep using the word inspirational, but it truly was. The world needs art like this right now.
Xo
Mika,
Seattle, WA
I'm glad that you found a personal connection with it. Nic Endo of ATR told me that the Kabuki books inspired her face paint and kanji look that she has. She said that in the mid-nineties a video director showed her Kabuki comics, and she did the face paint for a video inspired by the books. She kept the look ever since as she performs around the world. Nic sent me music she based on Kabuki. I did some paintings of her. But I do create some characters inspired from real people. The Character Akemi was named after a real person. And Link & Fumiko the cat were named after real people.

David,
Thanks not only for a very informative and inspiring visit to my class but also for your candid sharing of your past experiences in our get together before. I feel that you made it possible to really know you--and I am fascinated by your spirit. I run the visions of your family background almost like a movie in my head. Thank you and bravo for shared experience! It makes life so much richer for me when I recognize and identify with another person's authentic background.
Barron Storey
California College of Arts
San Francisco, CA

Dear David,
About 10 years ago a video director, had shown me a *Kabuki* book, because he'd suggested a face paint for a video we were then about to shoot with Atari Teenage Riot (my band) and I loved the idea. I decided to draw the Kanji for 'Teiko', meaning resistance on my face. To this day I'm wearing it whenever I am performing live and since then I have collected all the books there are from *Kabuki* - I even have a *Kabuki* statue on my work desk. I relate to her - I guess with special regards to *Kabuki*'s inner conflicts about her origin. The exceptional story line and the mood of *Kabuki* have fascinated and inspired me tremendously especially in my musical works. It is a great honor for me to be able to thank you for your continuous inspiration in person!
Nic Endo

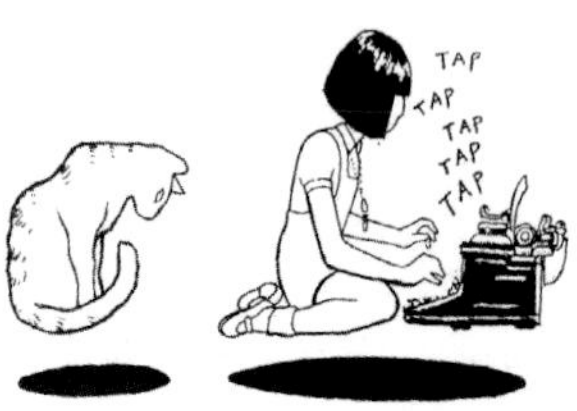
TAP
TAP
TAP
TAP
TAP

Atari Teenage Riot
Berlin, Germany

Hi Mr. Mack,
My son was lucky enough to attend your workshop in Austin, TX at St. Edwards University. I know it will seem odd that a mom is writing to you for a college student, but I wanted you to know that your time with my son was a great investment. He has always enjoyed working on his art & your time with him inspired him to continue working on his craft. I know you are very busy but appreciate you taking the time to give back. You are paying it forward and I really appreciate it. Sylvester has always marched to his own drummer- on this day- you made him feel like he was on the right track.
Sincerely,
Lonnie Sanchez

Happy Holidays, Dave!
My boy chose *Shy Creatures* to take to read to the whole class. He was very proud that he picked the most favored book (It really was!). Thanks for putting us on your Xmas card list. I love it.
Love,
Lucy Lawless.

Dear Mr. Mack,
I was so glad to be able to see you at Baltimore Comicon. You were amazingly kind & open to talk with. I was elated that you liked my "Flying Dutchman" tattoo of your work. Seeing my tattoo in Reflections #11 was really exciting and satisfying. I always thought I would be a part of the David Mack tattoo network, and seeing my picture in your Reflections book made it official! When I was showing my friend the new Reflections, she mentioned that her dad read *Kabuki*. It made him start drawing, and for the last two years, he's been drawing. Your work not only motivates me but everyone who comes into contact with it. And that's apparently a lot of people. It's wonderful that you're doing gallery showings of your work. I always thought your work should be in a gallery. Maybe one day I'll be able to go to one.
Love & good wishes,
Sarah Gibson

Dear David,
I don't know when you'll see this or if you ever will. You might not even remember me to be honest But I use to live next door to you, my friends and I would always have box wars with you lmao. During that time I don't know if you knew or not but my mother had just lost custody of me and that's why I was with Doug and Linda at the time. I remember sitting outside on your steps drawing pictures, yours better than mine obviously But I just wanted you to know that you helped me be happy, probably without even knowing it. You always had a smile on your face and would always be ready to laugh. You inspired me to be a writer and illustrate as well. Seeing how you could just imagine anything you wanted and make it life on paper was the coolest thing that I have ever seen. I also want to be someone that puts a smile on others faces just as you did for me. I know it's been a while since we last spoke, I wanted to thank you for changing my life. FOREVER
Dylan James

Dear Mr. David Mack,
I was given *The Alchemy* at a tumultuous, crucial point in my life, and the Conversations in the Air chapter steeled my resolve to stop studying Engineering, which I was good at, but not genuinely interested in; and instead pursue my lifelong dream of designing clothing and costumes for a living. I recently moved to New York City to study fashion design. I stopped in at Cosmic Comics & I picked up Dream Logic. When I got home, I started to flip through *The Alchemy* as well, and the chapter where Akemi is corresponding with *Kabuki* from a certain address in America (NY) which happens to be rather close to where I live now. In a strange fit of boldness and spontaneity, I walked over to NYC's own "House 13" - the First Zen Institute of America. I wasn't sure what I'd find there, or even sure of what I wanted to find there (perhaps a real life Buddha and the Psy-Chics?), but I met some wonderful people who remember you. They invited me to join in their Wednesday meditation, and I met Michael Holtz, Ian, another David & Peter (the biofeedback inventor). Synchronicities were found, new friendships were started. Now here's why I am nervous about this letter: I also learned that there is a Fumiko, & there was a cat, but they're not the same (Kabuki named her cat Fumiko). I learned that Fumiko is the (great?) granddaughter of the founder of the Zen Institute (which I just found mention of in the letterssection, as well as three of her letters), & she is half-black, half-Japanese. I suppose I'm intensely curious about inspiration & the mind of a favorite artist. I notice that many of your recent paintings (the Tarot featured in Dream Logic, for example) bear the likeness of a striking young black woman with interesting features. I feel strange about bringing all this up. I flip through the comics, click a picture on DavidMackGuide.com. I'm not sure what I want to know. Even though I might never know the full story (mysteries are some of the most beautiful things), I will be spending more time at the Zen Institute - it is full of wonderful people and beautiful things. Know that you have become your own Akemi - the book is a self-fulfilling prophecy, both for the author and the readers, in creation & in consumption. Perhaps one day, my art can be the same way. Maybe (like M. C. Square) I'll make a dry-erase smock dress for "Becoming the Idea..."
Love and Blessings,
Naomi, a fan
NY, NY

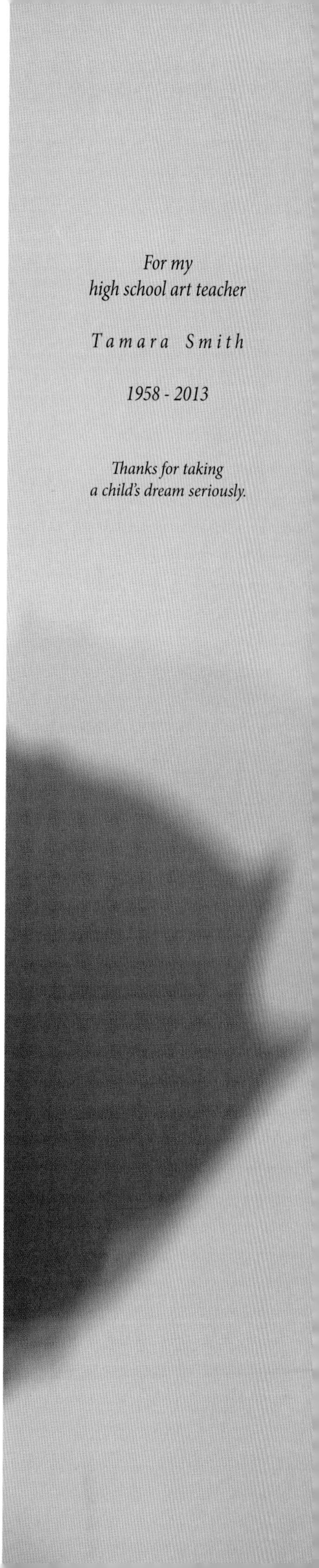

*For my
high school art teacher*

T a m a r a   S m i t h

1958 - 2013

*Thanks for taking
a child's dream seriously.*

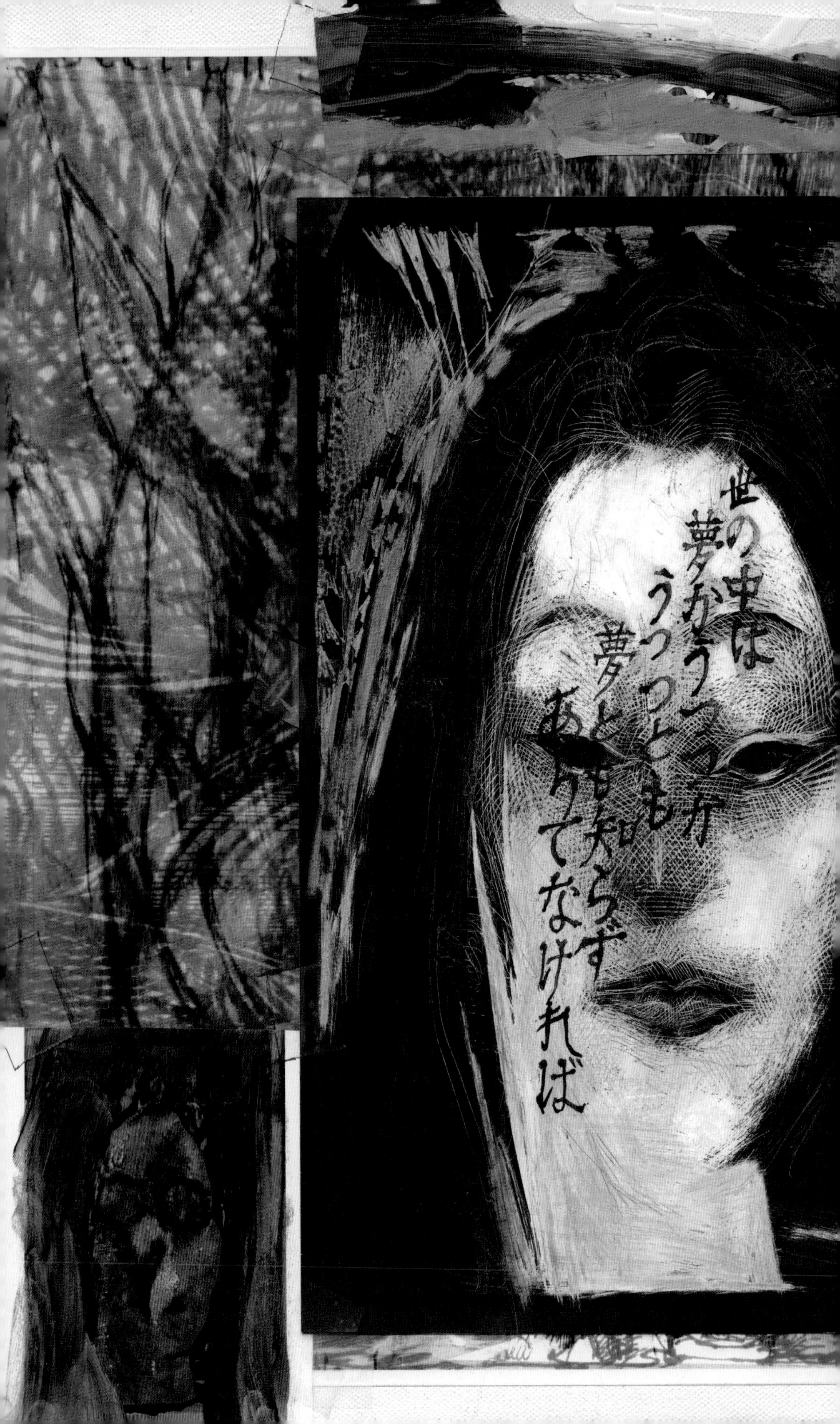
世の中は
夢かうつつか
うつつとも
夢とも知らず
ありてなければ

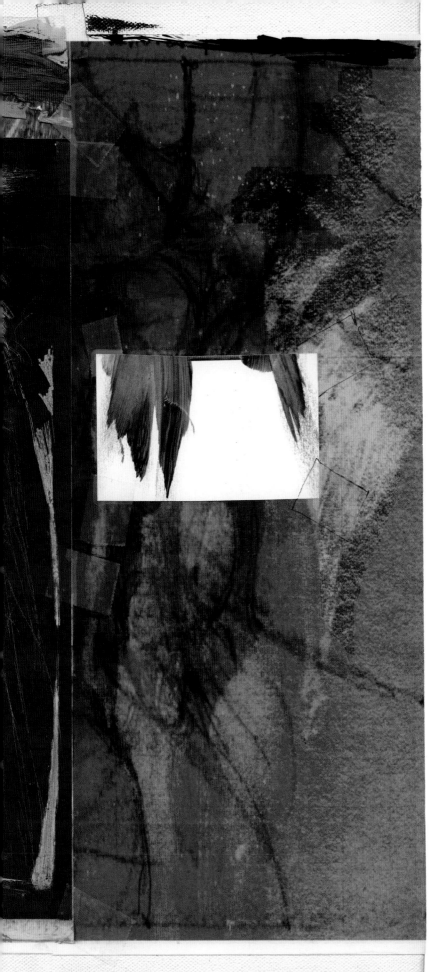

KABUKI

by legendary artist
and educator
Barron Storey.

I've had the honor to
speak at Barron Storey's
Sequential Art class at
California College of the Arts
several times.
His award winning carreer
in fine art and illustration has
spanned six decades. He
earned an Eisner Award for
his work on *Sandman*, and
his teaching & influence is
proudly claimed by such
luminaries as Kent Williams,
Bill Sienkiewicz & Dave
McKean.

I was honored to share art
exhibits with Barron in
galleries in Paris & Brussels,
and the Los Angeles
Temple of Art exhibit (and
documentary film)
& to write the introduction
to the new printing of his
legendary *Marat/Sade
Journals*.

Following pages:

KABUKI by
Kent Williams
Greg Spalenka

Both of these artists are
also influences on my work
and Kent has been a dear
friend and mentor.

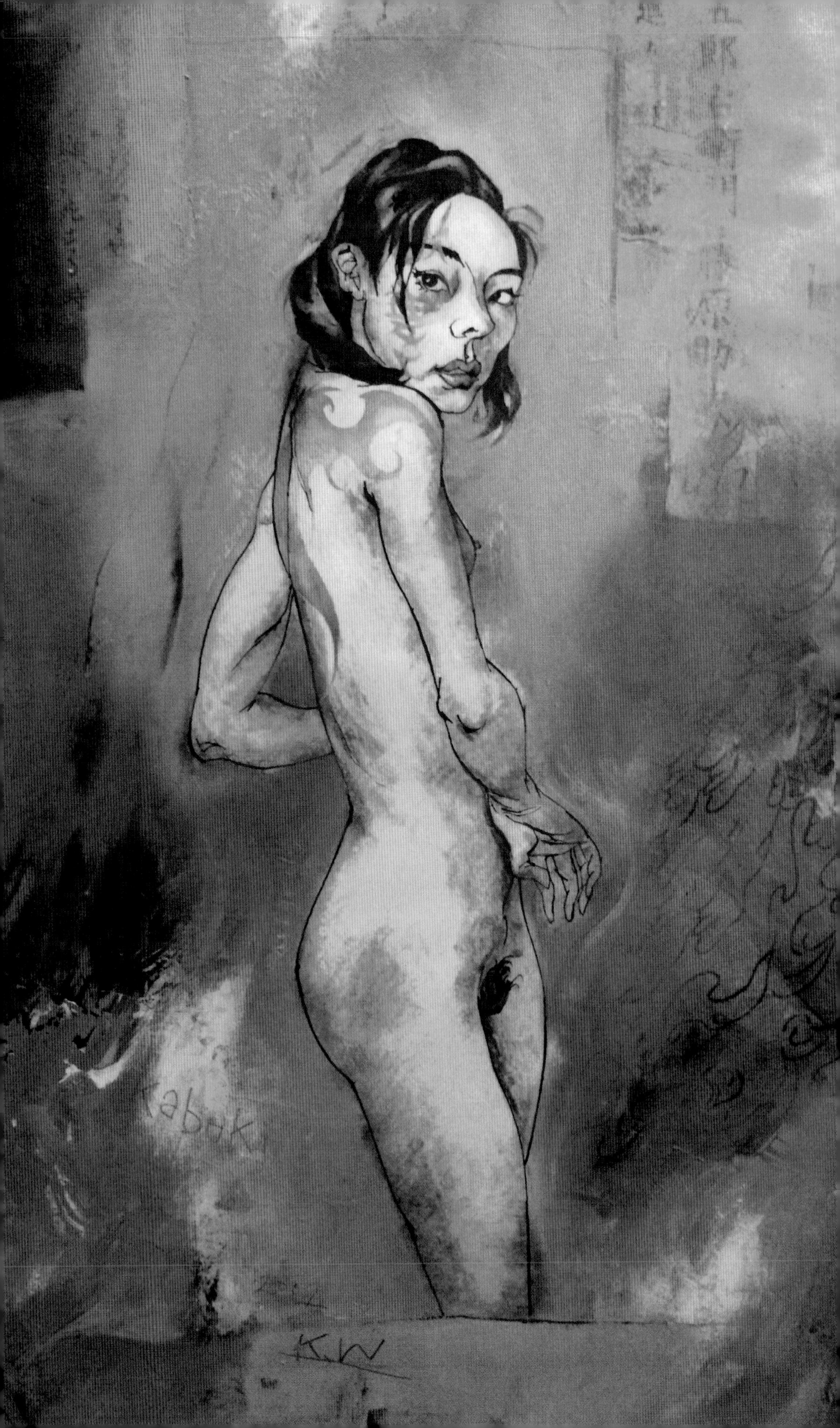
K.W

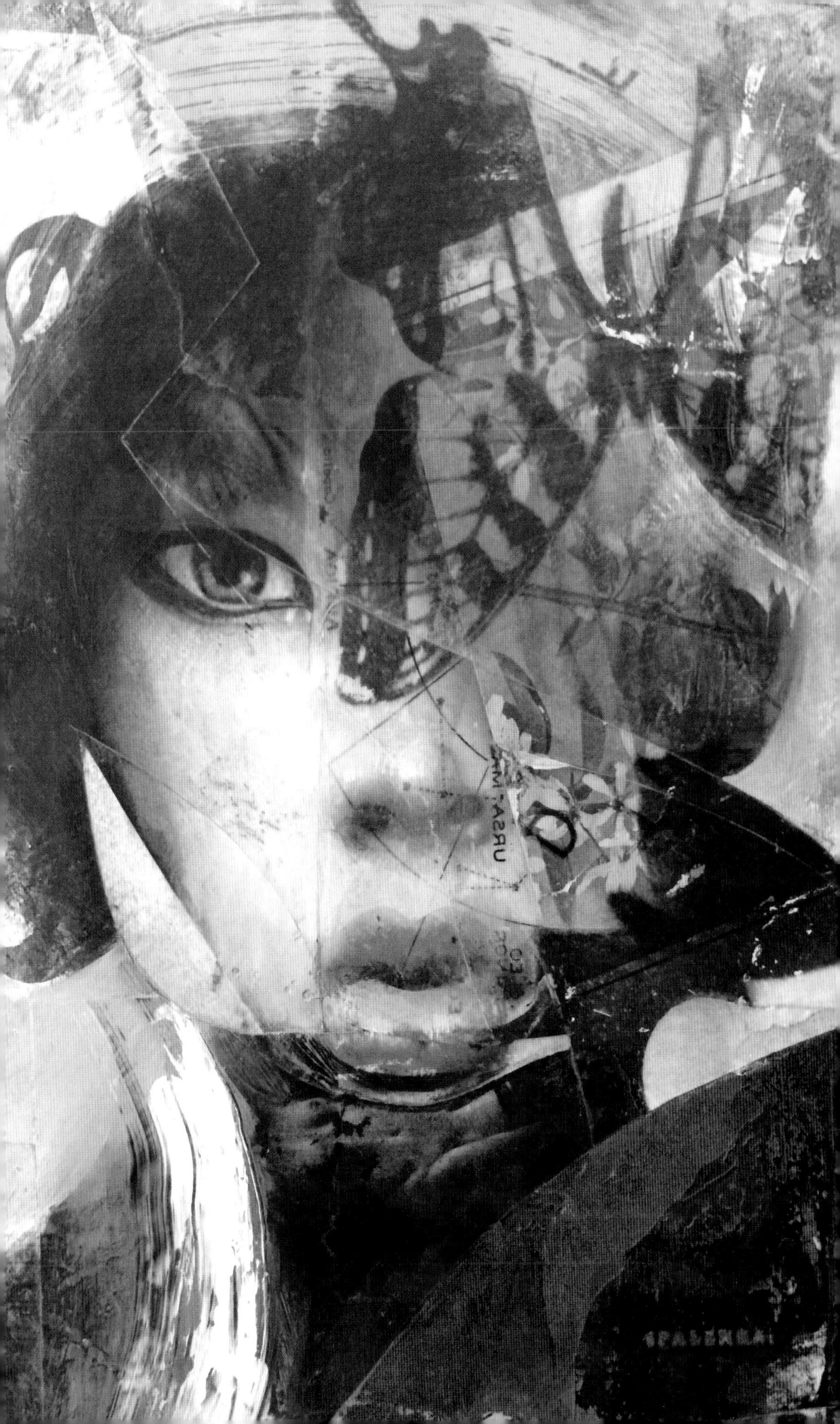

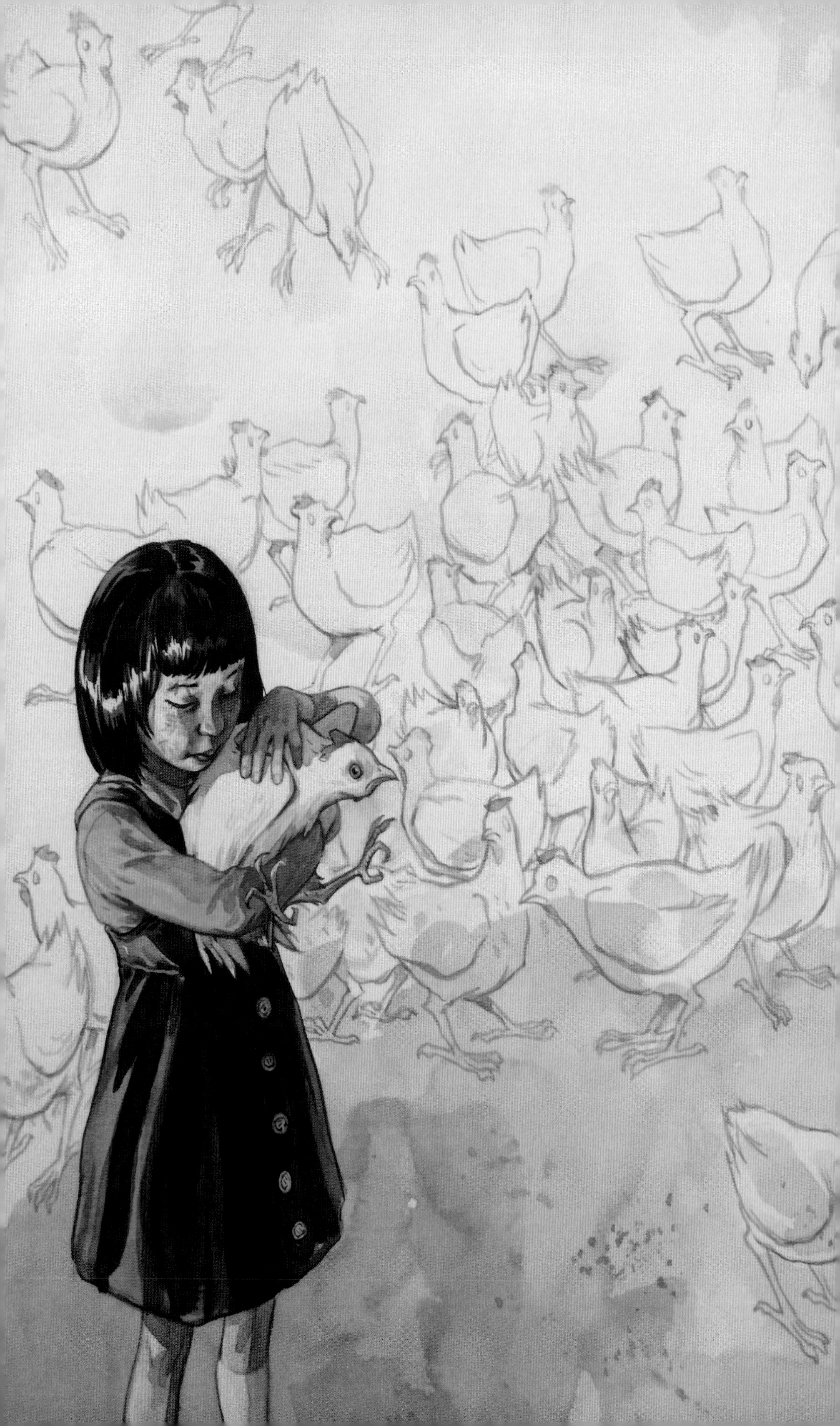

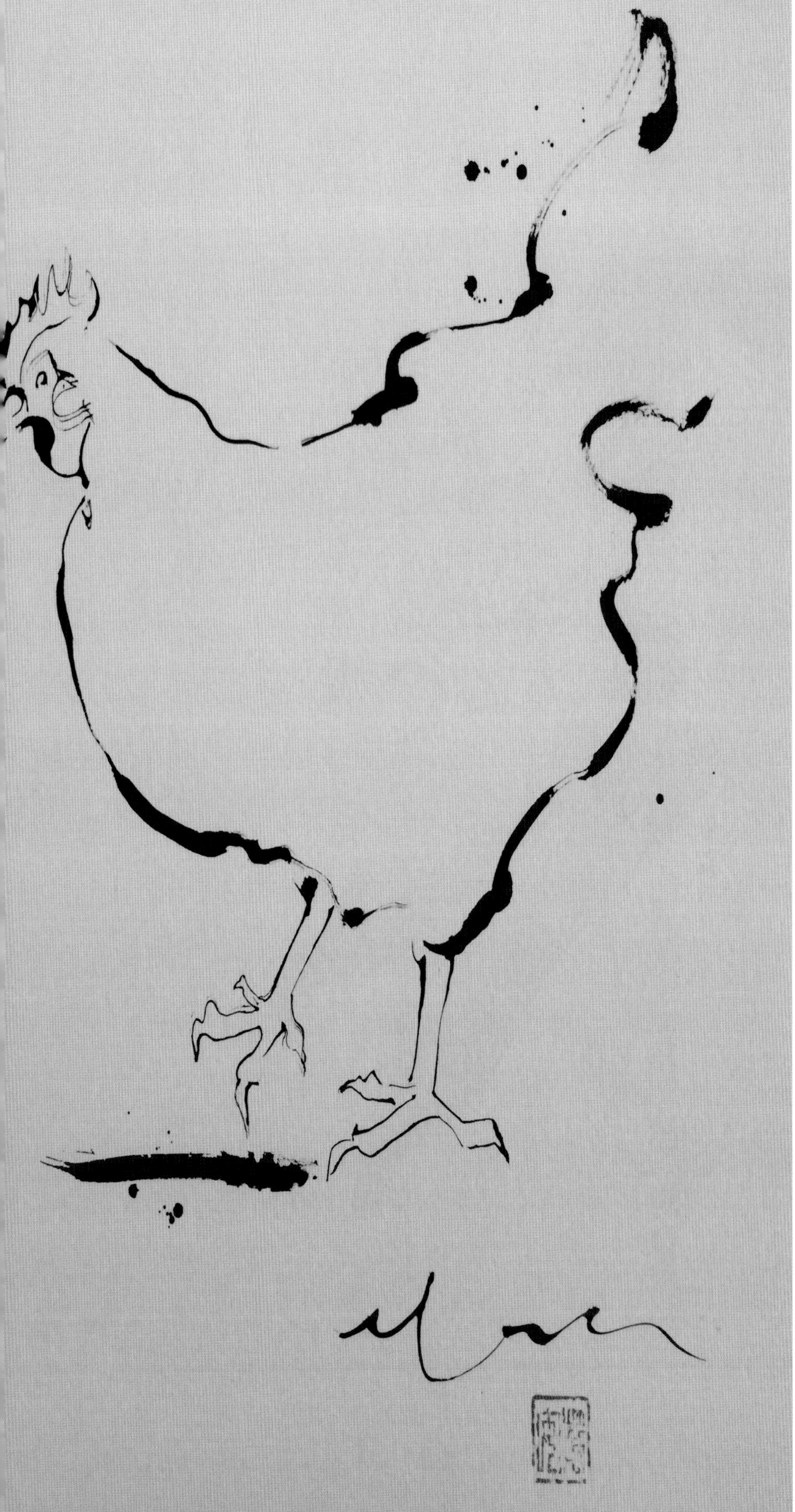

Opposite:

KABUKI by
Jill Thompson.

You may know her work from *Scary Godmother* and *Sandman*. I've always loved that she chose a moment of this era of Kabuki's life with the chickens. I see it as a live chicken in her arms and the ghosts of chickens past.

This page:

Brush & ink
For a private collector.

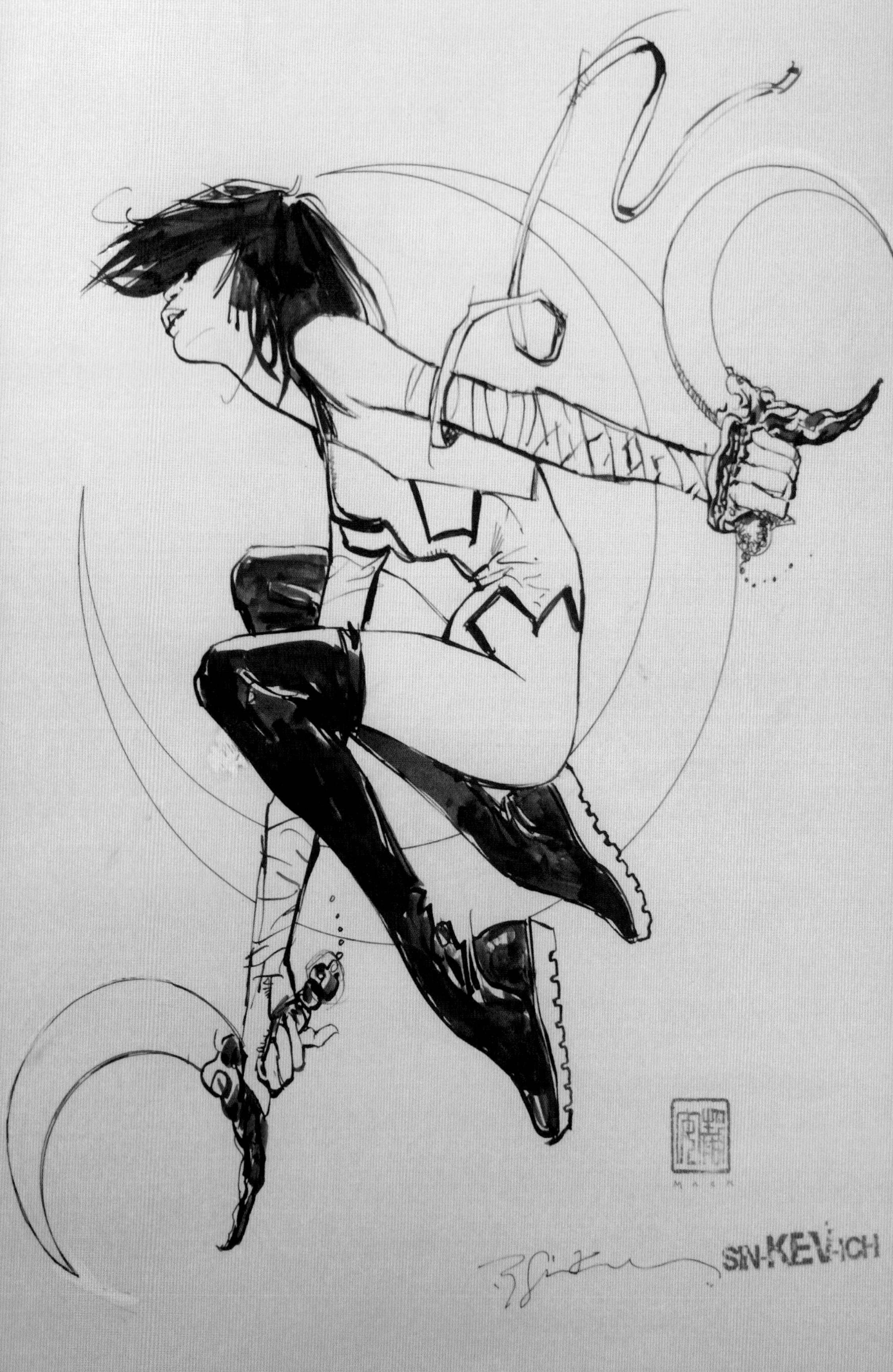
MACK
SIN-KEV-ICH

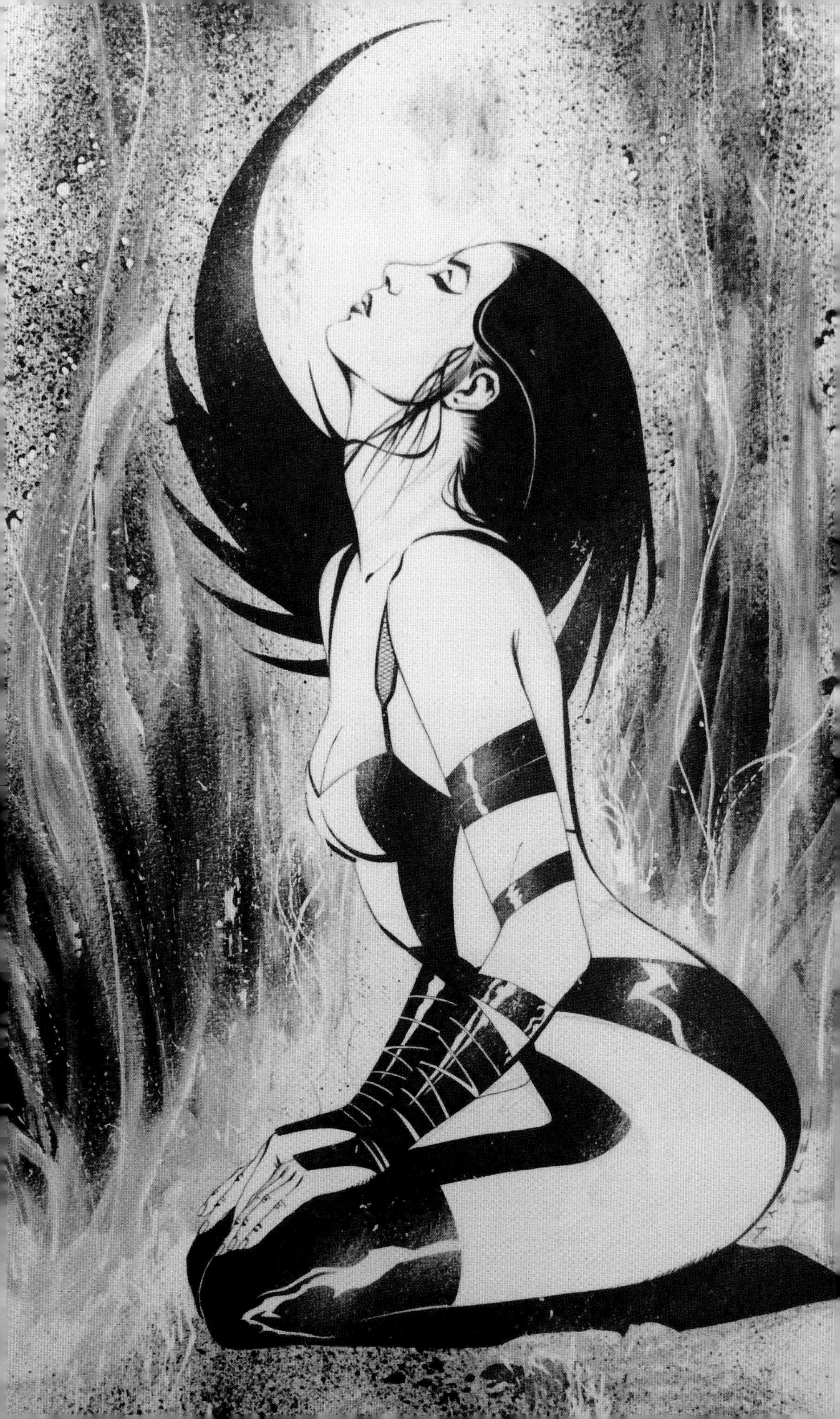

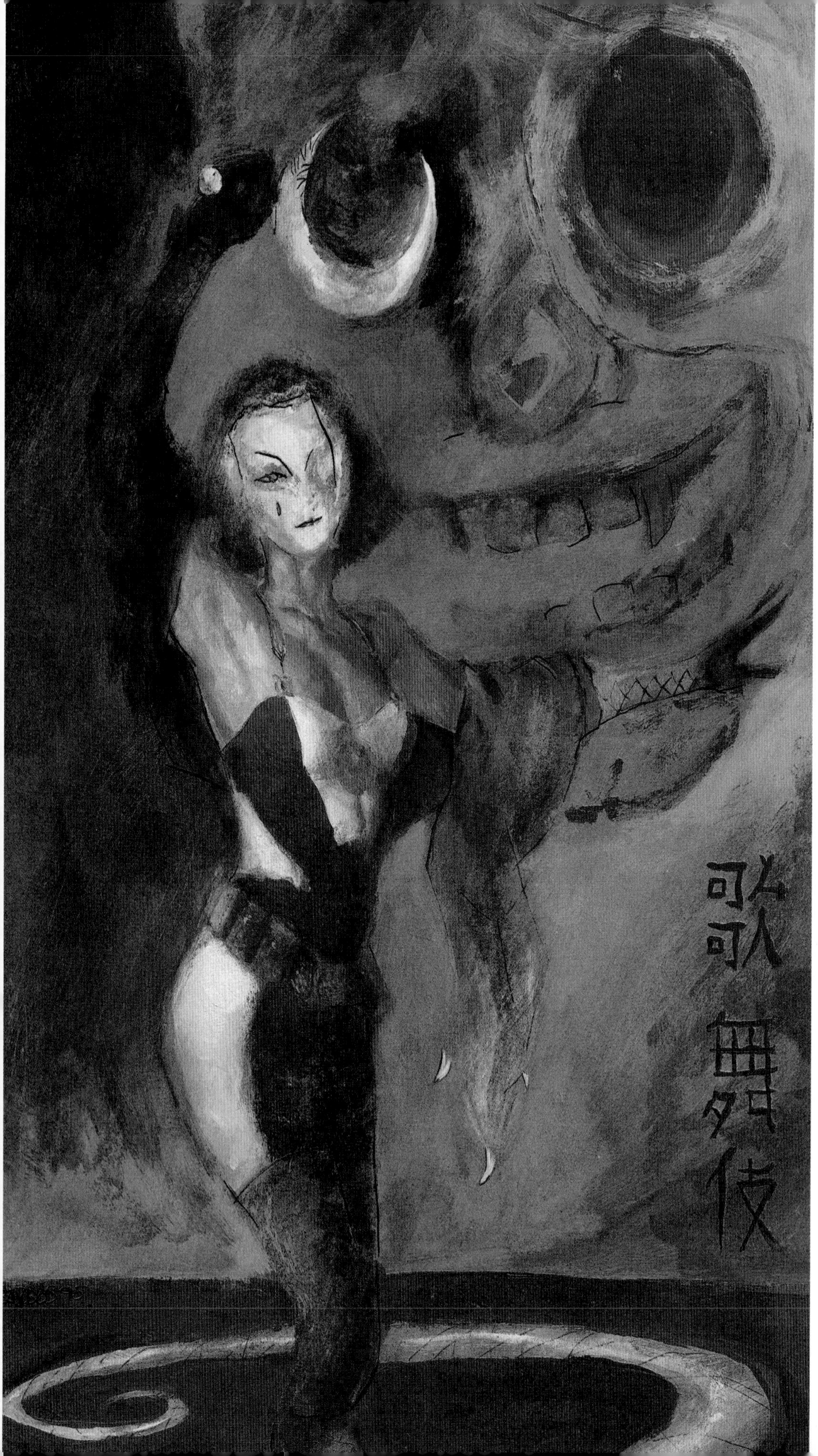
歌舞伎

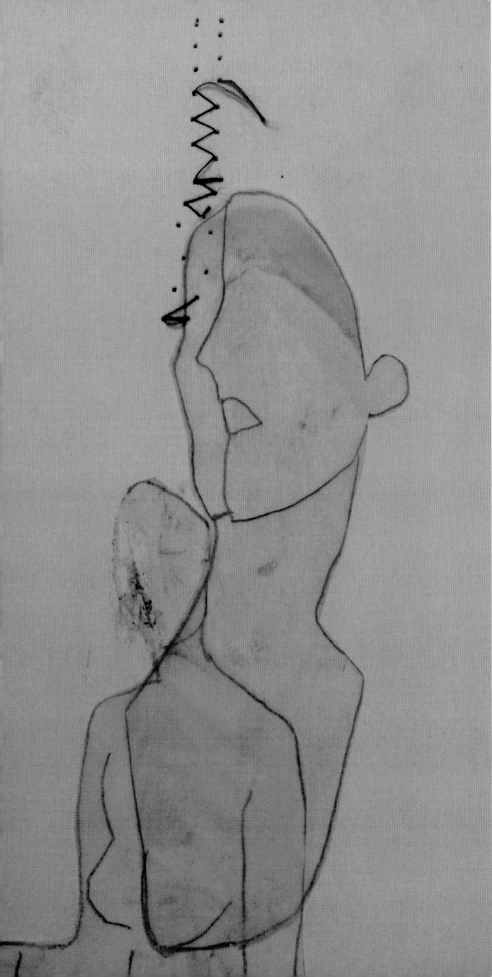

Previous pages:

Bill Sienkiewicz inks over my *KABUKI* drawing. It's been an honor to collaborate with Bill on *Daredevil: End of Days*, *Temple of Art*, *Dexter*, & more. A dear friend & mentor.

KABUKI cover by Jae Lee.

Opposite:

KABUKI by Michael Gaydos. We collaborated on Marvel's *Jessica Jones* comic book called *Alias* written by Bendis. It is now a TV series on Netflix. I created art for the opening titles of the Netflix series with Imaginary Forces. For the original comic, Gaydos was the interior artist and I did all of the cover art. I've always loved this take of his on Kabuki.

This page:

KABUKI by Anh Tran.

Anh colored *The Shy Creatures* and *Lil' KABUKI in Dreamland*. She co-founded Modern Makers which exhibits her multi-media art, fashion & design.

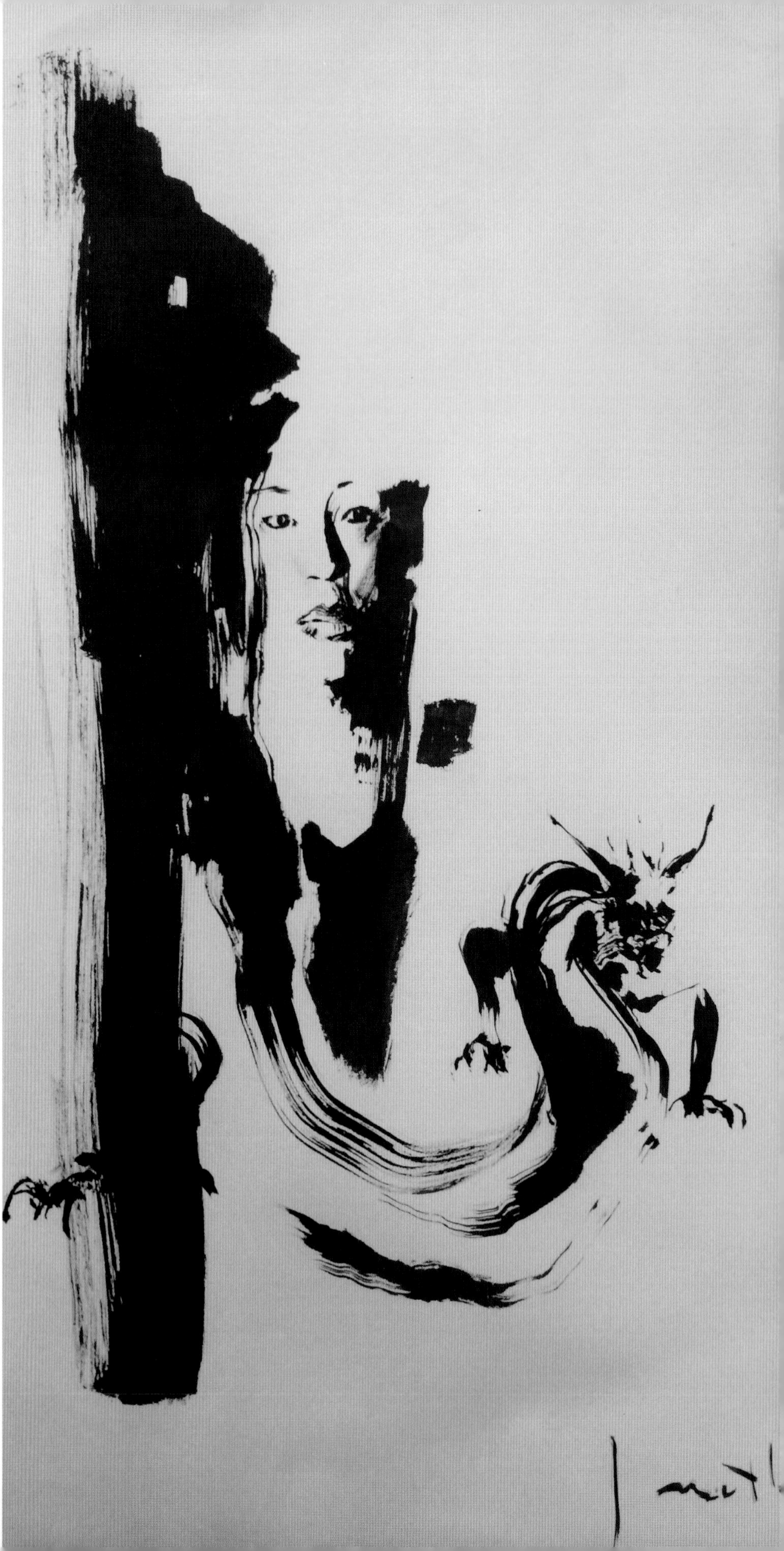

This page:

KABUKI.
Jon Muth.

Now known for his children's books, in comics Jon is known for his work on *Sandman* and his art on *Wolverine-Havoc: Meltdown* with Kent Williams.

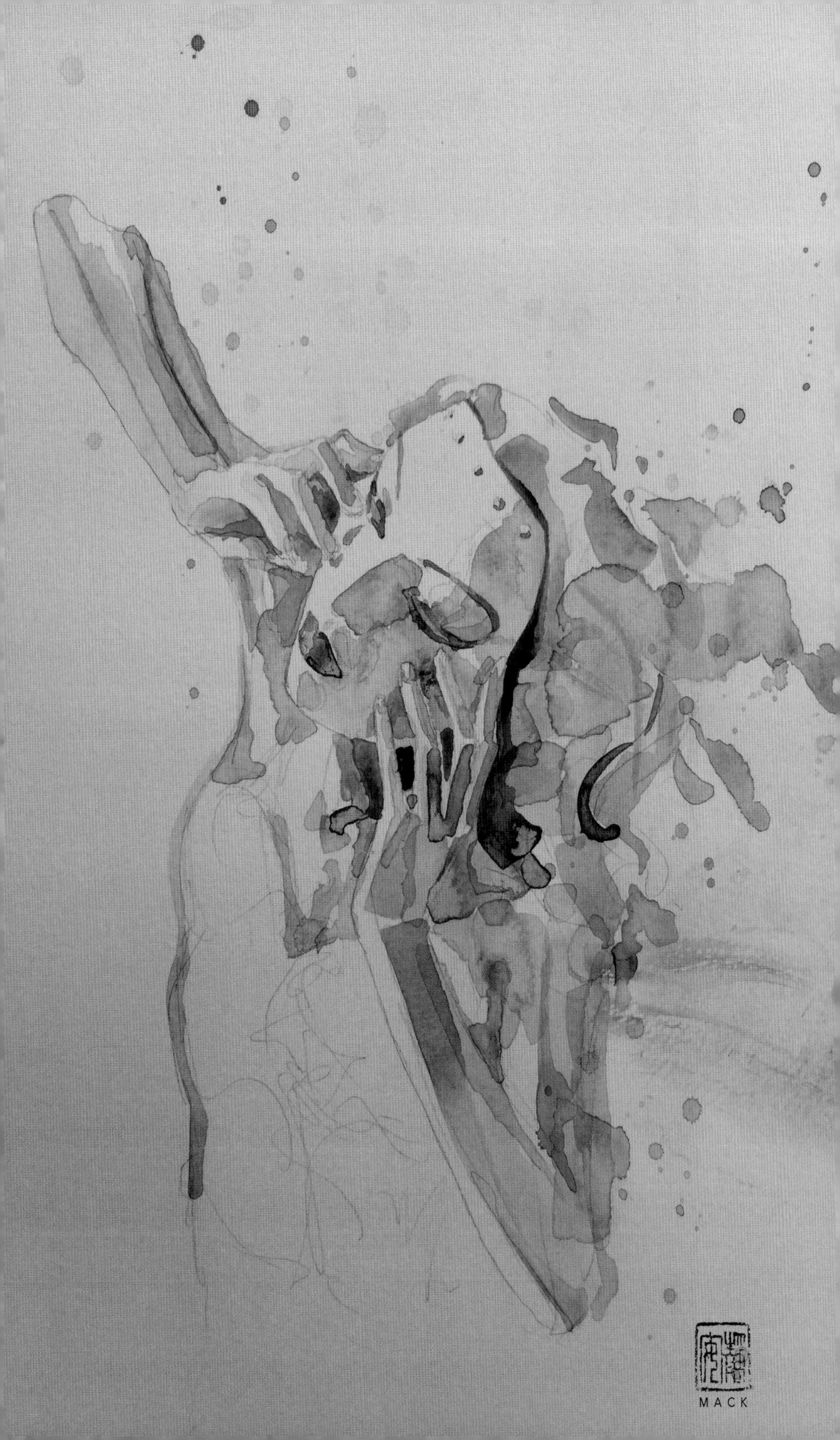
MACK

The Alchemy
Issue One.

The original script that I began with. From this I made countless layout ideas for the pages & panels followed by script modifications in response to the layout ideas.
You can see that some sequences here are different (or in a different order) than the printed version.

NOTE
For aspiring writers:
This is not the proper full script format that I use when writiing for another artist or for Marvel.
This is how I wrote this story knowing that I would draw it myself.
For an example of how I write a script for other artists to draw from there are script pages in the collection of *Daredevil: End of Days.*

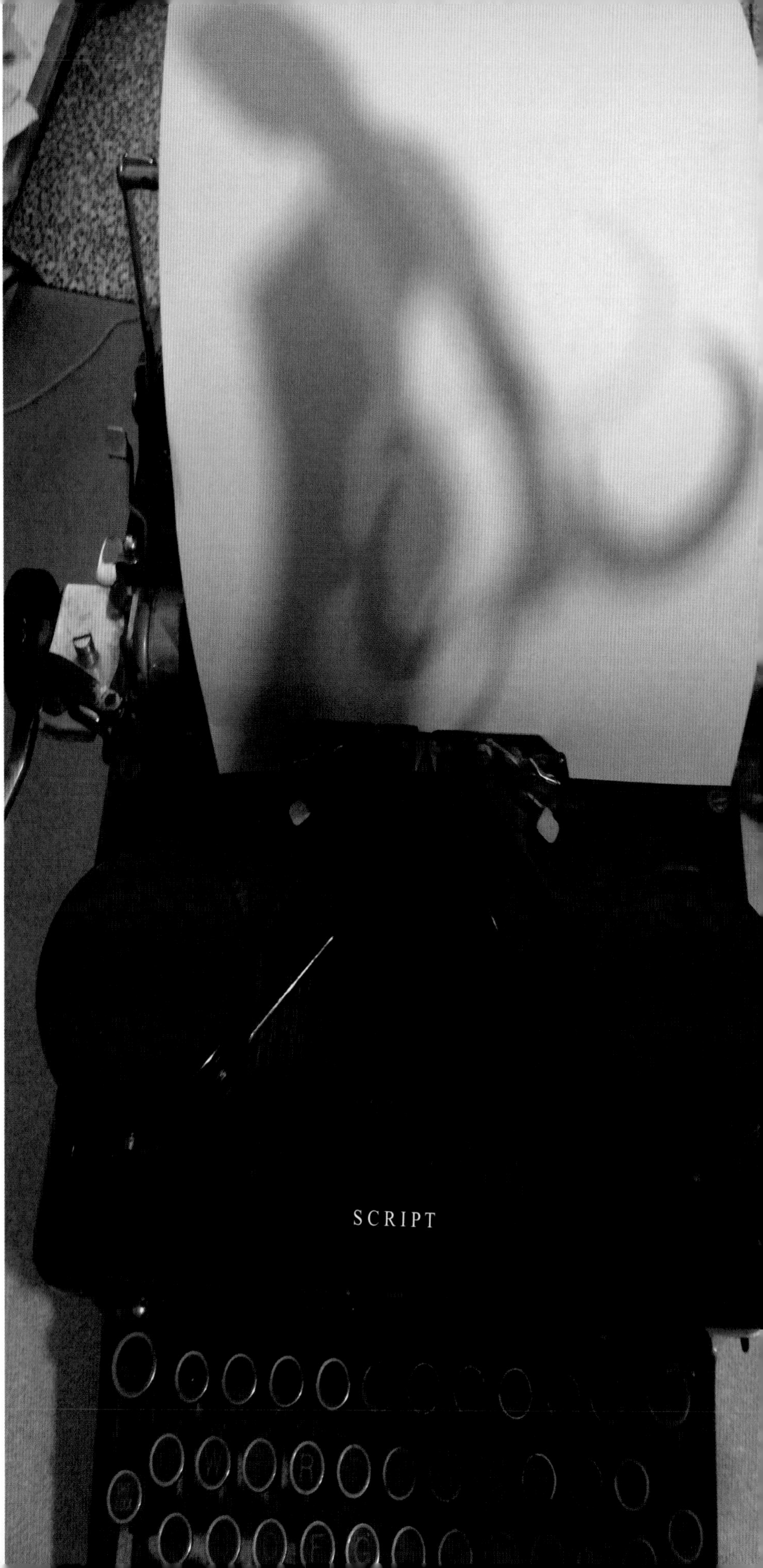

SCRIPT

KABUKI
The Alchemy
#1

(On IFC give readers a bit of an update. Can start here. Starting new life. If want to know previous life, read these books…)

Pg 1

ART- Hands unfolding Akemi note. Show multi paper squares. Different colors. Written on inside from out as unfolded.

Or her sitting on subway   some other close up. Paper collage?

(cut or move??) SCRIPT   All you need to know is that there is a scar on my face that says Kabuki. I'm starting a new life, and I have a friend that is helping me.

Akemi writes on notes that are folded into origami creatures. Her philosophy is all about transformation. Turning 2D into 3D. Taking an(a written) idea and folding it into reality.

This is the last note that she gave me. It includes eight different squares of paper. (for eight side of cube: the 6 surfaces sides and the inside and outside) Multi-faceted for my cubist life. Different from every angle you view it. I do my best to put them in order.

There are messages written in Akemi's own language. And a map of where to go to get a new paper identity and a plane ticket out of the country.

Pg 2

ART- on Subway. Handwritten notes that say she is on subway. Or train. Mention salary men catching last train of night back to their homes. Or hand write wonders if someone is following her. Smears of Rainy Japan passing by window at times? (cut in her as kid doing calligraphy or reading children's books? Or drawing mother?)

Pg 1
Script- (BEGIN HERE?)
"Don't believe in death as an end. There is no such thing. Believe in new beginnings. Fresh perspectives. Every exit is an entrance somewhere else.

CUT?-(Death of the 2D square of paper is the birth of the 3D origami animal. The unfolding of the origami creature is not the end of it's life but the birth of the message within it to be read).

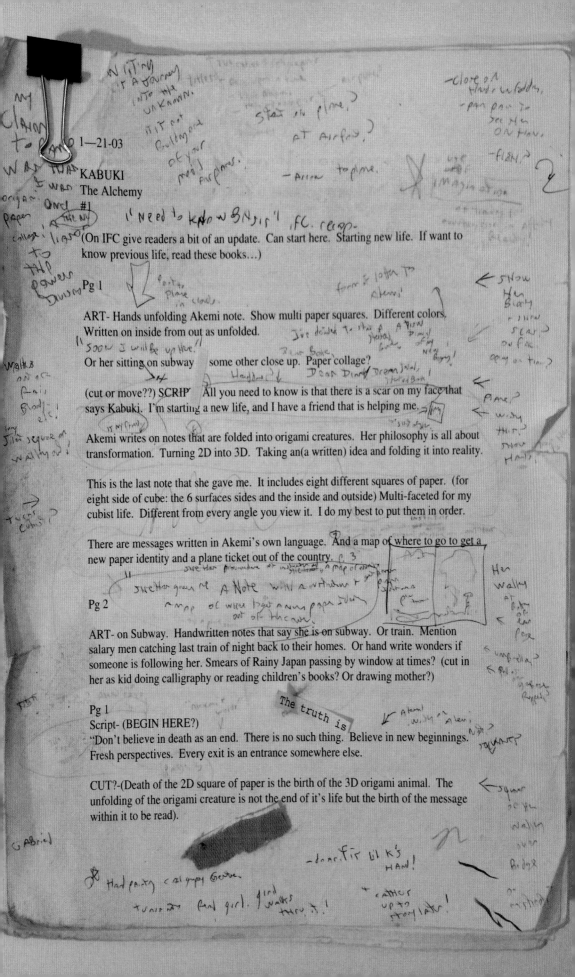

Pg 2

The Chinese calligraphers used to change their names mid career so they could start over as someone else.
They would change their signature, their identity, so they could remain free to evolve artistically, unconfined by the public's expectation for them to continue with a certain style or subject matter they had previously been known for.

ART- second part of page 2?(show folded note?) last part do calligraphy type?)
Script- My friend tells me this in a note. (the words are on toilet paper).
The note is folded into the shape of a dragon fly. The name of the shape isn't so much a description as it is a sentence with a noun and a verb explaining what I should do next.
Dragon – Fly (N&V underneath and underlined. Conjugated on kid writing paper. "Unfold wings and fly"). What does it mean when you find yourself conjugating the grammar of shapes?

It seems that the formerly inscrutable scrawls of physical reality have made themselves legible to me.

(I see the harmony in things. Everything is alive with the magic that you (your perception imbues it with) imbue it with.)

Pg 3 (her on train?)

This moment is the closest I've ever come to understanding the concept of reincarnation. Religion. Buddhism. Christianity.
The hollow constructs of dogma peeled away to reveal the actual meanings that (the words?) they once stood for.
I see the particles of the divine that exist in myself and everyone else. (or- in others and even myself). (I see that we are all individual cells of the same organism. Each peforming a different function of the same body).

I understand the term "born again". I understand the idea of forgiveness. For myself and others. I can even grasp the concept of someone dying for my sins that I may have new life. A chance to start over with a clean slate.
I see that death has no meaning and no weight for me. I no longer think in terms of death or other limitations, labels or finite categorizations.
I believe in new beginnings. I believe in the never ending dance and conversion of matter and energy.

This is the closest I've ever come to truly understanding reincarnation. Transmutation.
The concept of high school and graduation.

Time to switch trains. Get my connection.

Pg 4?

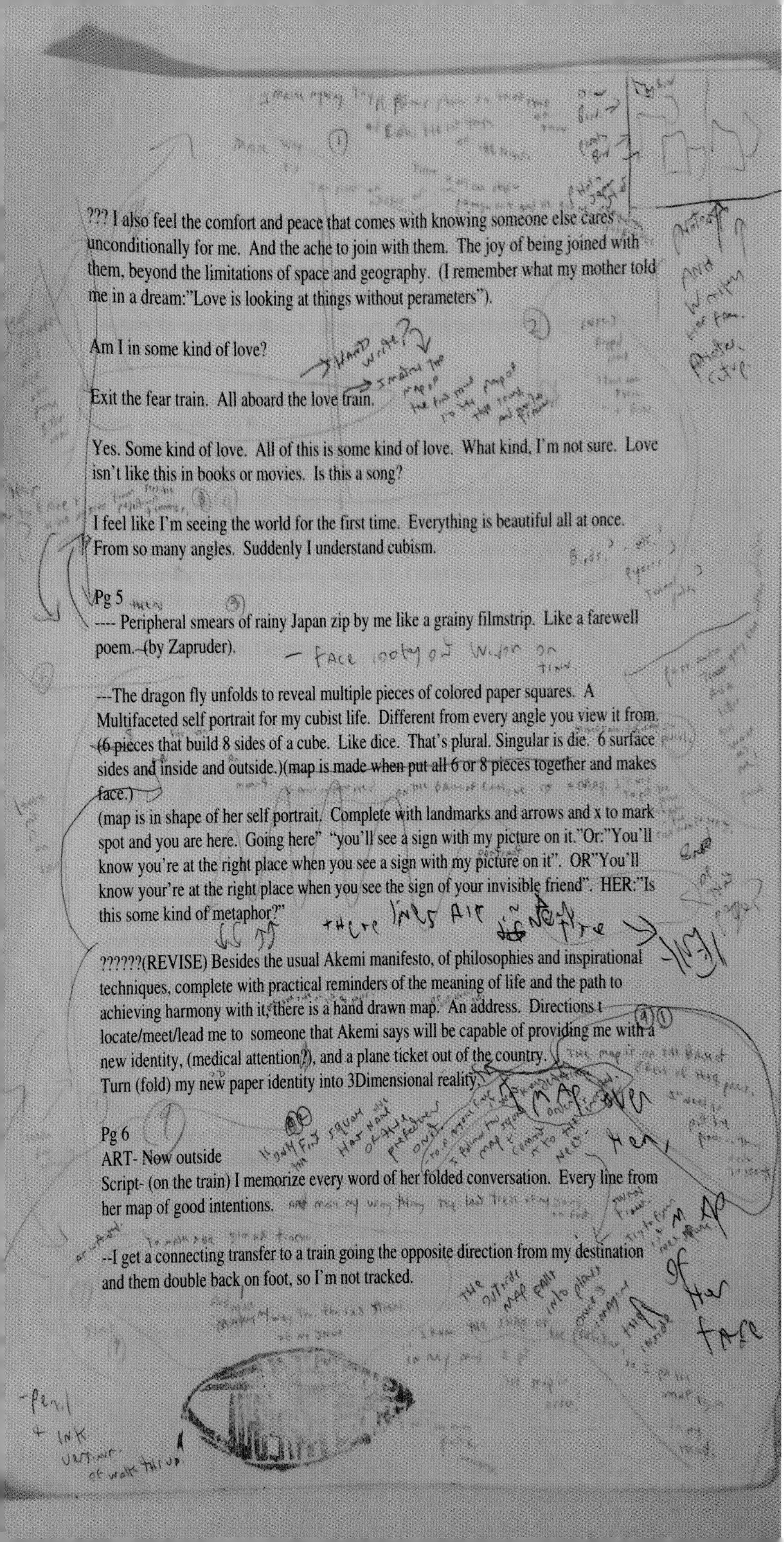

??? I also feel the comfort and peace that comes with knowing someone else cares unconditionally for me. And the ache to join with them. The joy of being joined with them, beyond the limitations of space and geography. (I remember what my mother told me in a dream:"Love is looking at things without perameters").

Am I in some kind of love?

Exit the fear train. All aboard the love train.

Yes. Some kind of love. All of this is some kind of love. What kind, I'm not sure. Love isn't like this in books or movies. Is this a song?

I feel like I'm seeing the world for the first time. Everything is beautiful all at once. From so many angles. Suddenly I understand cubism.

Pg 5

---- Peripheral smears of rainy Japan zip by me like a grainy filmstrip. Like a farewell poem. (by Zapruder).

---The dragon fly unfolds to reveal multiple pieces of colored paper squares. A Multifaceted self portrait for my cubist life. Different from every angle you view it from. (6 pieces that build 8 sides of a cube. Like dice. That's plural. Singular is die. 6 surface sides and inside and outside.)(map is made when put all 6 or 8 pieces together and makes face.)

(map is in shape of her self portrait. Complete with landmarks and arrows and x to mark spot and you are here. Going here" "you'll see a sign with my picture on it."Or:"You'll know you're at the right place when you see a sign with my picture on it". OR"You'll know your're at the right place when you see the sign of your invisible friend". HER:"Is this some kind of metaphor?"

??????(REVISE) Besides the usual Akemi manifesto, of philosophies and inspirational techniques, complete with practical reminders of the meaning of life and the path to achieving harmony with it, there is a hand drawn map. An address. Directions t locate/meet/lead me to someone that Akemi says will be capable of providing me with a new identity, (medical attention?), and a plane ticket out of the country. Turn (fold) my new paper identity into 3Dimensional reality.

Pg 6

ART- Now outside

Script- (on the train) I memorize every word of her folded conversation. Every line from her map of good intentions.

--I get a connecting transfer to a train going the opposite direction from my destination and them double back on foot, so I'm not tracked.

The handwritten notes on the pages are indcations to change the order of the panels or reorder the text. I changed the order of the first couple of pages several times. Early on, the airplane page that is the last page in issue 2 was originally the first page in issue 1. The art began with Kabuki on an airplane writing to Akemi. It wasn't until the issue was completely finished that I took that page from issue 1 and put it as the last page in #2.

--I've ripped the inside lining of the jacket out to wrap the cut on my arm so it doesn't /didn't soak through and draw attention (on the train).   Now the rain makes the jacket stick to my body like a second skin.

These are the early fertile moments of my new life. Wet and bloody like birth tends to be.

When I leave the train/subway, I'm a different person than when I went in. Like Clark Kent's phonebooth. Or Houdini's water chamber. I leave as a different creature. Unfolded like me dragon fly. I understand Superman. I understand Houdini.

CUT?--??Or—(name to look up address in phone book. It's in the business section.) (I stop at a lighted phone booth and look up the address of the name of my destination. It's in the business section. WHen I leave the phone booth I'm a different person. A different creature. Unfolded like my dragon fly. I understand how superman feels. I understand Houdini.

I understand the Chinese Caligraphers.

Pg 7
Art-changing styles?

I have evolved, (artistically). Grown. Moved on. Transformed. Possessed by a new set of aesthetics and personal subject matter. I'm ready to change my style. I'm ready to work in new mediums. I leave my previous name and my early work behind me.

Pg 8
?????(REVISE) But here's the great part. Here is the big question. Here is what college kids and working adults wrestle with everyday. Here is the quest. The adventure. The heart of the matter. What do I do now? Now that I finally realize that the choice is mine to make of this life what I want, just what is that and how do I do it? How do you turn your ideas and thoughts and dreams and perceptions of what is beautiful and wonderous in the world, into the actual live itself. Into a life worth living. Into a live that is the action of the art.

ART- Her as kid looking at a book of herself? Her walking at bottom of page? Sideways.

I'm exhilarated at the thought of it. This is the most dangerous, unpredictable and worthy mission(other word? Operation?) that I've ever been on. I feel just like a kid about to open a present. It's like a brand new choose your own adventure book.

So now I have to decide. What will I do in life? I know that it will be something that will enable me to encourage and inspire others the way Akemi has helped me.

(If you choose to respect Kabuki's decision to help others the way she feels enriched by Akemi, go on to the next page. If you're confused or apprehensive about her new

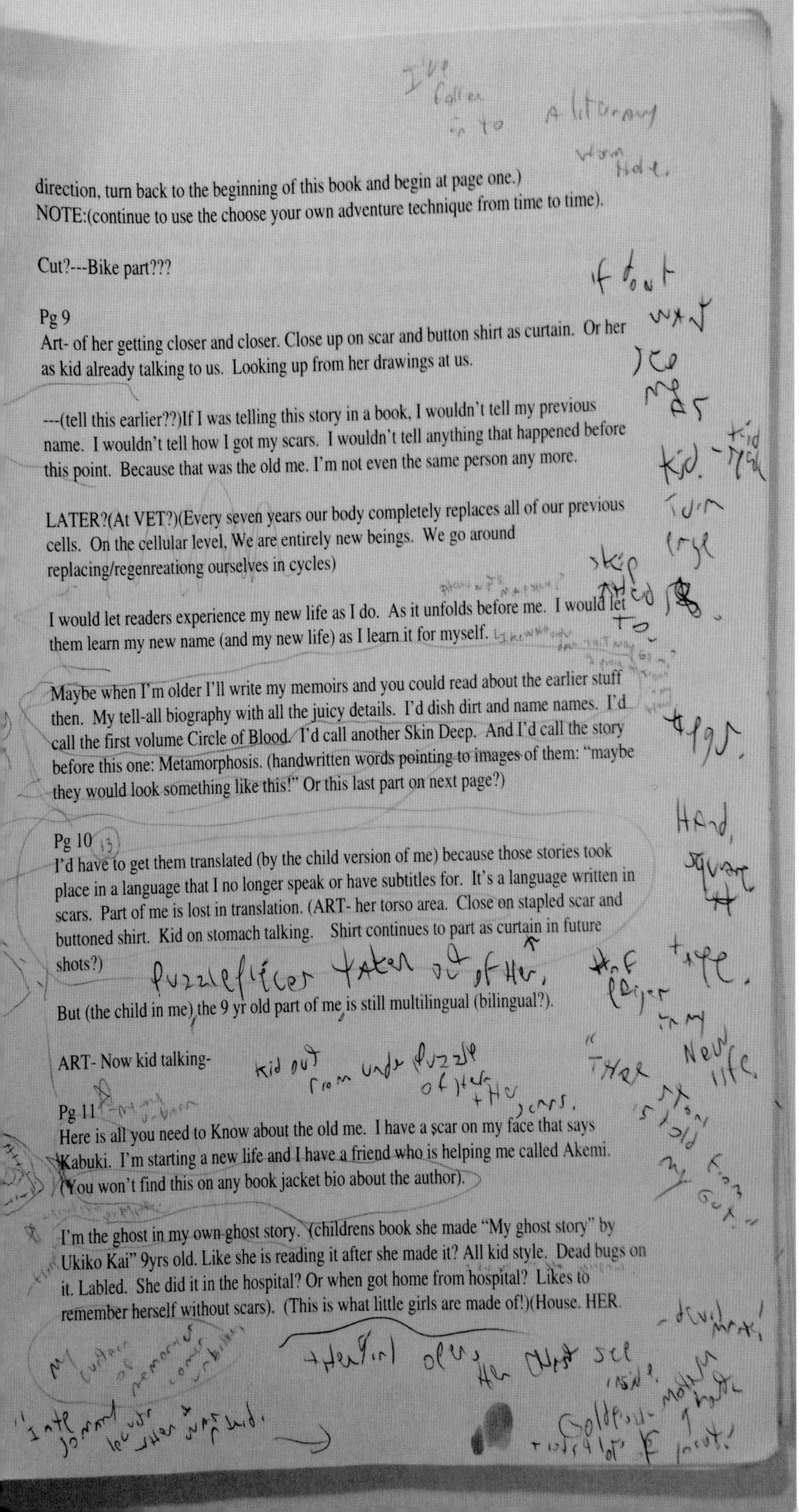
direction, turn back to the beginning of this book and begin at page one.)
NOTE:(continue to use the choose your own adventure technique from time to time).

Cut?---Bike part???

Pg 9
Art- of her getting closer and closer. Close up on scar and button shirt as curtain. Or her as kid already talking to us. Looking up from her drawings at us.

---(tell this earlier??)If I was telling this story in a book, I wouldn't tell my previous name. I wouldn't tell how I got my scars. I wouldn't tell anything that happened before this point. Because that was the old me. I'm not even the same person any more.

LATER?(At VET?)(Every seven years our body completely replaces all of our previous cells. On the cellular level, We are entirely new beings. We go around replacing/regenreationg ourselves in cycles)

I would let readers experience my new life as I do. As it unfolds before me. I would let them learn my new name (and my new life) as I learn it for myself.

Maybe when I'm older I'll write my memoirs and you could read about the earlier stuff then. My tell-all biography with all the juicy details. I'd dish dirt and name names. I'd call the first volume Circle of Blood. I'd call another Skin Deep. And I'd call the story before this one: Metamorphosis. (handwritten words pointing to images of them: "maybe they would look something like this!" Or this last part on next page?)

Pg 10
I'd have to get them translated (by the child version of me) because those stories took place in a language that I no longer speak or have subtitles for. It's a language written in scars. Part of me is lost in translation. (ART- her torso area. Close on stapled scar and buttoned shirt. Kid on stomach talking. Shirt continues to part as curtain in future shots?)

But (the child in me) the 9 yr old part of me is still multilingual (bilingual?).

ART- Now kid talking-

Pg 11
Here is all you need to Know about the old me. I have a scar on my face that says Kabuki. I'm starting a new life and I have a friend who is helping me called Akemi. (You won't find this on any book jacket bio about the author).

I'm the ghost in my own ghost story. (childrens book she made "My ghost story" by Ukiko Kai" 9yrs old. Like she is reading it after she made it? All kid style. Dead bugs on it. Labled. She did it in the hospital? Or when got home from hospital? Likes to remember herself without scars). (This is what little girls are made of!)(House. HER.

Early sketches on the script of the sequence of her buttoned shirt turning into the rising curtains of her memories to reveal Ukiko narrating as a child.

I had written many sections of this story over a period of time before putting it in script form. When working on one story, I will have ideas for future stories. So I've deveoloped a system of jotting those ideas down, and putting them in a folder for the future project.

When working on previous Kabuki stories I had made notes for this one as they came. Moments and sequences that I saw the character engaged in.

When it came to write this story, I pulled out the file and it was filled with hundres of little papers, napkins, post its, with ideas jotted on them.

Doors. House frame and labels with her in it. Goldfish and other stuff from her "HOUSE OF MEMORY")(Shirt curtain around house, or house is inside and curtain comes unbuttoned. "MY memory comes unbuttoned/My memories come unbuttoned. Come undone. "My Quiet place.". "House of reality" I build it brick by brick. Beam by beam") Stitches in time. Saves nine. (even do the bug collection of her own evolution. Latin name for her. (Kabukis metamorphosis)"Stages of the Kabuki Dragon fly" (grows wings on back).(Embryo, larva, egg, pupa, chrysalis, adult, dreamer, new ID) End, part is burnt paper.

"My family tree" By Ukiko Kai. 8 1/2 yrs old. (Or 9yrs)
(On inside cover, art of family tree pointing to mother and father, General, goldfish, her as fetus. "who is my real daddy?" "Mommy is gone").

My father was Japanese. My mother was Ainu (the indigenous people of Japan).

Pg 12
My mother loved me very much. But she died when I was born.

When I was 8 yrs old, my goldfish died.

Pg 13
When I was 9 yrs old I died for a few minutes. I'm not going to say how it happened. I don't talk about that. I'm not supposed to.

I found my mother on the other side. I mean when I was dead.

She spoke to me. She told me her secrets.

(NEW PAGE? Word balloon from mother.) I wanted to stay with her. But she told me to come back. "You must be a ghost. like (in the Kabuki plays)"

I fulfilled my obligations as a ghost writer for my mother's unfinished story. A vehicle for her unfinished business on the physical plane.

Pg 14
The doctors brought me back. I had bandages on my face. When they took them off, there were scars. I was labeled.

(ART- Book closed. Now her talking?)

Later I am given a mask to hid my scars. I learn to deal with the world only through the security of this mask.

!!!!(PUT BUG CHART OF HER HERE)

Pg 15

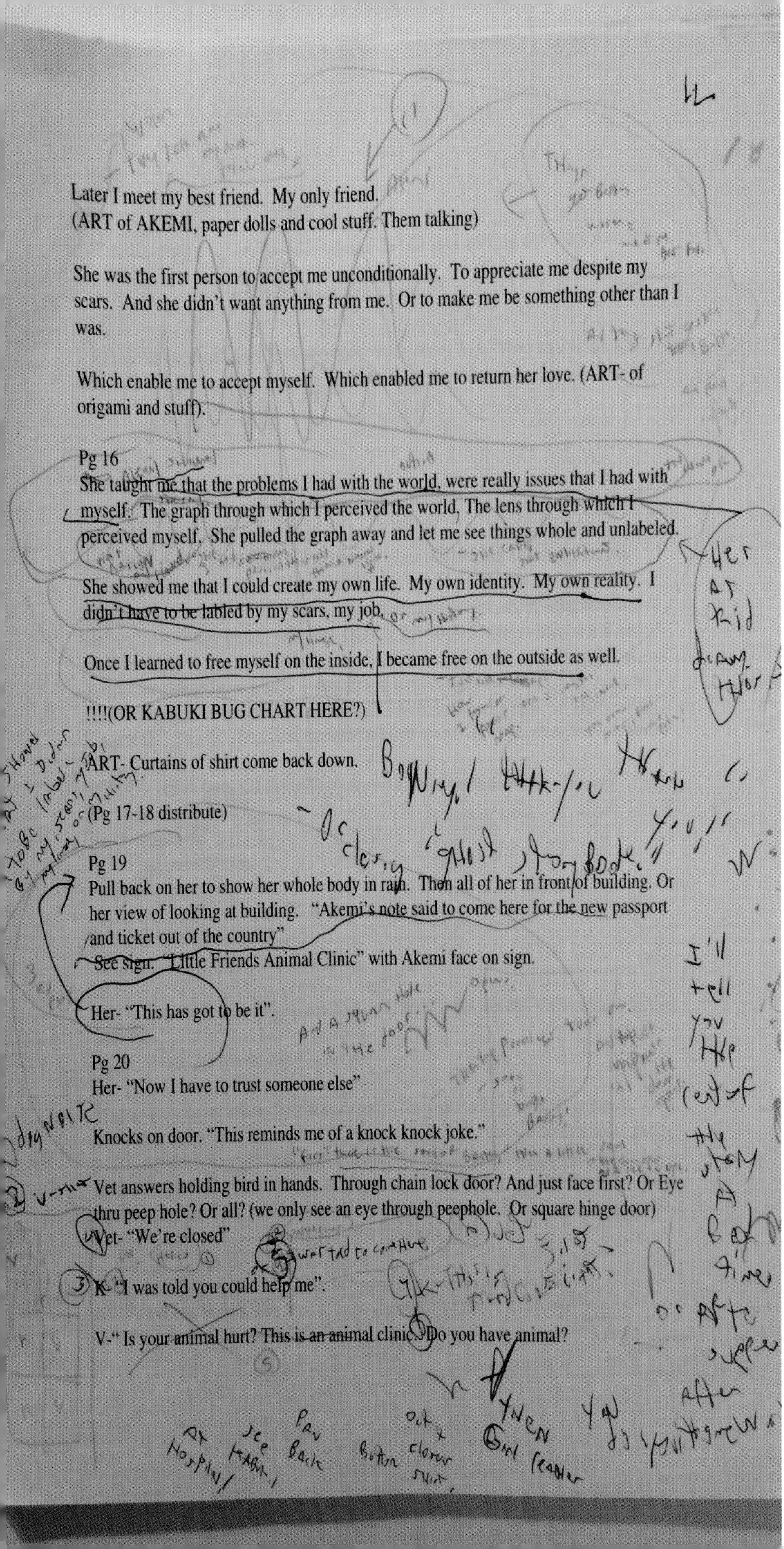
Later I meet my best friend. My only friend.
(ART of AKEMI, paper dolls and cool stuff. Them talking)

She was the first person to accept me unconditionally. To appreciate me despite my scars. And she didn't want anything from me. Or to make me be something other than I was.

Which enable me to accept myself. Which enabled me to return her love. (ART- of origami and stuff).

Pg 16
She taught me that the problems I had with the world, were really issues that I had with myself. The graph through which I perceived the world, The lens through which I perceived myself. She pulled the graph away and let me see things whole and unlabeled.

She showed me that I could create my own life. My own identity. My own reality. I didn't have to be labled by my scars, my job,

Once I learned to free myself on the inside, I became free on the outside as well.

!!!!(OR KABUKI BUG CHART HERE?)

ART- Curtains of shirt come back down.

(Pg 17-18 distribute)

Pg 19
Pull back on her to show her whole body in rain. Then all of her in front of building. Or her view of looking at building. "Akemi's note said to come here for the new passport and ticket out of the country"
See sign. "Little Friends Animal Clinic" with Akemi face on sign.

Her- "This has got to be it".

Pg 20
Her- "Now I have to trust someone else"

Knocks on door. "This reminds me of a knock knock joke."

Vet answers holding bird in hands. Through chain lock door? And just face first? Or Eye thru peep hole? Or all? (we only see an eye through peephole. Or square hinge door)
Vet- "We're closed"

K- "I was told you could help me".

V-" Is your animal hurt? This is an animal clinic. Do you have animal?

The challenge was then to find an order to these notes and ideas. To type them up into something I could use as an outline that suggested what things may happen in what chapters.

From the outline, I created an early script form that I jotted down more ideas & notes. There was quite a bit of finessing to in reordering panels and pages and moments.

Much of the surgical reordering of script has to do with letting the characters breathe and move in their own way, and then re-ordering the dialogue & penels to accomodate the natural instincts and quirks of the characters.

For the "bug chart" in the script, I had been saving dead bugs in a labled envelope for years to use for this sequence.

Script Note:

The final page of the first issue of *The Alchemy* is Kabuki holding the Akemi face paper square. The same composition as when Akemi first appeared to Kabuki and shows her self Portrait on the square note. When M. C. Square appears in #6, that page reveals her in the same composition. The final page of *Skin Deep* ended with Scarab's face in this composition. I knew this chapter would end with Kabuki appearing to another person in the same way that Akemi appeared to her.

Opposite:

Painting for the final page of the story. I had cut this page and other pages out of the final issue when it was released as a single issue. I felt that three pages at the end didn't work with the chapter on its own, but completely worked in the format of all the chapters together in one book. So I brought two of these pages back when this story was collected in its original hardcover and paperback. And I included all three in this collection with their originally intended page order.

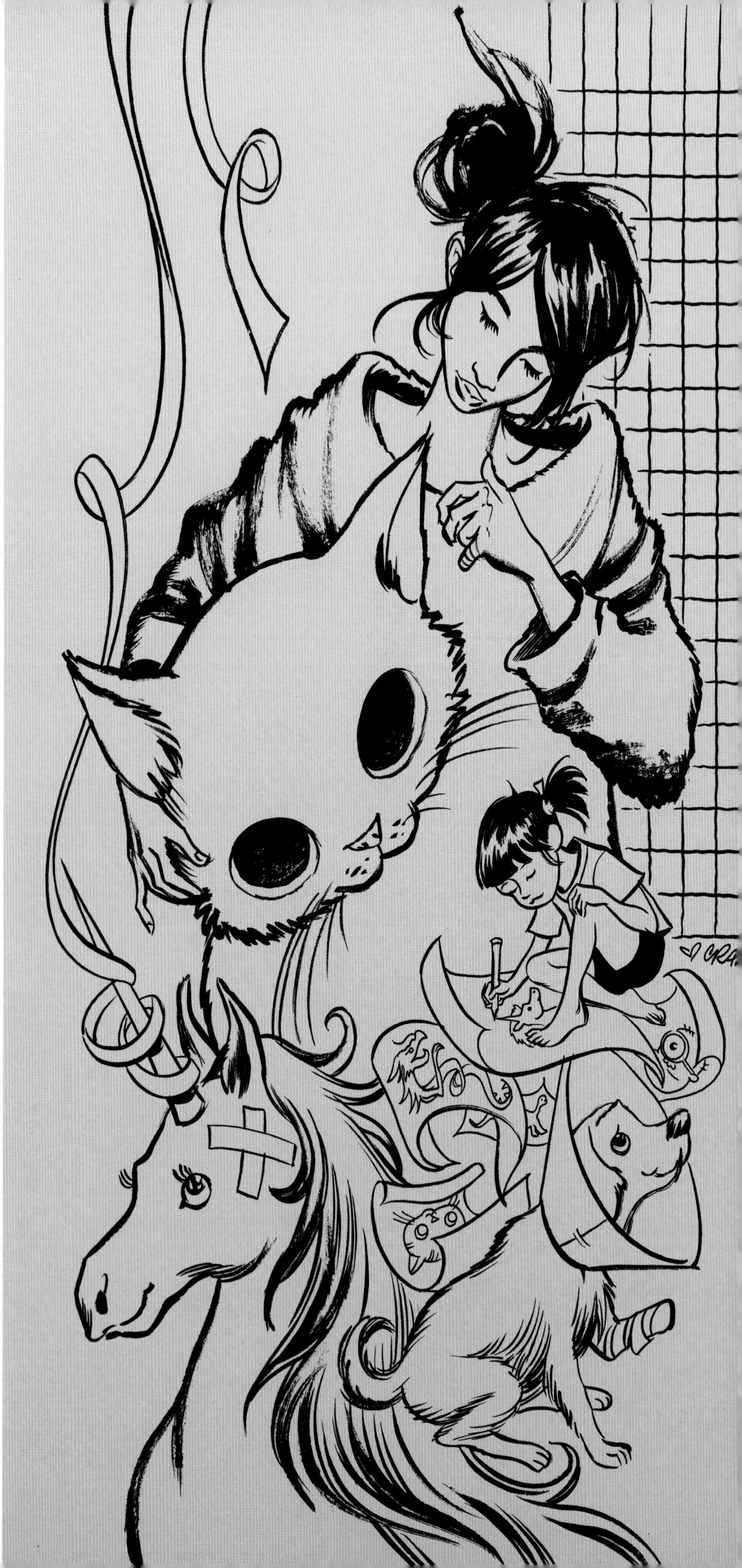

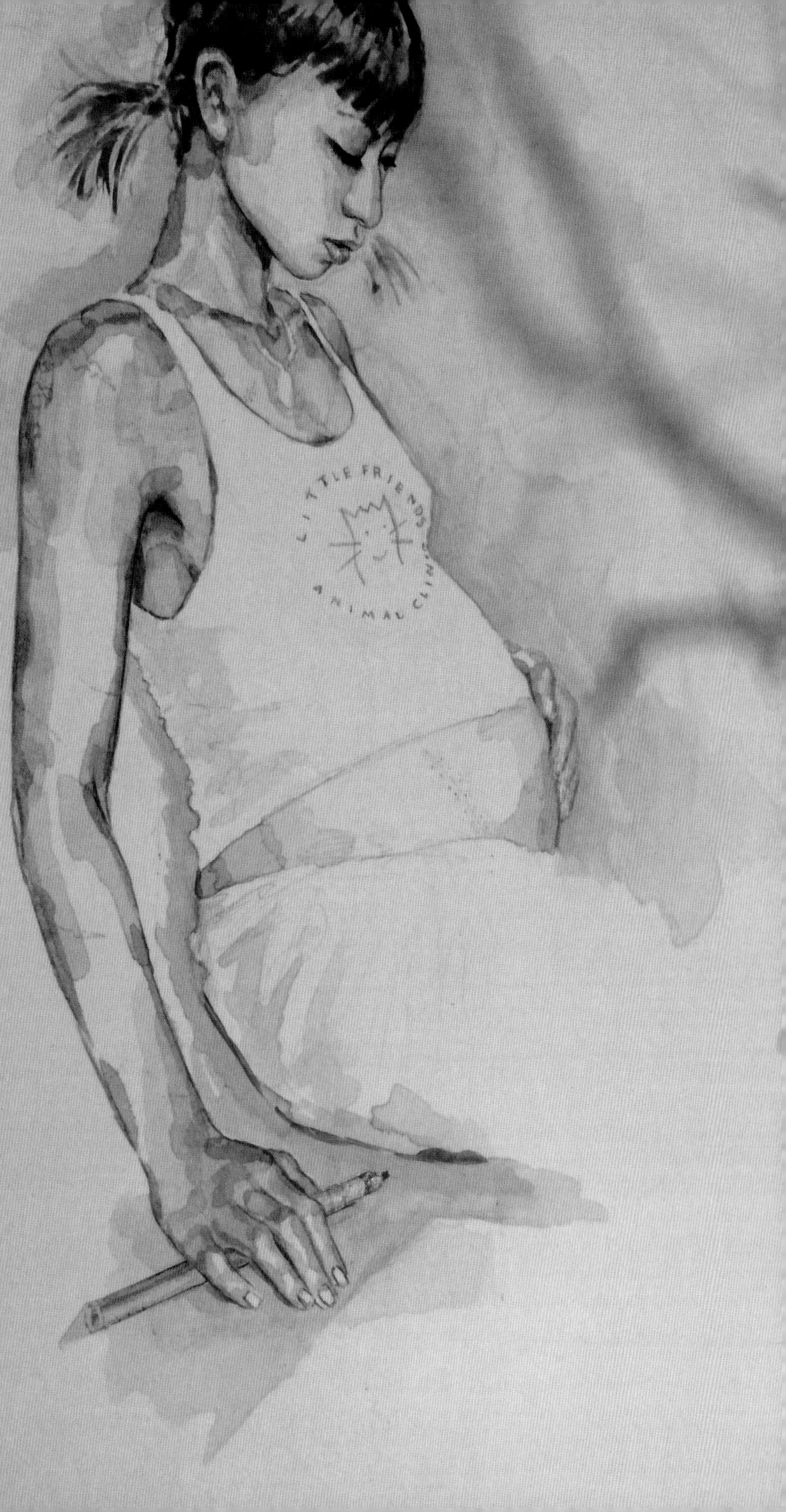
LITTLE FRIENDS
ANIMAL

)pposite:

(ABUKI
& Shy Creatures
by
Craig Thompson
Author of
Blankets,
Habibi, &
Space Dumplins.

Lil' KABUKI
in Dreamland

From Nemo:
Dream Another Dr

LIL KABUKI IN DREAMLAND

MAMA? AM I ASLEEP?

YES.

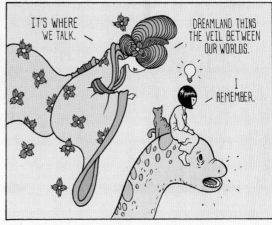

IT'S WHERE WE TALK.

DREAMLAND THINS THE VEIL BETWEEN OUR WORLDS.

I REMEMBER.

THE DREAM MEMORIES SHINE LIKE...

WHO ARE YOU?

I'M YOU IN THE FUTURE.

THINGS WILL GET CRAZY.

WHEN YOUR HUMAN COSTUME GETS HARD TO BREATHE IN...

CHANGE COSTUMES.

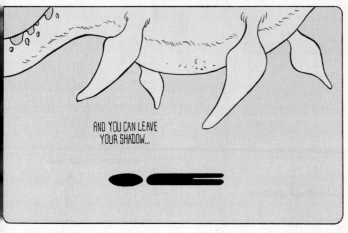

AND YOU CAN LEAVE YOUR SHADOW...

WHAT YOU LEARN IN THE DREAM WORLD, YOU CAN APPLY TO THE WAKING ONE.

KABUKI ™ © David Mack DAVIDMACK.NET

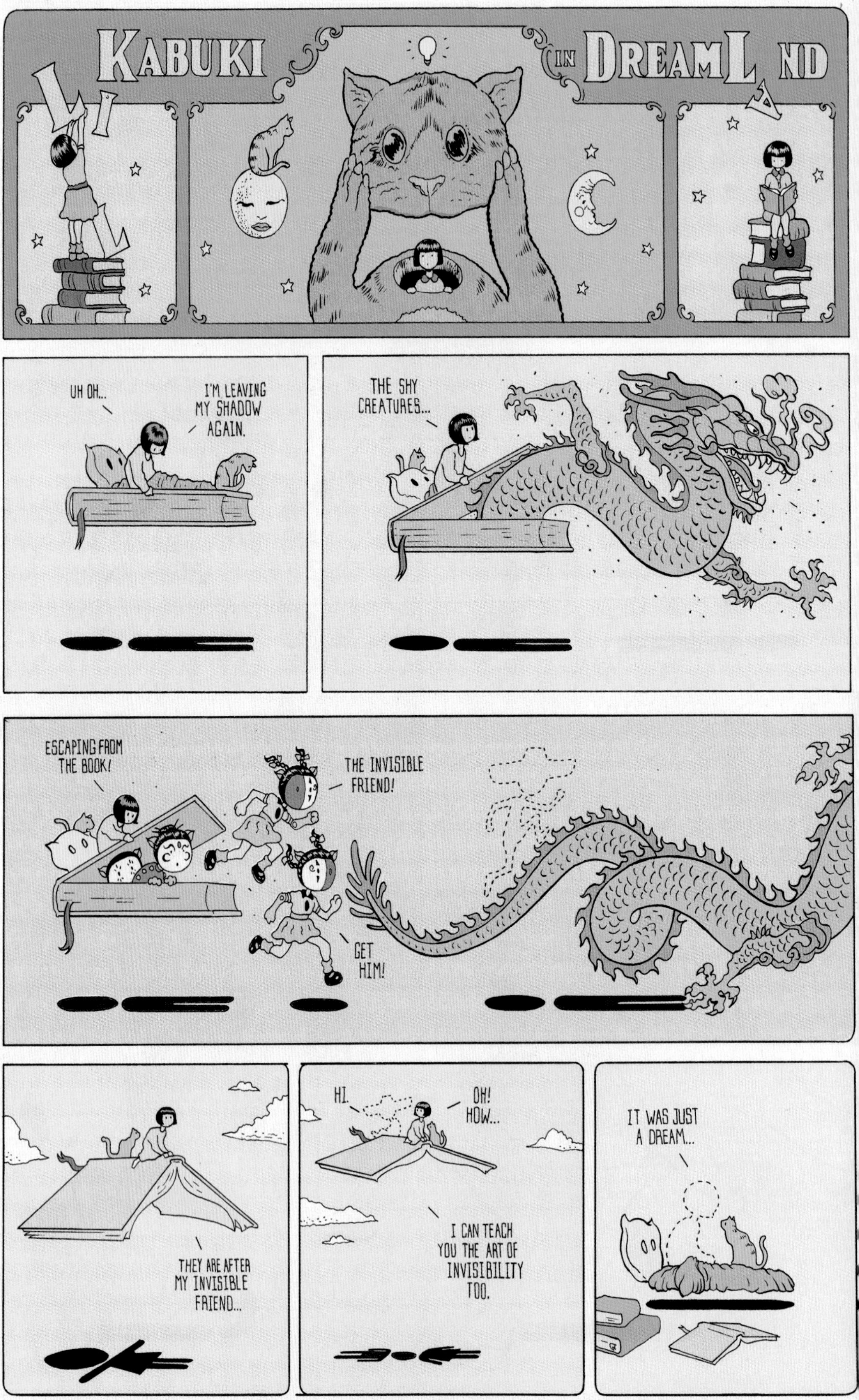
KABUKI IN DREAMLAND
UH OH...
I'M LEAVING MY SHADOW AGAIN.
THE SHY CREATURES...
ESCAPING FROM THE BOOK!
THE INVISIBLE FRIEND!
GET HIM!
THEY ARE AFTER MY INVISIBLE FRIEND...
HI.
OH! HOW...
I CAN TEACH YOU THE ART OF INVISIBILITY TOO.
IT WAS JUST A DREAM...

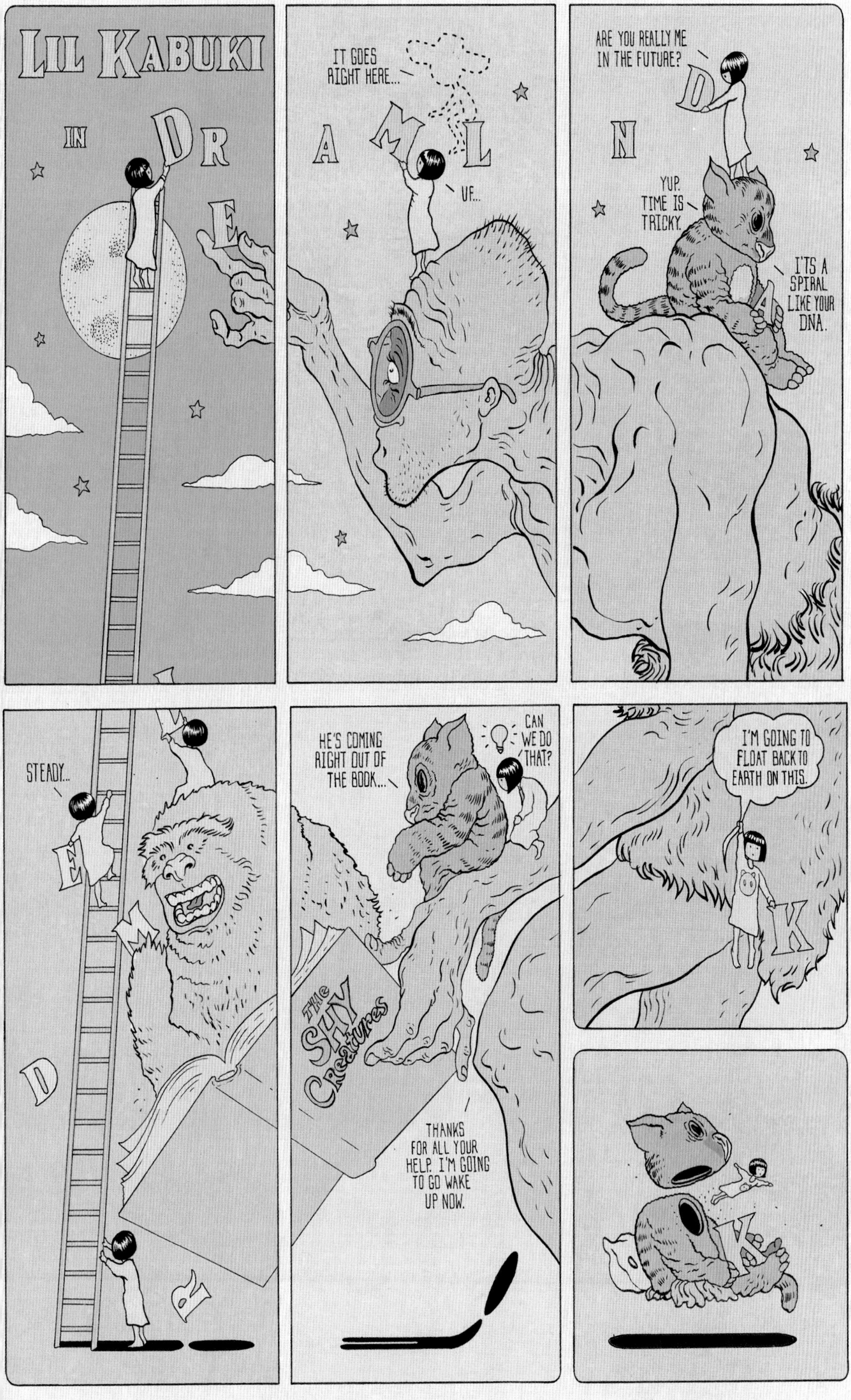
LIL KABUKI
IN
IT GOES RIGHT HERE...
UF...
ARE YOU REALLY ME IN THE FUTURE?
YUP. TIME IS TRICKY.
I'TS A SPIRAL LIKE YOUR DNA.
STEADY...
HE'S COMING RIGHT OUT OF THE BOOK...
CAN WE DO THAT?
THE SHY Creatures
THANKS FOR ALL YOUR HELP. I'M GOING TO GO WAKE UP NOW.
I'M GOING TO FLOAT BACK TO EARTH ON THIS.

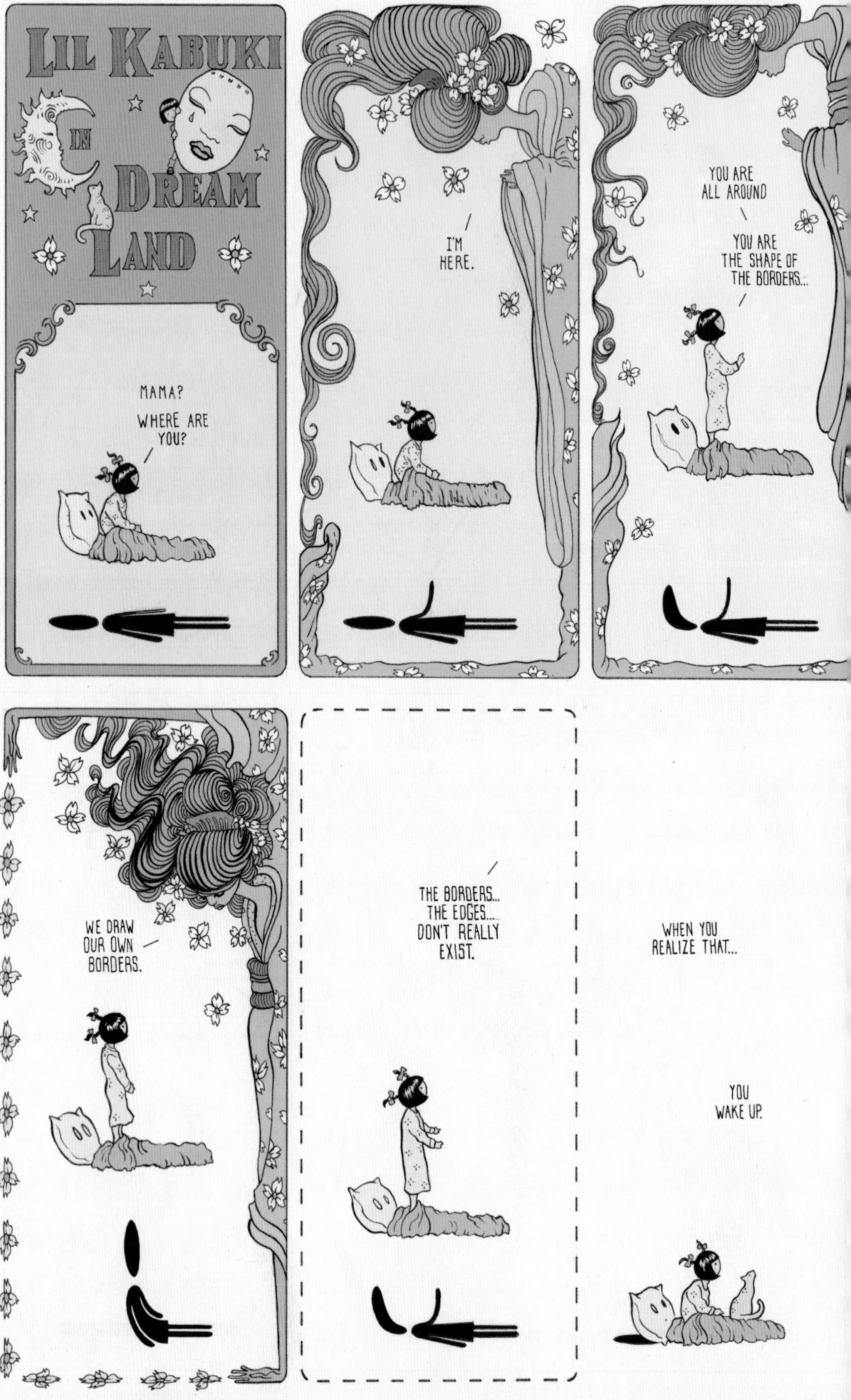
LIL KABUKI
IN
DREAM
LAND
MAMA?
WHERE ARE YOU?
I'M HERE.
YOU ARE ALL AROUND
YOU ARE THE SHAPE OF THE BORDERS...
WE DRAW OUR OWN BORDERS.
THE BORDERS... THE EDGES... DON'T REALLY EXIST.
WHEN YOU REALIZE THAT...
YOU WAKE UP.

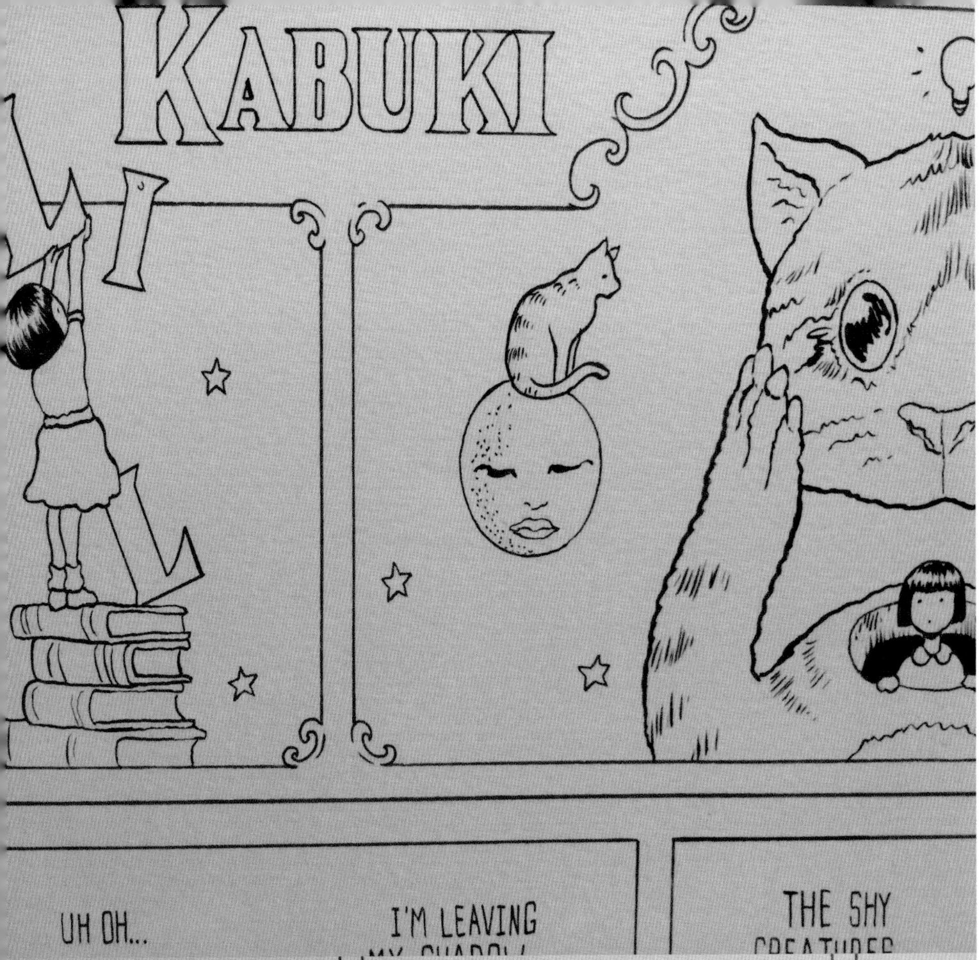
KABUKI
UH OH...
I'M LEAVING
THE SHY

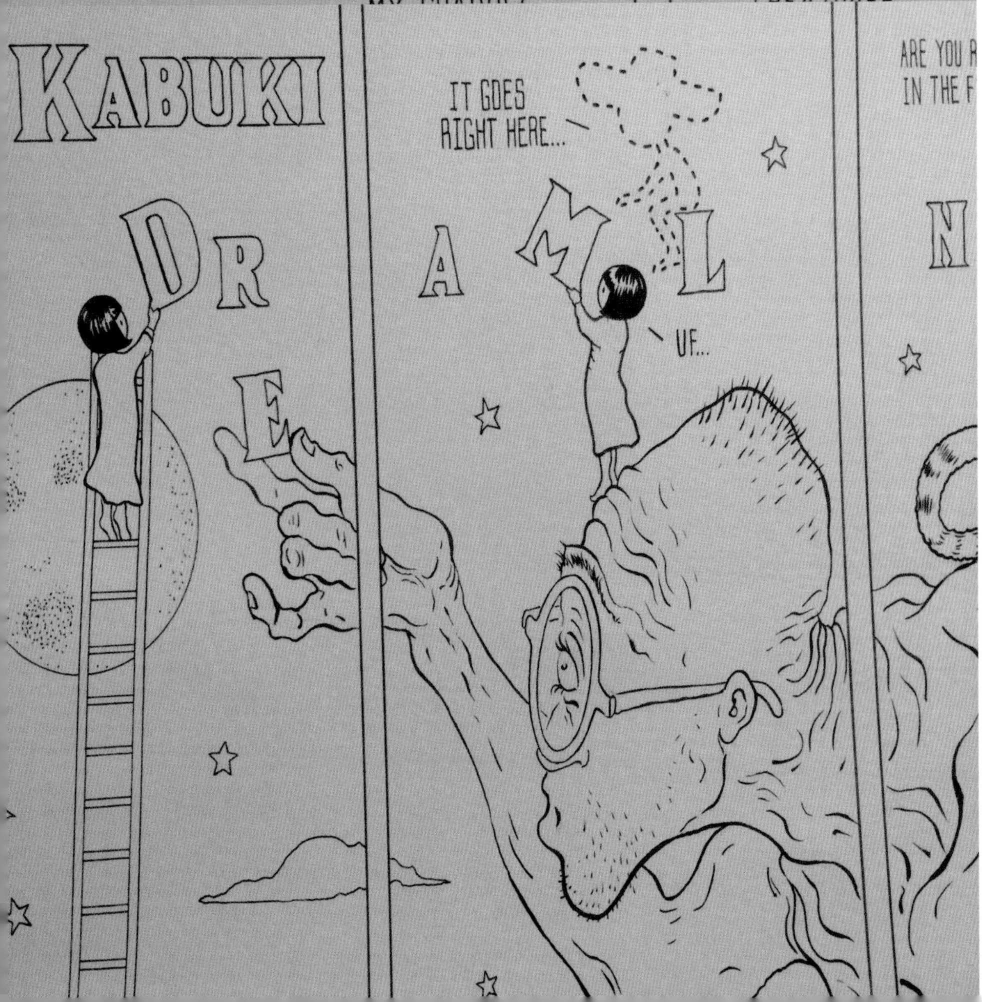
KABUKI
IT GOES RIGHT HERE...
UF...

LiL KABUKI in Dream Land.

Ink.
From
Nemo: Dream Another Dream.

The oversize book edition of creators asked to contribute homages to the great Windsor McKay and his newspaper strip from over a hundred years ago: *Little Nemo In Slumberland.*

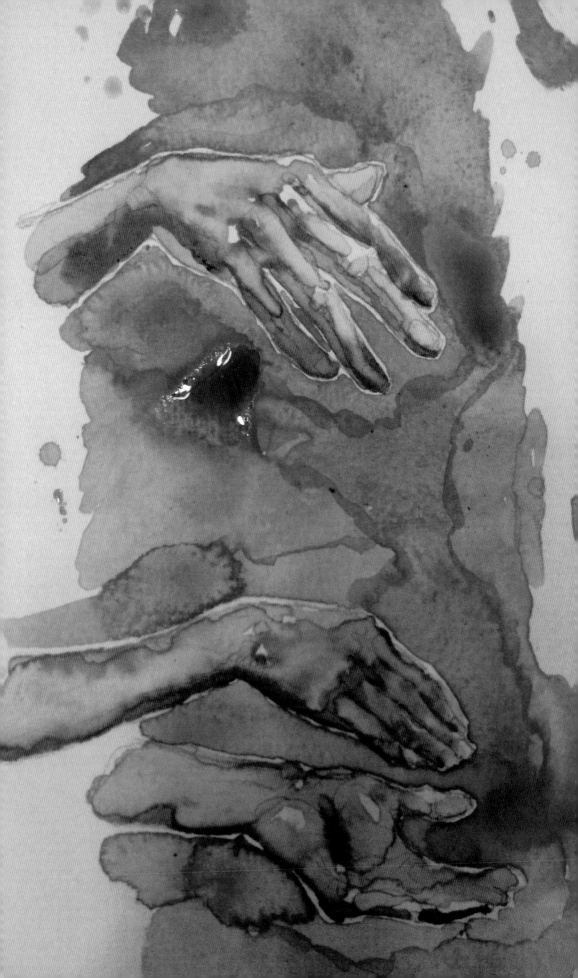

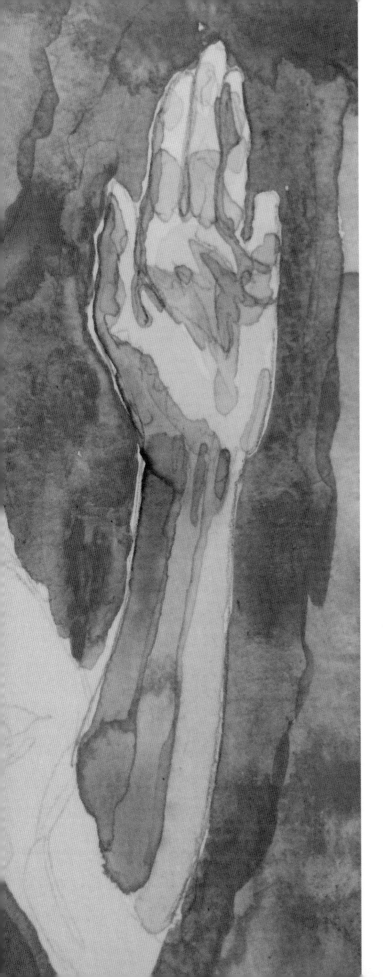

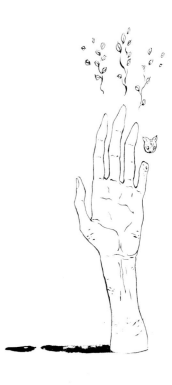

FOURTH MIND

As these *KABUKI* Library Editions and my art books *Dream Logic* & *Reflections* were being published by Dark Horse, they asked me to contribute a new *KABUKI* story to the new launch of *Dark Horse Presents* #1.

I went through my notes for the future *KABUKI* stories, to find a sequence that might work for that. In the process I found myself immersed in the notes and in visualizing new scenes while tinkering with the story arcs and outlines. I got caught up in chartacers and the joy of the scenes and stories fleshing out and taking shape.

An especially enjoyable scene I found myself detailng and making versions of was Kabuki and Tigerlily's next meeting. Here Kabuki meets someone else.

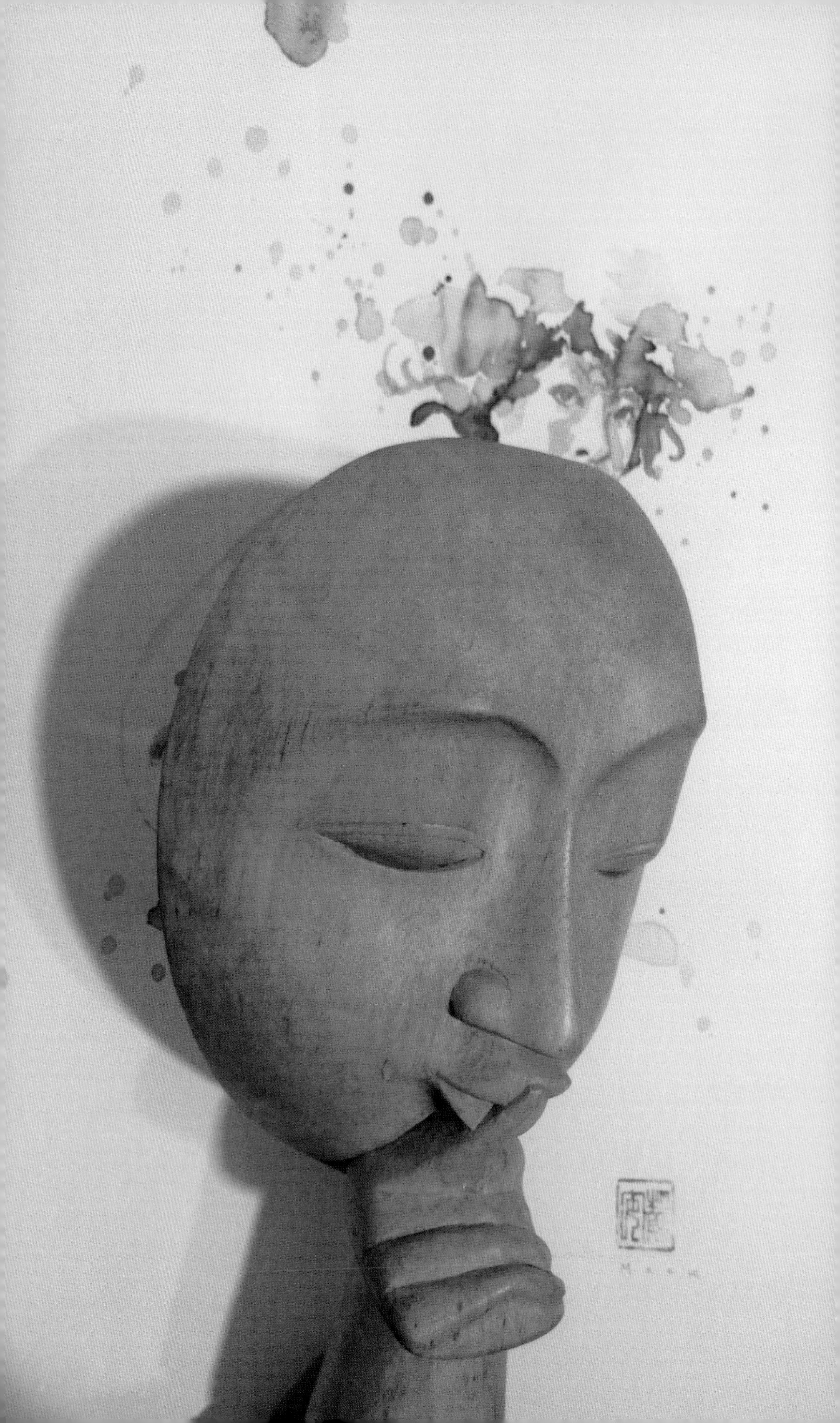

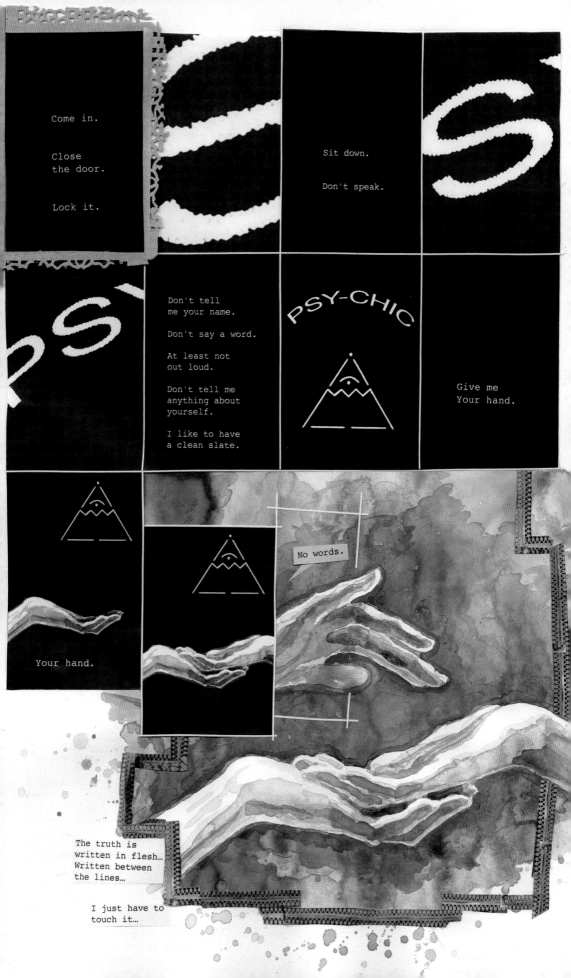

Come in.

Close
the door.

Lock it.

Sit down.

Don't speak.

Don't tell
me your name.

Don't say a word.

At least not
out loud.

Don't tell me
anything about
yourself.

I like to have
a clean slate.

PSY-CHIC

Give me
Your hand.

No words.

Your hand.

The truth is
written in flesh...
Written between
the lines...

I just have to
touch it...

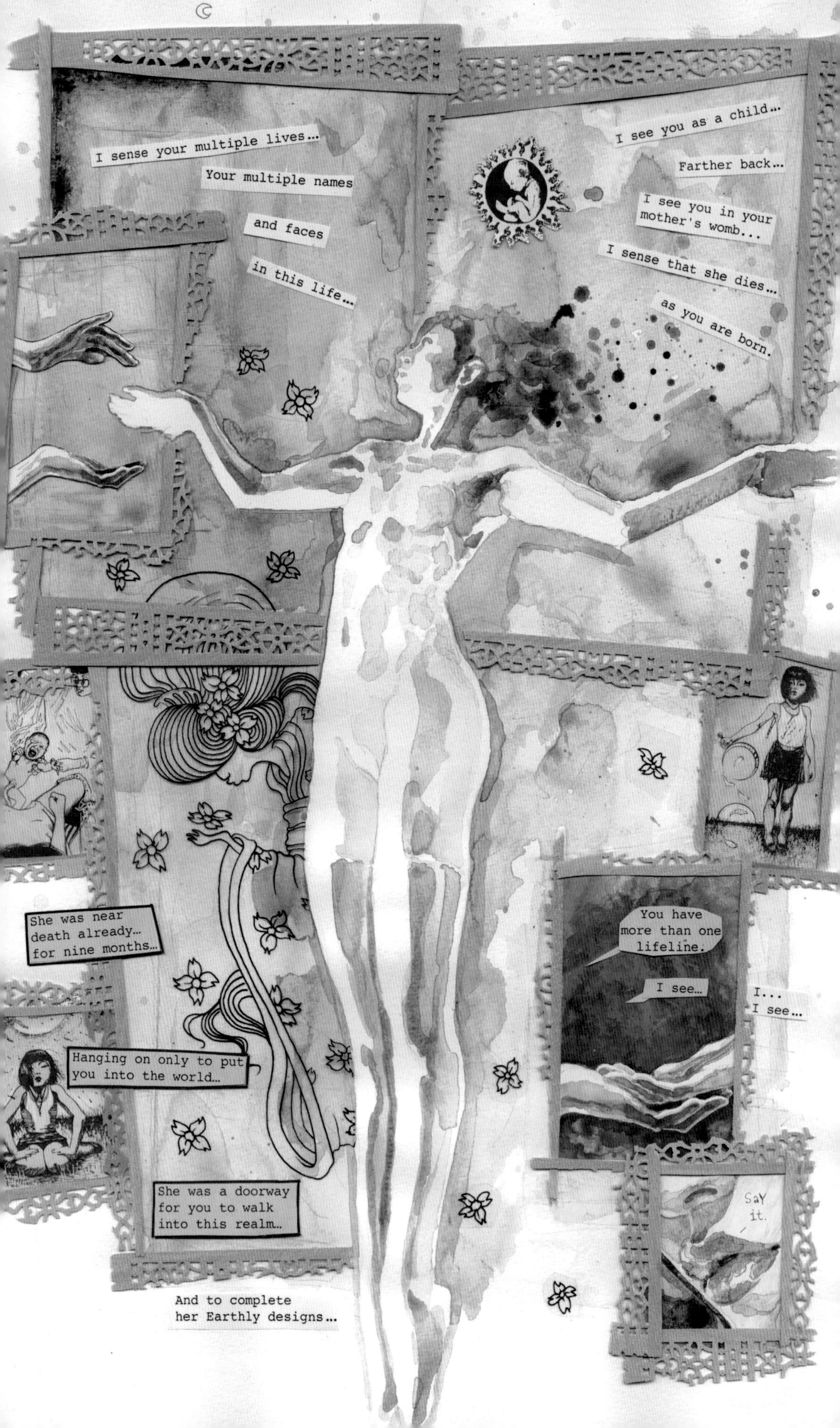

I sense your multiple lives...
Your multiple names
and faces
in this life...
I see you as a child...
Farther back...
I see you in your mother's womb...
I sense that she dies...
as you are born.
She was near death already... for nine months...
Hanging on only to put you into the world...
She was a doorway for you to walk into this realm...
And to complete her Earthly designs...
You have more than one lifeline.
I see...
I... I see...
SaY it.

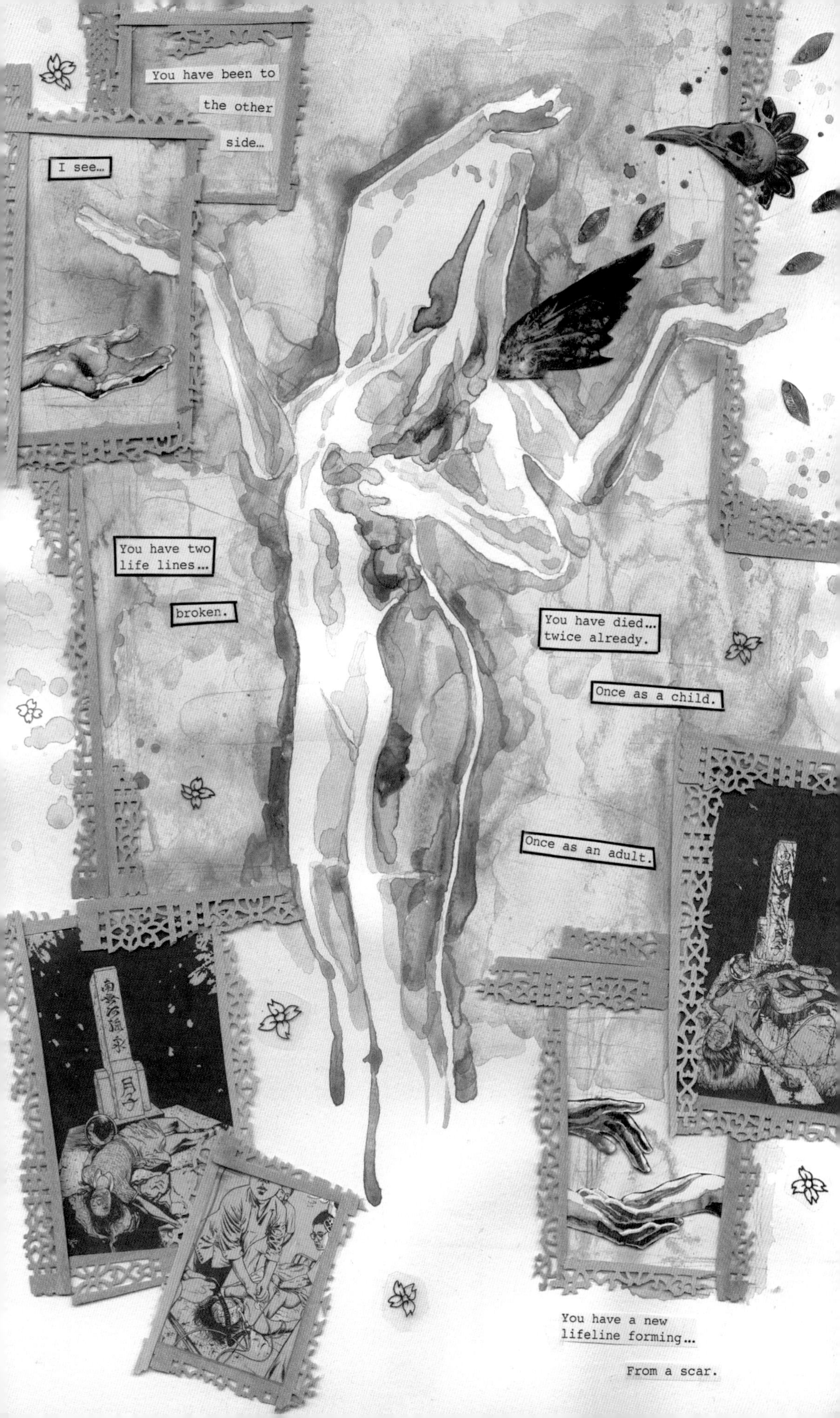

You have been to the other side...
I see...
You have two life lines...
broken.
You have died... twice already.
Once as a child.
Once as an adult.
You have a new lifeline forming...
From a scar.

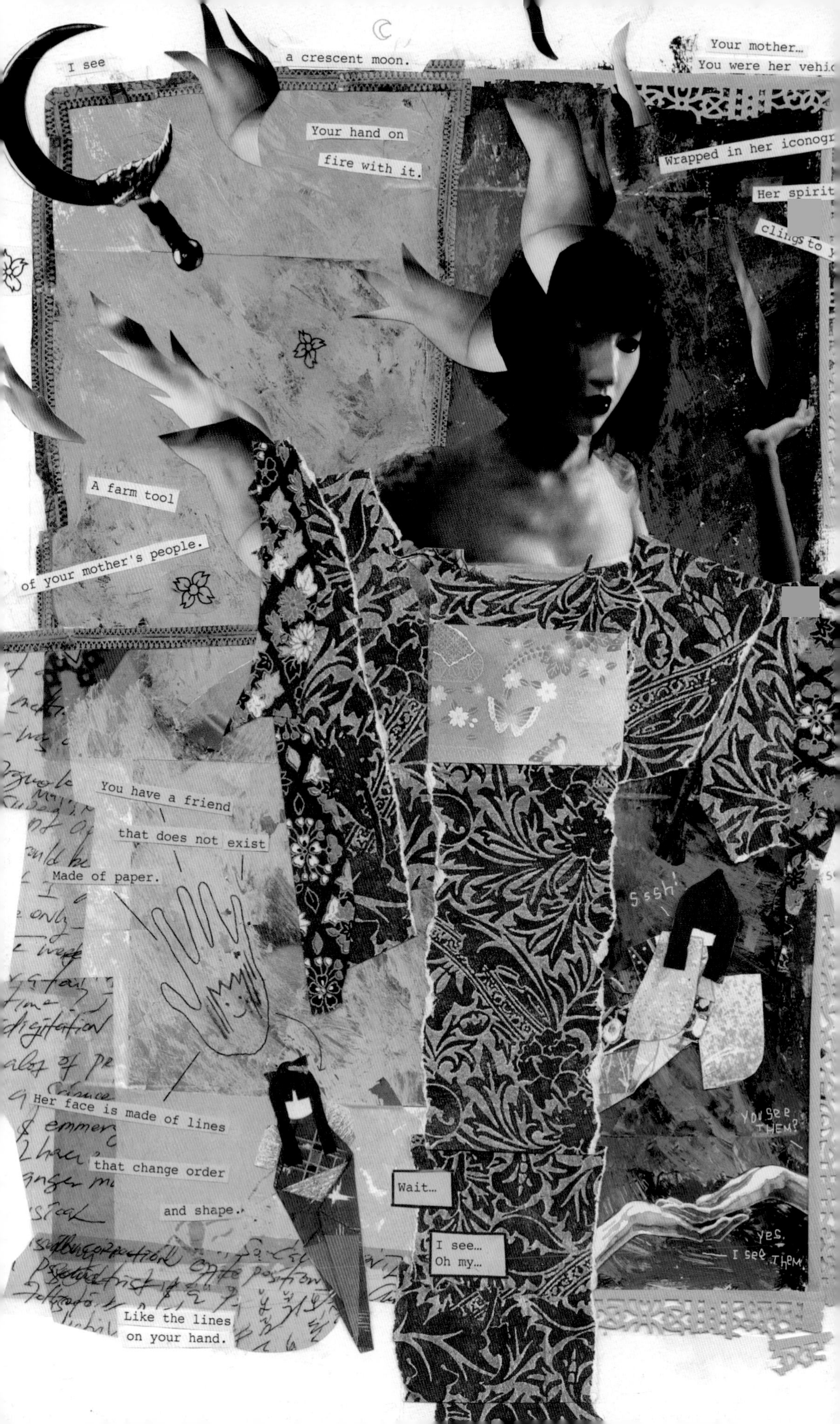
I see
a crescent moon.
Your hand on
fire with it.
A farm tool
of your mother's people.
Your mother...
You were her vehic
Wrapped in her iconogr
Her spirit
clings to y
You have a friend
that does not exist
Made of paper.
Sssh!
Her face is made of lines
that change order
and shape.
Like the lines
on your hand.
Wait...
I see...
Oh my...
You see THEM?
Yes.
I see THEM.

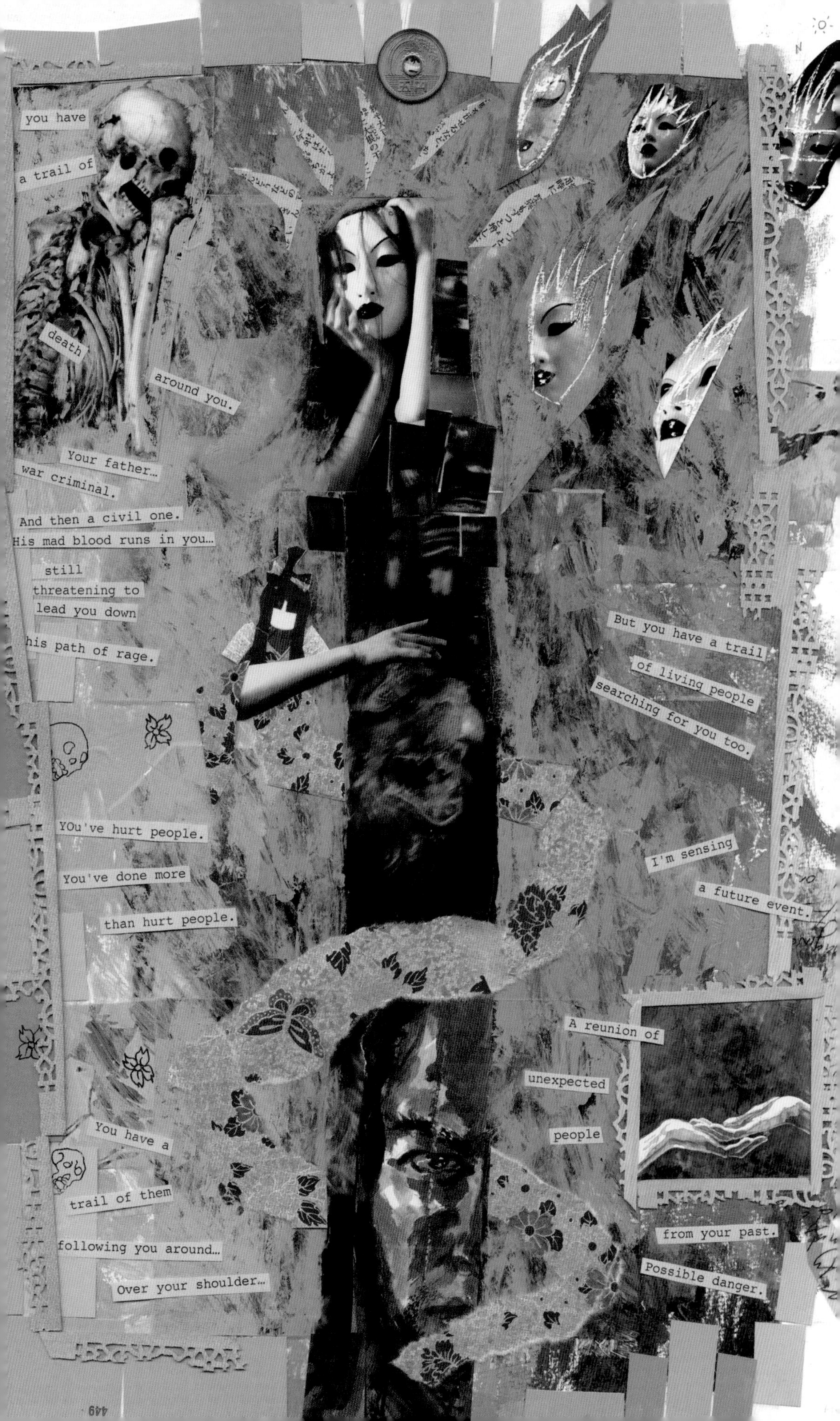
you have
a trail of
death
around you.
Your father...
war criminal.
And then a civil one.
His mad blood runs in you...
still
threatening to
lead you down
his path of rage.
But you have a trail
of living people
searching for you too.
YOu've hurt people.
You've done more
than hurt people.
I'm sensing
a future event.
A reunion of
unexpected
people
from your past.
Possible danger.
You have a
trail of them
following you around...
Over your shoulder...

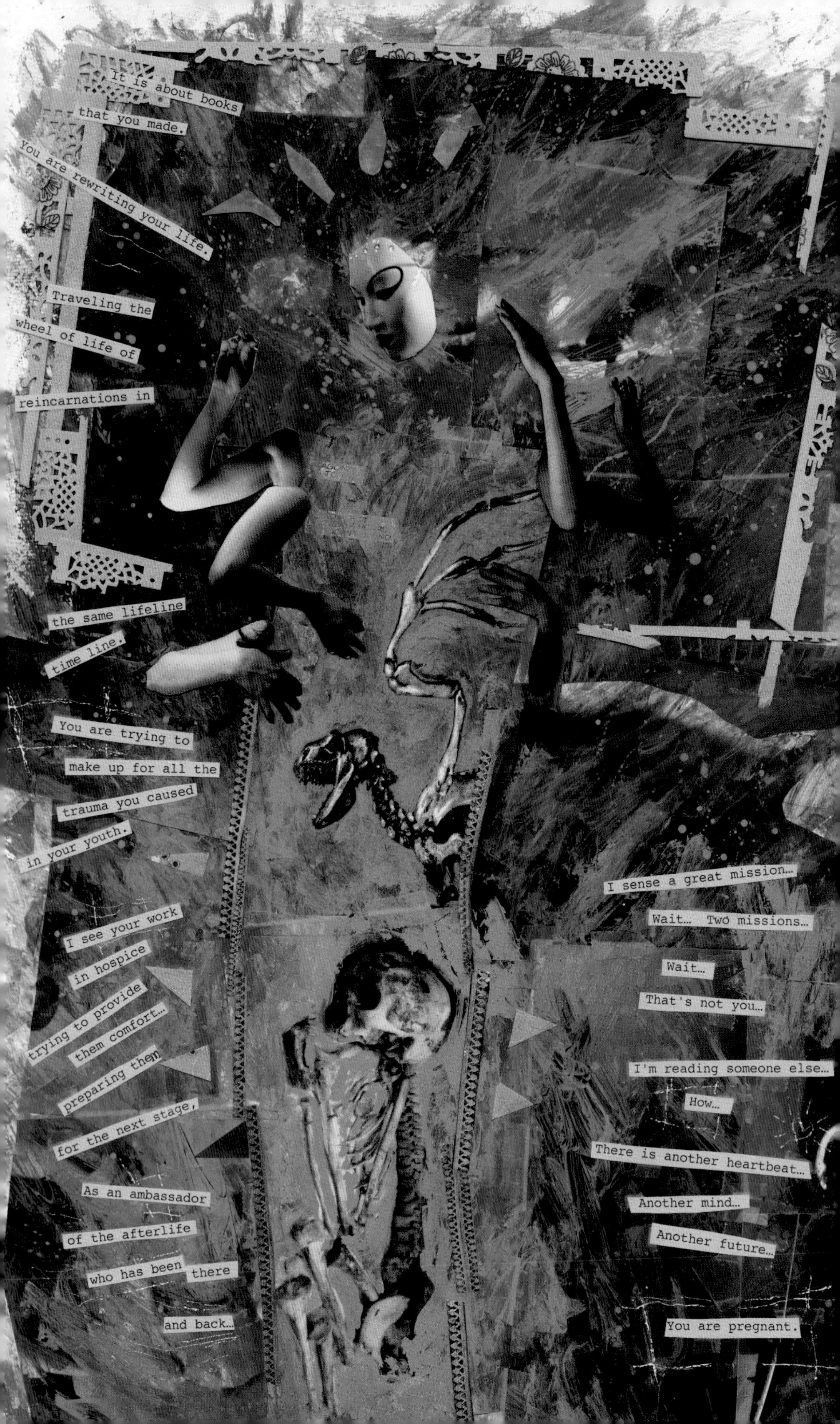
It is about books
that you made.
You are rewriting your life.
Traveling the
wheel of life of
reincarnations in
the same lifeline
time line.
You are trying to
make up for all the
trauma you caused
in your youth.
I see your work
in hospice
trying to provide
them comfort…
preparing them
for the next stage,
As an ambassador
of the afterlife
who has been there
and back…
I sense a great mission…
Wait… Two missions…
Wait…
That's not you…
I'm reading someone else…
How…
There is another heartbeat…
Another mind…
Another future…
You are pregnant.

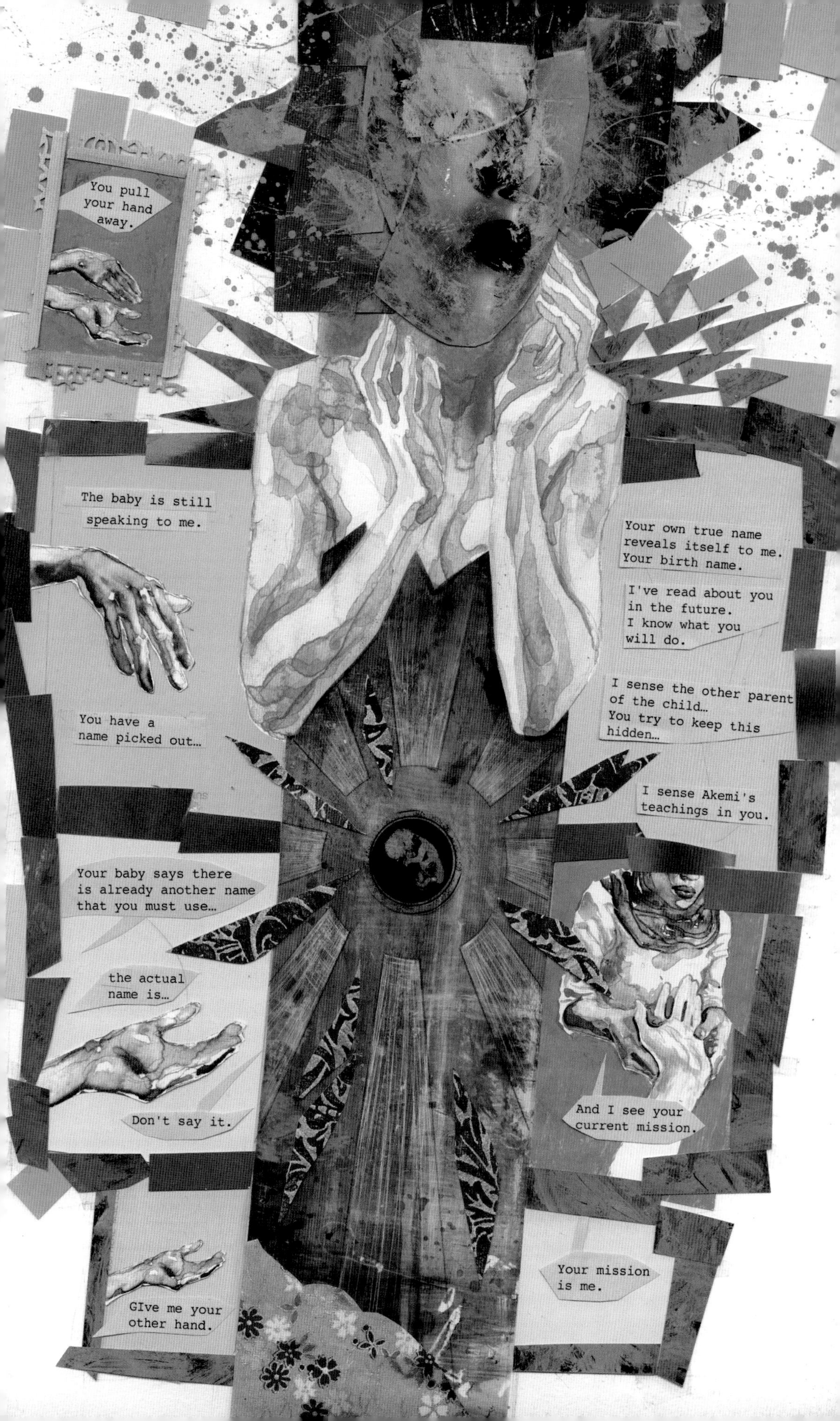
You pull your hand away.
The baby is still speaking to me.
You have a name picked out…
Your baby says there is already another name that you must use…
the actual name is…
Don't say it.
GIve me your other hand.
Your own true name reveals itself to me. Your birth name.
I've read about you in the future. I know what you will do.
I sense the other parent of the child… You try to keep this hidden…
I sense Akemi's teachings in you.
And I see your current mission.
Your mission is me.

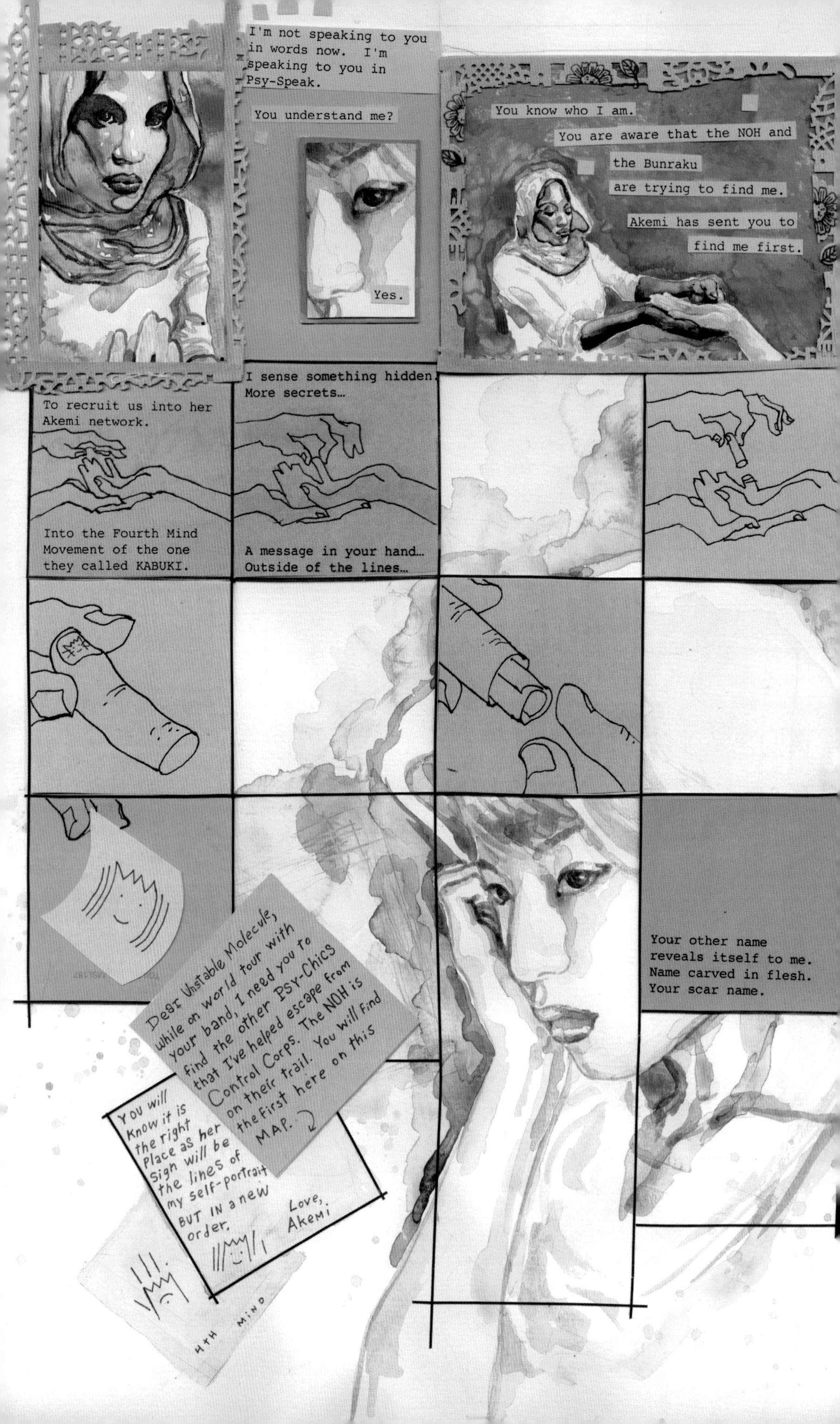

I'm not speaking to you in words now. I'm speaking to you in Psy-Speak.
You understand me?
Yes.
You know who I am.
You are aware that the NOH and
the Bunraku
are trying to find me.
Akemi has sent you to
find me first.
To recruit us into her Akemi network.
Into the Fourth Mind Movement of the one they called KABUKI.
I sense something hidden. More secrets...
A message in your hand... Outside of the lines...
Your other name reveals itself to me. Name carved in flesh. Your scar name.
Dear Unstable Molecule, while on world tour with your band, I need you to find the other PSY-CHICS that I've helped escape from Control Corps. The NOH is on their trail. You will find the First here on this MAP.
You will know it is the right place as her sign will be the lines of my self-portrait BUT IN a new order.
Love, Akemi
4TH MIND

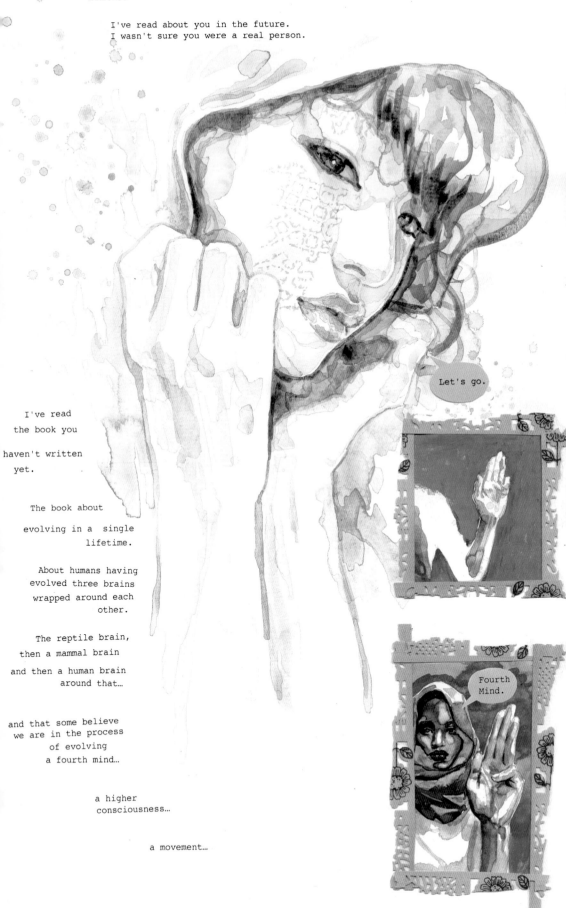

KABUKI.

I've read about you in the future.
I wasn't sure you were a real person.

I've read
the book you

haven't written
yet.

The book about

evolving in a single
lifetime.

About humans having
evolved three brains
wrapped around each
other.

The reptile brain,
then a mammal brain
and then a human brain
around that...

and that some believe
we are in the process
of evolving
a fourth mind...

a higher
consciousness...

a movement...

Let's go.

Fourth
Mind.

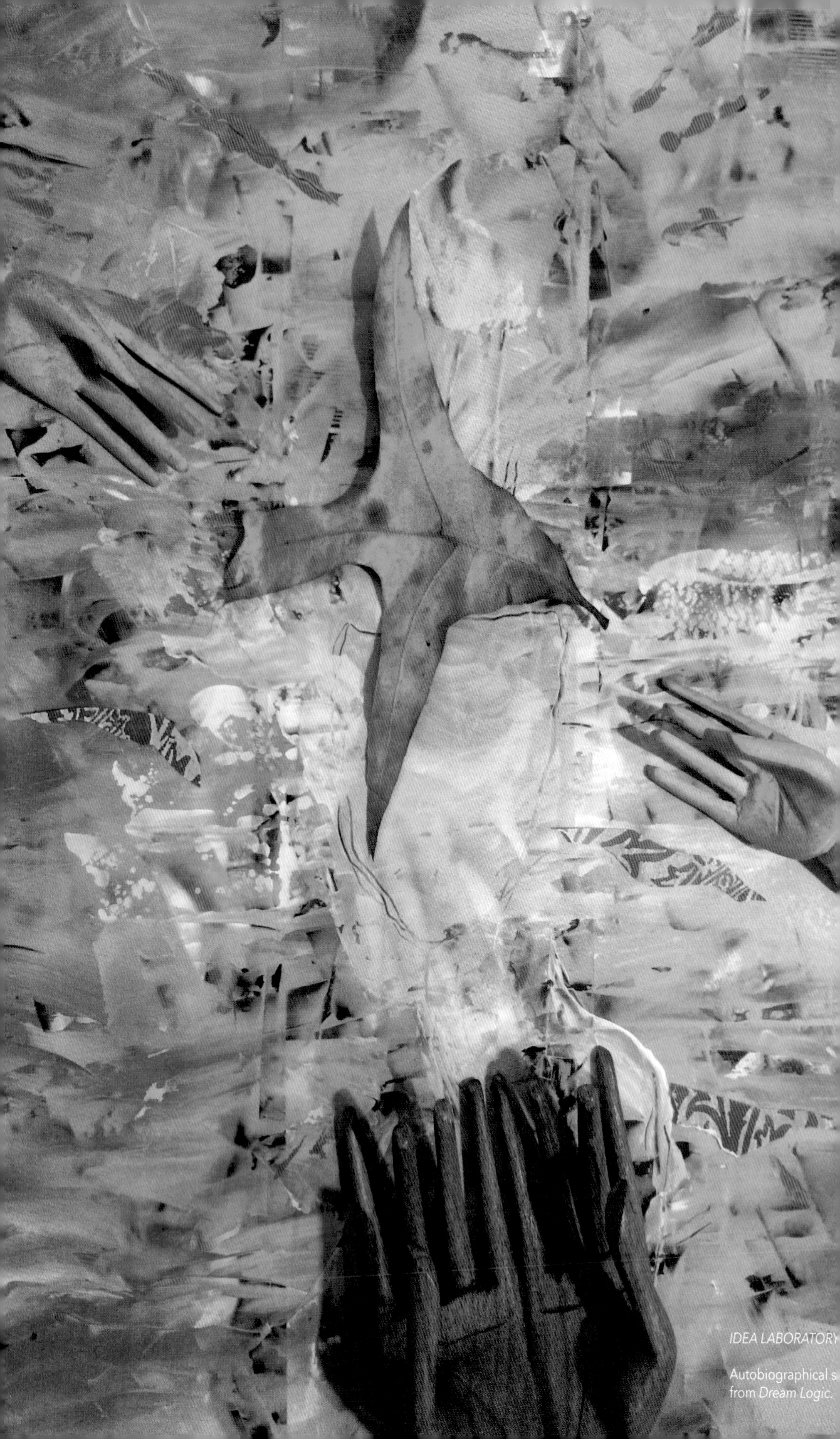

IDEA LABORATORY

Autobiographical s
from *Dream Logic.*

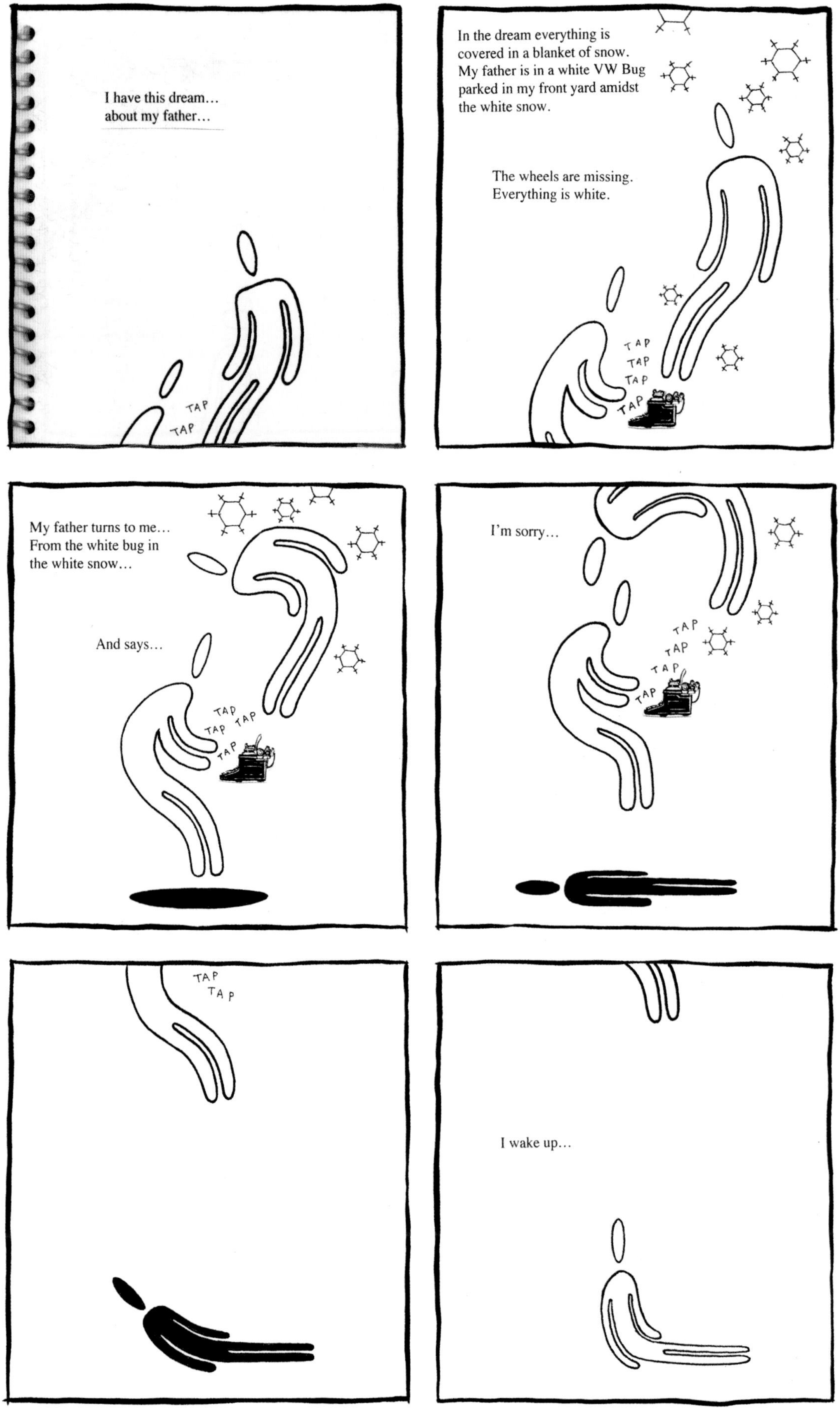
I have this dream…
about my father…
TAP
TAP
In the dream everything is covered in a blanket of snow. My father is in a white VW Bug parked in my front yard amidst the white snow.
The wheels are missing. Everything is white.
TAP
TAP
TAP
TAP
My father turns to me… From the white bug in the white snow…
And says…
TAP
TAP
TAP
TAP
I'm sorry…
TAP
TAP
TAP
TAP
TAP
TAP
I wake up…

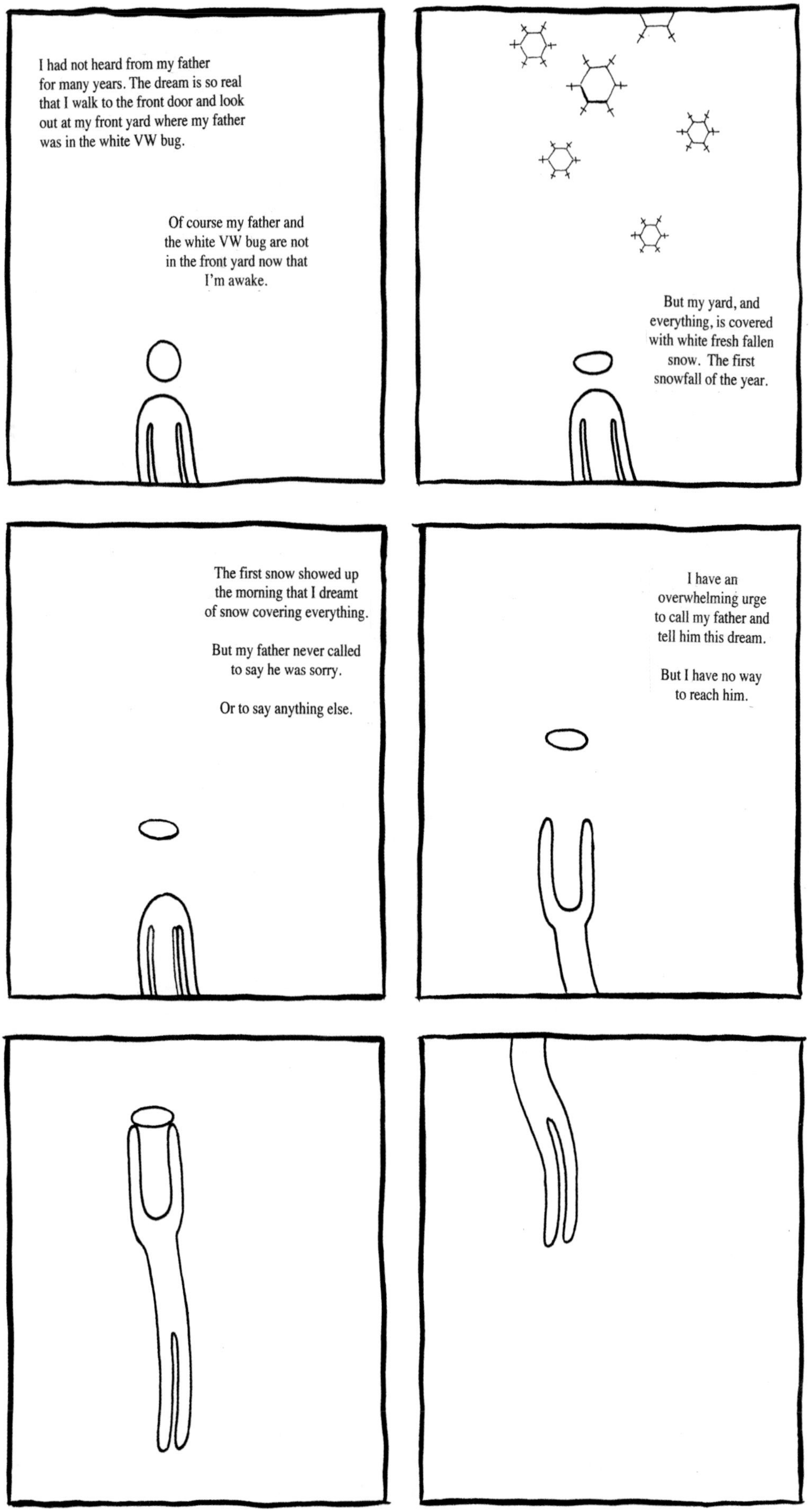
I had not heard from my father for many years. The dream is so real that I walk to the front door and look out at my front yard where my father was in the white VW bug.
Of course my father and the white VW bug are not in the front yard now that I'm awake.
But my yard, and everything, is covered with white fresh fallen snow. The first snowfall of the year.
The first snow showed up the morning that I dreamt of snow covering everything.
But my father never called to say he was sorry.
Or to say anything else.
I have an overwhelming urge to call my father and tell him this dream.
But I have no way to reach him.

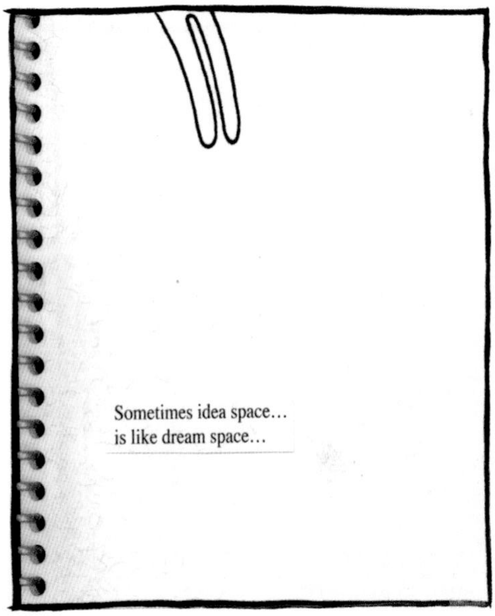
Sometimes idea space…
is like dream space…

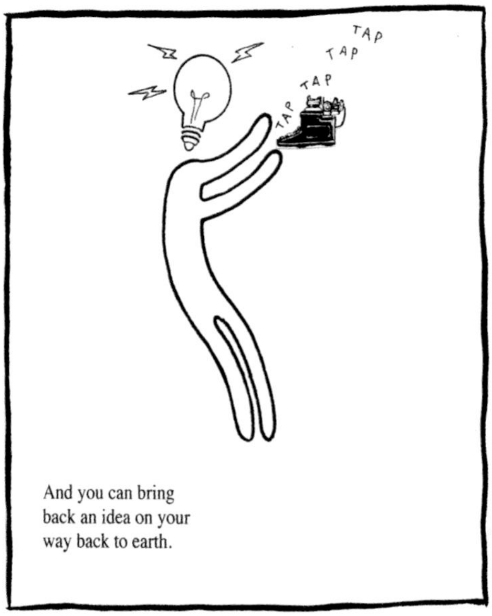
TAP
TAP
TAP
TAP
And you can bring
back an idea on your
way back to earth.

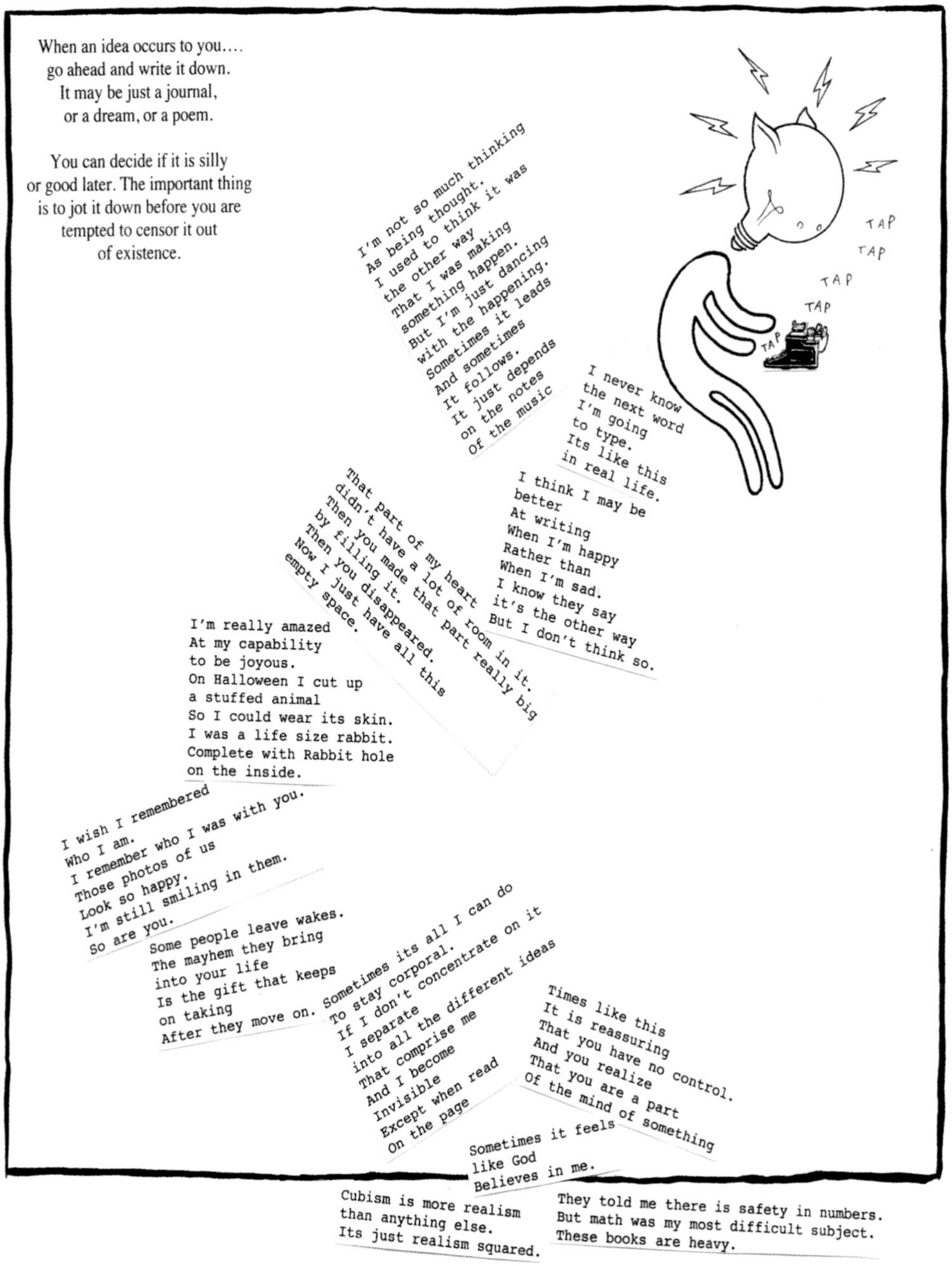
When an idea occurs to you….
go ahead and write it down.
It may be just a journal,
or a dream, or a poem.
You can decide if it is silly
or good later. The important thing
is to jot it down before you are
tempted to censor it out
of existence.
TAP
TAP
TAP
TAP
TAP
I'm not so much thinking
As being thought.
I used to think it was
the other way
That I was making
something happen.
But I'm just dancing
with the happening.
Sometimes it leads
And sometimes
It follows.
It just depends
on the notes
Of the music
I never know
the next word
I'm going
to type.
Its like this
in real life.
I think I may be
better
At writing
When I'm happy
Rather than
When I'm sad.
I know they say
it's the other way
But I don't think so.
That part of my heart
didn't have a lot of room in it.
Then you made that part really big
by filling it.
Then you disappeared.
Now I just have all this
empty space.
I'm really amazed
At my capability
to be joyous.
On Halloween I cut up
a stuffed animal
So I could wear its skin.
I was a life size rabbit.
Complete with Rabbit hole
on the inside.
I wish I remembered
Who I am.
I remember who I was with you.
Those photos of us
Look so happy.
I'm still smiling in them.
So are you.
Some people leave wakes.
The mayhem they bring
into your life
Is the gift that keeps
on taking
After they move on.
Sometimes its all I can do
To stay corporal.
If I don't concentrate on it
I separate
into all the different ideas
That comprise me
And I become
Invisible
Except when read
On the page
Times like this
It is reassuring
That you have no control.
And you realize
That you are a part
Of the mind of something
Sometimes it feels
like God
Believes in me.
Cubism is more realism
than anything else.
Its just realism squared.
They told me there is safety in numbers.
But math was my most difficult subject.
These books are heavy.

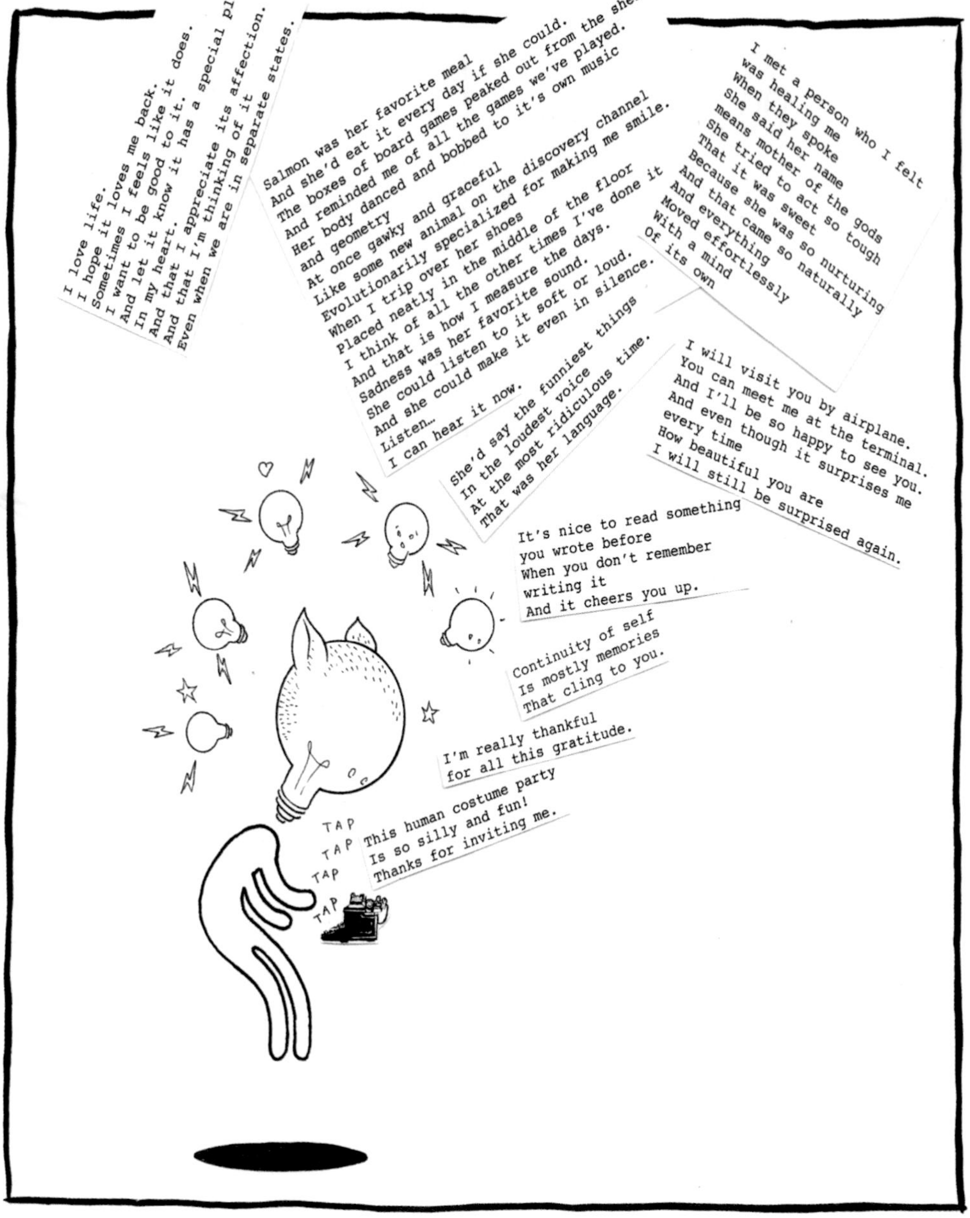
I love life.
I hope it loves me back.
Sometimes I feels like it does.
I want to be good to it.
And let it know it has a special place
In my heart.
And that I appreciate its affection.
And that I'm thinking of it
Even when we are in separate states.
Salmon was her favorite meal
And she'd eat it every day if she could.
The boxes of board games peaked out from the shelf
And reminded me of all the games we've played.
Her body danced and bobbed to it's own music
and geometry
At once gawky and graceful
Like some new animal on the discovery channel
Evolutionarily specialized for making me smile.
When I trip over her shoes
Placed neatly in the middle of the floor
I think of all the other times I've done it
And that is how I measure the days.
Sadness was her favorite sound.
She could listen to it soft or loud.
And she could make it even in silence.
Listen…
I can hear it now.
I met a person who I felt
was healing me
When they spoke
She said her name
means mother of the gods
She tried to act so tough
That it was sweet
Because she was so nurturing
And that came so naturally
And everything
Moved effortlessly
With a mind
Of its own
She'd say the funniest things
In the loudest voice
At the most ridiculous time.
That was her language.
I will visit you by airplane.
You can meet me at the terminal.
And I'll be so happy to see you.
And even though it surprises me
every time
How beautiful you are
I will still be surprised again.
It's nice to read something
you wrote before
When you don't remember
writing it
And it cheers you up.
Continuity of self
Is mostly memories
That cling to you.
I'm really thankful
for all this gratitude.
TAP
TAP
TAP
TAP
This human costume party
Is so silly and fun!
Thanks for inviting me.

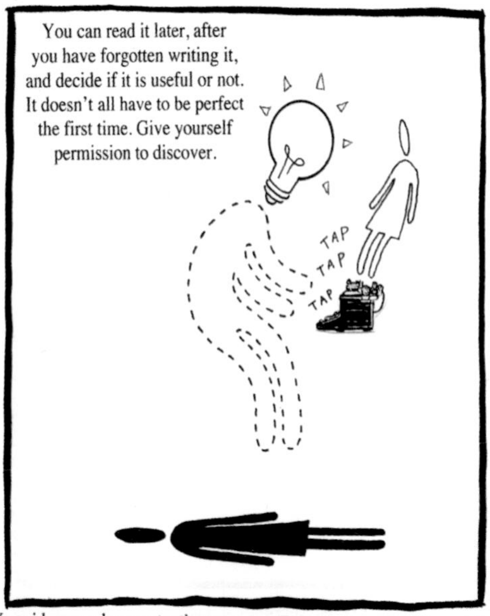
You can read it later, after you have forgotten writing it, and decide if it is useful or not. It doesn't all have to be perfect the first time. Give yourself permission to discover.
TAP
TAP
TAP

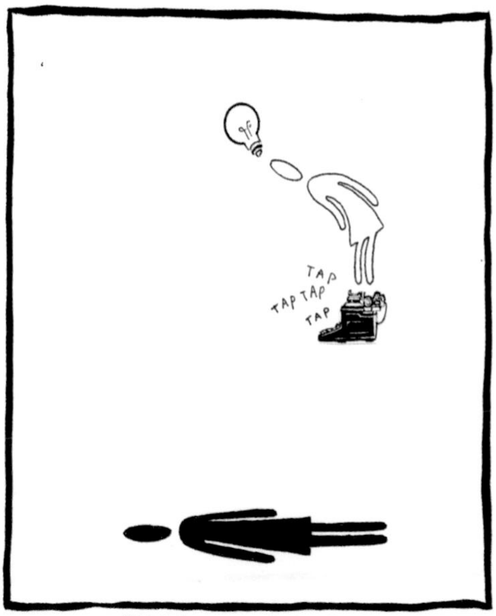
TAP
TAP TAP
TAP

Your ideas can be smarter than you are. They can have a life beyond you.

This is just an experiment. This is our playground.

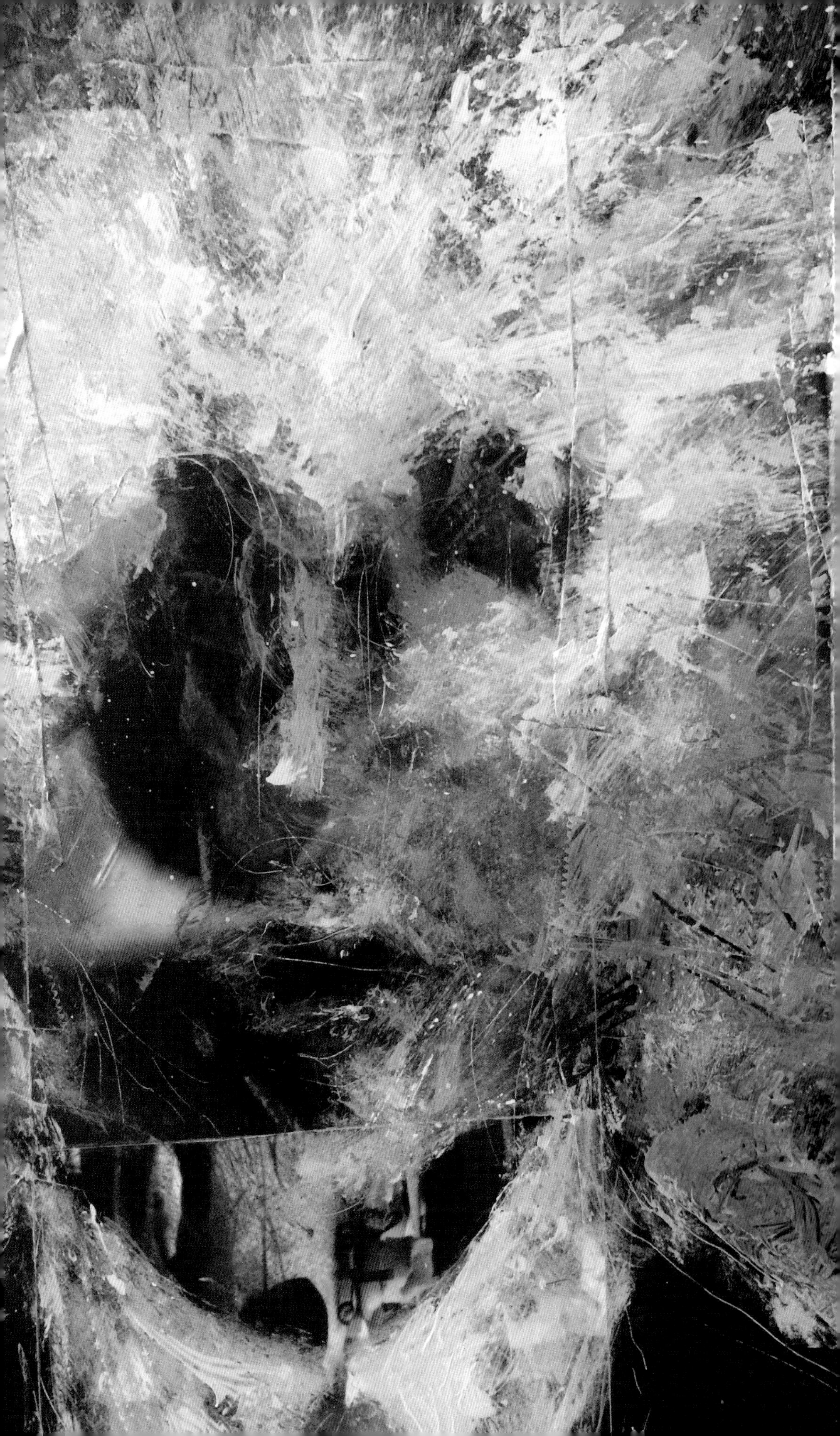

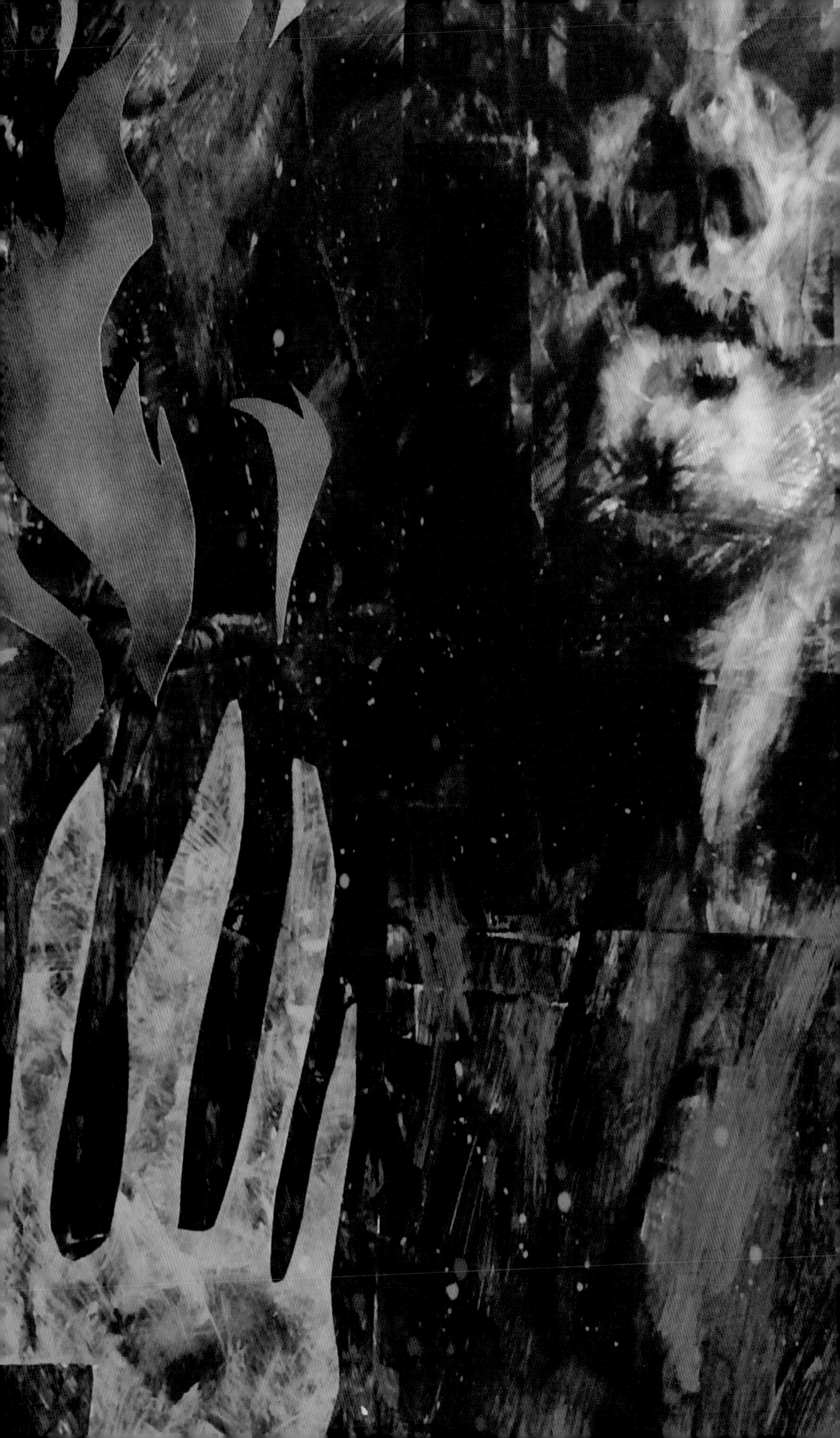

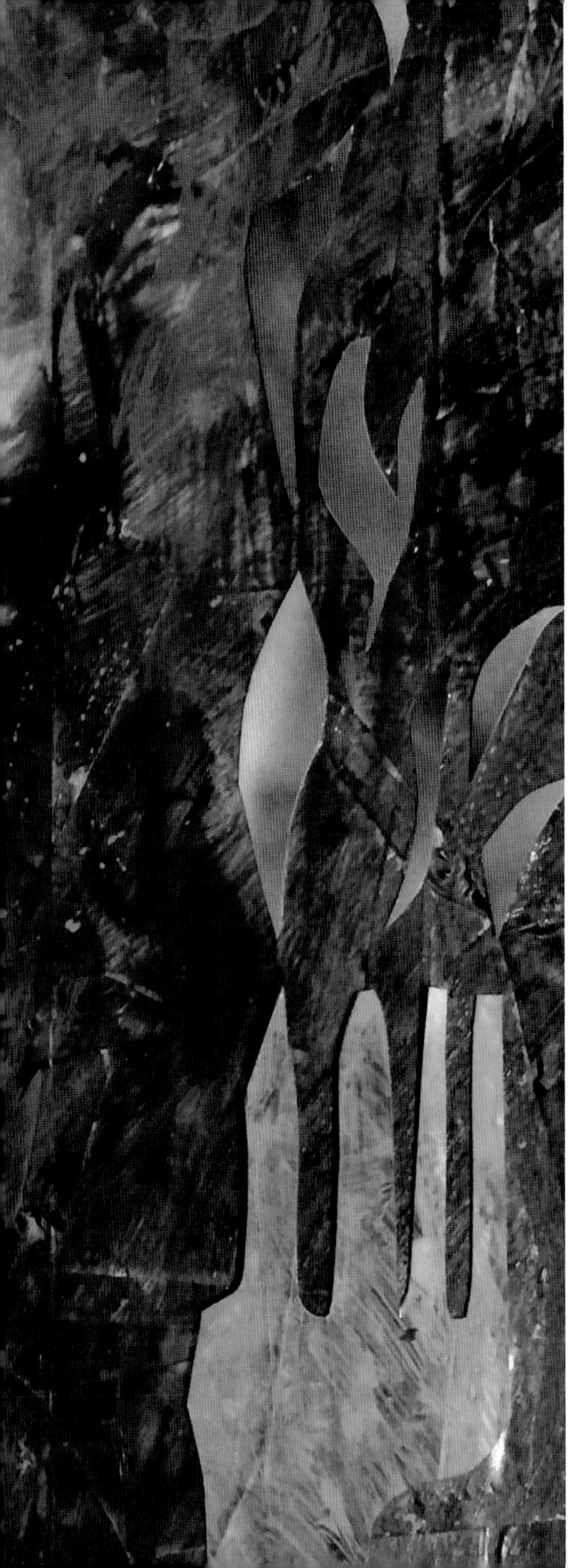

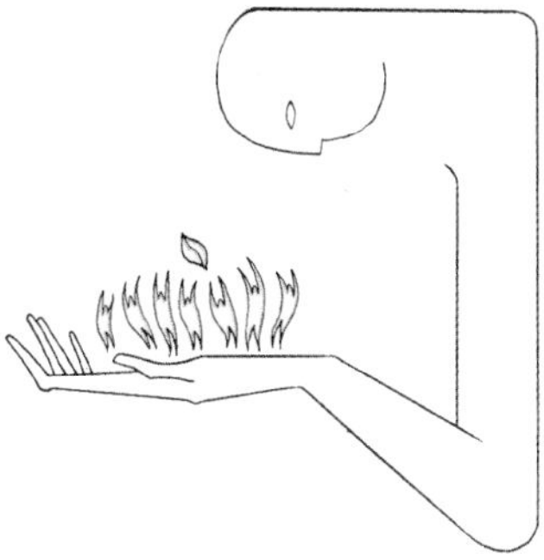

PROMETHEUS
ETERNAL

Commisioned by the Philadelphia Museum of Art for inclusion in their exhibit of the works of Michelangelo, Titian, and Rubens with the mythical Prometheus as their subject.

The museum contacted Locust Moon which had published my *Lil Kabuki story in Nemo: Dream Another Dream.*

Locust Moon published the *Prometheus Eternal* book with the Museum and both the book and the original art are on exhibit at the museum with the works of the masters.

A talk was held at the museum with myself, Bill Sienkiewicz and Yuko Shimizu for us to discuss our works in the exhibit and book.
Grant Morrison, Dave McKean, Paul Pope, Farel Dalrymple also contributed stories to the book about this mythical story of the creative spark.

Here is mine.

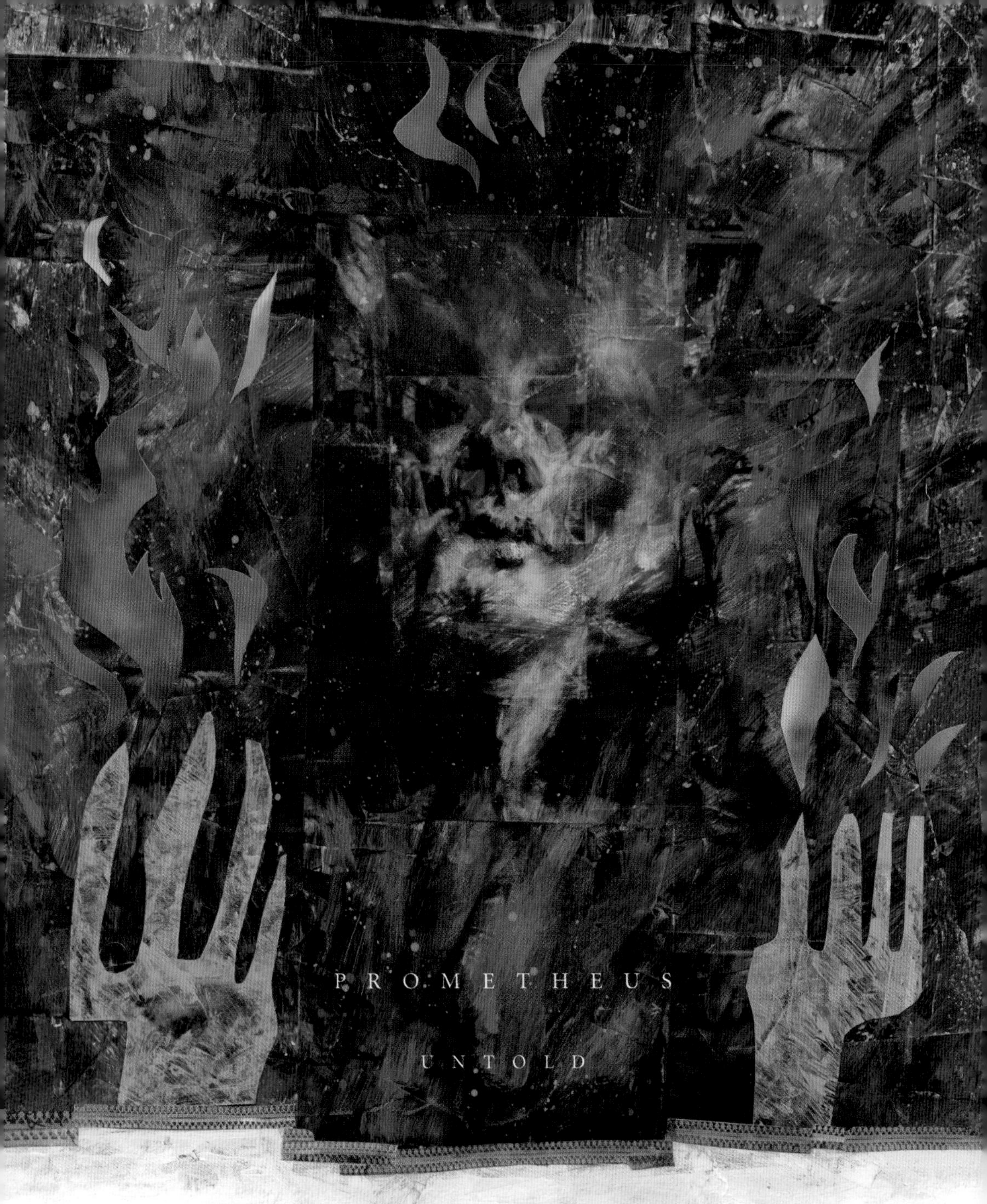
P R O M E T H E U S
U N T O L D

by DAVID MACK

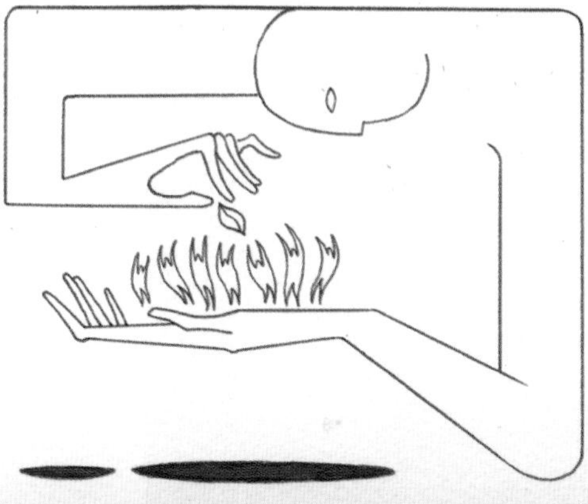

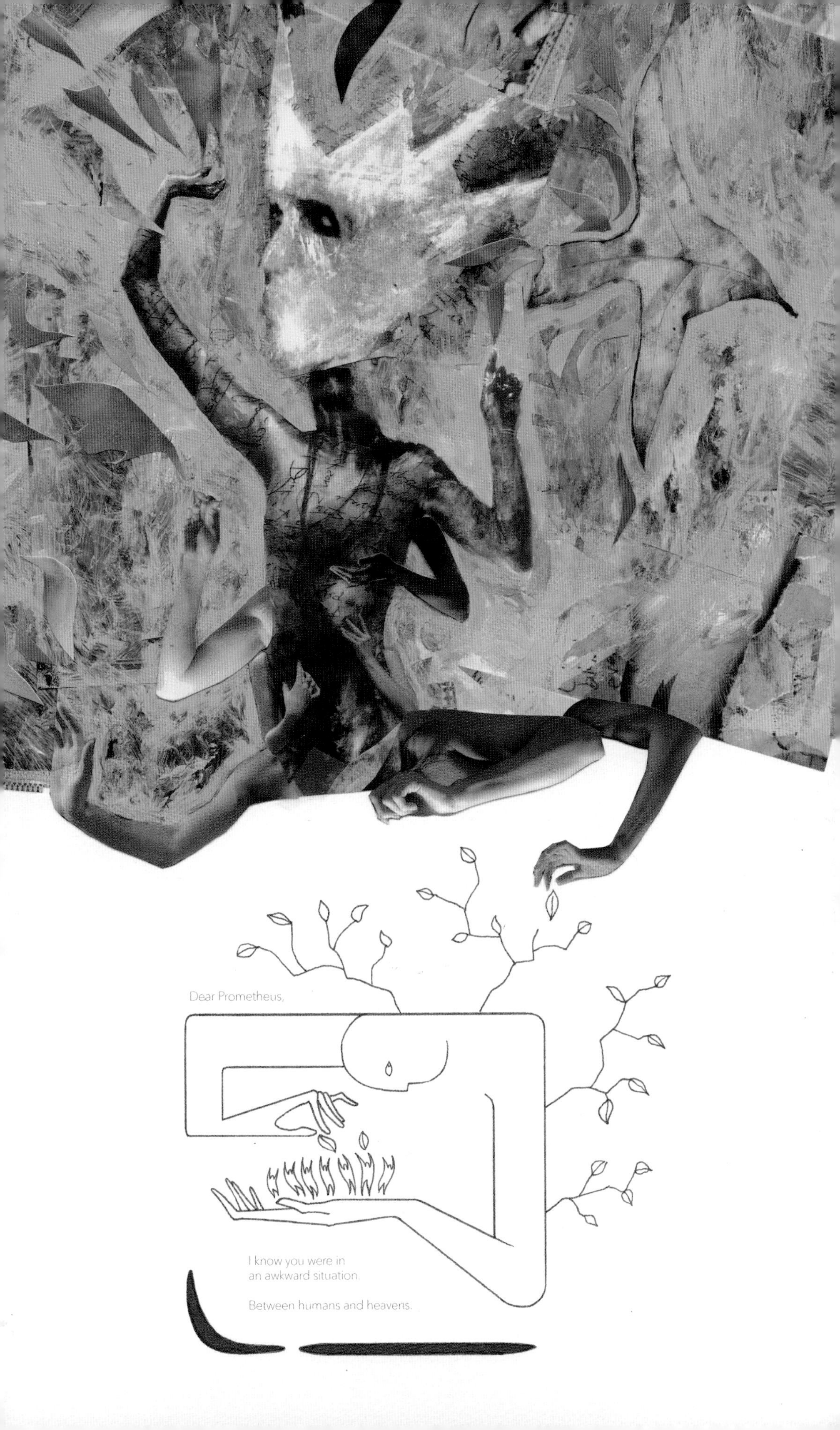
Dear Prometheus,
I know you were in
an awkward situation.
Between humans and heavens.

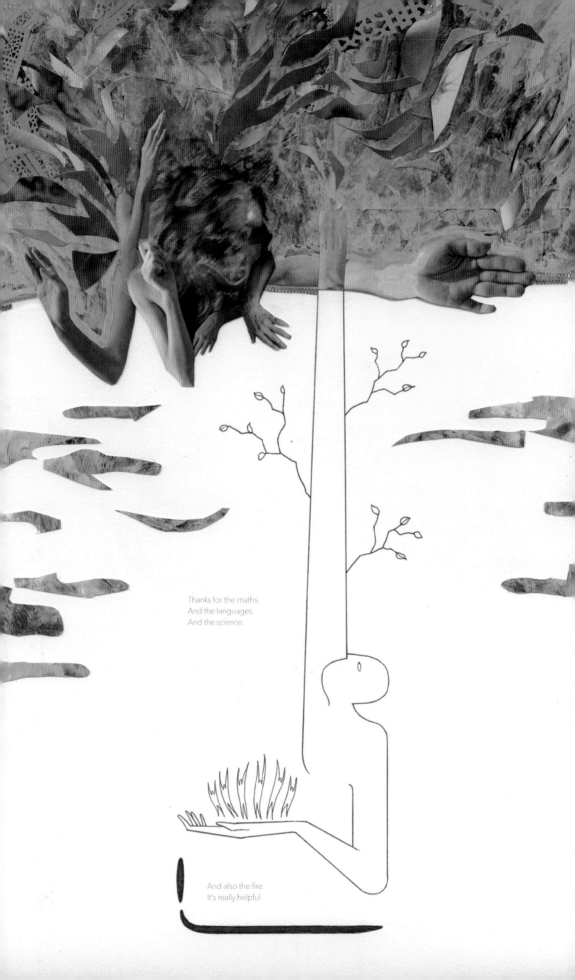

Thanks for the maths.
And the languages.
And the science.

And also the fire.
It's really helpful.

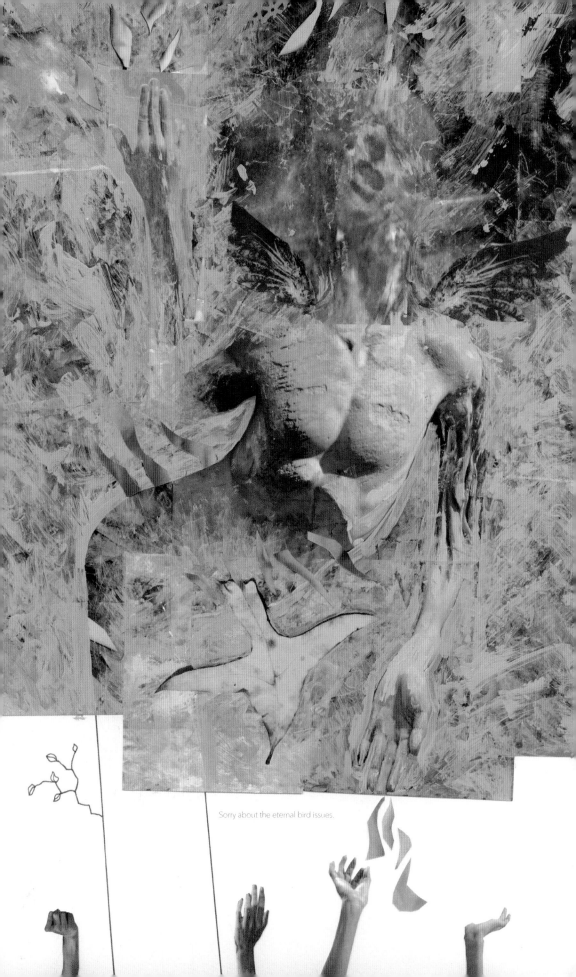

Sorry about the eternal bird issues.

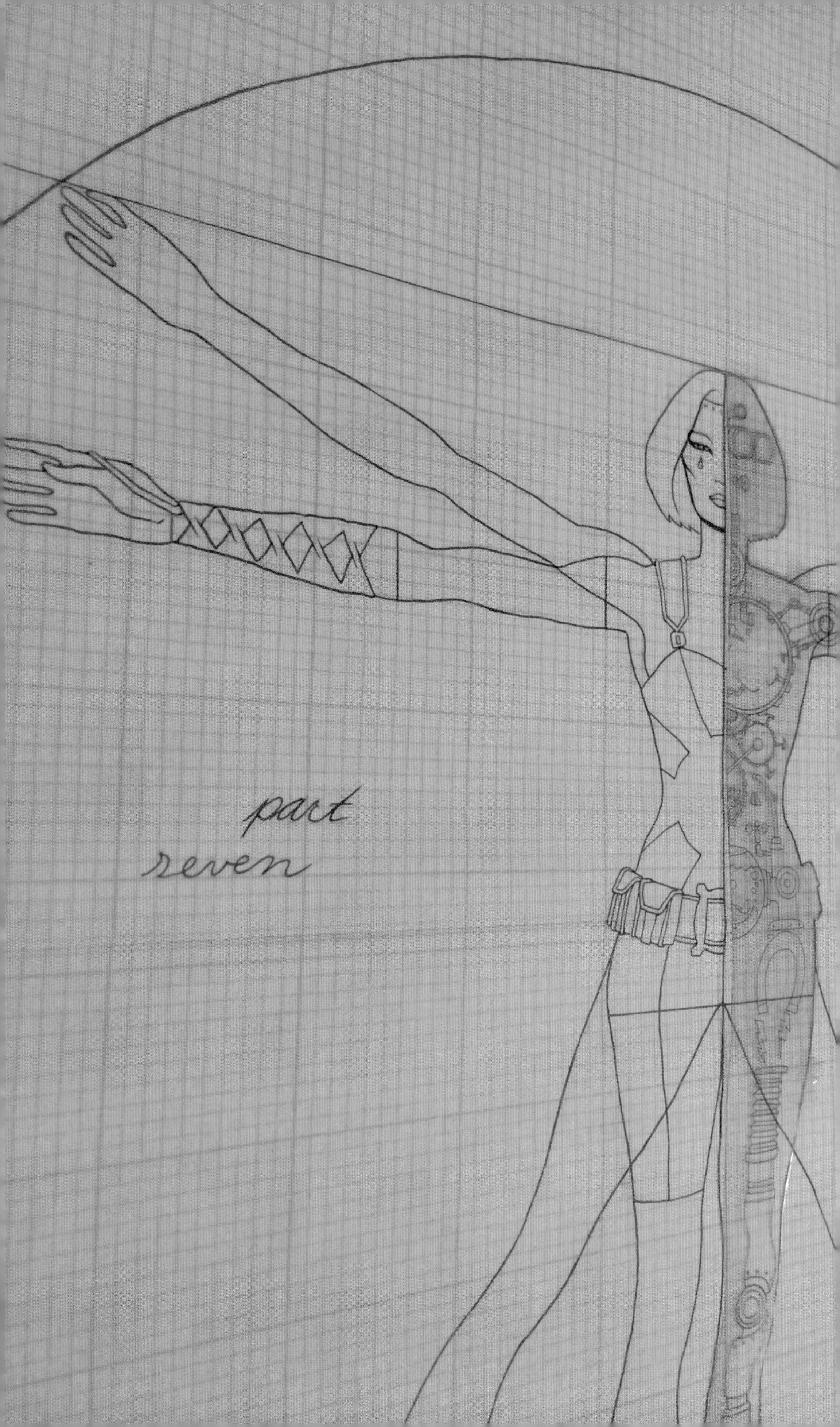
part
seven

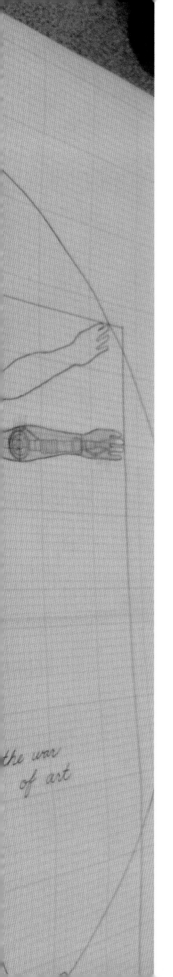

The Shaping of Things Electric

[S t o r i e s & M i n d s]

David Mack Afterword to Philip K. Dick's
"*Do Androids Dream of Electric Sheep?*"

July 1984: I'm 11 years old when I see *Blade Runner* on cable TV at a friend's house. I can never un-see it. I watched this film at such a young age, such a formative time in my hard-wiring, that I cannot escape it having an integral (even unconscious) lasting effect on me. In the same way that The Bible was my introduction to literature as a very young child, my mother reading Bible stories to me at night... I cannot escape the structure and archetypes of its stories in terms of how I tell my own stories and interpret others.

Watching *Blade Runner* at this early stage is compounded by the fact that I grew up in a house with no television, and I had no access to the cinema. I had little experience of common television and popular film culture, let alone preparation for this level of vision brought to screen. So even though I saw this film two years after it came out, on a tiny television in my childhood friend's kitchen, at eleven years old... I was moved.

January 1993: I begin work on my first creator-owned comic series *Kabuki*. By now I know that the film *Blade Runner* was adapted from the book *Do Androids Dream of Electric Sheep* and I had an appreciation for Philip K. Dick's use of science fiction to turn the volume up on the quintessential human questions. You can use the future to comment on the present. You can use something non-human as a metaphor to get to the essence of the truly human questions.

November 1994: *Kabuki* is published. Taking place in near-future Japan, there are nods to *Blade Runner* in the story (the visuals of "*Future Noir*", and the combination of this with what Joseph Campbell would call the classic "Hero's Journey", the quest to meet your maker, to discover your true destiny [or programming], the search for your true identity and role in the world). There are conscious nods. And probably unconscious ripple effects on the page as well. And those ripple effects keep happening. Even off of the page. A synchronicity that has its own "organizing principle."

June 2003: I get a phone call from the producer of the film *Waking Life* (and producer of the Philip K. Dick film adaptation *A Scanner Darkly*). His name is Tommy Pallotta. He has picked up *Kabuki* (Vol 5: *Metamorphosis*) at a bookstore in New York and asks me to collaborate with Hampton Fancher (*Blade Runner* Screenwriter) and novelist Jonathon Lethem (who also happens to be a PKD scholar) on a project. *Blade Runner* screenwriter Hampton Fancher & I (with Tommy as producer) are to adapt Jonathon Letham's novel *Amnesia Moon* into a kind of animated story.

November 2007: Fast forward. Portland. Bagdad Theater. I'm at lunch with *Fight Club* author Chuck Palahniuk. We are discussing Philip K. Dick, F. Scott Fitzgerald, the filming of the adaptation of Chuck's novel *Choke*, and an adaptation of Philip K. Dick's *Electric Ant* that I have been asked to write... That Philip K. Dick's daughters personally have asked me to write. Also we discuss where ideas come from and how projects take shape (including where Philip K. Dick believed his ideas came from). We'll get back to this.

July 2003: Rewind. The project with Hampton Fancher & Jonathan Lethem (I think it was for Microsoft) doesn't make it to the finished stage. Also I'm in the middle of writing and drawing *Daredevil* at Marvel Comics and my publishing schedule obligations limit how much extra work I can do. Producer Tommy Pallotta says we will work on something else in the future.

September 2006: The future. Tommy Pallotta emails me. He has just finished filming the Philip K. Dick film adaptation of *A Scanner Darkly* (also directed by *Waking Life* director Richard Linklater). Tommy wants to discuss collaborating on *Kabuki* as his next film.

April 1982: I am 9 years old. My mother turns to me in the car and tells me that aliens cannot be trusted. That they are evil. I'm upset by this.

October 2006: Tommy Pallotta & I meet in Los Angeles to discuss. After 20th Century Fox buying the film option for *Kabuki* four times in a row, hiring me to write the treatment and work with Academy Award winning screenwriter John Sayles on the script, after HBO envisioning *Kabuki* as a television series, after Quentin Tarantino's brilliant producer Lawrence Bender proposed a fantastic outside-the-box solution for filming *Kabuki* in Japan... Tommy and I discuss the possibilities of working together on the *Kabuki* film.

We also discuss childhood experiences: him

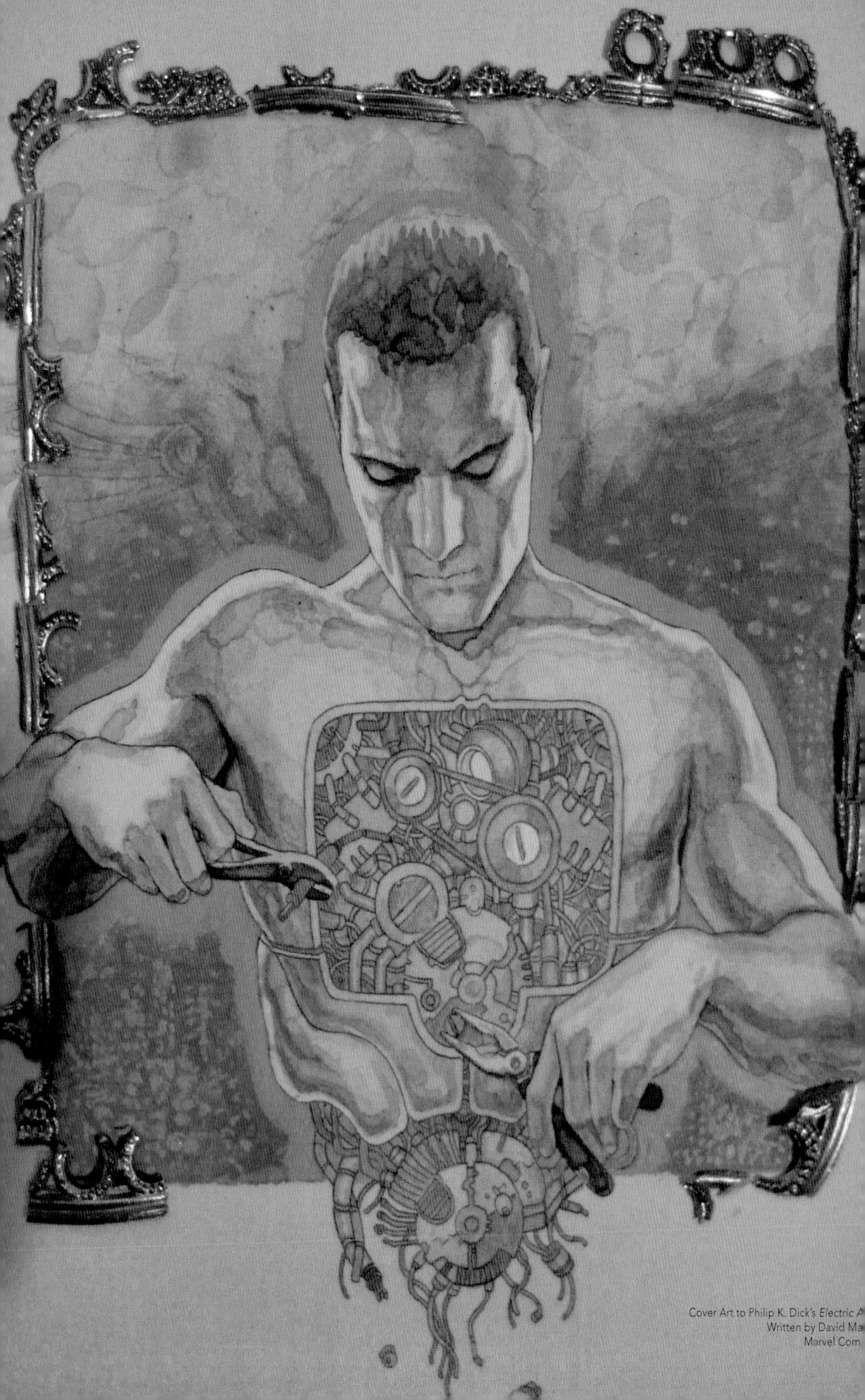

Cover Art to Philip K. Dick's *Electric A*
Written by David Ma
Marvel Com

being tested and cultivated for psychic powers as a child by an organization in Friendswood, Texas (I know the place because my uncle who works at NASA lives there.)… And my childhood growing up with a mother who became a prayer-healer, a Book of Revelation interpreter, and survivalist preparing for the end-times in a religious movement of her own making.

We also discuss Philip K. Dick.

January 2007: I'm reading a biography of Philip K. Dick, while in the process of working on KABUKI: The Alchemy. I saw the PKD biography by chance at a bookstore and bought it on impulse to read after working on The Alchemy at night before I fall asleep. It is while reading this biography that Tommy Pallotta calls me and says that Philip K. Dick's daughters Isa and Laura would like to meet me. I had just been reading about them being born in the PKD biography. Ripple effects are happening. Dots are connecting.

April 1982: I am 9 years old. I ask my mother if the Aliens can still go to Heaven when they die. My mother tells me no. She says the aliens cannot go to Heaven.

February 2007: Santa Monica, California I am at lunch with Isa and Laura, Philip K. Dick's daughters who run Electric Shepherd Productions. Tommy had given them my Kabuki books. He has asked me if I would be interested in adapting PKD into comics and graphic novels. Isa and Laura tell me they like my work in Kabuki and would entrust me to adapt their father's work.

July 1984: I'm 11 yrs old. Watching Blade Runner on a small television in a friend's kitchen in Kentucky.

February 2007: Santa Monica. Tommy and I Bike-riding along the beach through Venice, Malibu, to Manhattan Beach in LA, all the while trying to figure out what will be the best way to adapt Philip K. Dick stories into comic book & graphic novel form. We enlist the help of novelist Jonathan Lethem (who has an incredible knowledge of PKD and his work), and the three of us comb through the works of Philip K. Dick in search of what we think can be the right PKD story to begin an original adaptation into comic book form. We all reach one conclusion. Electric Ant.

A Tale of Ants & Sheep (The Electric Variety): Electric Ant is a story by Philip K. Dick that was published in 1969. The germ of the idea of Electric Ant became the DNA for Do Androids Dream of Electric Sheep on which the film Blade Runner was based. Philip K. Dick would at times build upon ideas explored in his short stories, and develop the concept in new directions, or from a different perspective, in the larger format of a novel.

We (novelist Jonathan Lethem, producer Tommy Pallotta, and myself) chose this story as our first choice for adaptation of PKD into comics because we felt the story has what we considered the classic quintessential Philip K. Dickian themes. The story asks the enduring existential questions: Who am I? Who created me? What was I created for? Do I have free will? Am I limited by my programming? Can I evolve into something beyond my original programming? What is reality? Is the way I perceive reality different than a fixed reality? Can I alter my perceptions to transcend my ego and programming limitations and see a pure reality? Does my internal reality affect the external reality? Which is more real?

It was most important to me to be respectful to Philip K.

Dick's story, to communicate the themes by taking advantage of the new opportunities that the comic book medium offers, and that my version would ring true to his daughters Laura and Isa. I cannot describe how happy I was that Philip K. Dick's daughters liked the script that I wrote. That meant everything to me.

From the beginning, the adaptation is planned to be very true to the original story, but there is more room to develop things in the comic book form that are only hinted at in the short story. In this case, that was one of the advantages of adapting a short story instead of a novel. In adapting a novel to film or graphic novel, you may have to edit it down. It can be a reductive process. With Electric Ant, I was able to let it develop organically into the new format in ways that expand on ideas and scenes that are only hinted at in the short story.

The moving parts of Electric Ant go like this: A man wakes up in the hospital from a traffic accident only to have the doctor tell him they cannot treat him because he is a robot. Naturally, this raises a lot of questions. Who made him? Who owns him? What is his program? Can he alter it? Has he been walking around seeing things differently than they really are? And once he learns how his reality functions… what if he begins to tinker with that? How much of reality does that really effect? What are the external ripple effects to what you change inside yourself?
All very human questions at their core… but made immediate and visceral through the metaphor of artificial intelligence. The metaphor itself asking the question: "What is artificial?" In terms of… "What is reality?"

I wrote the script adaptation of Electric Ant that I would write if I were turning the story into a film. It is not planned to be identical to the short story, but we decided early on that it was going to be very true to the source material. We did not want to change it into a different story with only minor similarities. Everything in the short story is adapted into this version, but things that are suggested in the original story are given more room to breathe and evolve. Some ideas and details that are mentioned only once at the beginning of the short story, now have room to return with a twist. And there is a sort of love story that developed. It is not an action story, though there is action in it. It became a kind of mystery, and a love story, with the mystery being the existential questions that are now made very real and immediate that the protagonist must strive to answer.

That is one of the fascinating opportunities in Science Fiction, particularly in how Philip K. Dick approached it: Take the existential questions of life, and through the metaphors of futurism, make them the practical, necessary, visceral, questions that propel the story and demand answers to satisfy the characters' immediate hierarchy of needs.

The biggest challenge of adaptation was that in the Electric Ant short story, the main character is mostly alone, thinking to himself (interestingly, this parallels how Screenwriter Hampton Fancher first envisioned the adaptation of Electric Sheep for the Blade Runner script). The characters of Danceman & Sarah are in the Electric Ant short story, but briefly. In my comic book adaptation, I let the characters of Sarah & Danceman develop more as they gave opportunity for the protagonist to voice his thoughts through interaction and discussion with these external characters, instead of him thinking most of the action the way it happened in the original short story. This afforded more visual opportunity for interaction between the characters and room for all of the characters to develop because of that, and it lead to the biggest change from the source material, in that there is a kind of love story that evolves in the adaptation. This lets the action externalize and lends itself to the visual language of the new medium.

Externalizing the world of the main character in *Electric Ant* also gave an opportunity to further flesh out the world in a kind of Philip K. Dick universe or continuum that alludes to other Dickian ideas, themes, names & nods to details from his other books (suggesting perhaps that there is a possible interconnection).

The term "Electric Ant" refers to the characters of artificial intelligence (who mostly do not know they are not the real McCoy). In my adaptation, that term (Electric Ant) is used as a slang or slur term for these characters by the biological population. Of course in order to do that, there needs to be a more clinical term that precedes the slang. I decided to not introduce an unrelated name, but instead keep the spelling of *Electric Ant* intact, but push the words together. I introduced the clinical term for the model as an "Electricant" (with "Electric Ant" being the slang variation). Just as the *Electric Ant* story was the precursor for the novel *Electric Sheep* which became Blade Runner… the "Electricant" is the earlier, less sophisticated robotic model of the "Replicant". As such, the term is an example of suggesting thru-lines to an external world of the story (and the literary and filmic world of PKD), taking into consideration that most people know of Philip K. Dick through *Blade Runner* as their port of entry to his work.

February 2007: Santa Monica, California. Laura and Isa tell me they like my take on *Electric Ant.* Over lunch they mention that some publishers have heard inside word that we are developing *Electric Ant* and that I am writing it, and they have received publishing offers for the project. As of yet I've been working only directly with the Dick Estate: Isa and Laura, with Tommy Pallotta orchestrating it all. No publishers are yet involved. I mention to Laura and Isa that Marvel has had success in adapting Stephen King to comic books published through Marvel Comics. I offer that Marvel is the largest comic book publisher in the States, that I write for Marvel, and my book *Kabuki* is published at Marvel, and it may be a great opportunity for Marvel to publish Philip K. Dick in the form of the *Electric Ant* story we have developed. Isa and Laura are intrigued and they give me their blessing to personally discuss the idea with Marvel.

February 2007: New York. The Marvel Comics offices. 417 Fifth Ave. 10th floor. It is the Monday after the New York Comicon. I've just left the Flat Iron Building from a meeting with my editor at Macmillan the publisher of my childrens' book *The Shy Creatures* (about a shy girl who is a veterinarian to mythological and cryptozoological creatures). I'm here for a meeting with Marvel Comics publisher Dan Buckley. I tell him our plan for *Electric Ant* and he likes it. The Marvel Comics House of Ideas and the Philip K. Dick estate / Electric Shepherd Productions are officially introduced. Thus begins months of legalese in terms of a publishing agreement.

November 2007: I'm given a green light for *Electric Ant* at Marvel. I meet with my dear friend, writer Brian Michael Bendis in Portland. He is enlisted on the team as a special editor on the project, and he gives me feedback that helps me finesse the script (we literally sit down at his house watching *Blade Runner* together including all the special features from the box set and discuss the mechanics of visual storytelling and adaptation). I know my artist friend Paul Pope is a big PKD fan so I ask if he would like to contribute art for the project. Pope is in for doing the covers. Artist Pascal Alixe from Paris is capable of drawing in a multitude of style variations and he is selected to do the art for the series because there are a variety of realities and reality changes in the story that can be reflected by his visual dexterity in art-style shifts.

I won't meet Pascal until I'm in Paris in 2010 when he comes to say hello at my gallery exhibit there, well after our work together on the story is completed.

I have late night discussions with my comic book godfather and mentor Jim Steranko. Like with Brian Michael Bendis, just talking to Steranko makes me smarter and gives invaluable perspective on whatever I am working on. Art pages of the script begins to come in. I rewrite the script to accommodate unforeseen artistic details. This project goes from coincidence, to synchronicity, to idea, to three-dimensional physical material reality. Kind of like the structure of the story of *Electric Ant* itself.

July 2008: Marvel editors Mark Paniccia & Charlie Beckerman email that

Marvel needs an advance image for *Electric Ant* to use for the cover and advance promotion (including a presence at San Diego Comicon). I do a painting for the cover of *Electric Ant;* the character tinkering with the internal gizmos in his chest.

The idea of programming in *Electric Ant*, that the character has an unwinding tape of what he perceives as reality preset inside of him, the idea that he has natural inclinations for what he is "hard wired" to do, to see, to enjoy, to pursue, is a metaphor that I think most humans can relate too. Also the idea that there are things in his program that are naturally edited out of his daily narrative before they make it to his conscious frontal awareness, is also, I think, comparable to the unconscious and conscious editing that happens with all of us on a daily basis.

Once we become aware that our reality is limited by these things: what we perceive, what we project, and that we have blind spots about things that we are not perceiving… that epiphany that we are not at all living in one objective linear reality because of our blind spots and our programming (from nature and nurture)… when we become aware of these things, and that our reality can indeed be influenced by our own thought and actions more than we realized, we then have a liberty and a responsibility, even a mission, to be more consciously intent about how we create the narrative of our lives. I think this surfaces as one of the themes in *Electric Ant* and I tried to crystallize that in the painting of the cover.

November 2007: Portland. Bagdad Theater. Lunch with Chuck Palaniuk. We discuss where ideas come from. Chuck says he has been writing his new book all morning as if he is in a trance. We discuss writing as a form of meditation. And as an idea that begins inside us then begins to affect our material world the more we act on it. The idea that we begin with a compulsion, and once the writing happens, the rest of the ideas show up. I mention that William Gibson said something to the effect that when he is writing, its not just the conscious version of him that is talking to you now, it is that person in collaboration with another part of him that he does not always have reliable access to but that hopefully shows up when he begins writing. I discuss with Chuck how Philip K. Dick crystallizes the concepts we are discussing… through his work, his work methods, his religious experience, and his vast body of work as a whole, having cascading influence into the realms of fiction and popular culture entertainment, and but also prescience of our culture as a whole and what it has become. It is as if you have your own personal ideas and conscious programming, but also an "organizing principle" that shows up when your conscious and unconscious programming are in sync.

That synchronicity of conscious and unconscious tends to occur when you are able to immerse yourself into a kind of focus or meditation. Writing can do this. So can painting, drawing, sculpture or the focused physical labor of a craft or exercise.

Also I ask Chuck about the character's mother's name of Ida in his book *Choke*. Because my mother's name was also Ida and there was a dynamic in that book with adventures of the mother & child living on the fringe of things that I related to.

June 2008: Los Angeles. Chateau Marmont. Tommy and I meet with Isa and Kalen of Electric Shepherd productions. Isa (Philip K. Dick's daughter) gives me the go ahead to begin writing a film treatment for *Electric Ant.*

April 1982: I am 9 years old. I ask my mother, "If the

Aliens pray to God and get "saved' can they then go to Heaven"? My mother tells me no. She says the aliens are evil and they cannot be "saved". She says they cannot go to heaven. I'm disappointed.

2010: *Electric Ant* the comic book comes out from Marvel. It's become real in the three dimensional material world. Then the Hardcover collection and now the paperback. Each book an idea delivery system of PKD's concepts to new readers across time.

April 2010: San Francsicso. Wondercon. I'm signing books at the convention. Isa stops by with her children. Philip K. Dick's grandchildren. They are a delight. I give them a copy of my children's book *The Shy Creatures*. We have our picture taken together. I remember that I was their age when I first saw *Blade Runner*. I lose myself in a moment fascinated by the ripple effects. I think of the metaphor in *Electric Ant* of changing your reality on the inside and seeing that manifest itself externally in the three dimensional material world.

April 1982: I'm 9 years old. Disappointed and confused about the aliens not being able to get into Heaven, I ask my mother: "What about robots? Can robots go to Heaven?"

David Mack

Idea Space

February 2011

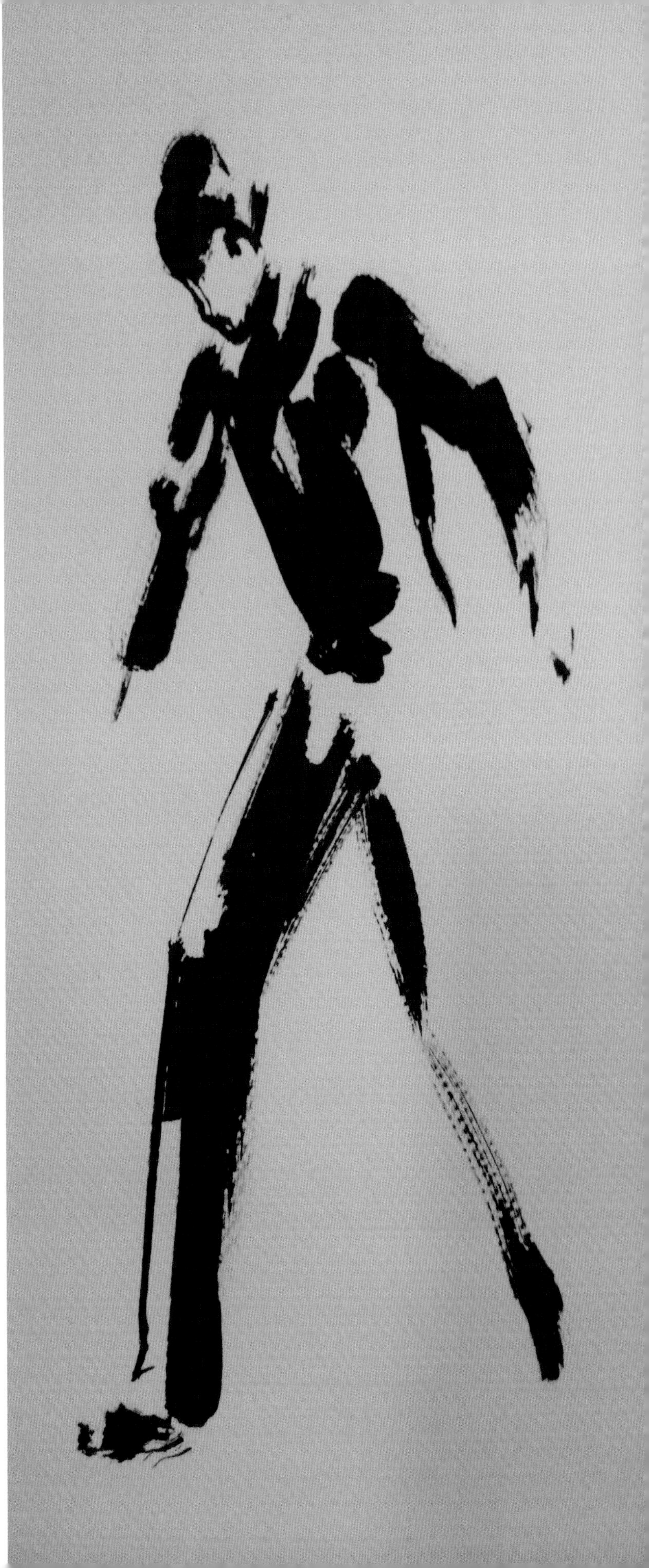

Facing page:

Flying Dutchman

Made with Tori Amos for her *Comic Book Tattoo* publication which won an Eisner Award at Comi-con International where Tori & I spoke at her panel about the book to a packed audience. The entire sequence collected here. I remember that I made this right after I had completed *The Alchemy*.

This page:

I painted Tori Amos for all of her calendars to benefit her RAINN charity. Some of my original paintings of her were auctioned off at the event for RAINN.

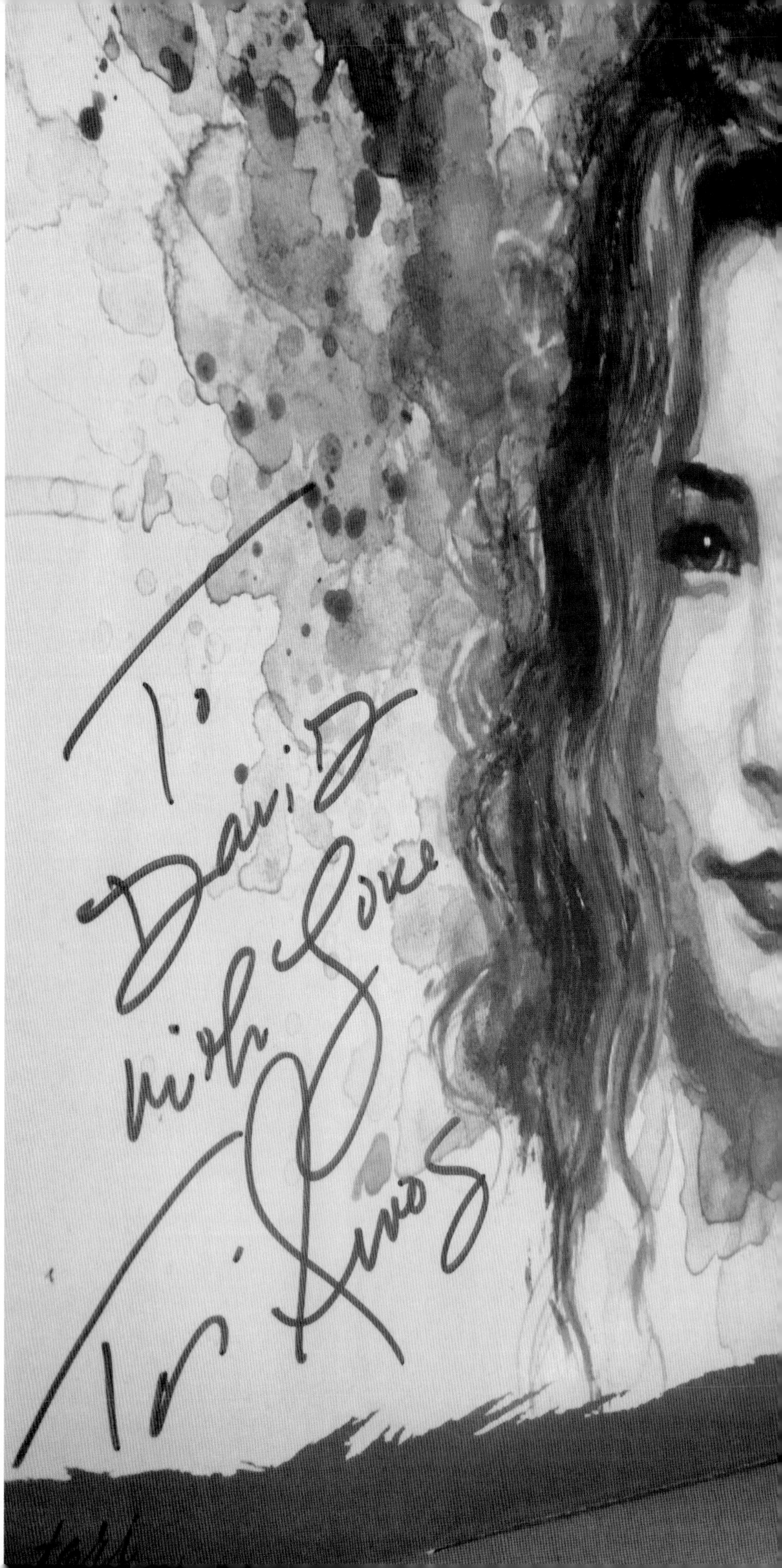
To David
with love
Tori Amos

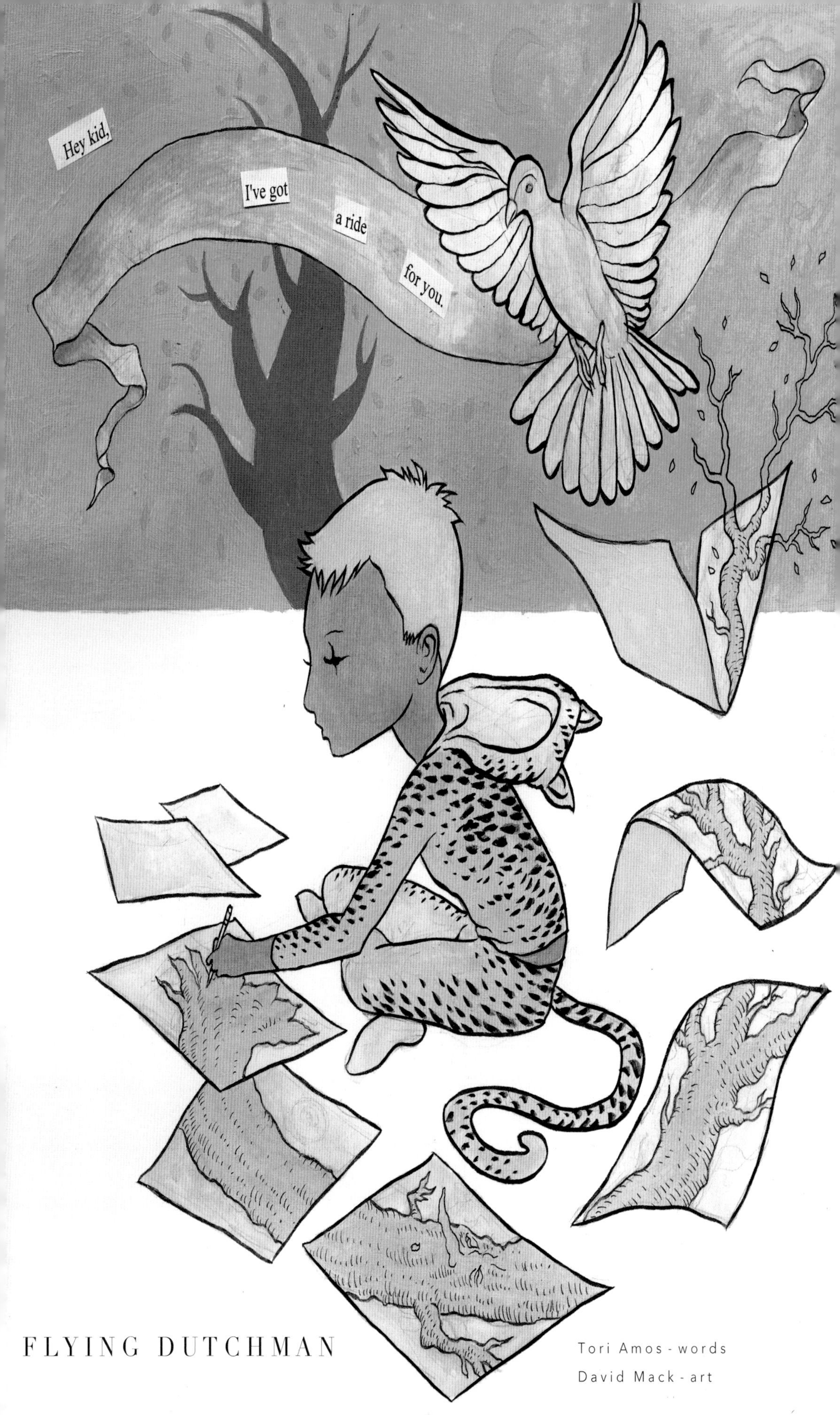
Hey kid,
I've got
a ride
for you.

FLYING DUTCHMAN

Tori Amos - words
David Mack - art

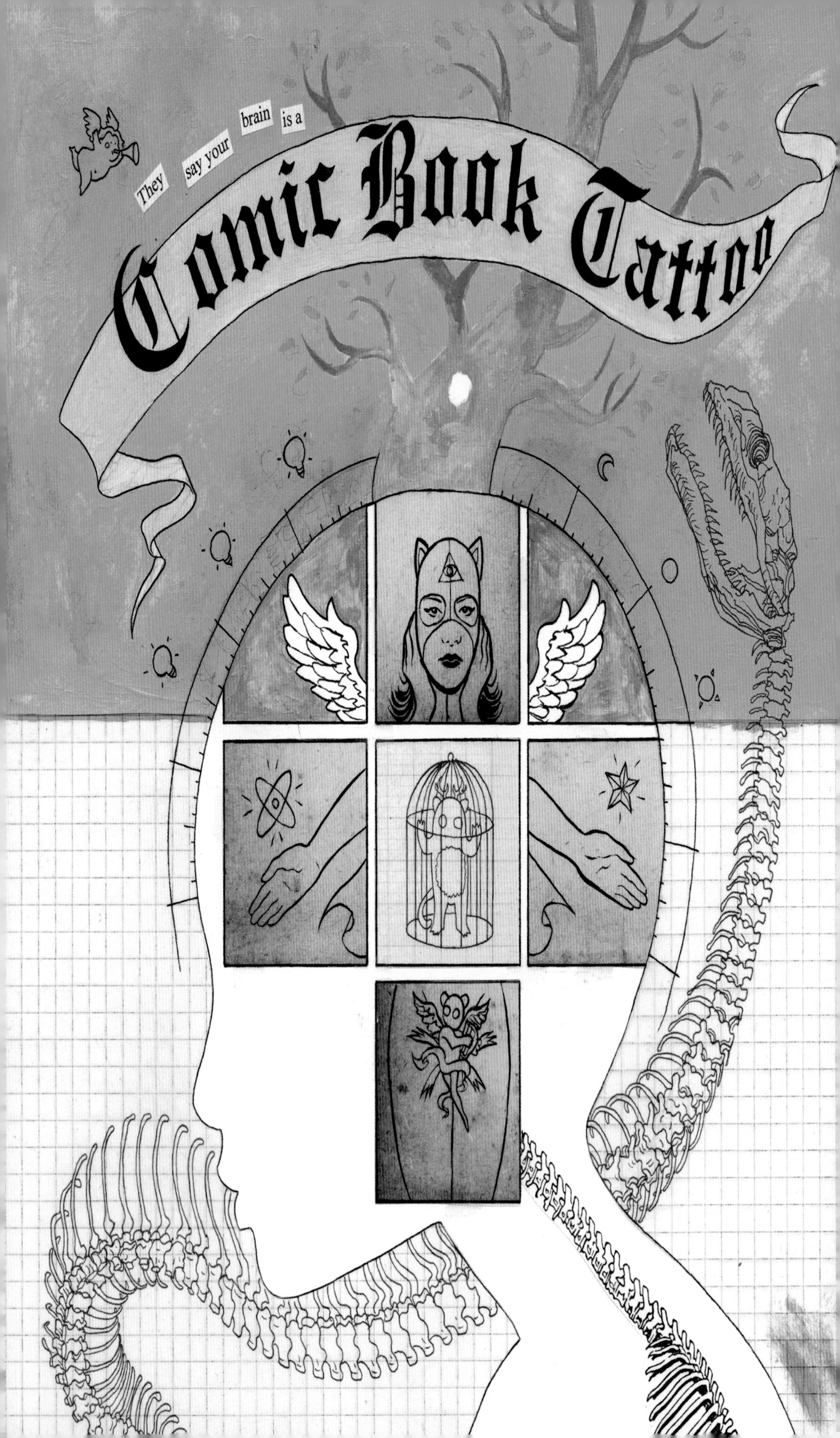
They say your brain is a
Comic Book Tattoo

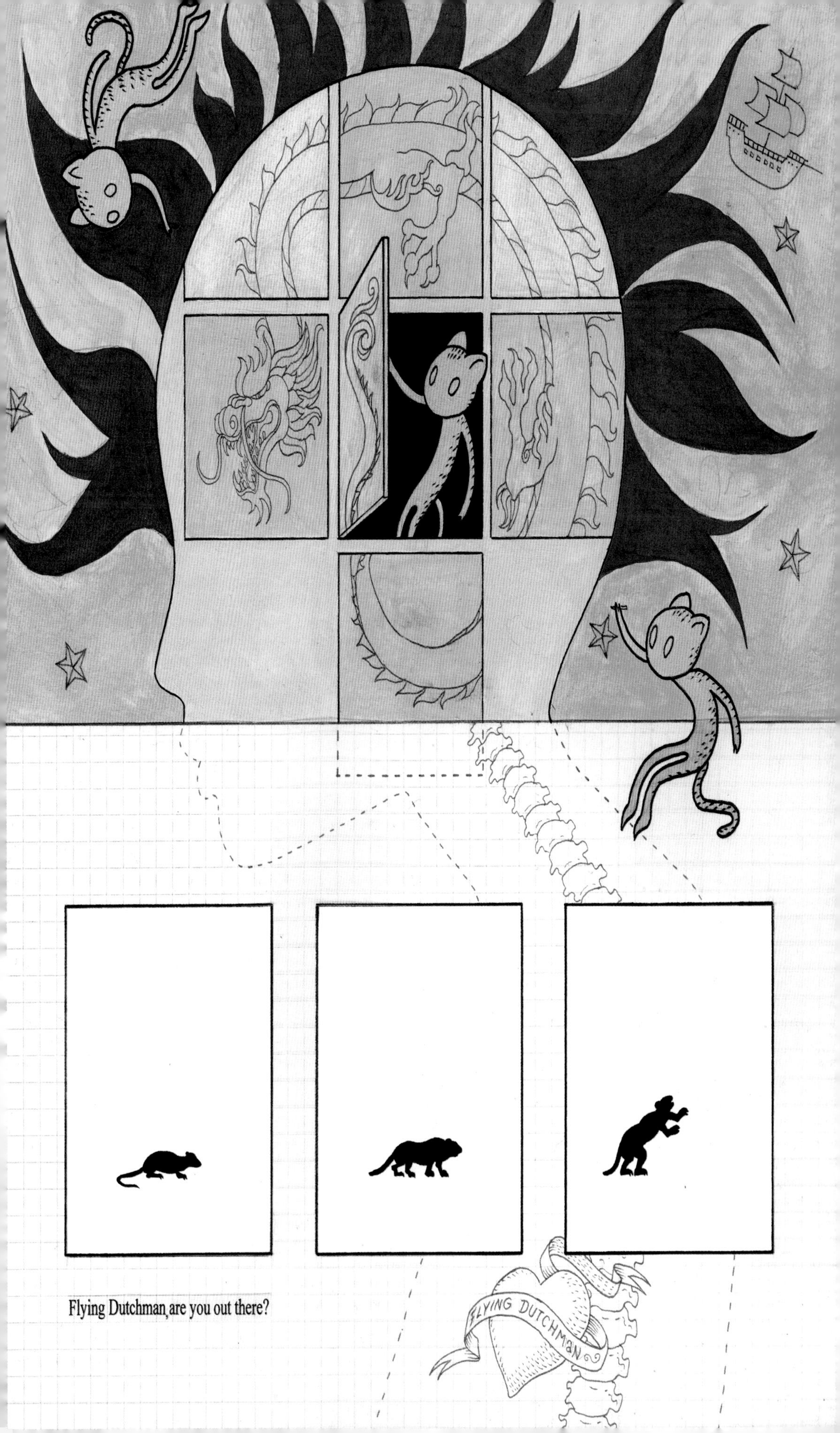
Flying Dutchman, are you out there?
FLYING DUTCHMAN

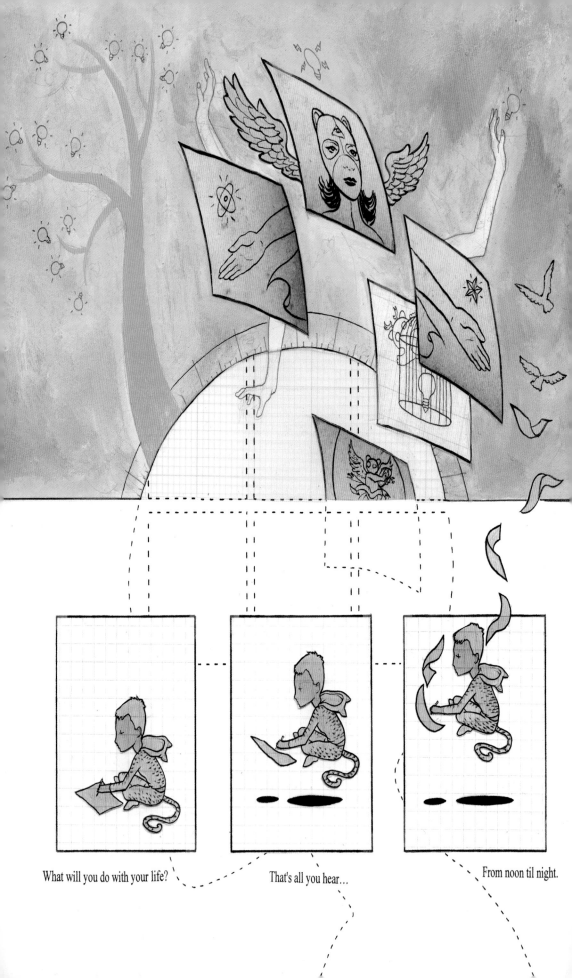

What will you do with your life?

That's all you hear…

From noon til night.

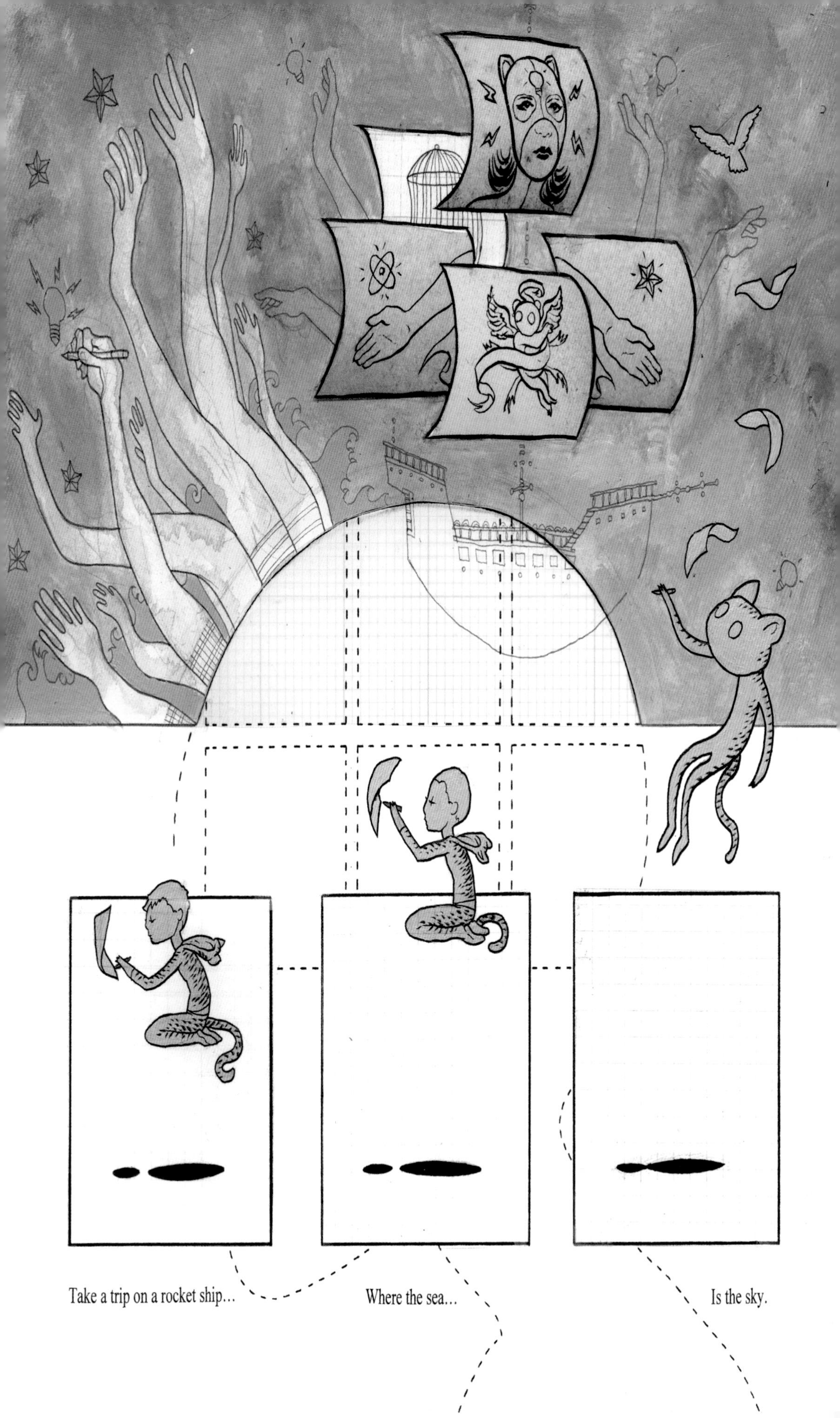
Take a trip on a rocket ship…
Where the sea…
Is the sky.

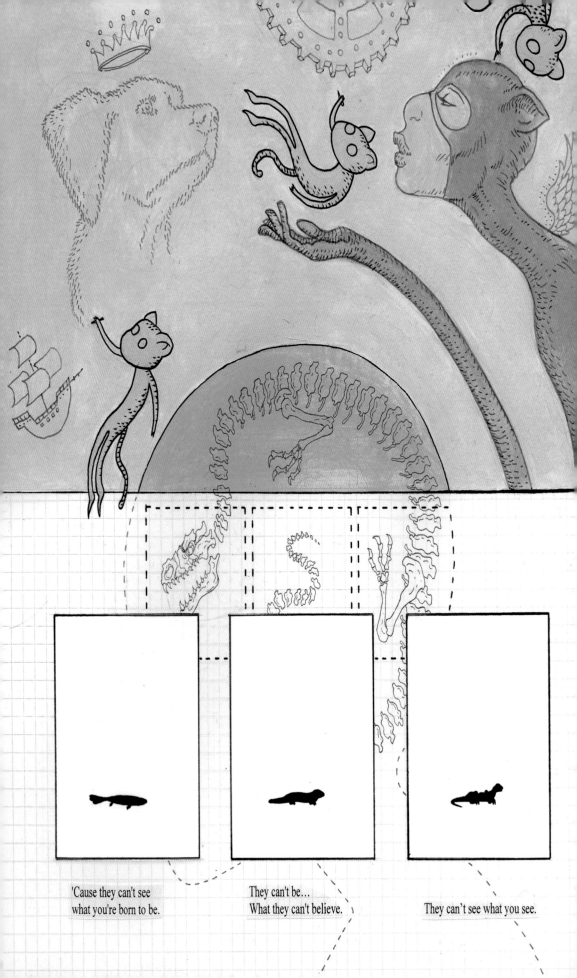

'Cause they can't see
what you're born to be.

They can't be...
What they can't believe.

They can't see what you see.

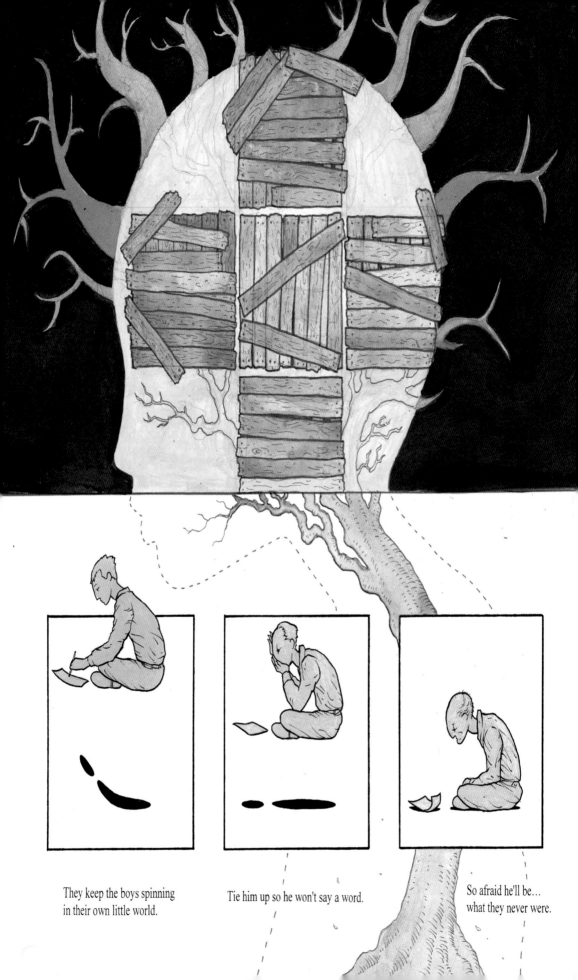

They keep the boys spinning
in their own little world.

Tie him up so he won't say a word.

So afraid he'll be...
what they never were.

2011 marked the opening of the DREAM LOGIC gallery show in Cincinnati at the P.A.C. Gallery. The entire large & small gallery spaces were filled with over 400 pieces.

These included the complete ALCHEMY story (all 9 chapters) as well as sculptures, other storytelling work, & drawings & paintings.

DAVID MACK
DREAM LOGIC

The original art pages of the entire *Alchemy* story in this book has been traveling as an exhibit at universities and libraries.

In 2011, NKU made *The Alchemy* the official book for its First Year program and issued as required

A close up of some pages of The Alchemy with their very three dimensional p

I found my place in life.

It is amazing how the universe answers you when you ask it the right questions, and state your intentions.

From the scrap parts that are too small to make into limbs for children…

I make customized prosthetics for people's pets.

It's a nice little cycle.

It gave me all the pieces…

And I fit them together.

negative intentions became disordered in structure & lost its magnificent patterning.

All that inspiration, catalyzed by line from a kid picture book on snowflakes.

As if the book itself passed on an organizing principle the way water molecules do.

Book as idea delivery system, imprinting on its reader, the pattern & nature of its subject.

You could actually read The Alchemy from beginning to end on the walls of the gallery, from room to room. It was if you were inside the story, as it surrounded you on every wall.

Each page is covered in glass so you can see the depth & texture.

I've resisted selling the original art of The Alchemy so that the story can be kept intact to be exhibited.

Some Alchemy exhibits include:
St Edwards University (Austin, TX 2008)
Salt Lake City Public Library (2009)
Ghent Castle (Ghent, Belgium 2009)
Floating World (Portland, Or 2010)
PAC Gallery (Cincinnati, OH 2011)
NKU Library (2011)
NKU Art Center (2011)

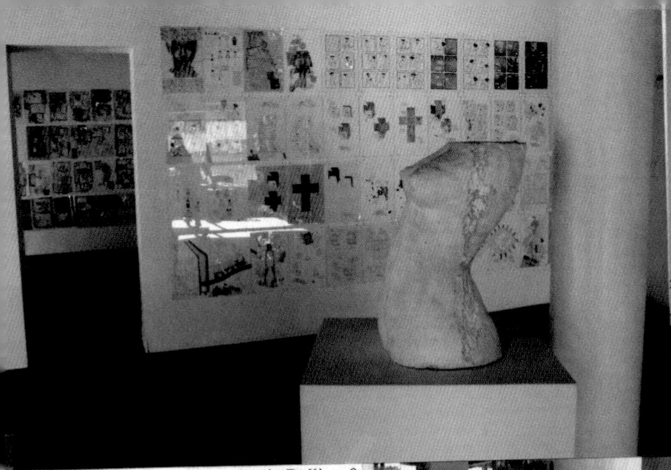

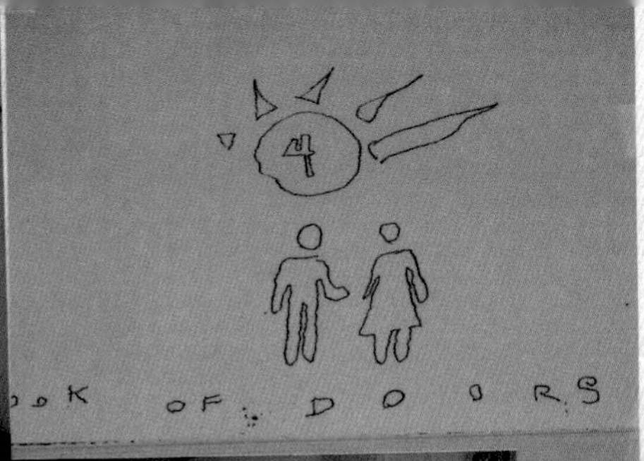

Thanks to PAC gallery owner Annie Bolling &
Jen Edwards, Natalie Jean, David Knight
& Emil Robinson

for their help in installing the show.

An exhibit like this gives readers the opportunity to experience the pages in their actual three dimensional form.

Sometimes I get used to seeing the print version of the books that I forget how textured and three-dimensional the actual pages are.

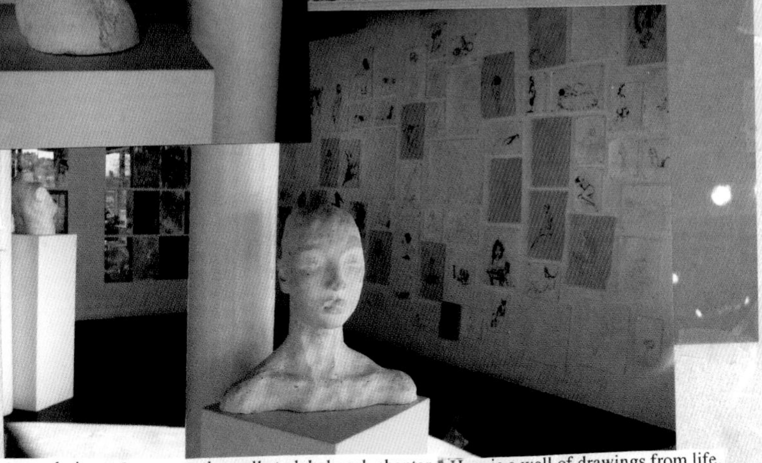

Many of the pages are as much sculpture as design. I wrote on the walls to label each chapter. Here is a wall of drawings from life.

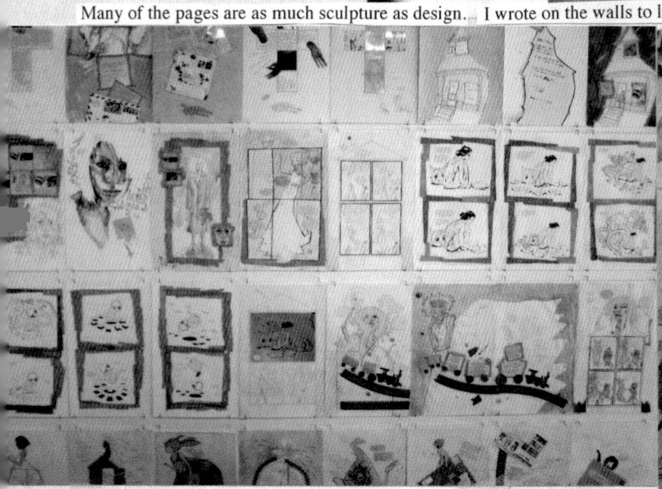

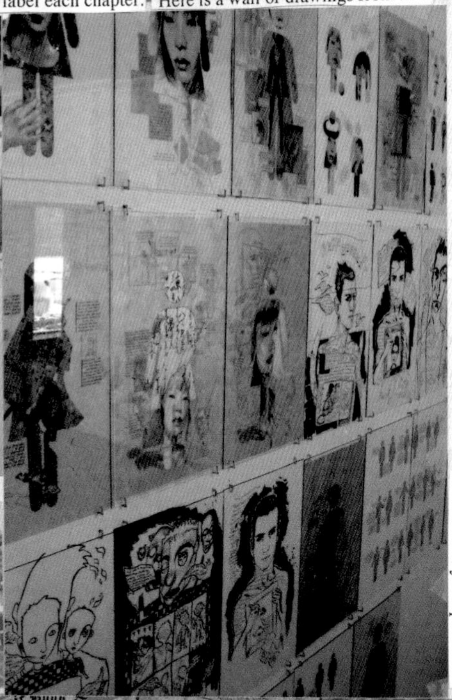

The Alchemy chapter four.

I did some talks at the gallery with Q & A.

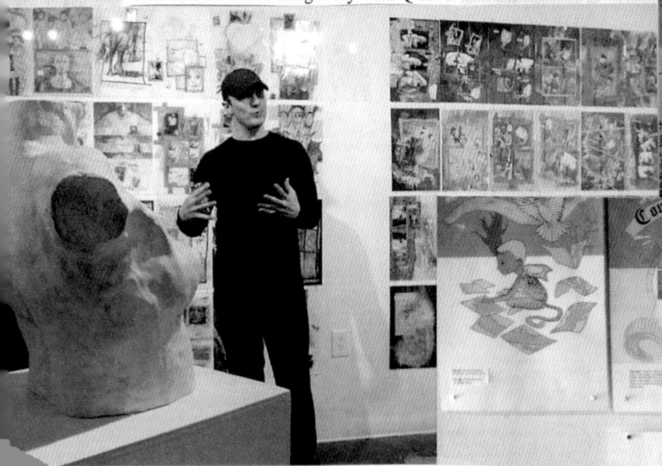

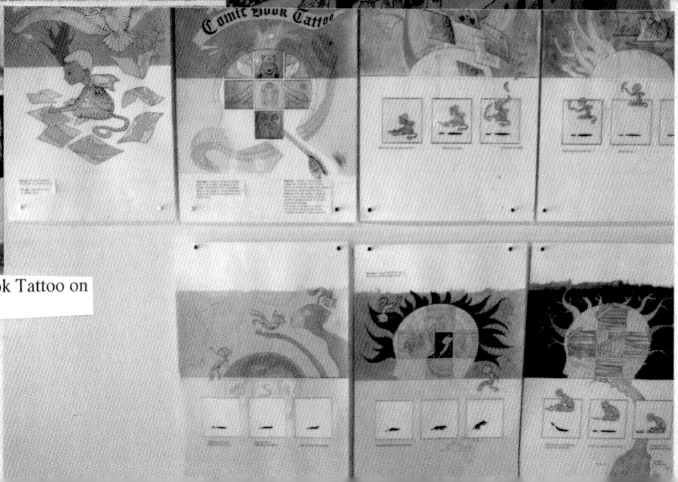
Comic Book Tattoo

The original pages of Tori Amos' Comic Book Tattoo on display.

Some of my life size sculptures on exhibit at each column in the gallery.

In 2013 Century Guild Gallery exhibited my drawings with the works of Gustav Klimt and Egon Schiele.
First there was a Chicago exhibit in June, and then a Los Angeles exhibit in July with an entirely different set of works of mine, Klimt, Schiele, Alphonse Mucha & Toulouse-Lautrec.

In October 2013 Century Guild presented a show of ink works of mine with Dave Mckean and Clive Barker.
In September 2014 the gallery presented a show of works with myself, Bill Sienkiewicz and Stephanie Inagaki.

The gallery then released a fine art book of my drawings from these shows called *MUSE*.
Here is a photo of the *MUSE* book at Century Guild in front of original Clive Barker paintings.

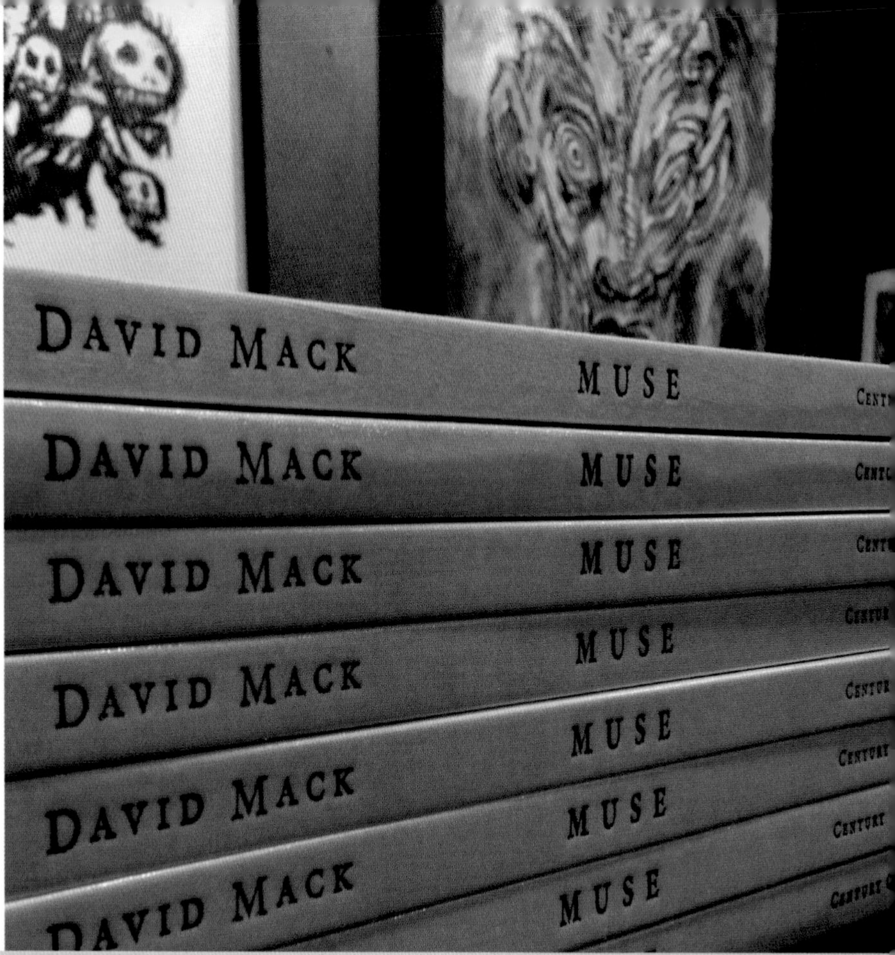
DAVID MACK
MUSE
DAVID MACK
MUSE
DAVID MACK
MUSE
DAVID MACK
MUSE
DAVID MACK
MUSE
DAVID MACK
MUSE
DAVID MACK
MUSE

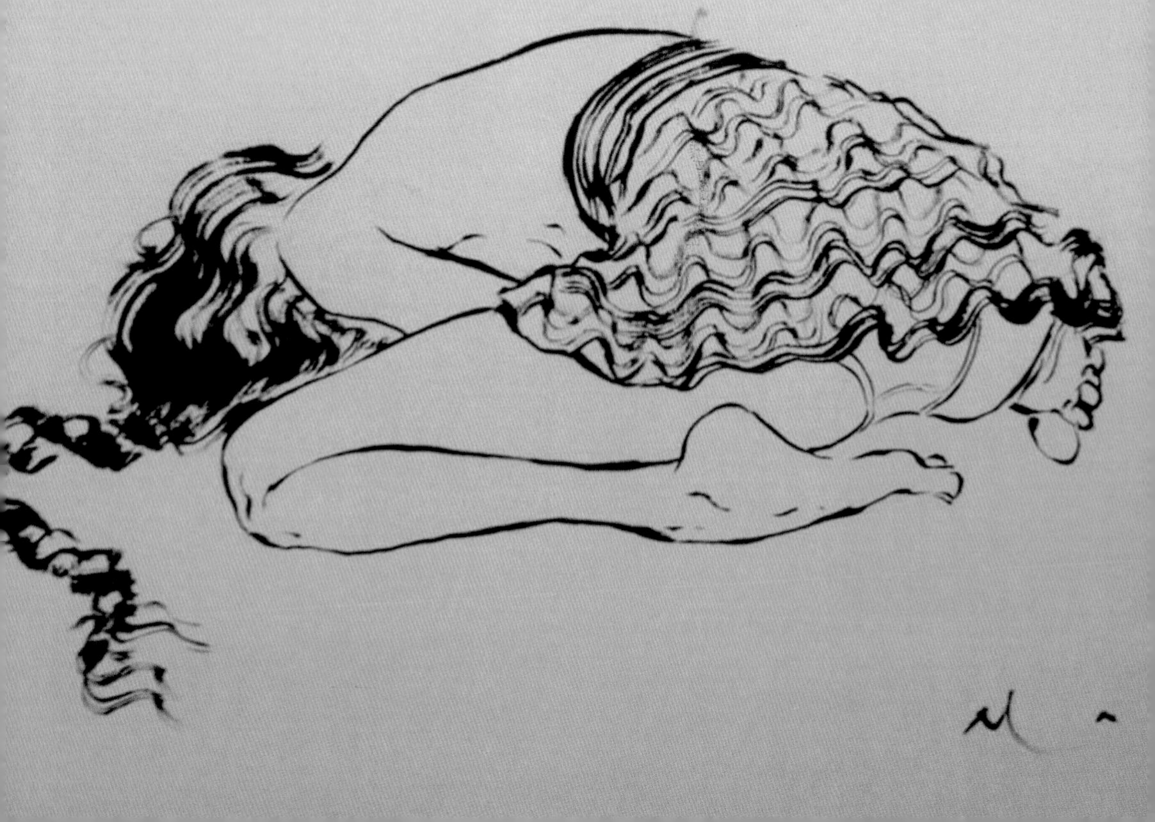

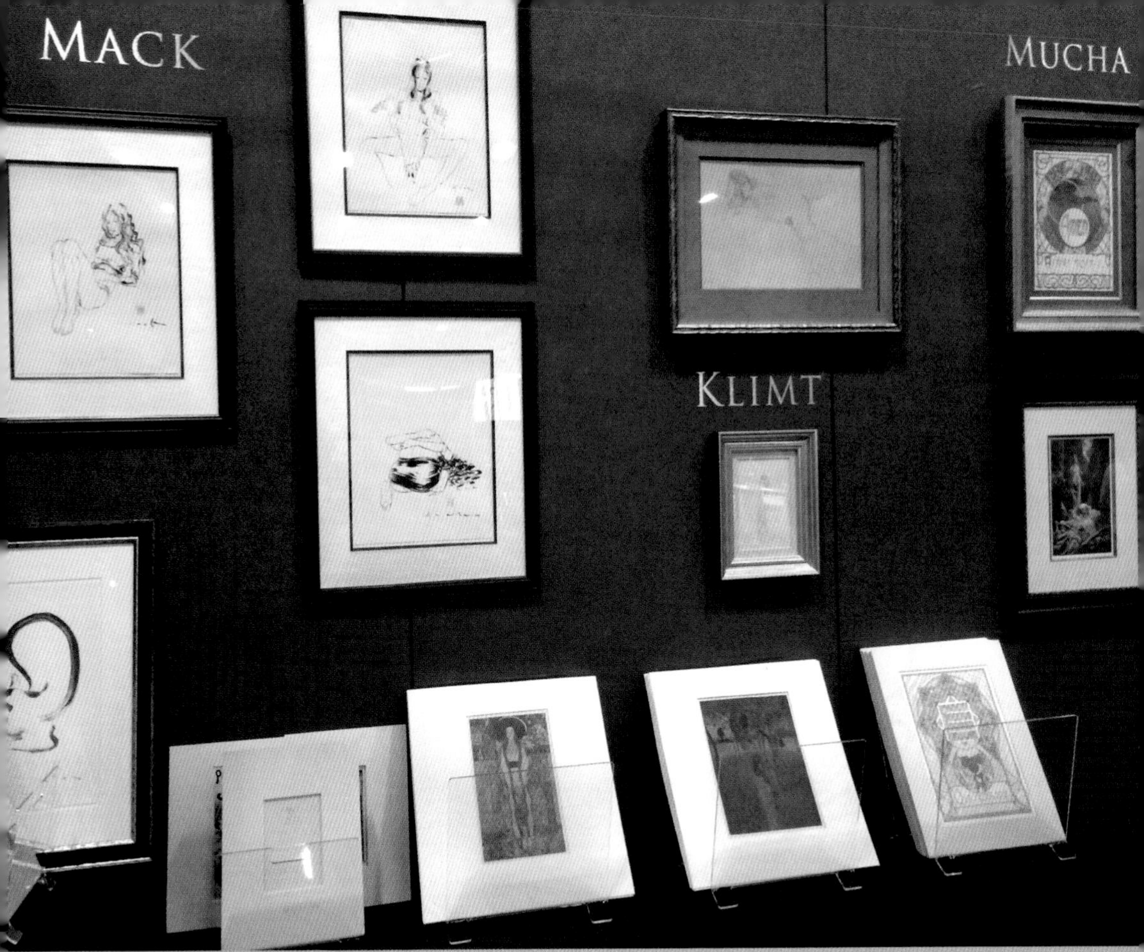
MACK
MUCHA
KLIMT
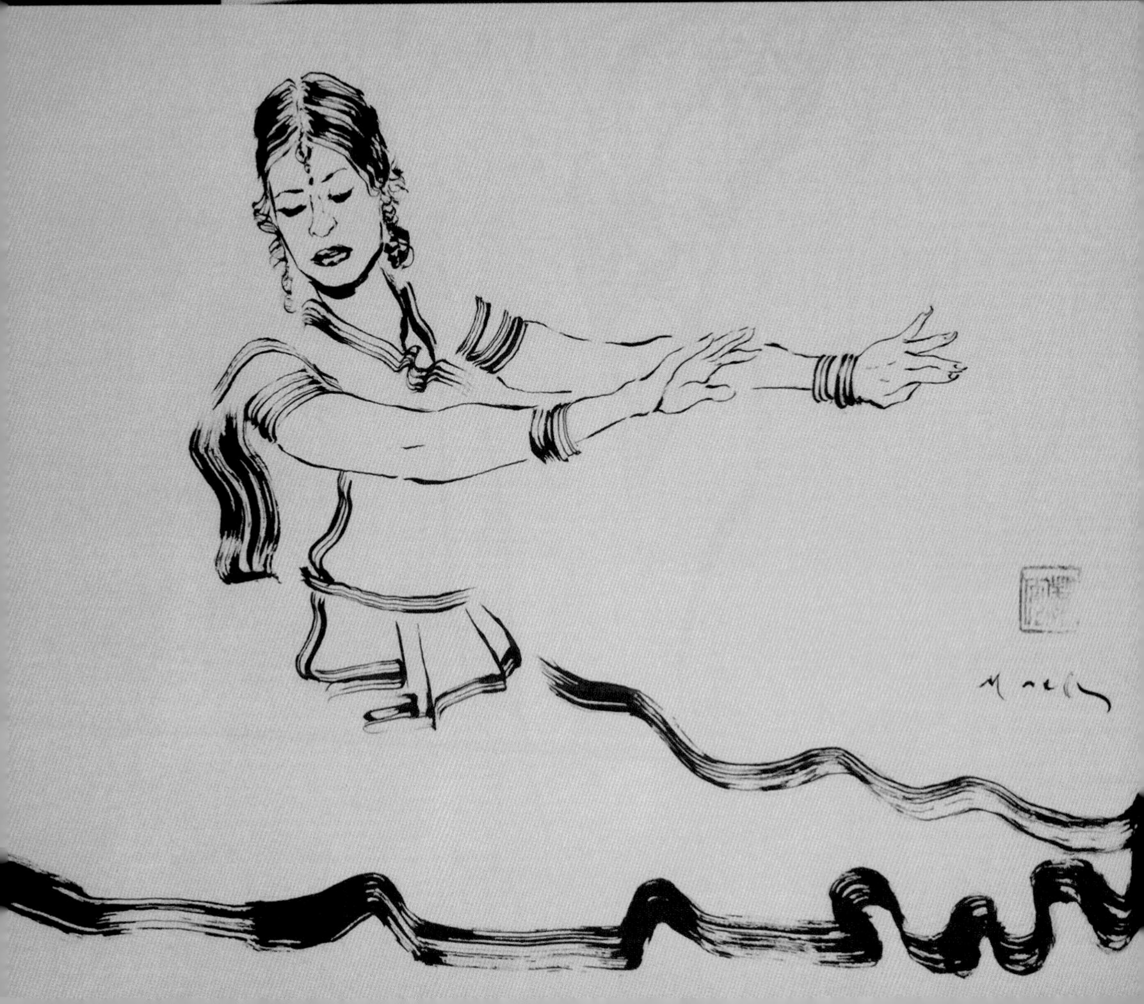

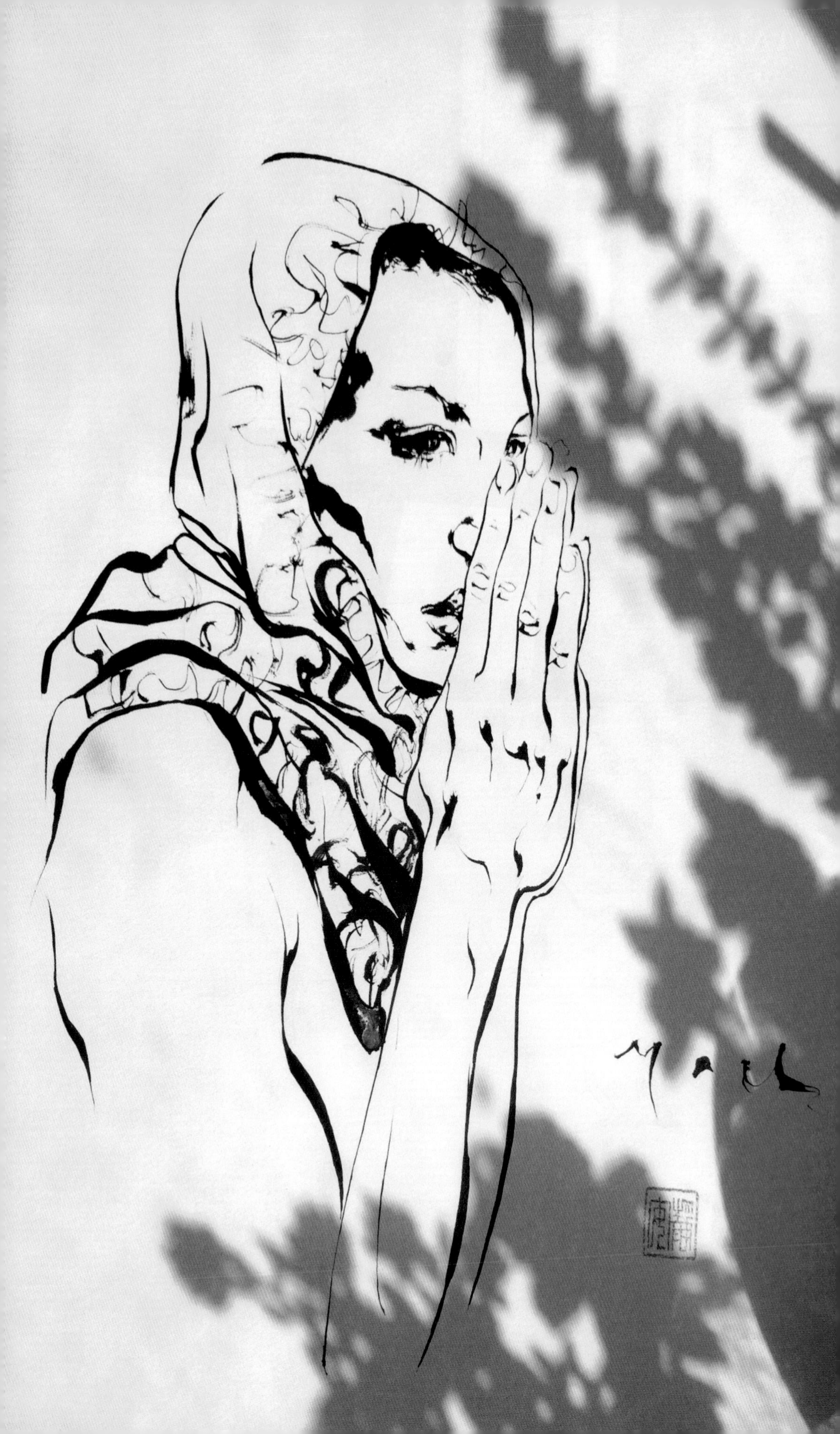

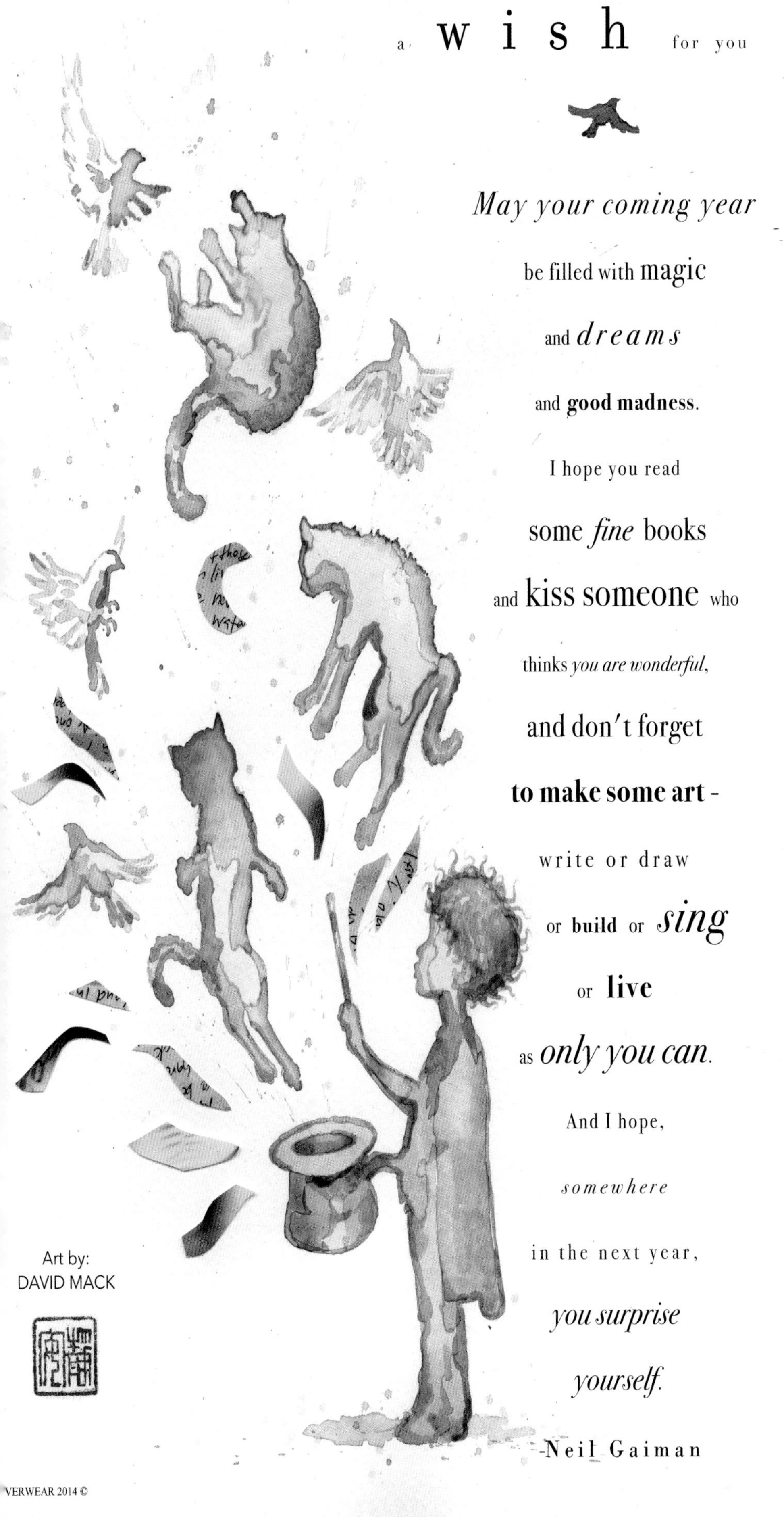
a wish for you
May your coming year
be filled with magic
and dreams
and good madness.
I hope you read
some fine books
and kiss someone who
thinks you are wonderful,
and don't forget
to make some art -
write or draw
or build or sing
or live
as only you can.
And I hope,
somewhere
in the next year,
you surprise
yourself.
-Neil Gaiman
Art by:
DAVID MACK
VERWEAR 2014 ©

Facing page:

Brush & ink. The model for the Psy-Chic in the *4th Mind* story.

This page:

The *WISH* print that I made with Neil Gaiman. Released in late 2014 from Neverwear.

"A book is a dream
that you hold
in your hands."

-NEIL GAIMAN

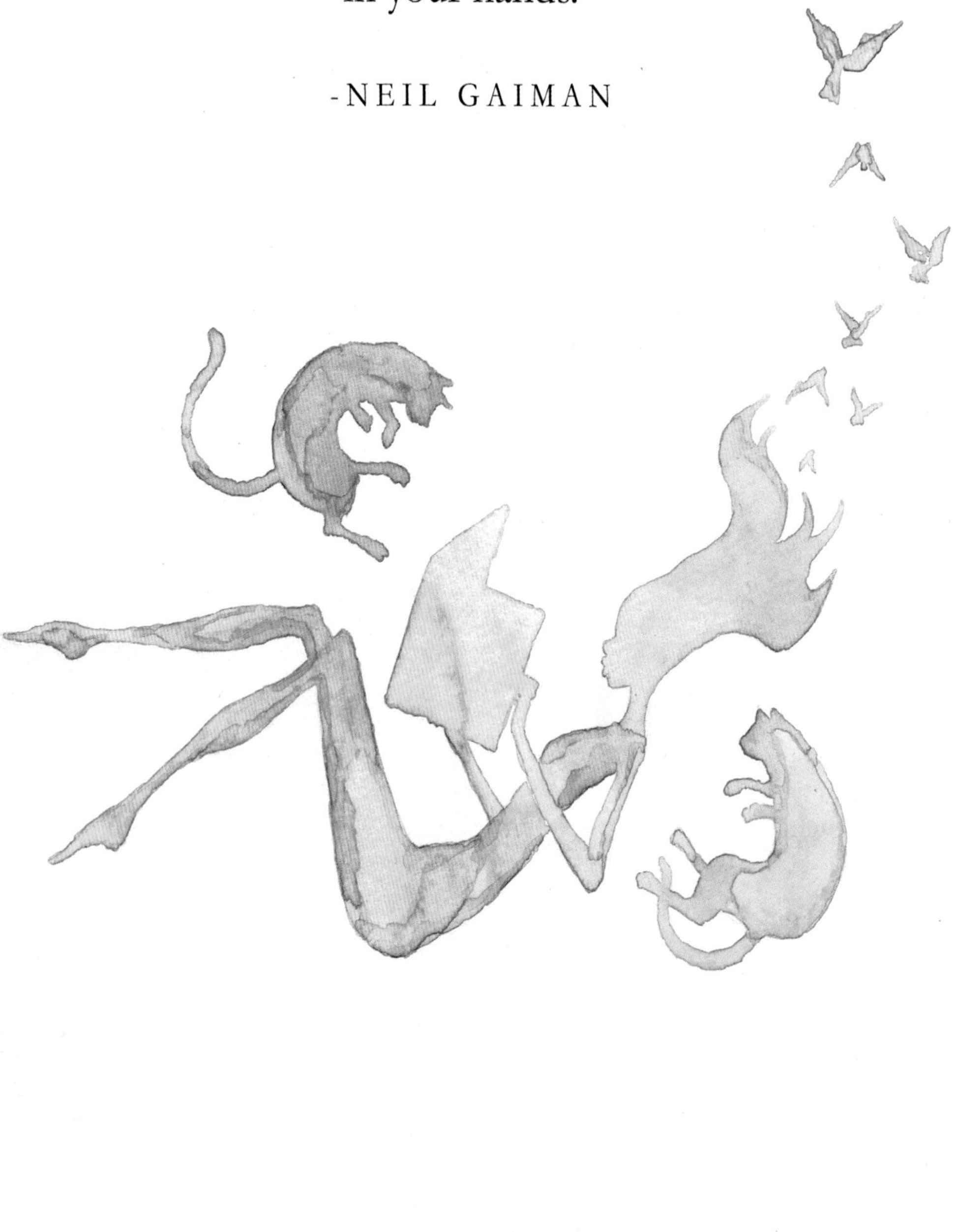

NEVERWEAR FIRST PRINTING 2015 ©

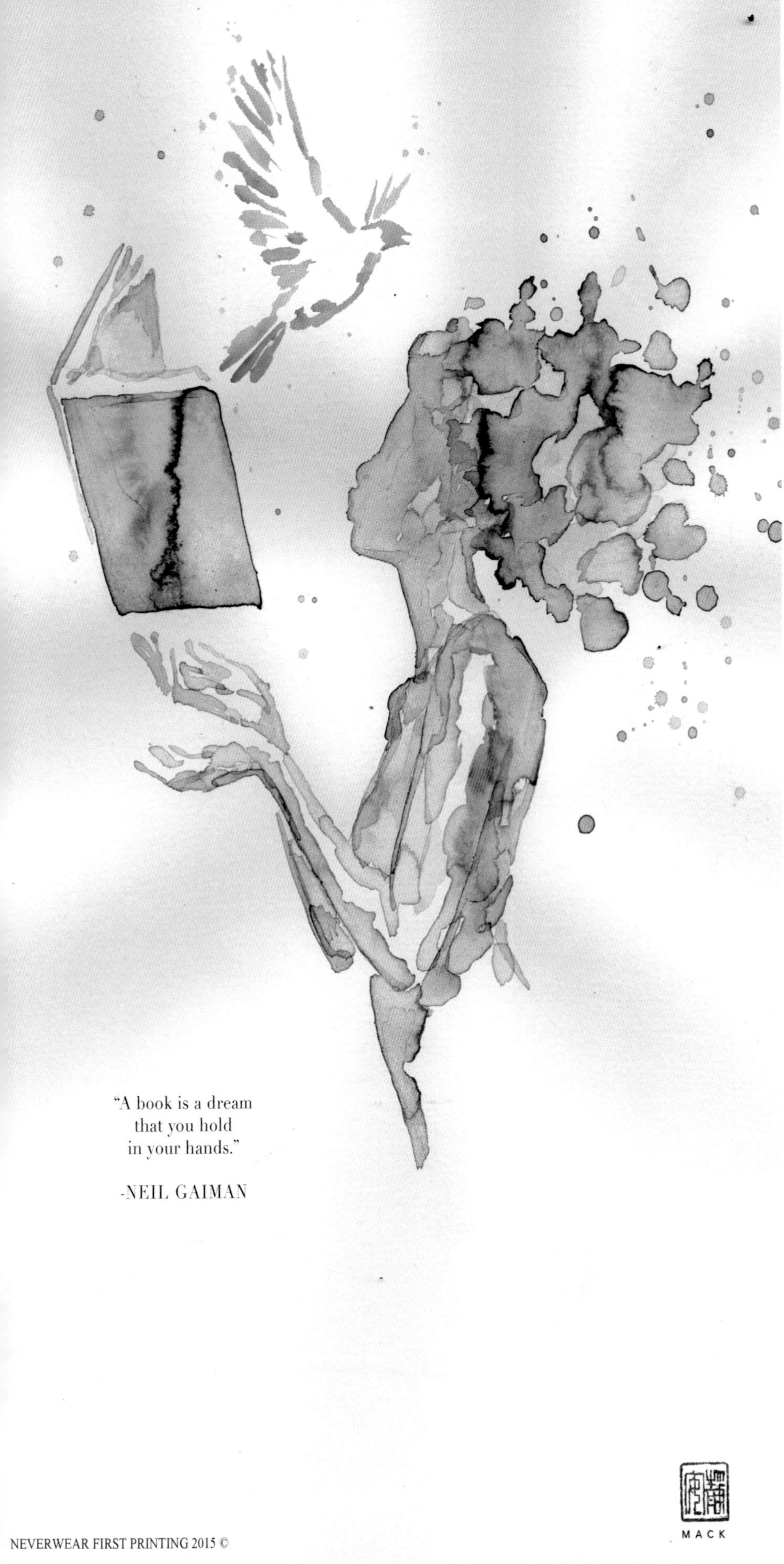
"A book is a dream
that you hold
in your hands."
-NEIL GAIMAN
NEVERWEAR FIRST PRINTING 2015 ©
MACK

Facing page:

The official *DREAM* print that I did with Neil Gaiman. Released from Neverwear in late 2015.

The 2012 and 2013 prints that I did with Neil Gaiman for Neverwear, *Words of Fire* & *The Goldfish Pool* are included in the *Dream Logic* hardcover with their origins and the process of creating the images.
I've been working with Cat Mihos of Neverwear in releasing these prints.
I've also been working with her to bring *The Shy Creatures* to the screen with Cat Mihos and her partner Rod Hamilton as producers and Neil Gaiman as Executive Producer.

This page:

This was another version that I created for this print.
Cat & Neil chose the version on the facing page as the official Neil Gaiman print from Neverwear and Cat told me that I could offer this version as an exclusive print.
I think of this as a companion piece to a figure and bird image that I included on the first page of this book. Sony had commisioned me to do a painting for Paul McCartney's *Blackbird* song, and combine the painting with the lyrics.
I painted them both from the same figure study session.

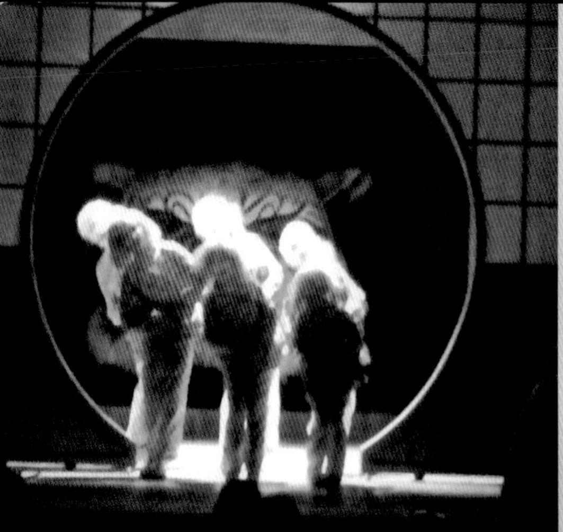

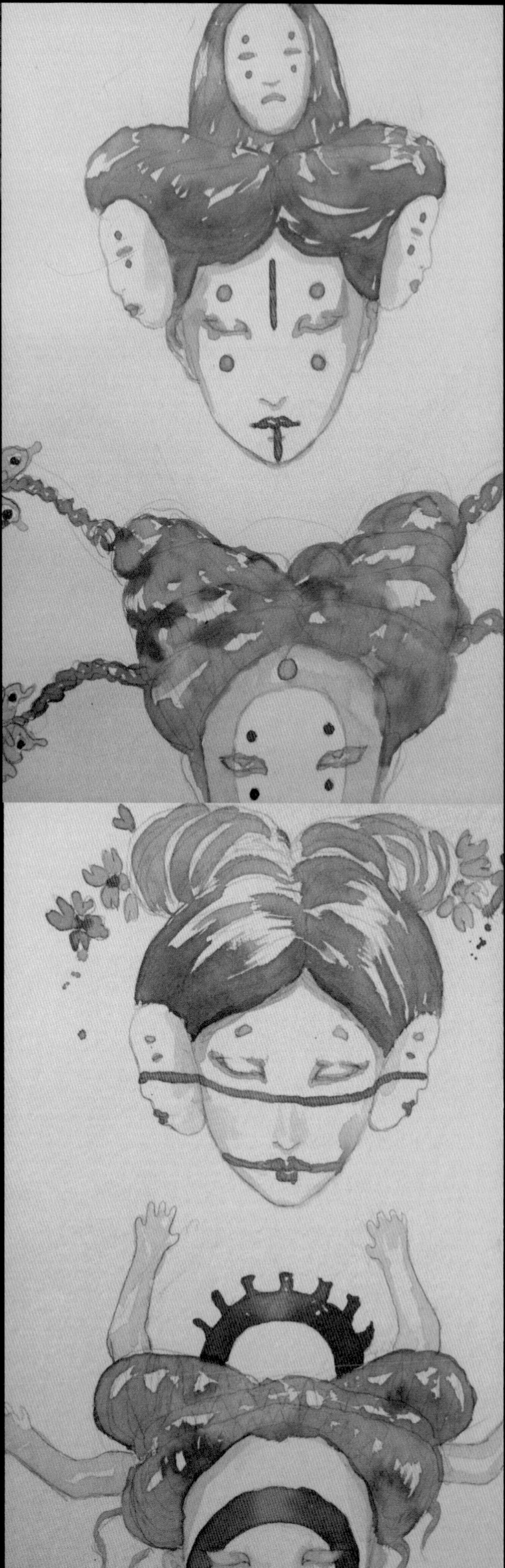

TENSHU

Based on my work in *Kabuki*,
I was asked to create the marquee art, title, poster, & character designs for the live theatrical production of the Japanese play *TENSHU*.

Japanese choreographer/director Hiromi Sakamoto brought the *TENSHU* theatrical production to America at Shadowbox Live in Columbus in 2015.

It was wonderful to see the designs come to life with the actors on the stage.

The production received Broadway World nominations & awards for:

Best Costume Design
Best Original Play
Best Choreography
Best Lighting Design
Best Leading Actress in a Musical
Best Musical

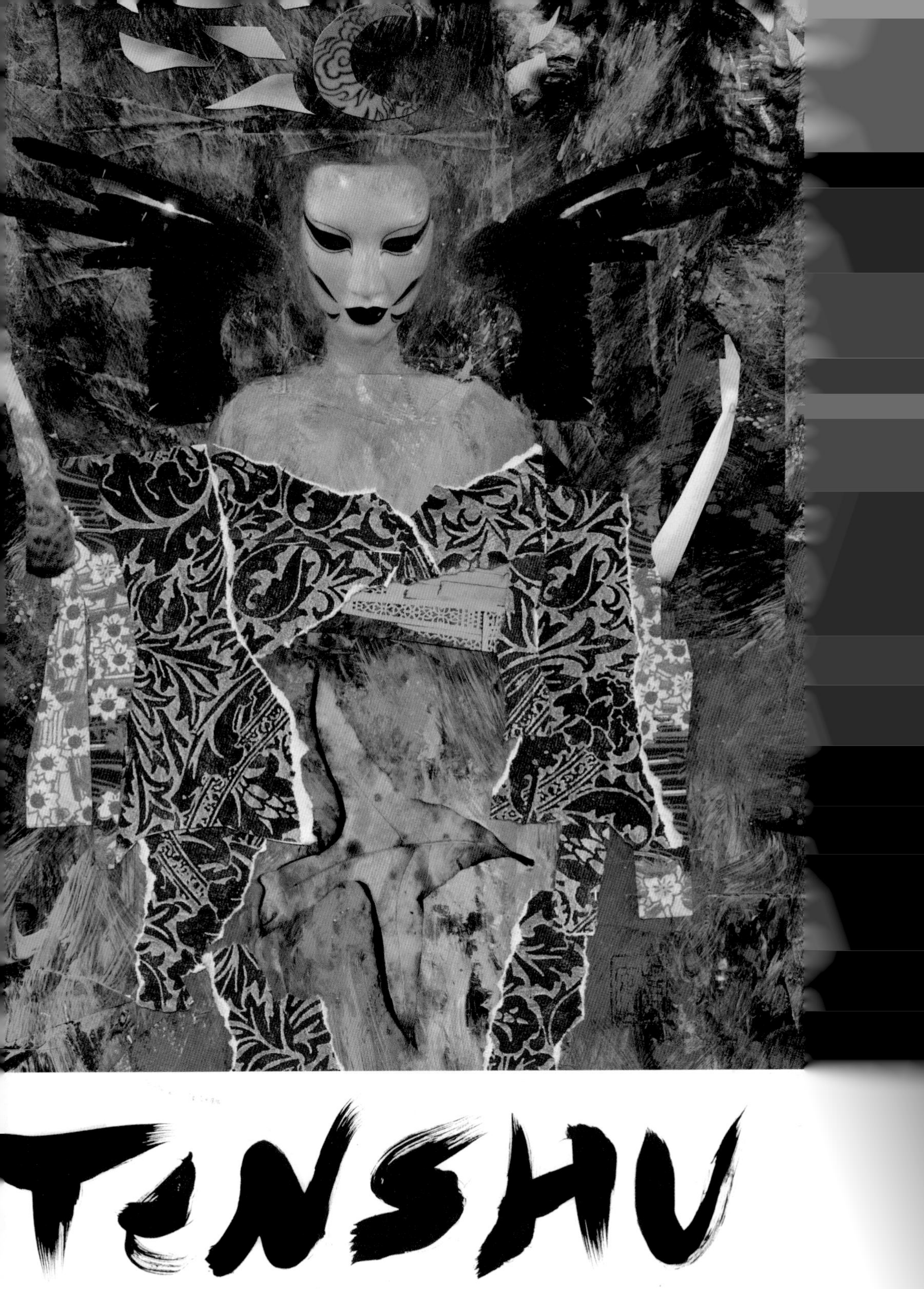

TENSHU

monogatari

a story of love and honor

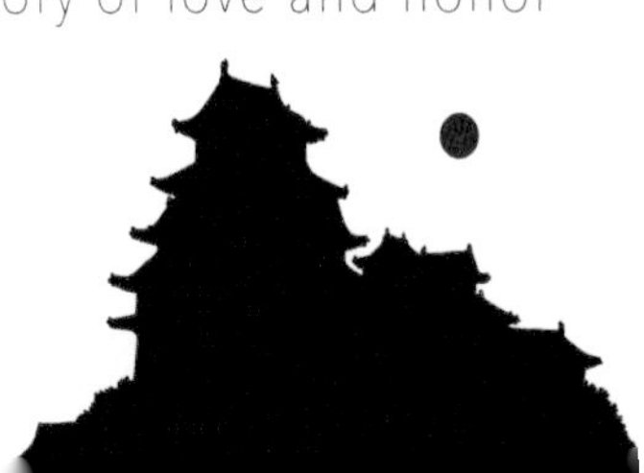

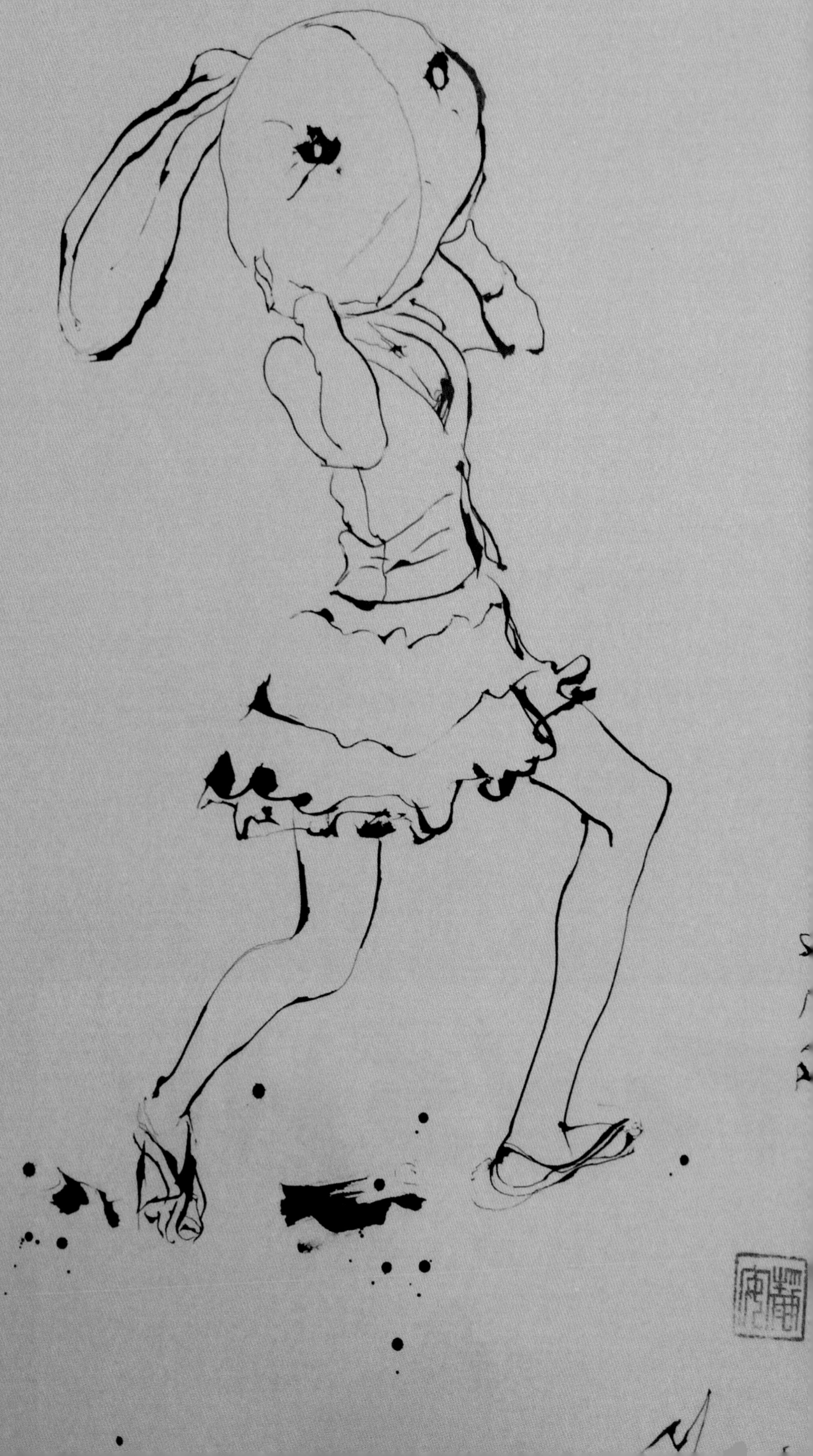

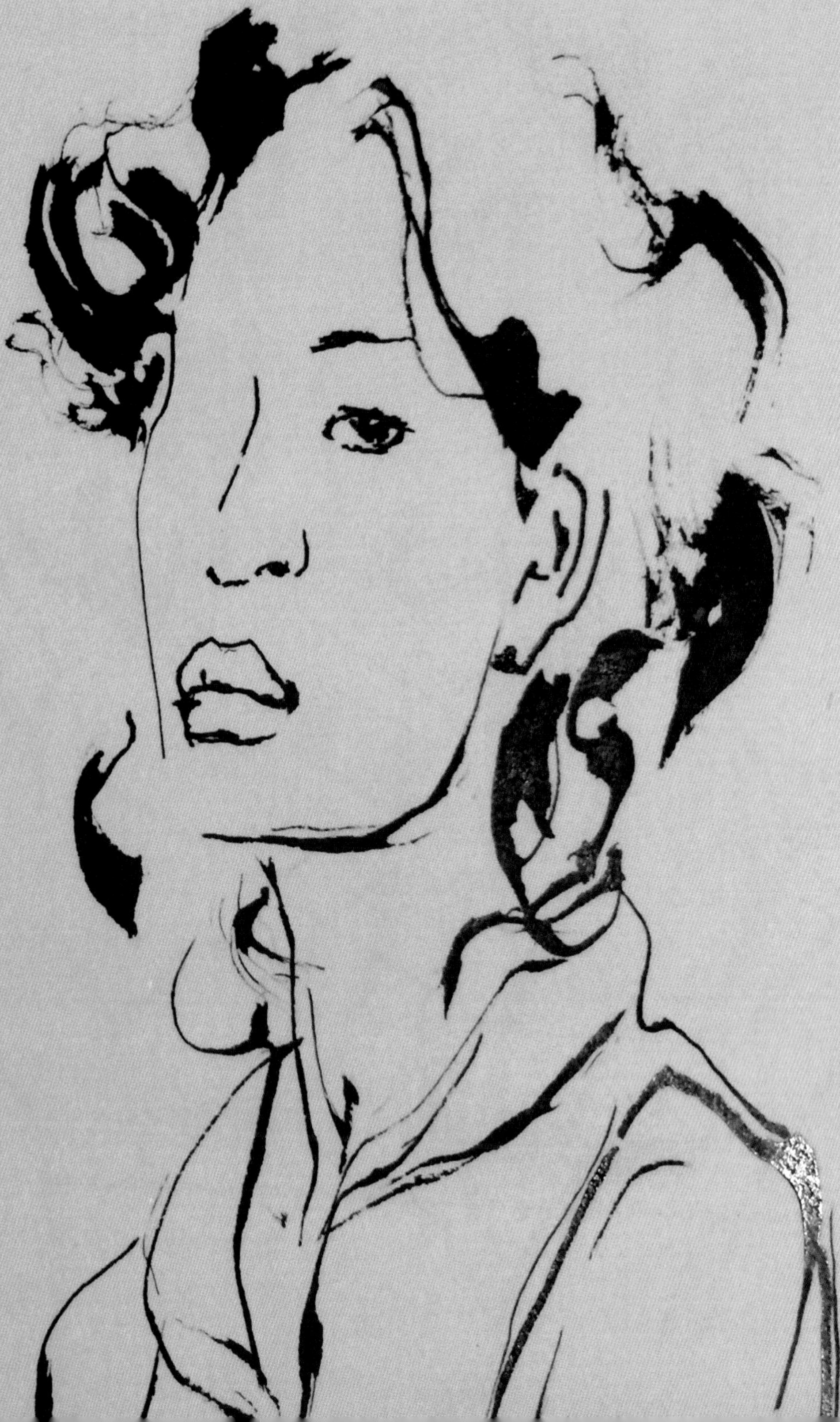

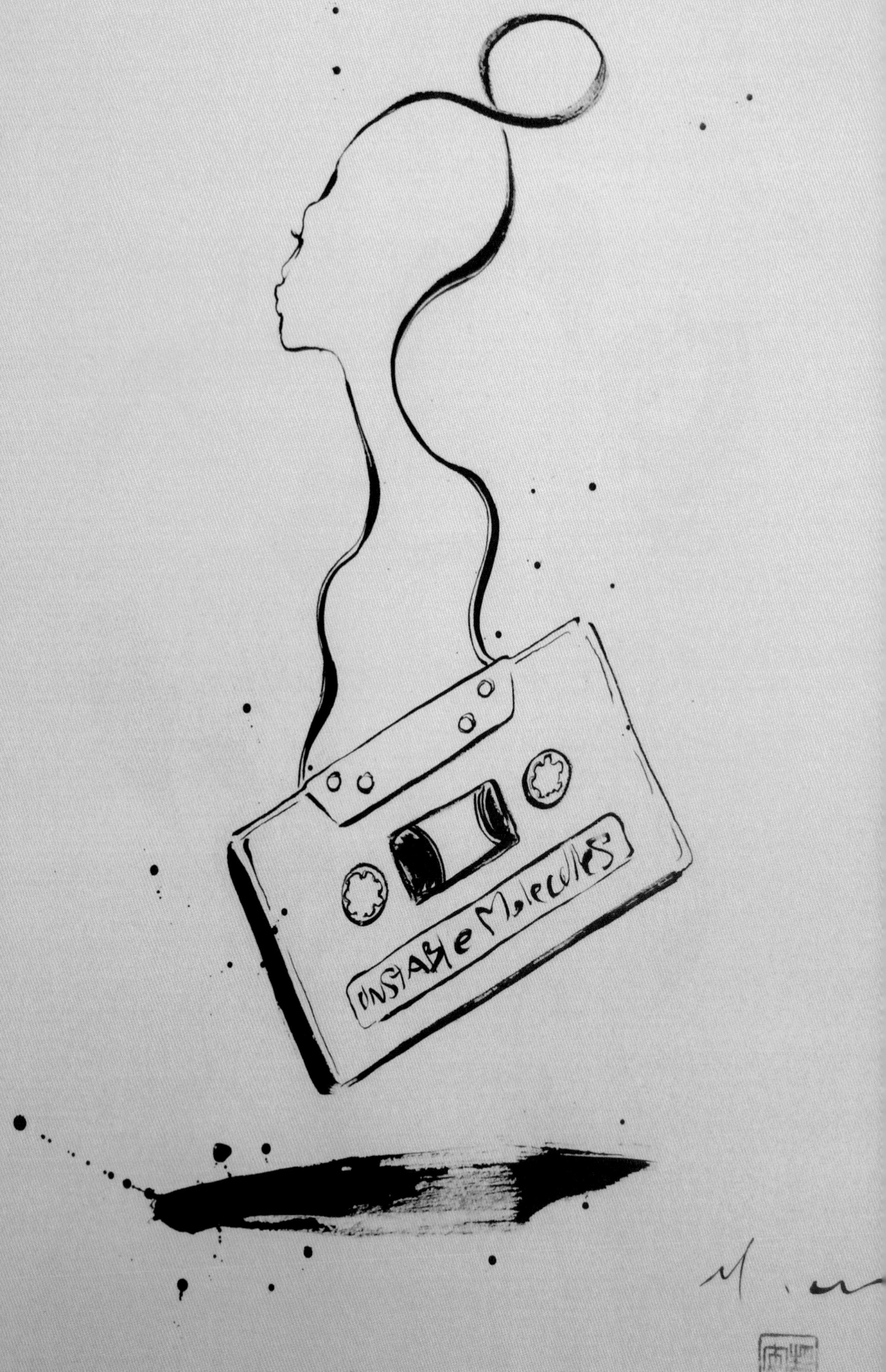
UNSTABLE Molecules

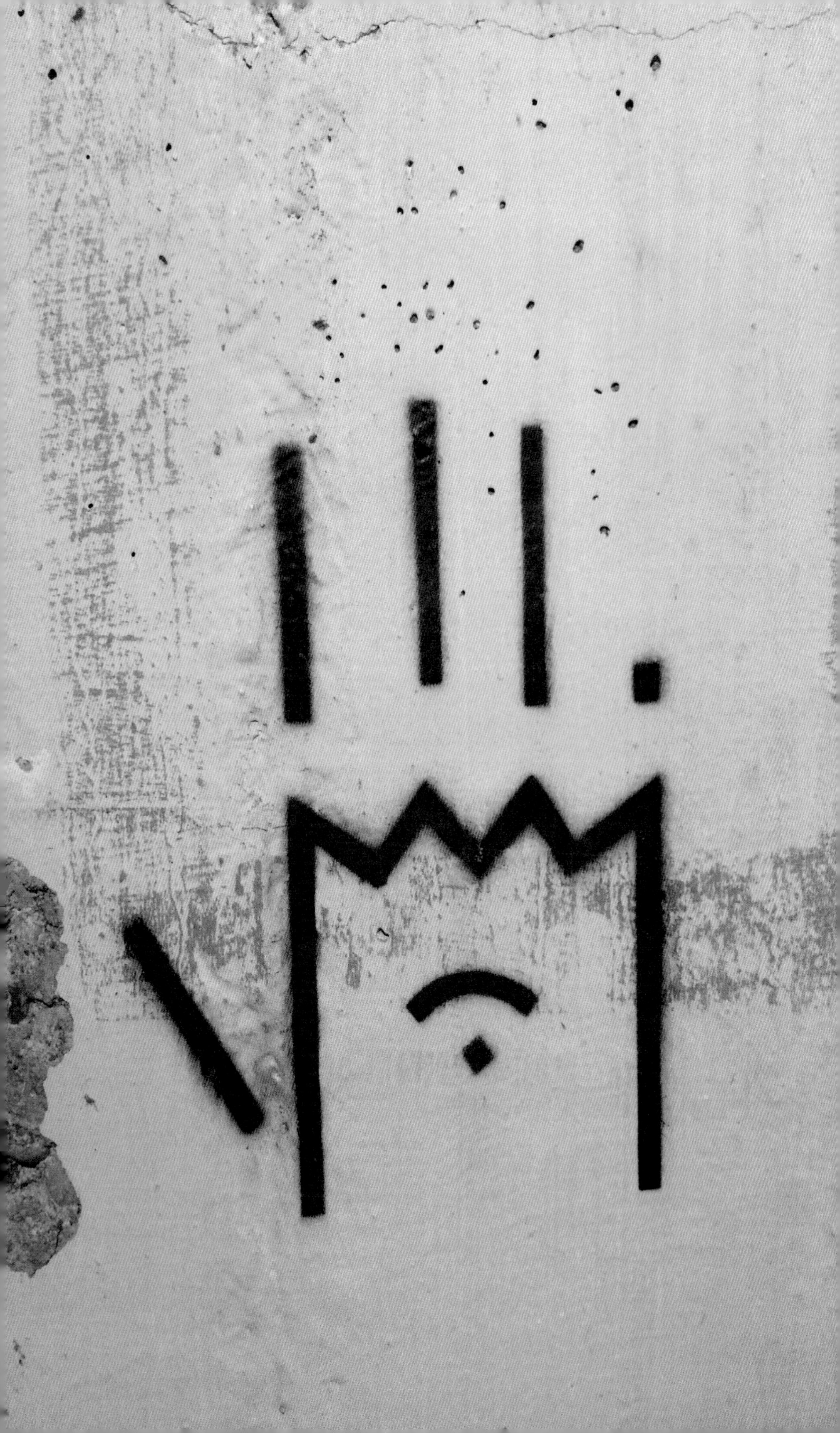

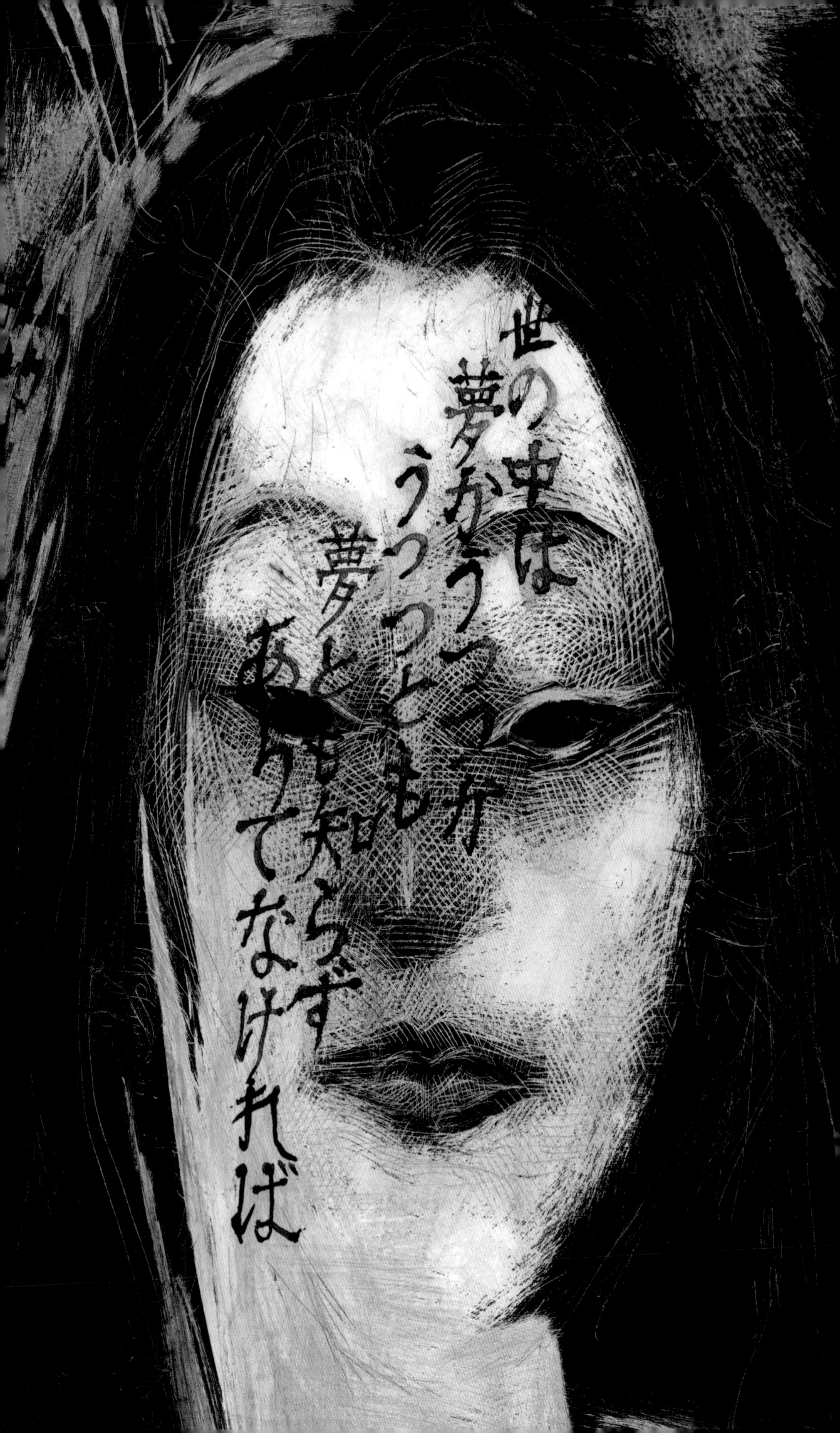
世の中は
夢かうつつか
うつつとも
夢とも知らず
ありてなければ

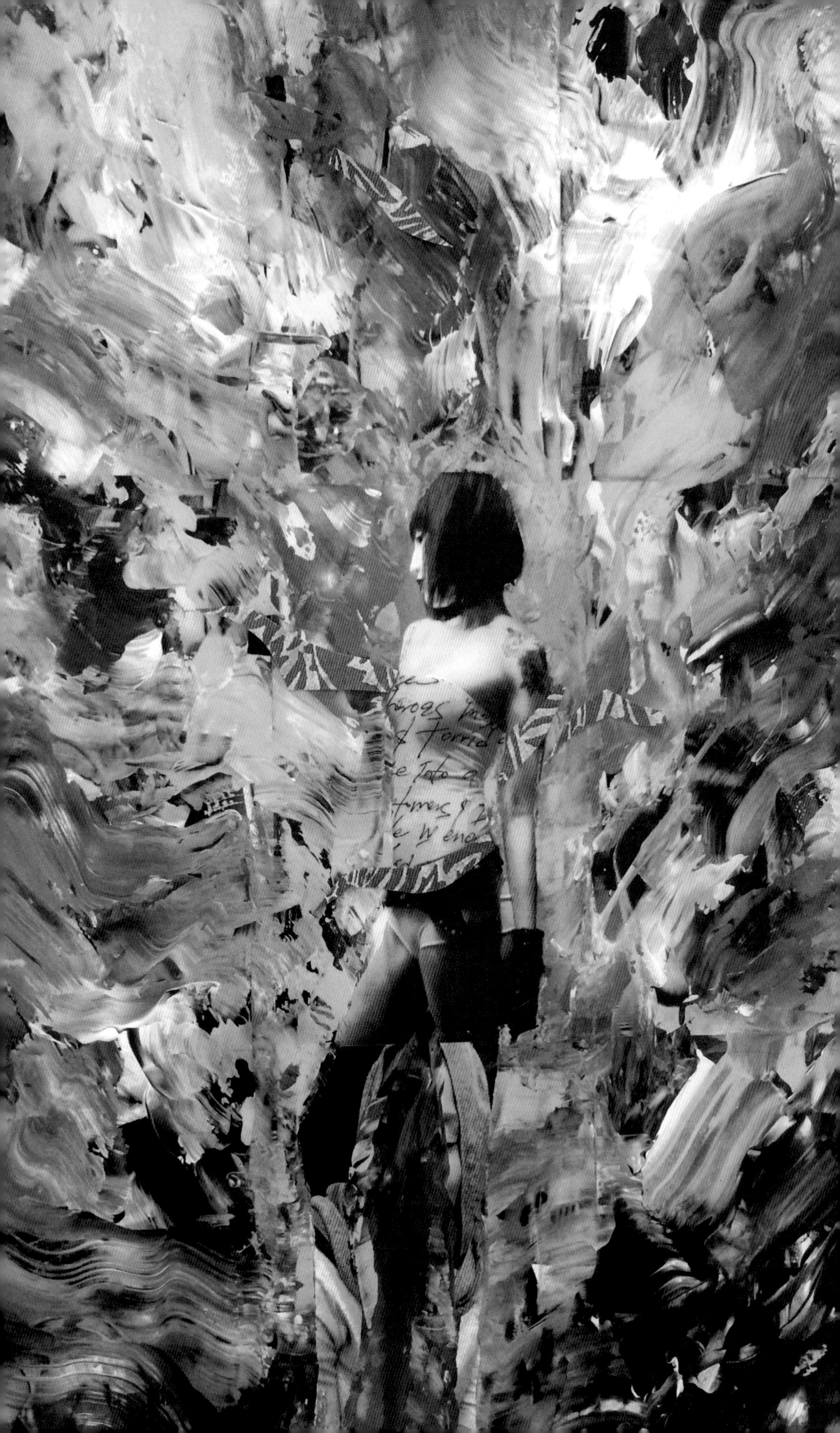

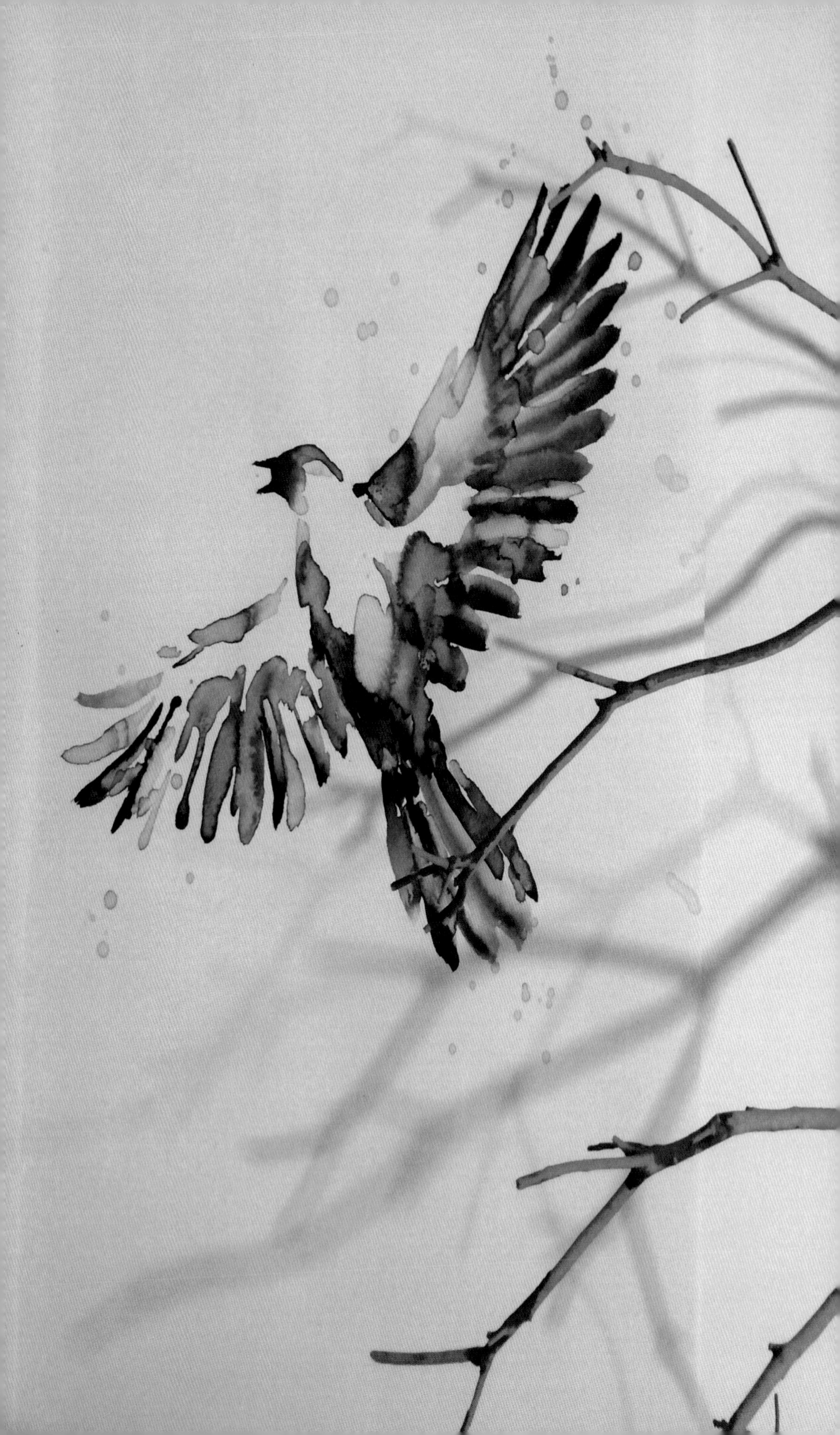

Thank you: To Anh Tran, Brian Michael Bendis, Mike Oeming, Alisa Bendis, Scott Allie, Cat Mihos, Neil Gaiman, Chuck Palahniuk, Shantel LaRocque, Jen Grunwald, Tim Daniel, David Gabriel, Dan Buckley, Andy Lee, Joe Quesada, Nanci Dakesian, Joe Martin, Olga Nunes, Bob & Mike Hickey, Steve Mack, Larry Woolum, Paul Mullins, Jim Valentino, Erik Larson, Gary Reed, Colleen Doran, Jim Steranko, David Thornton, Larry Woolum, Steven Mack, Evelyn Smith, Ean Kramer, Nick Barucci, Allen Spiegal, Caro, Kent Williams, Bill Sienkiewicz, Allan Amato, Satine Phoenix, Justin Cheung, Ron McElman, David Engel, Paul Mullins, Lee Hester, Paul & Burcu Ragsdale, Tori Amos, Rantz Hosely, Tommy Pallotta, Isa & Laura, Ian Punnett, Nick Barucci, Bill Marlowe, Matt Defoe, Tony Beuke, Ryan Liebowitz, Joe Ferrara, Mike Malve, Jim Valentino, Wilson Mack, Jeff Amano, Clay Moore, Nishan Patel, Chris Parnel, Tom Negovan, Rita Magnus, Elias Ortiz, Jaime Daez, Xochitl, Pooja, Carl Wyckaert, Stacie Boord, Tamara Smith, all the book stores that have supported my books over the years, beginning with my early student work of *Kabuki*, to all the readers that have given my work a chance and watched it evolve from the humble beginnings, of a college project with all its quirks of a beginner figuring out his way. You came to this book through word of mouth and there is no way I can express my gratitude for your support of this story over the last twenty years through all of its evolutions.

Art thanks: To Anh Tran for her editing, Shy Creatures coloring and design assistance, and for modeling as Kabuki, Miss Fumiko of the First Zen Institute of America for her inspiring mail and gifts (some of which I collaged into the artwork of this book), Brian Michael Bendis & Mike Oeming for their advice & friendship, Caro for the advice & bird leaf, Miho Suzuki, Brittany Bao for modeling, Mia Matsumiya for modeling, Mandy Amano, Quinn for modeling as the Psy-Chic, Wendy Lin for modeling, Christine Adams for modeling, Zu for modeling & art advice, Stephanie Inagaki, & Allan Amato.

Color credit: *The Shy Creatures & Lil KABUKI in Dream Land* colored by Anh Tran.

Book design by David Mack

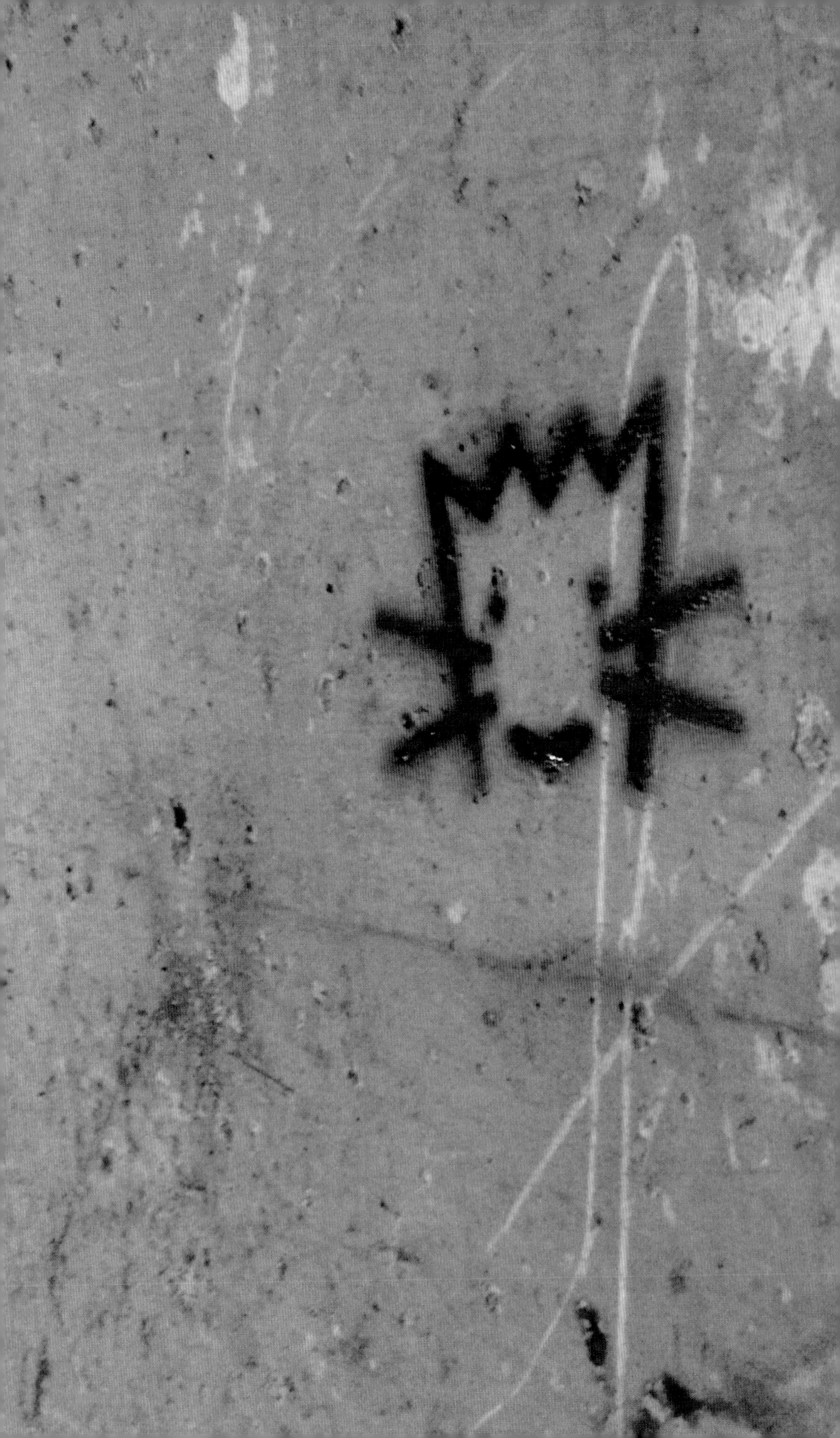

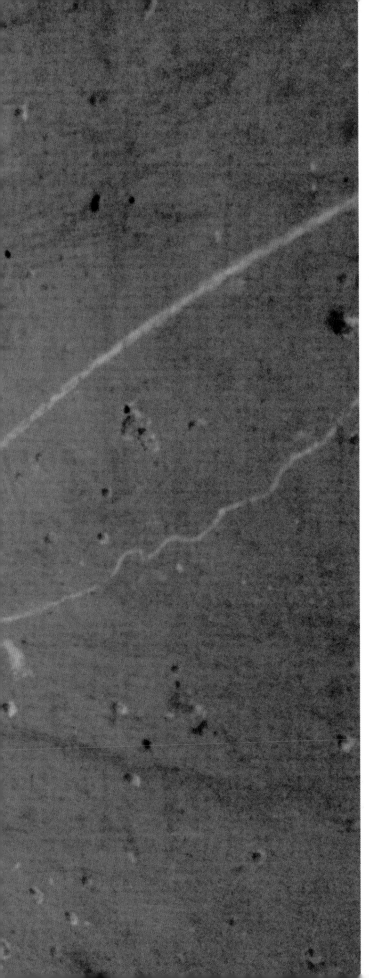

Acknowledgements:
(Chapter by chapter)

9. To *Fight Club* author Chuck Palahniuk for sending me gifts that I collaged into the art of pages in this book & a letter he wrote me that I referenced & quoted in this chapter, to the work of Dr. Masura Emoto, Nikola Tesla, Claire Wendling a sushi dinner conversation with Neil Gaiman that inspired the Akemi "Kiss" conversation, the Charlie Rose Show which I watched regularly while making this story, to Kathryn White, Lisa Cyr, Arie Brass & Ms. Fumiko whose gifts & stamps I collaged into this issue, to Allen Speigel, Liz Zsabla, & Jean Feiwell for their help in making *The Shy Creatures* a reality.

8. To the works of Steranko, Jack Kirby, R. Crumb, Ivan Brunetti, Art Spiegelman, Silvestre, Jorge Marin, Claire Wendling, Michael Brandt, Rila Fukushima, Scott Thorpe's *How to Think Like Einstein*.

7. To Katsuhiro Otomo, Leonardo Da Vinci, Nikola Tesla, Steven Pressfield's *The War of Art* that Akemi referenced & quoted in this issue, Silvestre, Hiromix, & Miss Fumiko of the first Zen Institute of America whose envelope I collaged into this issue.

6. To the works of Nikola Tesla, Albert Einstein, quotes from author Scott Thorpe's book *How to Think Like Einstein*, John Lienhard's *The Engines of Our Ingenuity* & Howard Zinn, Hiromix, Alan Moore, to Miss Fumiko of the first Zen Institute of America & Michelle Julia Bergin whose envelopes to me where collaged into this issue.

5. To the works of origami master Jodi Fukumoto, Hiromix, Claire Wendling, origami master John Montroll, stamps & letters that I collaged into this issue sent to me from Miss Fumiko of the First Zen Institute of America, Danna Batangbacal, Robin Hotter, Jason Chau, Bryan Goff, Daniel Winters & many more.

4. To the works of origami master Robert J. Lange, Hiromix, Walter Murch, Mike Oeming (whose depiction of NYPD Detective D.M. from his *Powers* Vol. 6 made a crossover appearance in the story), Miss Fumiko who's letters where collaged into the artwork of the story, a photo of the farm sickle from the actual farm in Pa. that my mother grew up on was collaged into this issue, and to Annie with the *Kabuki* Tattoo that I collaged into this issue.

3. To Dr. Seuss, Dr. Doolittle, to Anh Tran for coloring my brush & ink drawings in *The Shy Creatures*, & *Scarab* art of Rick Mays.

2. To the work of painter & physician Lian Quan Zhen, Gustav Klimt, Chagall, Jean-Michel Basquiat, Picasso, Miyamoto Musashi, to *Orthopaedic Biomechanics* by Dr. Victor H. Frankel & Dr. Albert H. Burstein, Ms Fumiko of the First Zen Institute of America (whose letters I collaged into the cover), Doug Merkle & Carolee for the photo reference of Carolee's arms, Joe and Traci Martin's dog Wyatt who modeled for the dog with the broken leg. Little Friends Animal Clinic was an actual animal hospital - my dad lived in the basement of the clinic and helped the doctor, and my brother and I would stay there on weekends -It is still a veterinary clinic but now with a different name.

1. To the works of origami master Robert J. Lange, Julian Schnabel, Eiko Ishikawa, Ms Fumiko of the First Zen Institute of America whose letters I collaged into the cover of this issue, Alice Lynch whose letters on origami paper I collaged into this issue.

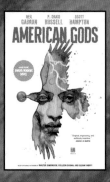

DREAM LOGIC
David Mack

Collecting the entire series of *Dream Logic* by David Mack, this hardcover includes original new stories, as well as a gallery of artwork, sketchbook section, and step-by-step art processes with commentary on Mack's cover work, the *Kabuki* series, and never-before-seen extras.

$34.99 | ISBN 978-1-61655-678-5

AMERICAN GODS
Neil Gaiman, P. Craig Russell, Scott Hampton, David Mack, and more!

This supernatural American road trip fantasy adapts the story of a war between the ancient and modern gods from Neil Gaiman's *American Gods* novel.

Collecting the comic book series, along with art process features, high res scans of original art, layouts, character designs, and variant covers by Becky Cloonan, Skottie Young, Fábio Moon, Dave McKean, and more!

Volume 1: The Shadows
$29.99 | ISBN 978-1-50670-386-2

Volume 2: My Ainsel
$29.99 | ISBN 978-1-50670-730-3

Volume 3: The Moment of the Storm
$29.99 | ISBN 978-1-50670-731-9

REFLECTIONS
David Mack

Collecting Marvel's *Reflections* series from multiple-Eisner-nominated creator David Mack. This format shows off a gorgeous collections of *Daredevil*, *Alias*, and *Kabuki* cover paintings, drawings, and step-by-step art processes.

$24.99 | ISBN 978-1-61655-676-1

FIGHT CLUB
Chuck Palahniuk, Cameron Stewart, and David Mack

Some imaginary friends never go away . . .

Ten years after starting Project Mayhem, he lives a mundane life. A kid, a wife. Pills to keep his destiny at bay. But it won't last long—the wife has seen to that. He's back where he started, but this go-round he's got more at stake than his own life. The time has arrived . . .

Fight Club 2 HC
$29.99 | ISBN 978-1-61655-945-8

Fight Club 2 TPB
$19.99 | ISBN 978-1-50670-628-3

Fight Club 3 HC
$39.99 | ISBN 978-1-50671-178-2

AVAILABLE AT YOUR LOCAL COMICS SHOP OR BOOKSTORE

TO FIND A COMICS SHOP IN YOUR AREA, VISIT COMICSHOPLOCATOR.COM • For more information or to order direct, visit DarkHorse.com

Dream Logic, Reflections © 2014, 2015 David Mack. American Gods™ © 2018, 2019 Neil Gaiman. Fight Club 2 © 2016, 2018 Chuck Palahniuk. Fight Club 3 © 2017, 2018, 2019, 2020 Chuck Palahniuk. Dark Horse Books® and the Dark Horse logo are registered trademarks of Dark Horse Comics LLC. All rights reserved.